Foolbert Funnies

FRANK STACK

(aka Foolbert Sturgeon)

Foolbert Funnies

HISTORIES AND OTHER FICTIONS

Foolbert Funnies: Histories and Other Fictions
By Frank Stack (aka Foolbert Sturgeon)

Editor: Kristy Valenti
Designer: Tony Ong
Production: Preston White
Proofreader: Janice Lee
Editorial Assistance: RJ Casey, Daniel Johnson, Caroline Sibila, and Althea Solis
Associate Publisher: Eric Reynolds
Publisher: Gary Groth

Foolbert Funnies: Histories and Other Fictions is copyright © 2015 Fantagraphics Books. All comics and text, including the cover, are copyright © 2015 Frank Stack, except the foreword "Sometimes the Only Thing" copyright © 2015 Bob Levin and "Rude: AWAKEning" copyright © 2015 Michael Price. All rights reserved. Published by Fantagraphics Books, 7563 Lake City Way NE, Seattle, WA 98115. Permission to reproduce for reviews and notices must be obtained from the publisher or the author. For a free full-color catalog of comics and cartooning, call 1-800-657-1100. Our books may be viewed—and purchased—on our website at www.fantagraphics.com.

First Fantagraphics Books edition: January 2015

ISBN 978-1-60699-808-3

Printed in Korea

TABLE OF CONTENTS

SOMETIMES THE ONLY THING

by Bob Levin

"Sometimes drawing cartoons is the only thing you can do."—Frank Stack (1996)

If you are as chowder-headed as me, all you know about Frank Stack is that (1) he cartooned *The New Adventures of Jesus*, which was—or maybe wasn't—the first underground comic; (2) he illustrated *Our Cancer Year*, in which the enjoyment of his work was somewhat hampered by having to digest a text which went down like 20W-50 motor oil; and (3) he taught art long enough at the University of Missouri to retire as a professor emeritus, a perhaps unprecedented end for an underground cartoonist, smacking as it does of numbing footnotes and mummifying committee meetings. So, boy, let me tell you, having devoured the volume you are holding, there are gaps in your knowledge as broad as Kansas and delights to be gained as bright as Oz.

Foolbert Funnies clears the chopped clams and cubed potatoes from the neural pathways with blasts from thirty years of Stack's comic work, ranging from single-page riffs to multi-leaf symphonies. Bubbles of bile boil over throughout, but the damn book should carry a product warning to protect members of the public who might be queasy about walking around with a smile permanently pressed upon their lips, a sharp cackle occasionally breaking through.

Stack has frequently cited "outrage" as the fuel firing his comic work, and while he does scorn such targets as authoritarianism, censorship, consumerism, mindless patriotism, the CIA, Richard Nixon, and George H. W. Bush, this seems fairly modest for a guy who has disclosed his displeasure with all "rotten, power-mongering, paper-shuffling assholes who think work is to buy cheap and sell dear" to Jim Ottaviani, in a *Comics Journal* interview. But Stack also believes that, whatever the ferocity of his feelings, he should leaven them with humor. "[T]he bottom line consideration about a cartoon," he added, "is that it's funny . . ."

Stack began creating comics in the 1960s, having shaped his sensibility through superheroes, ECs, classic newspaper strips, and movie serials. He was in his early twenties; and the future, his own, the nation's, and—under the shadow of The Bomb—the world's, seemed problematic. While headed for a career in High Art, he was attracted to comics because their "thoroughly disrespectful aspect" left him free to express his doubts, assault his enemies, and prick pomposity's balloons. Then, there was the additional liberating factor that, by aiming for an audience of a few like-minded friends, nothing he wrote and drew would be published anyway. When *New Adventures* proved his market analysis shallow, Stack kept producing. Times might change, but his indignation kept rolling.

"You choose a medium for what it does well," Stack once said, explaining the disparate nature of his work to an inquiring reporter. And while his pen-and-ink drawings, watercolors, and oils would earn him a career retrospective at the State Historical Society of Missouri, he would regularly lay out a gridded page for what he could not otherwise suitably express.

These pages offer expressions for everyone—especially those among the "every" who can guffaw at post–Harvey Kurtzman kidding of superheroes; are open to loopy conspiratorial thinking; may be tickled by the idea of an $89 time machine at Sears ($239.88 from Spiegel), with indecipherable instructions in Japanese; enjoy gawking at naked Amazons and Athenians grappling outside the walls of Troy, while griping about "smartass bitches" and "dumb grunt dog face asshole jock straps";

and don't mind laughing at a cut-rate ($10/hour), obese, thick-lipped, Sambo-talking black psychiatrist who smokes cigars, sports a derby, and stomps rats as they scurry, mid-session, across his floor.

To me, three stories merit special attention. All are biographical; all occur in different centuries and in different lands. "No Hope. No Fear." recounts the life of Caravaggio; "The Bard Must Die!" speculatively fills in gaps in what is known about Shakespeare's; and "The Lying Ear" imaginatively tackles van Gogh's time in Arles with Paul Gauguin. Stack is a masterful visual artist. He is, as well, a fine writer, who takes delight in the imaginative use of language. (It is not uncommon for words to occupy half the space his page offers.) And these stories, with their broad scope and serious subject matter, permit the full display of his chops.

All three stories required extensive research for them to ring with authenticity. The text had to be factually correct in order to suit the time and place depicted (save for some humorous dollops of anachronistic dialogue, as in "cashflow problems," "redneck chiseler," and "In your dreams, fatboy" from "No Hope No Fear.") and to be consistent with the known personalities of the principals. Then, once the "known" had been assessed, Stack had to think out and fill in the "unknown" in ways that, while in accord with the reality he had established, would jostle/jolt/jab his readers sufficiently to surprise/delight/provoke them. In each case, he succeeded smashingly.

Stack succeeded equally with his visuals. He came of age as an artist at a time when the taste-making pooh-bahs were pulling away from valuing the mastery of eye-pleasing technical skills—what Duchamp dismissed as "retinal art"—for work that, even if slapdash or crass, engaged more cognitively wired segments of the noggin. The illustrative stopped ringing the cash registers at Sotheby's or dominating column inches in *Artforum*. But in the comic book forum, the better Stack drew, the more his effort mattered. His skill with pencil and ink drew his readers more deeply into his stories. It tellingly strengthened mood, developed emotion, enriched sense of place, and deepened insight into character. The fluctuations of his panels' layouts enhanced the fluctuations between fact and imagination, memory and wish, and desire and polemic, that make up recorded history.

These stories, one surmises, must have been a hoot for Stack to deliver. He took the opportunity they provided to render cityscapes of early-seventeenth-century London, churches of late-sixteenth-century Italy, Paris in 1888, and Whitechapel's slum when the Ripper stalked it. He got to costume royalty and clergy in different centuries and portray sword and knife fights, severed heads (one shrunken), and hallucinated demons. He got to take a pass at capturing Caravaggio's *The Death of the Virgin*, the title page of the original King James Bible, Gauguin's Samoan nudes, and, most deliciously, subject matter that would show up on van Gogh's easel before the artist knew he would attempt it.

It is always gratifying to see an artist who has long worked with skill and seriousness of purpose, uncompromised by commercial considerations and celebrated with appreciative attention. It is good for that artist. It is good for others artist laboring with similar commitment, often wondering, "Why the fuck bother?" And it is good for a society, which can only benefit by keeping these artists pursuing their personal visions for the enrichment of thought and culture some of them—OK, some few of them—will provide.

So hats off to Frank Stack and Fantagraphics for this addition to the parade.

INTRODUCTION

by Frank Stack

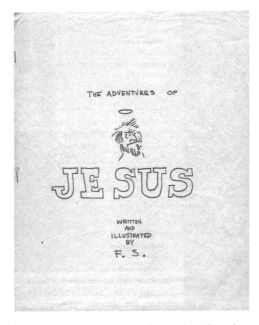

By 1962, I thought my comics career was over. I had drawn comics in high school for three years, publishing my first cartoons at age fourteen, and spent another three working for a monthly humor magazine at the University of Texas (UT). But, after a false start as an editorial cartoonist for a big city daily newspaper and as a whiz in an advertising agency, I had gone back to graduate school for painting when the Army decided it wanted me. I found myself stationed on Governor's Island in New York Harbor. It seemed that I was at an impasse.

THE ADVENTURES OF
JE SUS
WRITTEN
AND
ILLUSTRATED
BY
F. S.

I was married, living off-post in a Manhattan apartment, and had some friends from UT—including Gilbert Shelton, Bill Helmer, and Lynn Ashby—and made more, until it was a pretty jolly circle. Shelton was working on a publishable version of *Wonder Warthog*, and I drew the first of my *New Adventures of Jesus* cartoons (assuming that they couldn't be published) and hung out with Harvey Kurtzman and his associate editor for *Help!*, Chuck Alverson. Terry Gilliam, later of Monty Python, was part of the group, among others. Exciting times for all of us, I think.

But when I got out of the Army, my wife, Robbie, and I just went back to Texas and then to Wyoming for graduate school. My contact with the world of publishing seemed to be over. I got the master's degree in art, looked for a university faculty position, and got one at the University of Missouri (MU) in September 1963, teaching drawing, painting, and printmaking. I stayed, got tenure, and finally retired, thirty-nine years later.

The university didn't know it in the '60s and '70s, but I was drawing cartoons all along, sending many of them to Gilbert Shelton. Shelton was determined to make what would become "underground comics" *[ed. note: 1960s–'70s self- or small press–published comics that defied taboos and were mainly distributed through tabloids, head shops, and the mail]* work, and finally he and his Texas pals plunged into the publishing business themselves with Rip Off Press in San Francisco. My comic book *The New Adventures of Jesus* ("if you liked the New Testament, you'll LOVE this new improved Testament") was their first publication. It was announced for 1968, but it didn't actually appear till January 1969.

Of course, the country was in major turmoil in those years: beginning with the Kennedy assassination just months after I began working at MU, followed by war protests, more assassinations, the Chicago 1968 Democratic National Convention, campus shootings, and multiplying outrages. I didn't do paintings about such things, but I drew cartoons. "The Chancellor!" was about a cruel and cowardly official at the University of Missouri who had called out the National Guard to deal with a peaceful student protest on the campus quadrangle.

After some tense disagreement with senior art faculty, I squeaked by and got tenure in 1969. I took a sabbatical leave with my family: wife Robbie and preschool-age children Joan and Robert. We went to Paris and stayed from August 1970 till June 1971. Inspired by the art that I saw, I painted some large figure compositions and oil and watercolor landscapes, and drew cartoons. The *Amazons* book was a response to the persistent theme in classical art, which I saw in the Louvre, of combat between male Greek soldiers and female warriors. I related the subject to the battle-of-the-

sexes dynamics I'd seen at work as a kid. On one level it was a critique of sports and locker room bullying as well.

Amazons is my second Amazon comic; the first, titled *Amazon Comics*, published by Rip Off Press in 1971, is now out of print. *Amazons* puts the super-macho Greek heroes of the Trojan War in direct, reluctant conflict with the Wonder Women of Greek legend. It was inspired partly by a no-girls-allowed scenario from my childhood (end result: Barbara Williams punched John Wesley's face

so hard he went home crying) and literary accounts of the Trojan War that describe Achilles fighting, and even falling in love with, the Amazon warrior Penthesilea. Because this version is *my* story, I took some fictional license and called the Amazon protagonist Hippolyta rather than Penthesilea. (Penthesilea was the heroine of my first book.) One *Amazons* art influence is Amazonamachy, which is drawing, painting, and sculpture depicting battles between Greeks and Amazons, including the wonderful, simple, clean-line vase drawings of the so-called Penthesilea Painter.

Though I doubt there was actually a race of women warriors, I think that folktales and persistent literary myths are based on something that sticks in people's minds—maybe like seeing a Barbara Williams knock a John Wesley flat on his butt and thinking it served him right, for believing that he could bully her just because she wasn't a guy.

Shelton and his pals at Rip Off, in 1971, seemed willing to publish my comics, and so I got excited and worked hard. The earlier Jesus cartoons were pretty casual drawing, but I had some pride in my craft and started working harder to make it look good. After all, I was a graduate school figure drawing teacher. Dick Evens, my masterful drawing teacher at Wyoming, looked at the Jesus book and said, "My God! I've never done that many drawings in my life!"

It wasn't long before I was thinking that drawing was drawing: no real difference among illustrations, cartoons, and so-called fine art. The first time I remember trying to use my fairly well developed sense of naturalistic landscape drawing in the comics was in "A True Story or a Paranoid Fantasy," where the action is set around my own house. I got a chuckle out of drawing my own bent-wire fence and the litter in my bedroom accurately, as backgrounds for the ridiculous action. The realism seemed to make it funnier to me. The other side of that coin was to simplify my drawing and painting to make it more graphic, as good comic drawing is. And I wasn't thinking of superhero stuff—even the better stuff, like Jack Kirby and Frank Frazetta—more like Roy Crane, Alex Raymond, Frank King, Burne Hogarth, Walt Kelly, and Hal Foster. My feeling was that my "fine art" drawing and painting was strengthened by the expressive influence of comics.

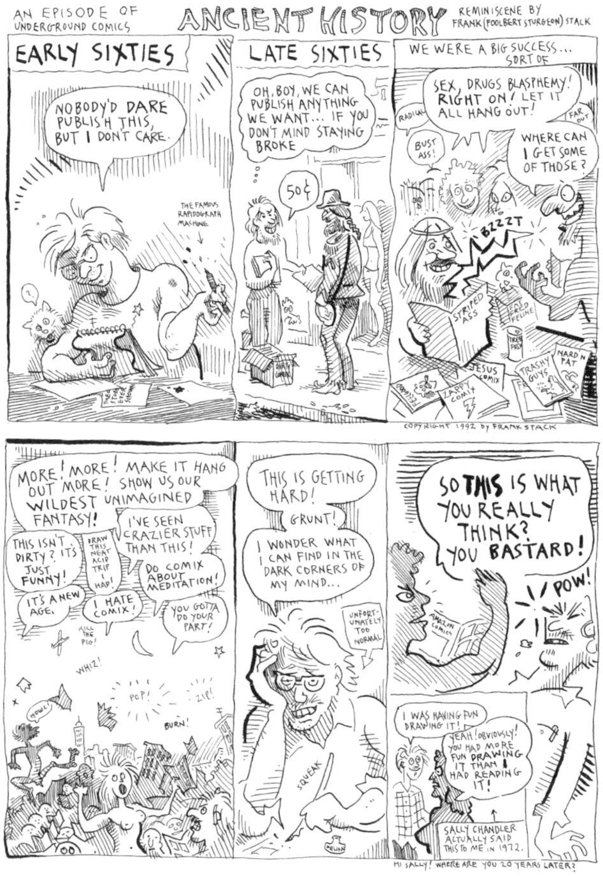

AN EPISODE OF UNDERGROUND COMICS
ANCIENT HISTORY
REMINISCENE BY FRANK (FOOLBERT STURGEON) STACK
EARLY SIXTIES
NOBODY'D DARE PUBLISH THIS, BUT I DON'T CARE.
THE FAMOUS RAPIDOGRAPH MACHINE
LATE SIXTIES
OH, BOY, WE CAN PUBLISH ANYTHING WE WANT... IF YOU DON'T MIND STAYING BROKE
50¢
DIRTY COMIX
WE WERE A BIG SUCCESS... SORT OF
SEX, DRUGS BLASPHEMY! RIGHT ON! LET IT ALL HANG OUT!
RADICAL
FAR OUT
BUST ASS!
WHERE CAN I GET SOME OF THOSE?
BZZZT
STRIPED ASS
FAT FRED FELINE
JESUS COMIX
ZAPPY COMIX
TRASHY GUYS
NARD N PAT
COPYRIGHT 1992 by FRANK STACK
MORE! MORE! MAKE IT HANG OUT MORE! SHOW US OUR WILDEST UNIMAGINED FANTASY!
I'VE SEEN CRAZIER STUFF THAN THIS!
THIS ISN'T DIRTY? IT'S JUST FUNNY!
DRAW THIS NEAT ACID TRIP I HAD!
DO COMIX ABOUT MEDITATION!
IT'S A NEW AGE.
I HATE COMIX!
YOU GOTTA DO YOUR PART!
KILL THE PIG!
WHIZ!
HOWL!
POP!
ZIP!
BURN!
THIS IS GETTING HARD!
GRUNT!
I WONDER WHAT I CAN FIND IN THE DARK CORNERS OF MY MIND...
UNFORTUNATELY TOO NORMAL
SQUEAK
SO THIS IS WHAT YOU REALLY THINK? YOU BASTARD!
POW!
AMAZON COMICS
I WAS HAVING FUN DRAWING IT!
YEAH! OBVIOUSLY! YOU HAD MORE FUN DRAWING IT THAN I HAD READING IT!
SALLY CHANDLER ACTUALLY SAID THIS TO ME IN 1972.
HI SALLY! WHERE ARE YOU 20 YEARS LATER?

The flame of the underground seemed to be burning hot in the early '70s. We were defying the Comics Code and actually drawing anything we wanted. We were the best in the world: Robert Crumb and S. Clay Wilson, Victor Moscoso, Gilbert Shelton—I hate to mention too many because then I'll get roasted for leaving out so many good ones. The great talents were coming to the underground, not to the world of museum and gallery art. In theory, at least, it was wide open to everyone. I think—feuding though there was—that the publishing opportunities that opened up to women and minorities played a major role in attracting attention to what good artists some of them were. Strange to consider women a minority since they are more than half of us.

It seemed a matter of principle that nothing was off-limits. There was a mantra of "let it all hang out!" and we tried. Unfortunately, there was a lot of offensive stuff. Well, of course there was. It was more about feeling than thinking. Actually seeing the violent bigotry, sexist and racist perversions, and other demons from the depths of the id laid out on cheap, already-disreputable comic book pages led to a rather general cry of "So, *that's* what you think! *You bastard!*"

I guess that's just how it goes. So, should the artists say, "Oh, I'm sorry to offend you. I apologize abjectly?"

Well, *no*.

What do I say about Doctor Feelgood? The character was based on a friend of mine from Kansas City named Don Douglass—a great, funny, free spirit, a good artist himself—and some of the stories were things he told me. The bit about stomping the rat was something that I witnessed a sergeant do in 1960, interrupting an indoctrination lecture. It's about contrasting racial stereotypes: a neurotic, white, intellectual patient looks for a bargain in therapy and finds a good-humored black person in a somewhat seedy professional practice giving psychological advice—simple common sense. It's a joke. Sorry. It is also an opportunity to parody adventure fantasies.

The "bright-burning flame" I spoke of was effectively, and I suspect purposefully, snuffed by the Great Newsprint Shortage of the mid-'70s. It was the end of marginally profitable publications, about which the involved publishers can speak better than I. The result was the end of the underground. The artists were obliged to go back to the much-hated Real World. Of course the end of the Vietnam War and the end of the compulsory draft played major roles in that development, too.

Rip Off Press, in the later part of the '70s, established The Rip Off Publishing Syndicate to serve the then-still-flourishing alternative press: little, intermittently published newspapers, often in connection with colleges and universities. Probably the most—or maybe only—wholesome series I ever did was the Pingy-Poo cartoons for Rip Off, which I did for about two years. It was about my own silly little dog, and the characters and settings are pretty much real: my wife and me, Tommy Cat—even the dog-sitter, Mattie—are real characters. The pooch was long-lived but suffered from systemic damage from an early bout with distemper. Macho guys seemed to hate him, but I got offers to keep it running in respectable venues if I'd just quit doing so many shit jokes. After he died I couldn't rouse any enthusiasm for making fun of him anymore.

My historical stories began with questions about well-known figures in art and literary history. In the case of "The Bard Must Die!" it was "Could William Shakespeare have been involved in writing the King James Version of the Bible?" And, necessarily following, "Who was he really, and why do we know so little about him?"

With "The Lying Ear: Vincent van Gogh and Paul Gauguin in Arles," I was curious about how Vincent van Gogh's "electric arguments" with Paul Gauguin could have led to his disastrous breakdown in the winter of 1888. What was going on in his hyperactive mind and imagination?

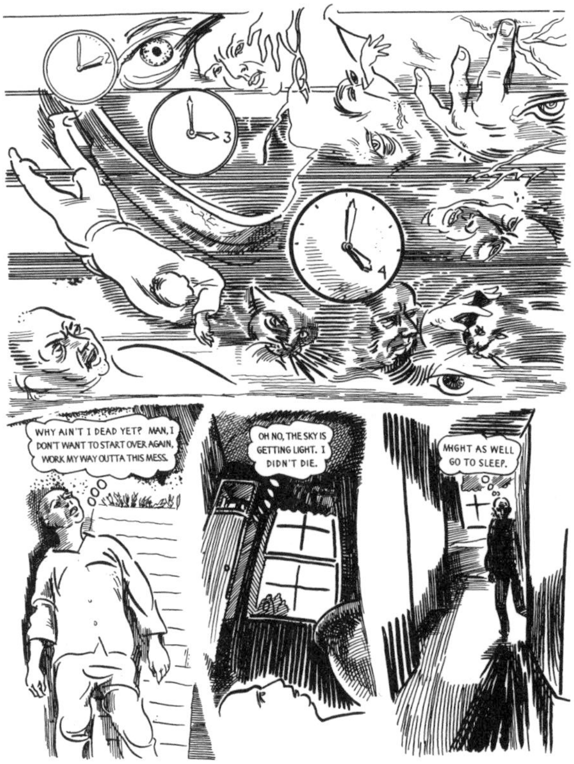
WHY AIN'T I DEAD YET? MAN, I DON'T WANT TO START OVER AGAIN, WORK MY WAY OUTTA THIS MESS.
OH NO, THE SKY IS GETTING LIGHT. I DIDN'T DIE.
MIGHT AS WELL GO TO SLEEP.

"No Hope. No Fear." focused on the ultimately fatal crisis in Michelangelo Merisi Caravaggio's career, which led to the killing, his murder conviction, and his permanent flight from Rome.

I did write and draw those stories and they are collected in this book. Others I planned but did not ultimately draw were about Michelangelo's possible forgery of the Laocoön Group, Benvenuto Cellini's story that he had saved the Pope's life during the Siege and Sack of Rome in 1527, and why Henri Matisse left Paris permanently to live out his life away from his family in the South of France. I would have liked to do these stories, but I wasn't able to sell a publisher on the ideas when I was still in a mood to take on big projects like those.

My notion of historical fiction is neither to illustrate a popular notion of

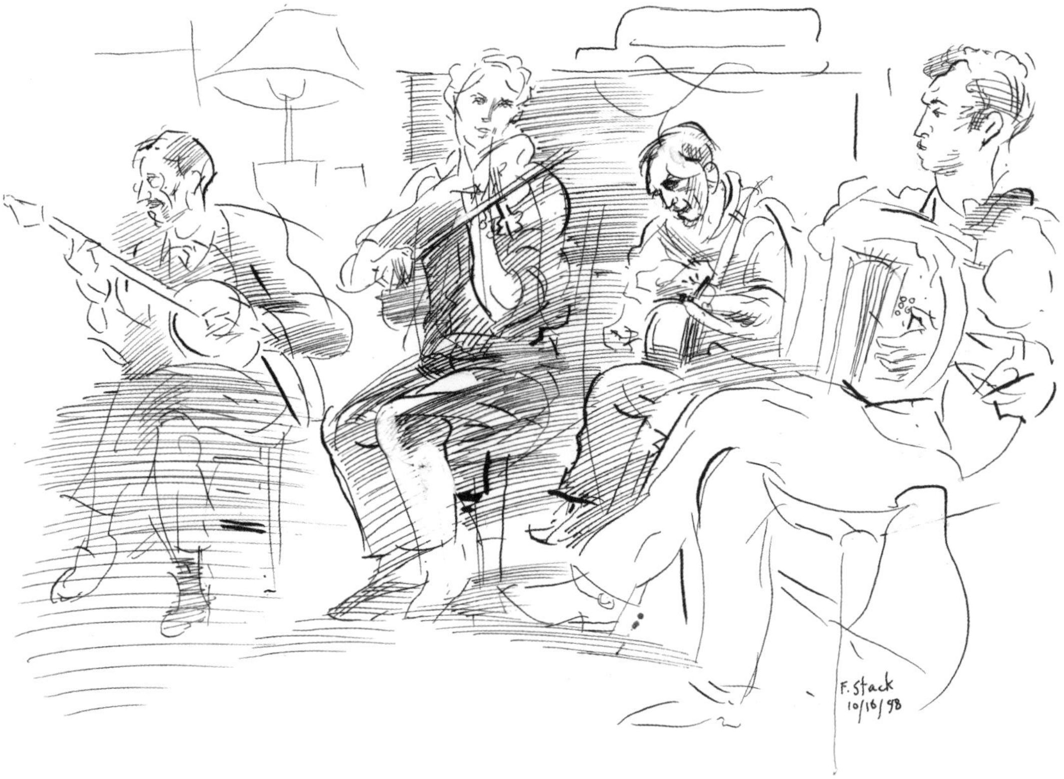
F. Stack
10/16/98

events nor to fabricate explanations by altering known facts, but to propose a feasible hypothesis to explain gaps in the established record.

Generally I have not done collaborations, but I have worked with Harvey Pekar many times for *American Splendor*, and with Pekar and Joyce Brabner for the graphic novel *Our Cancer Year*. The comic zombie story "Rude: AWAKEning" by Michael H. Price, here collected, is another exception to the rule. I worked on a couple of other stories with him that I think have not been published. I'd just been teaching anatomical drawing, so drawing the revenant's body coming to pieces was a lot of fun. Price did the titles, lettering, and breakdowns. I drew the pictures.

Like almost everybody who grew up in the South, I am saturated by popular culture trash, and I both love it because it's mine and hate it because it's trash, so I've made fun of it all my life.

Alley Oop was my favorite daily continuity strip, and V. T. Hamlin was one of the first artists I learned by name. Years later, in the '80s, I finally met him and helped get his work reprinted. I am still listed as the editor of *Alley Oop* magazine, published in Colorado by Andy Feighery.

The Adventures of the Phanty was pretty much a joke I drew in a sketchbook while I was staying in Sauve, France, mostly to amuse Pete Poplaski and Robert Crumb. Poplaski pretended to take offense, saying, "What a bad mood you must be in, to make fun of your boyhood heroes!"

While in Sauve I drew Crumb playing with a group of his friends.

The last movie serials (chapter plays) were made in the early '50s, so few living fans would even remember them, but the cliffhanger was part of my cherished upbringing. "How can they possibly get out of *this* fix?"

I had to wait about forty years to find out how the Phantom escaped from the gladiatorial duel with a gorilla who was breaking his back at the end of a chapter. It seemed like a good format for a series of comic book episodes, so I drew the first chapter of *The Adventures of Dirty Diana*, in which she apparently gets speared to death at the end of an eight-page story. It lay around for years before *Mineshaft* agreed to publish it. They've done six chapters in subsequent issues.

About the political cartoons: I suppose all cartoonists draw them, whether they are published or not. Paddy Booshwah is, of course, George Herbert Walker Bush, expostulating my notion that he was sort of a goofy CIA agent from the get-go. Do you really think that bunch would have allowed anybody to get appointed head of the agency who wasn't already in their pocket? "Patriotism for Dummies" was my response to the country's disgustingly shallow, flag-flapping response to 9/11. "Never forget!"

Never forget what? To be afraid.

Can't we make up our minds whether we are brave or we are cowards?

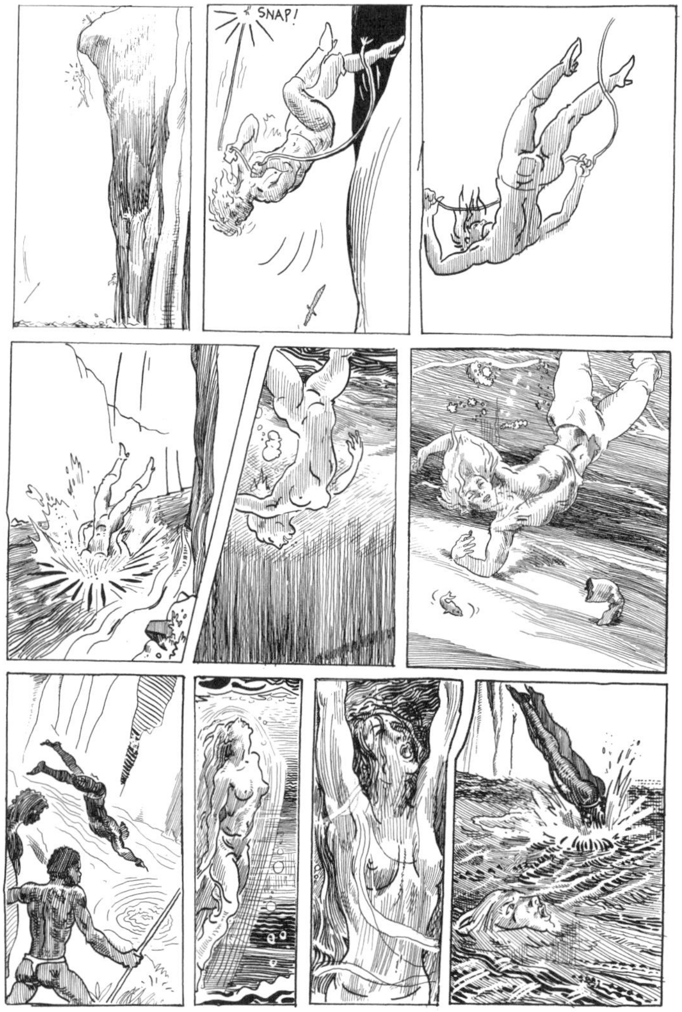
SNAP!

CHRONOLOGY

1937   Born October 31, 1937 at St. Joseph's Hospital, Houston, Texas, to Norma and Maurice Stack. Lived in Houston till age three and a half.

1941   Moved to Monahans in West Texas.

1943   Birth of my only sibling, brother Stephen, February 1943.

1944   Started first grade in Monahans, September 1944. Moved back to Houston, resumed first grade in North Houston, then in South Houston. On a visit to relatives in Center, in East Texas, contracted typhoid fever from a contaminated well, as did my mother and brother. Quarantined and missed two months of first grade.

1944–
1952   Continued public school in South Houston through eighth grade. Moved to Corpus Christi, Texas, the summer of 1952.

1952–
1955   Ninth through eleventh grades at W. B. Ray High School in Corpus Christi: published cartoons in the semiweekly high school newspaper, *El Tejano*. Moved to Midland, Texas, for last year of high school.

1955–
1956   Published drawings for weekly high school newspaper the *Bulldog*. Worked at Womack and Snelson Advertising Agency, and as the Wilson Supply Company warehouse gofer in Odessa. Began as a freshman at University of Texas in Austin, fall 1956. Immediately joined the *Texas Ranger* staff, writing stories and drawing cartoons. Associate editor 1957–1958, editor 1958–1959. Remained in Austin summers and never lived with my parents again. Met Gilbert Shelton 1959 and graduated with a bachelor of fine arts that year.

1959   Married Mildred Roberta Powell, June 1959. Moved to Houston to take job with the *Houston Chronicle* as associate arts editor. Took and passed Army physical as 1-A. Joined Army Reserve, was called up and sent to basic training, ending *Chronicle* job. Never lived in Houston again. Basic training at Fort Ord, California, and then posted to Presidio of San Francisco.

1960   Returned for summer in Austin when Robbie was in graduate school for master's degree in English. September 1960: went to Chicago for a year at the School of the Art Institute of Chicago and studied painting, drawing, and printmaking. Robbie taught junior high school in suburb of Argo, Illinois. Applied for graduate assistantships at other schools for graduate school in art: accepted offer from University of Wyoming in Laramie.

1961   Summer 1961 in Austin. Never lived in Texas again. Began grad school at Laramie, but in October 1961 was called up by Army Reserve for the Berlin Wall Crisis, and attached to a data processing unit posted to Governor's Island in New York Harbor. Drew first Jesus cartoons and showed them to Gilbert Shelton, and he showed me his new Wonder Warthog stories. Remained in Army and New York until June 1962.

1962–
1963   Returned to Laramie to finish graduate school, 1962–1963. Accepted offer to teach at University of Missouri and moved to Columbia, Missouri, June 1963. Shelton, in Austin, published first version of *The New Adventures of Jesus* by "FS." Had been working at MU only three months before Kennedy Assassination.

1965–
1971   Daughter Joan Elaine born 1965 and son Robert Huntington in 1966. More Jesus cartoons, some published in Shelton's magazine *The Austin Iconoclastic Newsletter* (aka *THE*). Taught watercolor, figure drawing, oil painting, and printmaking. First trip to Europe, summer of 1968: Amsterdam, Paris, and London. Tenure in 1969: Rip Off Press in San Francisco published *The New Adventures of Jesus*. Sabbatical leave to Paris with family, August 1970 to June 1971: lived at 12 rue Monge.

1972–
1988   *Feelgood* and *Amazon Comics* published 1972. *Dorman's Doggie* comic strip for Rip Off Publishing Syndicate 1977–1978. *The New Adventures of Jesus* collected 1979, most copies of which were destroyed in Rip Off's warehouse fire.
　　　　Lots of university duties, including chair of art department 1977–1983. *Feelgood Funnies* #2 was published in 1983. First collaborated with Harvey Pekar in 1987. Began teaching comics class at University of Missouri in 1988.

1991–
1992   For *Blab!*: "The Lying Ear" (1991), "The Bard Must Die" (1991), "No Hope. No Fear." (1992).

1993   *Our Cancer Year*.

1998   Death of wife, Robbie.

2000   Retired.

2002   Taught last classes.

2014   Still alive.

Juvenilia

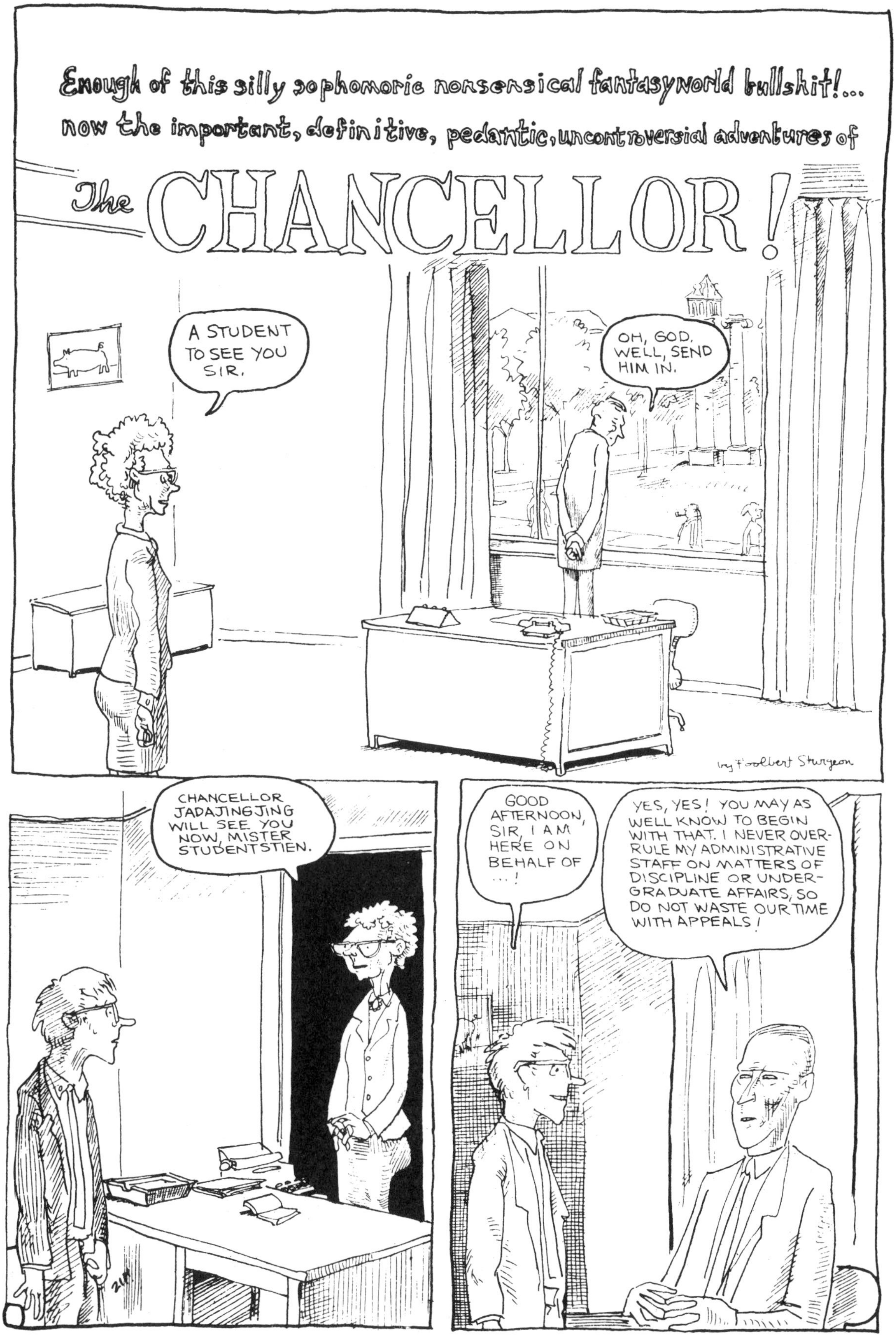
Enough of this silly sophomoric nonsensical fantasyworld bullshit!...
now the important, definitive, pedantic, uncontroversial adventures of
The CHANCELLOR!
A STUDENT TO SEE YOU SIR.
OH, GOD. WELL, SEND HIM IN.
by Foolbert Sturgeon
CHANCELLOR JADAJINGJING WILL SEE YOU NOW, MISTER STUDENTSTIEN.
GOOD AFTERNOON, SIR, I AM HERE ON BEHALF OF ...!
YES, YES! YOU MAY AS WELL KNOW TO BEGIN WITH THAT. I NEVER OVER-RULE MY ADMINISTRATIVE STAFF ON MATTERS OF DISCIPLINE OR UNDER-GRADUATE AFFAIRS, SO DO NOT WASTE OUR TIME WITH APPEALS!

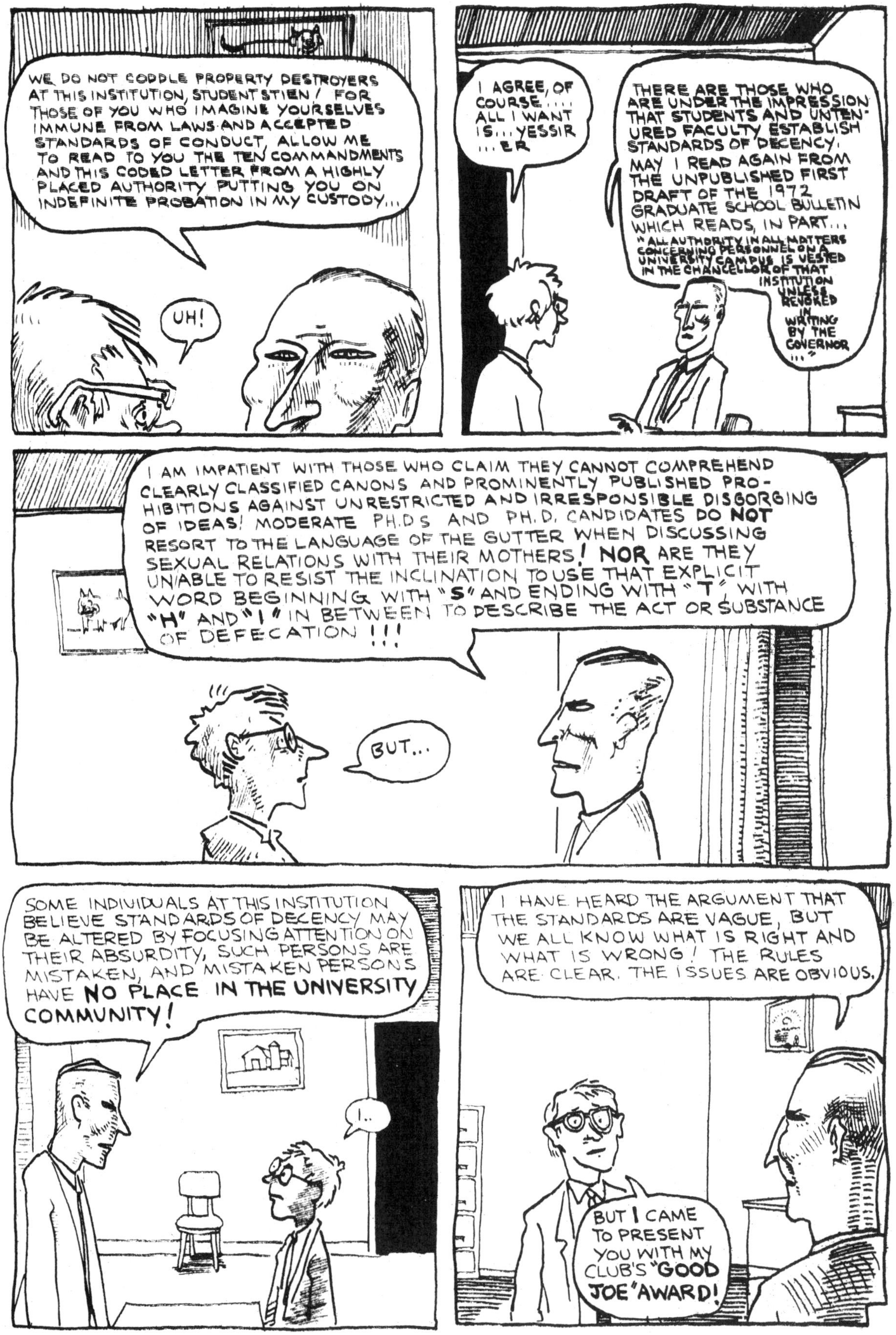

WE DO NOT CODDLE PROPERTY DESTROYERS AT THIS INSTITUTION, STUDENT STIEN! FOR THOSE OF YOU WHO IMAGINE YOURSELVES IMMUNE FROM LAWS AND ACCEPTED STANDARDS OF CONDUCT, ALLOW ME TO READ TO YOU THE TEN COMMANDMENTS AND THIS CODED LETTER FROM A HIGHLY PLACED AUTHORITY PUTTING YOU ON INDEFINITE PROBATION IN MY CUSTODY...
UH!
I AGREE, OF COURSE.... ALL I WANT IS... YESSIR ...ER
THERE ARE THOSE WHO ARE UNDER THE IMPRESSION THAT STUDENTS AND UNTENURED FACULTY ESTABLISH STANDARDS OF DECENCY. MAY I READ AGAIN FROM THE UNPUBLISHED FIRST DRAFT OF THE 1972 GRADUATE SCHOOL BULLETIN WHICH READS, IN PART... "ALL AUTHORITY IN ALL MATTERS CONCERNING PERSONNEL ON A UNIVERSITY CAMPUS IS VESTED IN THE CHANCELLOR OF THAT INSTITUTION UNLESS REVOKED IN WRITING BY THE GOVERNOR..."
I AM IMPATIENT WITH THOSE WHO CLAIM THEY CANNOT COMPREHEND CLEARLY CLASSIFIED CANONS AND PROMINENTLY PUBLISHED PROHIBITIONS AGAINST UNRESTRICTED AND IRRESPONSIBLE DISGORGING OF IDEAS! MODERATE PH.D'S AND PH.D. CANDIDATES DO NOT RESORT TO THE LANGUAGE OF THE GUTTER WHEN DISCUSSING SEXUAL RELATIONS WITH THEIR MOTHERS! NOR ARE THEY UNABLE TO RESIST THE INCLINATION TO USE THAT EXPLICIT WORD BEGINNING WITH "S" AND ENDING WITH "T" WITH "H" AND "I" IN BETWEEN TO DESCRIBE THE ACT OR SUBSTANCE OF DEFECATION!!!
BUT...
SOME INDIVIDUALS AT THIS INSTITUTION BELIEVE STANDARDS OF DECENCY MAY BE ALTERED BY FOCUSING ATTENTION ON THEIR ABSURDITY. SUCH PERSONS ARE MISTAKEN, AND MISTAKEN PERSONS HAVE NO PLACE IN THE UNIVERSITY COMMUNITY!
I..
I HAVE HEARD THE ARGUMENT THAT THE STANDARDS ARE VAGUE, BUT WE ALL KNOW WHAT IS RIGHT AND WHAT IS WRONG! THE RULES ARE CLEAR. THE ISSUES ARE OBVIOUS.
BUT I CAME TO PRESENT YOU WITH MY CLUB'S "GOOD JOE" AWARD!

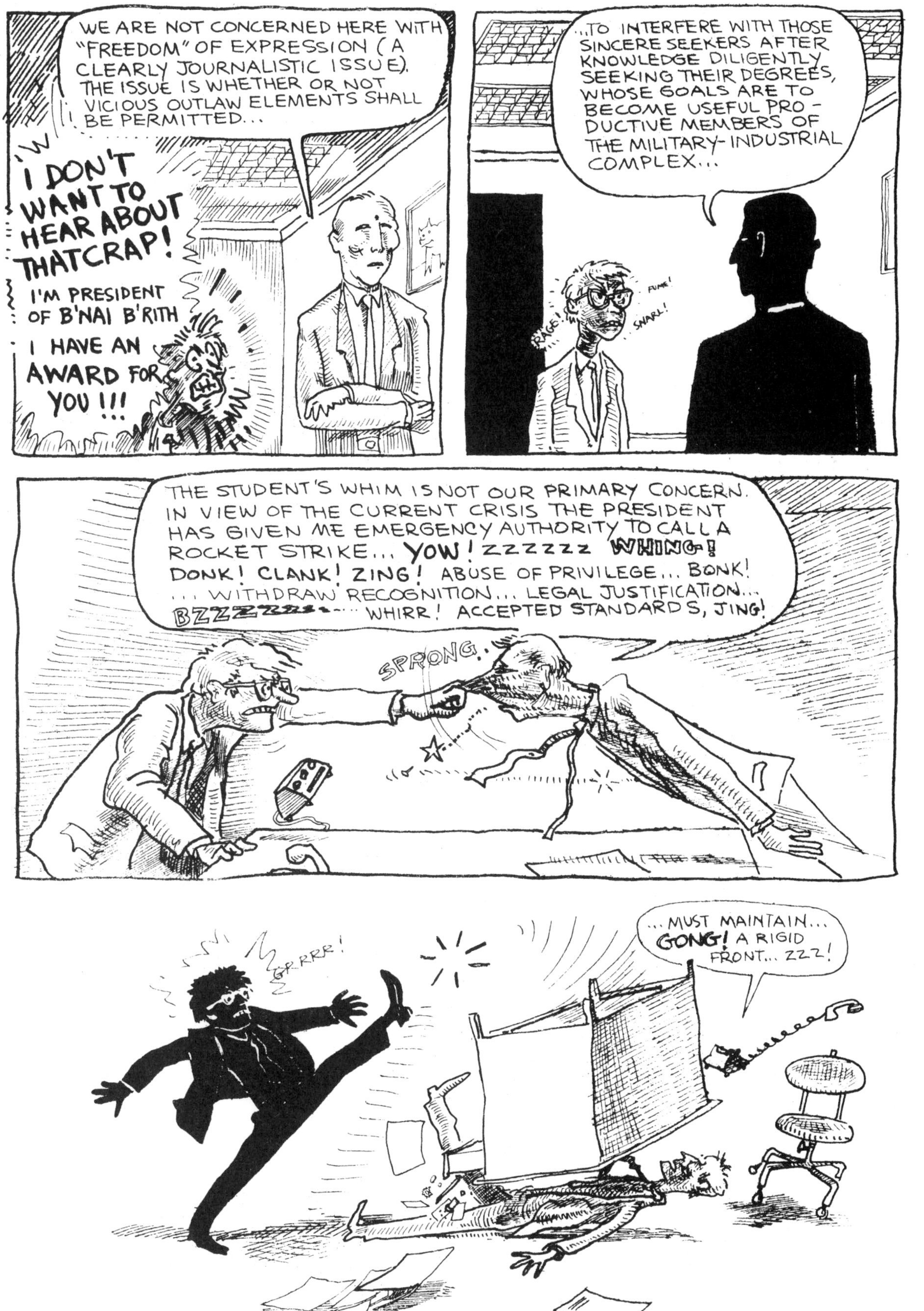
WE ARE NOT CONCERNED HERE WITH "FREEDOM" OF EXPRESSION (A CLEARLY JOURNALISTIC ISSUE). THE ISSUE IS WHETHER OR NOT VICIOUS OUTLAW ELEMENTS SHALL BE PERMITTED...
I DON'T WANT TO HEAR ABOUT THATCRAP!
I'M PRESIDENT OF B'NAI B'RITH
I HAVE AN AWARD FOR YOU!!!
...TO INTERFERE WITH THOSE SINCERE SEEKERS AFTER KNOWLEDGE DILIGENTLY SEEKING THEIR DEGREES, WHOSE GOALS ARE TO BECOME USEFUL PRODUCTIVE MEMBERS OF THE MILITARY-INDUSTRIAL COMPLEX...
RAGE!
FUME!
SNARL!
THE STUDENT'S WHIM IS NOT OUR PRIMARY CONCERN. IN VIEW OF THE CURRENT CRISIS THE PRESIDENT HAS GIVEN ME EMERGENCY AUTHORITY TO CALL A ROCKET STRIKE... YOW! ZZZZZZ WHING! DONK! CLANK! ZING! ABUSE OF PRIVILEGE... BONK! ... WITHDRAW RECOGNITION... LEGAL JUSTIFICATION... BZZZZZZZ... WHIRR! ACCEPTED STANDARDS, JING!
SPRONG
GRRRR!
...MUST MAINTAIN... GONG! A RIGID FRONT... ZZZ!

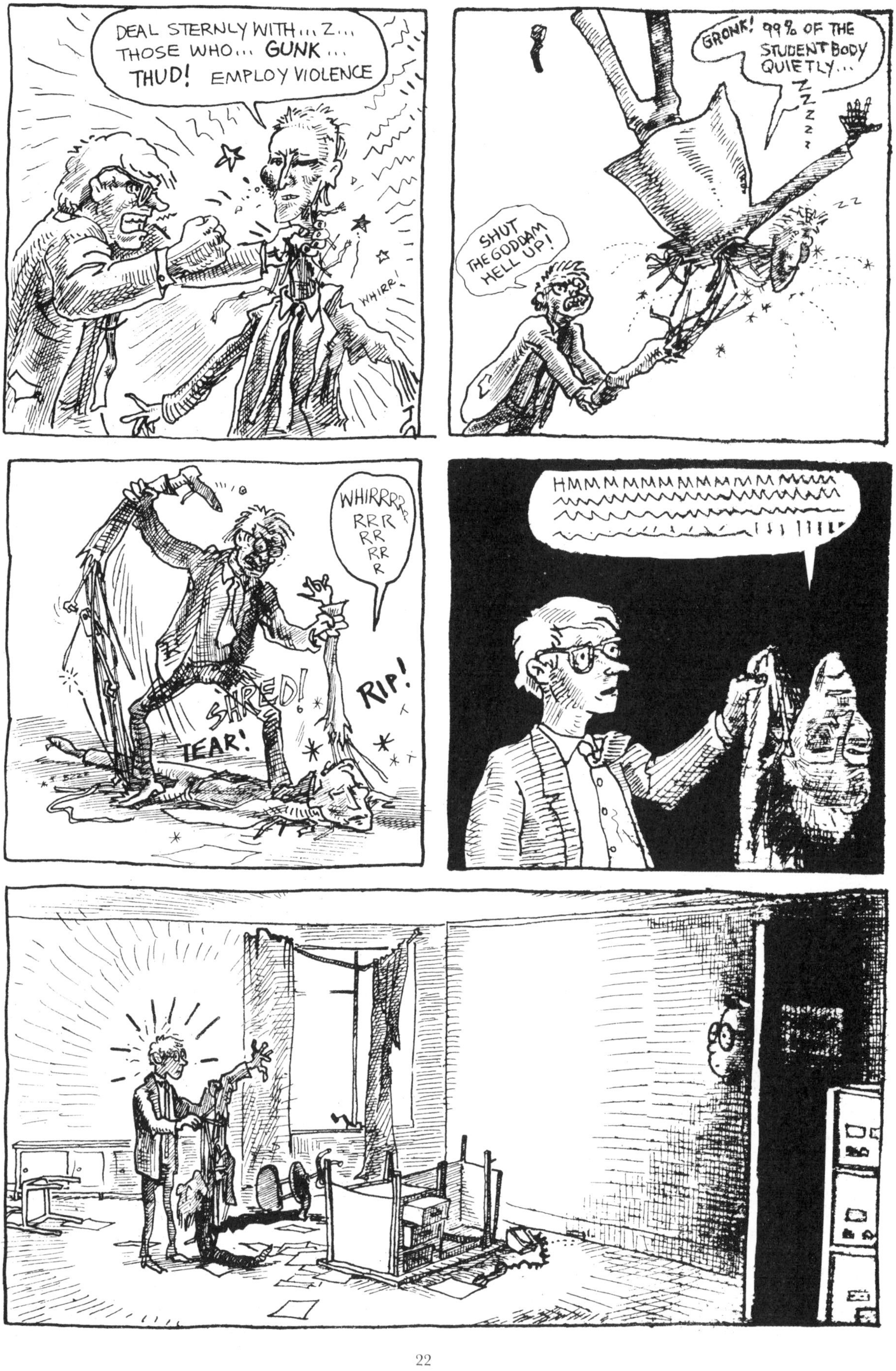
DEAL STERNLY WITH... Z... THOSE WHO... GUNK... THUD! EMPLOY VIOLENCE
WHIRR!
GRONK! 99% OF THE STUDENT BODY QUIETLY...
ZZZZ
SHUT THE GODDAM HELL UP!
WHIRRRRR RRR RR RR R
SHRED!
RIP!
TEAR!
HMMMMMMMMMMMM

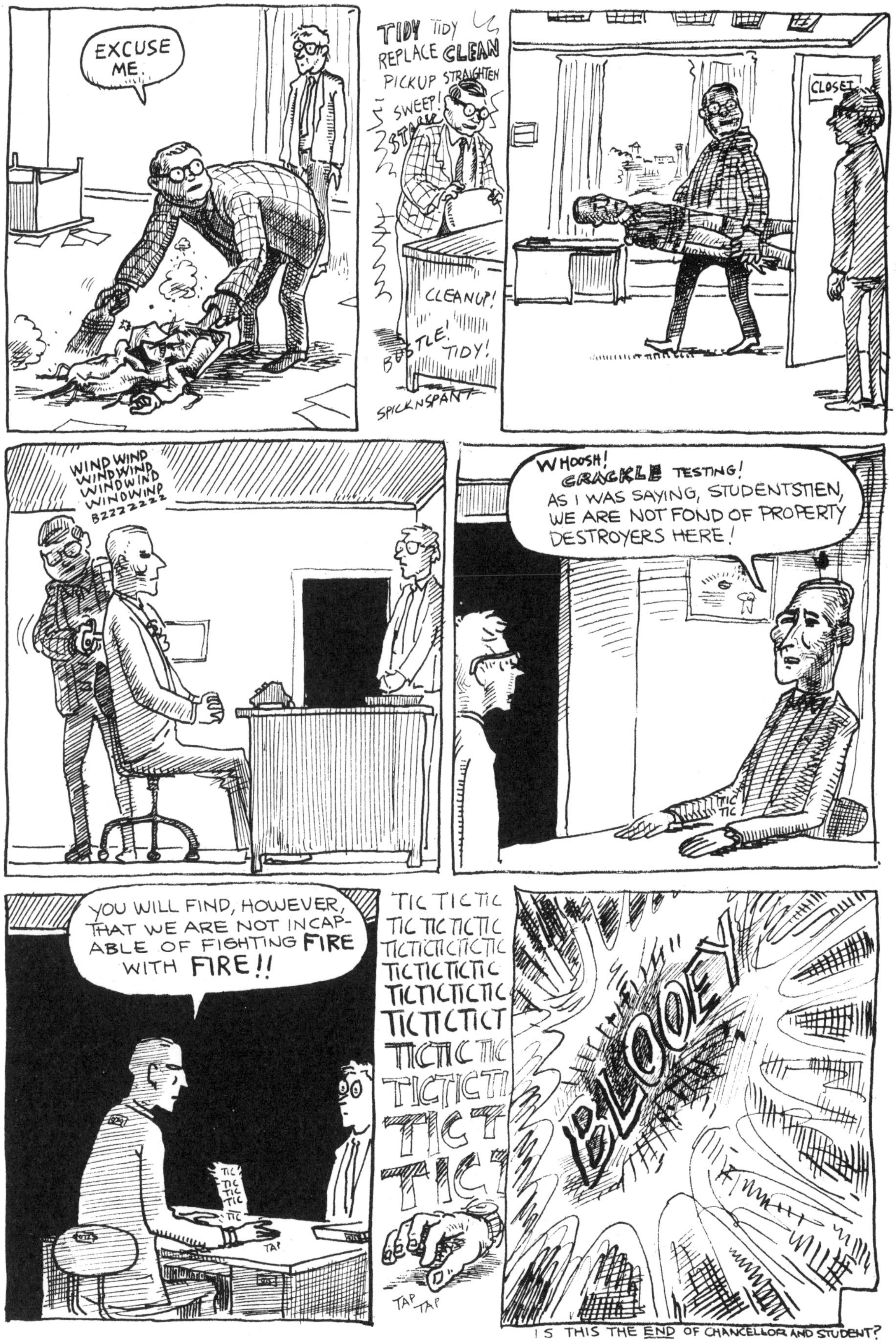
EXCUSE ME.
TIDY TIDY
REPLACE CLEAN
PICKUP STRAIGHTEN
SWEEP!
CLEANUP!
BUSTLE! TIDY!
SPICKNSPANT
CLOSET
WINDWIND WINDWIND WINDWIND WINDWIND BZZZZZZZ
WHOOSH! CRACKLE TESTING! AS I WAS SAYING, STUDENTSTIEN, WE ARE NOT FOND OF PROPERTY DESTROYERS HERE!
TIC TIC
YOU WILL FIND, HOWEVER, THAT WE ARE NOT INCAPABLE OF FIGHTING FIRE WITH FIRE!!
TIC TIC TIC TIC
TAP
TIC TIC TIC TIC TICTICTIC TICTICTICTIC TICTICTICTIC TICTICTICTIC TICTICTICT TICTICTIC TICTICTICTI TICT TICT
TAP TAP
BLOOEY

IS THIS THE END OF CHANCELLOR AND STUDENT?

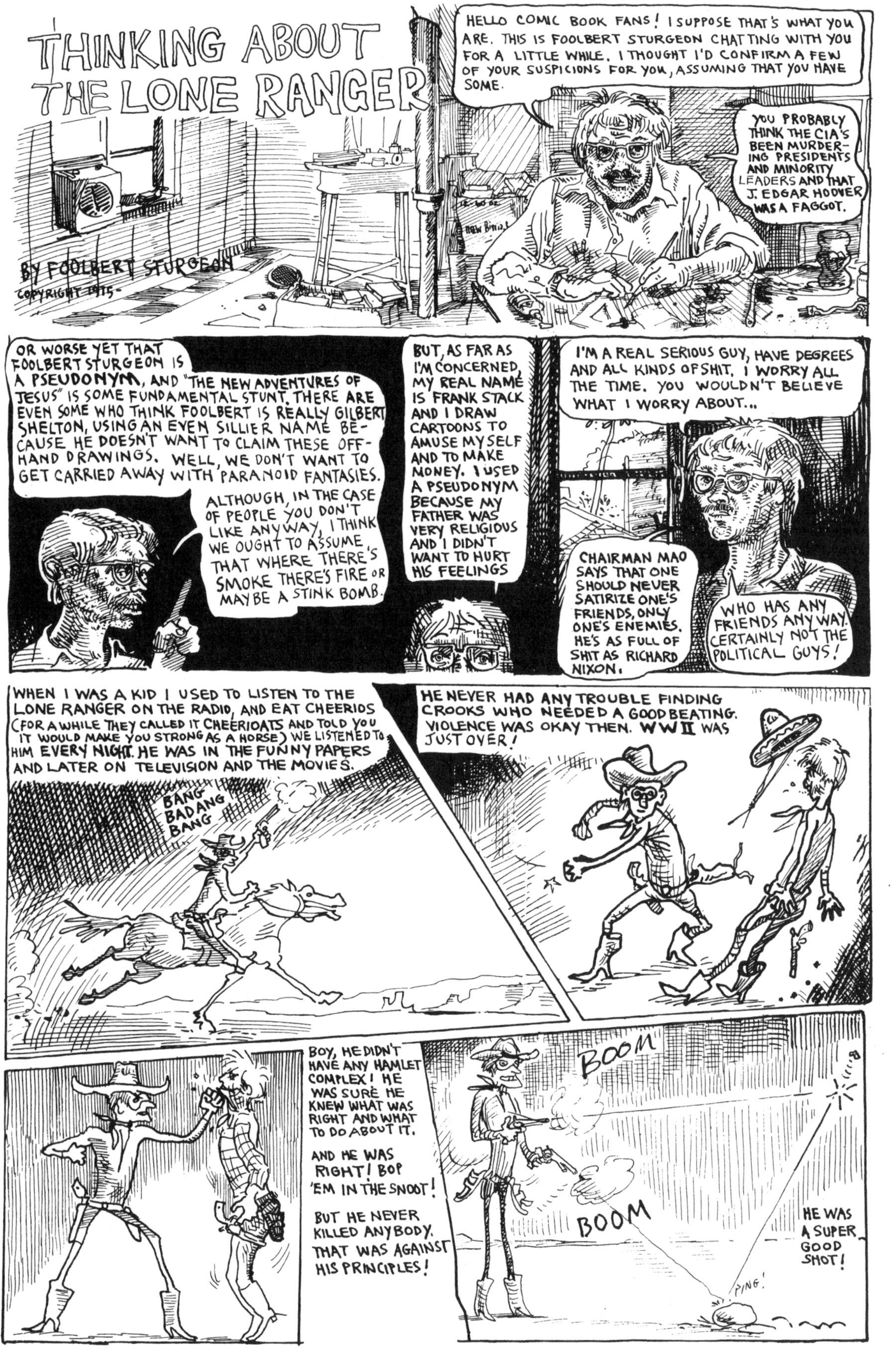
THINKING ABOUT THE LONE RANGER
BY FOOLBERT STURGEON
COPYRIGHT 1975.
HELLO COMIC BOOK FANS! I SUPPOSE THAT'S WHAT YOU ARE. THIS IS FOOLBERT STURGEON CHATTING WITH YOU FOR A LITTLE WHILE. I THOUGHT I'D CONFIRM A FEW OF YOUR SUSPICIONS FOR YOU, ASSUMING THAT YOU HAVE SOME.
YOU PROBABLY THINK THE CIA'S BEEN MURDERING PRESIDENTS AND MINORITY LEADERS AND THAT J. EDGAR HOOVER WAS A FAGGOT.
OR WORSE YET THAT FOOLBERT STURGEON IS A PSEUDONYM, AND "THE NEW ADVENTURES OF JESUS" IS SOME FUNDAMENTAL STUNT. THERE ARE EVEN SOME WHO THINK FOOLBERT IS REALLY GILBERT SHELTON, USING AN EVEN SILLIER NAME BECAUSE HE DOESN'T WANT TO CLAIM THESE OFF-HAND DRAWINGS. WELL, WE DON'T WANT TO GET CARRIED AWAY WITH PARANOID FANTASIES.
ALTHOUGH, IN THE CASE OF PEOPLE YOU DON'T LIKE ANYWAY, I THINK WE OUGHT TO ASSUME THAT WHERE THERE'S SMOKE THERE'S FIRE OR MAYBE A STINK BOMB.
BUT, AS FAR AS I'M CONCERNED, MY REAL NAME IS FRANK STACK AND I DRAW CARTOONS TO AMUSE MYSELF AND TO MAKE MONEY. I USED A PSEUDONYM BECAUSE MY FATHER WAS VERY RELIGIOUS AND I DIDN'T WANT TO HURT HIS FEELINGS
I'M A REAL SERIOUS GUY, HAVE DEGREES AND ALL KINDS OF SHIT. I WORRY ALL THE TIME. YOU WOULDN'T BELIEVE WHAT I WORRY ABOUT...
CHAIRMAN MAO SAYS THAT ONE SHOULD NEVER SATIRIZE ONE'S FRIENDS, ONLY ONE'S ENEMIES. HE'S AS FULL OF SHIT AS RICHARD NIXON.
WHO HAS ANY FRIENDS ANYWAY. CERTAINLY NOT THE POLITICAL GUYS!
WHEN I WAS A KID I USED TO LISTEN TO THE LONE RANGER ON THE RADIO, AND EAT CHEERIOS (FOR A WHILE THEY CALLED IT CHEERIOATS AND TOLD YOU IT WOULD MAKE YOU STRONG AS A HORSE) WE LISTENED TO HIM EVERY NIGHT. HE WAS IN THE FUNNY PAPERS AND LATER ON TELEVISION AND THE MOVIES.
BANG BADANG BANG
HE NEVER HAD ANY TROUBLE FINDING CROOKS WHO NEEDED A GOOD BEATING. VIOLENCE WAS OKAY THEN. WW II WAS JUST OVER!
BOY, HE DIDN'T HAVE ANY HAMLET COMPLEX! HE WAS SURE HE KNEW WHAT WAS RIGHT AND WHAT TO DO ABOUT IT.
AND HE WAS RIGHT! BOP 'EM IN THE SNOOT!
BUT HE NEVER KILLED ANYBODY. THAT WAS AGAINST HIS PRINCIPLES!
BOOM
BOOM
PING!
HE WAS A SUPER GOOD SHOT!

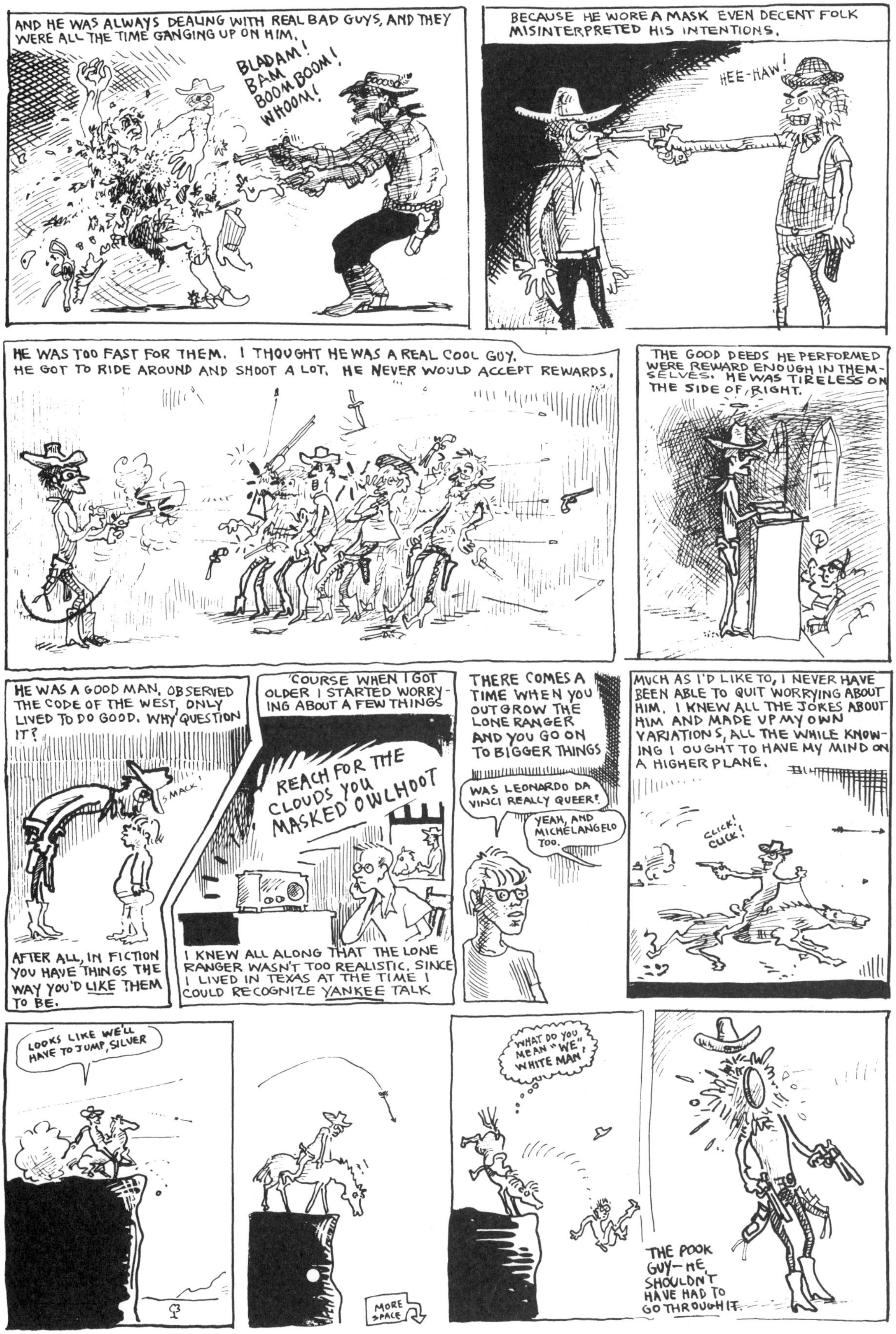
AND HE WAS ALWAYS DEALING WITH REAL BAD GUYS, AND THEY WERE ALL THE TIME GANGING UP ON HIM.
BLADAM! BAM BOOM BOOM! WHOOM!
BECAUSE HE WORE A MASK EVEN DECENT FOLK MISINTERPRETED HIS INTENTIONS.
HEE-HAW!
HE WAS TOO FAST FOR THEM. I THOUGHT HE WAS A REAL COOL GUY. HE GOT TO RIDE AROUND AND SHOOT A LOT. HE NEVER WOULD ACCEPT REWARDS.
THE GOOD DEEDS HE PERFORMED WERE REWARD ENOUGH IN THEMSELVES. HE WAS TIRELESS ON THE SIDE OF RIGHT.
HE WAS A GOOD MAN, OBSERVED THE CODE OF THE WEST, ONLY LIVED TO DO GOOD. WHY QUESTION IT?
SMACK!
AFTER ALL, IN FICTION YOU HAVE THINGS THE WAY YOU'D LIKE THEM TO BE.
'COURSE WHEN I GOT OLDER I STARTED WORRYING ABOUT A FEW THINGS
REACH FOR THE CLOUDS YOU MASKED OWLHOOT
I KNEW ALL ALONG THAT THE LONE RANGER WASN'T TOO REALISTIC. SINCE I LIVED IN TEXAS AT THE TIME I COULD RECOGNIZE YANKEE TALK
THERE COMES A TIME WHEN YOU OUTGROW THE LONE RANGER AND YOU GO ON TO BIGGER THINGS
WAS LEONARDO DA VINCI REALLY QUEER?
YEAH, AND MICHELANGELO TOO.
MUCH AS I'D LIKE TO, I NEVER HAVE BEEN ABLE TO QUIT WORRYING ABOUT HIM. I KNEW ALL THE JOKES ABOUT HIM AND MADE UP MY OWN VARIATIONS, ALL THE WHILE KNOWING I OUGHT TO HAVE MY MIND ON A HIGHER PLANE.
CLICK! CLICK!
LOOKS LIKE WE'LL HAVE TO JUMP, SILVER
MORE SPACE
WHAT DO YOU MEAN "WE" WHITE MAN?
THE POOR GUY—HE SHOULDN'T HAVE HAD TO GO THROUGH IT.

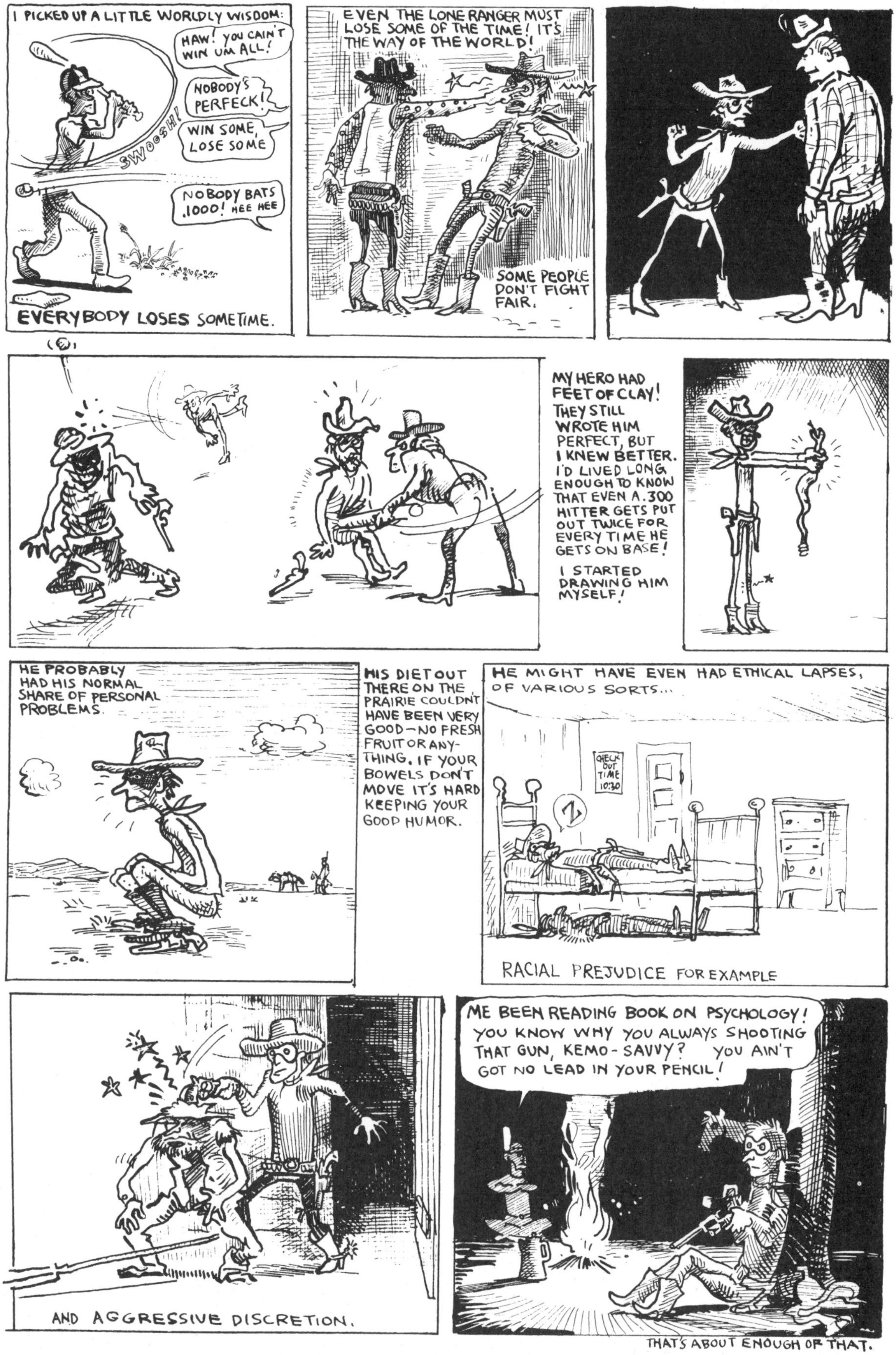
I PICKED UP A LITTLE WORLDLY WISDOM:
HAW! YOU CAIN'T WIN UM ALL!
NOBODY'S PERFECK!
WIN SOME, LOSE SOME
SWOOSH!
NOBODY BATS .1000! HEE HEE
EVERYBODY LOSES SOMETIME.
EVEN THE LONE RANGER MUST LOSE SOME OF THE TIME! IT'S THE WAY OF THE WORLD!
SOME PEOPLE DON'T FIGHT FAIR.
MY HERO HAD FEET OF CLAY! THEY STILL WROTE HIM PERFECT, BUT I KNEW BETTER. I'D LIVED LONG ENOUGH TO KNOW THAT EVEN A .300 HITTER GETS PUT OUT TWICE FOR EVERY TIME HE GETS ON BASE!
I STARTED DRAWING HIM MYSELF!
HE PROBABLY HAD HIS NORMAL SHARE OF PERSONAL PROBLEMS.
HIS DIET OUT THERE ON THE PRAIRIE COULDN'T HAVE BEEN VERY GOOD—NO FRESH FRUIT OR ANYTHING. IF YOUR BOWELS DON'T MOVE IT'S HARD KEEPING YOUR GOOD HUMOR.
HE MIGHT HAVE EVEN HAD ETHICAL LAPSES, OF VARIOUS SORTS...
CHECK OUT TIME 10:30
Z
RACIAL PREJUDICE FOR EXAMPLE
AND AGGRESSIVE DISCRETION.
ME BEEN READING BOOK ON PSYCHOLOGY! YOU KNOW WHY YOU ALWAYS SHOOTING THAT GUN, KEMO-SAVVY? YOU AIN'T GOT NO LEAD IN YOUR PENCIL!
THAT'S ABOUT ENOUGH OF THAT.

Character Work

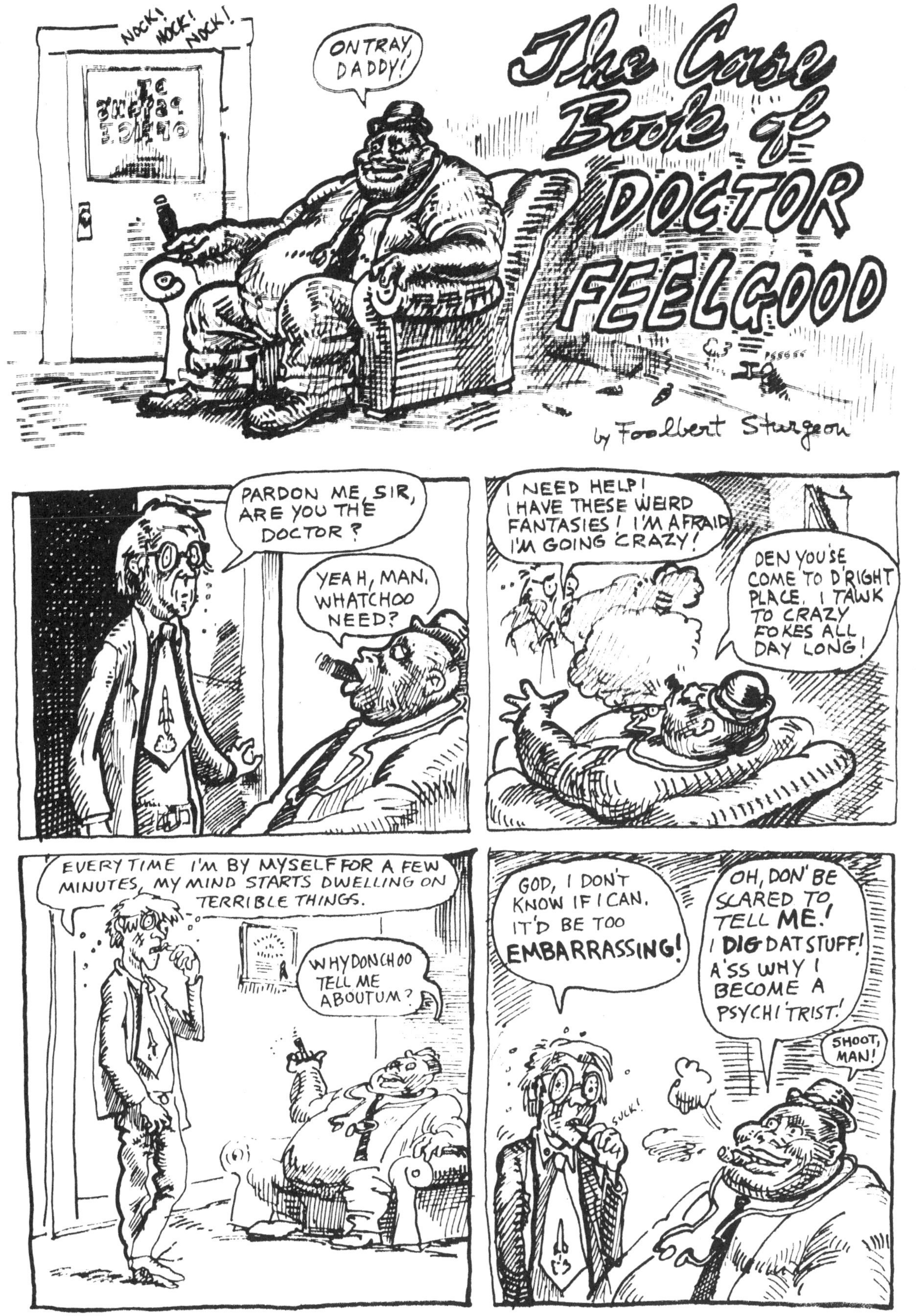
NOCK! NOCK! NOCK!
ONTRAY, DADDY!
The Case Book of DOCTOR FEELGOOD
by Foolbert Sturgeon
PARDON ME, SIR, ARE YOU THE DOCTOR?
YEAH, MAN, WHATCHOO NEED?
I NEED HELP! I HAVE THESE WEIRD FANTASIES! I'M AFRAID I'M GOING CRAZY!
DEN YOU'SE COME TO D'RIGHT PLACE. I TAWK TO CRAZY FOKES ALL DAY LONG!
EVERY TIME I'M BY MYSELF FOR A FEW MINUTES, MY MIND STARTS DWELLING ON TERRIBLE THINGS.
WHYDONCHOO TELL ME ABOUTUM?
GOD, I DON'T KNOW IF I CAN. IT'D BE TOO EMBARRASSING!
OH, DON' BE SCARED TO TELL ME! I DIG DAT STUFF! A'SS WHY I BECOME A PSYCHI'TRIST!
SHOOT, MAN!
SUCK!

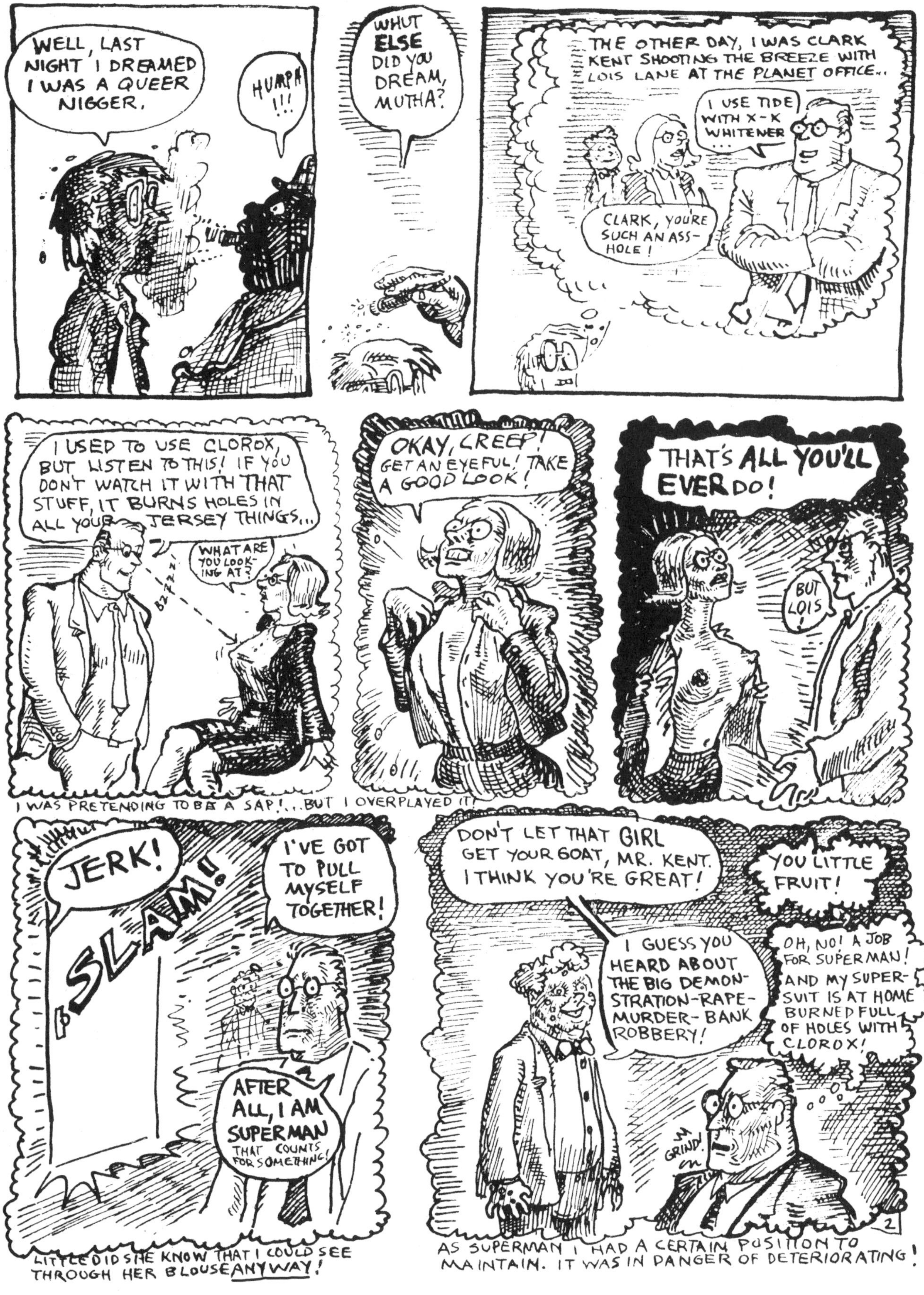

WELL, LAST NIGHT I DREAMED I WAS A QUEER NIGGER.
HUMPH !!!
WHUT ELSE DID YOU DREAM, MUTHA?
THE OTHER DAY, I WAS CLARK KENT SHOOTING THE BREEZE WITH LOIS LANE AT THE PLANET OFFICE..
I USE TIDE WITH X-K WHITENER ...
CLARK, YOU'RE SUCH AN ASS-HOLE!
I USED TO USE CLOROX, BUT LISTEN TO THIS! IF YOU DON'T WATCH IT WITH THAT STUFF, IT BURNS HOLES IN ALL YOUR JERSEY THINGS...
WHAT ARE YOU LOOKING AT?
BZZZZ!
OKAY, CREEP! GET AN EYEFUL! TAKE A GOOD LOOK!
THAT'S ALL YOU'LL EVER DO!
BUT LOIS!
I WAS PRETENDING TO BE A SAP!...BUT I OVERPLAYED IT!
JERK!
SLAM!
I'VE GOT TO PULL MYSELF TOGETHER!
AFTER ALL, I AM SUPERMAN THAT COUNTS FOR SOMETHING!
LITTLE DID SHE KNOW THAT I COULD SEE THROUGH HER BLOUSE ANYWAY!
DON'T LET THAT GIRL GET YOUR GOAT, MR. KENT. I THINK YOU'RE GREAT!
YOU LITTLE FRUIT!
I GUESS YOU HEARD ABOUT THE BIG DEMON-STRATION-RAPE-MURDER-BANK ROBBERY!
OH, NO! A JOB FOR SUPERMAN! AND MY SUPER-SUIT IS AT HOME BURNED FULL OF HOLES WITH CLOROX!
GRIND!
2
AS SUPERMAN I HAD A CERTAIN POSITION TO MAINTAIN. IT WAS IN DANGER OF DETERIORATING!

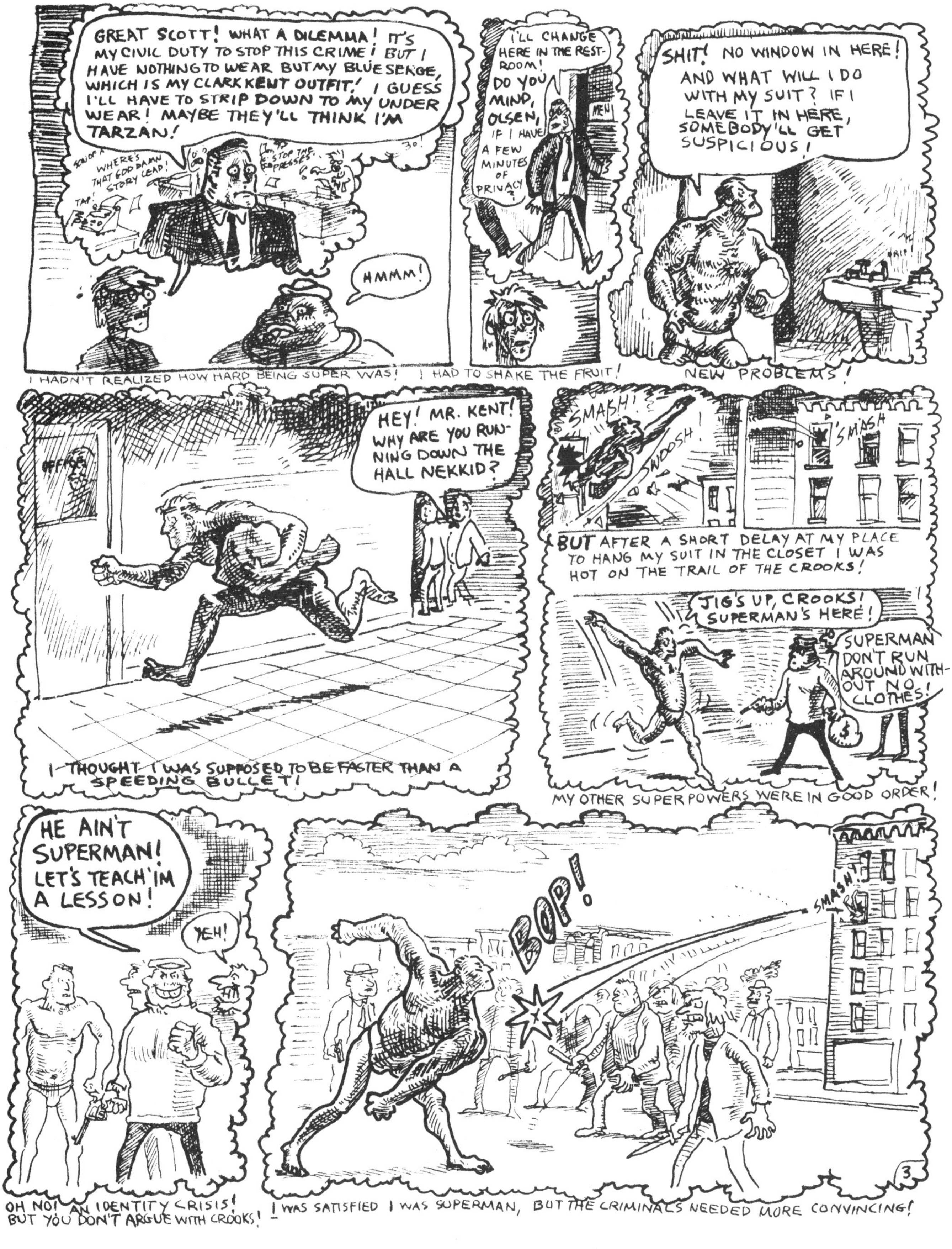
GREAT SCOTT! WHAT A DILEMMA! IT'S MY CIVIC DUTY TO STOP THIS CRIME! BUT I HAVE NOTHING TO WEAR BUT MY BLUE SERGE, WHICH IS MY CLARK KENT OUTFIT! I GUESS I'LL HAVE TO STRIP DOWN TO MY UNDER WEAR! MAYBE THEY'LL THINK I'M TARZAN!
SON OF A
WHERE'S THAT GOD DAMN STORY LEAD!
STOP THE PRESSES!
TAP!
30!
HMMM!
I HADN'T REALIZED HOW HARD BEING SUPER WAS!
I'LL CHANGE HERE IN THE REST-ROOM! DO YOU MIND, OLSEN, IF I HAVE A FEW MINUTES OF PRIVACY?
MEN
I HAD TO SHAKE THE FRUIT!
SHIT! NO WINDOW IN HERE!
AND WHAT WILL I DO WITH MY SUIT? IF I LEAVE IT IN HERE, SOMEBODY'LL GET SUSPICIOUS!
DRIP
NEW PROBLEMS!
HEY! MR. KENT! WHY ARE YOU RUNNING DOWN THE HALL NEKKID?
I THOUGHT I WAS SUPPOSED TO BE FASTER THAN A SPEEDING BULLET!
SMASH!
WOOSH!
SMASH
BUT AFTER A SHORT DELAY AT MY PLACE TO HANG MY SUIT IN THE CLOSET I WAS HOT ON THE TRAIL OF THE CROOKS!
JIG'S UP, CROOKS! SUPERMAN'S HERE!
SUPERMAN DON'T RUN AROUND WITHOUT NO CLOTHES!
MY OTHER SUPER POWERS WERE IN GOOD ORDER!
HE AIN'T SUPERMAN! LET'S TEACH 'IM A LESSON!
YEH!
OH NO! AN IDENTITY CRISIS! BUT YOU DON'T ARGUE WITH CROOKS!
BOP!
SMASH!
3
I WAS SATISFIED I WAS SUPERMAN, BUT THE CRIMINALS NEEDED MORE CONVINCING!

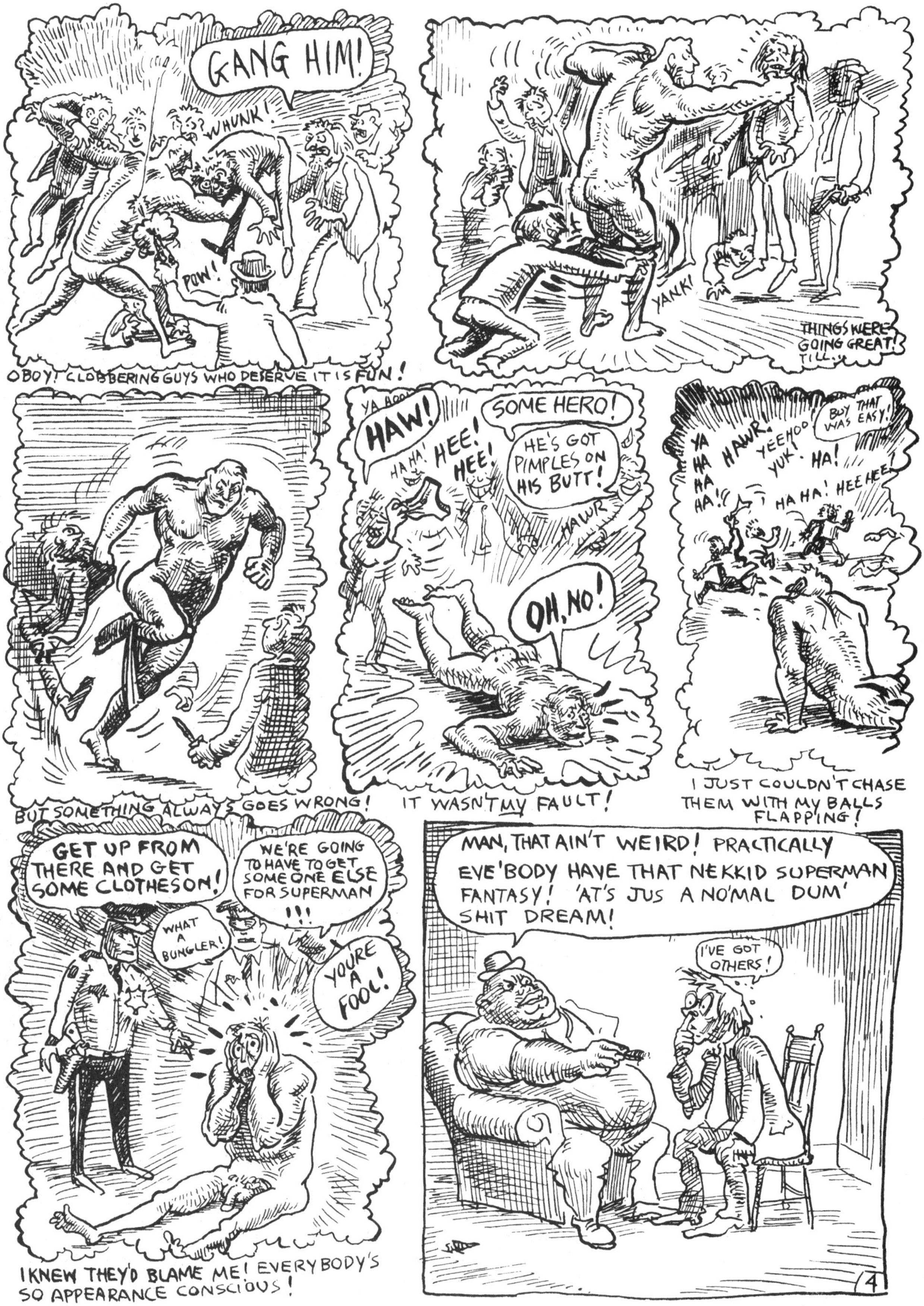
GANG HIM!
?? WHUNK!
POW!
OBOY! CLOBBERING GUYS WHO DESERVE IT IS FUN!
YANK!
THINGS WERE GOING GREAT! TILL...
BUT SOMETHING ALWAYS GOES WRONG!
HAW!
SOME HERO!
HA HA! HEE! HEE!
HE'S GOT PIMPLES ON HIS BUTT!
HAWR
OH, NO!
IT WASN'T MY FAULT!
YA HA HA HA!
HAWR.
YEEHOO!
BOY THAT WAS EASY!
YUK. HA!
HA HA! HEE HEE!
I JUST COULDN'T CHASE THEM WITH MY BALLS FLAPPING!
GET UP FROM THERE AND GET SOME CLOTHES ON!
WE'RE GOING TO HAVE TO GET SOMEONE ELSE FOR SUPERMAN !!!
WHAT A BUNGLER!
YOU'RE A FOOL!
I KNEW THEY'D BLAME ME! EVERYBODY'S SO APPEARANCE CONSCIOUS!
MAN, THAT AIN'T WEIRD! PRACTICALLY EVE'BODY HAVE THAT NEKKID SUPERMAN FANTASY! 'AT'S JUS A NO'MAL DUM' SHIT DREAM!
I'VE GOT OTHERS!
4

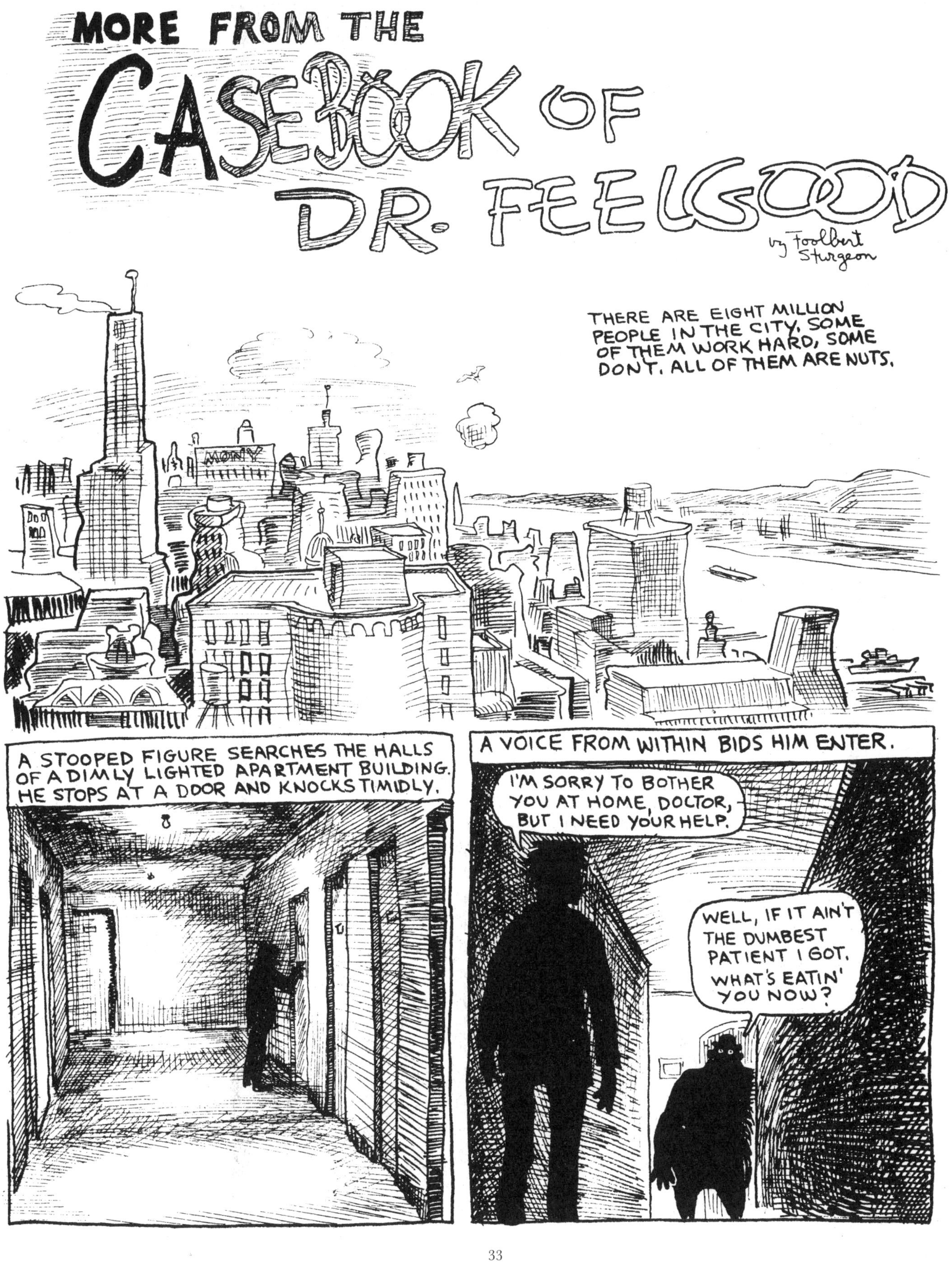
MORE FROM THE
CASEBOOK OF
DR. FEELGOOD
by Toolbert Sturgeon
THERE ARE EIGHT MILLION PEOPLE IN THE CITY. SOME OF THEM WORK HARD, SOME DON'T. ALL OF THEM ARE NUTS.
MONY
A STOOPED FIGURE SEARCHES THE HALLS OF A DIMLY LIGHTED APARTMENT BUILDING. HE STOPS AT A DOOR AND KNOCKS TIMIDLY.
A VOICE FROM WITHIN BIDS HIM ENTER.
I'M SORRY TO BOTHER YOU AT HOME, DOCTOR, BUT I NEED YOUR HELP.
WELL, IF IT AIN'T THE DUMBEST PATIENT I GOT. WHAT'S EATIN' YOU NOW?

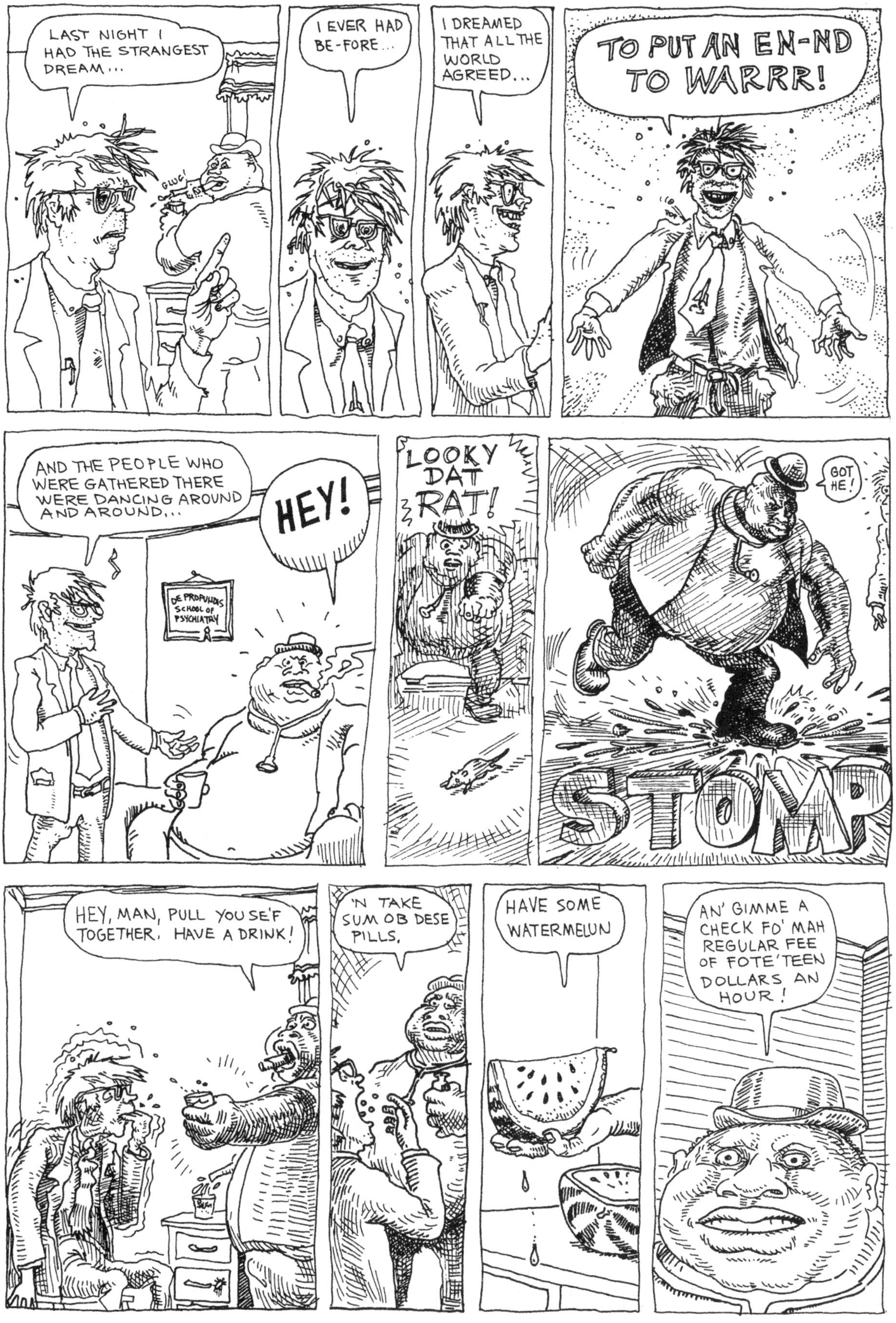
LAST NIGHT I HAD THE STRANGEST DREAM...
GLUG!
I EVER HAD BE-FORE...
I DREAMED THAT ALL THE WORLD AGREED...
TO PUT AN EN-ND TO WARRR!
AND THE PEOPLE WHO WERE GATHERED THERE WERE DANCING AROUND AND AROUND...
HEY!
DE PROFUNDIS SCHOOL OF PSYCHIATRY
LOOKY DAT RAT!
GOT HE!
STOMP
HEY, MAN, PULL YOU SE'F TOGETHER. HAVE A DRINK!
'N TAKE SUM OB DESE PILLS.
HAVE SOME WATERMELUN
AN' GIMME A CHECK FO' MAH REGULAR FEE OF FOTE'TEEN DOLLARS AN HOUR!

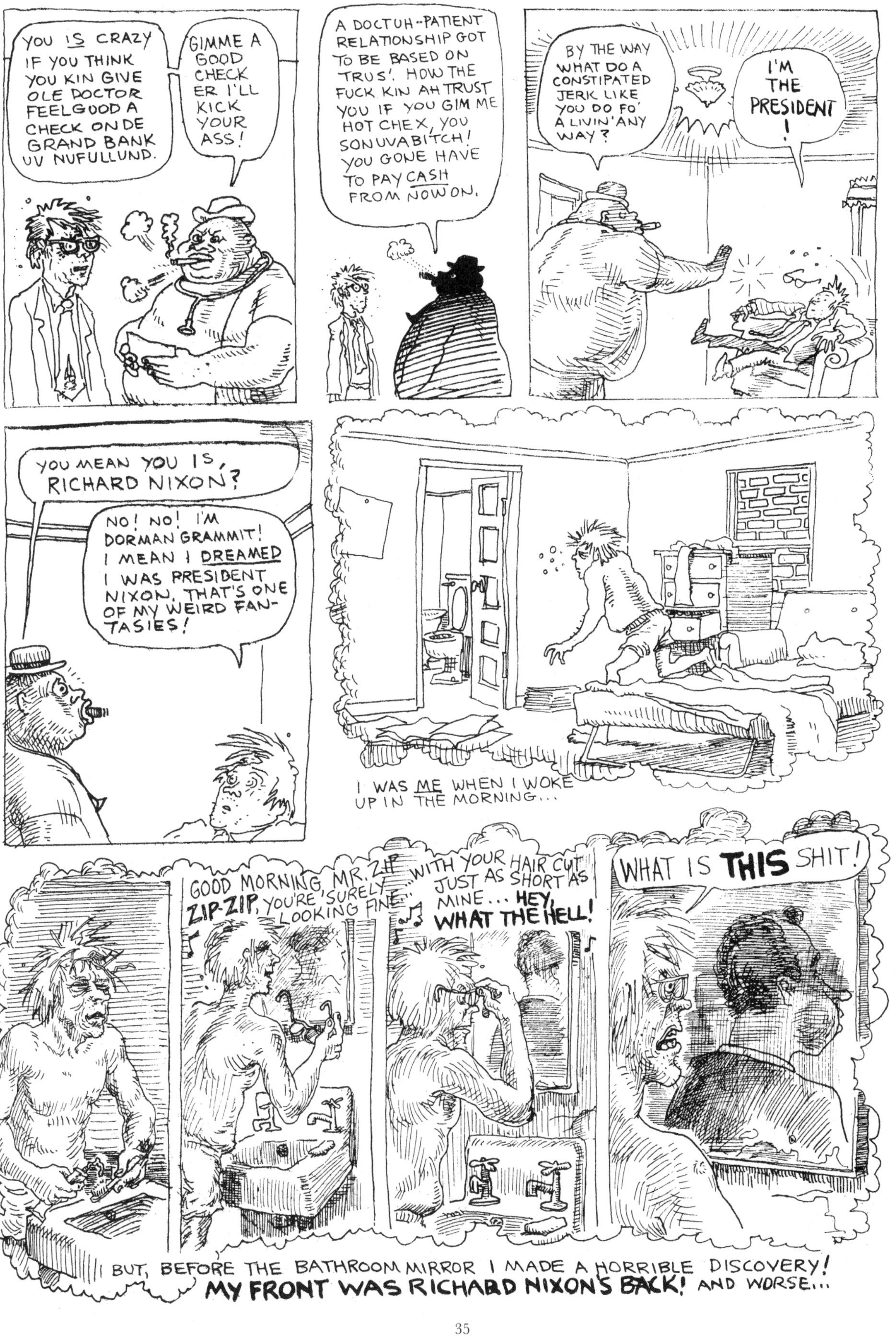
YOU IS CRAZY IF YOU THINK YOU KIN GIVE OLE DOCTOR FEELGOOD A CHECK ON DE GRAND BANK UV NUFULLUND.
GIMME A GOOD CHECK ER I'LL KICK YOUR ASS!
A DOCTUH-PATIENT RELATIONSHIP GOT TO BE BASED ON TRUS'. HOW THE FUCK KIN AH TRUST YOU IF YOU GIM ME HOT CHEX, YOU SONUVABITCH! YOU GONE HAVE TO PAY CASH FROM NOW ON.
BY THE WAY WHAT DO A CONSTIPATED JERK LIKE YOU DO FO' A LIVIN' ANY WAY?
I'M THE PRESIDENT!
YOU MEAN YOU IS, RICHARD NIXON?
NO! NO! I'M DORMAN GRAMMIT! I MEAN I DREAMED I WAS PRESIDENT NIXON, THAT'S ONE OF MY WEIRD FANTASIES!
I WAS ME WHEN I WOKE UP IN THE MORNING...
GOOD MORNING, MR. ZIP ZIP-ZIP, YOU'RE SURELY LOOKING FINE...
WITH YOUR HAIR CUT JUST AS SHORT AS MINE... HEY, WHAT THE HELL!
WHAT IS THIS SHIT!
BUT, BEFORE THE BATHROOM MIRROR I MADE A HORRIBLE DISCOVERY!
MY FRONT WAS RICHARD NIXON'S BACK! AND WORSE...

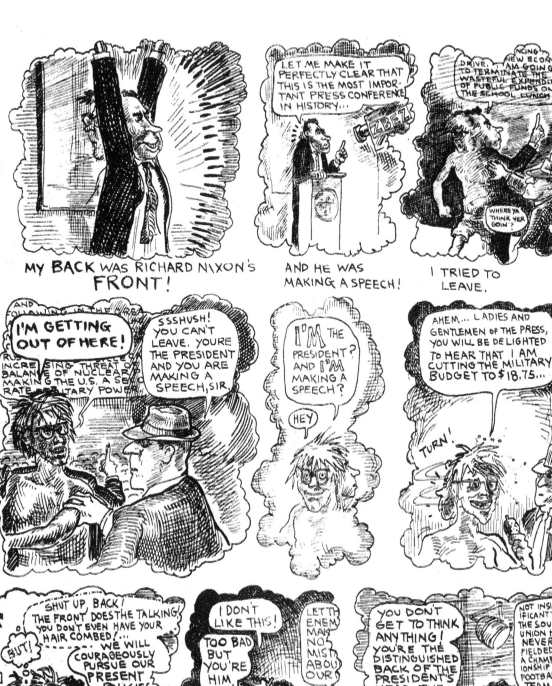

MY BACK WAS RICHARD NIXON'S FRONT!
LET ME MAKE IT PERFECTLY CLEAR THAT THIS IS THE MOST IMPORTANT PRESS CONFERENCE IN HISTORY...
AND HE WAS MAKING A SPEECH!
WHERE YA THINK YER GOIN'?
I TRIED TO LEAVE.
I'M GETTING OUT OF HERE!
SSSHUSH! YOU CAN'T LEAVE. YOURE THE PRESIDENT AND YOU ARE MAKING A SPEECH, SIR.
I'M THE PRESIDENT? AND I'M MAKING A SPEECH?
HEY
AHEM... LADIES AND GENTLEMEN OF THE PRESS, YOU WILL BE DELIGHTED TO HEAR THAT I AM CUTTING THE MILITARY BUDGET TO $18.75...
TURN!
SHUT UP, BACK! THE FRONT DOES THE TALKING! YOU DON'T EVEN HAVE YOUR HAIR COMBED!...
BUT!
WE WILL COURAGEOUSLY PURSUE OUR PRESENT POLICIES. YA YA YO YO...
SHUSH!
I DON'T LIKE THIS!
TOO BAD BUT YOU'RE HIM NOW!
I WANTA BE ME! I WANT TO SAY WHAT I THINK!
YOU DON'T GET TO THINK ANYTHING! YOU'RE THE DISTINGUISHED BACK OF THE PRESIDENT'S HEAD. THE OFFICIAL MOUTH IS ON THE OTHER SIDE!
NOT INSIGNIFICANT THAT THE SOVIET UNION HAS NEVER FIELDED A CHAMPIONSHIP FOOTBALL TEAM...

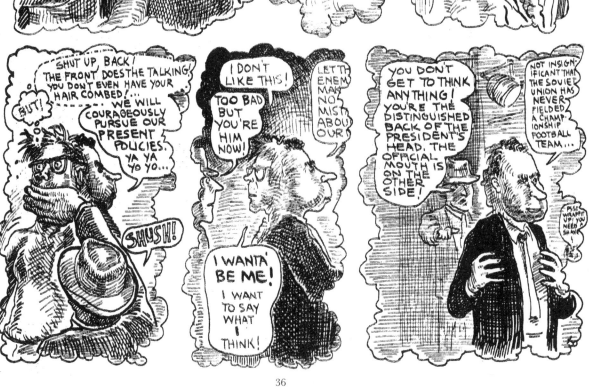

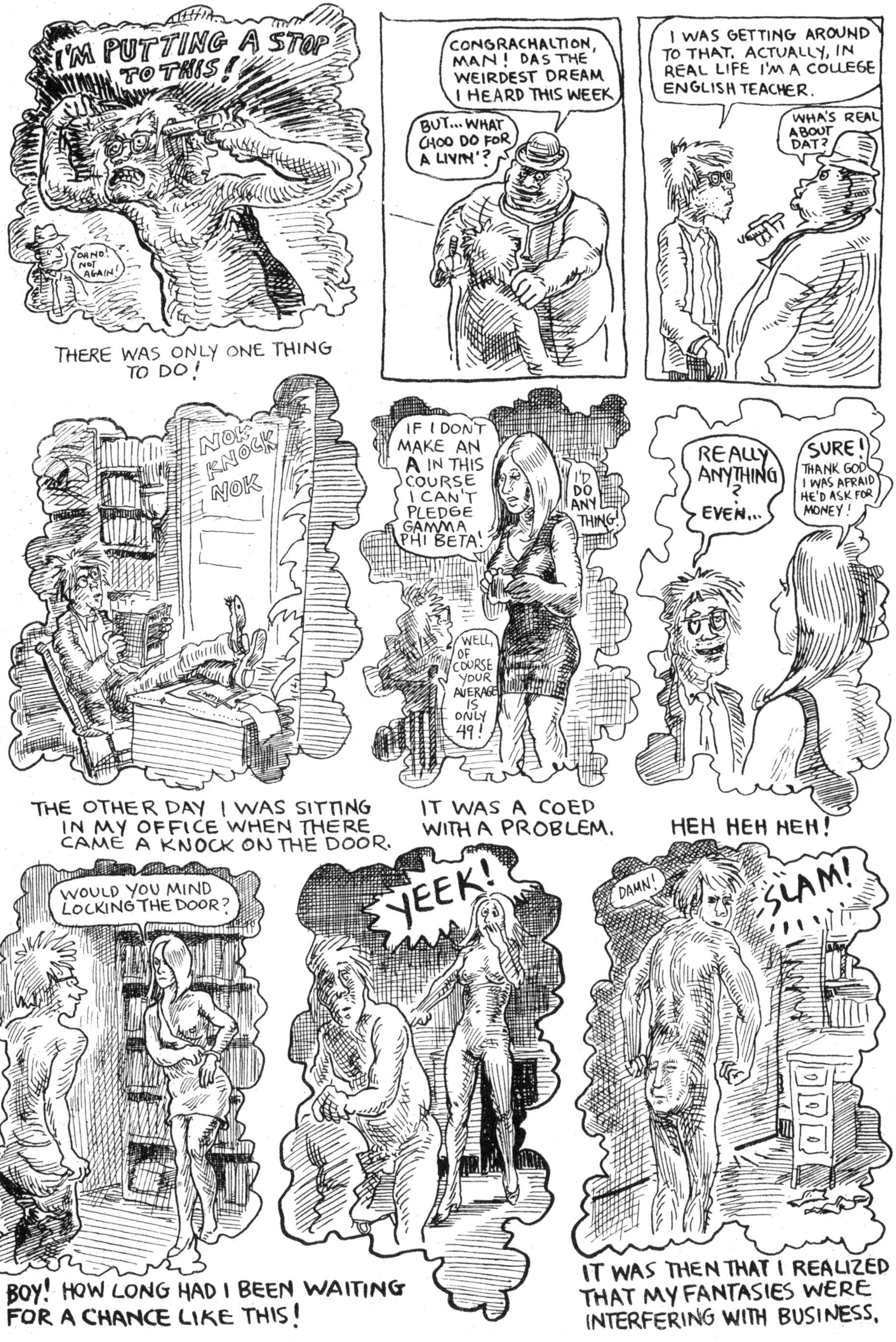
I'M PUTTING A STOP TO THIS!
OH NO! NOT AGAIN!
THERE WAS ONLY ONE THING TO DO!
CONGRACHALTION, MAN! DAS THE WEIRDEST DREAM I HEARD THIS WEEK
BUT... WHAT CHOO DO FOR A LIVIN'?
I WAS GETTING AROUND TO THAT. ACTUALLY, IN REAL LIFE I'M A COLLEGE ENGLISH TEACHER.
WHA'S REAL ABOUT DAT?
NOK KNOCK NOK
THE OTHER DAY I WAS SITTING IN MY OFFICE WHEN THERE CAME A KNOCK ON THE DOOR.
IF I DON'T MAKE AN A IN THIS COURSE I CAN'T PLEDGE GAMMA PHI BETA!
I'D DO ANY THING!
WELL, OF COURSE YOUR AVERAGE IS ONLY 49!
IT WAS A COED WITH A PROBLEM.
REALLY ANYTHING? EVEN...
SURE! THANK GOD I WAS AFRAID HE'D ASK FOR MONEY!
HEH HEH HEH!
WOULD YOU MIND LOCKING THE DOOR?
BOY! HOW LONG HAD I BEEN WAITING FOR A CHANCE LIKE THIS!
YEEK!
DAMN!
SLAM!
IT WAS THEN THAT I REALIZED THAT MY FANTASIES WERE INTERFERING WITH BUSINESS.

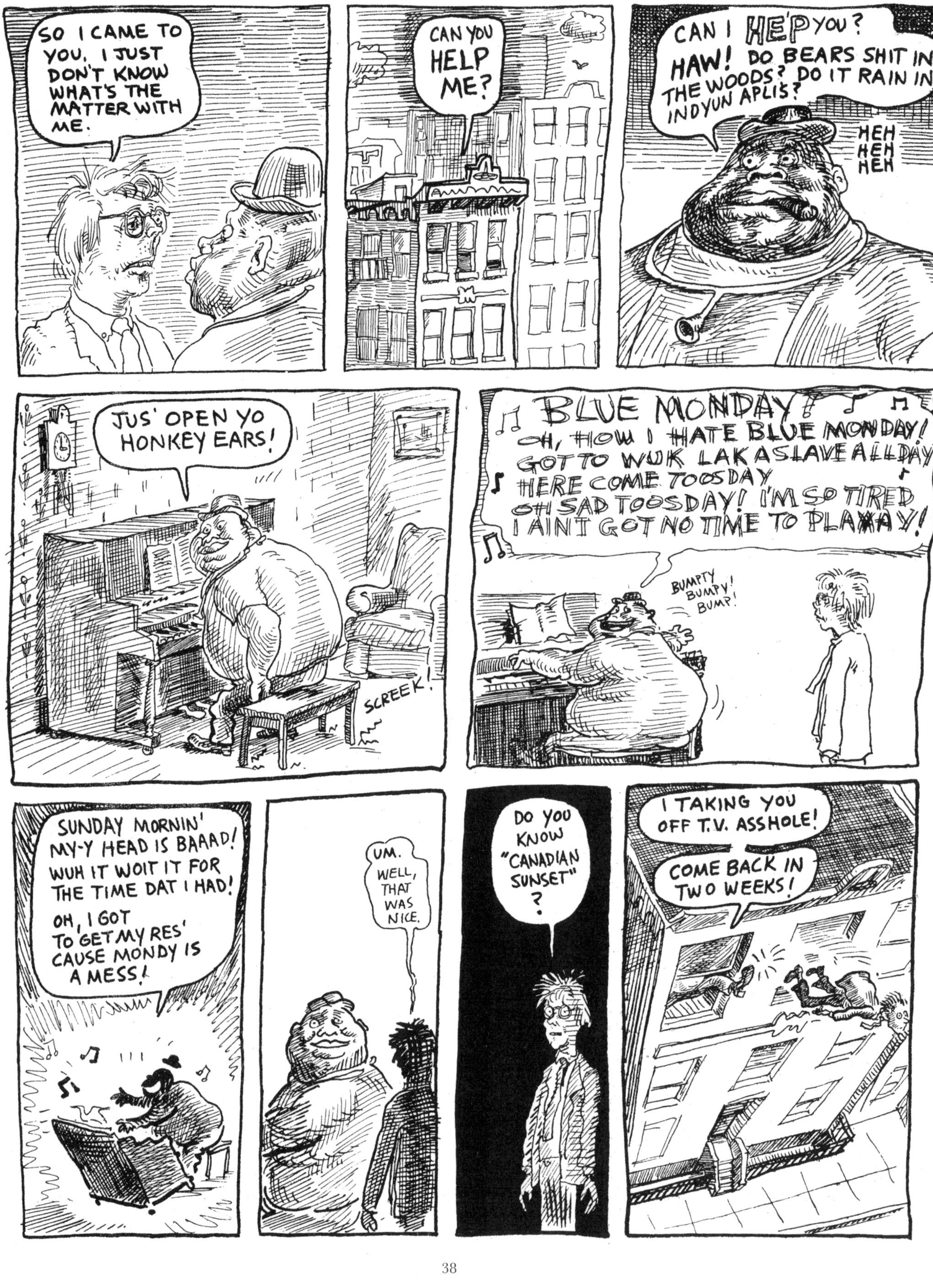
SO I CAME TO YOU. I JUST DON'T KNOW WHAT'S THE MATTER WITH ME.
CAN YOU HELP ME?
CAN I HEP YOU? HAW! DO BEARS SHIT IN THE WOODS? DO IT RAIN IN INDYUN APLIS?
HEH HEH HEH
JUS' OPEN YO HONKEY EARS!
SCREEK!
BLUE MONDAY! OH, HOW I HATE BLUE MONDAY! GOT TO WUK LAK A SLAVE ALL DAY HERE COME TOOSDAY OH SAD TOOSDAY! I'M SO TIRED I AINT GOT NO TIME TO PLAY AY!
BUMPTY BUMPY! BUMP!
SUNDAY MORNIN' MY-Y HEAD IS BAAAD! WUH IT WOIT IT FOR THE TIME DAT I HAD! OH, I GOT TO GET MY RES' CAUSE MONDY IS A MESS!
UM.
WELL, THAT WAS NICE.
DO YOU KNOW "CANADIAN SUNSET"?
I TAKING YOU OFF T.V. ASSHOLE!
COME BACK IN TWO WEEKS!

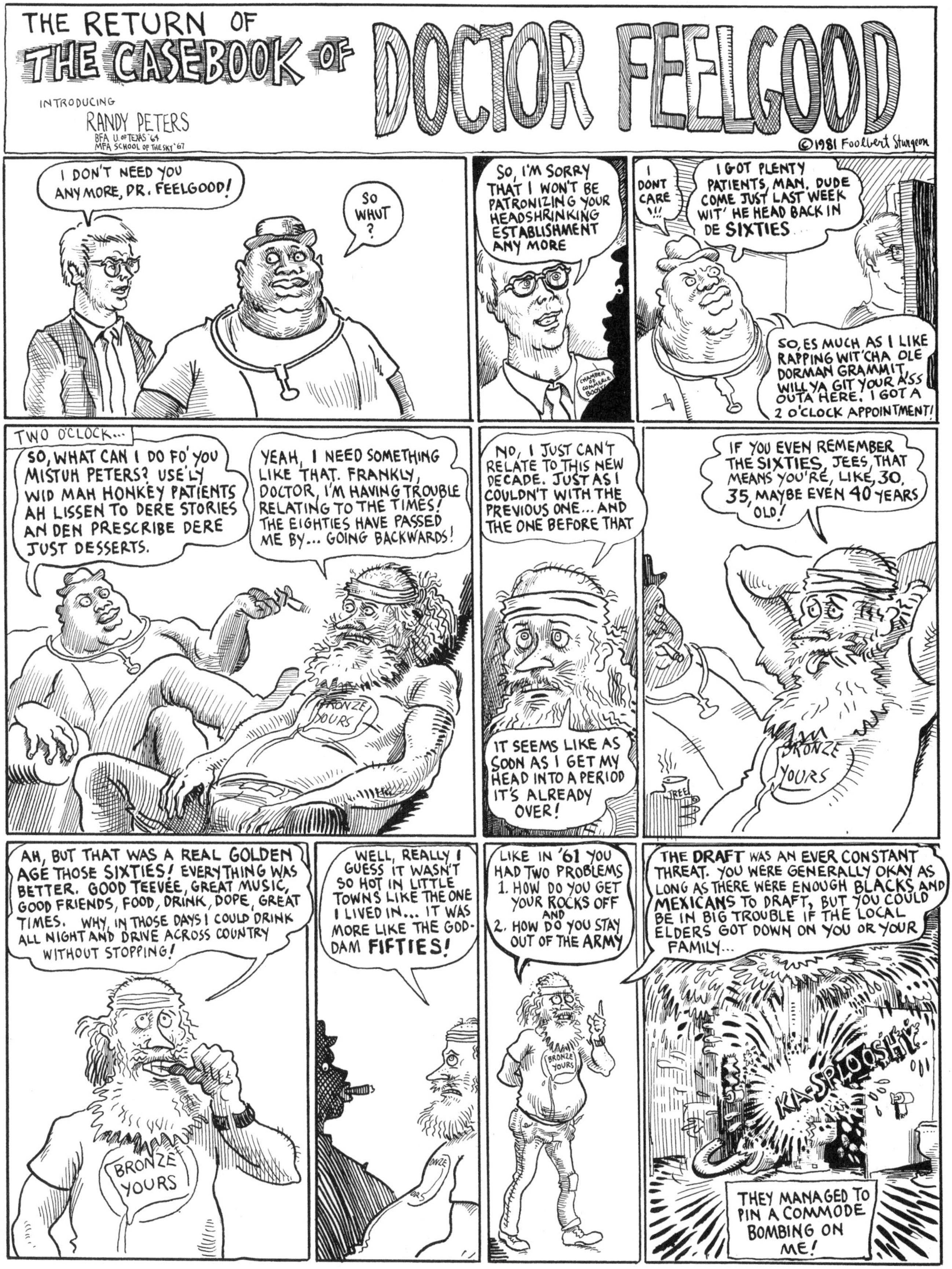
THE RETURN OF THE CASEBOOK OF DOCTOR FEELGOOD
INTRODUCING RANDY PETERS BFA U. OF TEXAS '64 MFA SCHOOL OF THE SKY '67
©1981 Foolbert Sturgeon
I DON'T NEED YOU ANYMORE, DR. FEELGOOD!
SO WHUT ?
SO, I'M SORRY THAT I WON'T BE PATRONIZING YOUR HEADSHRINKING ESTABLISHMENT ANY MORE
CHAMBER OF COMMERCE BOOSTER
I DONT CARE !!!
I GOT PLENTY PATIENTS, MAN. DUDE COME JUST LAST WEEK WIT' HE HEAD BACK IN DE SIXTIES
SO, ES MUCH AS I LIKE RAPPING WIT'CHA OLE DORMAN GRAMMIT, WILL YA GIT YOUR ASS OUTA HERE. I GOT A 2 O'CLOCK APPOINTMENT!
TWO O'CLOCK...
SO, WHAT CAN I DO FO' YOU MISTUH PETERS? USE'LY WID MAH HONKEY PATIENTS AH LISSEN TO DERE STORIES AN DEN PRESCRIBE DERE JUST DESSERTS.
YEAH, I NEED SOMETHING LIKE THAT. FRANKLY, DOCTOR, I'M HAVING TROUBLE RELATING TO THE TIMES! THE EIGHTIES HAVE PASSED ME BY... GOING BACKWARDS!
BRONZE YOURS
NO, I JUST CAN'T RELATE TO THIS NEW DECADE. JUST AS I COULDN'T WITH THE PREVIOUS ONE... AND THE ONE BEFORE THAT
IT SEEMS LIKE AS SOON AS I GET MY HEAD INTO A PERIOD IT'S ALREADY OVER!
IF YOU EVEN REMEMBER THE SIXTIES, JEES, THAT MEANS YOU'RE, LIKE, 30, 35, MAYBE EVEN 40 YEARS OLD!
TREE
BRONZE YOURS
AH, BUT THAT WAS A REAL GOLDEN AGE THOSE SIXTIES! EVERYTHING WAS BETTER. GOOD TEEVÉE, GREAT MUSIC, GOOD FRIENDS, FOOD, DRINK, DOPE, GREAT TIMES. WHY, IN THOSE DAYS I COULD DRINK ALL NIGHT AND DRIVE ACROSS COUNTRY WITHOUT STOPPING!
BRONZE YOURS
WELL, REALLY I GUESS IT WASN'T SO HOT IN LITTLE TOWNS LIKE THE ONE I LIVED IN... IT WAS MORE LIKE THE GOD-DAM FIFTIES!
LIKE IN '61 YOU HAD TWO PROBLEMS 1. HOW DO YOU GET YOUR ROCKS OFF AND 2. HOW DO YOU STAY OUT OF THE ARMY
BRONZE YOURS
THE DRAFT WAS AN EVER CONSTANT THREAT. YOU WERE GENERALLY OKAY AS LONG AS THERE WERE ENOUGH BLACKS AND MEXICANS TO DRAFT, BUT YOU COULD BE IN BIG TROUBLE IF THE LOCAL ELDERS GOT DOWN ON YOU OR YOUR FAMILY...
KA-SPLOOSH!
THEY MANAGED TO PIN A COMMODE BOMBING ON ME!
FEELGOOD & PETERS' P. 1

CAN'T I GET A COLLEGE DEFERMENT OR SOMETHING

I GUESS THAT'S OKAY!

JUST BE SURE YOU LEAVE TOWN!

U.S. ARMY CRUITME CENTER

SO I WENT TO COLLEGE

OBOY! AUSTIN!

I'LL STUDY ENGINEERING SO I CAN GET A GOOD JOB WHEN I GET OUT!

ENGINEERS MAKE LOTS OF MONEY, AND GET ALL THE GIRLS!

I'D NEVER SEEN SO MANY GIRLS WITH GORGEOUS KNOCKERS

BUT THERE WERE NO GIRLS IN ENGINEERING SCHOOL... AND THE ENGINEERS SURE WEREN'T SCORING MUCH!

ARE YOU GETTING ANY LATELY?

HAD A GOOD BEAVER SHOT TUESDAY!

I'M GOING OVER TO THE GIRLS GYM AND WATCH VOLLEY BALL PRACTICE!

LOOKIT THAT QUEER WEARING A BOAT NECK SWEATER!

YOUR GIRL FRIEND IS FLAT!

I HEAR THEY GOT NOOD MODELS IN ART DRAWING CLASSES IN THE ART BUILDING!

I'M GOING HOME AND BEAT OFF TO THE NEW PLAYBOY CENTER FOLD!

IT'S FRUITY TO WEAR JOCKEY SHORTS INSTEAD OF BOXERS!

YOURS IS A BOW-WOW!

WHERE'S THAT AT?

LOOK AT THE PANSY CARRYING A BRIEFCASE!

FUCK YOU!

SAME TO YOU!

ENGINEERING

SO I CHANGED MAJORS... SEVERAL TIMES.

THERE THEY WERE, EVERY WHERE YOU LOOKED, BUT SEEING THEM AND GETTING THEM WERE TWO DIFFERENT THINGS

HOW EMBARRASSING!

I WASN'T SURE I COULD STAND IT!

HOW ABOUT A COKE DATE?

DROP DEAD, CREEP!

IT SEEMED LIKE THE GOOD ONES ONLY WENT OUT WITH BMOC'S (BIG MEN ON CAMPUS) FRAT RATS, AND...

FOOTBALL PLAYERS.

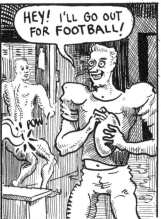

HEY! I'LL GO OUT FOR FOOTBALL!

POW

I WAS A GOOD ATHLETE! 175 LBS OF HARD MUSCLE. I COULD MAJOR IN PHYSICAL EDUCATION!

I WAS QUICK, FAST AND SMART... BUT NOT QUICK OR FAST ENOUGH, AND MAYBE NOT SO SMART AFTER ALL...

HANG ON TO THE BALL, NUMBNUTS!

63

FEELGOOD & PETERS P. 2.

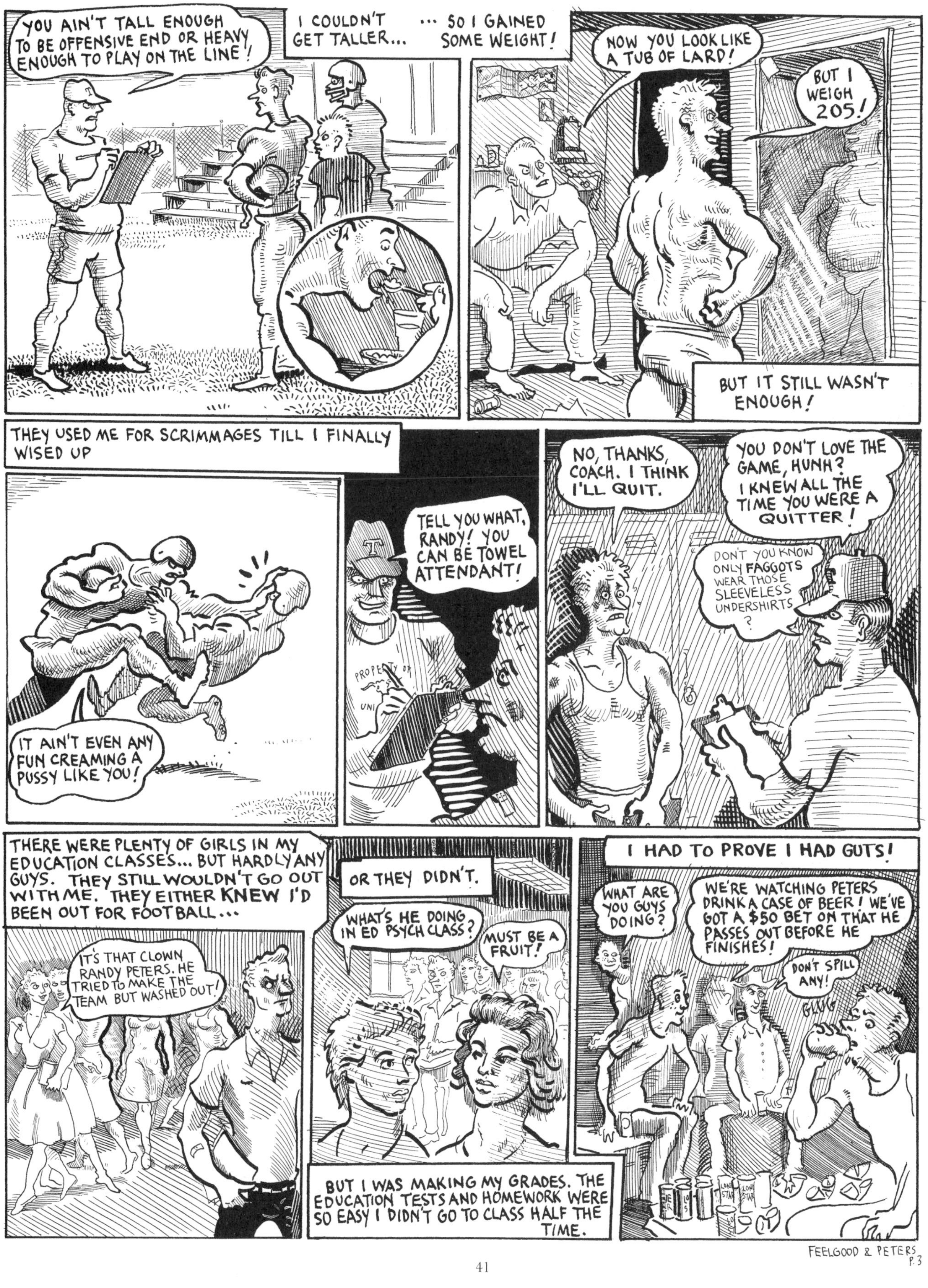
YOU AIN'T TALL ENOUGH TO BE OFFENSIVE END OR HEAVY ENOUGH TO PLAY ON THE LINE!
I COULDN'T GET TALLER...
...SO I GAINED SOME WEIGHT!
NOW YOU LOOK LIKE A TUB OF LARD!
BUT I WEIGH 205!
BUT IT STILL WASN'T ENOUGH!
THEY USED ME FOR SCRIMMAGES TILL I FINALLY WISED UP
IT AIN'T EVEN ANY FUN CREAMING A PUSSY LIKE YOU!
TELL YOU WHAT, RANDY! YOU CAN BE TOWEL ATTENDANT!
NO, THANKS, COACH. I THINK I'LL QUIT.
YOU DON'T LOVE THE GAME, HUNH? I KNEW ALL THE TIME YOU WERE A QUITTER!
DON'T YOU KNOW ONLY FAGGOTS WEAR THOSE SLEEVELESS UNDERSHIRTS?
THERE WERE PLENTY OF GIRLS IN MY EDUCATION CLASSES... BUT HARDLY ANY GUYS. THEY STILL WOULDN'T GO OUT WITH ME. THEY EITHER KNEW I'D BEEN OUT FOR FOOTBALL...
IT'S THAT CLOWN RANDY PETERS. HE TRIED TO MAKE THE TEAM BUT WASHED OUT!
OR THEY DIDN'T.
WHAT'S HE DOING IN ED PSYCH CLASS?
MUST BE A FRUIT!
BUT I WAS MAKING MY GRADES. THE EDUCATION TESTS AND HOMEWORK WERE SO EASY I DIDN'T GO TO CLASS HALF THE TIME.
I HAD TO PROVE I HAD GUTS!
WHAT ARE YOU GUYS DOING?
WE'RE WATCHING PETERS DRINK A CASE OF BEER! WE'VE GOT A $50 BET ON THAT HE PASSES OUT BEFORE HE FINISHES!
DON'T SPILL ANY!
GLUG
FEELGOOD & PETERS P. 3

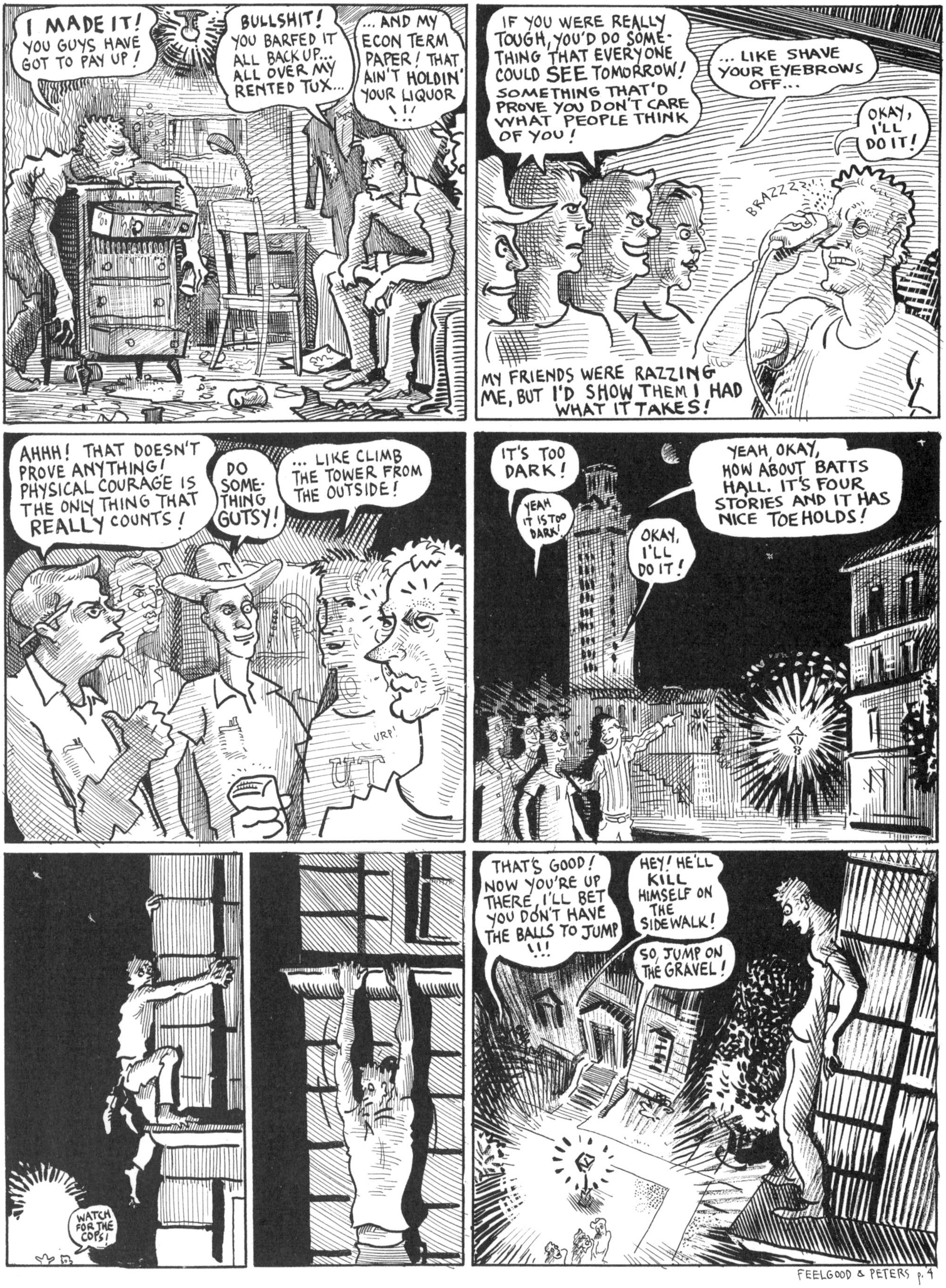
I MADE IT! YOU GUYS HAVE GOT TO PAY UP!
BULLSHIT! YOU BARFED IT ALL BACK UP... ALL OVER MY RENTED TUX...
...AND MY ECON TERM PAPER! THAT AIN'T HOLDIN' YOUR LIQUOR !!!
IF YOU WERE REALLY TOUGH, YOU'D DO SOMETHING THAT EVERYONE COULD SEE TOMORROW! SOMETHING THAT'D PROVE YOU DON'T CARE WHAT PEOPLE THINK OF YOU!
...LIKE SHAVE YOUR EYEBROWS OFF...
OKAY, I'LL DO IT!
BRAZZZZ
MY FRIENDS WERE RAZZING ME, BUT I'D SHOW THEM I HAD WHAT IT TAKES!
AHHH! THAT DOESN'T PROVE ANYTHING! PHYSICAL COURAGE IS THE ONLY THING THAT REALLY COUNTS!
DO SOMETHING GUTSY!
...LIKE CLIMB THE TOWER FROM THE OUTSIDE!
URP!
U.T
IT'S TOO DARK!
YEAH IT IS TOO DARK!
YEAH, OKAY, HOW ABOUT BATTS HALL. IT'S FOUR STORIES AND IT HAS NICE TOEHOLDS!
OKAY, I'LL DO IT!
WATCH FOR THE COPS!
THAT'S GOOD! NOW YOU'RE UP THERE, I'LL BET YOU DON'T HAVE THE BALLS TO JUMP !!!
HEY! HE'LL KILL HIMSELF ON THE SIDEWALK!
SO, JUMP ON THE GRAVEL!

FEELGOOD & PETERS p. 4

SO I DID IT.

WOW, MAN

THAT'S WHAT I CALL INTESTINAL FORTITUDE, MOXIE, AND CHUTZPA!

I'M NOT IMPRESSED

HOW COME, MAN?

HE WAS DRUNK! IN HIS BEFUDDLED CONDITION HE DIDN'T REALIZE HOW MUCH IT WOULD HURT!

HE WAS PRETTY BOMBED!

THE HELL I DIDN'T!

I'VE DONE STUFF LIKE THIS LOTS OF TIMES BEFORE !!!

I'LL BET YOU WOULD'NT DO IT AGAIN!

SO I DID IT AGAIN.

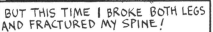

BUT THIS TIME I BROKE BOTH LEGS AND FRACTURED MY SPINE!

MAN, ARE YOU LUCKY! NOW YOU'LL BE 4-F. EVEN IF YOU FLUNK OUT THEY WON'T DRAFT YOU!

HE JUST DID IT BECAUSE HE WAS TOO CHICKENSHIT TO GET DRAFTED.

I AWREADY GOT MY NOTICE

SO, ONE OF MY BIG PROBLEMS WAS TAKEN CARE OF... BUT THE OTHER ONE HAD GOTTEN WORSE!

YER HOUR'S UP, MAN! I KIN SEE THE GRAVITY OF DAT SITCH'ATION, 'CAUSE I KIN SEE HOW YOU TURNED OUT. I GONNA PRESCRIBE JOGGIN' FO' YA!

JOGGING?

BRONZE HOURS

YEAH, JOG DOWN TO THE CORNER AN BUY ME A SIX-PACK OF TREE-FROG BEER AND JOG BACK!

MORE TO FOLLOW ABOUT RANDY PETERS AND SEX IN THE SIXTIES IN THE CASEBOOK OF DR. FEELGOOD!

FEELGOOD & PETERS p.5

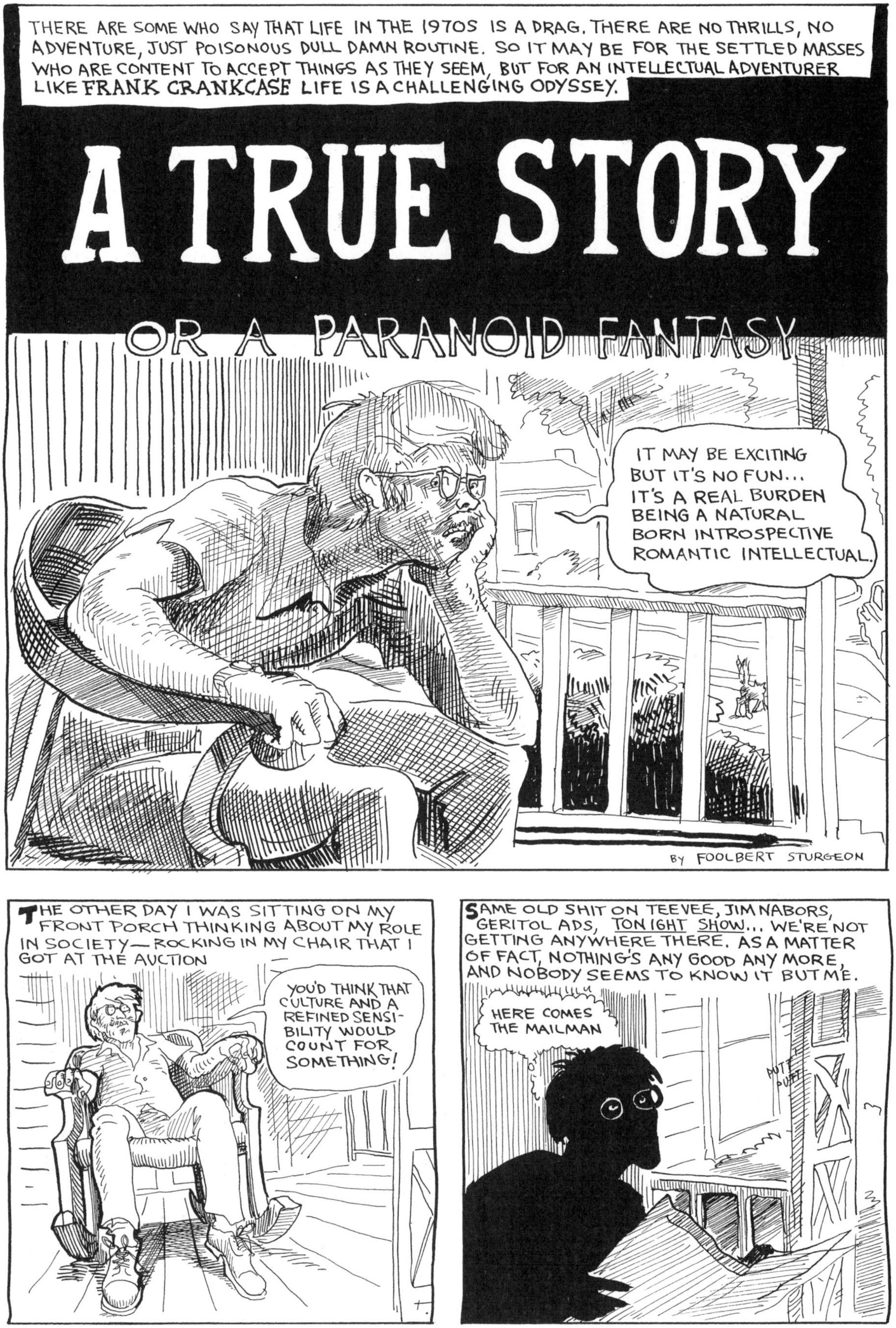
THERE ARE SOME WHO SAY THAT LIFE IN THE 1970S IS A DRAG. THERE ARE NO THRILLS, NO ADVENTURE, JUST POISONOUS DULL DAMN ROUTINE. SO IT MAY BE FOR THE SETTLED MASSES WHO ARE CONTENT TO ACCEPT THINGS AS THEY SEEM, BUT FOR AN INTELLECTUAL ADVENTURER LIKE FRANK CRANKCASE LIFE IS A CHALLENGING ODYSSEY.
A TRUE STORY
OR A PARANOID FANTASY
IT MAY BE EXCITING BUT IT'S NO FUN... IT'S A REAL BURDEN BEING A NATURAL BORN INTROSPECTIVE ROMANTIC INTELLECTUAL.
BY FOOLBERT STURGEON
THE OTHER DAY I WAS SITTING ON MY FRONT PORCH THINKING ABOUT MY ROLE IN SOCIETY— ROCKING IN MY CHAIR THAT I GOT AT THE AUCTION
YOU'D THINK THAT CULTURE AND A REFINED SENSI-BILITY WOULD COUNT FOR SOMETHING!
SAME OLD SHIT ON TEEVEE, JIM NABORS, GERITOL ADS, TONIGHT SHOW... WE'RE NOT GETTING ANYWHERE THERE. AS A MATTER OF FACT, NOTHING'S ANY GOOD ANY MORE, AND NOBODY SEEMS TO KNOW IT BUT ME.
HERE COMES THE MAILMAN
PUFF PUFF

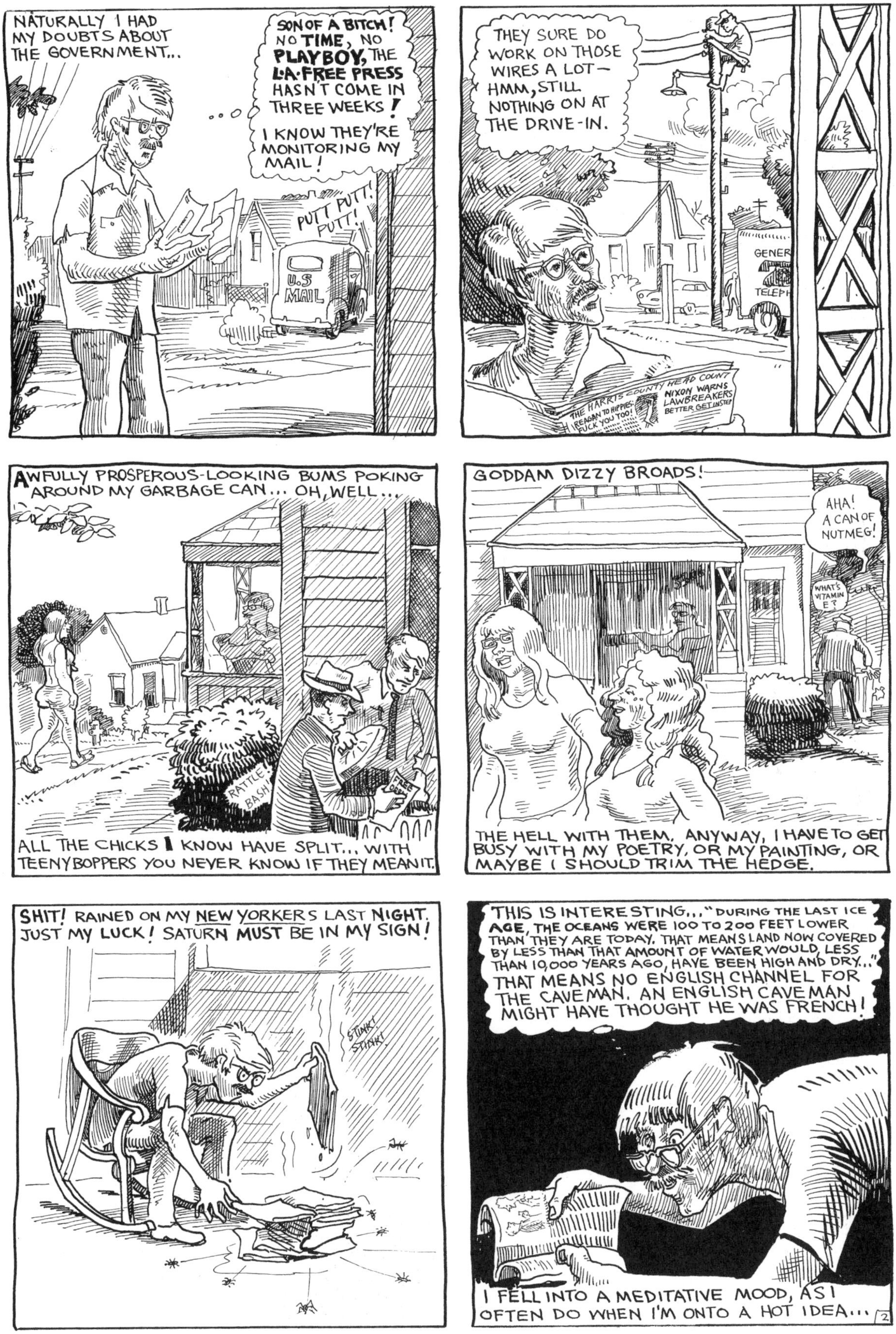
NATURALLY I HAD MY DOUBTS ABOUT THE GOVERNMENT...
SON OF A BITCH! NO TIME, NO PLAYBOY, THE L.A. FREE PRESS HASN'T COME IN THREE WEEKS!
I KNOW THEY'RE MONITORING MY MAIL!
PUTT PUTT! PUTT!
U.S MAIL
THEY SURE DO WORK ON THOSE WIRES A LOT— HMM, STILL NOTHING ON AT THE DRIVE-IN.
THE HARRIS COUNTY HEAD COUNT
REAGAN TO HIPPIES: FUCK YOU TOO!
NIXON WARNS LAWBREAKERS BETTER GET INSTEP
AWFULLY PROSPEROUS-LOOKING BUMS POKING AROUND MY GARBAGE CAN... OH, WELL...
RATTLE BASH
ALL THE CHICKS I KNOW HAVE SPLIT... WITH TEENYBOPPERS YOU NEVER KNOW IF THEY MEAN IT.
GODDAM DIZZY BROADS!
AHA! A CAN OF NUTMEG!
WHAT'S VITAMIN E?
THE HELL WITH THEM, ANYWAY, I HAVE TO GET BUSY WITH MY POETRY, OR MY PAINTING, OR MAYBE I SHOULD TRIM THE HEDGE.
SHIT! RAINED ON MY NEW YORKERS LAST NIGHT. JUST MY LUCK! SATURN MUST BE IN MY SIGN!
STINK! STINK!
THIS IS INTERESTING... "DURING THE LAST ICE AGE, THE OCEANS WERE 100 TO 200 FEET LOWER THAN THEY ARE TODAY. THAT MEANS LAND NOW COVERED BY LESS THAN THAT AMOUNT OF WATER WOULD, LESS THAN 10,000 YEARS AGO, HAVE BEEN HIGH AND DRY..." THAT MEANS NO ENGLISH CHANNEL FOR THE CAVEMAN. AN ENGLISH CAVEMAN MIGHT HAVE THOUGHT HE WAS FRENCH!
I FELL INTO A MEDITATIVE MOOD, AS I OFTEN DO WHEN I'M ONTO A HOT IDEA...
2

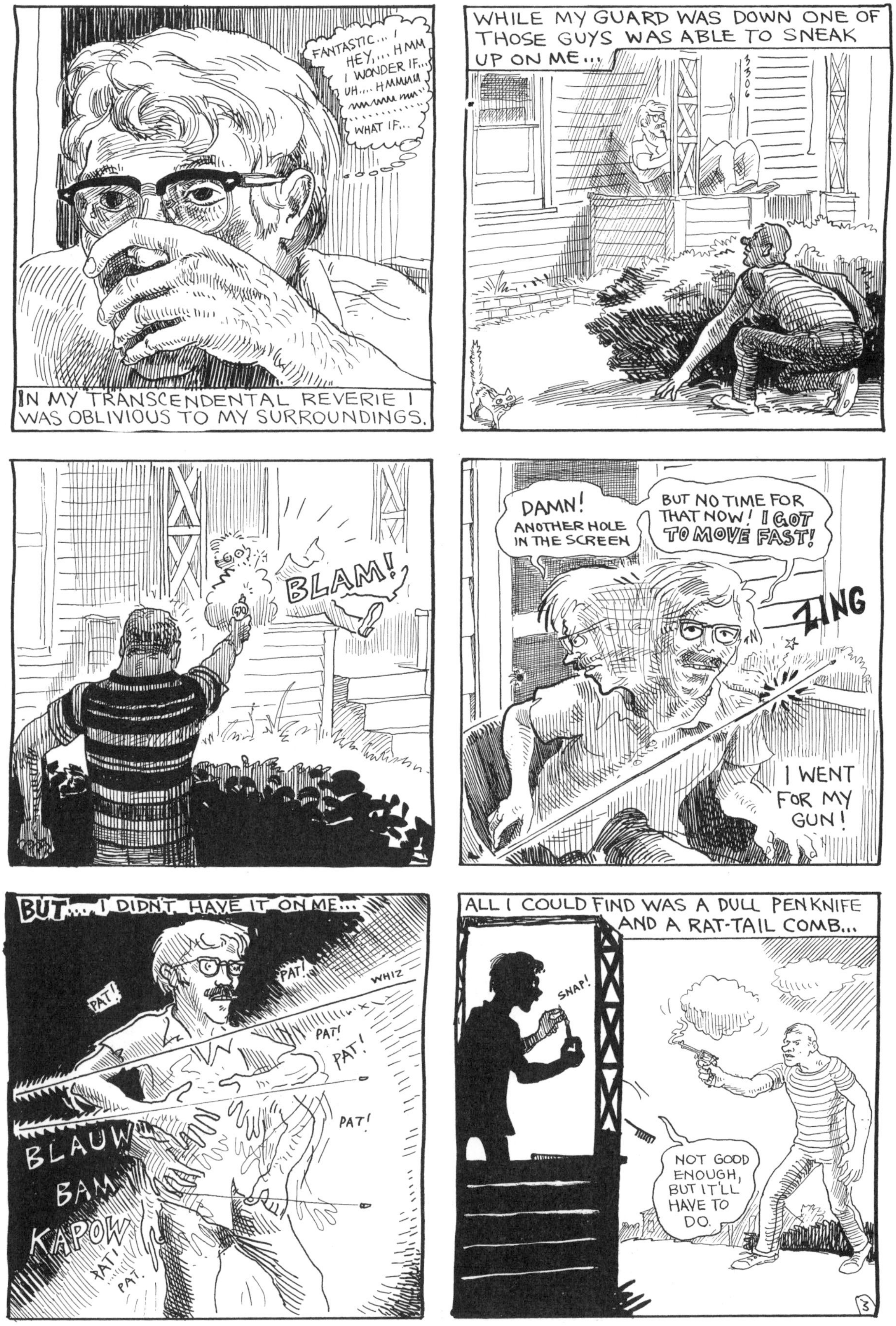
FANTASTIC... ! HEY,... HMM I WONDER IF... UH.... HMMM
WHAT IF...
IN MY TRANSCENDENTAL REVERIE I WAS OBLIVIOUS TO MY SURROUNDINGS.
WHILE MY GUARD WAS DOWN ONE OF THOSE GUYS WAS ABLE TO SNEAK UP ON ME...
3306
BLAM!
DAMN! ANOTHER HOLE IN THE SCREEN
BUT NO TIME FOR THAT NOW! I GOT TO MOVE FAST!
ZING
I WENT FOR MY GUN!
BUT... I DIDN'T HAVE IT ON ME...
PAT!
WHIZ
PAT!
PAT!
PAT!
PAT!
BLAUW
BAM
KAPOW
PAT!
PAT.
ALL I COULD FIND WAS A DULL PEN KNIFE AND A RAT-TAIL COMB...
SNAP!
NOT GOOD ENOUGH, BUT IT'LL HAVE TO DO.
3

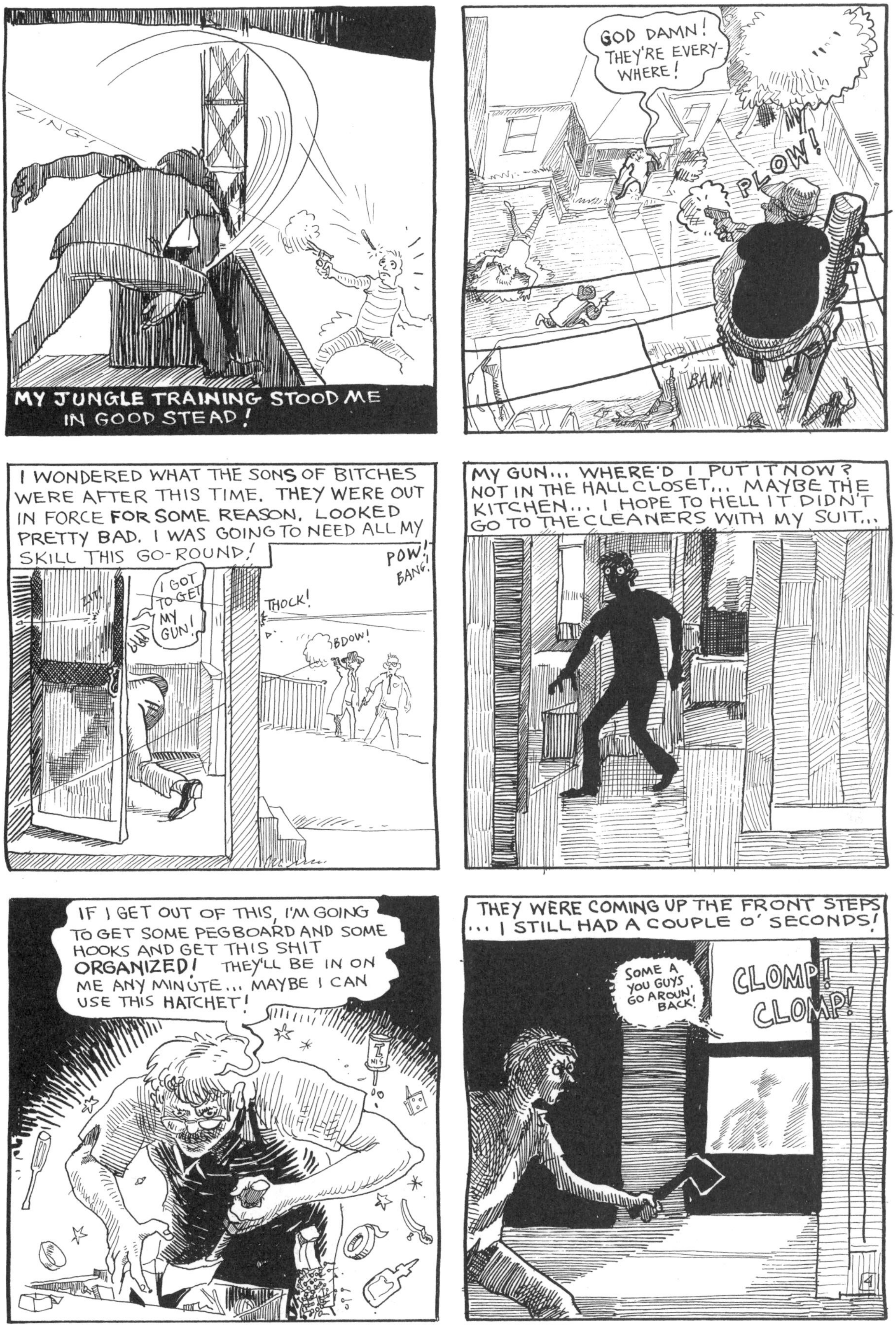
ZING!
MY JUNGLE TRAINING STOOD ME IN GOOD STEAD!
GOD DAMN! THEY'RE EVERY-WHERE!
PLOW!
BAM!
I WONDERED WHAT THE SONS OF BITCHES WERE AFTER THIS TIME. THEY WERE OUT IN FORCE FOR SOME REASON. LOOKED PRETTY BAD. I WAS GOING TO NEED ALL MY SKILL THIS GO-ROUND!
POW!
BANG!
I GOT TO GET MY GUN!
THOCK!
BDOW!
MY GUN... WHERE'D I PUT IT NOW? NOT IN THE HALL CLOSET... MAYBE THE KITCHEN... I HOPE TO HELL IT DIDN'T GO TO THE CLEANERS WITH MY SUIT...
IF I GET OUT OF THIS, I'M GOING TO GET SOME PEGBOARD AND SOME HOOKS AND GET THIS SHIT ORGANIZED! THEY'LL BE IN ON ME ANY MINUTE... MAYBE I CAN USE THIS HATCHET!
THEY WERE COMING UP THE FRONT STEPS ... I STILL HAD A COUPLE O' SECONDS!
SOME A YOU GUYS GO AROUN' BACK!
CLOMP! CLOMP!
4

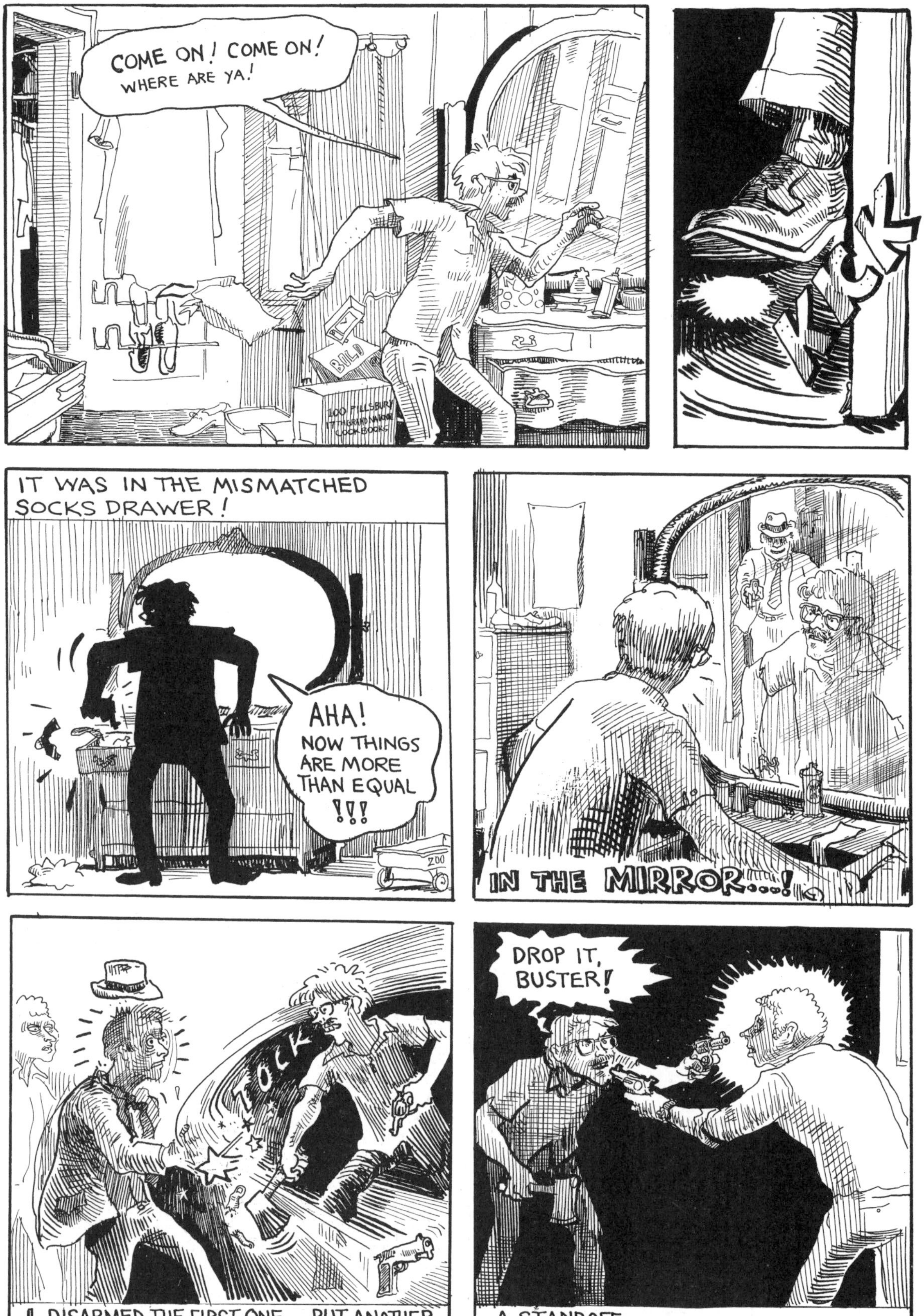
COME ON! COME ON!
WHERE ARE YA!
IT WAS IN THE MISMATCHED SOCKS DRAWER!
AHA! NOW THINGS ARE MORE THAN EQUAL !!!
IN THE MIRROR...!
TOCK
I DISARMED THE FIRST ONE... BUT ANOTHER GUY WAS JUST BEHIND!
DROP IT, BUSTER!
A STANDOFF... WHO HAD THE BEST NERVES?

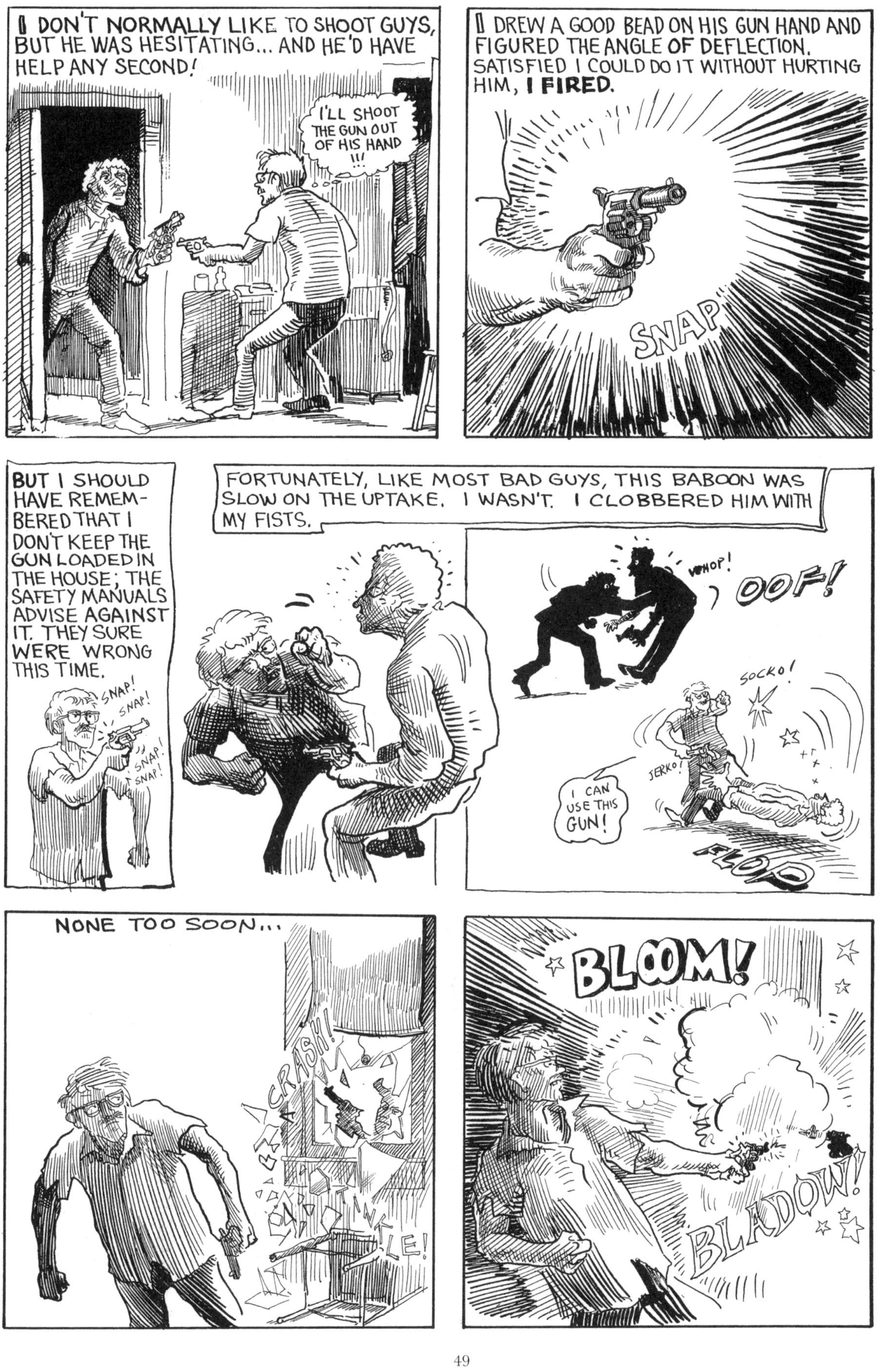

I DON'T NORMALLY LIKE TO SHOOT GUYS, BUT HE WAS HESITATING... AND HE'D HAVE HELP ANY SECOND!
I'LL SHOOT THE GUN OUT OF HIS HAND !!!
I DREW A GOOD BEAD ON HIS GUN HAND AND FIGURED THE ANGLE OF DEFLECTION. SATISFIED I COULD DO IT WITHOUT HURTING HIM, I FIRED.
SNAP
BUT I SHOULD HAVE REMEMBERED THAT I DON'T KEEP THE GUN LOADED IN THE HOUSE; THE SAFETY MANUALS ADVISE AGAINST IT. THEY SURE WERE WRONG THIS TIME.
SNAP! SNAP!
SNAP! SNAP!
FORTUNATELY, LIKE MOST BAD GUYS, THIS BABOON WAS SLOW ON THE UPTAKE. I WASN'T. I CLOBBERED HIM WITH MY FISTS.
WHOP!
OOF!
SOCKO!
JERKO!
I CAN USE THIS GUN!
FLOP
NONE TOO SOON...
CRASH!
BLOOM!
BLADOW!

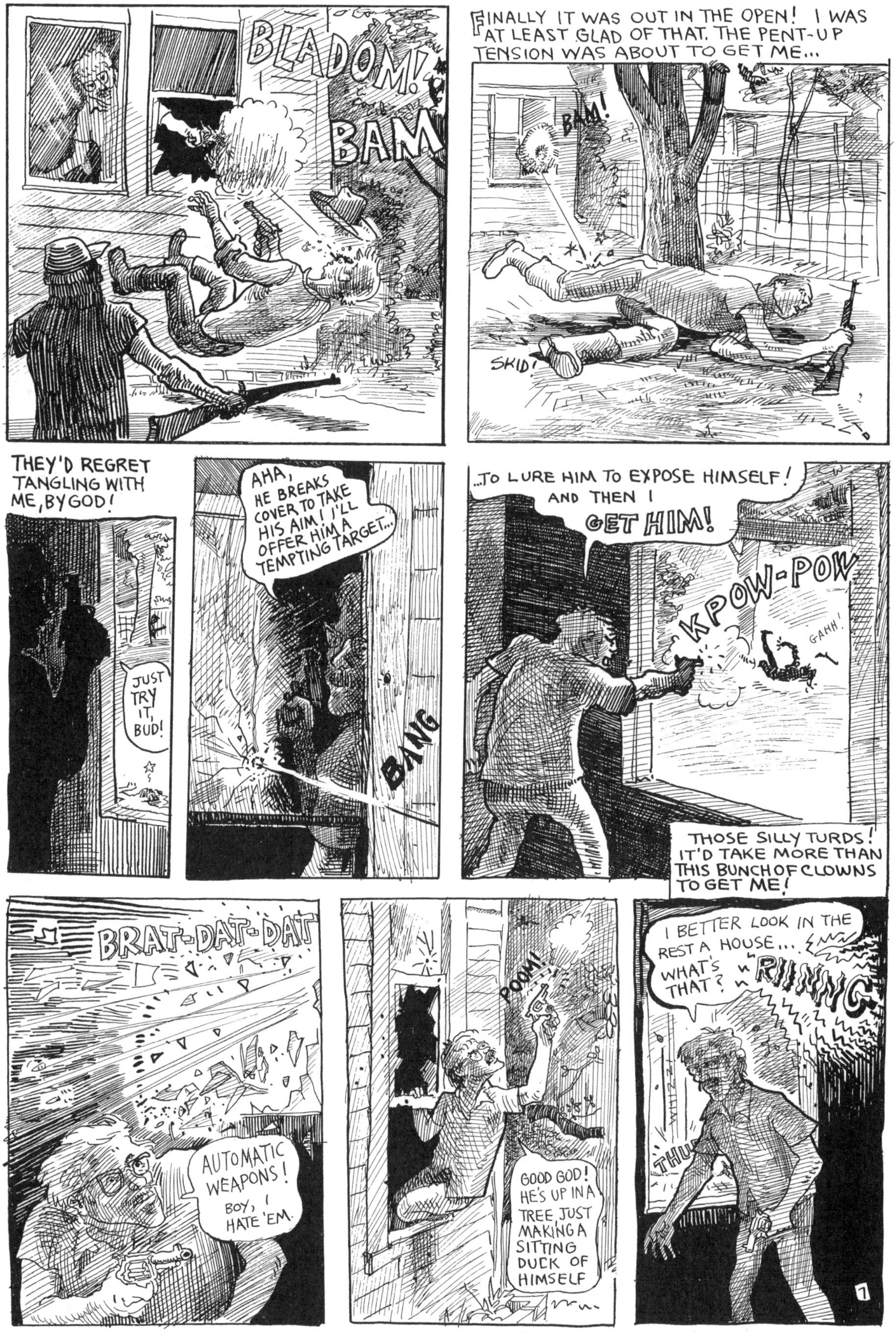
BLADOM!
BAM
FINALLY IT WAS OUT IN THE OPEN! I WAS AT LEAST GLAD OF THAT. THE PENT-UP TENSION WAS ABOUT TO GET ME...
BAM!
SKID!
THEY'D REGRET TANGLING WITH ME, BY GOD!
JUST TRY IT, BUD!
AHA, HE BREAKS COVER TO TAKE HIS AIM! I'LL OFFER HIM A TEMPTING TARGET...
BANG
...TO LURE HIM TO EXPOSE HIMSELF! AND THEN I
GET HIM!
KPOW-POW
GAHH!
THOSE SILLY TURDS! IT'D TAKE MORE THAN THIS BUNCH OF CLOWNS TO GET ME!
BRAT-DAT-DAT
AUTOMATIC WEAPONS!
BOY, I HATE 'EM.
POOM!
GOOD GOD! HE'S UP IN A TREE JUST MAKING A SITTING DUCK OF HIMSELF
I BETTER LOOK IN THE REST A HOUSE... WHAT'S THAT?
RIIING
7

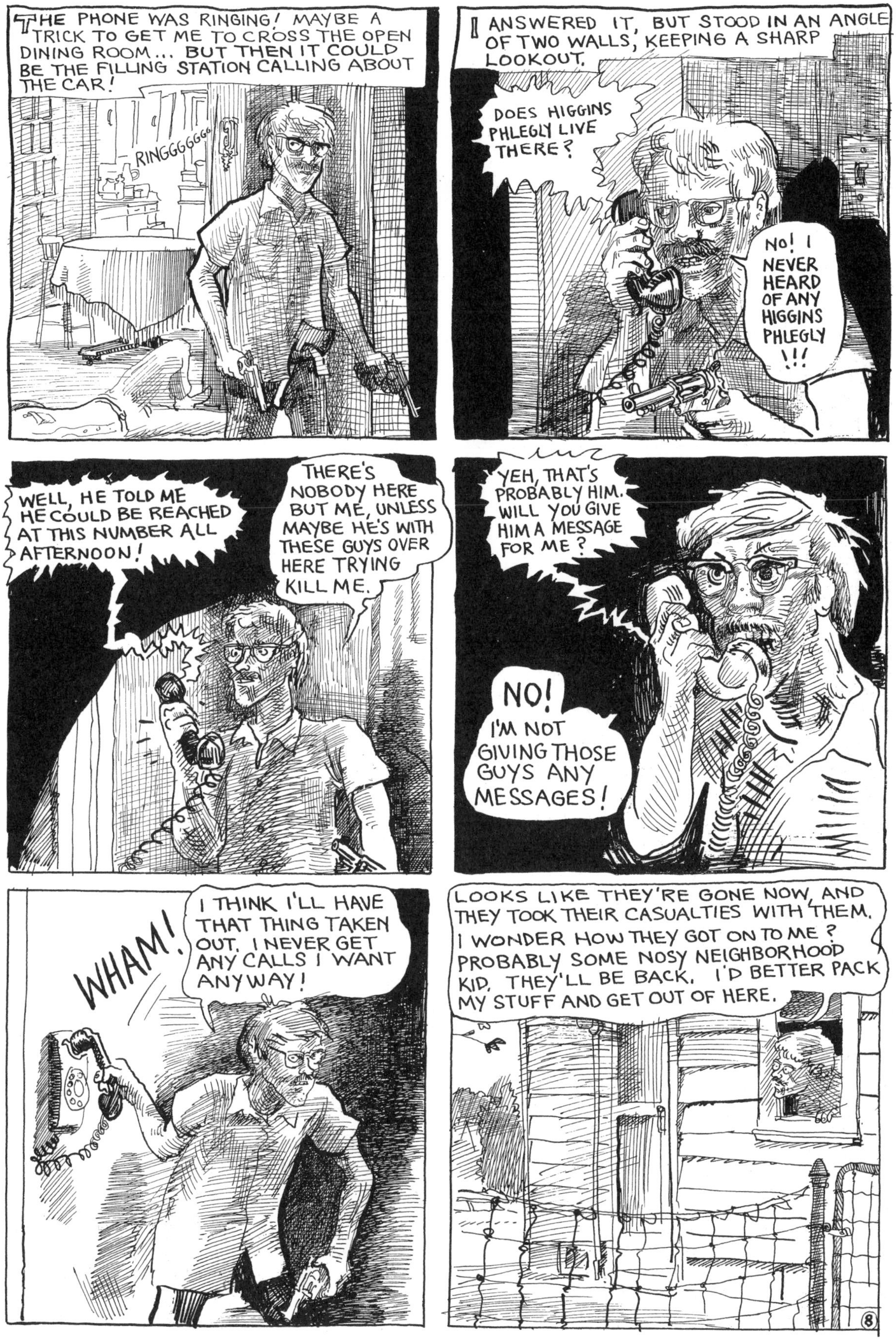
THE PHONE WAS RINGING! MAYBE A TRICK TO GET ME TO CROSS THE OPEN DINING ROOM... BUT THEN IT COULD BE THE FILLING STATION CALLING ABOUT THE CAR!
RINGGGGGGG
I ANSWERED IT, BUT STOOD IN AN ANGLE OF TWO WALLS, KEEPING A SHARP LOOKOUT.
DOES HIGGINS PHLEGLY LIVE THERE?
NO! I NEVER HEARD OF ANY HIGGINS PHLEGLY !!!
WELL, HE TOLD ME HE COULD BE REACHED AT THIS NUMBER ALL AFTERNOON!
THERE'S NOBODY HERE BUT ME, UNLESS MAYBE HE'S WITH THESE GUYS OVER HERE TRYING KILL ME.
YEH, THAT'S PROBABLY HIM. WILL YOU GIVE HIM A MESSAGE FOR ME?
NO! I'M NOT GIVING THOSE GUYS ANY MESSAGES!
WHAM!
I THINK I'LL HAVE THAT THING TAKEN OUT. I NEVER GET ANY CALLS I WANT ANYWAY!
LOOKS LIKE THEY'RE GONE NOW, AND THEY TOOK THEIR CASUALTIES WITH THEM. I WONDER HOW THEY GOT ON TO ME? PROBABLY SOME NOSY NEIGHBORHOOD KID. THEY'LL BE BACK. I'D BETTER PACK MY STUFF AND GET OUT OF HERE.
8

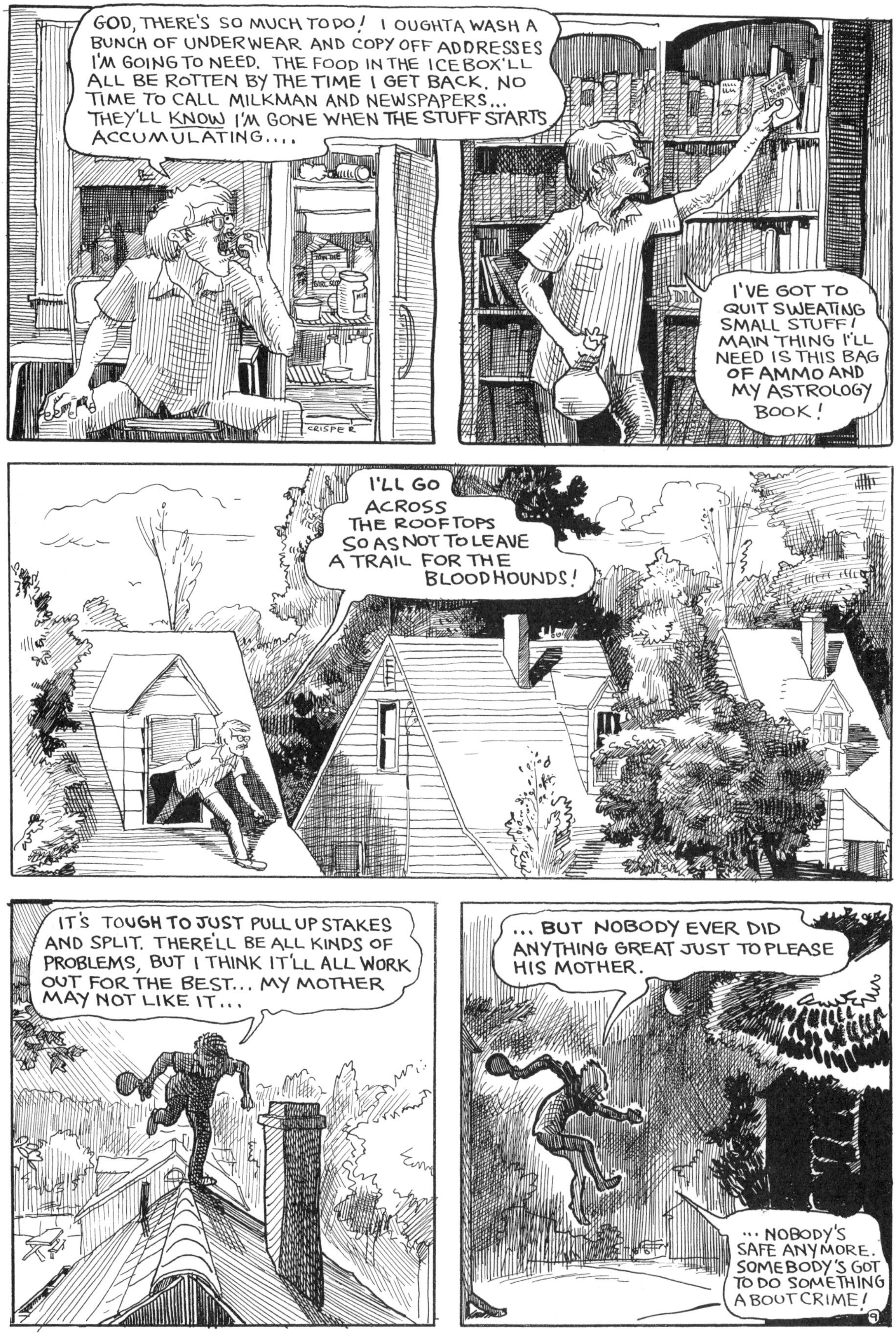

GOD, THERE'S SO MUCH TO DO! I OUGHTA WASH A BUNCH OF UNDERWEAR AND COPY OFF ADDRESSES I'M GOING TO NEED. THE FOOD IN THE ICEBOX'LL ALL BE ROTTEN BY THE TIME I GET BACK. NO TIME TO CALL MILKMAN AND NEWSPAPERS... THEY'LL KNOW I'M GONE WHEN THE STUFF STARTS ACCUMULATING....
CRISPER
I'VE GOT TO QUIT SWEATING SMALL STUFF! MAIN THING I'LL NEED IS THIS BAG OF AMMO AND MY ASTROLOGY BOOK!
I'LL GO ACROSS THE ROOFTOPS SO AS NOT TO LEAVE A TRAIL FOR THE BLOODHOUNDS!
IT'S TOUGH TO JUST PULL UP STAKES AND SPLIT. THERE'LL BE ALL KINDS OF PROBLEMS, BUT I THINK IT'LL ALL WORK OUT FOR THE BEST... MY MOTHER MAY NOT LIKE IT...
... BUT NOBODY EVER DID ANYTHING GREAT JUST TO PLEASE HIS MOTHER.
... NOBODY'S SAFE ANYMORE. SOMEBODY'S GOT TO DO SOMETHING ABOUT CRIME!
9

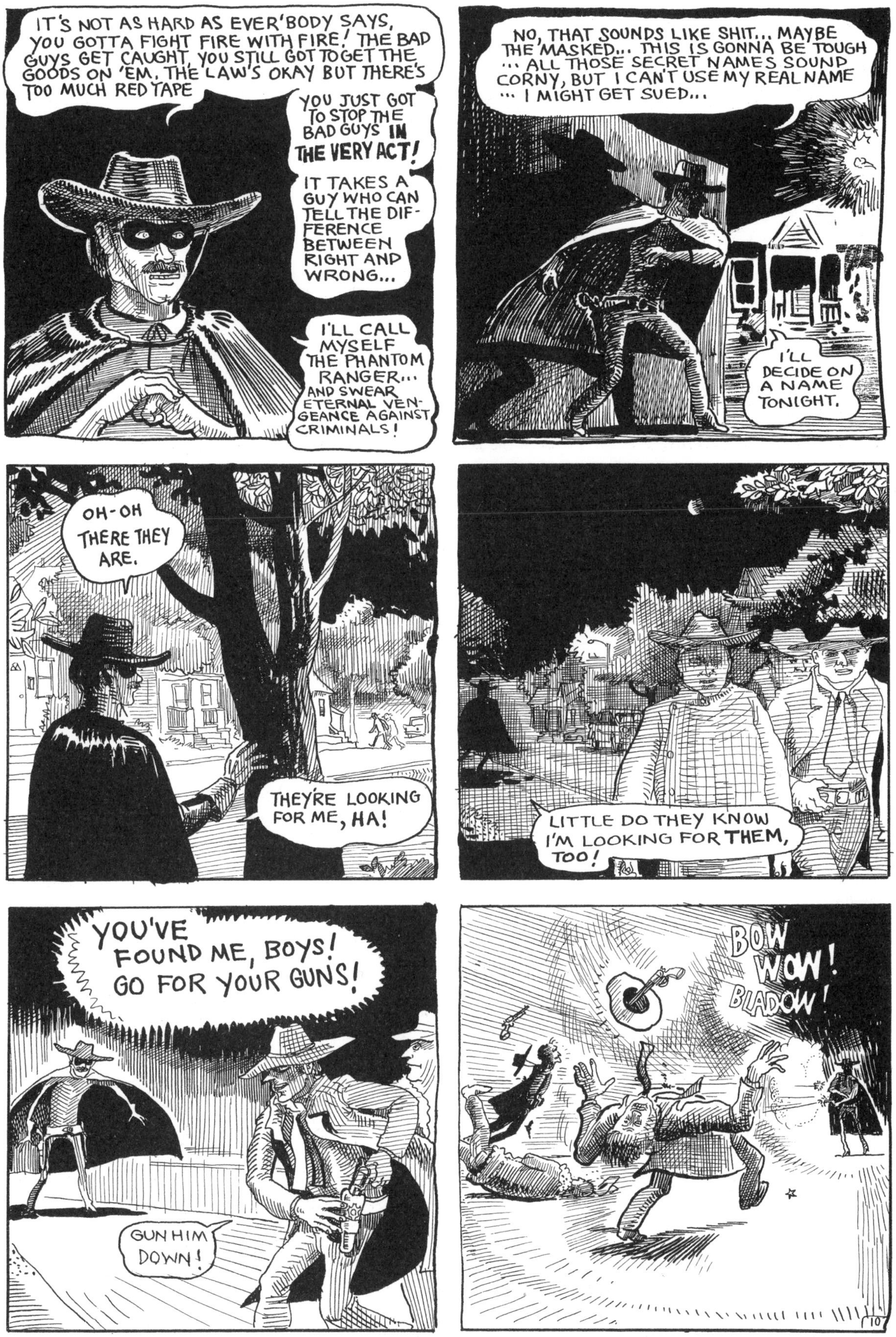

IT'S NOT AS HARD AS EVER'BODY SAYS, YOU GOTTA FIGHT FIRE WITH FIRE! THE BAD GUYS GET CAUGHT, YOU STILL GOT TO GET THE GOODS ON 'EM. THE LAW'S OKAY BUT THERE'S TOO MUCH RED TAPE
YOU JUST GOT TO STOP THE BAD GUYS IN THE VERY ACT!
IT TAKES A GUY WHO CAN TELL THE DIFFERENCE BETWEEN RIGHT AND WRONG...
I'LL CALL MYSELF THE PHANTOM RANGER... AND SWEAR ETERNAL VENGEANCE AGAINST CRIMINALS!
NO, THAT SOUNDS LIKE SHIT... MAYBE THE MASKED... THIS IS GONNA BE TOUGH ... ALL THOSE SECRET NAMES SOUND CORNY, BUT I CAN'T USE MY REAL NAME ... I MIGHT GET SUED...
I'LL DECIDE ON A NAME TONIGHT.
OH-OH THERE THEY ARE.
THEY'RE LOOKING FOR ME, HA!
LITTLE DO THEY KNOW I'M LOOKING FOR THEM, TOO!
YOU'VE FOUND ME, BOYS! GO FOR YOUR GUNS!
GUN HIM DOWN!
BOW WOW! BLADOW!
10

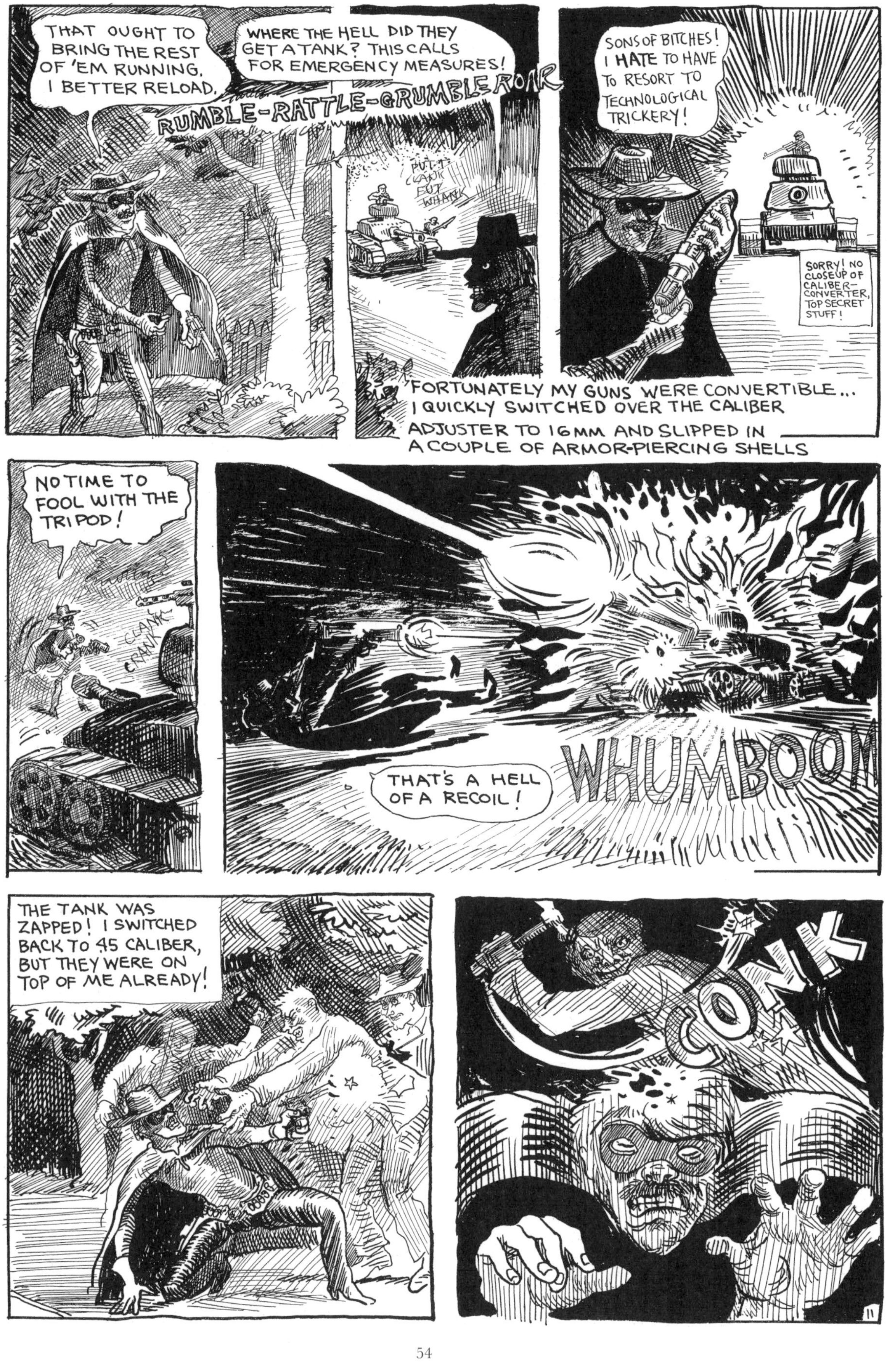
THAT OUGHT TO BRING THE REST OF 'EM RUNNING. I BETTER RELOAD.
WHERE THE HELL DID THEY GET A TANK? THIS CALLS FOR EMERGENCY MEASURES!
RUMBLE-RATTLE-GRUMBLE-ROAR
PUT-T- CLANK PUT WHANK
SONS OF BITCHES! I HATE TO HAVE TO RESORT TO TECHNOLOGICAL TRICKERY!
SORRY! NO CLOSEUP OF CALIBER-CONVERTER, TOP SECRET STUFF!
FORTUNATELY MY GUNS WERE CONVERTIBLE... I QUICKLY SWITCHED OVER THE CALIBER ADJUSTER TO 16MM AND SLIPPED IN A COUPLE OF ARMOR-PIERCING SHELLS
NO TIME TO FOOL WITH THE TRIPOD!
CLANK CRANK
THAT'S A HELL OF A RECOIL!
WHUMBOOM
THE TANK WAS ZAPPED! I SWITCHED BACK TO .45 CALIBER, BUT THEY WERE ON TOP OF ME ALREADY!
CONK
11

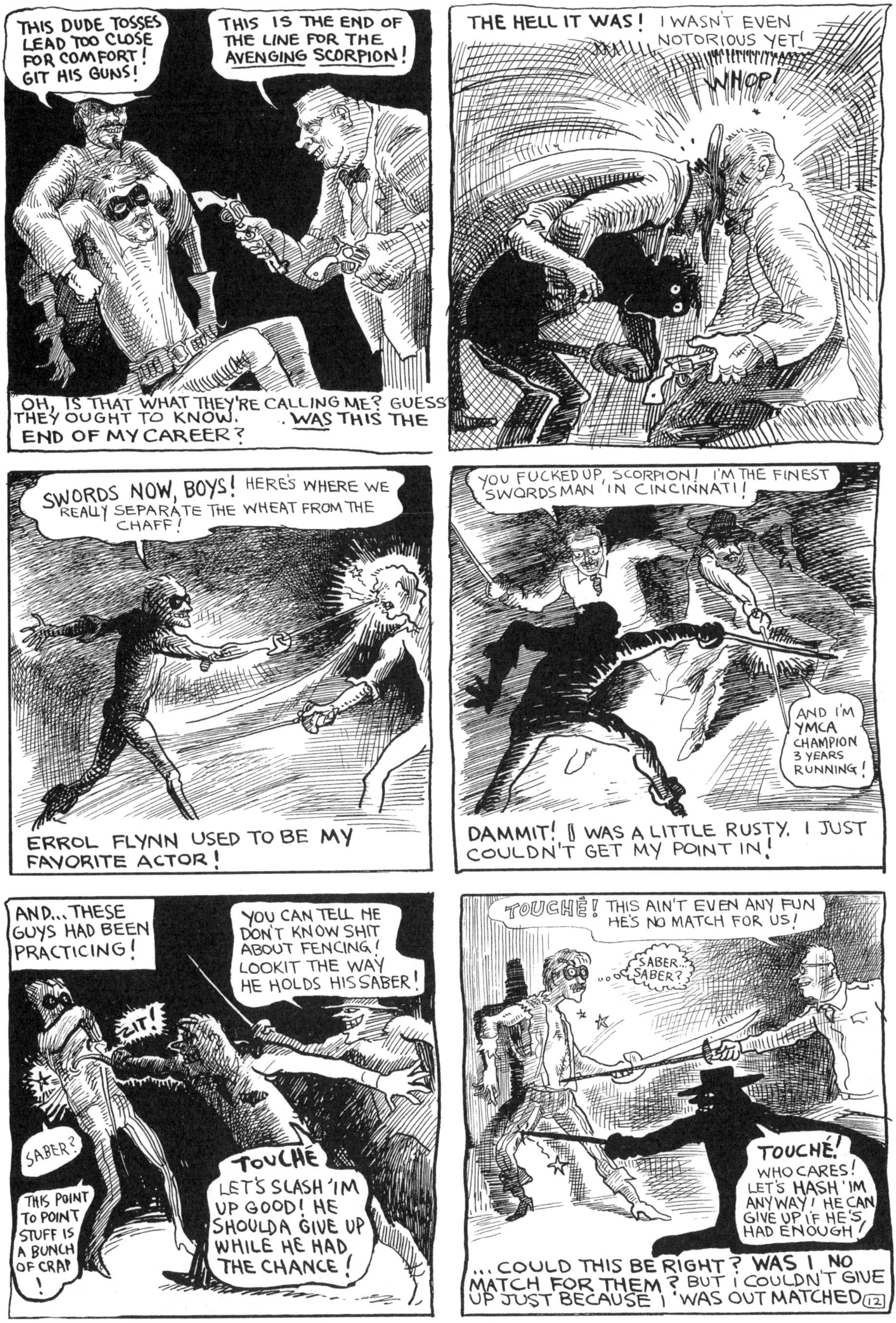
THIS DUDE TOSSES LEAD TOO CLOSE FOR COMFORT! GIT HIS GUNS!
THIS IS THE END OF THE LINE FOR THE AVENGING SCORPION!
OH, IS THAT WHAT THEY'RE CALLING ME? GUESS THEY OUGHT TO KNOW. . WAS THIS THE END OF MY CAREER?
THE HELL IT WAS! I WASN'T EVEN NOTORIOUS YET!
WHOP!
SWORDS NOW, BOYS! HERE'S WHERE WE REALLY SEPARATE THE WHEAT FROM THE CHAFF!
ERROL FLYNN USED TO BE MY FAVORITE ACTOR!
YOU FUCKED UP, SCORPION! I'M THE FINEST SWORDSMAN IN CINCINNATI!
AND I'M YMCA CHAMPION 3 YEARS RUNNING!
DAMMIT! I WAS A LITTLE RUSTY. I JUST COULDN'T GET MY POINT IN!
AND... THESE GUYS HAD BEEN PRACTICING!
YOU CAN TELL HE DON'T KNOW SHIT ABOUT FENCING! LOOKIT THE WAY HE HOLDS HIS SABER!
ZIT!
SABER?
THIS POINT TO POINT STUFF IS A BUNCH OF CRAP!
TOUCHÉ LET'S SLASH 'IM UP GOOD! HE SHOULDA GIVE UP WHILE HE HAD THE CHANCE!
TOUCHÉ! THIS AIN'T EVEN ANY FUN HE'S NO MATCH FOR US!
SABER... SABER?
TOUCHÉ! WHO CARES! LET'S HASH 'IM ANYWAY! HE CAN GIVE UP IF HE'S HAD ENOUGH!
...COULD THIS BE RIGHT? WAS I NO MATCH FOR THEM? BUT I COULDN'T GIVE UP JUST BECAUSE I WAS OUT MATCHED
12

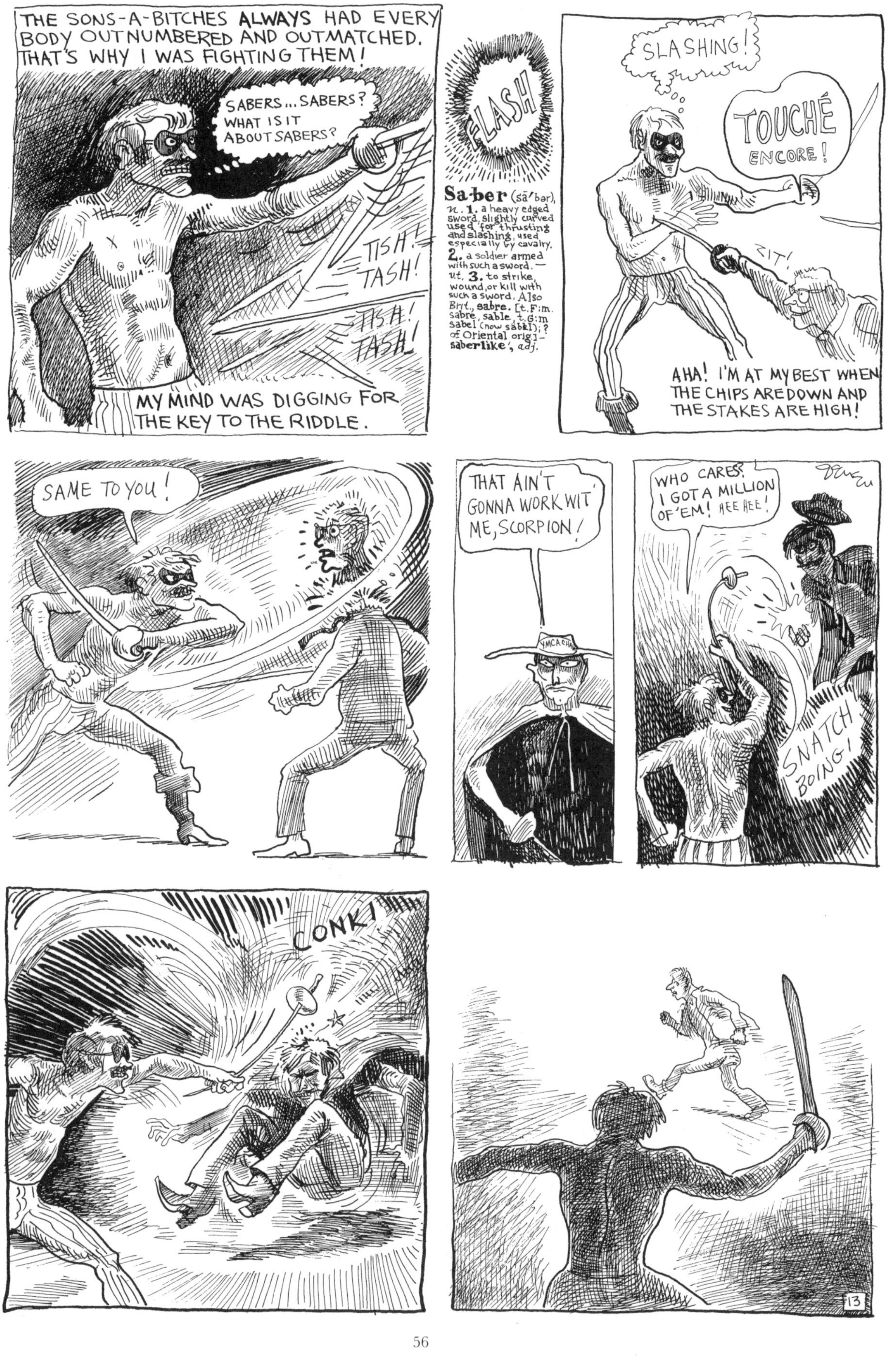

THE SONS-A-BITCHES ALWAYS HAD EVERY BODY OUTNUMBERED AND OUTMATCHED. THAT'S WHY I WAS FIGHTING THEM!
SABERS... SABERS? WHAT IS IT ABOUT SABERS?
TISH! TASH!
TISH! TASH!
MY MIND WAS DIGGING FOR THE KEY TO THE RIDDLE.
FLASH
Sa·ber (sā′bər), n. 1. a heavy edged sword, slightly curved used for thrusting and slashing, used especially by cavalry. 2. a soldier armed with such a sword. —v.t. 3. to strike, wound, or kill with such a sword. Also Brit., sabre. [t. F: m. sabre, sable, t. G: m sabel (now säbel); ? of Oriental orig.] —saberlike′, adj.
SLASHING!
TOUCHÉ ENCORE!
ZIT!
AHA! I'M AT MY BEST WHEN THE CHIPS ARE DOWN AND THE STAKES ARE HIGH!
SAME TO YOU!
THAT AIN'T GONNA WORK WIT' ME, SCORPION!
YMCA
WHO CARES? I GOT A MILLION OF 'EM! HEE HEE!
SNATCH! BOING!
CONK!
13

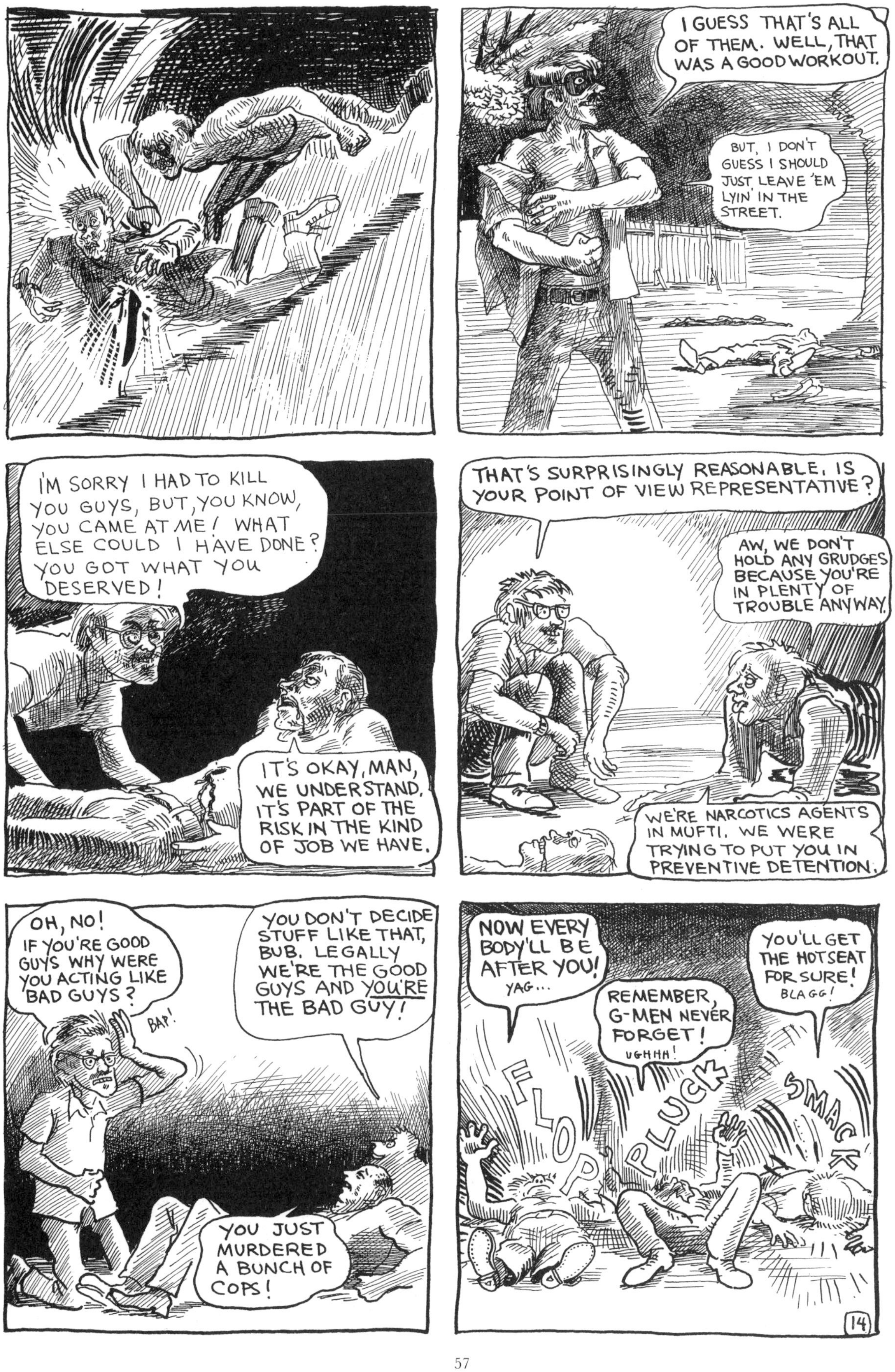
I GUESS THAT'S ALL OF THEM. WELL, THAT WAS A GOOD WORKOUT.
BUT, I DON'T GUESS I SHOULD JUST LEAVE 'EM LYIN' IN THE STREET.
I'M SORRY I HAD TO KILL YOU GUYS, BUT, YOU KNOW, YOU CAME AT ME! WHAT ELSE COULD I HAVE DONE? YOU GOT WHAT YOU DESERVED!
IT'S OKAY, MAN, WE UNDERSTAND, IT'S PART OF THE RISK IN THE KIND OF JOB WE HAVE.
THAT'S SURPRISINGLY REASONABLE. IS YOUR POINT OF VIEW REPRESENTATIVE?
AW, WE DON'T HOLD ANY GRUDGES BECAUSE YOU'RE IN PLENTY OF TROUBLE ANYWAY.
WE'RE NARCOTICS AGENTS IN MUFTI. WE WERE TRYING TO PUT YOU IN PREVENTIVE DETENTION.
OH, NO! IF YOU'RE GOOD GUYS WHY WERE YOU ACTING LIKE BAD GUYS?
BAP!
YOU DON'T DECIDE STUFF LIKE THAT, BUB. LEGALLY WE'RE THE GOOD GUYS AND YOU'RE THE BAD GUY!
YOU JUST MURDERED A BUNCH OF COPS!
NOW EVERY BODY'LL BE AFTER YOU!
YAG...
REMEMBER, G-MEN NEVER FORGET!
UGHHH!
YOU'LL GET THE HOTSEAT FOR SURE!
BLAGG!
FLOP
PLUCK
SMACK
14

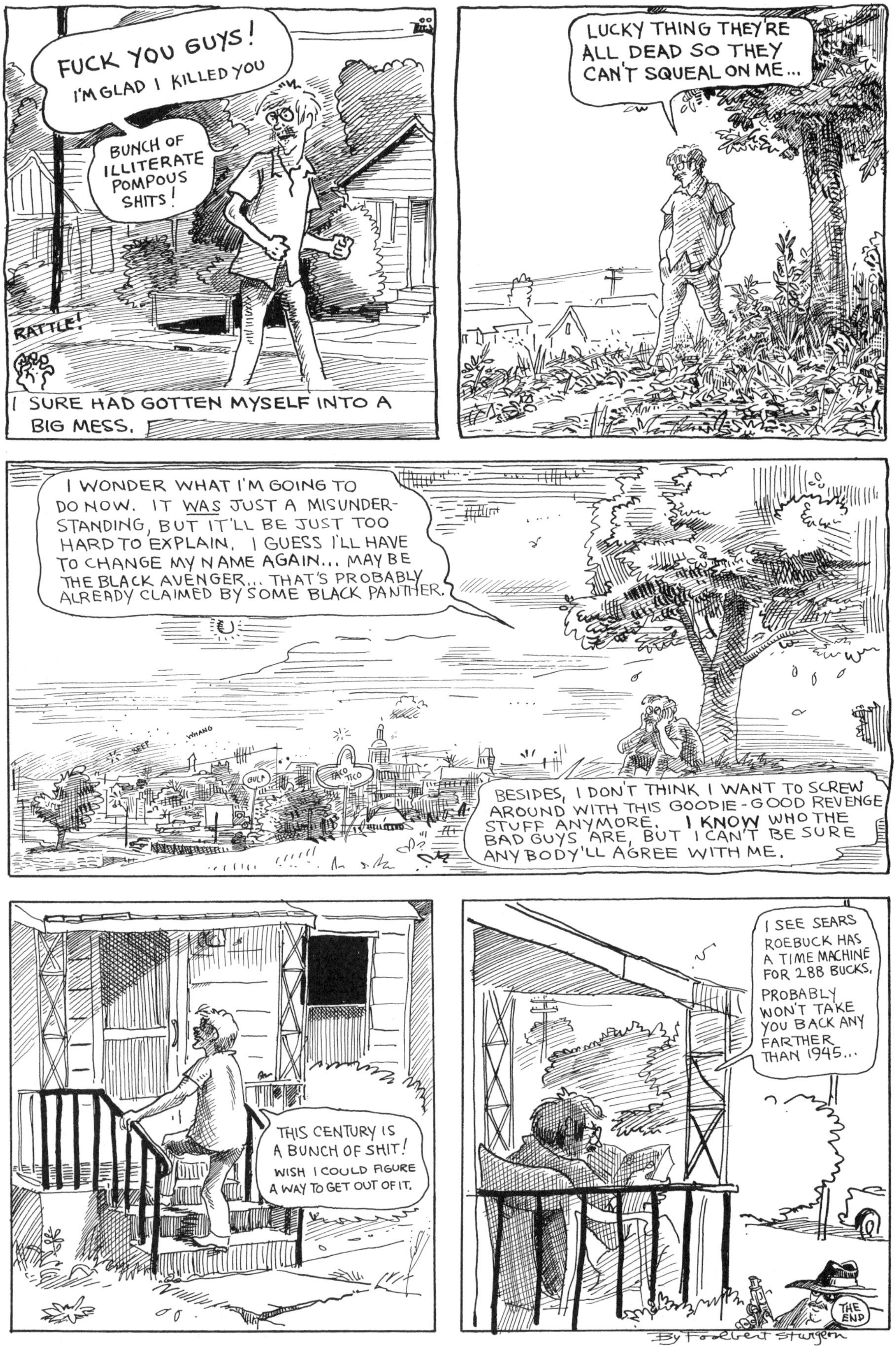
FUCK YOU GUYS! I'M GLAD I KILLED YOU
BUNCH OF ILLITERATE POMPOUS SHITS!
RATTLE!
I SURE HAD GOTTEN MYSELF INTO A BIG MESS.
LUCKY THING THEY'RE ALL DEAD SO THEY CAN'T SQUEAL ON ME...
I WONDER WHAT I'M GOING TO DO NOW. IT WAS JUST A MISUNDERSTANDING, BUT IT'LL BE JUST TOO HARD TO EXPLAIN. I GUESS I'LL HAVE TO CHANGE MY NAME AGAIN... MAYBE THE BLACK AVENGER... THAT'S PROBABLY ALREADY CLAIMED BY SOME BLACK PANTHER.
BEEP
WHANG
GULP
TACO TICO
BESIDES, I DON'T THINK I WANT TO SCREW AROUND WITH THIS GOODIE-GOOD REVENGE STUFF ANYMORE. I KNOW WHO THE BAD GUYS ARE, BUT I CAN'T BE SURE ANYBODY'LL AGREE WITH ME.
THIS CENTURY IS A BUNCH OF SHIT! WISH I COULD FIGURE A WAY TO GET OUT OF IT.
I SEE SEARS ROEBUCK HAS A TIME MACHINE FOR 288 BUCKS.
PROBABLY WON'T TAKE YOU BACK ANY FARTHER THAN 1945...
THE END
By Foolbert Sturgeon

FRANK CRANKCASE'S
Time Machine
by foolbert sturgeon

THE SEVENTIES WERE **DULL** IF NOT WORSE. ARE THE EIGHTIES GOING TO BE BETTER? LET'S GET THE HELL OUT OF HERE!

IT'S MAILTIME AT THE HOME OF MIDWESTERN INTELLECTUAL FRANK CRANKCASE!

JUNK MAIL! AT LEAST THE OVERDRAFTS AREN'T COMING OUT YET!

HEY! SEARS SALE CATALOG LISTS A TIME MACHINE FOR ONLY 89 BUCKS! I'VE ALWAYS WANTED ONE!

BUT "WHOLE EARTH CATALOG" SAID THAT MACHINE WAS REAL CRUMMY. I DON'T WANT TO GET BURNED...

CONSUMER GUIDE SAYS YOU'VE GOT TO SPEND AS MUCH ON A TIME MACHINE AS YOU'D PAY FOR A LAWN MOWER!

JUST AS I THOUGHT! EPA RECALLED THAT MODEL LAST YEAR! IT KEPT GETTING STUCK ON 1968!

I'M NOT GONNA BUY THAT PIECE OF **JUNK!** WHAT A STOOPID IDEA ANYWAY, BUYING A TIME MACHINE FROM SEARS!

HOW DUMB DO THEY THINK I AM? I'VE LEARNED A FEW THINGS OVER THE YEARS!

I'M NO PIGEON* !!!

I'LL BUY THE DELUXE MODEL FROM WOOLCO!

$240! I'LL PUT IT ON MASTERCHARGE THEN GET GET A BILLPAYER LOAN FROM PHILANTHROPIC PHINANCE COMPANY!

Frank Stack

* FRANK CRANKCASE DOES **NOT KEEP UP** ON HIS STREET SLANG!

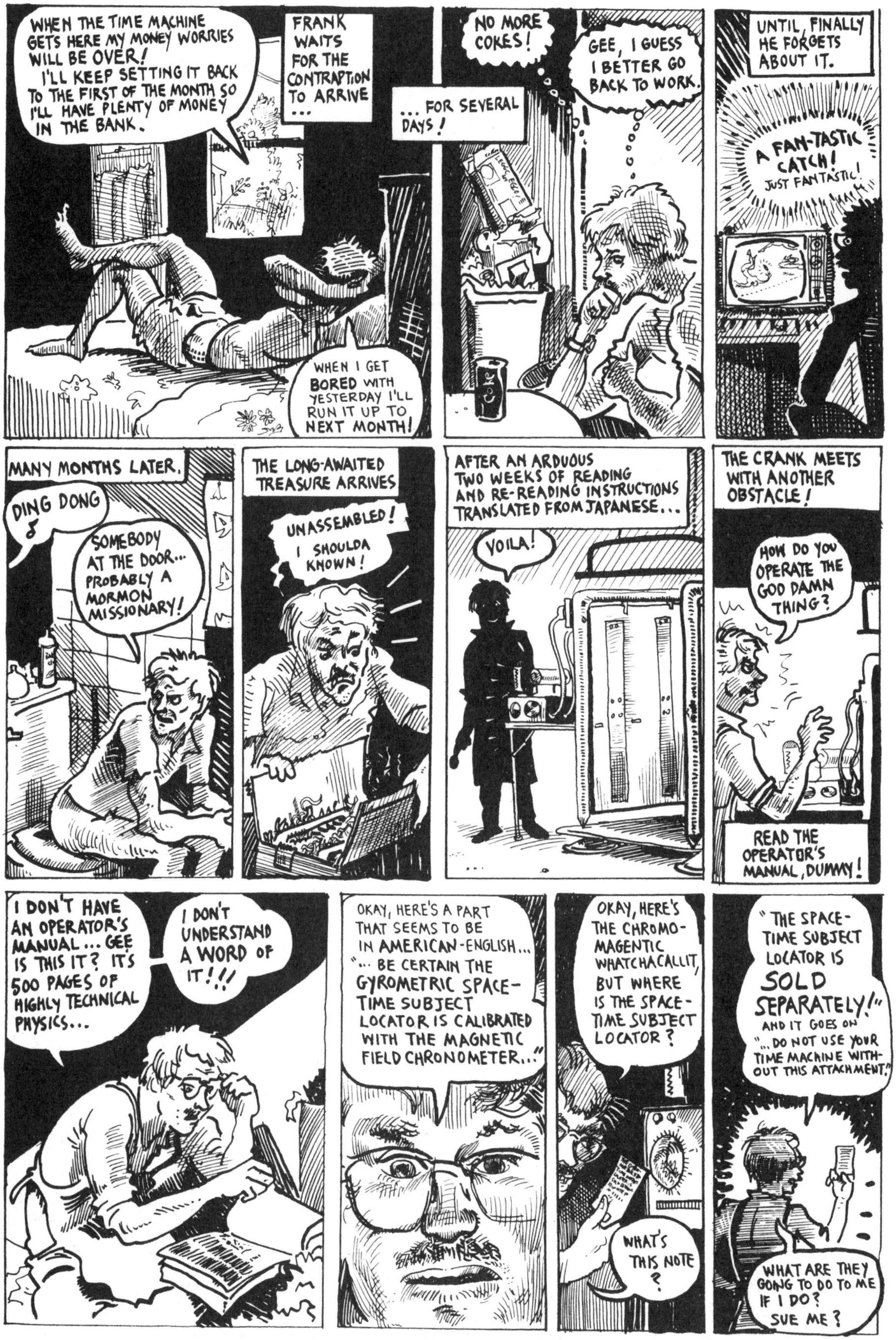
WHEN THE TIME MACHINE GETS HERE MY MONEY WORRIES WILL BE OVER! I'LL KEEP SETTING IT BACK TO THE FIRST OF THE MONTH SO I'LL HAVE PLENTY OF MONEY IN THE BANK.
FRANK WAITS FOR THE CONTRAPTION TO ARRIVE ...
WHEN I GET BORED WITH YESTERDAY I'LL RUN IT UP TO NEXT MONTH!
NO MORE COKES!
... FOR SEVERAL DAYS!
GEE, I GUESS I BETTER GO BACK TO WORK.
UNTIL, FINALLY HE FORGETS ABOUT IT.
A FAN-TASTIC CATCH! JUST FANTASTIC!
MANY MONTHS LATER.
DING DONG
SOMEBODY AT THE DOOR... PROBABLY A MORMON MISSIONARY!
THE LONG-AWAITED TREASURE ARRIVES
UNASSEMBLED! I SHOULDA KNOWN!
AFTER AN ARDUOUS TWO WEEKS OF READING AND RE-READING INSTRUCTIONS TRANSLATED FROM JAPANESE...
VOILA!
THE CRANK MEETS WITH ANOTHER OBSTACLE!
HOW DO YOU OPERATE THE GOD DAMN THING?
READ THE OPERATOR'S MANUAL, DUMMY!
I DON'T HAVE AN OPERATOR'S MANUAL... GEE IS THIS IT? IT'S 500 PAGES OF HIGHLY TECHNICAL PHYSICS...
I DON'T UNDERSTAND A WORD OF IT!!!
OKAY, HERE'S A PART THAT SEEMS TO BE IN AMERICAN-ENGLISH... "... BE CERTAIN THE GYROMETRIC SPACE-TIME SUBJECT LOCATOR IS CALIBRATED WITH THE MAGNETIC FIELD CHRONOMETER..."
OKAY, HERE'S THE CHROMO-MAGENTIC WHATCHACALLIT, BUT WHERE IS THE SPACE-TIME SUBJECT LOCATOR?
WHAT'S THIS NOTE?
"THE SPACE-TIME SUBJECT LOCATOR IS SOLD SEPARATELY!" AND IT GOES ON "...DO NOT USE YOUR TIME MACHINE WITH-OUT THIS ATTACHMENT."
WHAT ARE THEY GOING TO DO TO ME IF I DO? SUE ME?

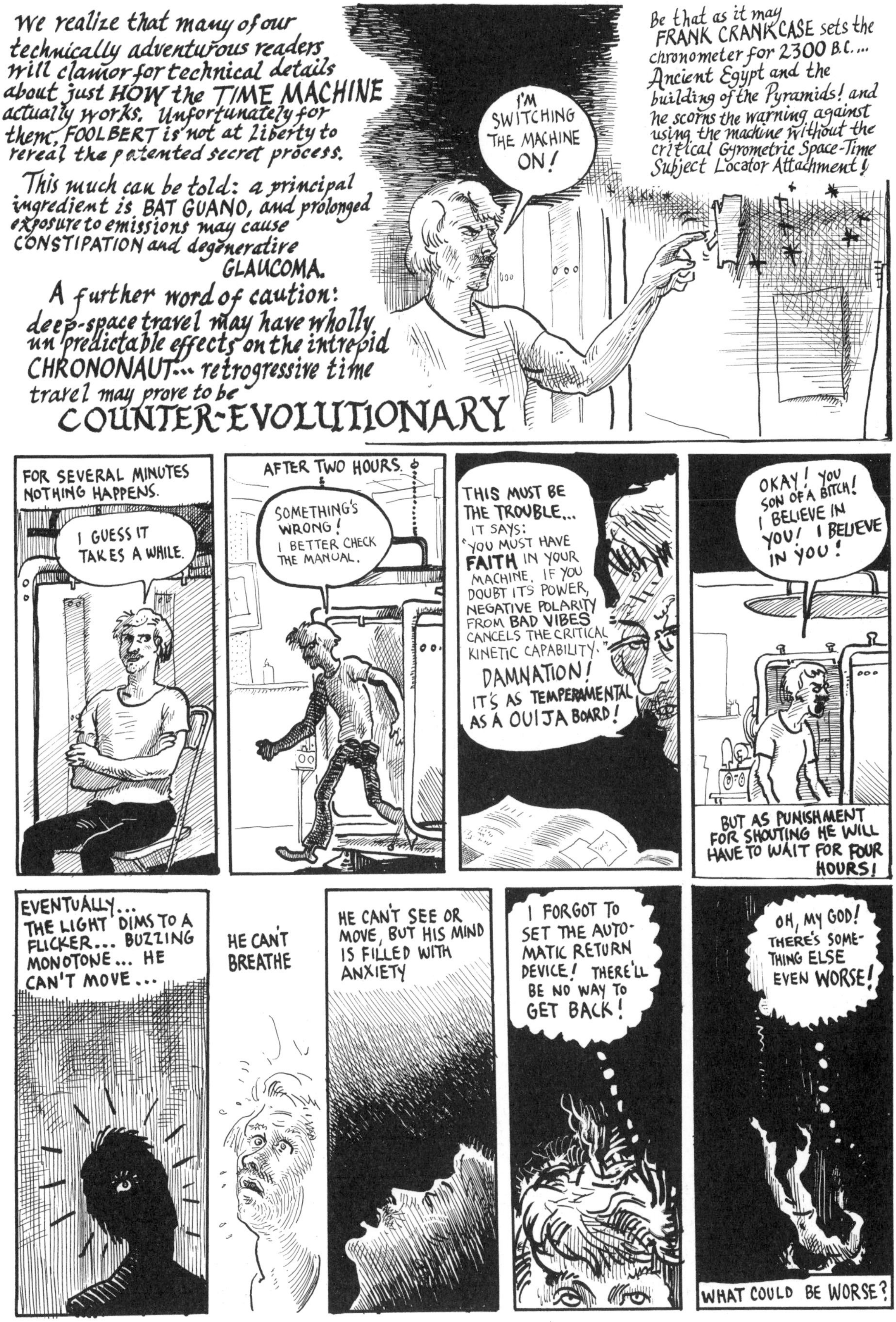
We realize that many of our technically adventurous readers will clamor for technical details about just HOW the TIME MACHINE actually works. Unfortunately for them, FOOLBERT is not at liberty to reveal the patented secret process.
This much can be told: a principal ingredient is BAT GUANO, and prolonged exposure to emissions may cause CONSTIPATION and degenerative GLAUCOMA.
A further word of caution: deep-space travel may have wholly unpredictable effects on the intrepid CHRONONAUT... retrogressive time travel may prove to be COUNTER-EVOLUTIONARY
I'M SWITCHING THE MACHINE ON!
Be that as it may FRANK CRANKCASE sets the chronometer for 2300 B.C.... Ancient Egypt and the building of the Pyramids! and he scorns the warning against using the machine without the critical Gyrometric Space-Time Subject Locator Attachment!
FOR SEVERAL MINUTES NOTHING HAPPENS.
I GUESS IT TAKES A WHILE.
AFTER TWO HOURS.
SOMETHING'S WRONG! I BETTER CHECK THE MANUAL.
THIS MUST BE THE TROUBLE... IT SAYS: "YOU MUST HAVE FAITH IN YOUR MACHINE. IF YOU DOUBT ITS POWER, NEGATIVE POLARITY FROM BAD VIBES CANCELS THE CRITICAL KINETIC CAPABILITY." DAMNATION! IT'S AS TEMPERAMENTAL AS A OUIJA BOARD!
OKAY! YOU SON OF A BITCH! I BELIEVE IN YOU! I BELIEVE IN YOU!
BUT AS PUNISHMENT FOR SHOUTING HE WILL HAVE TO WAIT FOR FOUR HOURS!
EVENTUALLY... THE LIGHT DIMS TO A FLICKER... BUZZING MONOTONE... HE CAN'T MOVE...
HE CAN'T BREATHE
HE CAN'T SEE OR MOVE, BUT HIS MIND IS FILLED WITH ANXIETY
I FORGOT TO SET THE AUTOMATIC RETURN DEVICE! THERE'LL BE NO WAY TO GET BACK!
OH, MY GOD! THERE'S SOMETHING ELSE EVEN WORSE!
WHAT COULD BE WORSE?

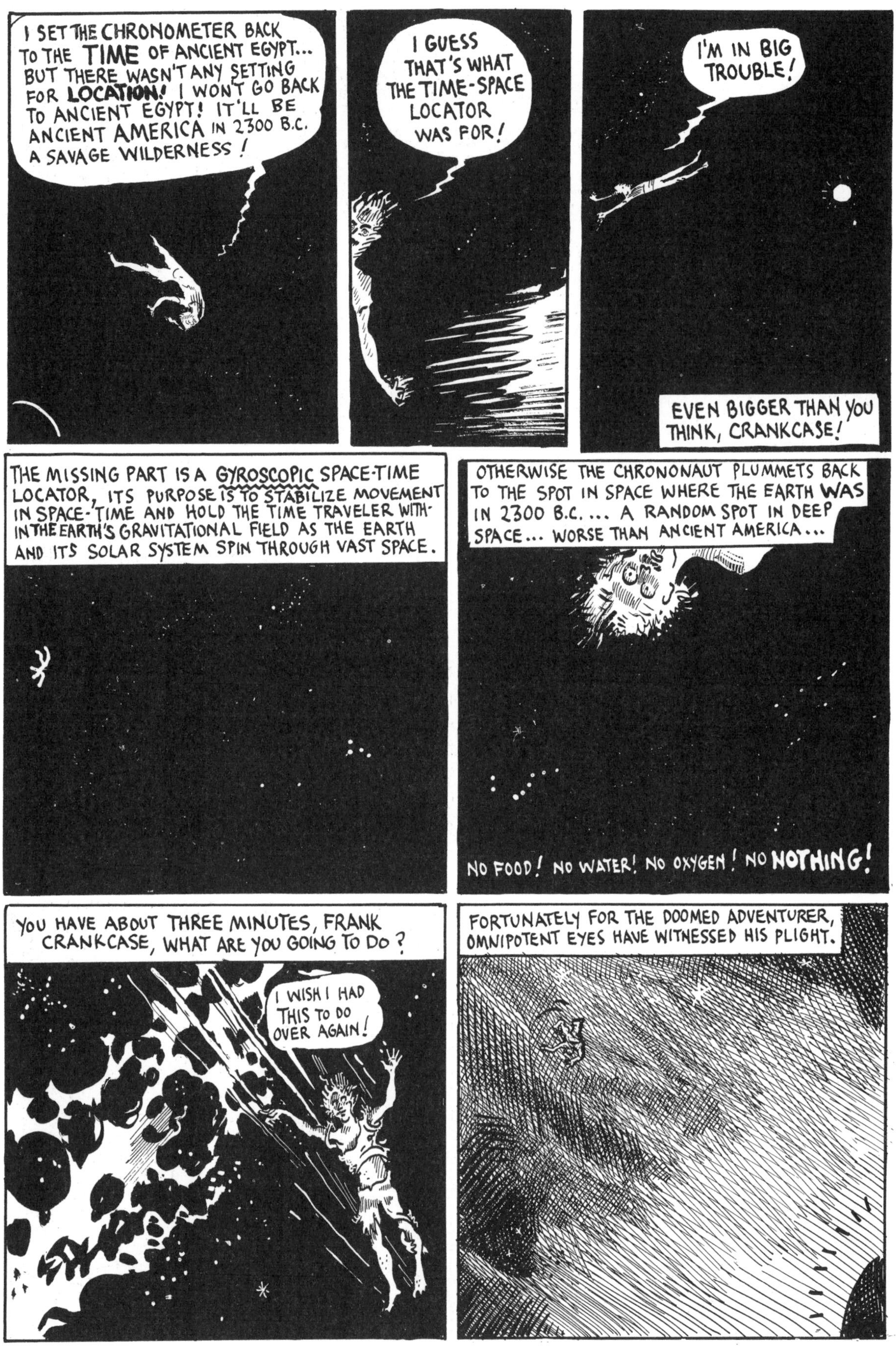
I SET THE CHRONOMETER BACK TO THE TIME OF ANCIENT EGYPT... BUT THERE WASN'T ANY SETTING FOR LOCATION! I WON'T GO BACK TO ANCIENT EGYPT! IT'LL BE ANCIENT AMERICA IN 2300 B.C. A SAVAGE WILDERNESS!
I GUESS THAT'S WHAT THE TIME-SPACE LOCATOR WAS FOR!
I'M IN BIG TROUBLE!
EVEN BIGGER THAN YOU THINK, CRANKCASE!
THE MISSING PART IS A GYROSCOPIC SPACE-TIME LOCATOR, ITS PURPOSE IS TO STABILIZE MOVEMENT IN SPACE-TIME AND HOLD THE TIME TRAVELER WITHIN THE EARTH'S GRAVITATIONAL FIELD AS THE EARTH AND ITS SOLAR SYSTEM SPIN THROUGH VAST SPACE.
OTHERWISE THE CHRONONAUT PLUMMETS BACK TO THE SPOT IN SPACE WHERE THE EARTH WAS IN 2300 B.C.... A RANDOM SPOT IN DEEP SPACE... WORSE THAN ANCIENT AMERICA...
NO FOOD! NO WATER! NO OXYGEN! NO NOTHING!
YOU HAVE ABOUT THREE MINUTES, FRANK CRANKCASE, WHAT ARE YOU GOING TO DO?
I WISH I HAD THIS TO DO OVER AGAIN!
FORTUNATELY FOR THE DOOMED ADVENTURER, OMNIPOTENT EYES HAVE WITNESSED HIS PLIGHT.

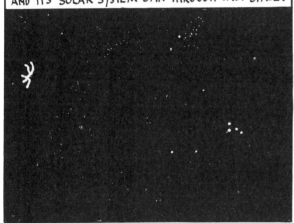

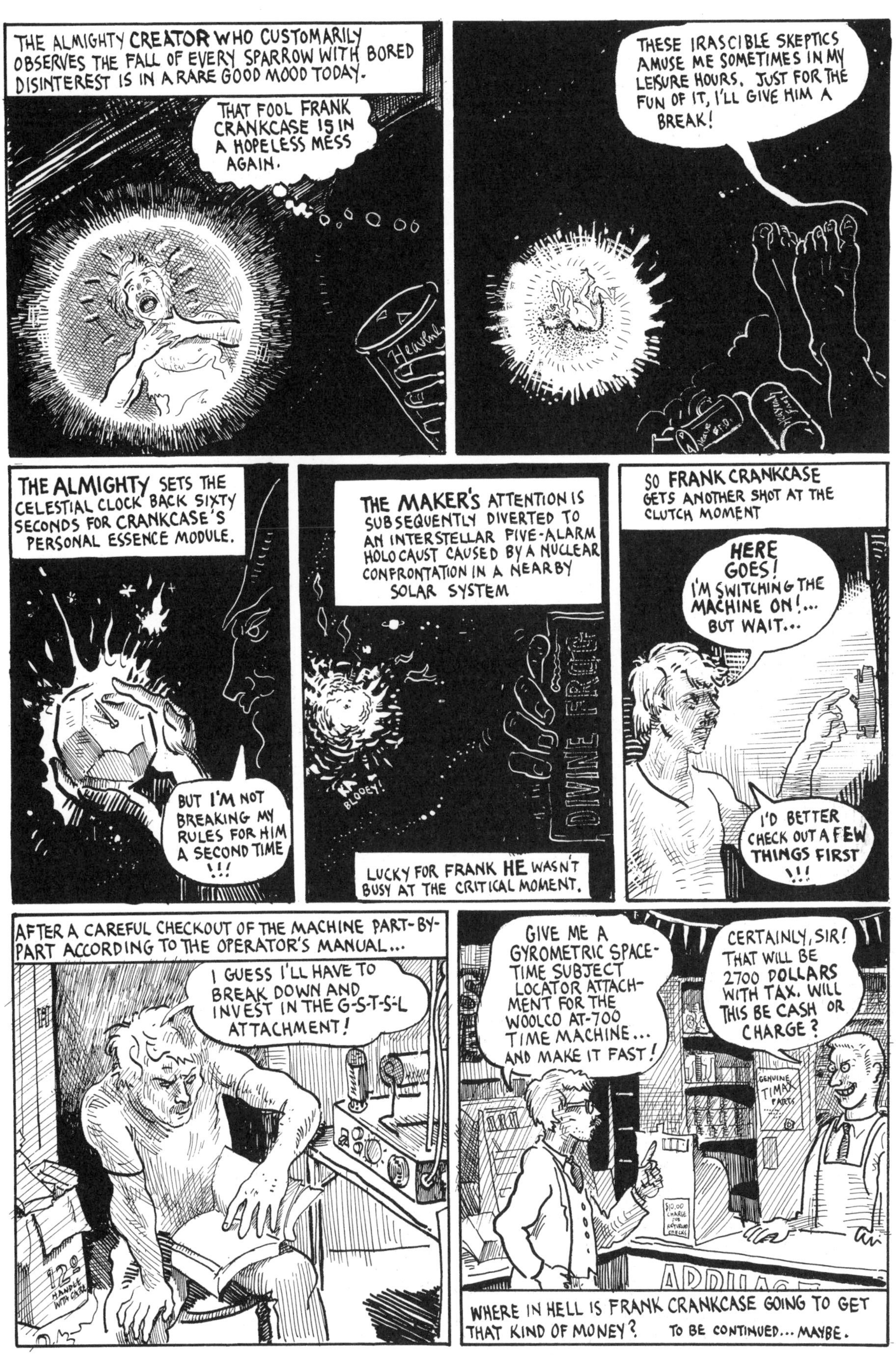
THE ALMIGHTY CREATOR WHO CUSTOMARILY OBSERVES THE FALL OF EVERY SPARROW WITH BORED DISINTEREST IS IN A RARE GOOD MOOD TODAY.
THAT FOOL FRANK CRANKCASE IS IN A HOPELESS MESS AGAIN.
THESE IRASCIBLE SKEPTICS AMUSE ME SOMETIMES IN MY LEISURE HOURS. JUST FOR THE FUN OF IT, I'LL GIVE HIM A BREAK!
THE ALMIGHTY SETS THE CELESTIAL CLOCK BACK SIXTY SECONDS FOR CRANKCASE'S PERSONAL ESSENCE MODULE.
BUT I'M NOT BREAKING MY RULES FOR HIM A SECOND TIME !!!
THE MAKER'S ATTENTION IS SUBSEQUENTLY DIVERTED TO AN INTERSTELLAR FIVE-ALARM HOLOCAUST CAUSED BY A NUCLEAR CONFRONTATION IN A NEARBY SOLAR SYSTEM
BLOOEY!
DIVINE FROG
LUCKY FOR FRANK HE WASN'T BUSY AT THE CRITICAL MOMENT.
SO FRANK CRANKCASE GETS ANOTHER SHOT AT THE CLUTCH MOMENT
HERE GOES! I'M SWITCHING THE MACHINE ON!... BUT WAIT...
I'D BETTER CHECK OUT A FEW THINGS FIRST !!!
AFTER A CAREFUL CHECKOUT OF THE MACHINE PART-BY-PART ACCORDING TO THE OPERATOR'S MANUAL...
I GUESS I'LL HAVE TO BREAK DOWN AND INVEST IN THE G-S-T-S-L ATTACHMENT!
12¢
HANDLE WITH CARE
GIVE ME A GYROMETRIC SPACE-TIME SUBJECT LOCATOR ATTACHMENT FOR THE WOOLCO AT-700 TIME MACHINE... AND MAKE IT FAST!
CERTAINLY, SIR! THAT WILL BE 2700 DOLLARS WITH TAX. WILL THIS BE CASH OR CHARGE?
GENUINE TIMAX PARTS
$10.00 CHARGE FOR RETURNED CHECKS
WHERE IN HELL IS FRANK CRANKCASE GOING TO GET THAT KIND OF MONEY?
TO BE CONTINUED... MAYBE.

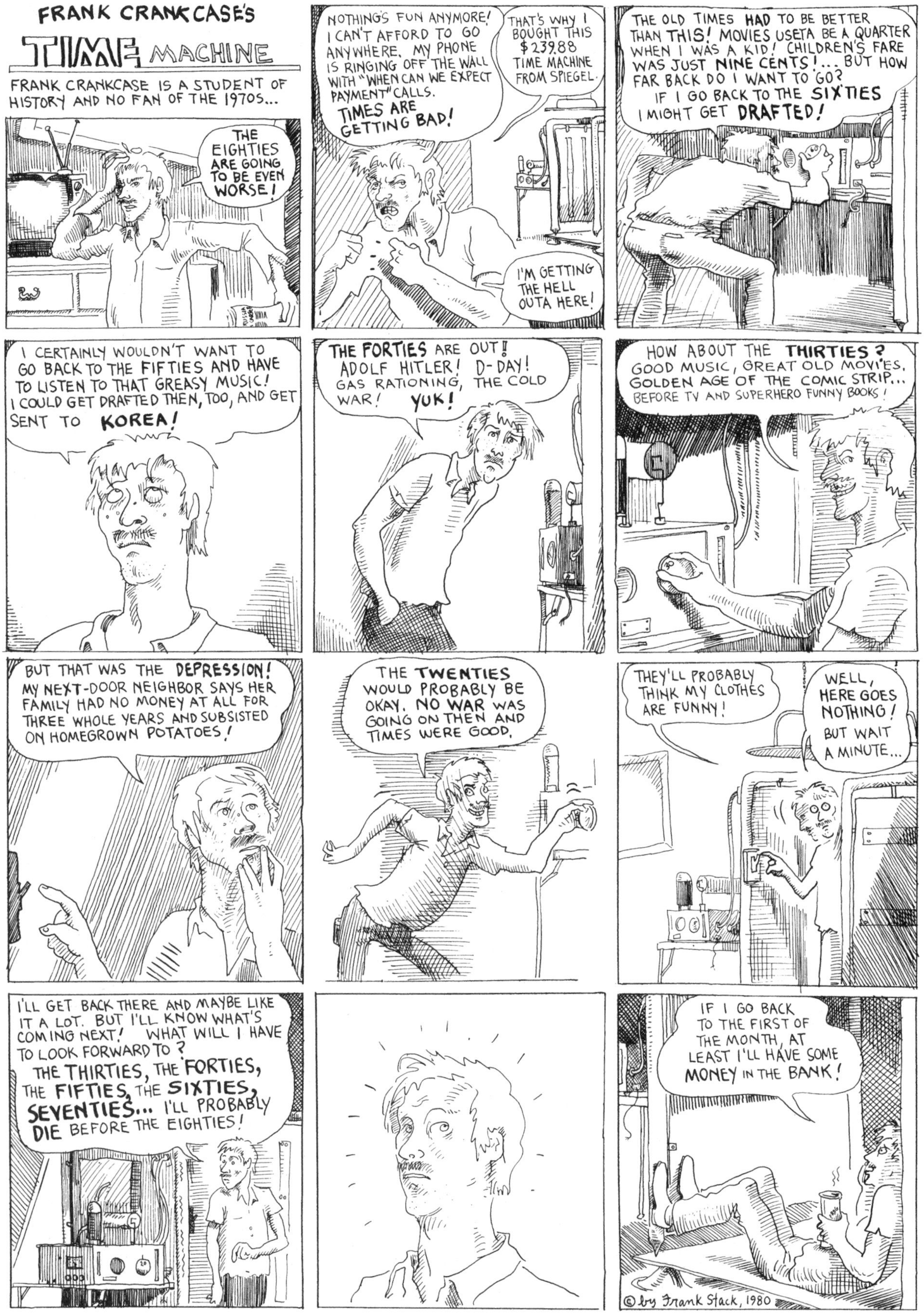
FRANK CRANKCASE'S
TIME MACHINE
FRANK CRANKCASE IS A STUDENT OF HISTORY AND NO FAN OF THE 1970S...
THE EIGHTIES ARE GOING TO BE EVEN WORSE!
NOTHING'S FUN ANYMORE! I CAN'T AFFORD TO GO ANYWHERE. MY PHONE IS RINGING OFF THE WALL WITH "WHEN CAN WE EXPECT PAYMENT" CALLS. TIMES ARE GETTING BAD!
THAT'S WHY I BOUGHT THIS $239.88 TIME MACHINE FROM SPIEGEL.
I'M GETTING THE HELL OUTA HERE!
THE OLD TIMES HAD TO BE BETTER THAN THIS! MOVIES USETA BE A QUARTER WHEN I WAS A KID! CHILDREN'S FARE WAS JUST NINE CENTS!... BUT HOW FAR BACK DO I WANT TO GO? IF I GO BACK TO THE SIXTIES I MIGHT GET DRAFTED!
I CERTAINLY WOULDN'T WANT TO GO BACK TO THE FIFTIES AND HAVE TO LISTEN TO THAT GREASY MUSIC! I COULD GET DRAFTED THEN, TOO, AND GET SENT TO KOREA!
THE FORTIES ARE OUT! ADOLF HITLER! D-DAY! GAS RATIONING, THE COLD WAR! YUK!
HOW ABOUT THE THIRTIES? GOOD MUSIC, GREAT OLD MOVIES, GOLDEN AGE OF THE COMIC STRIP... BEFORE TV AND SUPERHERO FUNNY BOOKS!
BUT THAT WAS THE DEPRESSION! MY NEXT-DOOR NEIGHBOR SAYS HER FAMILY HAD NO MONEY AT ALL FOR THREE WHOLE YEARS AND SUBSISTED ON HOMEGROWN POTATOES!
THE TWENTIES WOULD PROBABLY BE OKAY. NO WAR WAS GOING ON THEN AND TIMES WERE GOOD.
THEY'LL PROBABLY THINK MY CLOTHES ARE FUNNY!
WELL, HERE GOES NOTHING! BUT WAIT A MINUTE...
I'LL GET BACK THERE AND MAYBE LIKE IT A LOT. BUT I'LL KNOW WHAT'S COMING NEXT! WHAT WILL I HAVE TO LOOK FORWARD TO? THE THIRTIES, THE FORTIES, THE FIFTIES, THE SIXTIES, SEVENTIES... I'LL PROBABLY DIE BEFORE THE EIGHTIES!
IF I GO BACK TO THE FIRST OF THE MONTH, AT LEAST I'LL HAVE SOME MONEY IN THE BANK!
© by Frank Stack, 1980

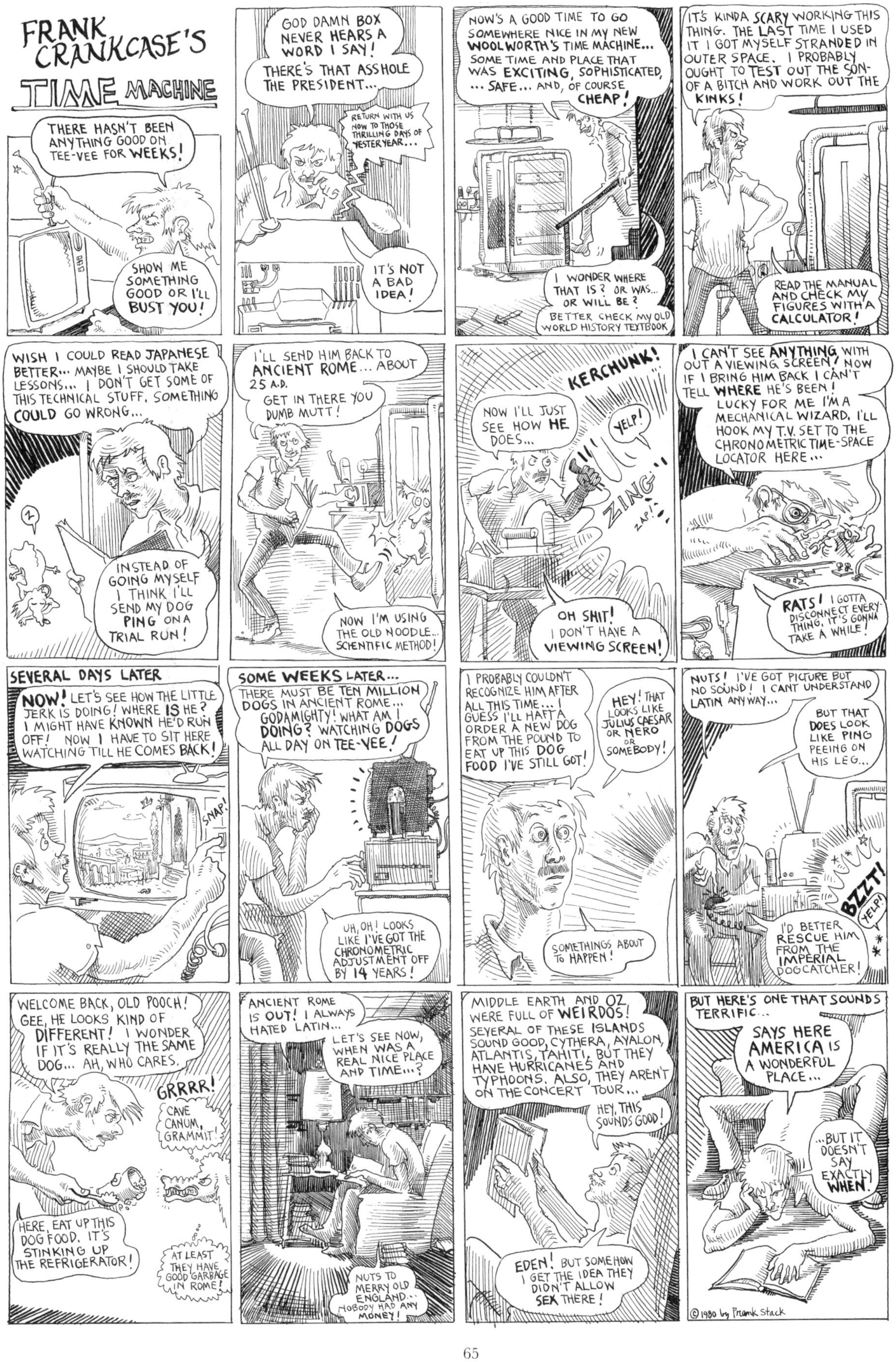
FRANK CRANKCASE'S TIME MACHINE
THERE HASN'T BEEN ANYTHING GOOD ON TEE-VEE FOR WEEKS!
SHOW ME SOMETHING GOOD OR I'LL BUST YOU!
GOD DAMN BOX NEVER HEARS A WORD I SAY!
THERE'S THAT ASSHOLE THE PRESIDENT...
RETURN WITH US NOW TO THOSE THRILLING DAYS OF YESTER YEAR...
IT'S NOT A BAD IDEA!
NOW'S A GOOD TIME TO GO SOMEWHERE NICE IN MY NEW WOOLWORTH'S TIME MACHINE... SOME TIME AND PLACE THAT WAS EXCITING, SOPHISTICATED, ... SAFE... AND, OF COURSE CHEAP!
I WONDER WHERE THAT IS? OR WAS... OR WILL BE?
BETTER CHECK MY OLD WORLD HISTORY TEXTBOOK
IT'S KINDA SCARY WORKING THIS THING. THE LAST TIME I USED IT I GOT MYSELF STRANDED IN OUTER SPACE. I PROBABLY OUGHT TO TEST OUT THE SON-OF A BITCH AND WORK OUT THE KINKS!
READ THE MANUAL AND CHECK MY FIGURES WITH A CALCULATOR!
WISH I COULD READ JAPANESE BETTER... MAYBE I SHOULD TAKE LESSONS... I DON'T GET SOME OF THIS TECHNICAL STUFF. SOMETHING COULD GO WRONG...
INSTEAD OF GOING MYSELF I THINK I'LL SEND MY DOG PING ON A TRIAL RUN!
I'LL SEND HIM BACK TO ANCIENT ROME... ABOUT 25 A.D.
GET IN THERE YOU DUMB MUTT!
NOW I'M USING THE OLD NOODLE... SCIENTIFIC METHOD!
KERCHUNK!
NOW I'LL JUST SEE HOW HE DOES...
YELP!
ZING
ZAP!
OH SHIT! I DON'T HAVE A VIEWING SCREEN!
I CAN'T SEE ANYTHING WITH OUT A VIEWING SCREEN! NOW IF I BRING HIM BACK I CAN'T TELL WHERE HE'S BEEN! LUCKY FOR ME I'M A MECHANICAL WIZARD. I'LL HOOK MY T.V. SET TO THE CHRONOMETRIC TIME-SPACE LOCATOR HERE...
RATS! I GOTTA DISCONNECT EVERY-THING, IT'S GONNA TAKE A WHILE!
SEVERAL DAYS LATER
NOW! LET'S SEE HOW THE LITTLE JERK IS DOING! WHERE IS HE? I MIGHT HAVE KNOWN HE'D RUN OFF! NOW I HAVE TO SIT HERE WATCHING TILL HE COMES BACK!
SNAP!
SOME WEEKS LATER...
THERE MUST BE TEN MILLION DOGS IN ANCIENT ROME... GODAMIGHTY! WHAT AM I DOING? WATCHING DOGS ALL DAY ON TEE-VEE!
UH, OH! LOOKS LIKE I'VE GOT THE CHRONOMETRIC ADJUSTMENT OFF BY 14 YEARS!
I PROBABLY COULDN'T RECOGNIZE HIM AFTER ALL THIS TIME... I GUESS I'LL HAFTA ORDER A NEW DOG FROM THE POUND TO EAT UP THIS DOG FOOD I'VE STILL GOT!
HEY! THAT LOOKS LIKE JULIUS CAESAR OR NERO OR SOMEBODY!
SOMETHINGS ABOUT TO HAPPEN!
NUTS! I'VE GOT PICTURE BUT NO SOUND! I CANT UNDERSTAND LATIN ANYWAY...
BUT THAT DOES LOOK LIKE PING PEEING ON HIS LEG...
BZZT!
YELP!
I'D BETTER RESCUE HIM FROM THE IMPERIAL DOGCATCHER!
WELCOME BACK, OLD POOCH! GEE, HE LOOKS KIND OF DIFFERENT! I WONDER IF IT'S REALLY THE SAME DOG... AH, WHO CARES.
GRRRR!
CAVE CANUM, GRAMMIT!
HERE, EAT UP THIS DOG FOOD. IT'S STINKING UP THE REFRIGERATOR!
AT LEAST THEY HAVE GOOD GARBAGE IN ROME!
ANCIENT ROME IS OUT! I ALWAYS HATED LATIN...
LET'S SEE NOW, WHEN WAS A REAL NICE PLACE AND TIME...?
NUTS TO MERRY OLD ENGLAND... NOBODY HAD ANY MONEY!
MIDDLE EARTH AND OZ WERE FULL OF WEIRDOS! SEVERAL OF THESE ISLANDS SOUND GOOD, CYTHERA, AVALON, ATLANTIS, TAHITI, BUT THEY HAVE HURRICANES AND TYPHOONS. ALSO, THEY AREN'T ON THE CONCERT TOUR...
HEY, THIS SOUNDS GOOD!
EDEN! BUT SOMEHOW I GET THE IDEA THEY DIDN'T ALLOW SEX THERE!
BUT HERE'S ONE THAT SOUNDS TERRIFIC...
SAYS HERE AMERICA IS A WONDERFUL PLACE...
...BUT IT DOESN'T SAY EXACTLY WHEN.
© 1980 by Frank Stack

Histories and Other Fictions

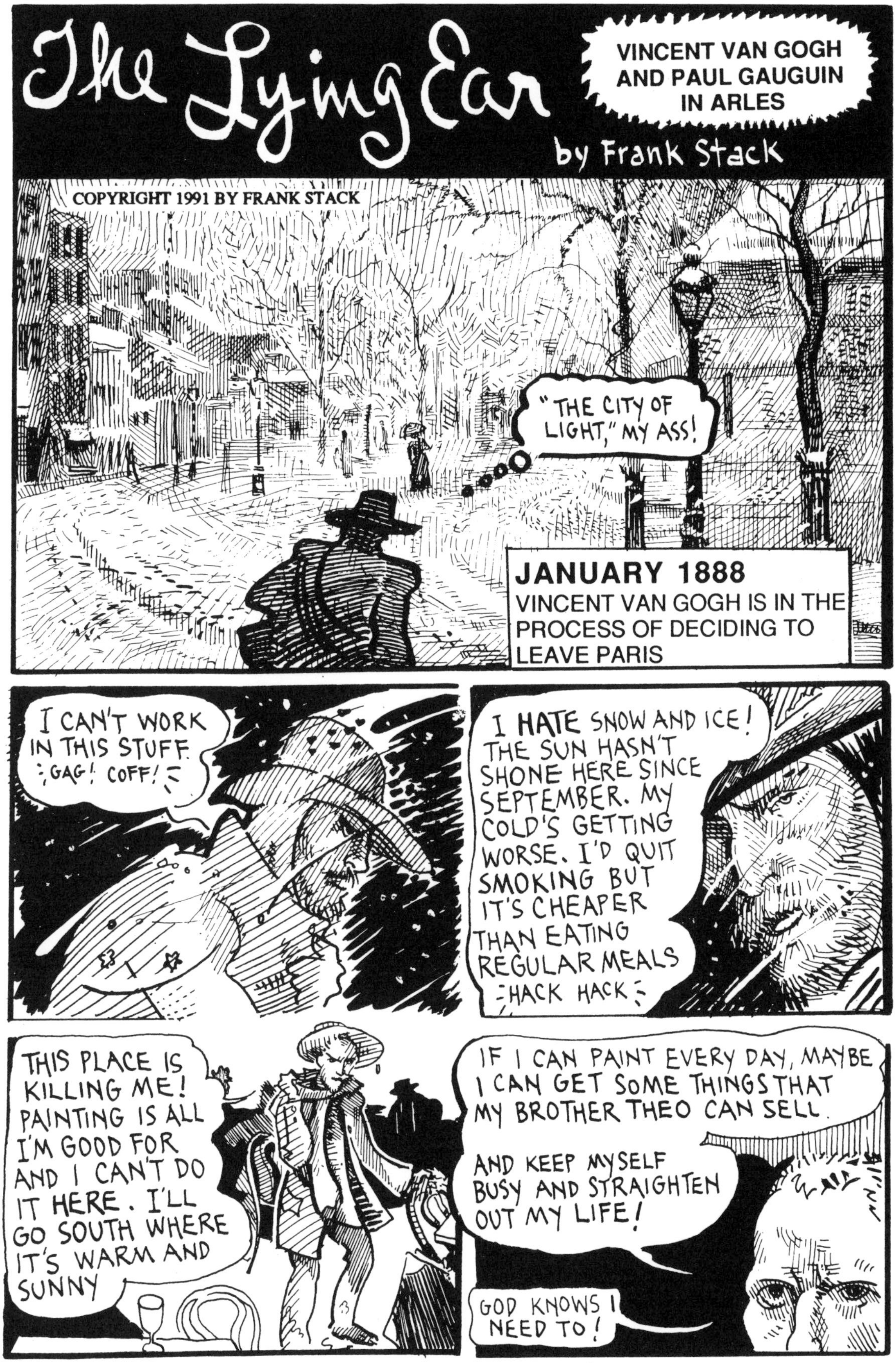
The Lying Ear
VINCENT VAN GOGH AND PAUL GAUGUIN IN ARLES
by Frank Stack
COPYRIGHT 1991 BY FRANK STACK
"THE CITY OF LIGHT," MY ASS!
JANUARY 1888
VINCENT VAN GOGH IS IN THE PROCESS OF DECIDING TO LEAVE PARIS
I CAN'T WORK IN THIS STUFF. GAG! COFF!
I HATE SNOW AND ICE! THE SUN HASN'T SHONE HERE SINCE SEPTEMBER. MY COLD'S GETTING WORSE. I'D QUIT SMOKING BUT IT'S CHEAPER THAN EATING REGULAR MEALS
HACK HACK
THIS PLACE IS KILLING ME! PAINTING IS ALL I'M GOOD FOR AND I CAN'T DO IT HERE. I'LL GO SOUTH WHERE IT'S WARM AND SUNNY
IF I CAN PAINT EVERY DAY, MAYBE I CAN GET SOME THINGS THAT MY BROTHER THEO CAN SELL
AND KEEP MYSELF BUSY AND STRAIGHTEN OUT MY LIFE!
GOD KNOWS I NEED TO!

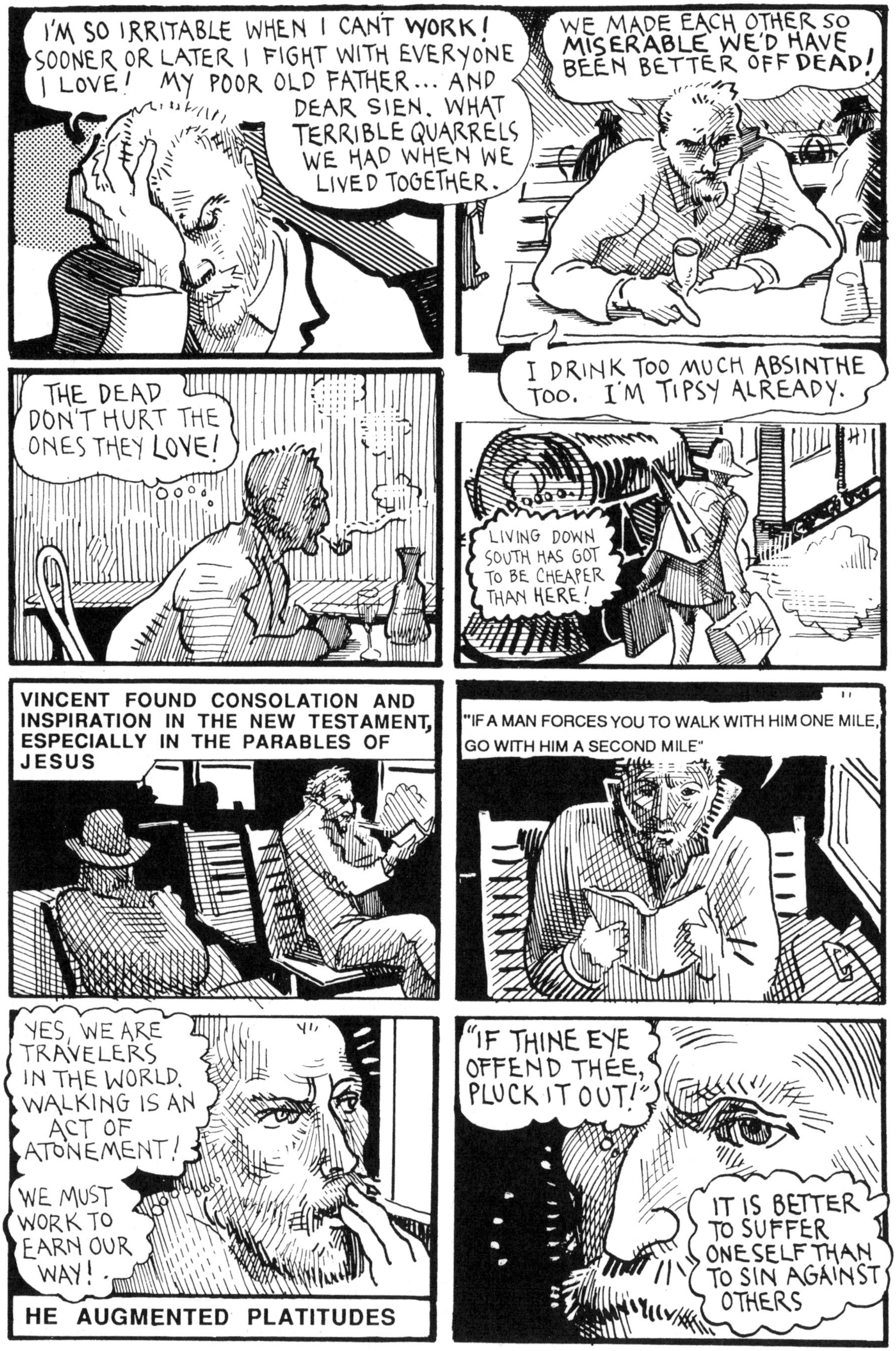
I'M SO IRRITABLE WHEN I CAN'T WORK! SOONER OR LATER I FIGHT WITH EVERYONE I LOVE! MY POOR OLD FATHER... AND DEAR SIEN. WHAT TERRIBLE QUARRELS WE HAD WHEN WE LIVED TOGETHER.
WE MADE EACH OTHER SO MISERABLE WE'D HAVE BEEN BETTER OFF DEAD!
I DRINK TOO MUCH ABSINTHE TOO. I'M TIPSY ALREADY.
THE DEAD DON'T HURT THE ONES THEY LOVE!
LIVING DOWN SOUTH HAS GOT TO BE CHEAPER THAN HERE!
VINCENT FOUND CONSOLATION AND INSPIRATION IN THE NEW TESTAMENT, ESPECIALLY IN THE PARABLES OF JESUS
"IF A MAN FORCES YOU TO WALK WITH HIM ONE MILE, GO WITH HIM A SECOND MILE"
YES, WE ARE TRAVELERS IN THE WORLD. WALKING IS AN ACT OF ATONEMENT!
WE MUST WORK TO EARN OUR WAY!
HE AUGMENTED PLATITUDES
"IF THINE EYE OFFEND THEE, PLUCK IT OUT!"
IT IS BETTER TO SUFFER ONESELF THAN TO SIN AGAINST OTHERS

WHEN HE LEFT PARIS, VINCENT HAD NOT DECIDED WHERE IN THE SOUTH HE PLANNED TO SETTLE, BUT HE WANTED TO SEE THE CITY OF ARLES, FAMOUS FOR ITS EXOTIC MONUMENTS AND BEAUTIFUL WOMEN. HE CHECKED INTO A HOTEL FOR A FEW DAYS.

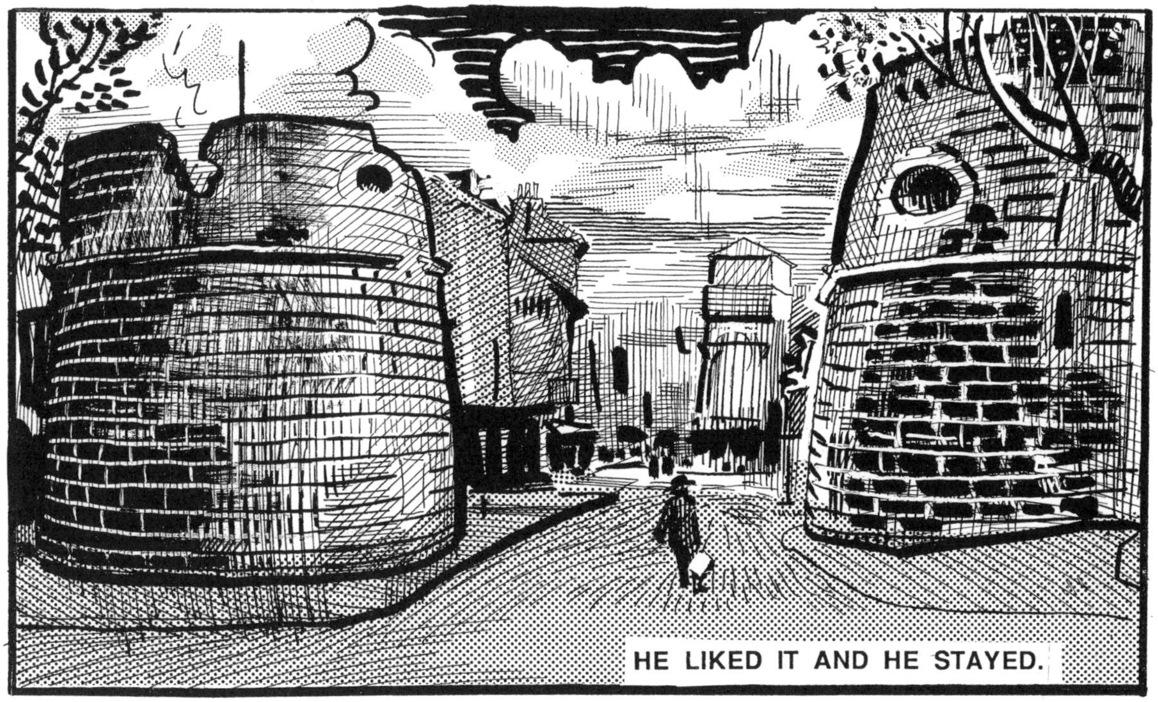
HE LIKED IT AND HE STAYED.

ONE OF HIS DREAMS WAS TO ESTABLISH AN ARTISTS' COLONY SOMEWHERE IN A SUNNY CLIMATE.

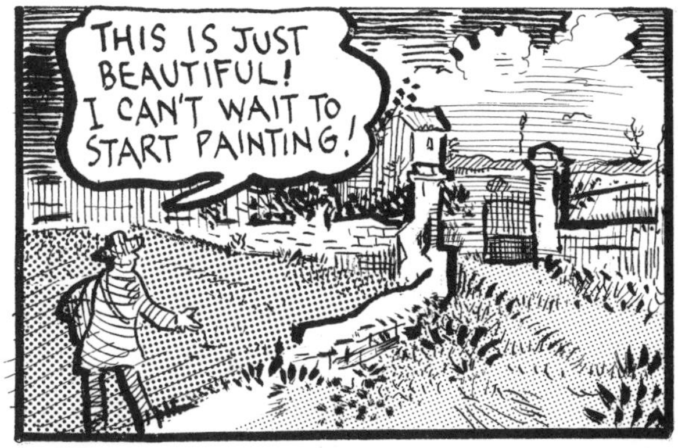
THIS IS JUST BEAUTIFUL! I CAN'T WAIT TO START PAINTING!

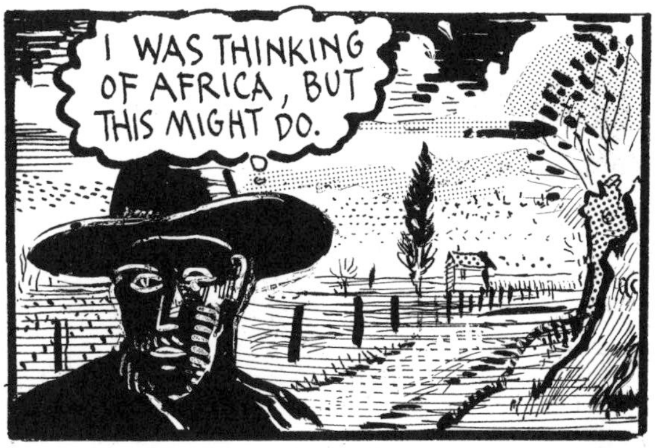
I WAS THINKING OF AFRICA, BUT THIS MIGHT DO.

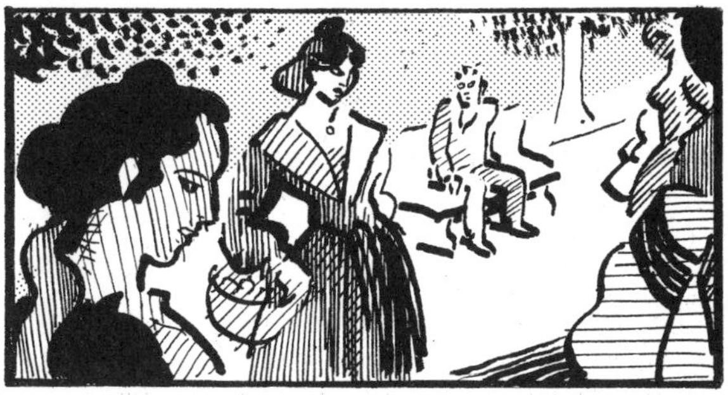

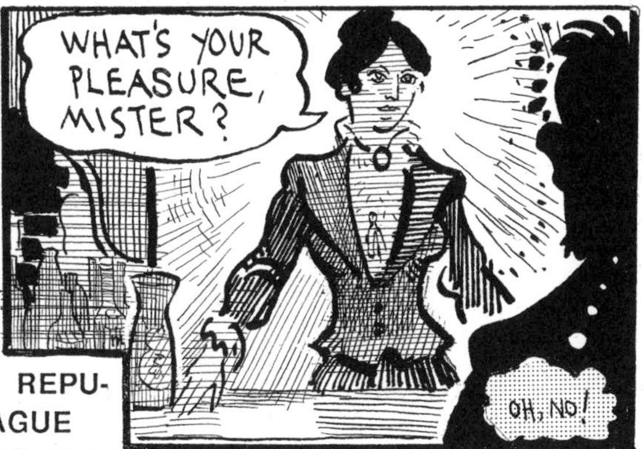
WHAT'S YOUR PLEASURE, MISTER?
OH, NO!

THE WOMEN OF ARLES DESERVED THEIR REPUTATION FOR BEAUTY. HE EVEN HAD A VAGUE FEELING THAT THEY WERE SEXUALLY AVAILABLE.

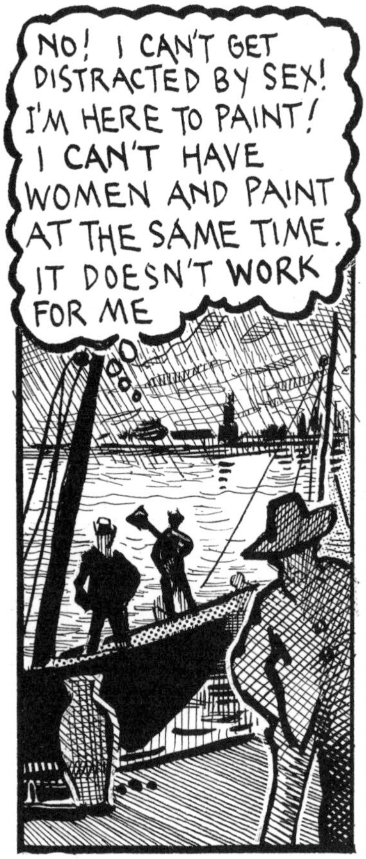
NO! I CAN'T GET DISTRACTED BY SEX! I'M HERE TO PAINT! I CAN'T HAVE WOMEN AND PAINT AT THE SAME TIME. IT DOESN'T WORK FOR ME

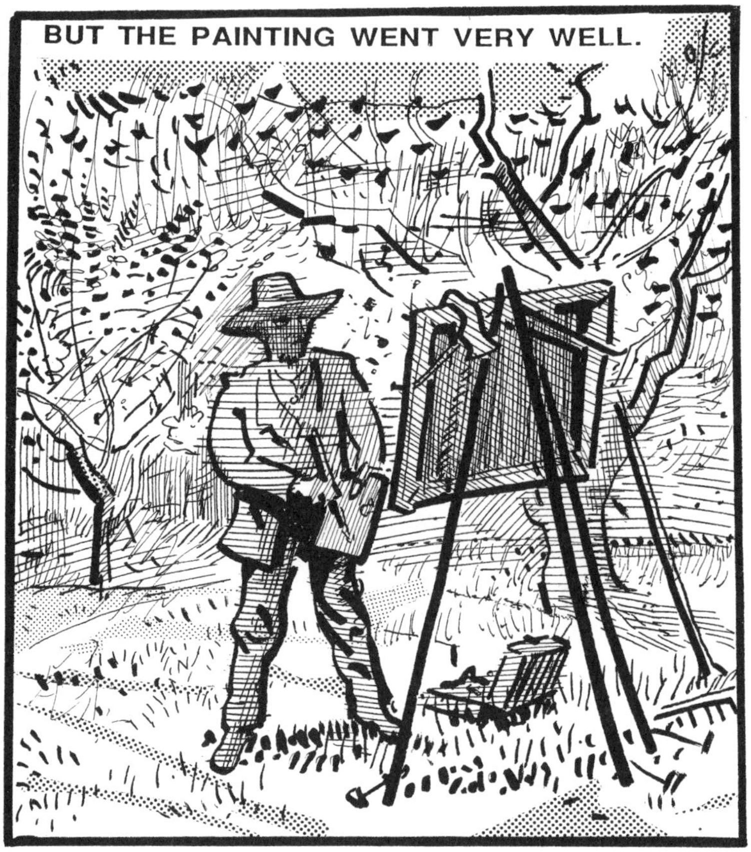
BUT THE PAINTING WENT VERY WELL.

THE LANDSCAPE REMINDED HIM OF HIS CHILDHOOD HOME.

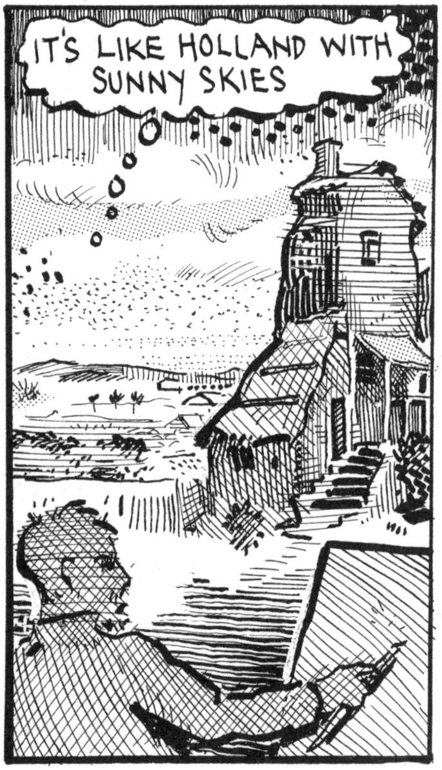
IT'S LIKE HOLLAND WITH SUNNY SKIES

HE SURPRISED HIMSELF AT BEING THRILLED BY THE SAVAGE SPECTACLE OF THE BULLFIGHTS HELD ON SUNDAYS IN THE ANCIENT ROMAN ARENA.

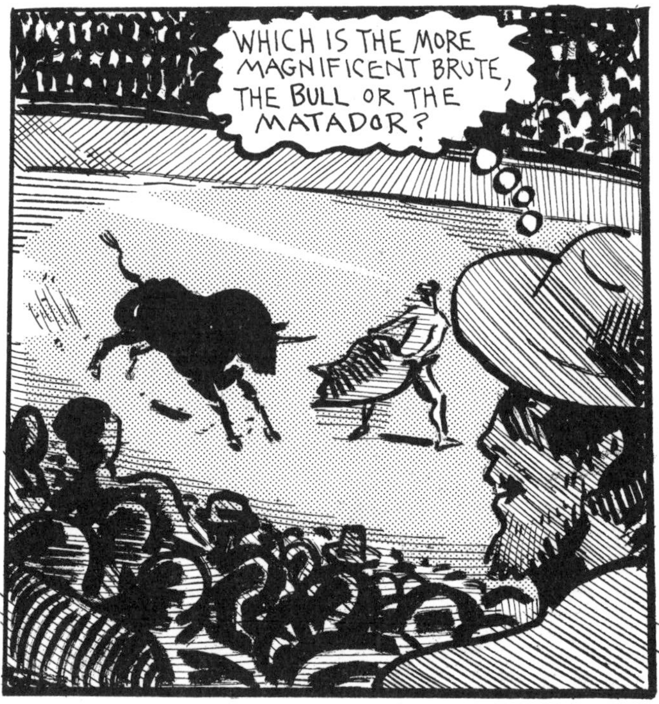
WHICH IS THE MORE MAGNIFICENT BRUTE, THE BULL OR THE MATADOR?

AS HE PLUNGED INTO HIS WORK, HE THOUGHT ABOUT HIS LIFE.

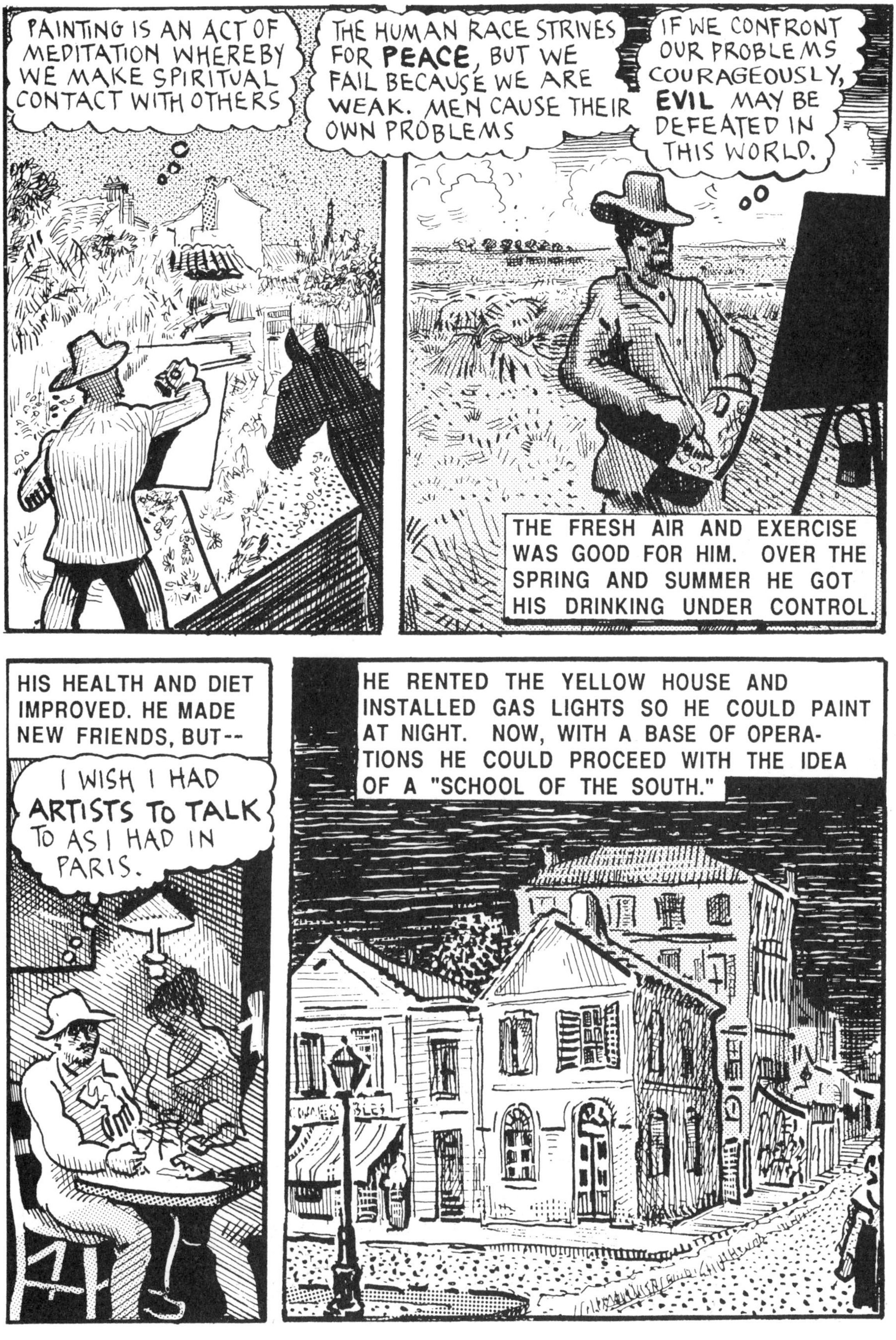
PAINTING IS AN ACT OF MEDITATION WHEREBY WE MAKE SPIRITUAL CONTACT WITH OTHERS
THE HUMAN RACE STRIVES FOR PEACE, BUT WE FAIL BECAUSE WE ARE WEAK. MEN CAUSE THEIR OWN PROBLEMS
IF WE CONFRONT OUR PROBLEMS COURAGEOUSLY, EVIL MAY BE DEFEATED IN THIS WORLD.
THE FRESH AIR AND EXERCISE WAS GOOD FOR HIM. OVER THE SPRING AND SUMMER HE GOT HIS DRINKING UNDER CONTROL.
HIS HEALTH AND DIET IMPROVED. HE MADE NEW FRIENDS, BUT--
I WISH I HAD ARTISTS TO TALK TO AS I HAD IN PARIS.
HE RENTED THE YELLOW HOUSE AND INSTALLED GAS LIGHTS SO HE COULD PAINT AT NIGHT. NOW, WITH A BASE OF OPERATIONS HE COULD PROCEED WITH THE IDEA OF A "SCHOOL OF THE SOUTH."

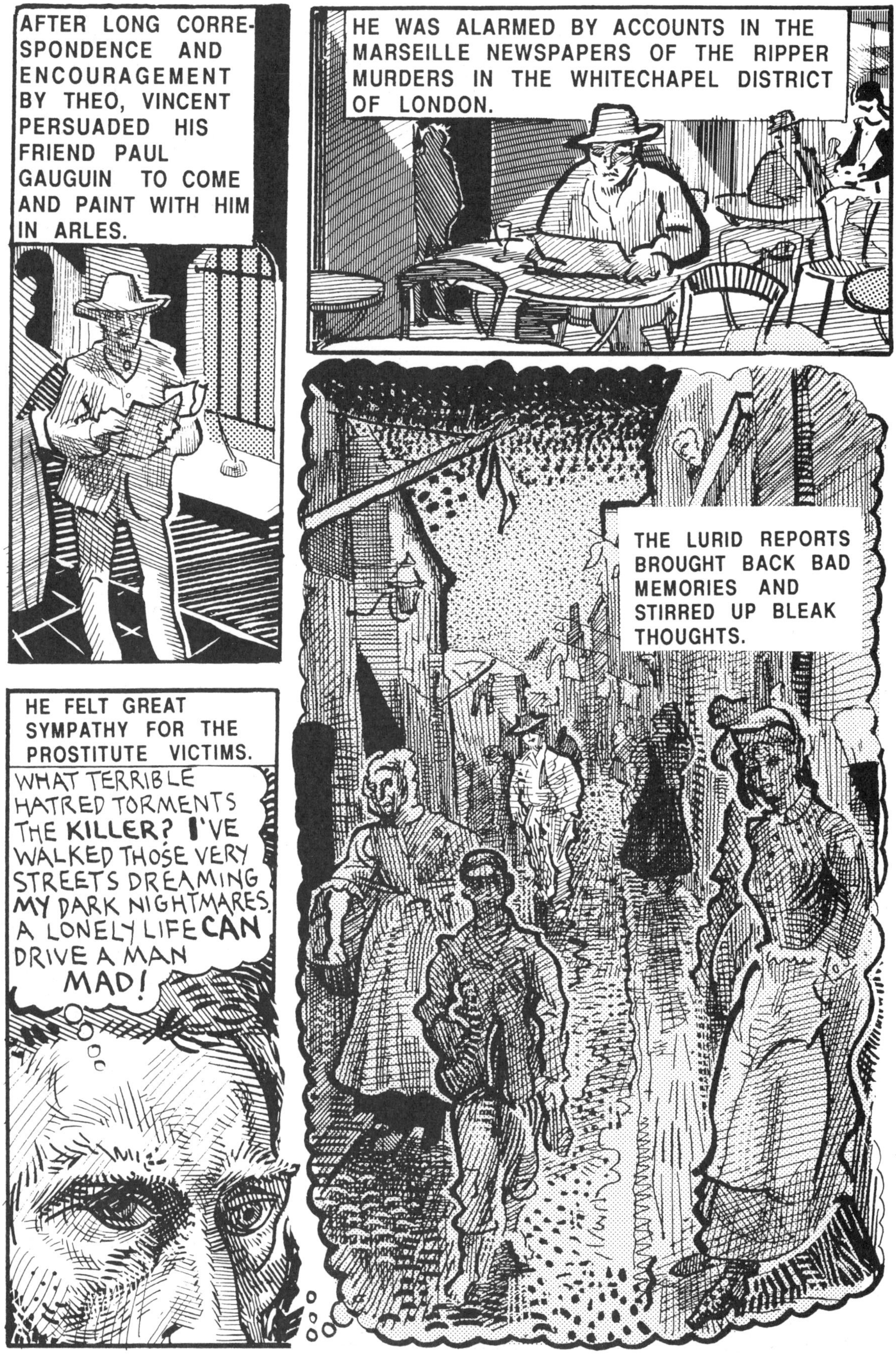
AFTER LONG CORRESPONDENCE AND ENCOURAGEMENT BY THEO, VINCENT PERSUADED HIS FRIEND PAUL GAUGUIN TO COME AND PAINT WITH HIM IN ARLES.
HE WAS ALARMED BY ACCOUNTS IN THE MARSEILLE NEWSPAPERS OF THE RIPPER MURDERS IN THE WHITECHAPEL DISTRICT OF LONDON.
HE FELT GREAT SYMPATHY FOR THE PROSTITUTE VICTIMS.
WHAT TERRIBLE HATRED TORMENTS THE KILLER? I'VE WALKED THOSE VERY STREETS DREAMING MY DARK NIGHTMARES. A LONELY LIFE CAN DRIVE A MAN MAD!
THE LURID REPORTS BROUGHT BACK BAD MEMORIES AND STIRRED UP BLEAK THOUGHTS.

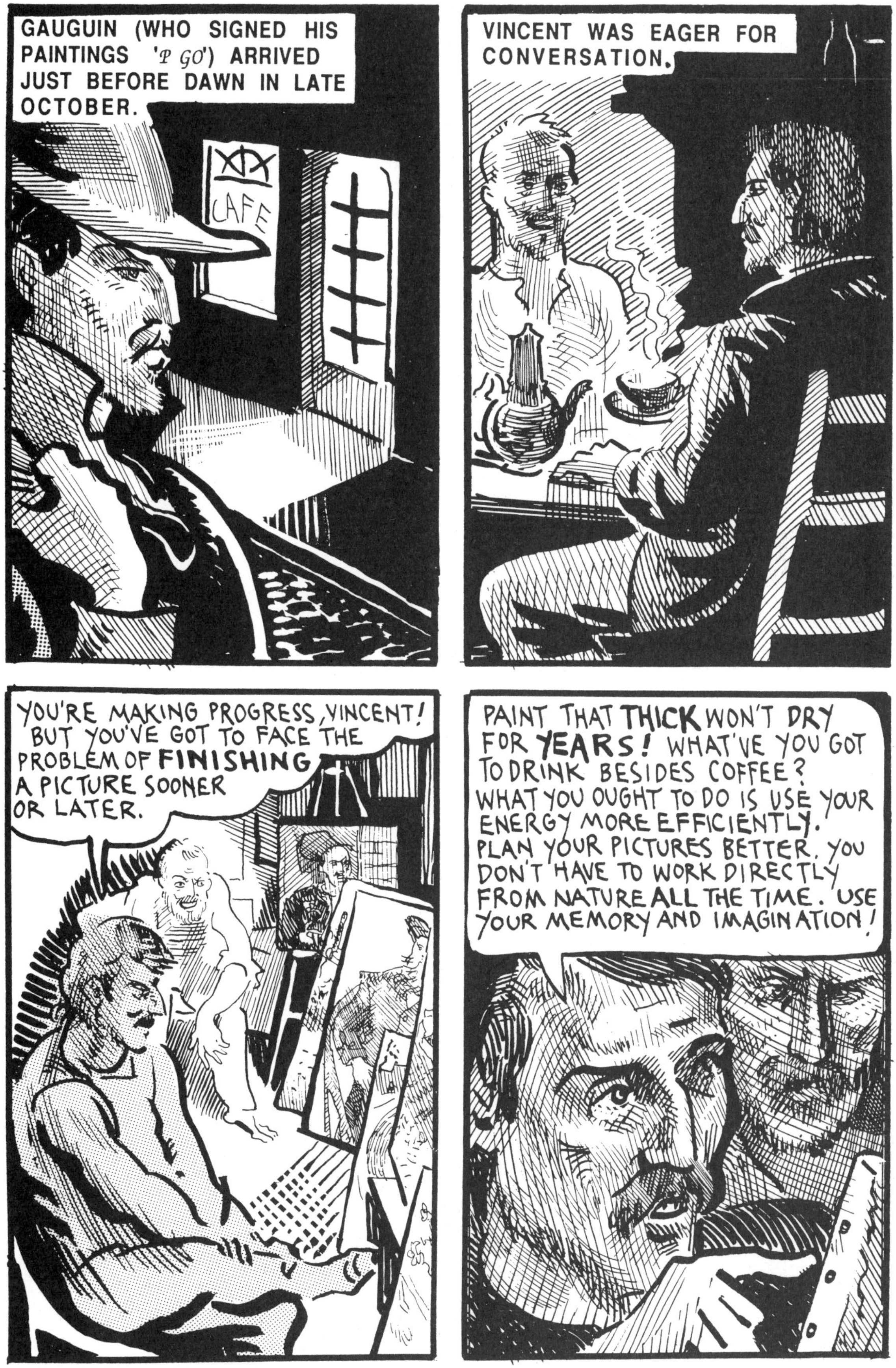
GAUGUIN (WHO SIGNED HIS PAINTINGS 'P GO') ARRIVED JUST BEFORE DAWN IN LATE OCTOBER.
CAFE
VINCENT WAS EAGER FOR CONVERSATION.
YOU'RE MAKING PROGRESS, VINCENT! BUT YOU'VE GOT TO FACE THE PROBLEM OF FINISHING A PICTURE SOONER OR LATER.
PAINT THAT THICK WON'T DRY FOR YEARS! WHAT'VE YOU GOT TO DRINK BESIDES COFFEE? WHAT YOU OUGHT TO DO IS USE YOUR ENERGY MORE EFFICIENTLY. PLAN YOUR PICTURES BETTER. YOU DON'T HAVE TO WORK DIRECTLY FROM NATURE ALL THE TIME. USE YOUR MEMORY AND IMAGINATION!

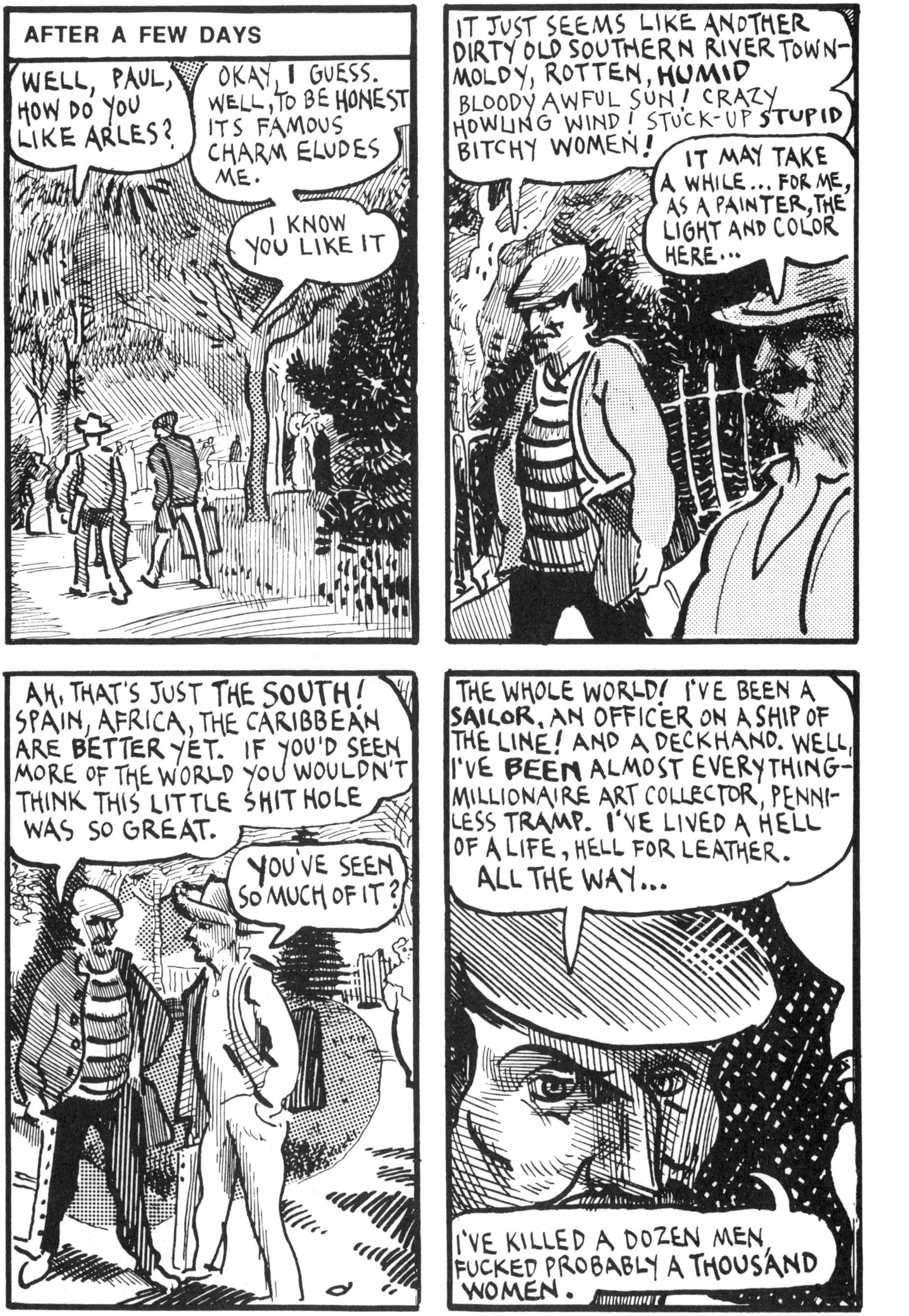
AFTER A FEW DAYS
WELL, PAUL, HOW DO YOU LIKE ARLES?
OKAY, I GUESS. WELL, TO BE HONEST ITS FAMOUS CHARM ELUDES ME.
I KNOW YOU LIKE IT
IT JUST SEEMS LIKE ANOTHER DIRTY OLD SOUTHERN RIVER TOWN- MOLDY, ROTTEN, HUMID BLOODY AWFUL SUN! CRAZY HOWLING WIND! STUCK-UP STUPID BITCHY WOMEN!
IT MAY TAKE A WHILE... FOR ME, AS A PAINTER, THE LIGHT AND COLOR HERE...
AH, THAT'S JUST THE SOUTH! SPAIN, AFRICA, THE CARIBBEAN ARE BETTER YET. IF YOU'D SEEN MORE OF THE WORLD YOU WOULDN'T THINK THIS LITTLE SHIT HOLE WAS SO GREAT.
YOU'VE SEEN SO MUCH OF IT?
THE WHOLE WORLD! I'VE BEEN A SAILOR, AN OFFICER ON A SHIP OF THE LINE! AND A DECKHAND. WELL, I'VE BEEN ALMOST EVERYTHING- MILLIONAIRE ART COLLECTOR, PENNILESS TRAMP. I'VE LIVED A HELL OF A LIFE, HELL FOR LEATHER. ALL THE WAY...
I'VE KILLED A DOZEN MEN, FUCKED PROBABLY A THOUSAND WOMEN.

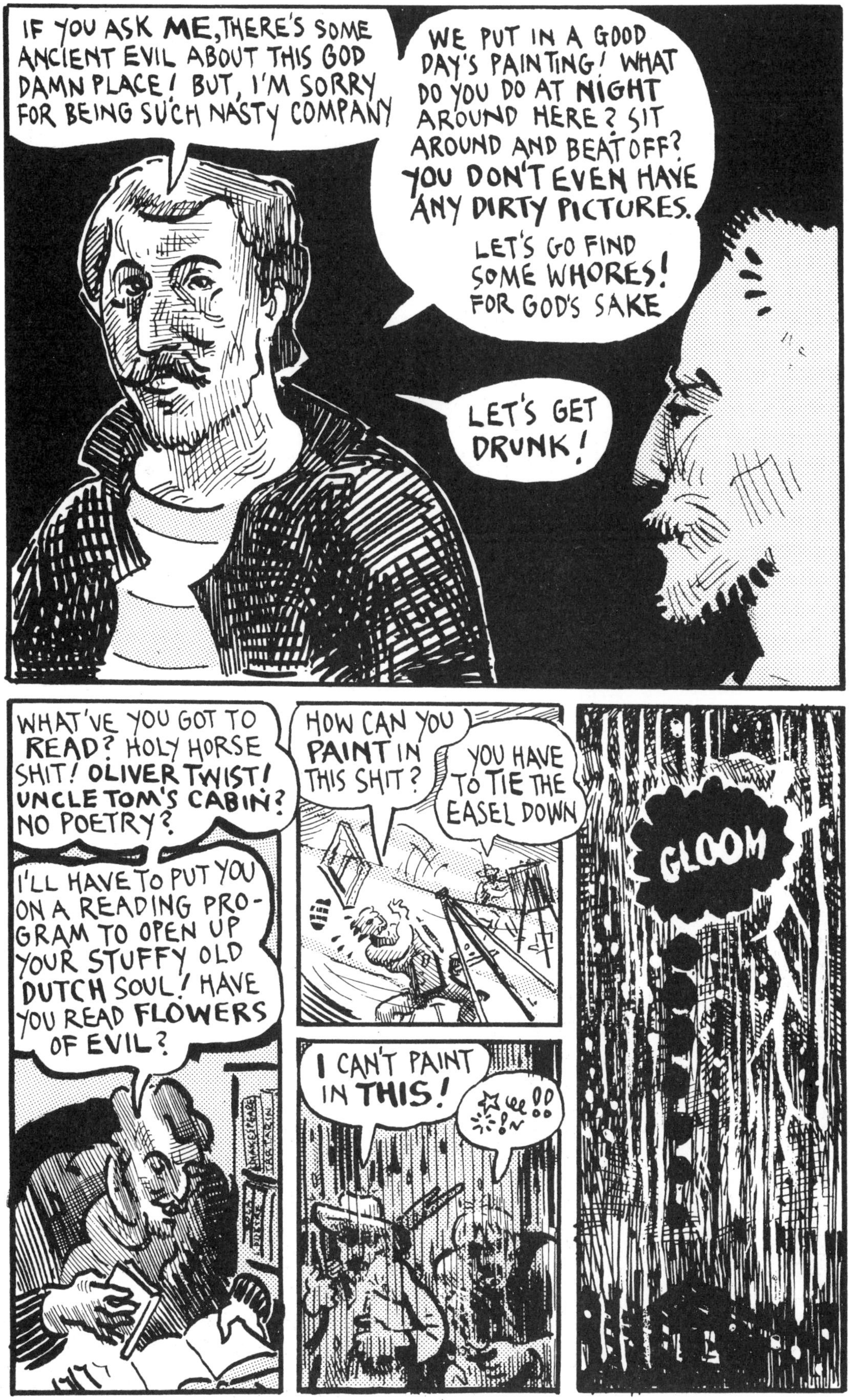
IF YOU ASK ME, THERE'S SOME ANCIENT EVIL ABOUT THIS GOD DAMN PLACE! BUT, I'M SORRY FOR BEING SUCH NASTY COMPANY
WE PUT IN A GOOD DAY'S PAINTING! WHAT DO YOU DO AT NIGHT AROUND HERE? SIT AROUND AND BEAT OFF? YOU DON'T EVEN HAVE ANY DIRTY PICTURES.
LET'S GO FIND SOME WHORES! FOR GOD'S SAKE
LET'S GET DRUNK!
WHAT'VE YOU GOT TO READ? HOLY HORSE SHIT! OLIVER TWIST! UNCLE TOM'S CABIN? NO POETRY?
I'LL HAVE TO PUT YOU ON A READING PROGRAM TO OPEN UP YOUR STUFFY OLD DUTCH SOUL! HAVE YOU READ FLOWERS OF EVIL?
HOW CAN YOU PAINT IN THIS SHIT?
YOU HAVE TO TIE THE EASEL DOWN
I CAN'T PAINT IN THIS!
GLOOM

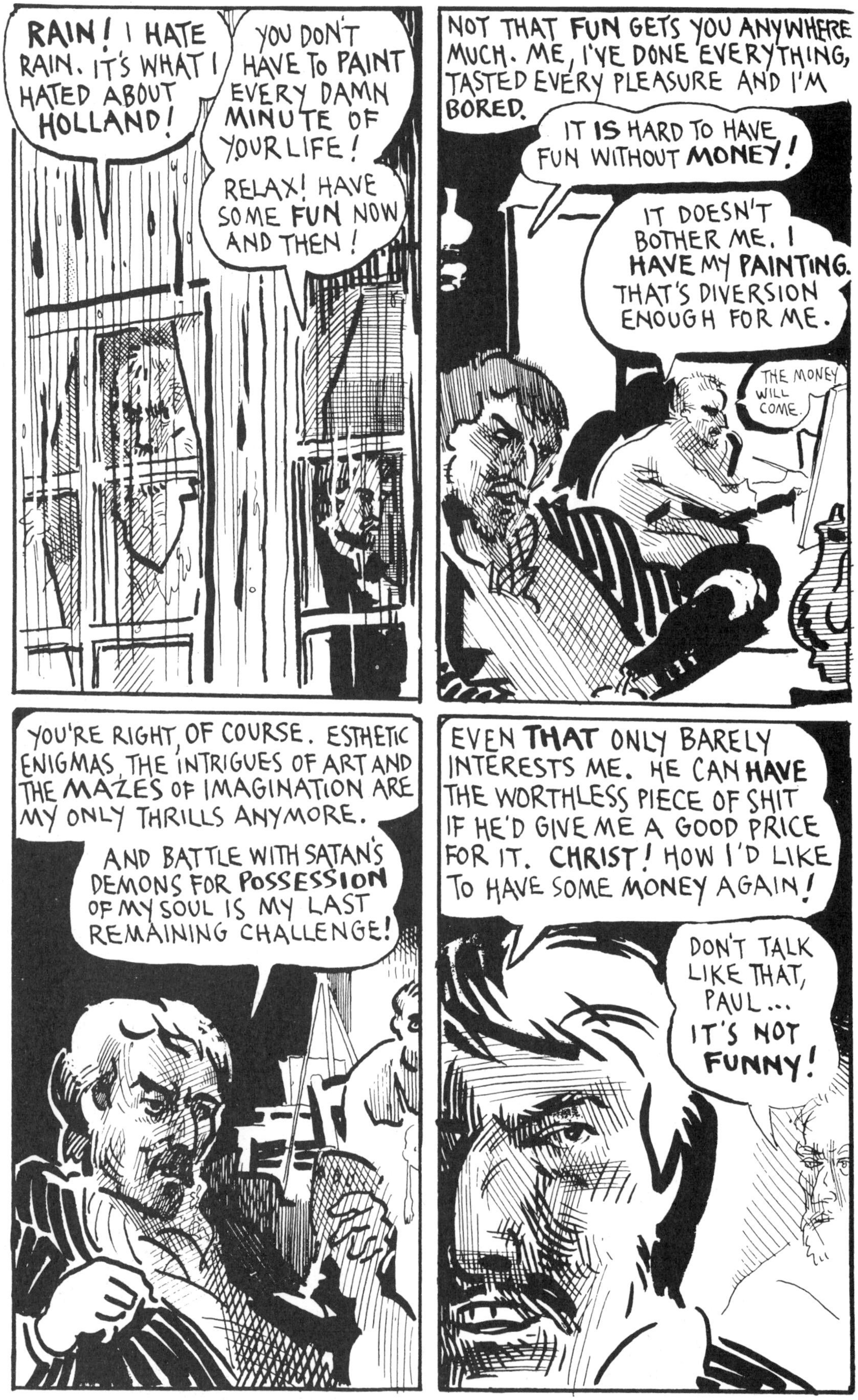
RAIN! I HATE RAIN. IT'S WHAT I HATED ABOUT HOLLAND!
YOU DON'T HAVE TO PAINT EVERY DAMN MINUTE OF YOUR LIFE!
RELAX! HAVE SOME FUN NOW AND THEN!
NOT THAT FUN GETS YOU ANYWHERE MUCH. ME, I'VE DONE EVERYTHING, TASTED EVERY PLEASURE AND I'M BORED.
IT IS HARD TO HAVE FUN WITHOUT MONEY!
IT DOESN'T BOTHER ME. I HAVE MY PAINTING. THAT'S DIVERSION ENOUGH FOR ME.
THE MONEY WILL COME.
YOU'RE RIGHT, OF COURSE. ESTHETIC ENIGMAS, THE INTRIGUES OF ART AND THE MAZES OF IMAGINATION ARE MY ONLY THRILLS ANYMORE.
AND BATTLE WITH SATAN'S DEMONS FOR POSSESSION OF MY SOUL IS MY LAST REMAINING CHALLENGE!
EVEN THAT ONLY BARELY INTERESTS ME. HE CAN HAVE THE WORTHLESS PIECE OF SHIT IF HE'D GIVE ME A GOOD PRICE FOR IT. CHRIST! HOW I'D LIKE TO HAVE SOME MONEY AGAIN!
DON'T TALK LIKE THAT, PAUL... IT'S NOT FUNNY!

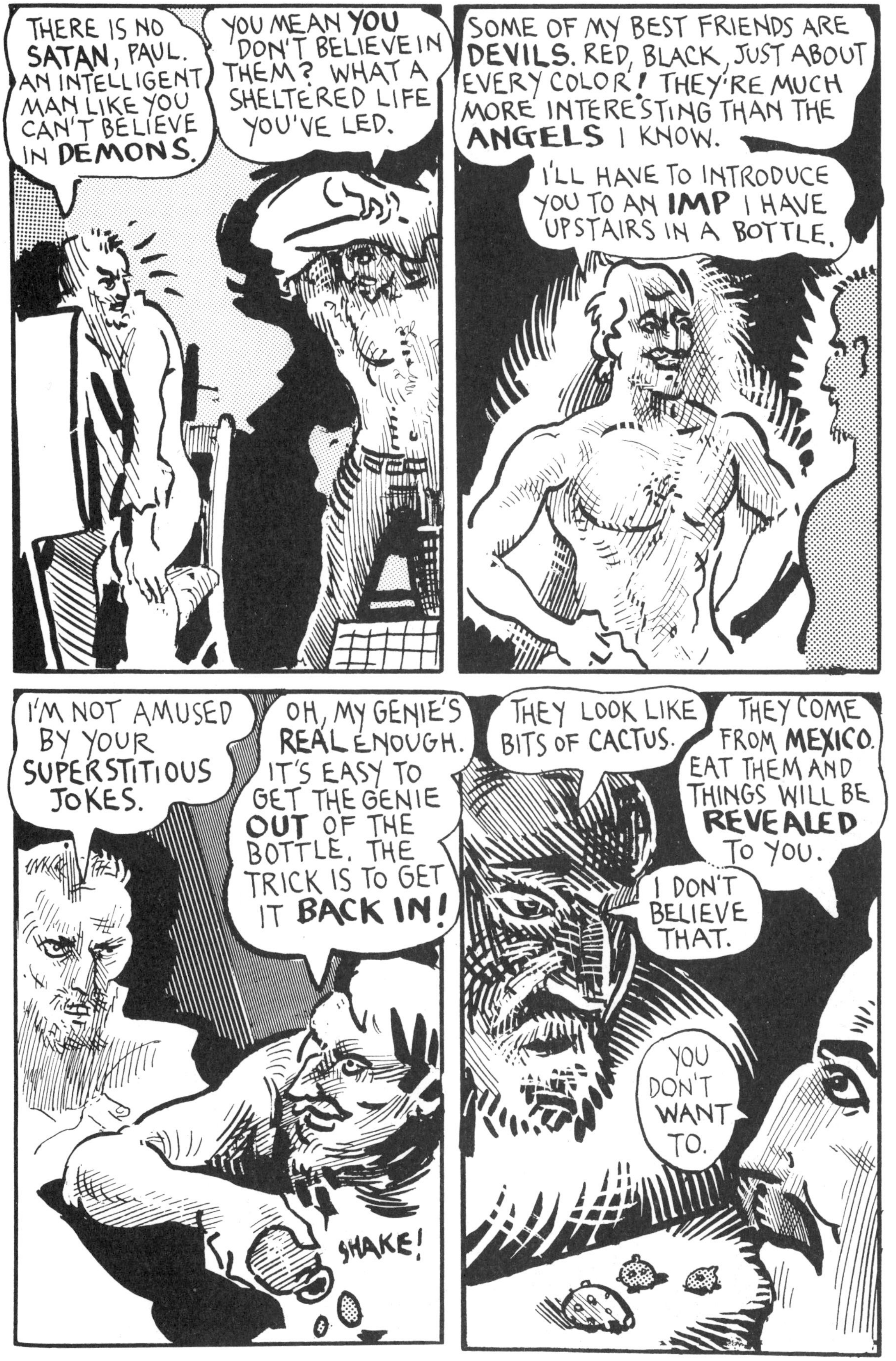
THERE IS NO SATAN, PAUL. AN INTELLIGENT MAN LIKE YOU CAN'T BELIEVE IN DEMONS.
YOU MEAN YOU DON'T BELIEVE IN THEM? WHAT A SHELTERED LIFE YOU'VE LED.
SOME OF MY BEST FRIENDS ARE DEVILS. RED, BLACK, JUST ABOUT EVERY COLOR! THEY'RE MUCH MORE INTERESTING THAN THE ANGELS I KNOW.
I'LL HAVE TO INTRODUCE YOU TO AN IMP I HAVE UPSTAIRS IN A BOTTLE.
I'M NOT AMUSED BY YOUR SUPERSTITIOUS JOKES.
OH, MY GENIE'S REAL ENOUGH. IT'S EASY TO GET THE GENIE OUT OF THE BOTTLE. THE TRICK IS TO GET IT BACK IN!
SHAKE!
THEY LOOK LIKE BITS OF CACTUS.
THEY COME FROM MEXICO. EAT THEM AND THINGS WILL BE REVEALED TO YOU.
I DON'T BELIEVE THAT.
YOU DON'T WANT TO.

BUT TO PROVE HE WASN'T AFRAID VINCENT ATE THE CACTUS.
HE SPENT THE NEXT SEVERAL HOURS IN THE AGONY OF AN UNUSUALLY HORRIBLE DRUG-INDUCED HALLUCINATION.

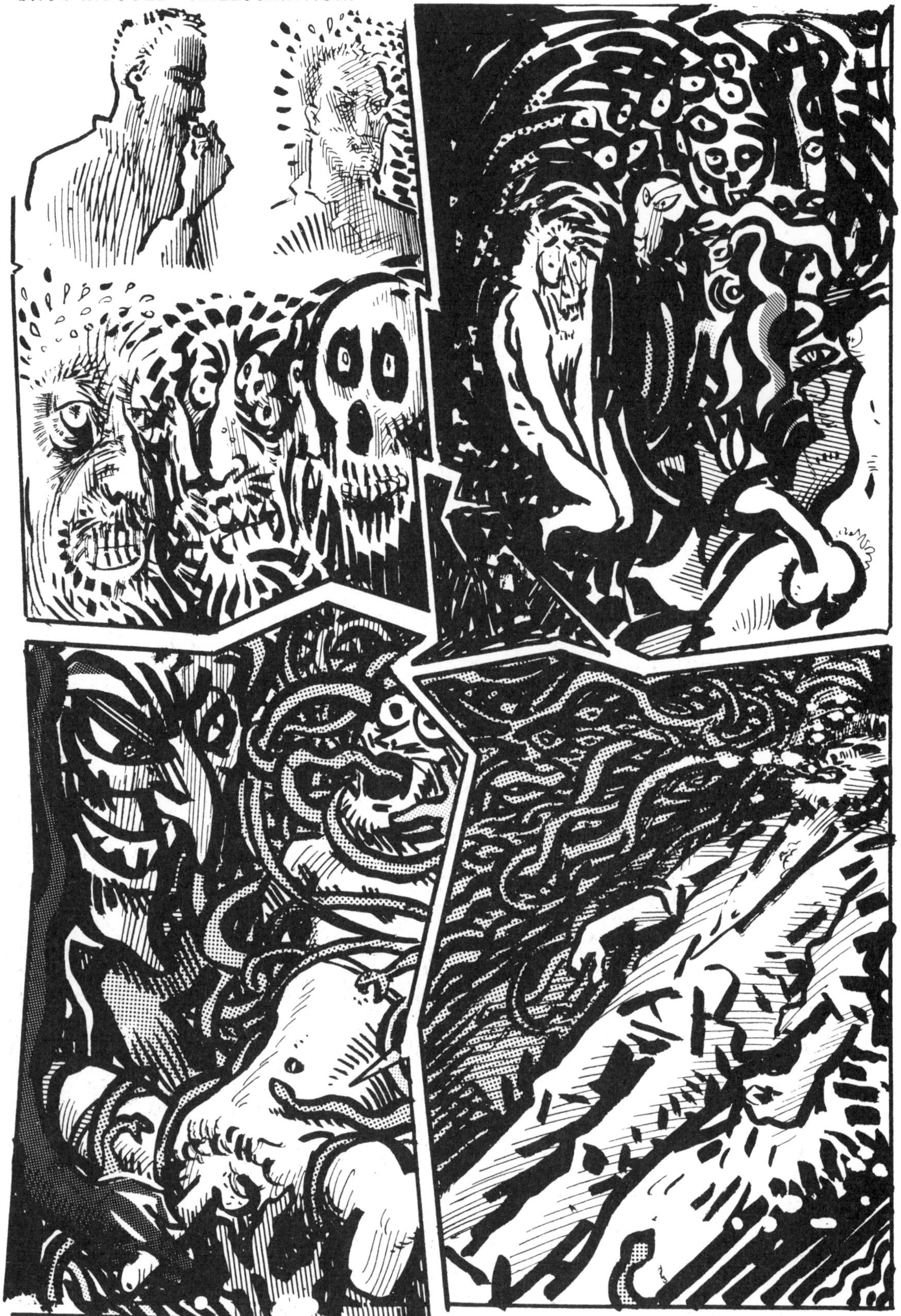

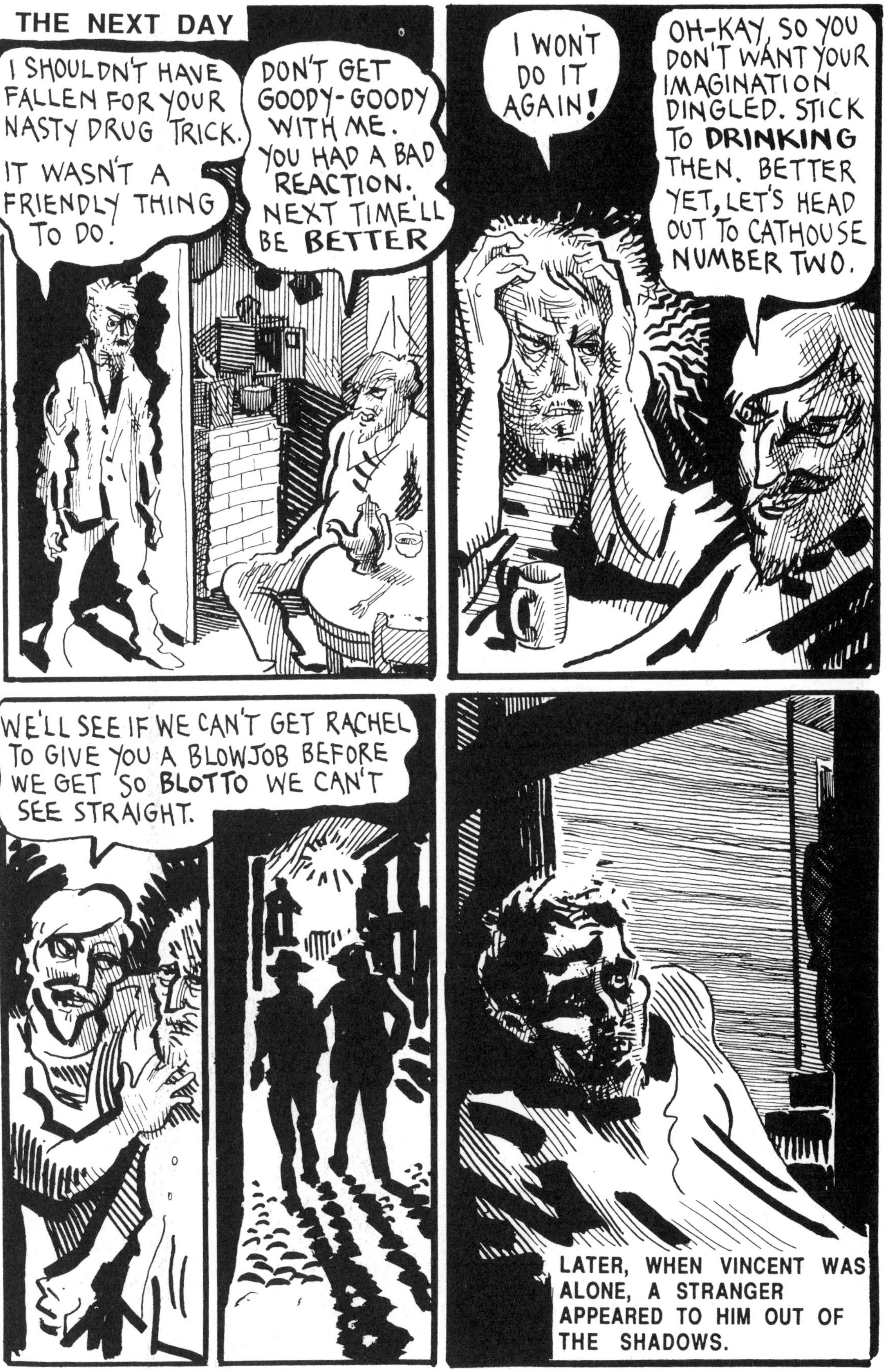
THE NEXT DAY
I SHOULDN'T HAVE FALLEN FOR YOUR NASTY DRUG TRICK. IT WASN'T A FRIENDLY THING TO DO.
DON'T GET GOODY-GOODY WITH ME. YOU HAD A BAD REACTION. NEXT TIME'LL BE BETTER
I WON'T DO IT AGAIN!
OH-KAY, SO YOU DON'T WANT YOUR IMAGINATION DINGLED. STICK TO DRINKING THEN. BETTER YET, LET'S HEAD OUT TO CATHOUSE NUMBER TWO.
WE'LL SEE IF WE CAN'T GET RACHEL TO GIVE YOU A BLOWJOB BEFORE WE GET SO BLOTTO WE CAN'T SEE STRAIGHT.
LATER, WHEN VINCENT WAS ALONE, A STRANGER APPEARED TO HIM OUT OF THE SHADOWS.

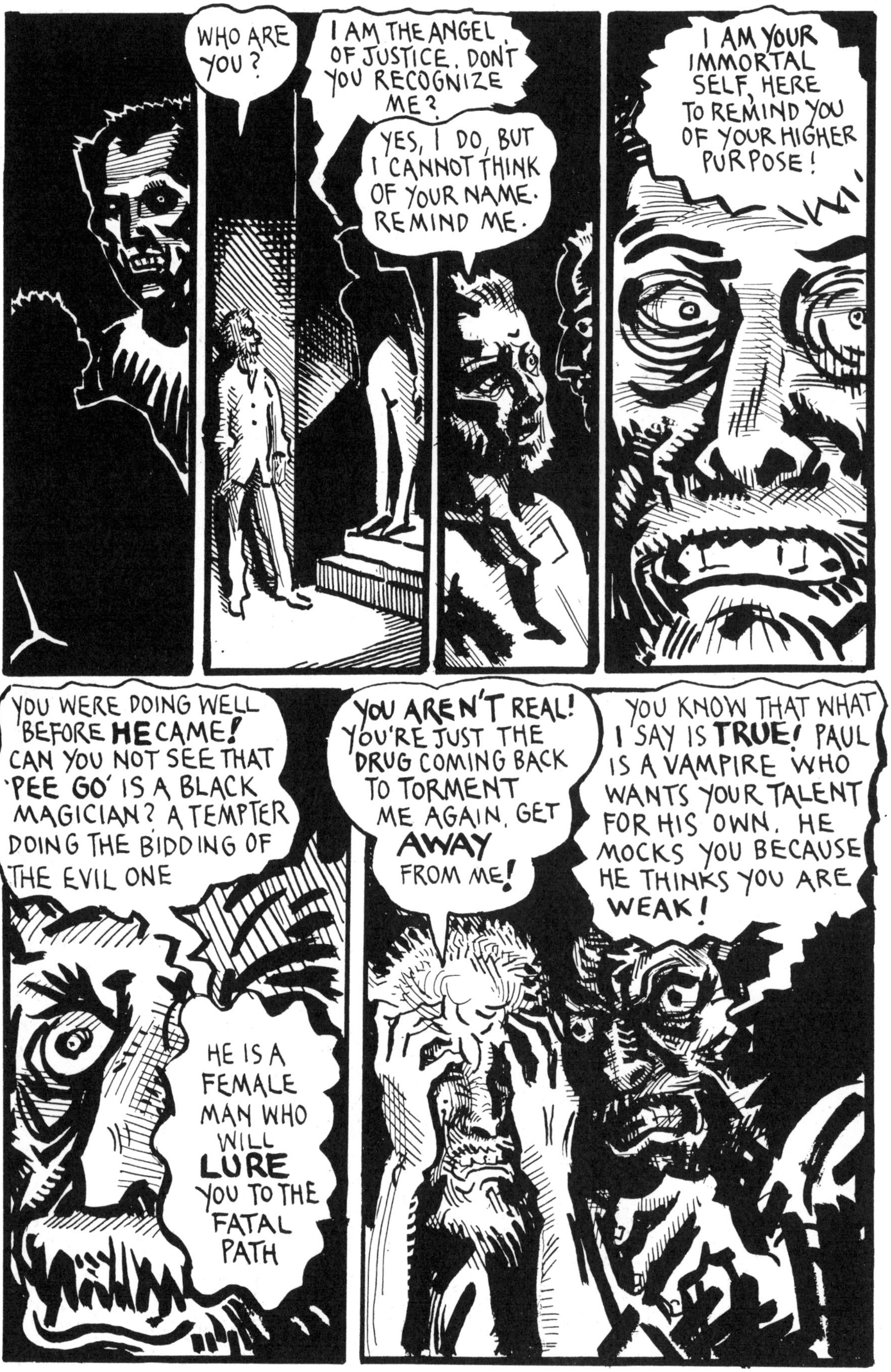
WHO ARE YOU?
I AM THE ANGEL OF JUSTICE. DON'T YOU RECOGNIZE ME?
YES, I DO, BUT I CANNOT THINK OF YOUR NAME. REMIND ME.
I AM YOUR IMMORTAL SELF, HERE TO REMIND YOU OF YOUR HIGHER PURPOSE!
YOU WERE DOING WELL BEFORE HE CAME! CAN YOU NOT SEE THAT 'PEE GO' IS A BLACK MAGICIAN? A TEMPTER DOING THE BIDDING OF THE EVIL ONE
HE IS A FEMALE MAN WHO WILL LURE YOU TO THE FATAL PATH
YOU AREN'T REAL! YOU'RE JUST THE DRUG COMING BACK TO TORMENT ME AGAIN. GET AWAY FROM ME!
YOU KNOW THAT WHAT I SAY IS TRUE! PAUL IS A VAMPIRE WHO WANTS YOUR TALENT FOR HIS OWN. HE MOCKS YOU BECAUSE HE THINKS YOU ARE WEAK!

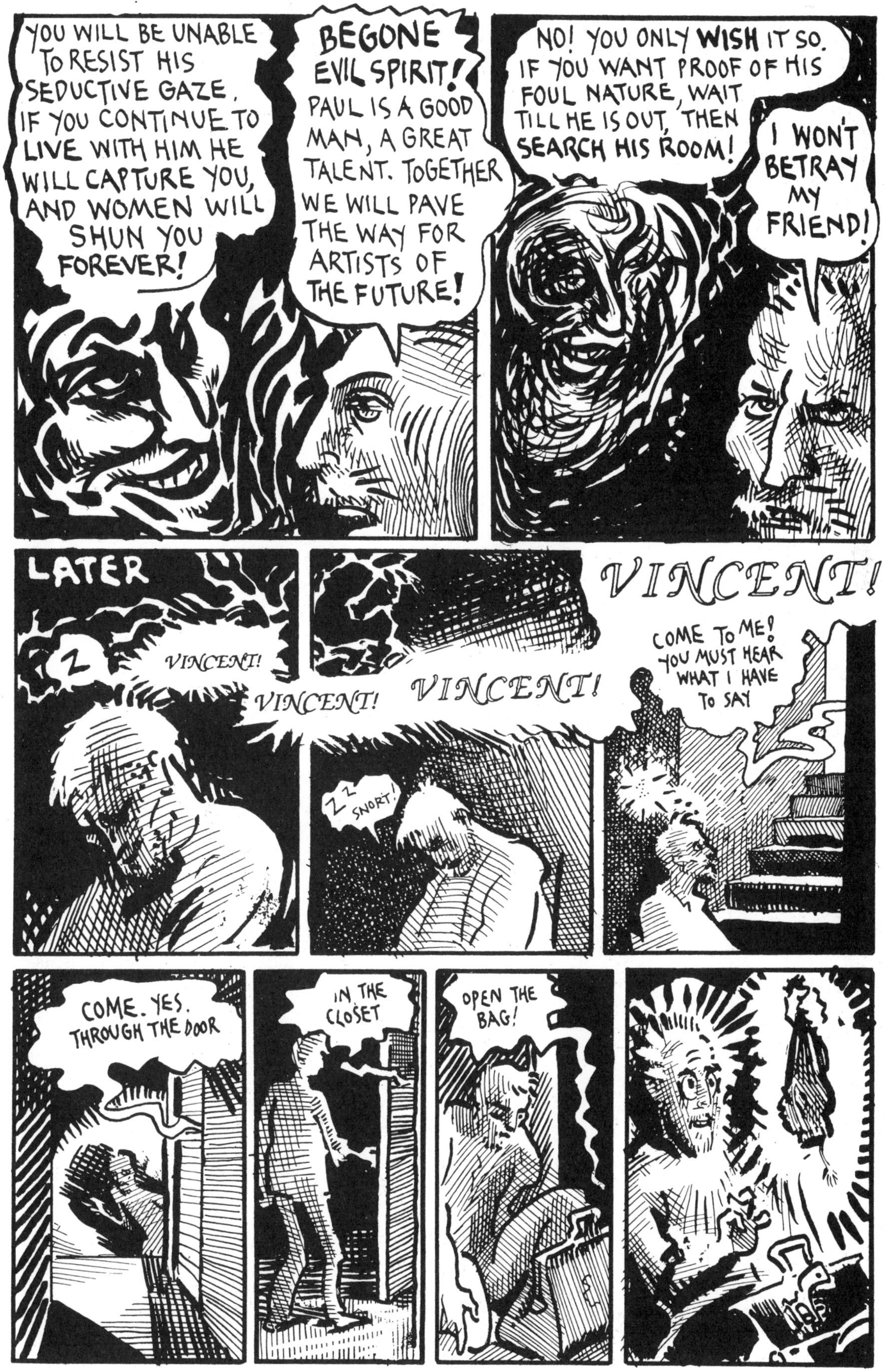
YOU WILL BE UNABLE TO RESIST HIS SEDUCTIVE GAZE. IF YOU CONTINUE TO LIVE WITH HIM HE WILL CAPTURE YOU, AND WOMEN WILL SHUN YOU FOREVER!
BEGONE EVIL SPIRIT! PAUL IS A GOOD MAN, A GREAT TALENT. TOGETHER WE WILL PAVE THE WAY FOR ARTISTS OF THE FUTURE!
NO! YOU ONLY WISH IT SO. IF YOU WANT PROOF OF HIS FOUL NATURE, WAIT TILL HE IS OUT, THEN SEARCH HIS ROOM!
I WON'T BETRAY MY FRIEND!
LATER
Z
VINCENT!
VINCENT!
VINCENT!
VINCENT!
Z Z SNORT!
COME TO ME! YOU MUST HEAR WHAT I HAVE TO SAY
COME. YES. THROUGH THE DOOR
IN THE CLOSET
OPEN THE BAG!

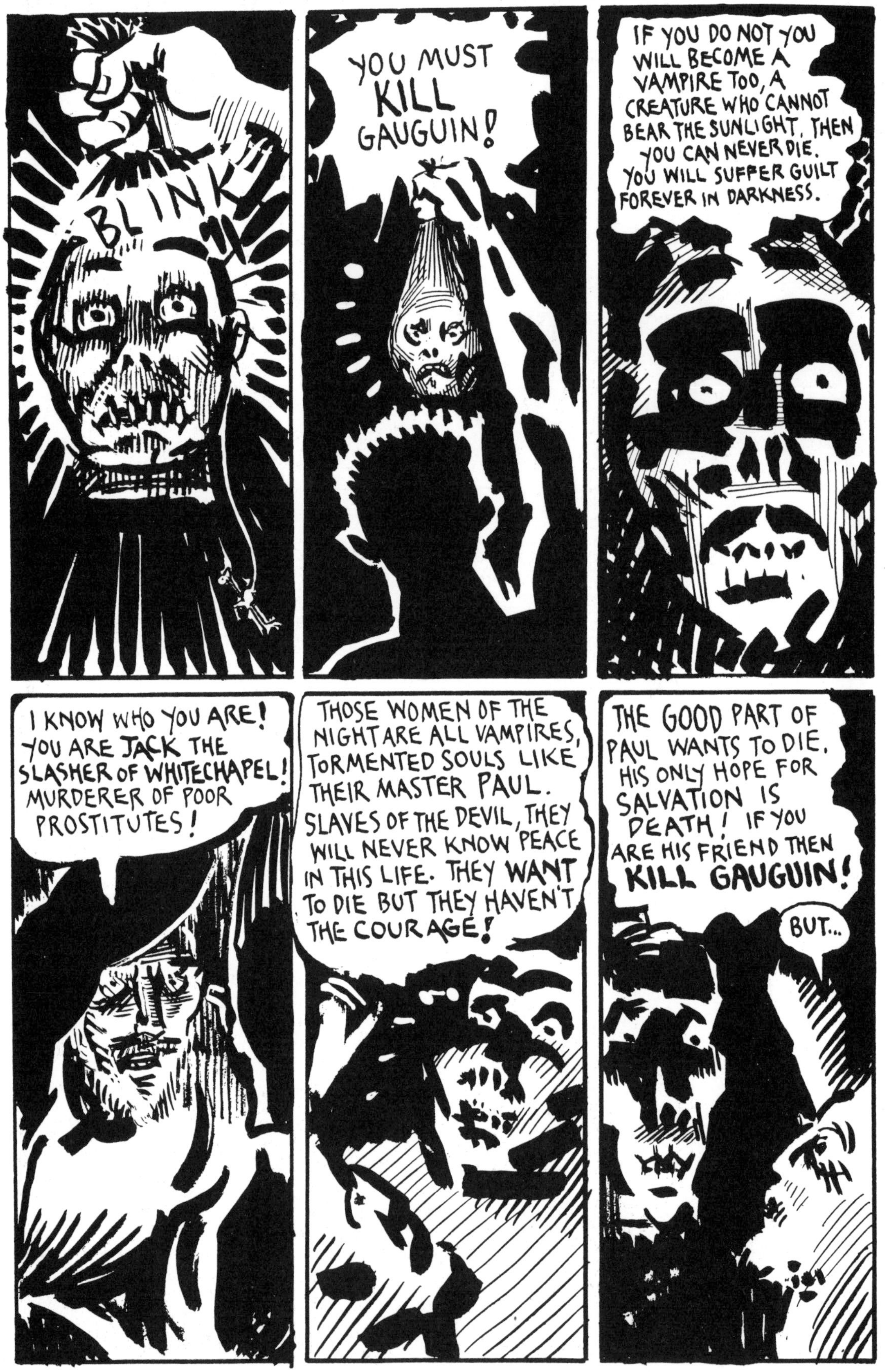
BLINK
YOU MUST KILL GAUGUIN!
IF YOU DO NOT YOU WILL BECOME A VAMPIRE TOO, A CREATURE WHO CANNOT BEAR THE SUNLIGHT. THEN YOU CAN NEVER DIE. YOU WILL SUFFER GUILT FOREVER IN DARKNESS.
I KNOW WHO YOU ARE! YOU ARE JACK THE SLASHER OF WHITECHAPEL! MURDERER OF POOR PROSTITUTES!
THOSE WOMEN OF THE NIGHT ARE ALL VAMPIRES, TORMENTED SOULS LIKE THEIR MASTER PAUL. SLAVES OF THE DEVIL, THEY WILL NEVER KNOW PEACE IN THIS LIFE. THEY WANT TO DIE BUT THEY HAVEN'T THE COURAGE!
THE GOOD PART OF PAUL WANTS TO DIE. HIS ONLY HOPE FOR SALVATION IS DEATH! IF YOU ARE HIS FRIEND THEN KILL GAUGUIN!
BUT...

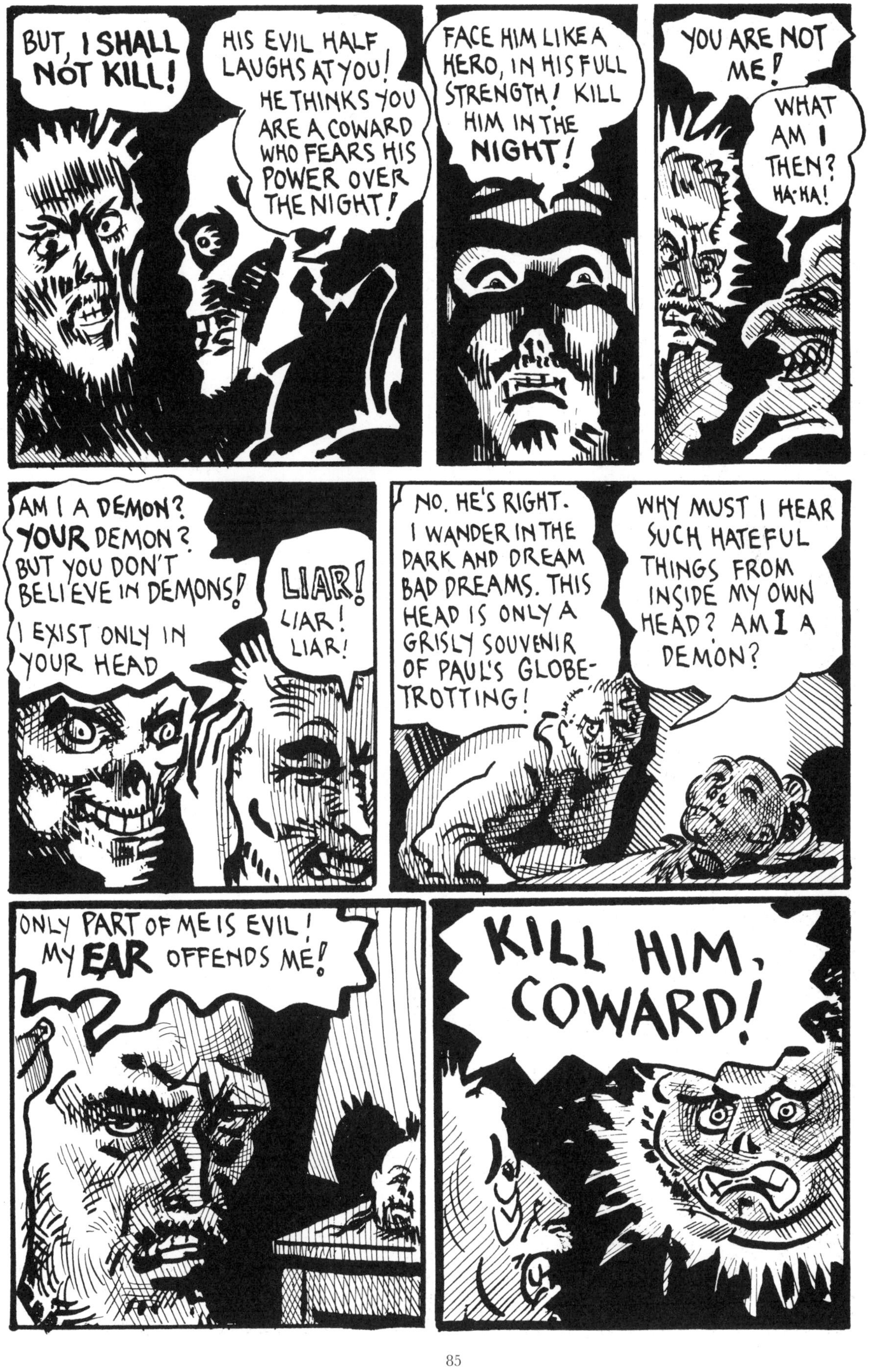
BUT, I SHALL NOT KILL!
HIS EVIL HALF LAUGHS AT YOU!
HE THINKS YOU ARE A COWARD WHO FEARS HIS POWER OVER THE NIGHT!
FACE HIM LIKE A HERO, IN HIS FULL STRENGTH! KILL HIM IN THE NIGHT!
YOU ARE NOT ME!
WHAT AM I THEN? HA-HA!
AM I A DEMON? YOUR DEMON? BUT YOU DON'T BELIEVE IN DEMONS!
I EXIST ONLY IN YOUR HEAD
LIAR! LIAR! LIAR!
NO. HE'S RIGHT. I WANDER IN THE DARK AND DREAM BAD DREAMS. THIS HEAD IS ONLY A GRISLY SOUVENIR OF PAUL'S GLOBE-TROTTING!
WHY MUST I HEAR SUCH HATEFUL THINGS FROM INSIDE MY OWN HEAD? AM I A DEMON?
ONLY PART OF ME IS EVIL! MY EAR OFFENDS ME!
KILL HIM, COWARD!

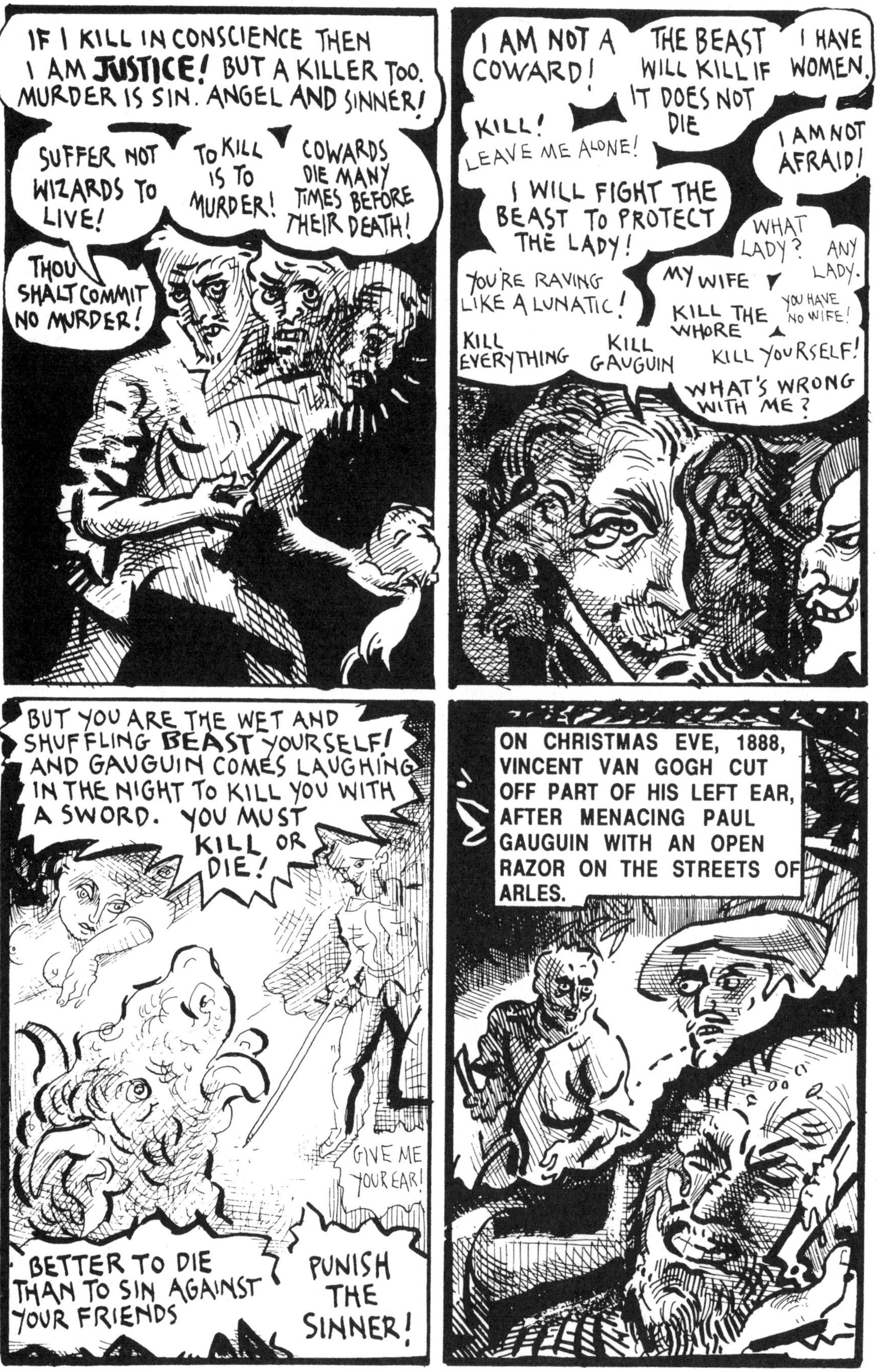
IF I KILL IN CONSCIENCE THEN I AM JUSTICE! BUT A KILLER TOO. MURDER IS SIN. ANGEL AND SINNER!
SUFFER NOT WIZARDS TO LIVE!
TO KILL IS TO MURDER!
COWARDS DIE MANY TIMES BEFORE THEIR DEATH!
THOU SHALT COMMIT NO MURDER!
I AM NOT A COWARD!
THE BEAST WILL KILL IF IT DOES NOT DIE
I HAVE WOMEN.
KILL!
LEAVE ME ALONE!
I AM NOT AFRAID!
I WILL FIGHT THE BEAST TO PROTECT THE LADY!
WHAT LADY?
ANY LADY.
YOU'RE RAVING LIKE A LUNATIC!
MY WIFE
YOU HAVE NO WIFE!
KILL THE WHORE
KILL EVERYTHING
KILL GAUGUIN
KILL YOURSELF!
WHAT'S WRONG WITH ME?
BUT YOU ARE THE WET AND SHUFFLING BEAST YOURSELF! AND GAUGUIN COMES LAUGHING IN THE NIGHT TO KILL YOU WITH A SWORD. YOU MUST KILL OR DIE!
GIVE ME YOUR EAR!
BETTER TO DIE THAN TO SIN AGAINST YOUR FRIENDS
PUNISH THE SINNER!
ON CHRISTMAS EVE, 1888, VINCENT VAN GOGH CUT OFF PART OF HIS LEFT EAR, AFTER MENACING PAUL GAUGUIN WITH AN OPEN RAZOR ON THE STREETS OF ARLES.

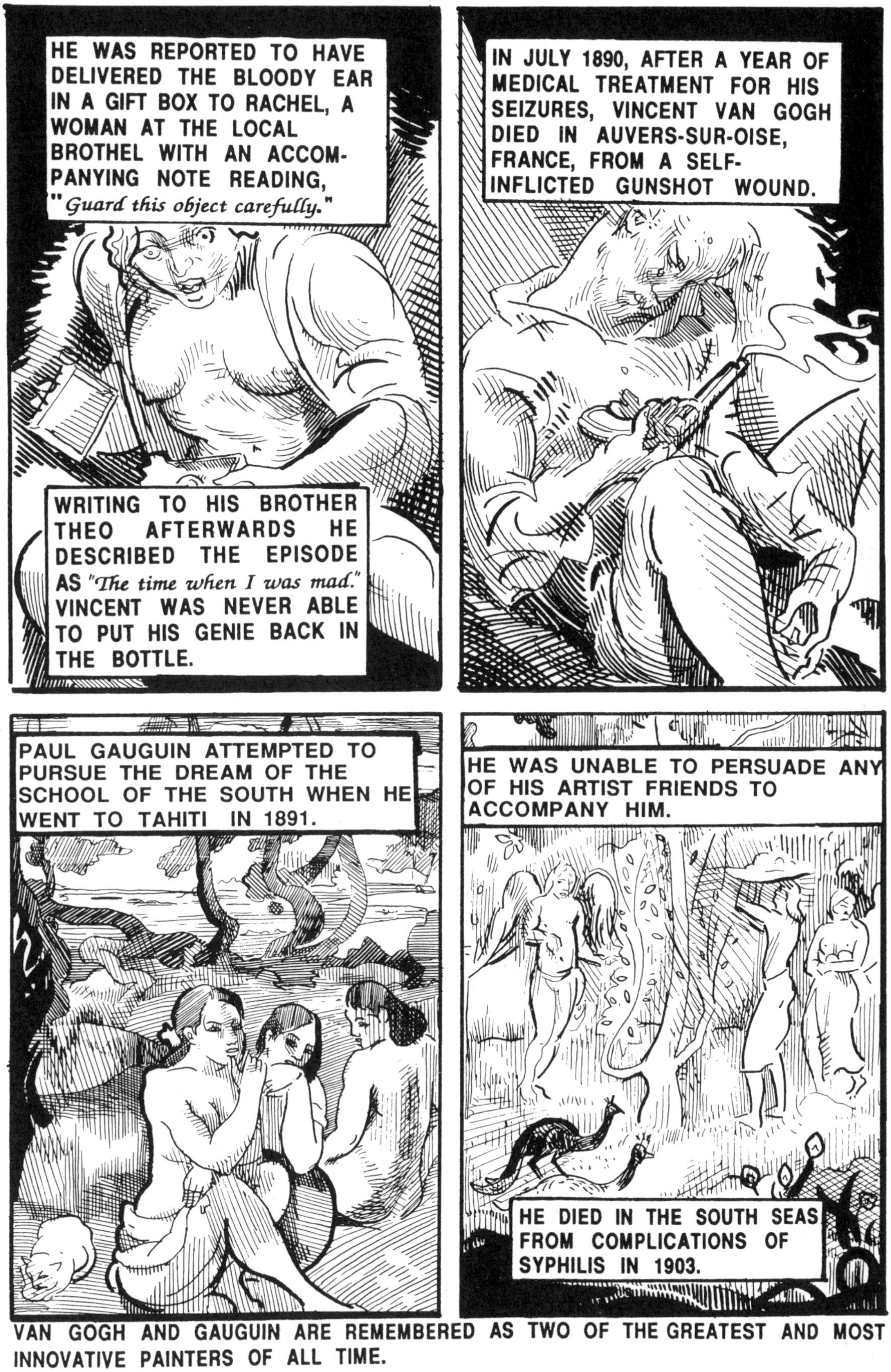
HE WAS REPORTED TO HAVE DELIVERED THE BLOODY EAR IN A GIFT BOX TO RACHEL, A WOMAN AT THE LOCAL BROTHEL WITH AN ACCOMPANYING NOTE READING, "*Guard this object carefully.*"
WRITING TO HIS BROTHER THEO AFTERWARDS HE DESCRIBED THE EPISODE AS "*The time when I was mad.*" VINCENT WAS NEVER ABLE TO PUT HIS GENIE BACK IN THE BOTTLE.
IN JULY 1890, AFTER A YEAR OF MEDICAL TREATMENT FOR HIS SEIZURES, VINCENT VAN GOGH DIED IN AUVERS-SUR-OISE, FRANCE, FROM A SELF-INFLICTED GUNSHOT WOUND.
PAUL GAUGUIN ATTEMPTED TO PURSUE THE DREAM OF THE SCHOOL OF THE SOUTH WHEN HE WENT TO TAHITI IN 1891.
HE WAS UNABLE TO PERSUADE ANY OF HIS ARTIST FRIENDS TO ACCOMPANY HIM.
HE DIED IN THE SOUTH SEAS FROM COMPLICATIONS OF SYPHILIS IN 1903.

VAN GOGH AND GAUGUIN ARE REMEMBERED AS TWO OF THE GREATEST AND MOST INNOVATIVE PAINTERS OF ALL TIME.

The Bard

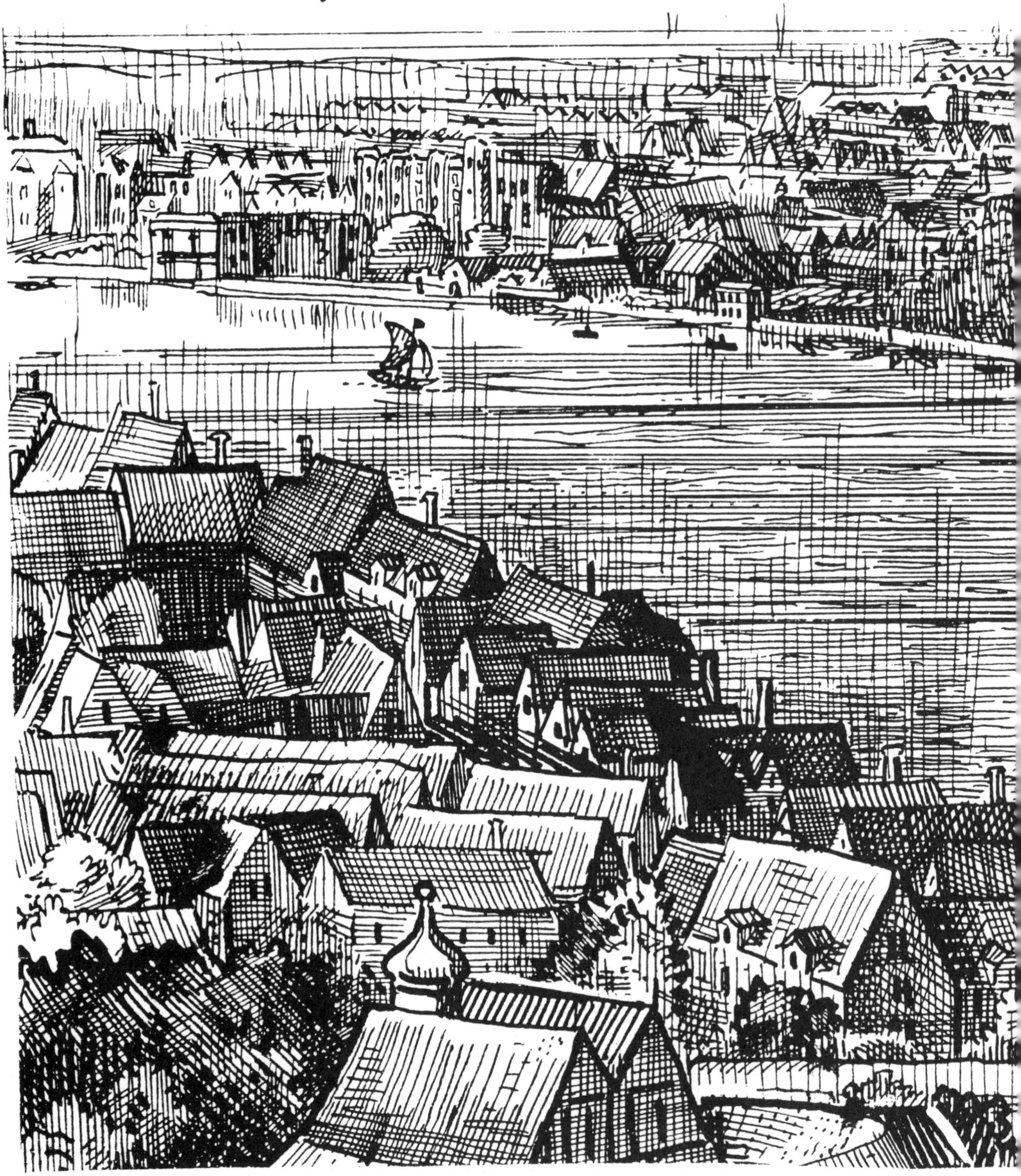

Must Die!

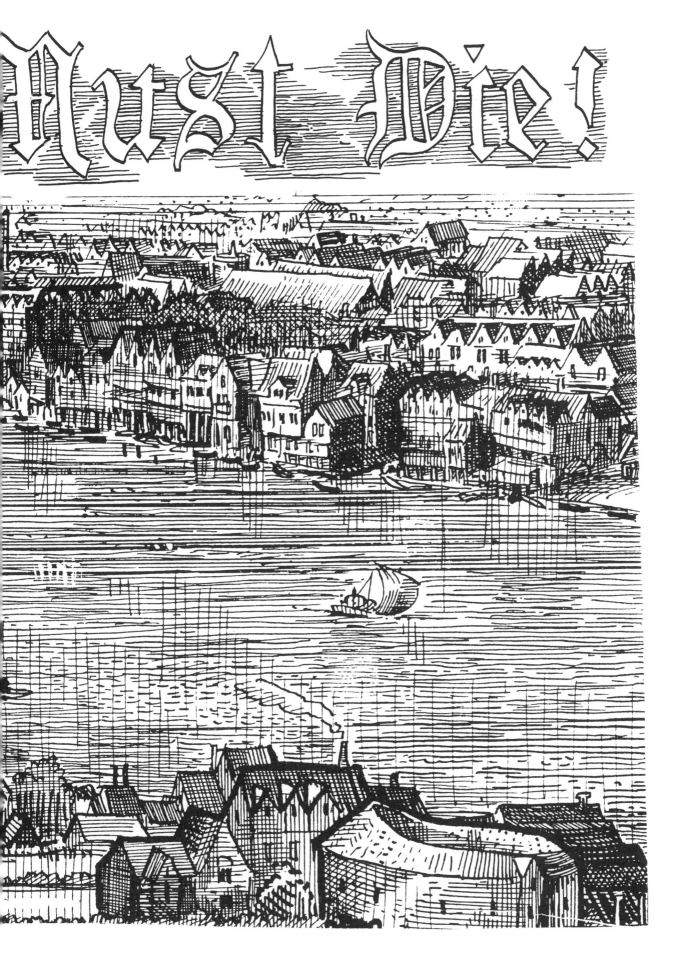

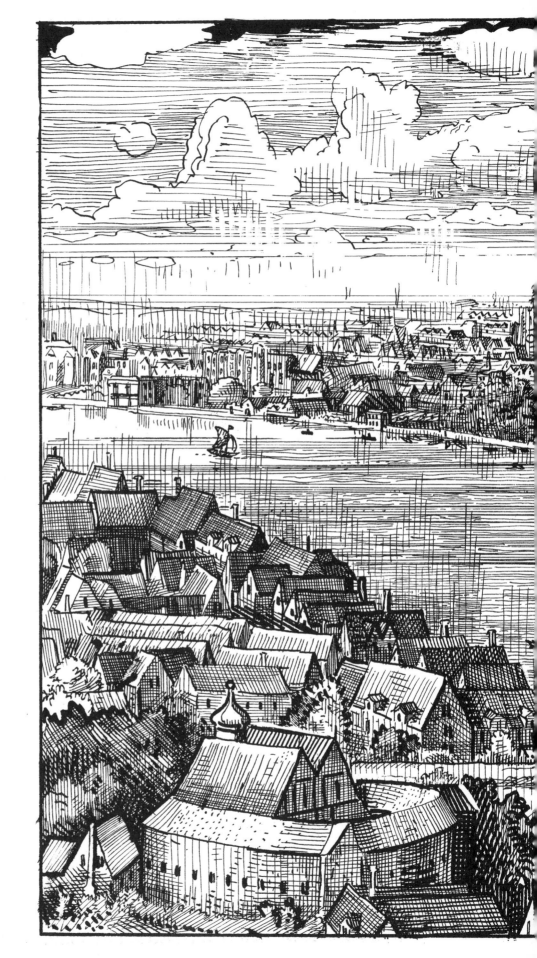

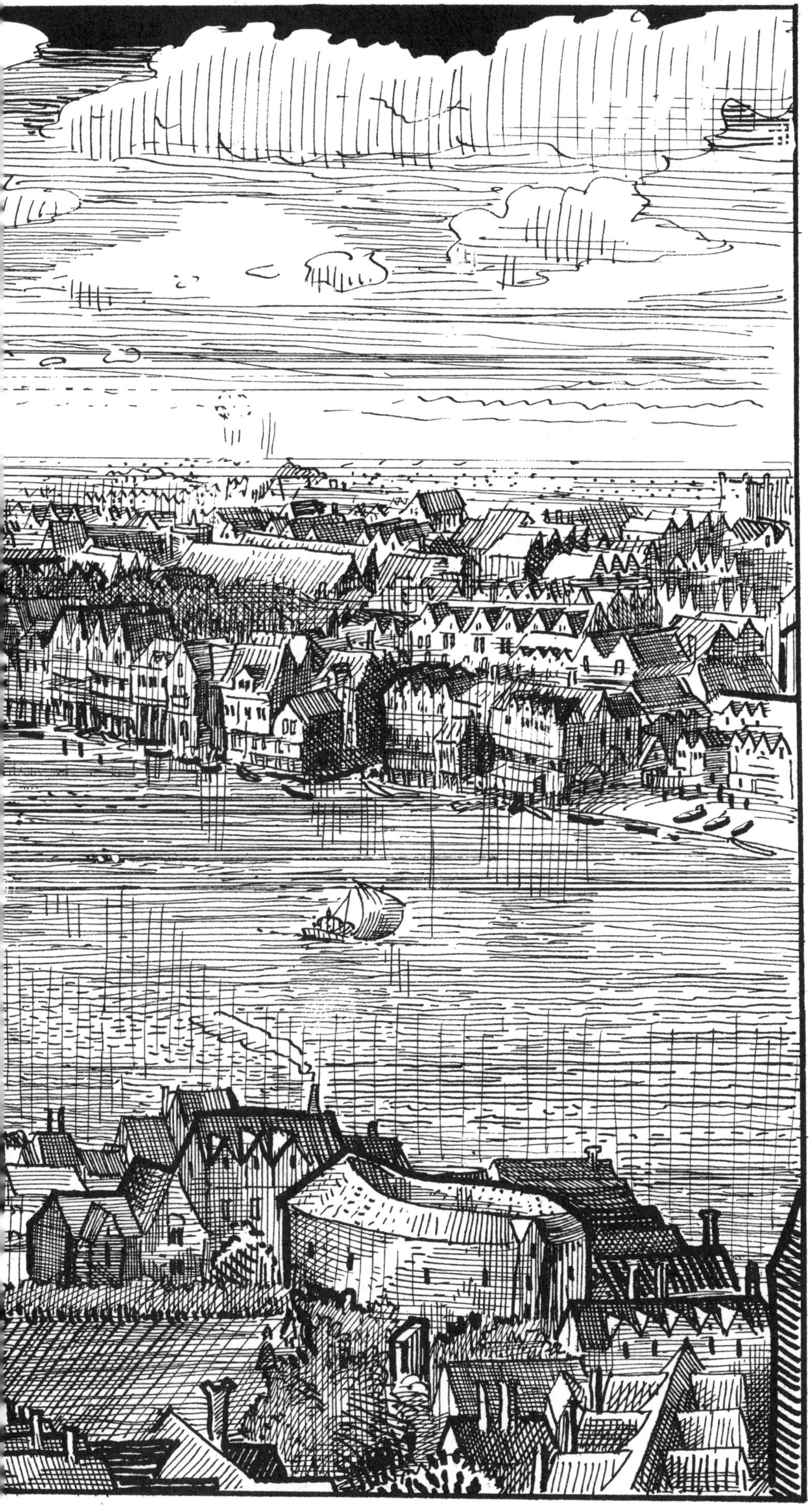

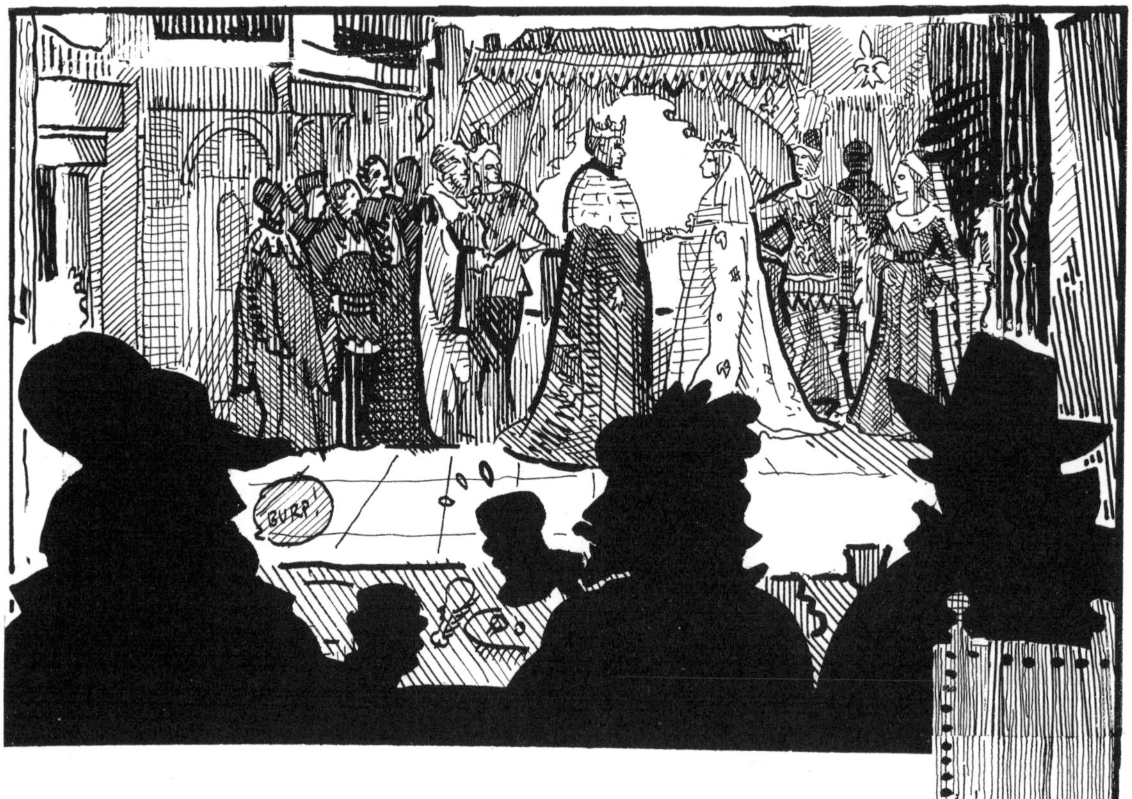
BURP!

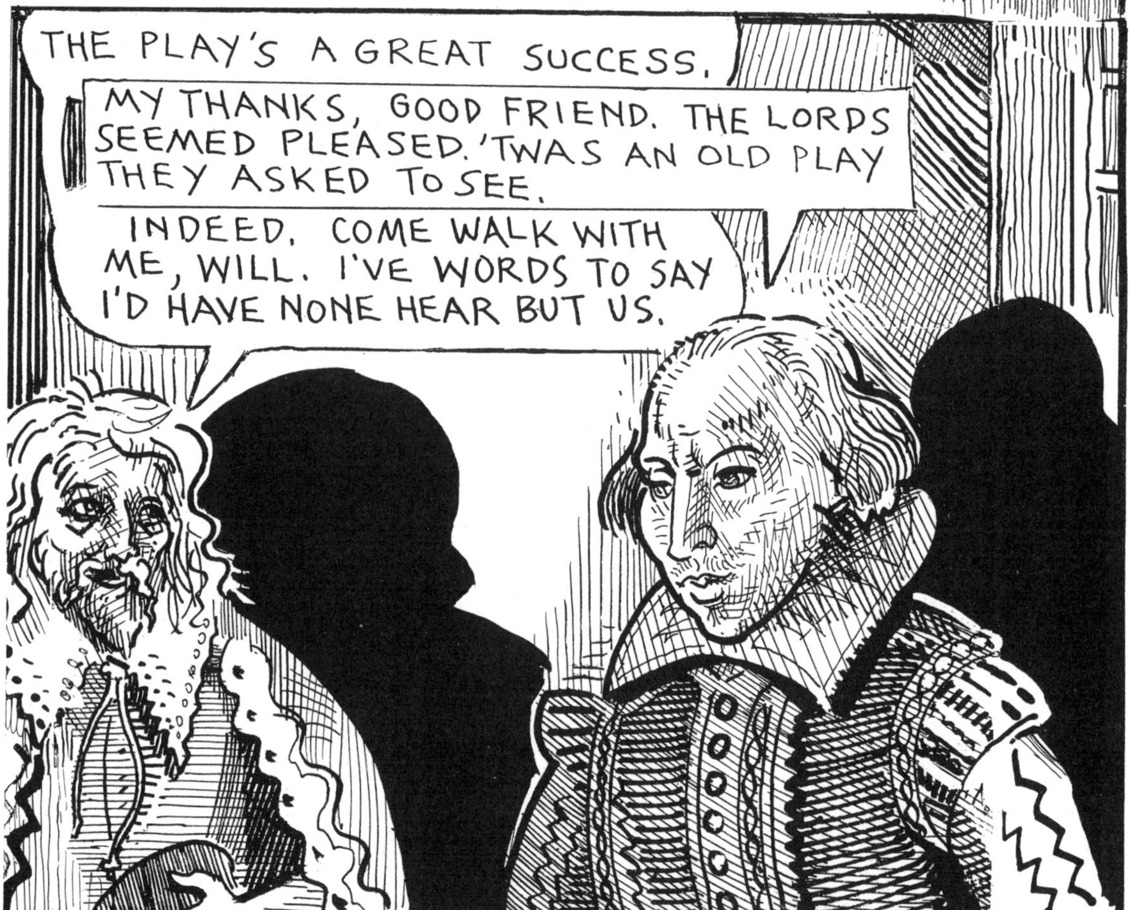
THE PLAY'S A GREAT SUCCESS.
MY THANKS, GOOD FRIEND. THE LORDS SEEMED PLEASED. 'TWAS AN OLD PLAY THEY ASKED TO SEE.
INDEED. COME WALK WITH ME, WILL. I'VE WORDS TO SAY I'D HAVE NONE HEAR BUT US.

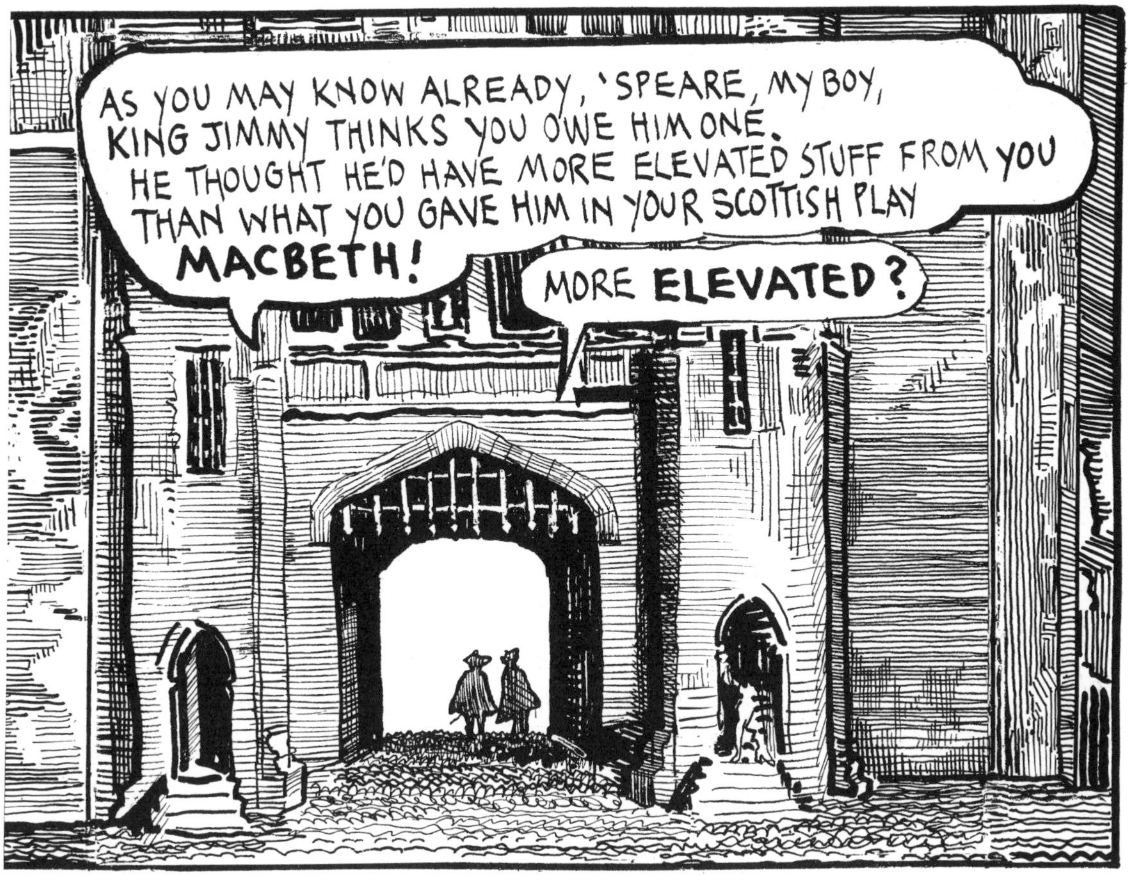
AS YOU MAY KNOW ALREADY, 'SPEARE, MY BOY, KING JIMMY THINKS YOU OWE HIM ONE. HE THOUGHT HE'D HAVE MORE ELEVATED STUFF FROM YOU THAN WHAT YOU GAVE HIM IN YOUR SCOTTISH PLAY MACBETH!
MORE ELEVATED?
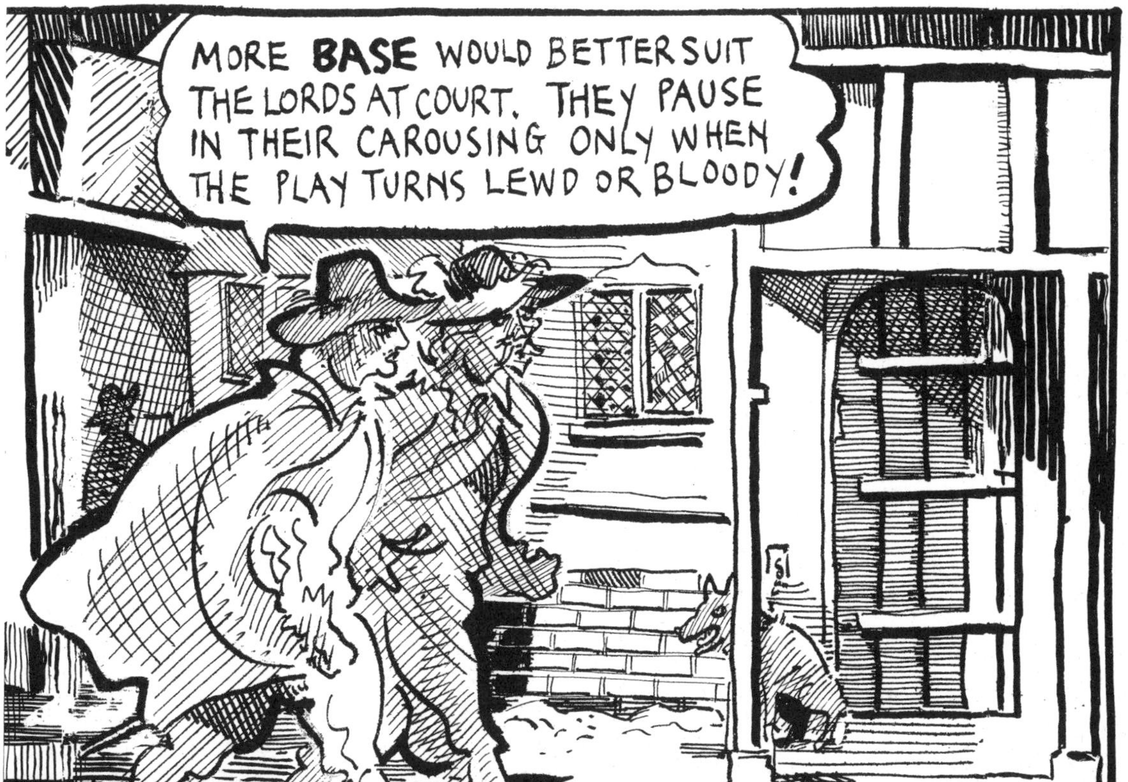
MORE BASE WOULD BETTER SUIT THE LORDS AT COURT. THEY PAUSE IN THEIR CAROUSING ONLY WHEN THE PLAY TURNS LEWD OR BLOODY!

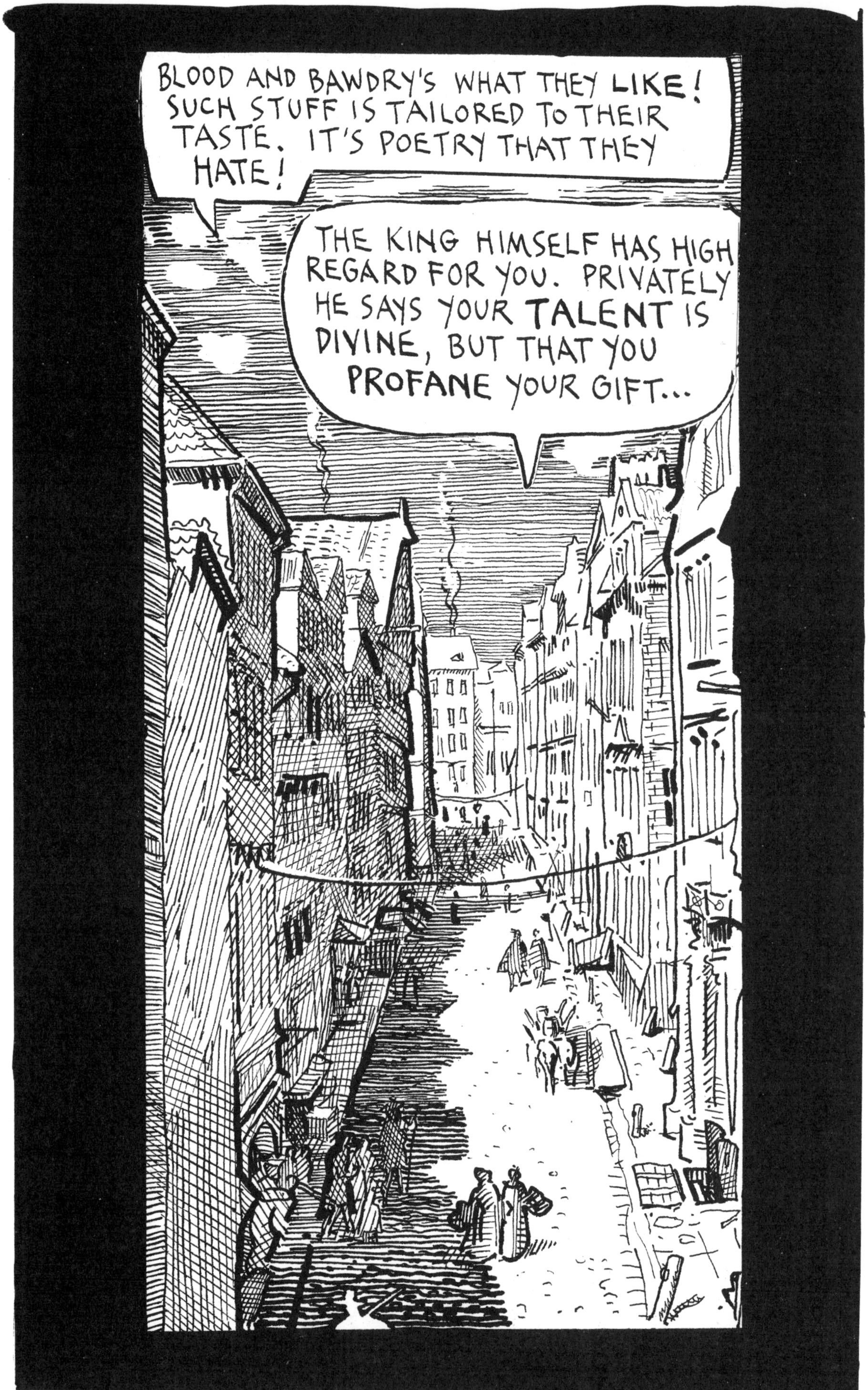
BLOOD AND BAWDRY'S WHAT THEY LIKE! SUCH STUFF IS TAILORED TO THEIR TASTE. IT'S POETRY THAT THEY HATE!
THE KING HIMSELF HAS HIGH REGARD FOR YOU. PRIVATELY HE SAYS YOUR TALENT IS DIVINE, BUT THAT YOU PROFANE YOUR GIFT...

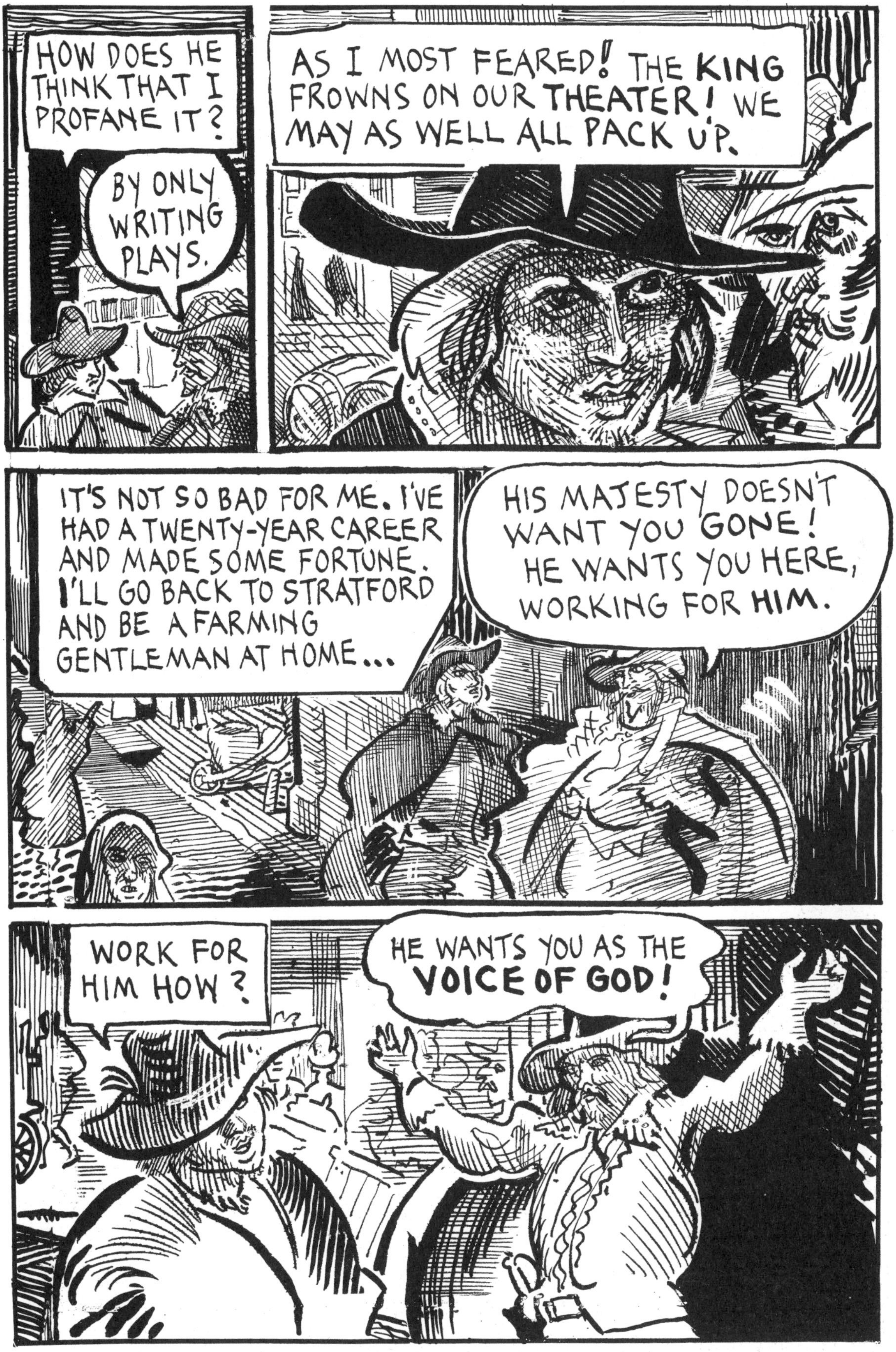
HOW DOES HE THINK THAT I PROFANE IT?
BY ONLY WRITING PLAYS.
AS I MOST FEARED! THE KING FROWNS ON OUR THEATER! WE MAY AS WELL ALL PACK UP.
IT'S NOT SO BAD FOR ME. I'VE HAD A TWENTY-YEAR CAREER AND MADE SOME FORTUNE. I'LL GO BACK TO STRATFORD AND BE A FARMING GENTLEMAN AT HOME...
HIS MAJESTY DOESN'T WANT YOU GONE! HE WANTS YOU HERE, WORKING FOR HIM.
WORK FOR HIM HOW?
HE WANTS YOU AS THE VOICE OF GOD!

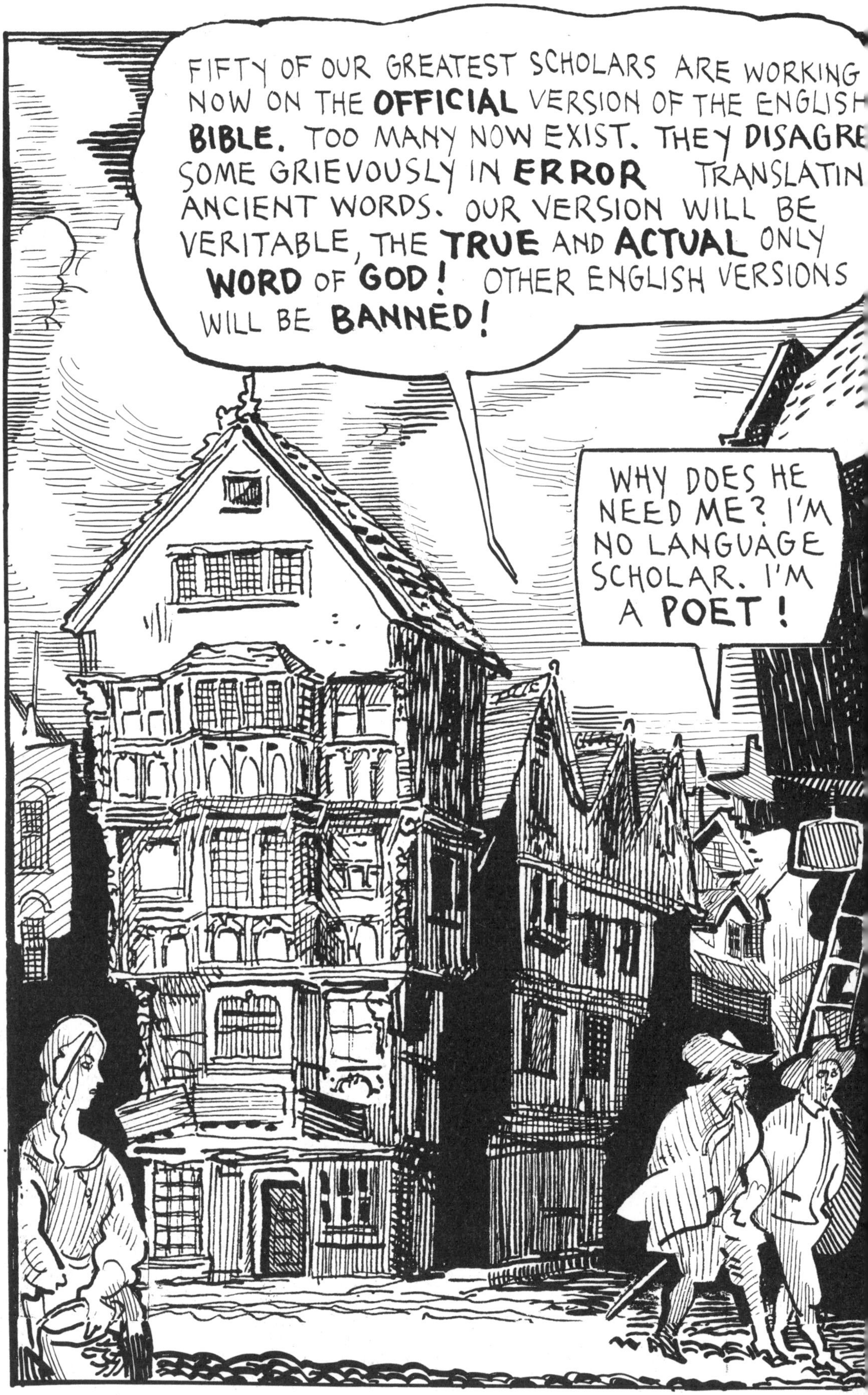
FIFTY OF OUR GREATEST SCHOLARS ARE WORKING NOW ON THE OFFICIAL VERSION OF THE ENGLISH BIBLE. TOO MANY NOW EXIST. THEY DISAGREE SOME GRIEVOUSLY IN ERROR TRANSLATING ANCIENT WORDS. OUR VERSION WILL BE VERITABLE, THE TRUE AND ACTUAL ONLY WORD OF GOD! OTHER ENGLISH VERSIONS WILL BE BANNED!
WHY DOES HE NEED ME? I'M NO LANGUAGE SCHOLAR. I'M A POET!

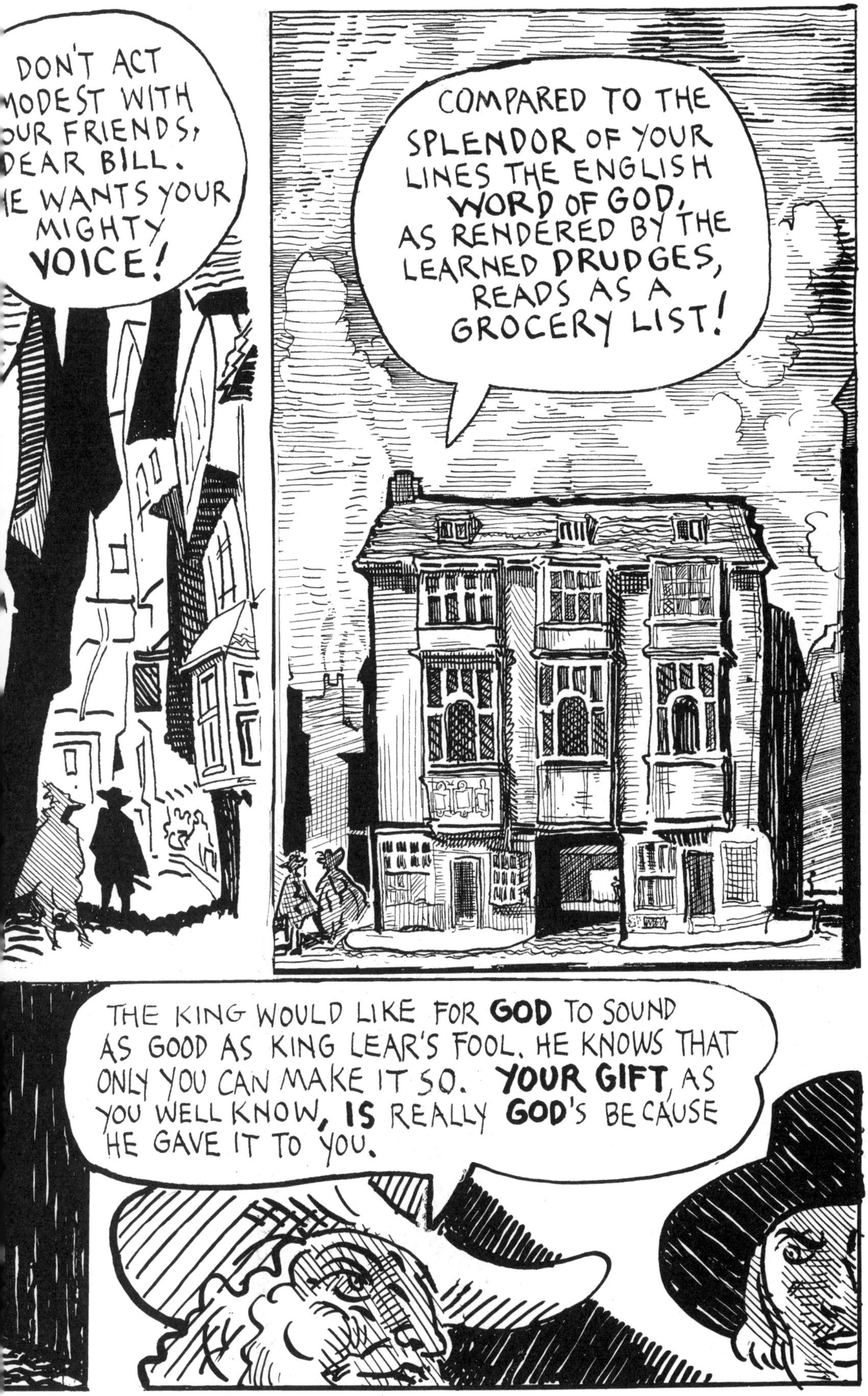
DON'T ACT MODEST WITH OUR FRIENDS, DEAR BILL. HE WANTS YOUR MIGHTY VOICE!
COMPARED TO THE SPLENDOR OF YOUR LINES THE ENGLISH WORD OF GOD, AS RENDERED BY THE LEARNED DRUDGES, READS AS A GROCERY LIST!
THE KING WOULD LIKE FOR GOD TO SOUND AS GOOD AS KING LEAR'S FOOL. HE KNOWS THAT ONLY YOU CAN MAKE IT SO. YOUR GIFT, AS YOU WELL KNOW, IS REALLY GOD'S BECAUSE HE GAVE IT TO YOU.

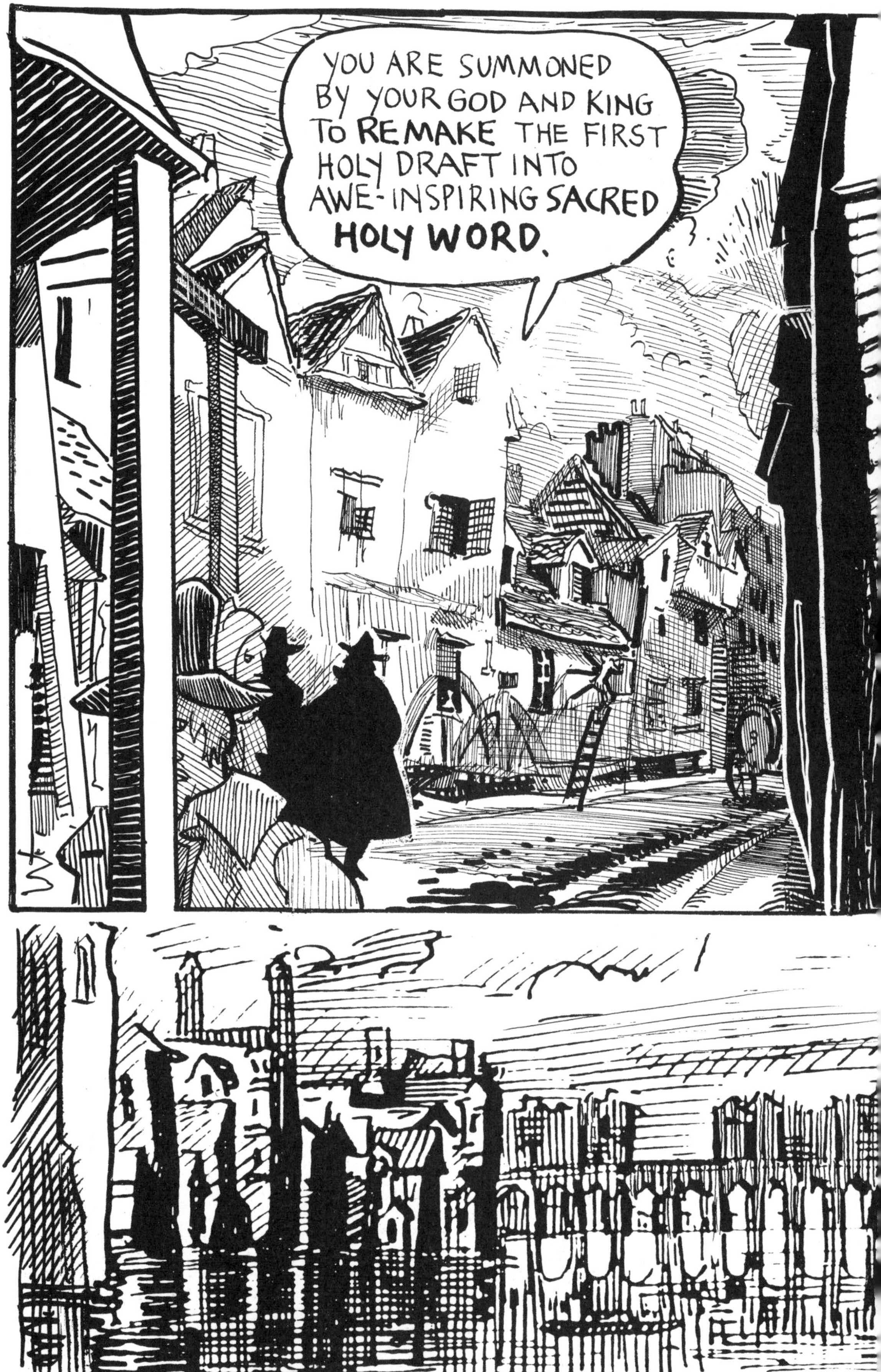
YOU ARE SUMMONED BY YOUR GOD AND KING TO REMAKE THE FIRST HOLY DRAFT INTO AWE-INSPIRING SACRED HOLY WORD.

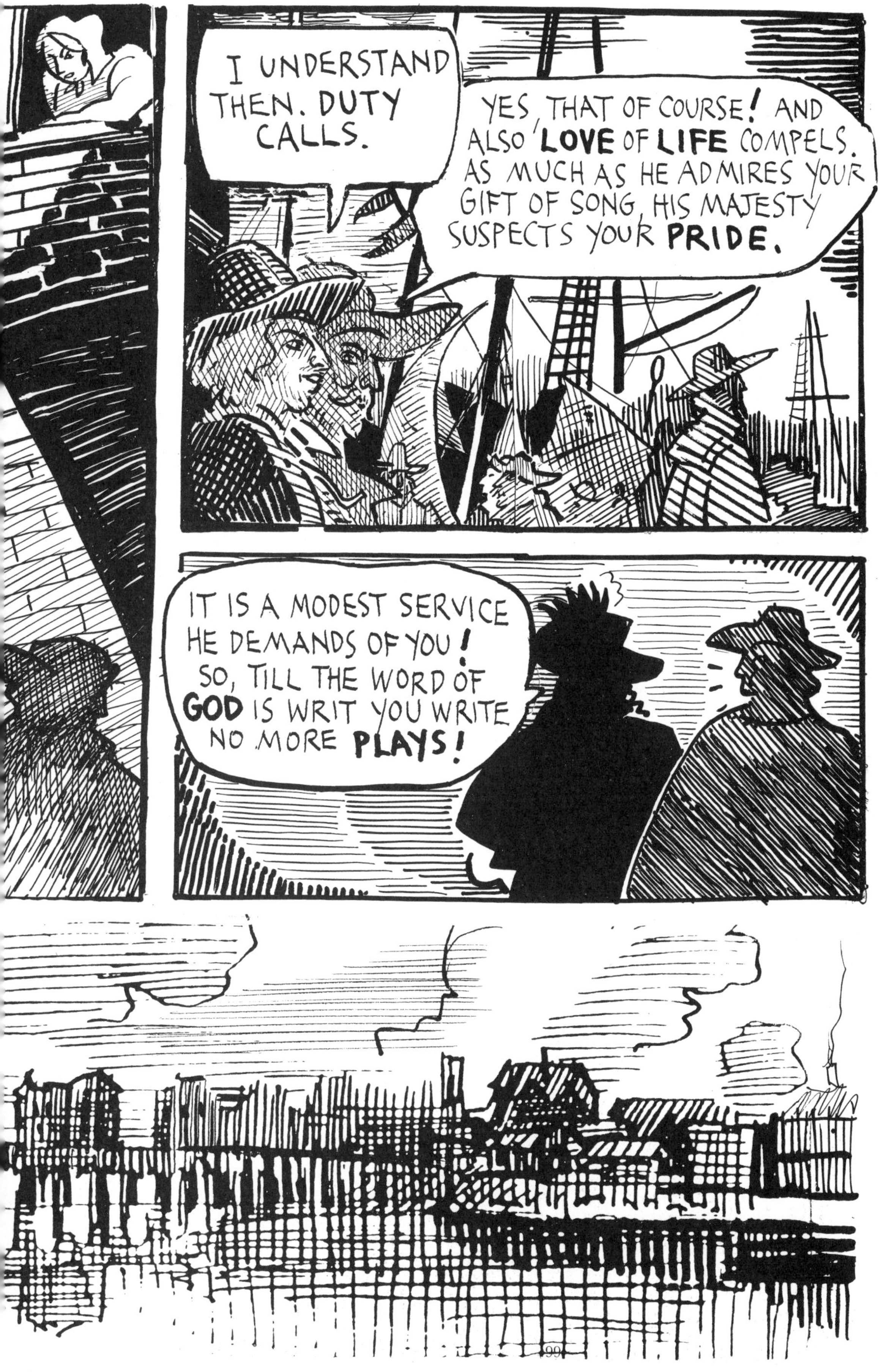
I UNDERSTAND THEN. DUTY CALLS.
YES, THAT OF COURSE! AND ALSO LOVE OF LIFE COMPELS. AS MUCH AS HE ADMIRES YOUR GIFT OF SONG, HIS MAJESTY SUSPECTS YOUR PRIDE.
IT IS A MODEST SERVICE HE DEMANDS OF YOU! SO, TILL THE WORD OF GOD IS WRIT YOU WRITE NO MORE PLAYS!

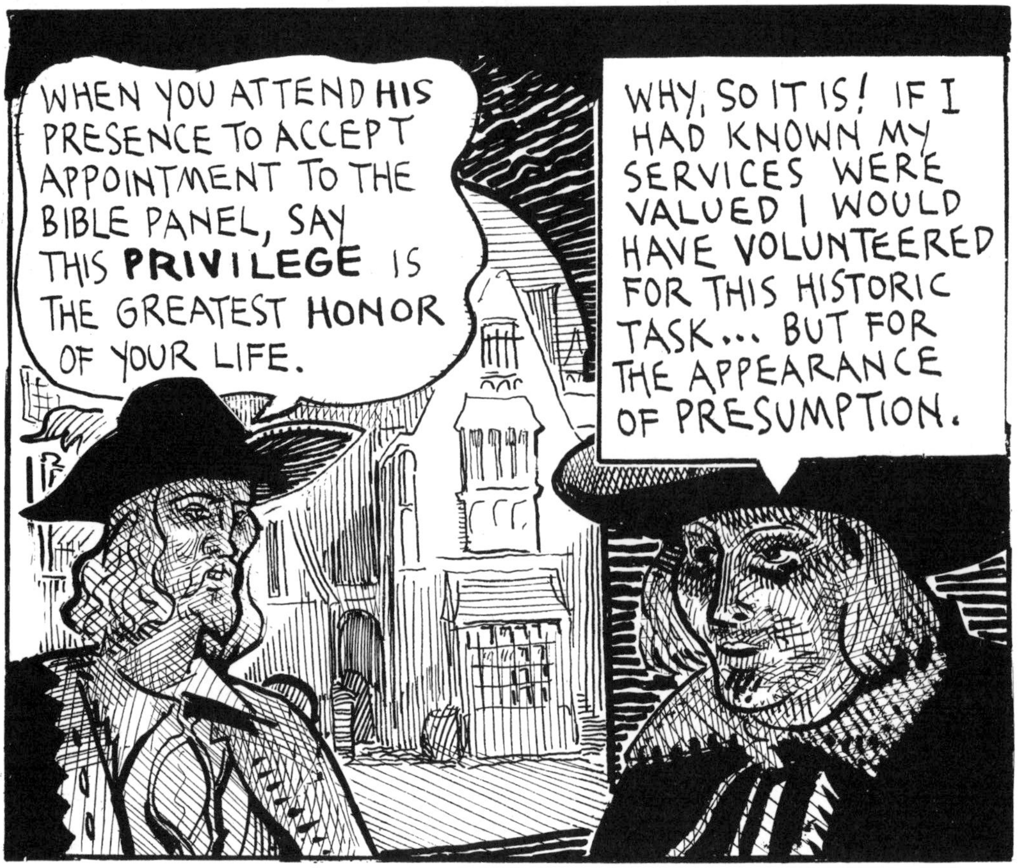
WHEN YOU ATTEND **HIS** PRESENCE TO ACCEPT APPOINTMENT TO THE BIBLE PANEL, SAY THIS **PRIVILEGE** IS THE GREATEST **HONOR** OF YOUR LIFE.
WHY, SO IT IS! IF I HAD KNOWN MY SERVICES WERE VALUED I WOULD HAVE VOLUNTEERED FOR THIS HISTORIC TASK... BUT FOR THE APPEARANCE OF PRESUMPTION.

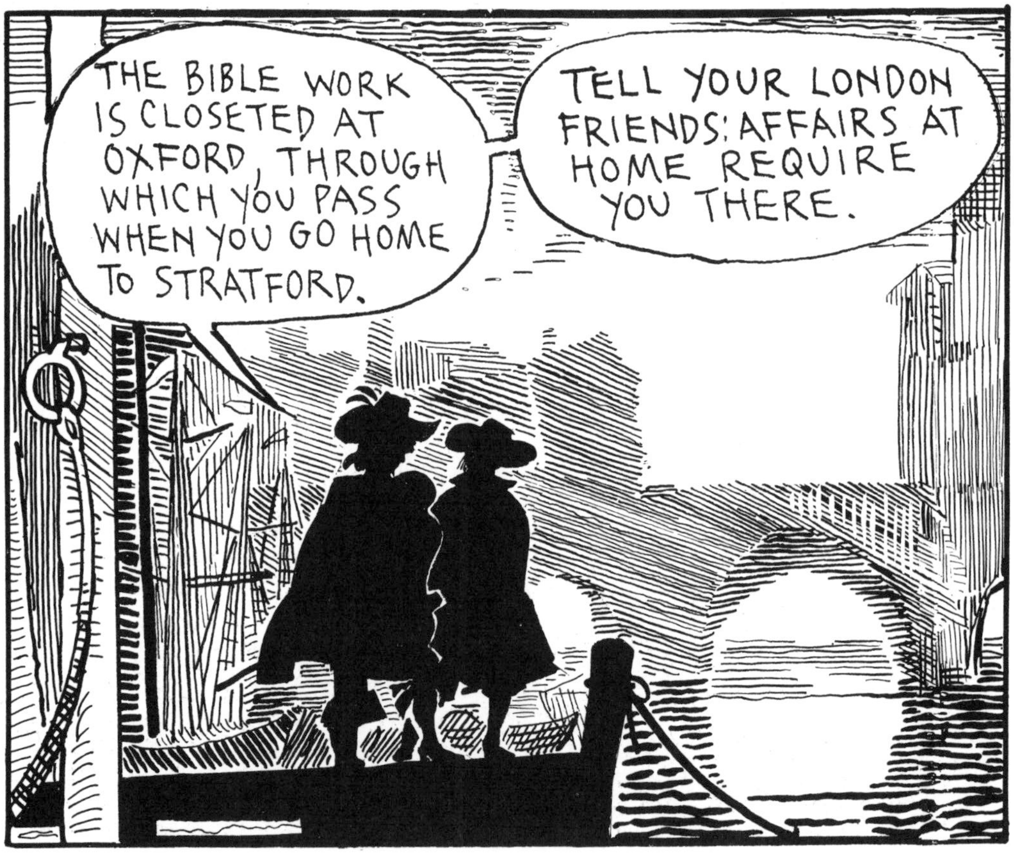
THE BIBLE WORK IS CLOSETED AT OXFORD, THROUGH WHICH YOU PASS WHEN YOU GO HOME TO STRATFORD.
TELL YOUR LONDON FRIENDS: AFFAIRS AT HOME REQUIRE YOU THERE.

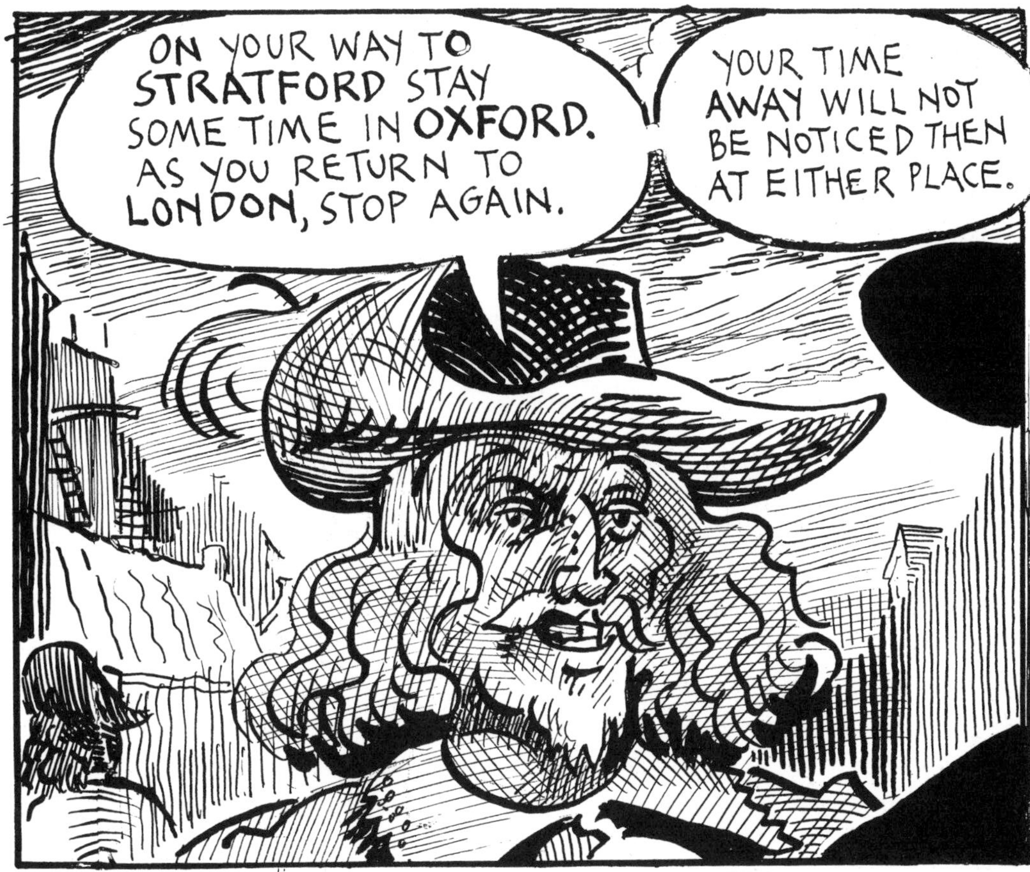
ON YOUR WAY TO STRATFORD STAY SOME TIME IN OXFORD. AS YOU RETURN TO LONDON, STOP AGAIN.
YOUR TIME AWAY WILL NOT BE NOTICED THEN AT EITHER PLACE.

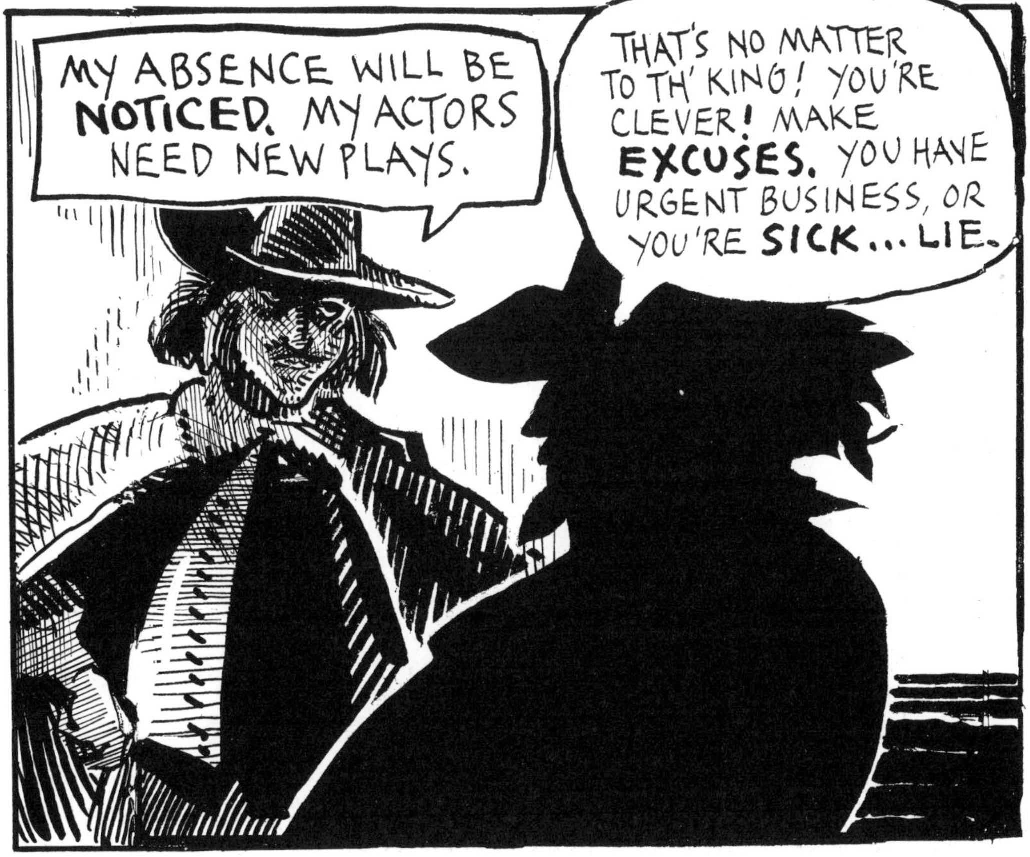
MY ABSENCE WILL BE NOTICED. MY ACTORS NEED NEW PLAYS.
THAT'S NO MATTER TO TH' KING! YOU'RE CLEVER! MAKE EXCUSES. YOU HAVE URGENT BUSINESS, OR YOU'RE SICK... LIE.

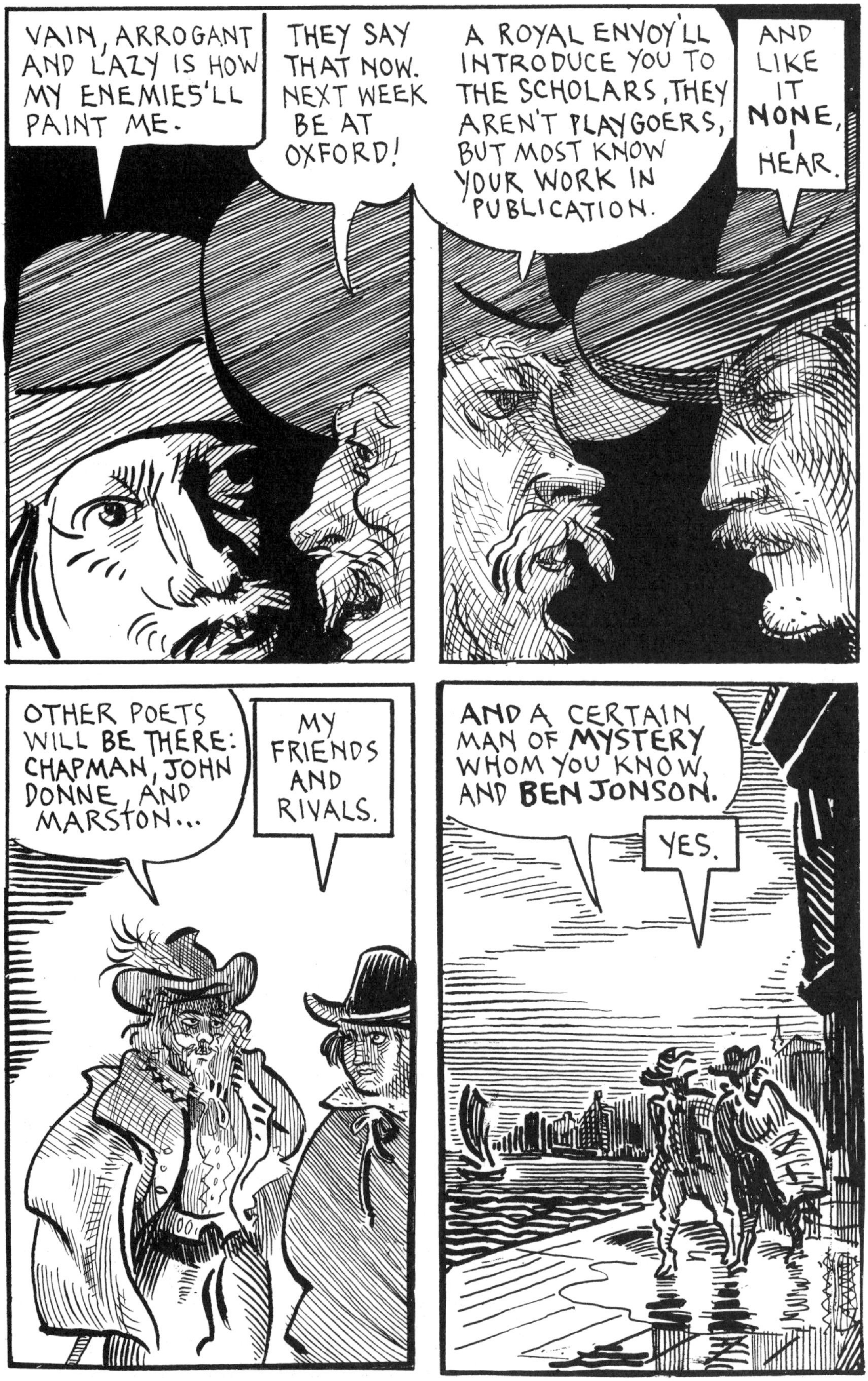
VAIN, ARROGANT AND LAZY IS HOW MY ENEMIES'LL PAINT ME.
THEY SAY THAT NOW. NEXT WEEK BE AT OXFORD!
A ROYAL ENVOY'LL INTRODUCE YOU TO THE SCHOLARS, THEY AREN'T PLAYGOERS, BUT MOST KNOW YOUR WORK IN PUBLICATION.
AND LIKE IT NONE, I HEAR.
OTHER POETS WILL BE THERE: CHAPMAN, JOHN DONNE AND MARSTON...
MY FRIENDS AND RIVALS.
AND A CERTAIN MAN OF MYSTERY WHOM YOU KNOW, AND BEN JONSON.
YES.

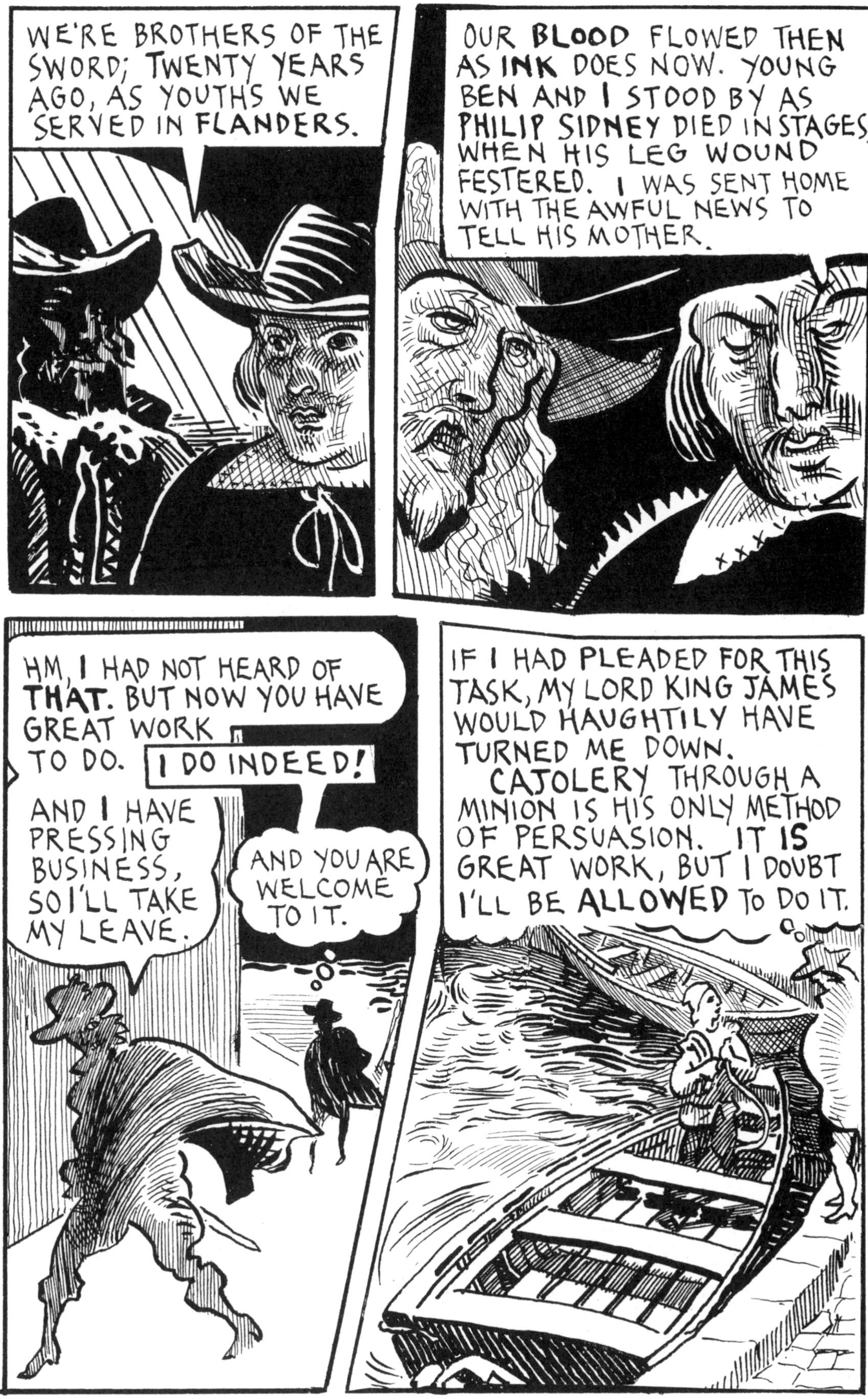
WE'RE BROTHERS OF THE SWORD; TWENTY YEARS AGO, AS YOUTHS WE SERVED IN FLANDERS.
OUR BLOOD FLOWED THEN AS INK DOES NOW. YOUNG BEN AND I STOOD BY AS PHILIP SIDNEY DIED IN STAGES, WHEN HIS LEG WOUND FESTERED. I WAS SENT HOME WITH THE AWFUL NEWS TO TELL HIS MOTHER.
HM, I HAD NOT HEARD OF THAT. BUT NOW YOU HAVE GREAT WORK TO DO.
I DO INDEED!
AND I HAVE PRESSING BUSINESS, SO I'LL TAKE MY LEAVE.
AND YOU ARE WELCOME TO IT.
IF I HAD PLEADED FOR THIS TASK, MY LORD KING JAMES WOULD HAUGHTILY HAVE TURNED ME DOWN.
CAJOLERY THROUGH A MINION IS HIS ONLY METHOD OF PERSUASION. IT IS GREAT WORK, BUT I DOUBT I'LL BE ALLOWED TO DO IT.

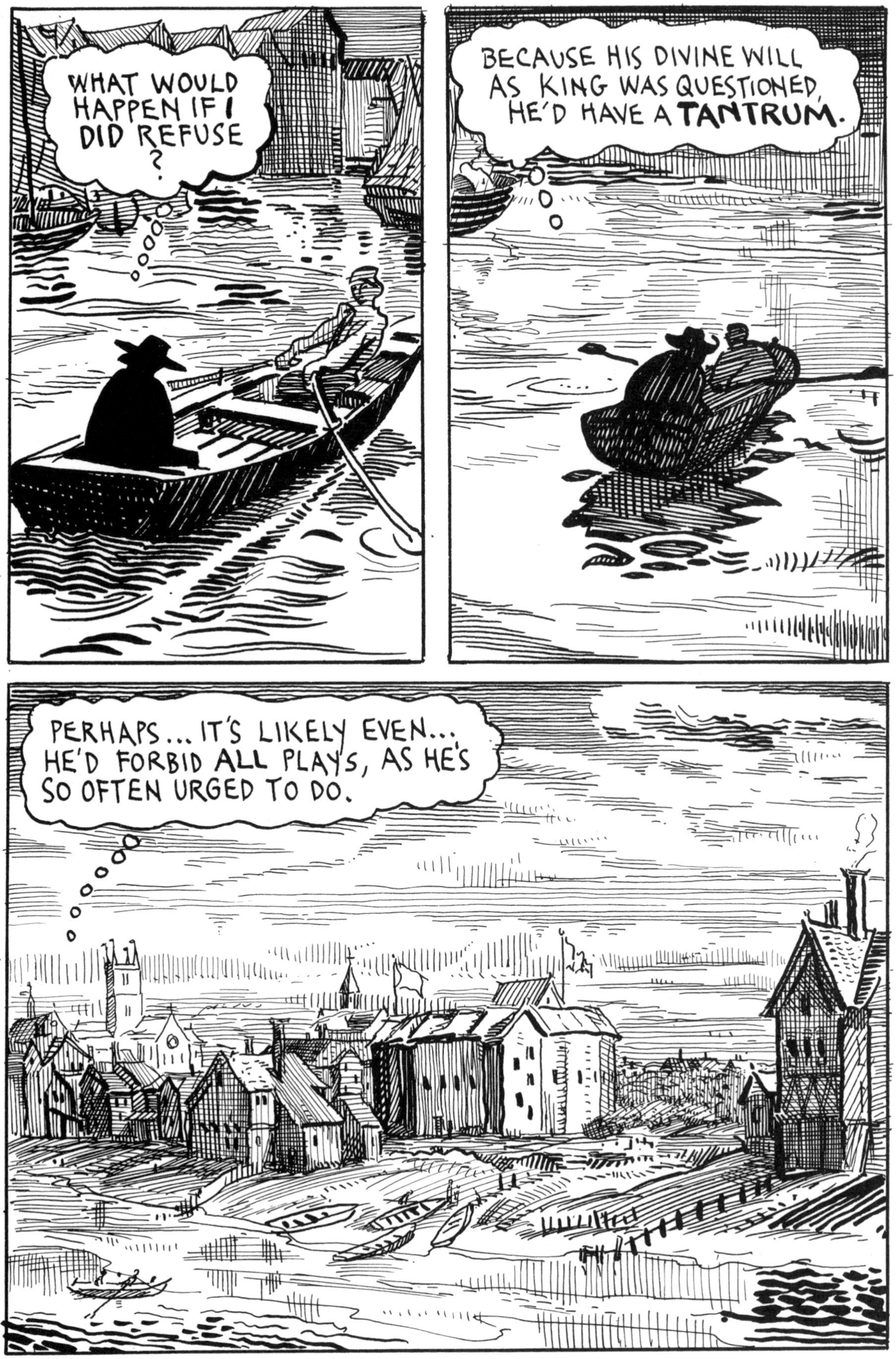
WHAT WOULD HAPPEN IF I DID REFUSE ?
BECAUSE HIS DIVINE WILL AS KING WAS QUESTIONED, HE'D HAVE A TANTRUM.
PERHAPS... IT'S LIKELY EVEN... HE'D FORBID ALL PLAYS, AS HE'S SO OFTEN URGED TO DO.

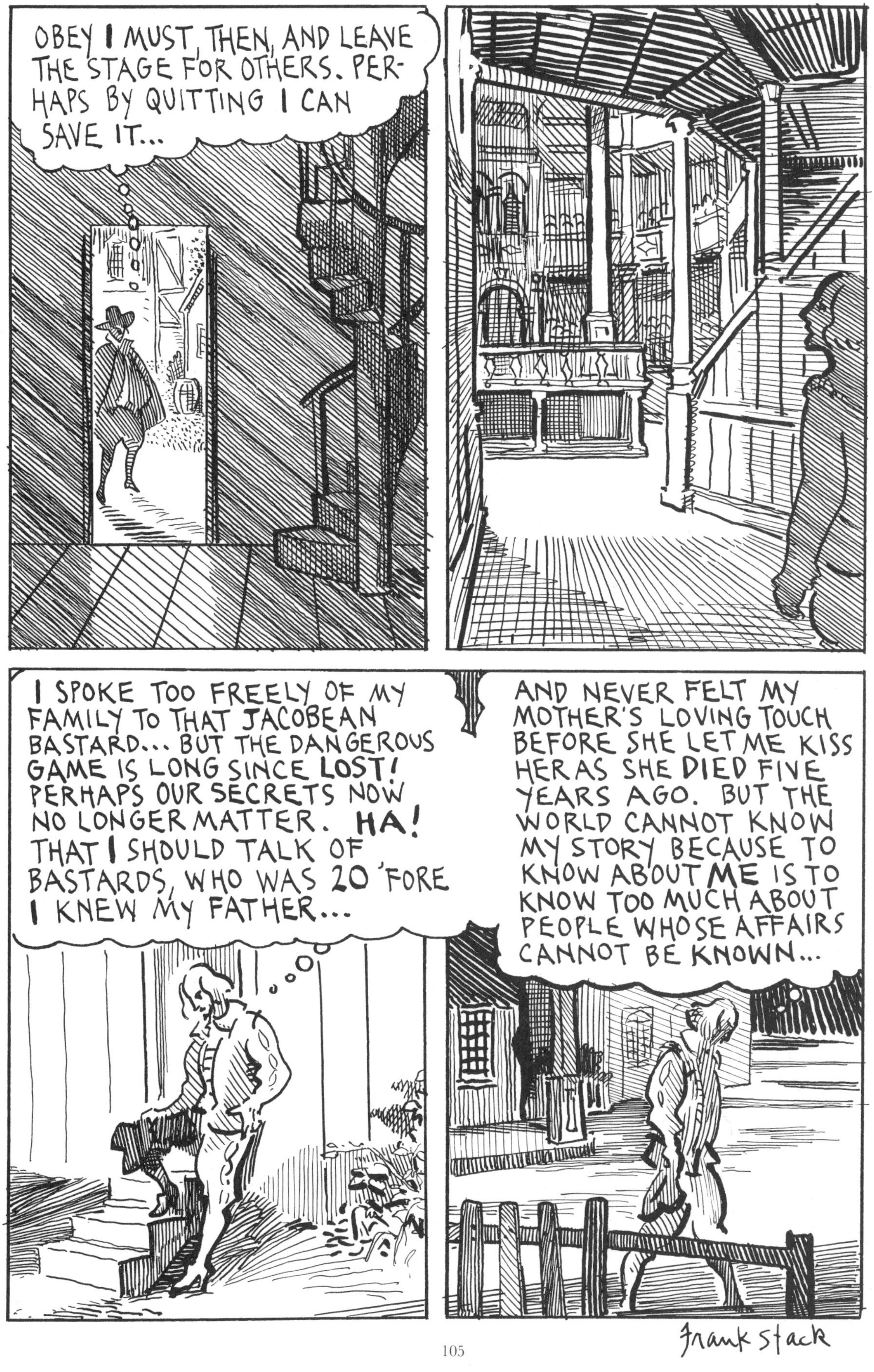
OBEY I MUST, THEN, AND LEAVE THE STAGE FOR OTHERS. PERHAPS BY QUITTING I CAN SAVE IT...
I SPOKE TOO FREELY OF MY FAMILY TO THAT JACOBEAN BASTARD... BUT THE DANGEROUS GAME IS LONG SINCE LOST! PERHAPS OUR SECRETS NOW NO LONGER MATTER. HA! THAT I SHOULD TALK OF BASTARDS, WHO WAS 20 'FORE I KNEW MY FATHER...
AND NEVER FELT MY MOTHER'S LOVING TOUCH BEFORE SHE LET ME KISS HER AS SHE DIED FIVE YEARS AGO. BUT THE WORLD CANNOT KNOW MY STORY BECAUSE TO KNOW ABOUT ME IS TO KNOW TOO MUCH ABOUT PEOPLE WHOSE AFFAIRS CANNOT BE KNOWN...
Frank Stack

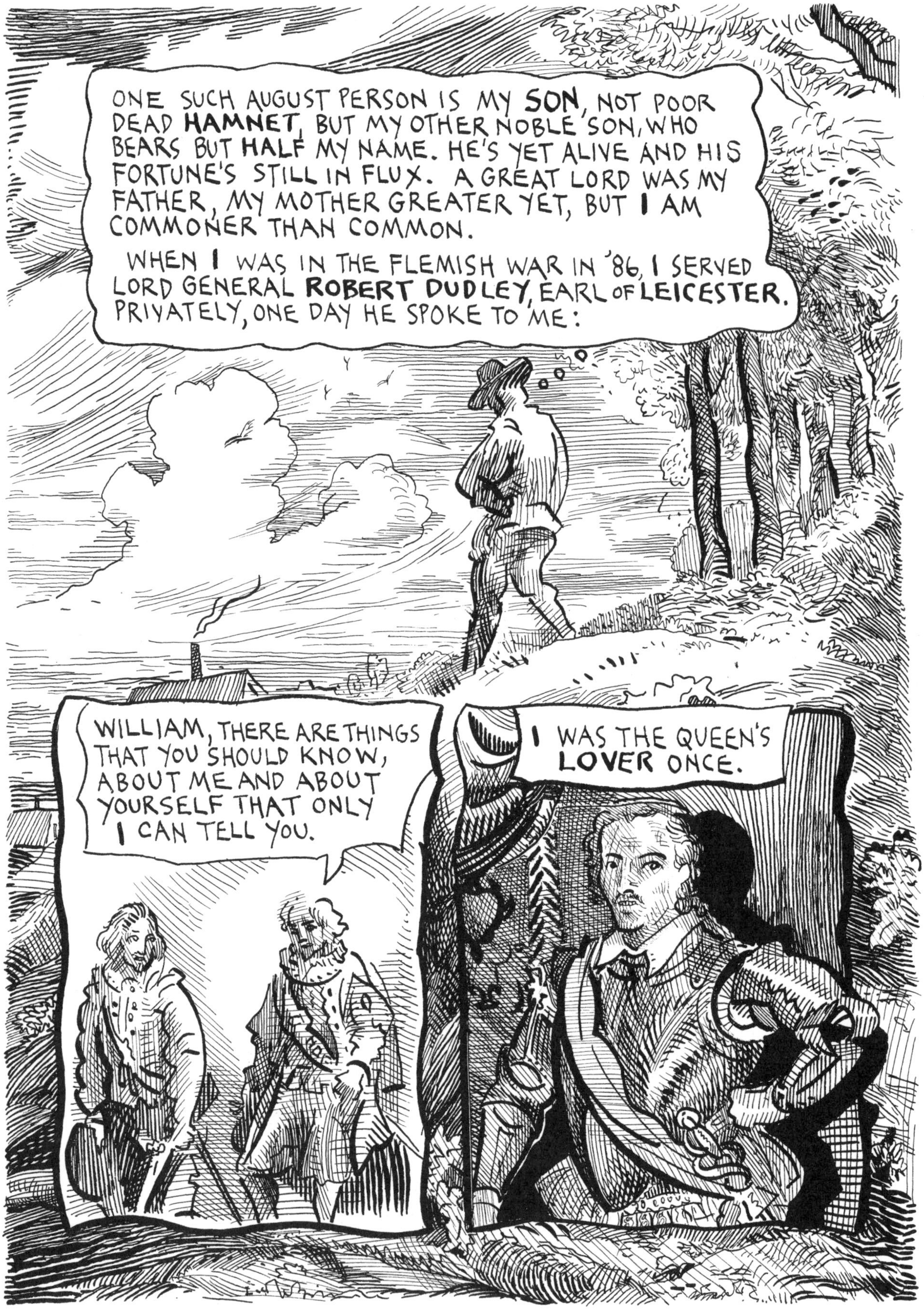
ONE SUCH AUGUST PERSON IS MY SON, NOT POOR DEAD HAMNET, BUT MY OTHER NOBLE SON, WHO BEARS BUT HALF MY NAME. HE'S YET ALIVE AND HIS FORTUNE'S STILL IN FLUX. A GREAT LORD WAS MY FATHER, MY MOTHER GREATER YET, BUT I AM COMMONER THAN COMMON.
WHEN I WAS IN THE FLEMISH WAR IN '86, I SERVED LORD GENERAL ROBERT DUDLEY, EARL OF LEICESTER. PRIVATELY, ONE DAY HE SPOKE TO ME:
WILLIAM, THERE ARE THINGS THAT YOU SHOULD KNOW, ABOUT ME AND ABOUT YOURSELF THAT ONLY I CAN TELL YOU.
I WAS THE QUEEN'S LOVER ONCE.

IT WAS SAID OF ME THAT WHAT I WANTED WAS THE CROWN, AND IT WAS THIS MUCH TRUE: WHAT I, AND ENGLAND, WANTED WAS AN ENGLISH MAN ON ENGLAND'S THRONE! NO SPANISH GRANDEE OR REGAL FROG AND CERTAIN NOT A THICK-TONGUE TOADY SCOT WHO'D ASK THE POPE FOR LEAVE TO TAKE A PISS! ANOTHER LORD OF ROYAL

BLOOD WOULD HAVE SERVED AS WELL BUT WHO ELSE WAS THERE WHEN BESS WAS QUEEN AND YOUNG ENOUGH TO BREED AN HEIR? AS THERE WAS NO BETTER MAN ABOUT, I MADE MY SUIT. WE'RE BOTH GRAY NOW, BUT WE WERE SPLENDID THEN! AND SHE LOVED ME.

IT WAS DIFFICULT TO BE ALONE, BUT WE FOUND WAYS: MIDNIGHT RENDEZVOUS. ONE OF MY ACTORS IMPERSONATED ME, SO I MIGHT DISAPPEAR AND GO TO HER. SHE HAD DOUBLES TOO. IT MAY BE THAT FEW WERE FOOLED, BUT NO ONE DARED OBJECT. WE WERE READY TO BE MARRIED...

BUT I HAD A WIFE ALREADY

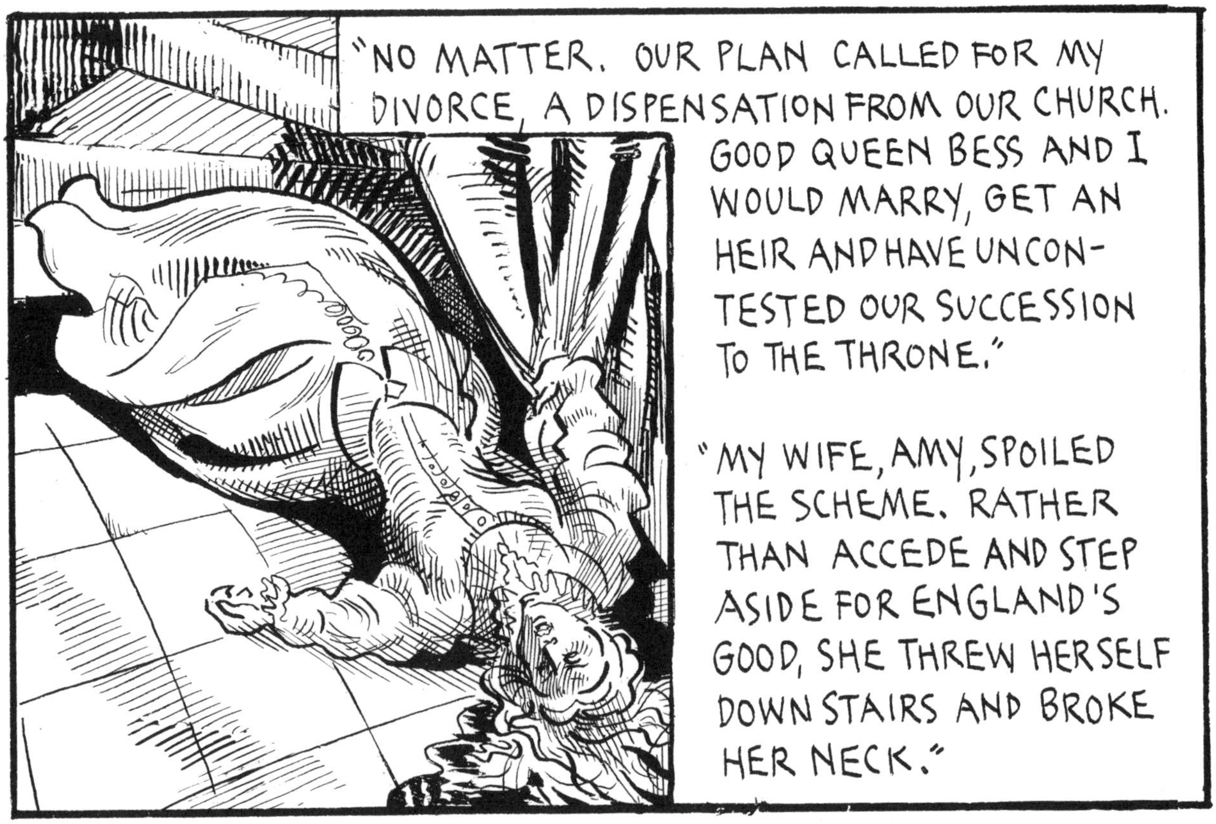
"NO MATTER. OUR PLAN CALLED FOR MY DIVORCE, A DISPENSATION FROM OUR CHURCH. GOOD QUEEN BESS AND I WOULD MARRY, GET AN HEIR AND HAVE UNCONTESTED OUR SUCCESSION TO THE THRONE."
"MY WIFE, AMY, SPOILED THE SCHEME. RATHER THAN ACCEDE AND STEP ASIDE FOR ENGLAND'S GOOD, SHE THREW HERSELF DOWN STAIRS AND BROKE HER NECK."

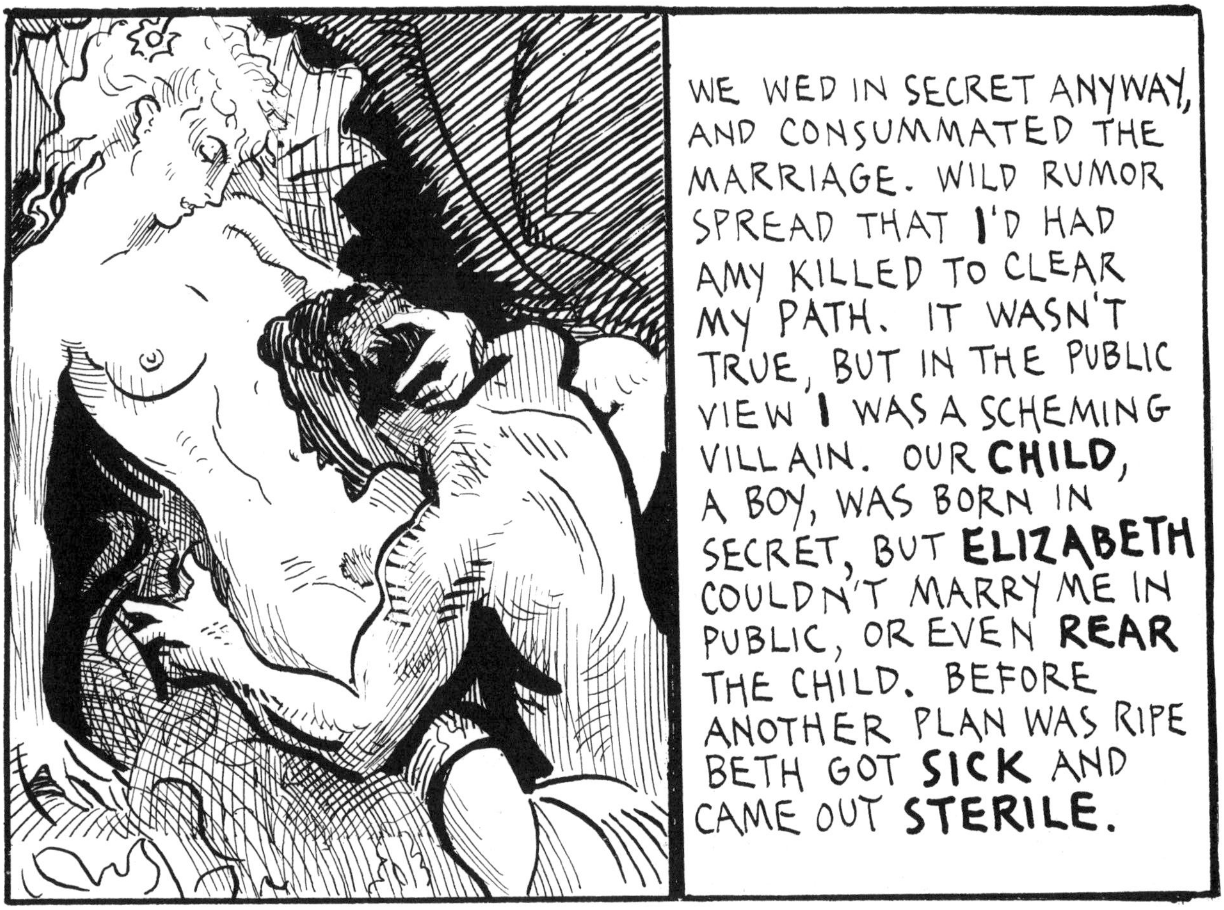
WE WED IN SECRET ANYWAY, AND CONSUMMATED THE MARRIAGE. WILD RUMOR SPREAD THAT I'D HAD AMY KILLED TO CLEAR MY PATH. IT WASN'T TRUE, BUT IN THE PUBLIC VIEW I WAS A SCHEMING VILLAIN. OUR CHILD, A BOY, WAS BORN IN SECRET, BUT ELIZABETH COULDN'T MARRY ME IN PUBLIC, OR EVEN REAR THE CHILD. BEFORE ANOTHER PLAN WAS RIPE BETH GOT SICK AND CAME OUT STERILE.

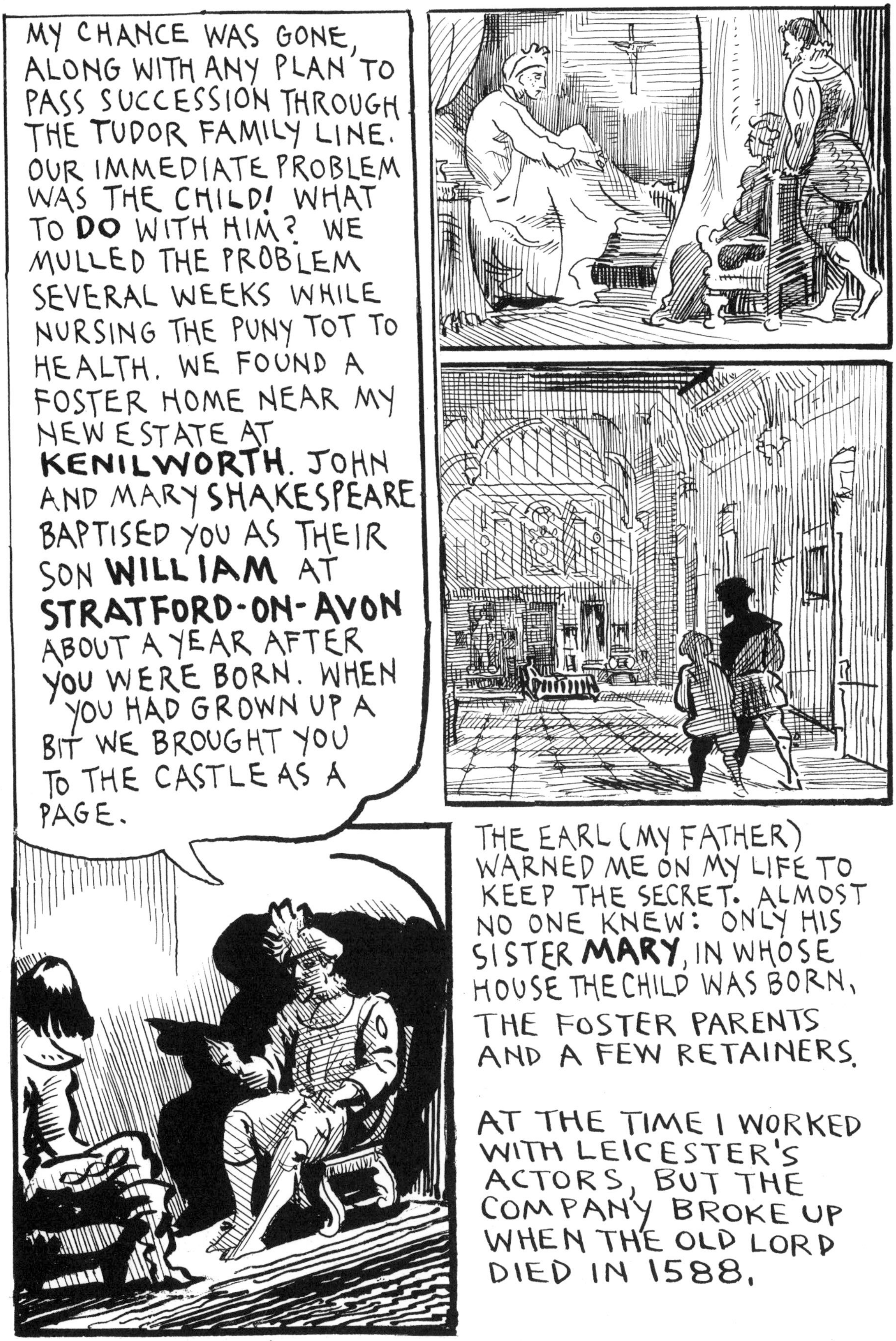
MY CHANCE WAS GONE, ALONG WITH ANY PLAN TO PASS SUCCESSION THROUGH THE TUDOR FAMILY LINE. OUR IMMEDIATE PROBLEM WAS THE CHILD! WHAT TO DO WITH HIM? WE MULLED THE PROBLEM SEVERAL WEEKS WHILE NURSING THE PUNY TOT TO HEALTH. WE FOUND A FOSTER HOME NEAR MY NEW ESTATE AT KENILWORTH. JOHN AND MARY SHAKESPEARE BAPTISED YOU AS THEIR SON WILLIAM AT STRATFORD-ON-AVON ABOUT A YEAR AFTER YOU WERE BORN. WHEN YOU HAD GROWN UP A BIT WE BROUGHT YOU TO THE CASTLE AS A PAGE.
THE EARL (MY FATHER) WARNED ME ON MY LIFE TO KEEP THE SECRET. ALMOST NO ONE KNEW: ONLY HIS SISTER MARY, IN WHOSE HOUSE THE CHILD WAS BORN, THE FOSTER PARENTS AND A FEW RETAINERS.
AT THE TIME I WORKED WITH LEICESTER'S ACTORS, BUT THE COMPANY BROKE UP WHEN THE OLD LORD DIED IN 1588.

AFTER THAT, I ACTED WITH AND WROTE SOME PLAYS FOR PEMBROKE'S MEN. THAT ACTING TROUPE WAS PATRONIZED IN TRUTH BY LADY MARY, MY OLDEST, TRUEST FRIEND.... I HAVE BEEN ASKED HOW I CAME TO BE A POET. IF I'M TO SPEAK OF THAT, I MUST TALK OF PHILIP AND MARY SIDNEY.

I MET THEM WHEN THEY CAME WITH THEIR MOTHER TO VISIT KENILWORTH. LEICESTER WAS HER BROTHER. THEIR FATHER WAS **SIR HENRY SIDNEY**, LORD HIGH CONSTABLE OF **IRELAND**. I, AS AN EXPERIENCED HOUSE-HOLD PAGE, BECAME THEIR GUIDE AROUND THE GREAT HOUSE AND GROUNDS. I'D BEEN THERE SINCE THE AGE OF EIGHT, ACTING SOMETIMES WITH THE RESIDENT **CHILDREN'S** ACTING COMPANY.

PHILIP SIDNEY, THEN 19, WAS A RISING STAR AT COURT—HANDSOME, ATHLETIC AND WELL SPOKEN. JUST DOWN FROM OXFORD, HE WAS PRE-PARING FOR HIS TRIP TO EUROPE AS DIPLOMATIC ENVOY FOR HIS QUEEN.

I WAS ONLY 10, TOO YOUNG TO INTEREST PHILIP, BUT I HIT IT OFF QUITE WELL WITH BOB, HIS YOUNGER BROTHER, JUST MY AGE. I LATER LEARNED WE WERE BORN IN THE SAME HOUSE, TWO MONTHS APART.

AND I WAS INFATUATED BY THEIR RADIANT SISTER **MARY**, THREE YEARS OUR SENIOR. SHE WAS WARM AND CLEVER, TOLERANT OF OUR YOUTHFUL PRANKS. THE BEST COMPANION, AND, THOUGH ONLY **12**, THE MOST BEAUTIFUL WOMAN IN ALL THE REALM.

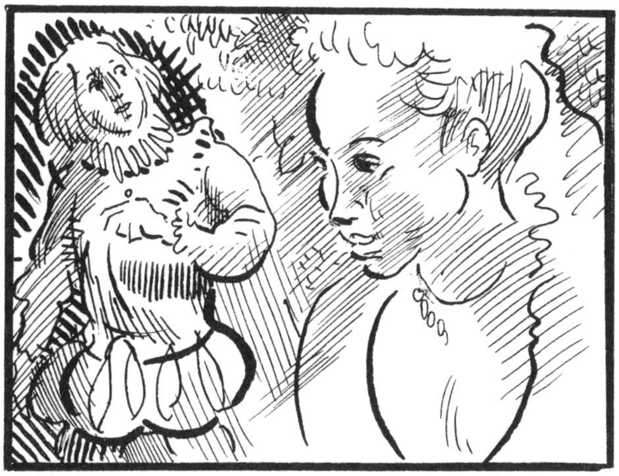

LATER, ROBERT SIDNEY ASKED FOR ME TO JOIN HIS SERVICE AND SERVE HIM AS A GENTLEMAN COMPANION WHEN HE WENT UP TO **OXFORD**. THOUGH LATER HE WAS FAMOUS AS A SCHOLAR, I WAS THE MORE APT STUDENT AND HELPED HIM PASS HIS COURSES.

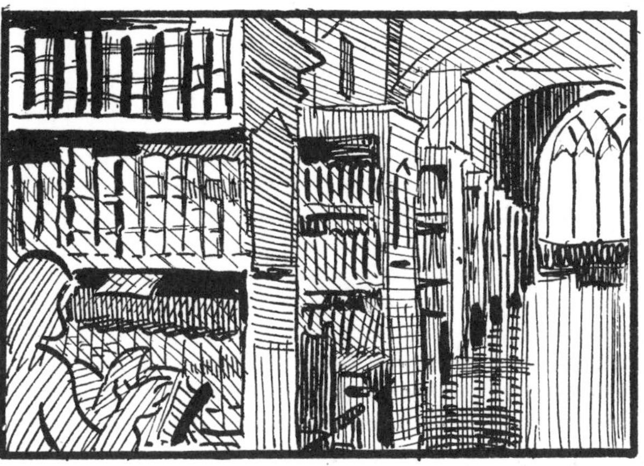

I WENT WITH HIM TOO ON HIS CONTINENTAL TOUR. IT WAS MY ONLY TIME IN **ITALY**. ROBERT STAYED ABROAD FOR SEVERAL YEARS, BUT SENT ME BACK WITH SECRET MESSAGES OF STATE.

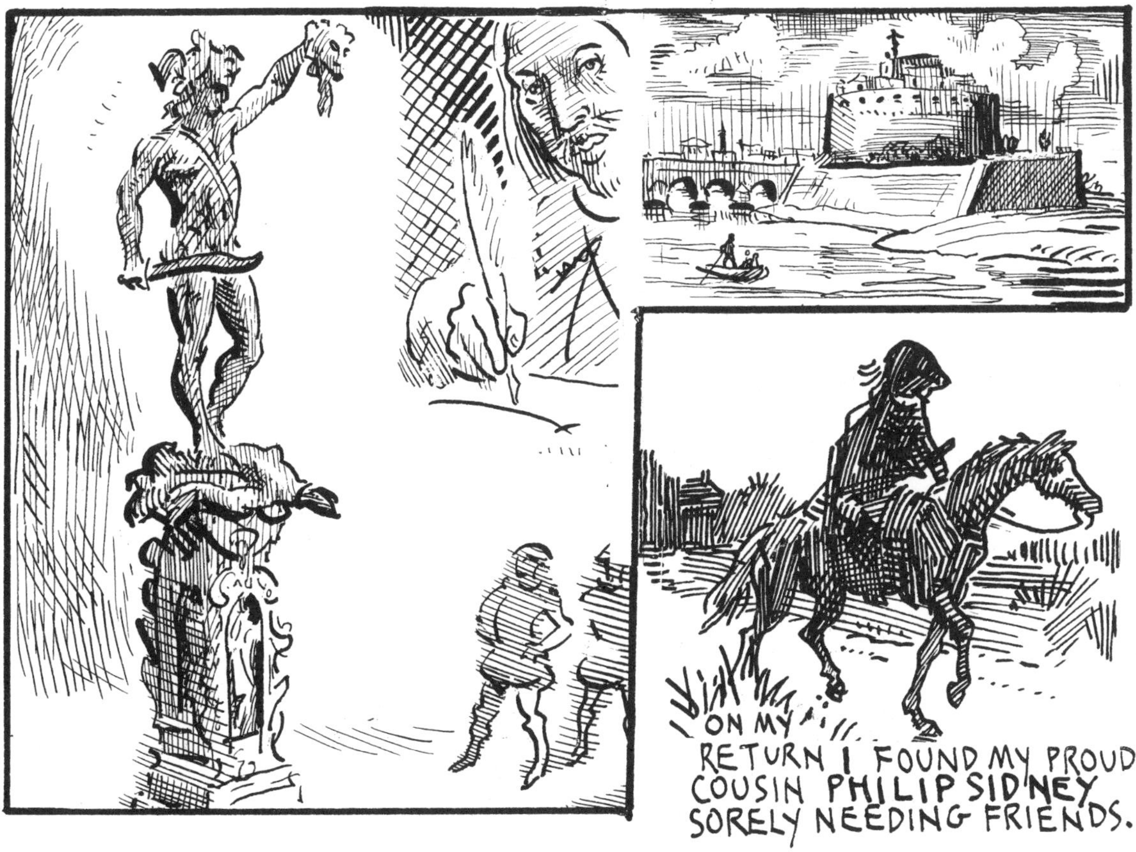

ON MY RETURN I FOUND MY PROUD COUSIN **PHILIP SIDNEY** SORELY NEEDING FRIENDS.

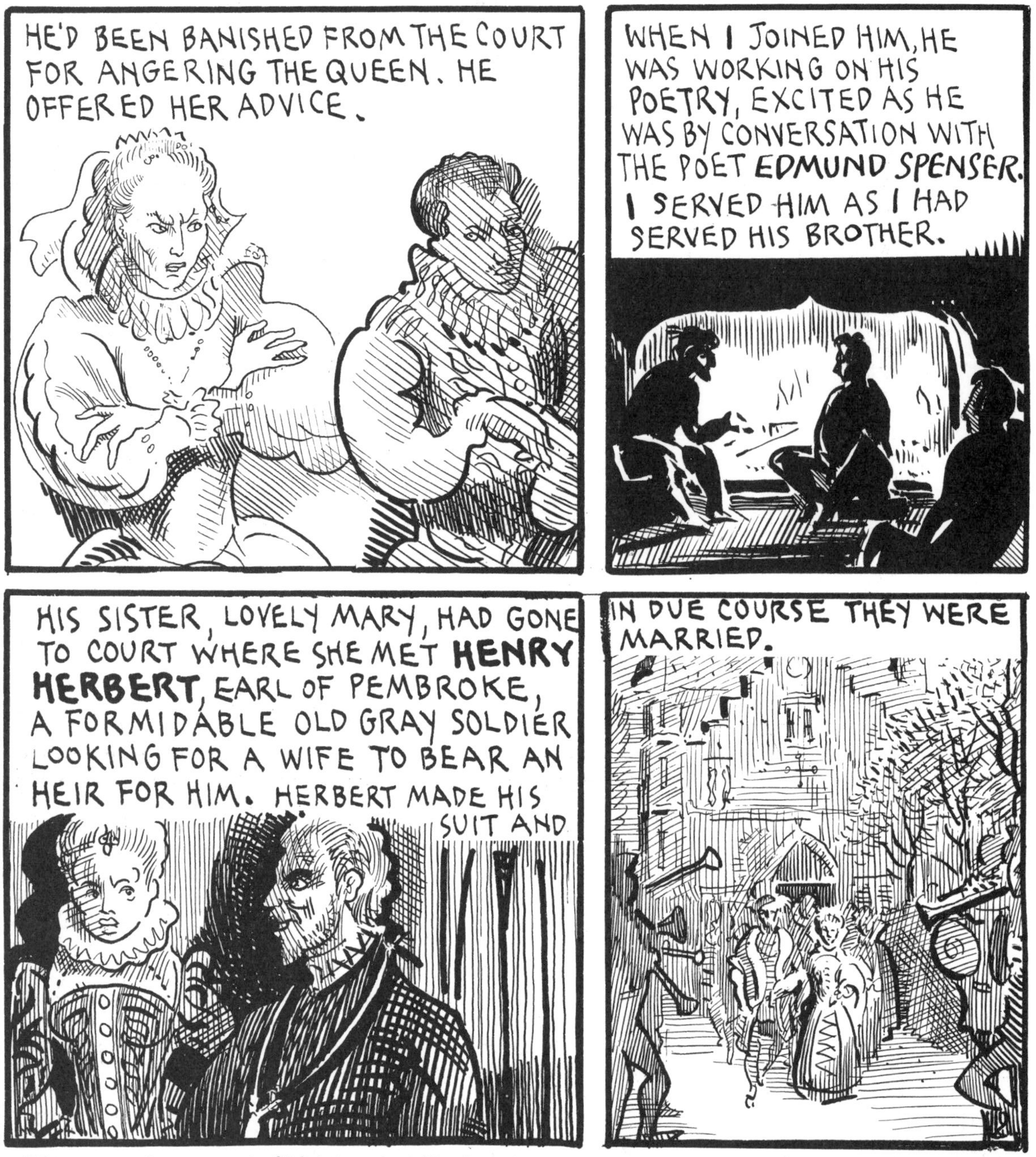
HE'D BEEN BANISHED FROM THE COURT FOR ANGERING THE QUEEN. HE OFFERED HER ADVICE.
WHEN I JOINED HIM, HE WAS WORKING ON HIS POETRY, EXCITED AS HE WAS BY CONVERSATION WITH THE POET **EDMUND SPENSER**. I SERVED HIM AS I HAD SERVED HIS BROTHER.
HIS SISTER, LOVELY MARY, HAD GONE TO COURT WHERE SHE MET **HENRY HERBERT**, EARL OF PEMBROKE, A FORMIDABLE OLD GRAY SOLDIER LOOKING FOR A WIFE TO BEAR AN HEIR FOR HIM. HERBERT MADE HIS SUIT AND
IN DUE COURSE THEY WERE MARRIED.

THEY LIVED AT **WILTON HOUSE** IN WILTSHIRE. I TAGGED ALONG WITH PHILIP WHEN HE WENT THERE AS A GUEST FOR THE SPRING AND SUMMER **1580.**
MARY WAS BLOOMING, OVER-RIPE AT 19, MARRIED **THREE** YEARS TO A MAN **25** YEARS HER SENIOR, NO MORE PREGNANT THAN SHE WAS BEFORE. SHE WAS GLAD TO SEE US.

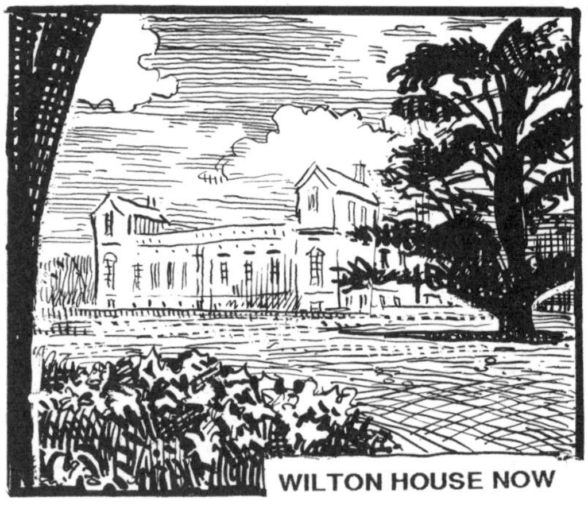

WILTON HOUSE NOW

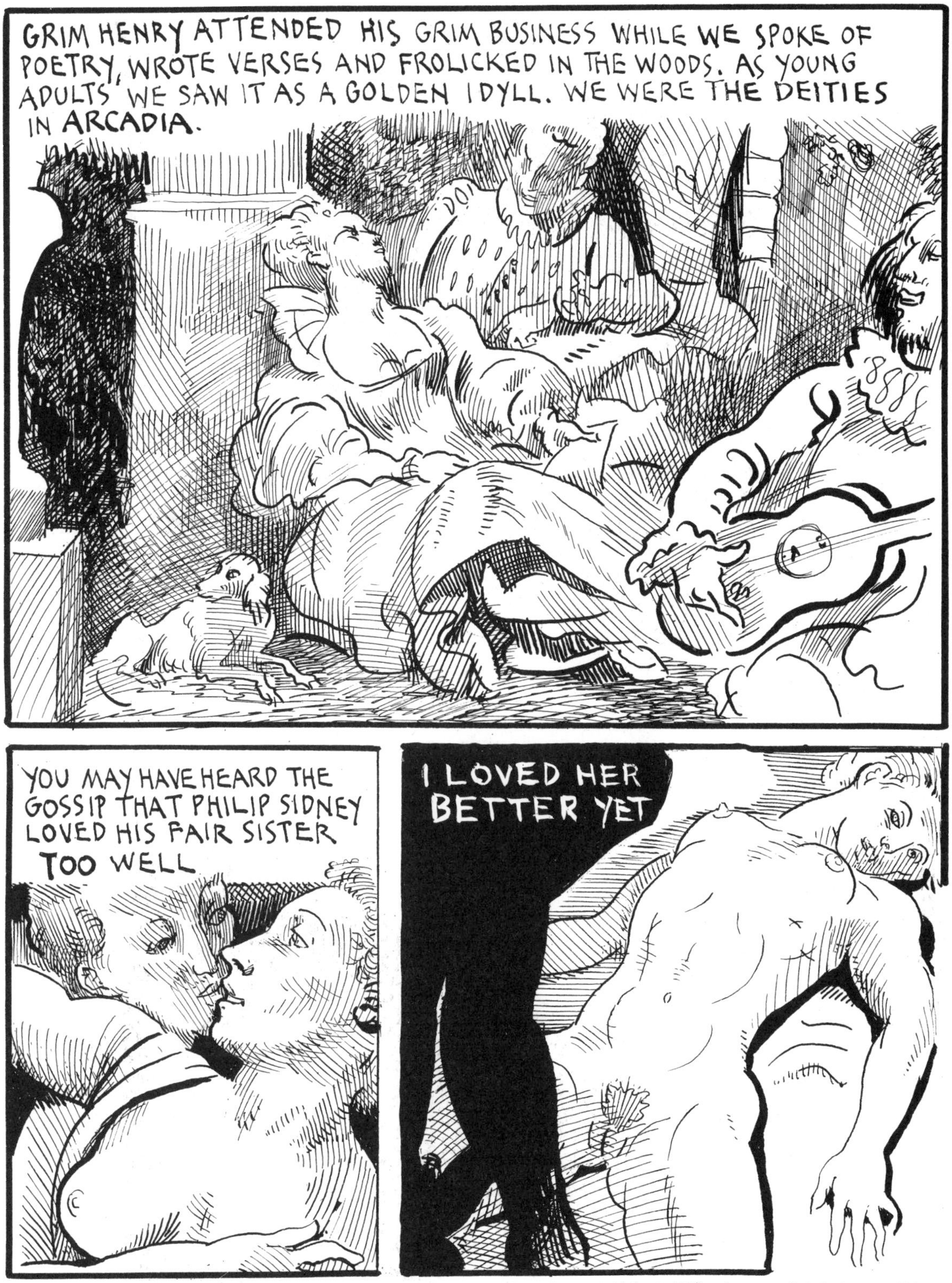
GRIM HENRY ATTENDED HIS GRIM BUSINESS WHILE WE SPOKE OF POETRY, WROTE VERSES AND FROLICKED IN THE WOODS. AS YOUNG ADULTS WE SAW IT AS A GOLDEN IDYLL. WE WERE THE DEITIES IN ARCADIA.
YOU MAY HAVE HEARD THE GOSSIP THAT PHILIP SIDNEY LOVED HIS FAIR SISTER TOO WELL
I LOVED HER BETTER YET

THE COUNTESS PEMBROKE BORE A CHILD **THAT FALL**. SHE NAMED HIM **WILLIAM**, SUPPOSEDLY FOR HIS GRANDFATHER, FIRST EARL OF PEMBROKE. HER NEXT CHILD'S NAME WAS **PHILIP**. MAKE WHAT YOU WILL OF **THAT**. MY **SONNETS**, PUBLISHED SOME YEARS **LATER** EXPRESSING LOVE FOR A YOUNG MAN, WERE WRITTEN, IN PART, TO MY SECRET SON, THIRD EARL OF PEMBROKE.

OLD HENRY HERBERT, IMPOTENT OF COURSE, ACCEPTED HIS WIFE MARY'S CHILD AS HIS. NONETHELESS HE CAUGHT US BARE TOGETHER, CHASTISED ME SEVERELY AND SENT ME BACK TO STRATFORD IN DISGRACE...

... WHERE I FOUND JOHN SHAKESPEARE, MY GOOD FOSTER FATHER, HAVING DIFFICULTY WITH HIS BUSINESS.

WHILE WORKING FOR THAT HONEST MAN (TO WHOM I OWE MY FONDEST LOYALTY) I WAS IN THRALL TO MY RASH YOUNG PASSIONS. HAVING, AS IT SEEMED TO ME THEN, NO BETTER PROSPECTS, I MARRIED **ANNE HATHAWAY**, THE BEST-LOOKING WOMAN IN THE COUNTY — AND SEV- ERAL YEARS MY ELDER. SHORTLY AFTER, IN 1582, LORD DUDLEY, EARL OF

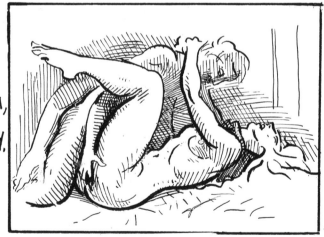

LEICESTER, SUMMONED ME BACK INTO HIS SERVICE, PROBABLY AT THE URGING OF THE **QUEEN** WHO KEPT A WATCHFUL, THOUGH PERIODIC EYE ON MY FORTUNES, BECAUSE I WAS HER BASTARD BOY. BECAUSE I DIDN'T KNOW HE MEANT TO AID MY CAREER, I DID NOT UNDER- STAND LORD DUDLEY'S ANGER WITH MY MARRIAGE. ALWAYS TO PRACTICAL DETAILS MOST ATTENTIVE, I WAS EMPLOYED BY LEICESTER FOR MANY PRACTICAL SERVICES.

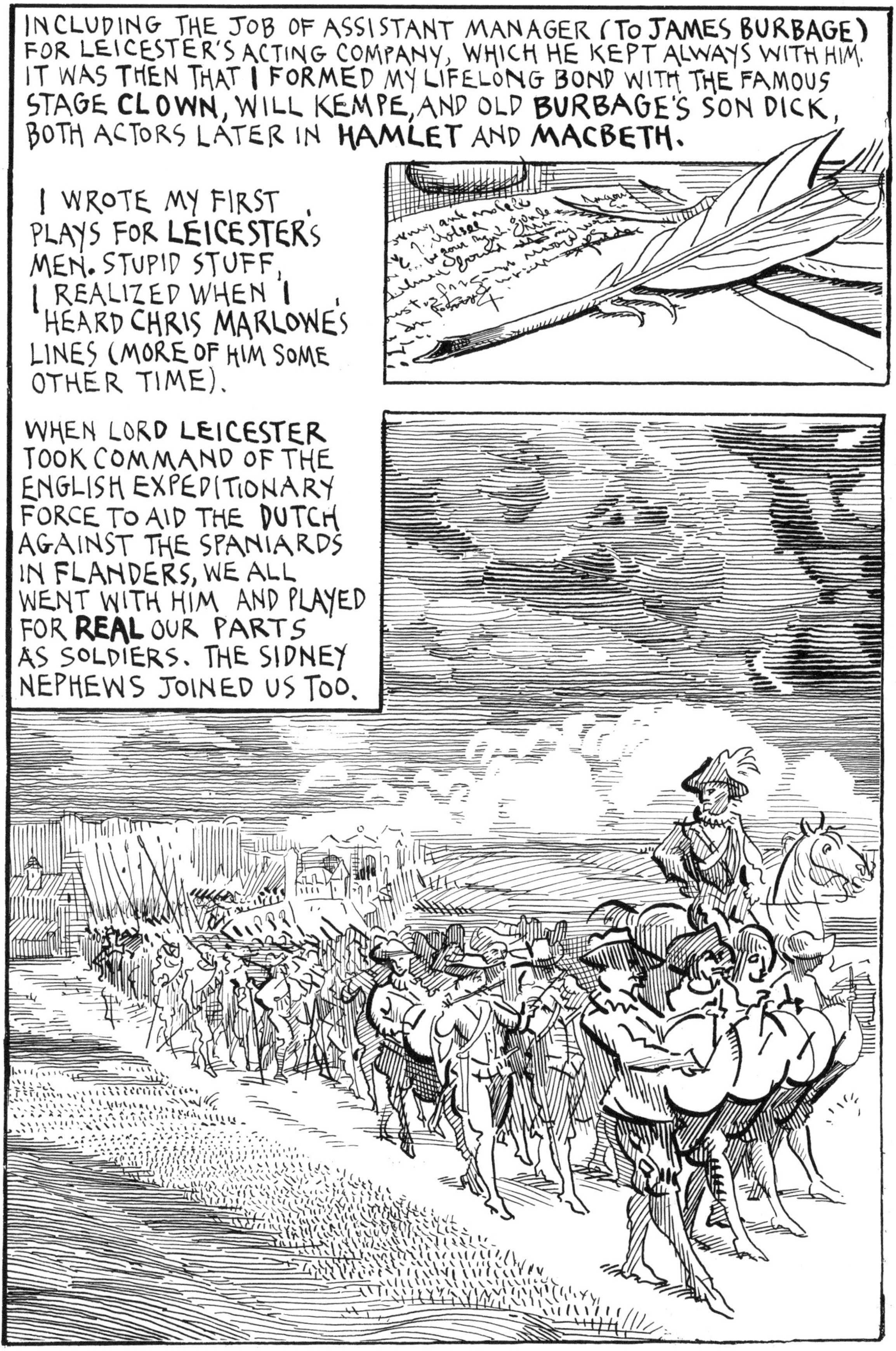
INCLUDING THE JOB OF ASSISTANT MANAGER (TO JAMES BURBAGE) FOR LEICESTER'S ACTING COMPANY, WHICH HE KEPT ALWAYS WITH HIM. IT WAS THEN THAT I FORMED MY LIFELONG BOND WITH THE FAMOUS STAGE CLOWN, WILL KEMPE, AND OLD BURBAGE'S SON DICK, BOTH ACTORS LATER IN HAMLET AND MACBETH.
I WROTE MY FIRST PLAYS FOR LEICESTER'S MEN. STUPID STUFF, I REALIZED WHEN I HEARD CHRIS MARLOWE'S LINES (MORE OF HIM SOME OTHER TIME).
WHEN LORD LEICESTER TOOK COMMAND OF THE ENGLISH EXPEDITIONARY FORCE TO AID THE DUTCH AGAINST THE SPANIARDS IN FLANDERS, WE ALL WENT WITH HIM AND PLAYED FOR REAL OUR PARTS AS SOLDIERS. THE SIDNEY NEPHEWS JOINED US TOO.

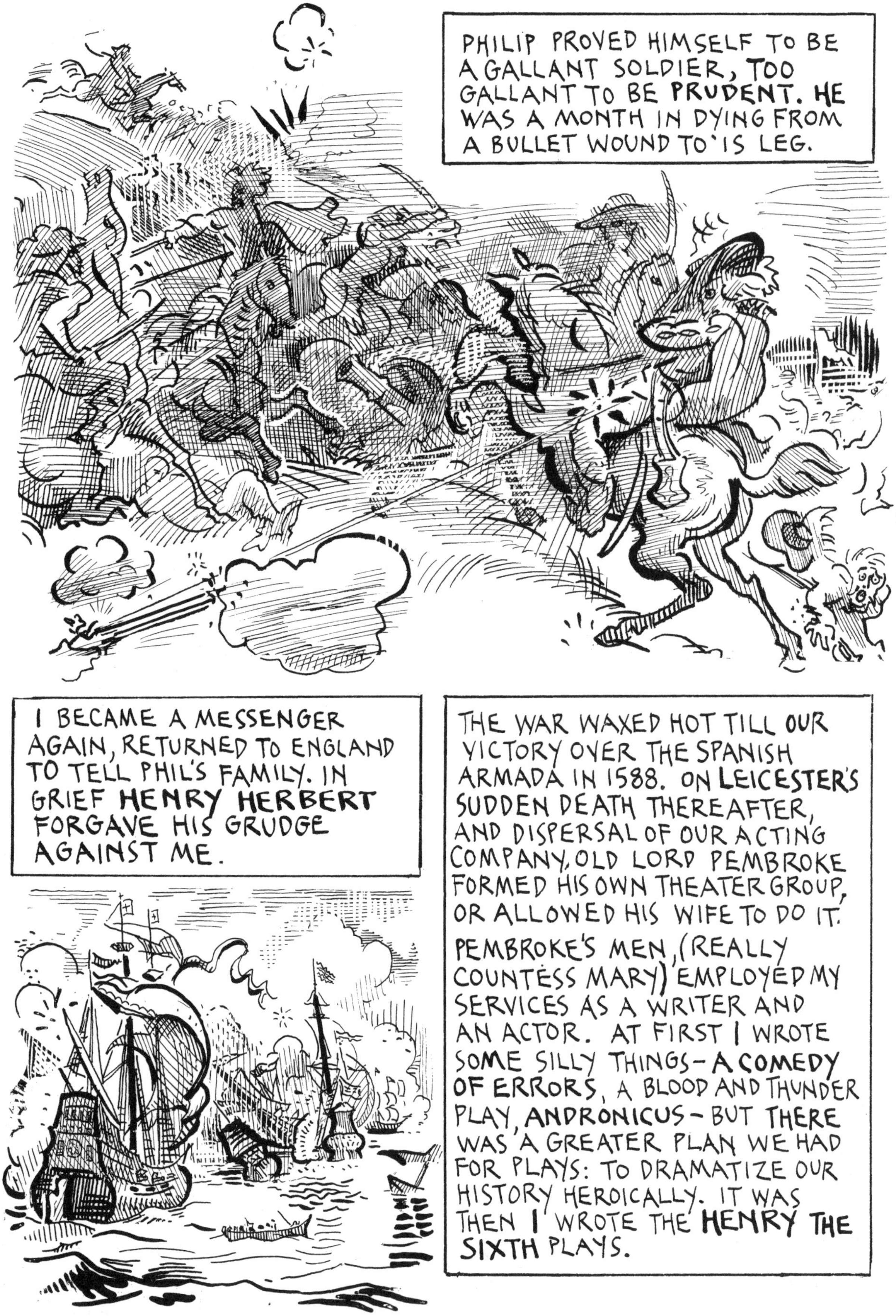
PHILIP PROVED HIMSELF TO BE A GALLANT SOLDIER, TOO GALLANT TO BE **PRUDENT. HE** WAS A MONTH IN DYING FROM A BULLET WOUND TO 'IS LEG.
I BECAME A MESSENGER AGAIN, RETURNED TO ENGLAND TO TELL PHIL'S FAMILY. IN GRIEF **HENRY HERBERT** FORGAVE HIS GRUDGE AGAINST ME.
THE WAR WAXED HOT TILL OUR VICTORY OVER THE SPANISH ARMADA IN 1588. ON **LEICESTER'S** SUDDEN DEATH THEREAFTER, AND DISPERSAL OF OUR ACTING COMPANY, OLD LORD PEMBROKE FORMED HIS OWN THEATER GROUP, OR ALLOWED HIS WIFE TO DO IT.
PEMBROKE'S MEN, (REALLY COUNTESS MARY) EMPLOYED MY SERVICES AS A WRITER AND AN ACTOR. AT FIRST I WROTE SOME SILLY THINGS – **A COMEDY OF ERRORS**, A BLOOD AND THUNDER PLAY, **ANDRONICUS** – BUT THERE WAS A GREATER PLAN WE HAD FOR PLAYS: TO DRAMATIZE OUR HISTORY HEROICALLY. IT WAS THEN I WROTE THE **HENRY THE SIXTH** PLAYS.

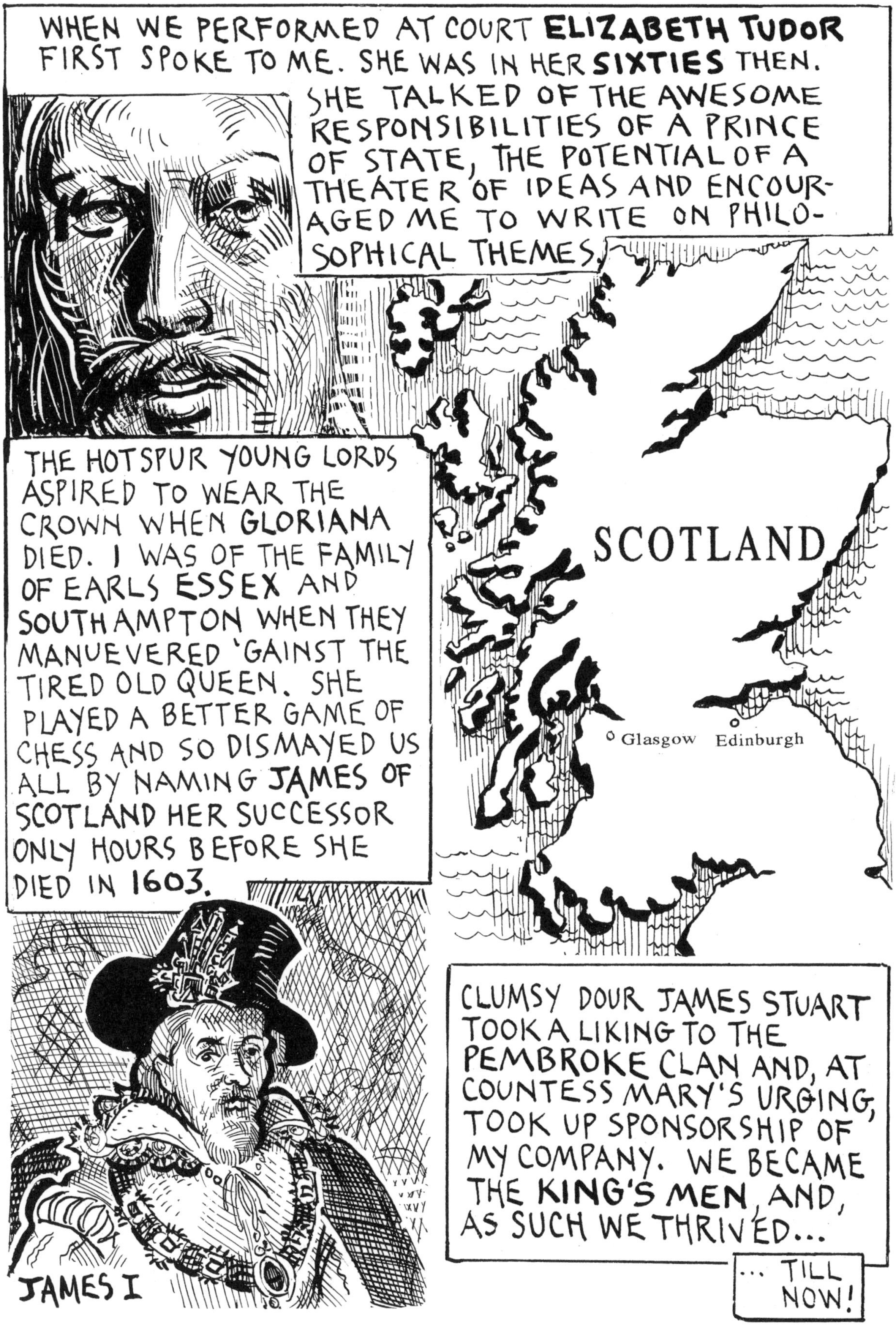
WHEN WE PERFORMED AT COURT ELIZABETH TUDOR FIRST SPOKE TO ME. SHE WAS IN HER SIXTIES THEN.
SHE TALKED OF THE AWESOME RESPONSIBILITIES OF A PRINCE OF STATE, THE POTENTIAL OF A THEATER OF IDEAS AND ENCOURAGED ME TO WRITE ON PHILOSOPHICAL THEMES.
SCOTLAND
Glasgow
Edinburgh
THE HOTSPUR YOUNG LORDS ASPIRED TO WEAR THE CROWN WHEN GLORIANA DIED. I WAS OF THE FAMILY OF EARLS ESSEX AND SOUTHAMPTON WHEN THEY MANUEVERED 'GAINST THE TIRED OLD QUEEN. SHE PLAYED A BETTER GAME OF CHESS AND SO DISMAYED US ALL BY NAMING JAMES OF SCOTLAND HER SUCCESSOR ONLY HOURS BEFORE SHE DIED IN 1603.
JAMES I
CLUMSY DOUR JAMES STUART TOOK A LIKING TO THE PEMBROKE CLAN AND, AT COUNTESS MARY'S URGING, TOOK UP SPONSORSHIP OF MY COMPANY. WE BECAME THE KING'S MEN, AND, AS SUCH WE THRIVED...
... TILL NOW!

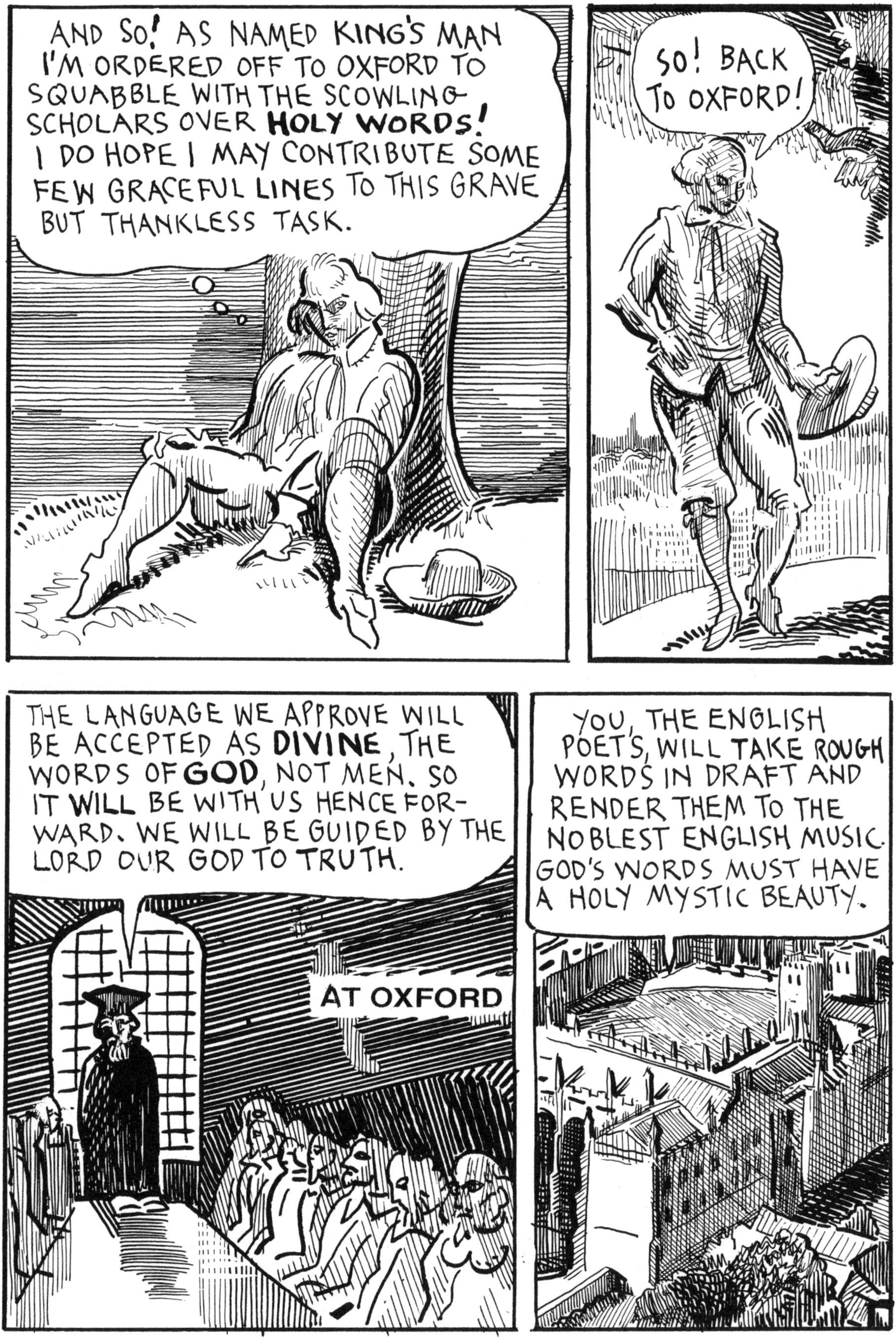

AND SO! AS NAMED KING'S MAN I'M ORDERED OFF TO OXFORD TO SQUABBLE WITH THE SCOWLING SCHOLARS OVER HOLY WORDS! I DO HOPE I MAY CONTRIBUTE SOME FEW GRACEFUL LINES TO THIS GRAVE BUT THANKLESS TASK.
SO! BACK TO OXFORD!
AT OXFORD
THE LANGUAGE WE APPROVE WILL BE ACCEPTED AS DIVINE, THE WORDS OF GOD, NOT MEN. SO IT WILL BE WITH US HENCE FORWARD. WE WILL BE GUIDED BY THE LORD OUR GOD TO TRUTH.
YOU, THE ENGLISH POET'S, WILL TAKE ROUGH WORDS IN DRAFT AND RENDER THEM TO THE NOBLEST ENGLISH MUSIC. GOD'S WORDS MUST HAVE A HOLY MYSTIC BEAUTY.

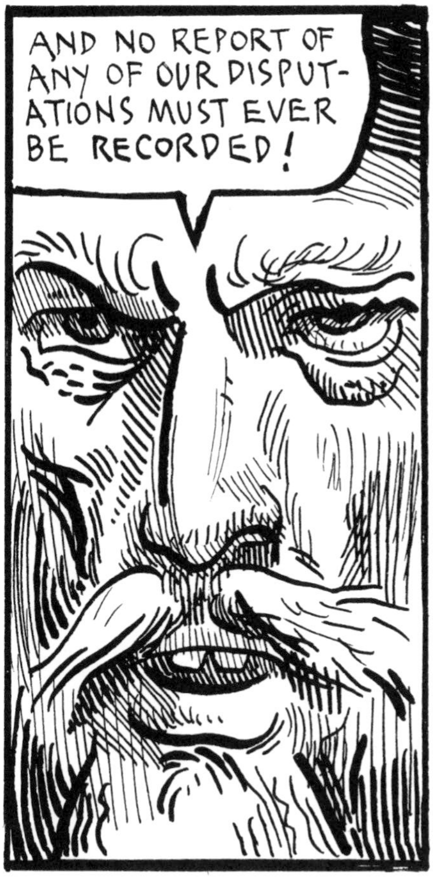
AND NO REPORT OF ANY OF OUR DISPUTATIONS MUST EVER BE RECORDED!

THE MUCH-DISCUSSED AND CAREFULLY CRAFTED TEXT WAS FINALLY APPROVED BY SCHOLARS, THEOLOGIANS, GOVERNMENT OFFICIALS AND THE **HOLY KING** HIMSELF (ACTUALLY LITTLE CHANGED FROM WILLIAM TYNDALE'S ENGLISH TRANSLATION FROM ALMOST 100 YEARS EARLIER). THE AUTHORIZED VERSION APPEARED IN **1611.**

The original title page to the 1611 edition

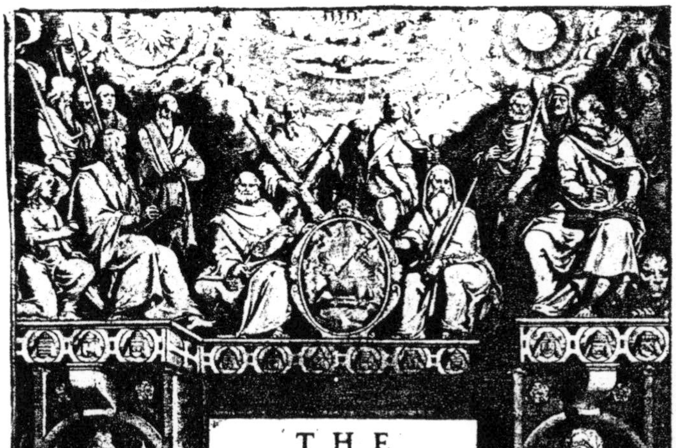
THE HOLY BIBLE,
Conteyning the Old Testament,
AND THE NEW:
Newly Translated out of the Originall tongues: & with the former Translations diligently compared and revised by his Maiesties speciall Comandement
Appointed to be read in Churches
Imprinted at London by Robert Barker, Printer to the Kings most Excellent Maiestie.
ANNO DOM 1611

BY THEN, SHAKESPEARE WAS WEARY AND ILL. HE FINISHED A FEW FINAL PLAYS: **CYMBELINE, THE WINTER'S TALE** AND **THE TEMPEST.**

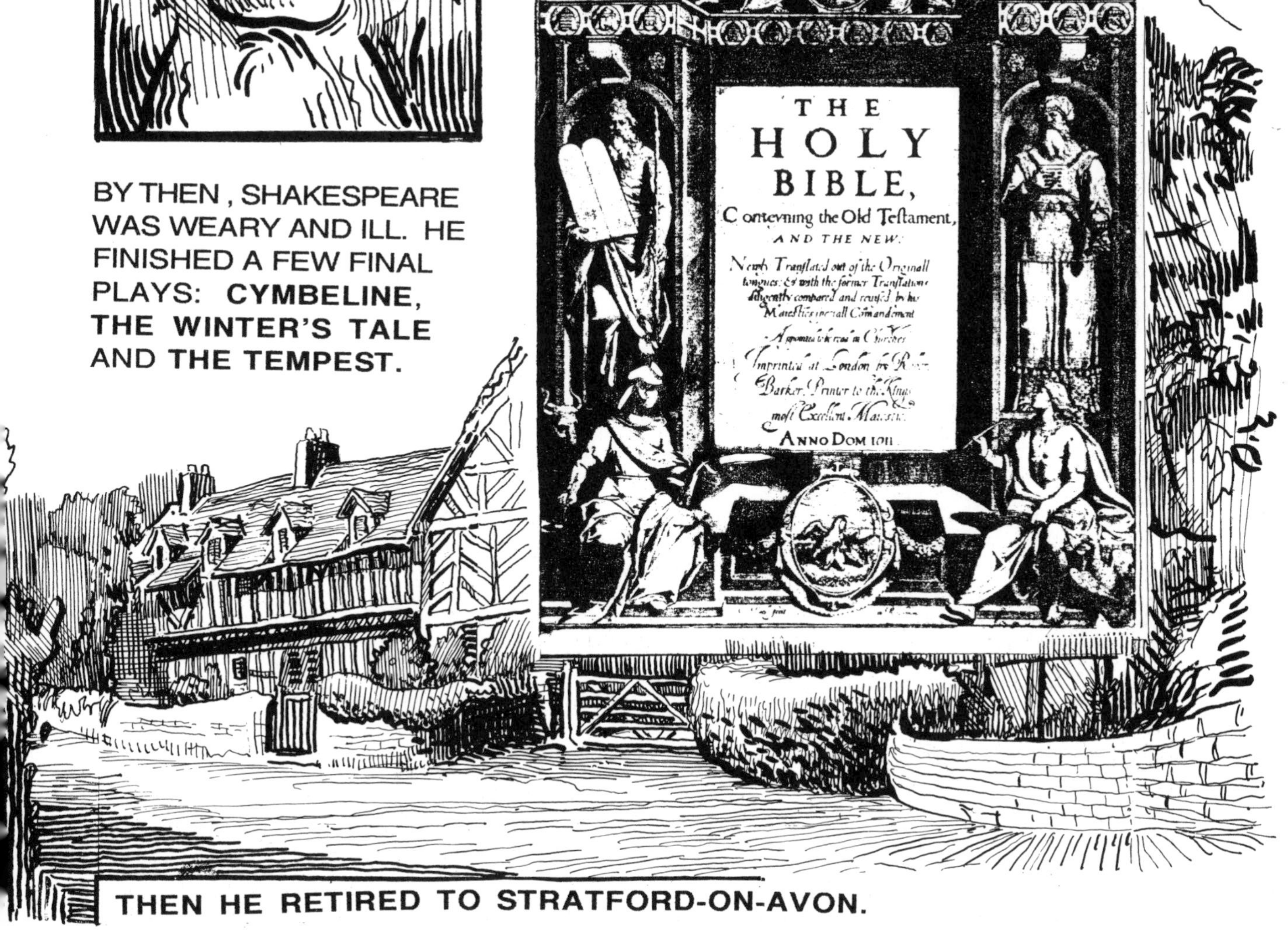

THEN HE RETIRED TO STRATFORD-ON-AVON.

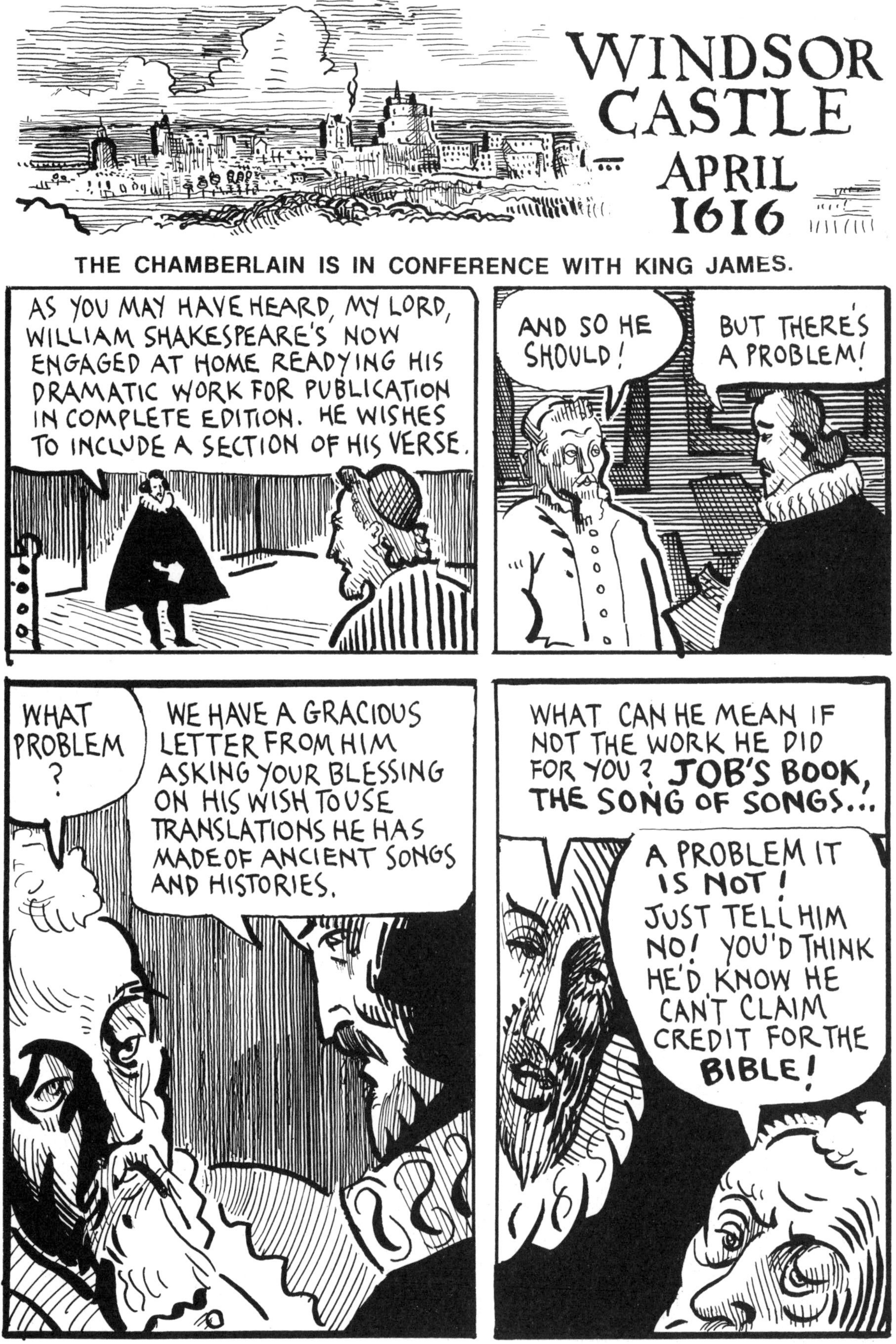
WINDSOR CASTLE
APRIL 1616
THE CHAMBERLAIN IS IN CONFERENCE WITH KING JAMES.
AS YOU MAY HAVE HEARD, MY LORD, WILLIAM SHAKESPEARE'S NOW ENGAGED AT HOME READYING HIS DRAMATIC WORK FOR PUBLICATION IN COMPLETE EDITION. HE WISHES TO INCLUDE A SECTION OF HIS VERSE.
AND SO HE SHOULD!
BUT THERE'S A PROBLEM!
WHAT PROBLEM?
WE HAVE A GRACIOUS LETTER FROM HIM ASKING YOUR BLESSING ON HIS WISH TO USE TRANSLATIONS HE HAS MADE OF ANCIENT SONGS AND HISTORIES.
WHAT CAN HE MEAN IF NOT THE WORK HE DID FOR YOU? JOB'S BOOK, THE SONG OF SONGS...
A PROBLEM IT IS NOT! JUST TELL HIM NO! YOU'D THINK HE'D KNOW HE CAN'T CLAIM CREDIT FOR THE BIBLE!

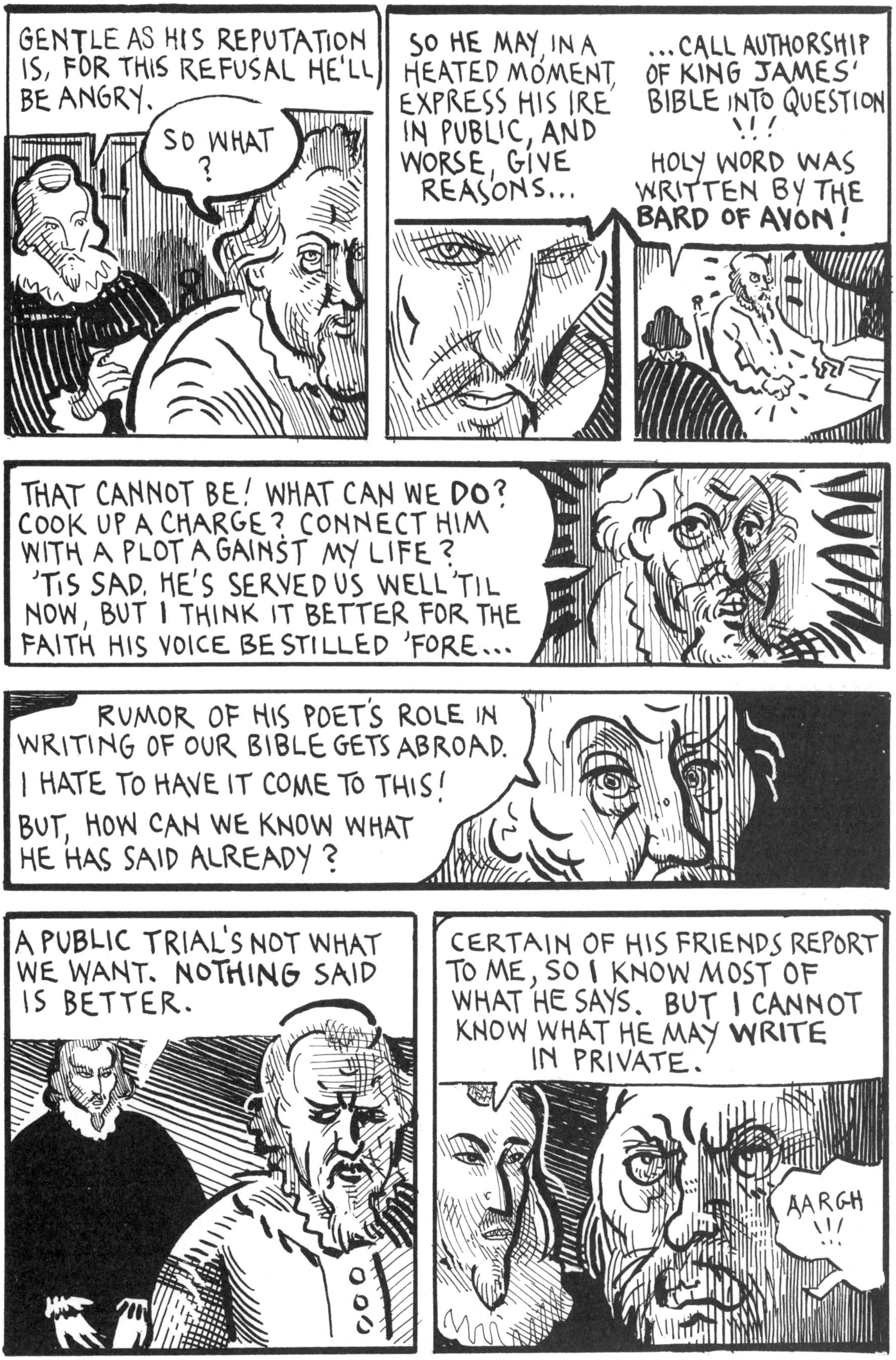
GENTLE AS HIS REPUTATION IS, FOR THIS REFUSAL HE'LL BE ANGRY.
SO WHAT ?
SO HE MAY, IN A HEATED MOMENT, EXPRESS HIS IRE IN PUBLIC, AND WORSE, GIVE REASONS...
...CALL AUTHORSHIP OF KING JAMES' BIBLE INTO QUESTION !!!
HOLY WORD WAS WRITTEN BY THE BARD OF AVON!
THAT CANNOT BE! WHAT CAN WE DO? COOK UP A CHARGE? CONNECT HIM WITH A PLOT AGAINST MY LIFE? 'TIS SAD. HE'S SERVED US WELL 'TIL NOW, BUT I THINK IT BETTER FOR THE FAITH HIS VOICE BE STILLED 'FORE...
RUMOR OF HIS POET'S ROLE IN WRITING OF OUR BIBLE GETS ABROAD.
I HATE TO HAVE IT COME TO THIS!
BUT, HOW CAN WE KNOW WHAT HE HAS SAID ALREADY?
A PUBLIC TRIAL'S NOT WHAT WE WANT. NOTHING SAID IS BETTER.
CERTAIN OF HIS FRIENDS REPORT TO ME, SO I KNOW MOST OF WHAT HE SAYS. BUT I CANNOT KNOW WHAT HE MAY WRITE IN PRIVATE.
AARGH !!!

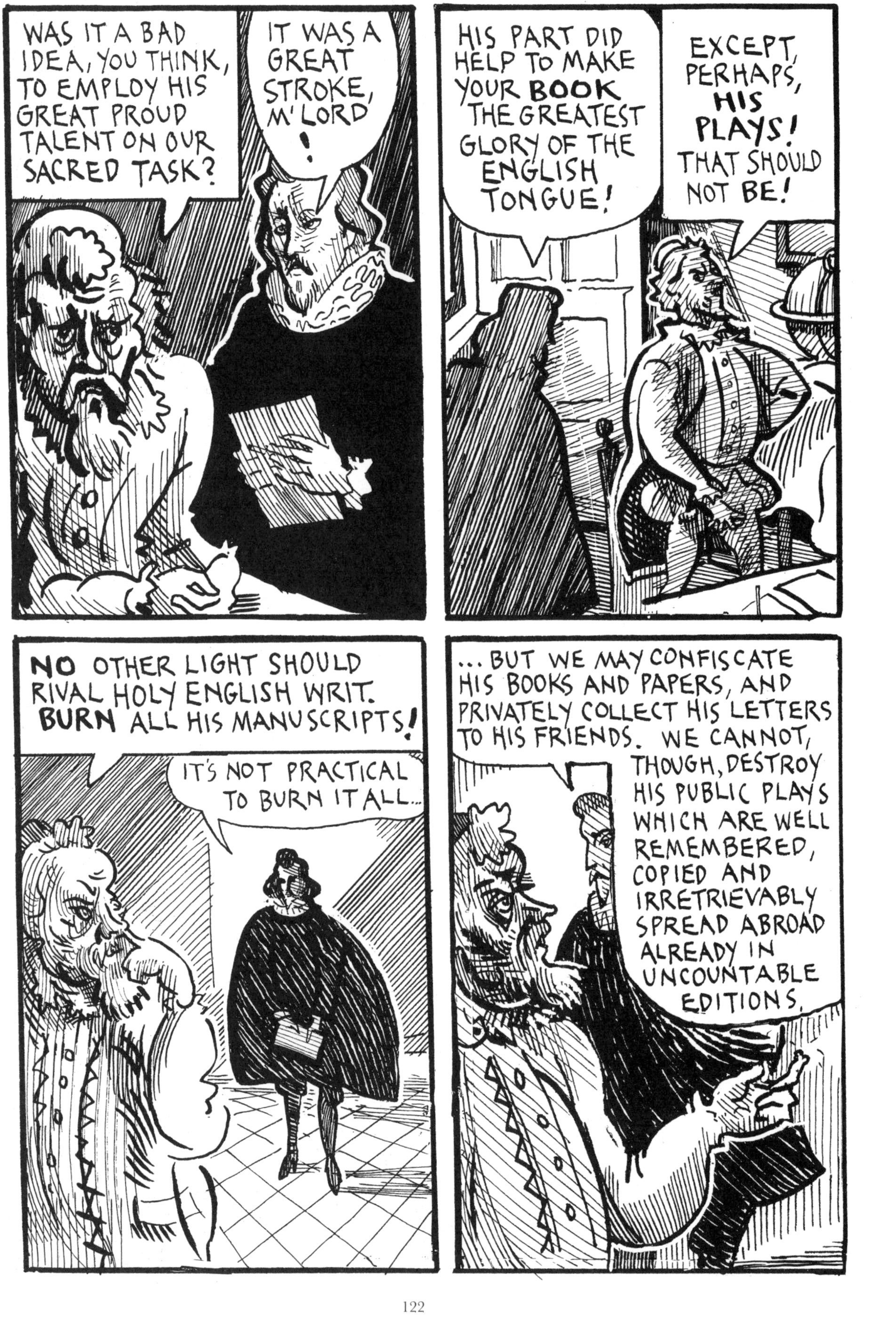
WAS IT A BAD IDEA, YOU THINK, TO EMPLOY HIS GREAT PROUD TALENT ON OUR SACRED TASK?
IT WAS A GREAT STROKE, M'LORD!
HIS PART DID HELP TO MAKE YOUR BOOK THE GREATEST GLORY OF THE ENGLISH TONGUE!
EXCEPT, PERHAPS, HIS PLAYS! THAT SHOULD NOT BE!
NO OTHER LIGHT SHOULD RIVAL HOLY ENGLISH WRIT. BURN ALL HIS MANUSCRIPTS!
IT'S NOT PRACTICAL TO BURN IT ALL...
... BUT WE MAY CONFISCATE HIS BOOKS AND PAPERS, AND PRIVATELY COLLECT HIS LETTERS TO HIS FRIENDS. WE CANNOT, THOUGH, DESTROY HIS PUBLIC PLAYS WHICH ARE WELL REMEMBERED, COPIED AND IRRETRIEVABLY SPREAD ABROAD ALREADY IN UNCOUNTABLE EDITIONS.

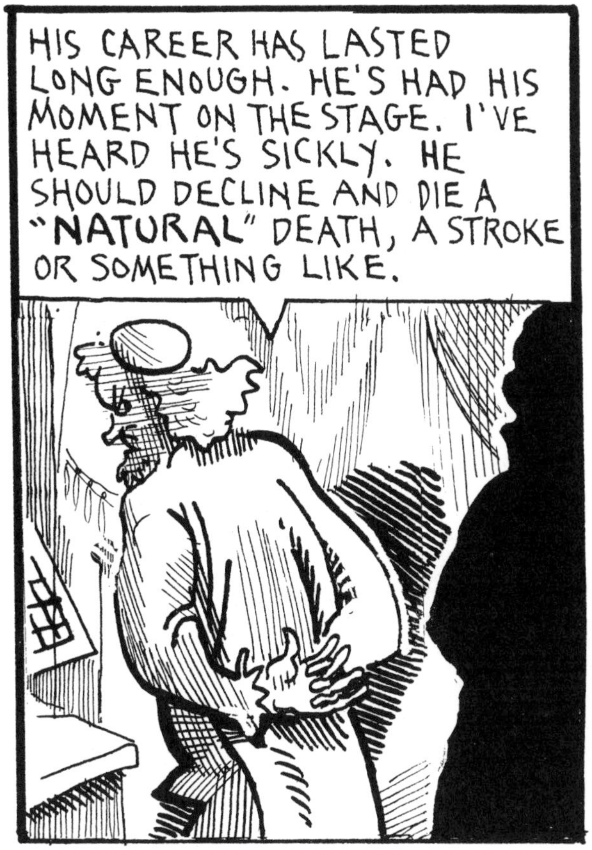
HIS CAREER HAS LASTED LONG ENOUGH. HE'S HAD HIS MOMENT ON THE STAGE. I'VE HEARD HE'S SICKLY. HE SHOULD DECLINE AND DIE A "NATURAL" DEATH, A STROKE OR SOMETHING LIKE.

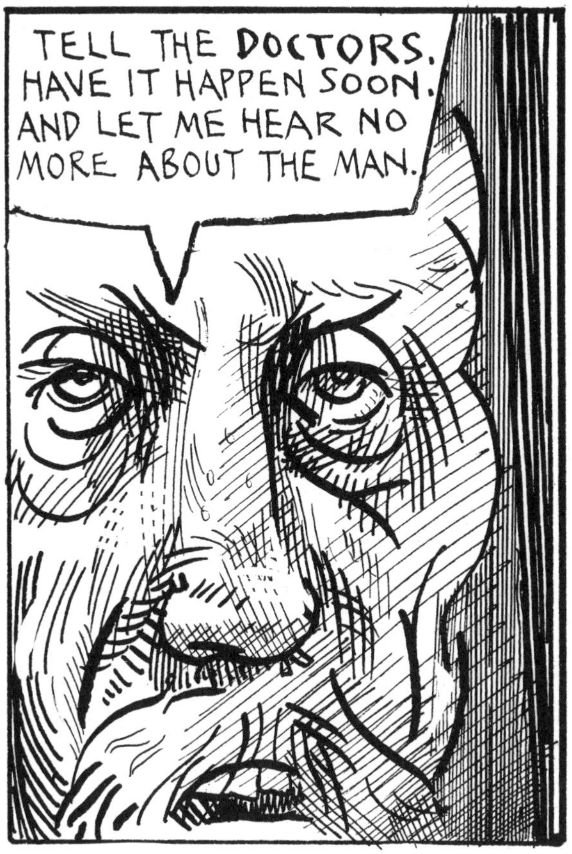
TELL THE DOCTORS. HAVE IT HAPPEN SOON. AND LET ME HEAR NO MORE ABOUT THE MAN.

ON APRIL 22, 1616, WILLIAM SHAKESPEARE RECEIVED AN UNEXPECTED VISIT FROM TWO WRITER FRIENDS.

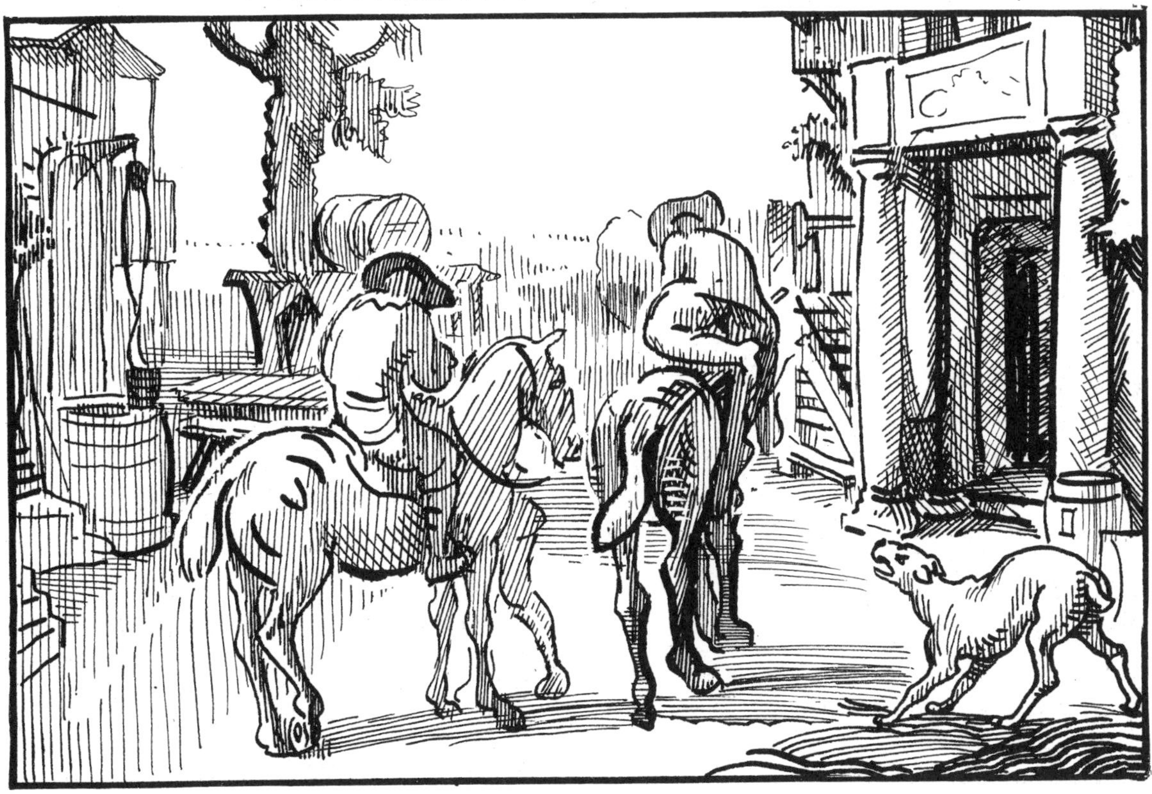

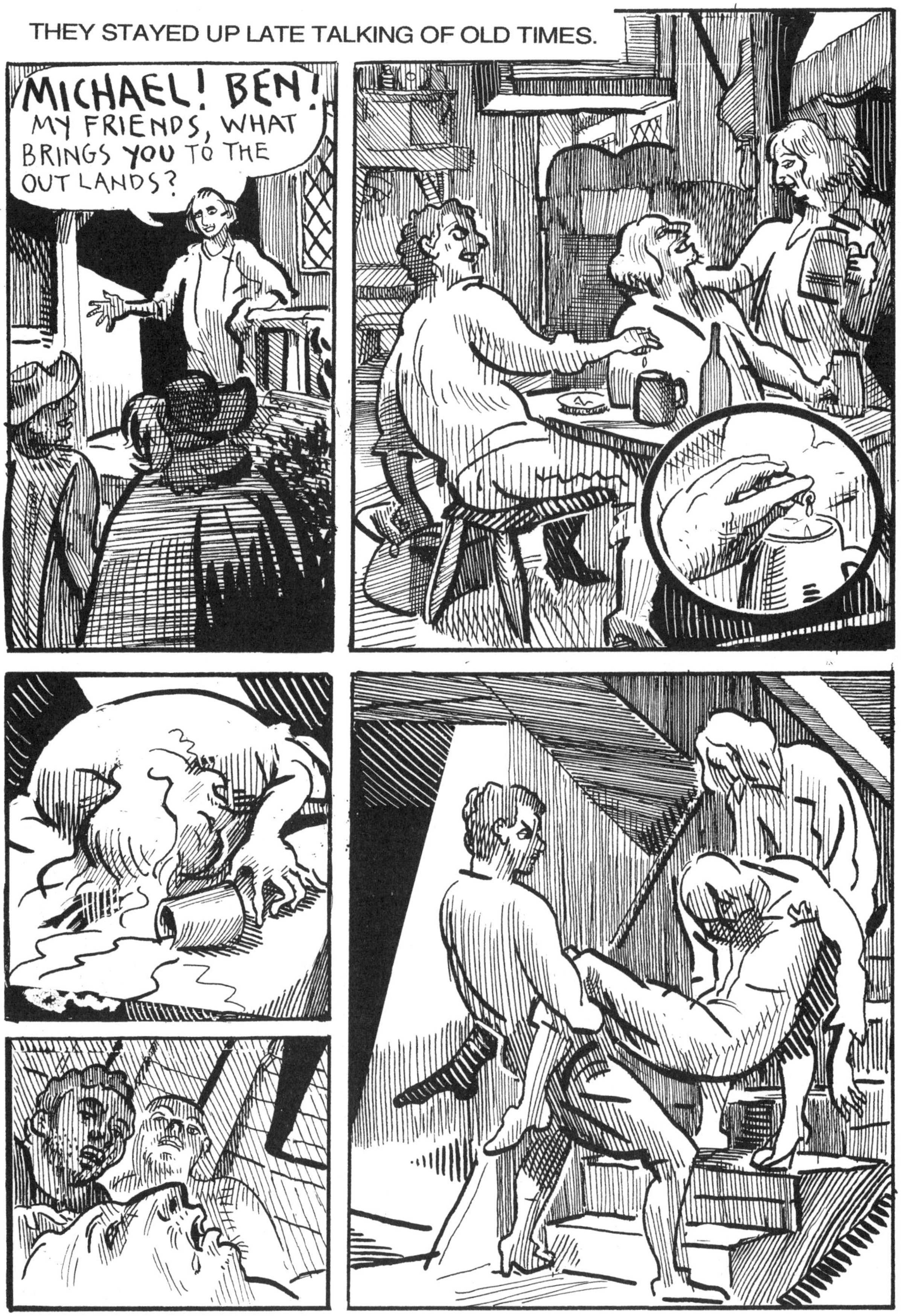
THEY STAYED UP LATE TALKING OF OLD TIMES.
MICHAEL! BEN! MY FRIENDS, WHAT BRINGS YOU TO THE OUTLANDS?

WILLIAM SHAKESPEARE DIED THE NEXT DAY, IT WAS SAID "OF A FEVER" CAUSED BY TOO MUCH DRINK.

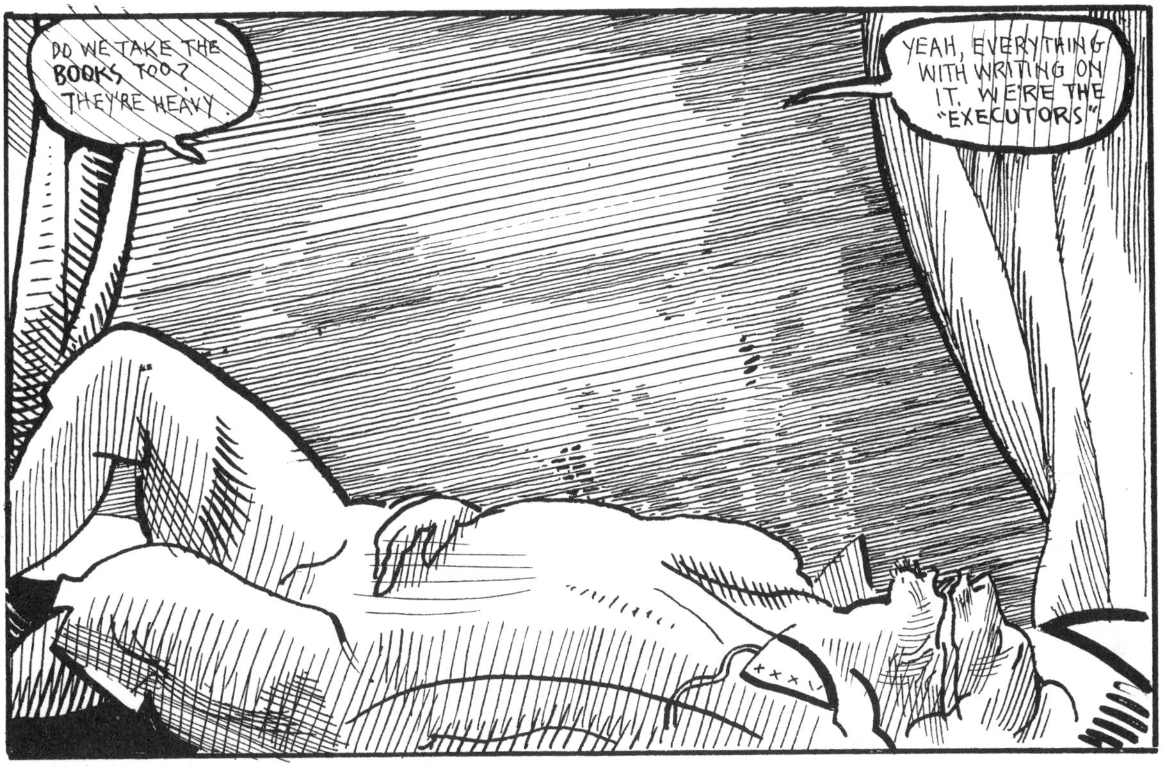
DO WE TAKE THE BOOKS, TOO? THEY'RE HEAVY.
YEAH, EVERYTHING WITH WRITING ON IT. WE'RE THE "EXECUTORS".

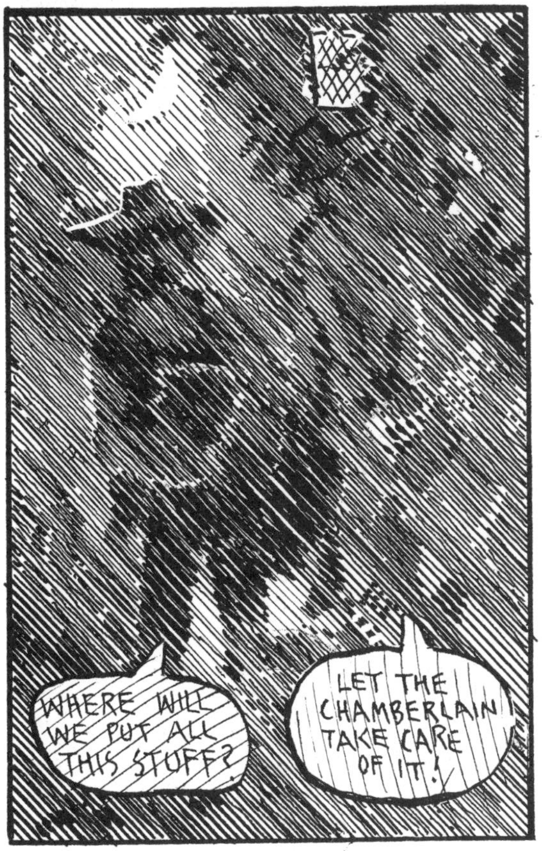
WHERE WILL WE PUT ALL THIS STUFF?
LET THE CHAMBERLAIN TAKE CARE OF IT!

HIS PLAYS WERE PUBLISHED IN 1623 IN A DELUXE FOLIO EDITION DEDICATED TO, AND PERHAPS PAID FOR BY, **WILLIAM HERBERT**, EARL OF PEMBROKE (SINCE 1603).

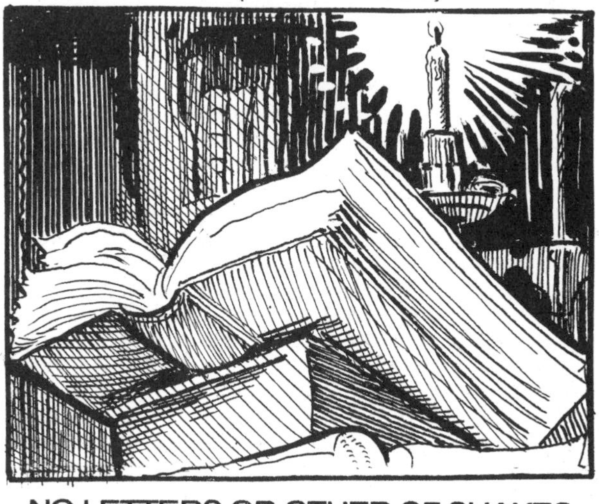

NO LETTERS OR OTHER OF SHAKESPEARE'S PERSONAL PAPERS HAVE EVER BEEN FOUND.

The End

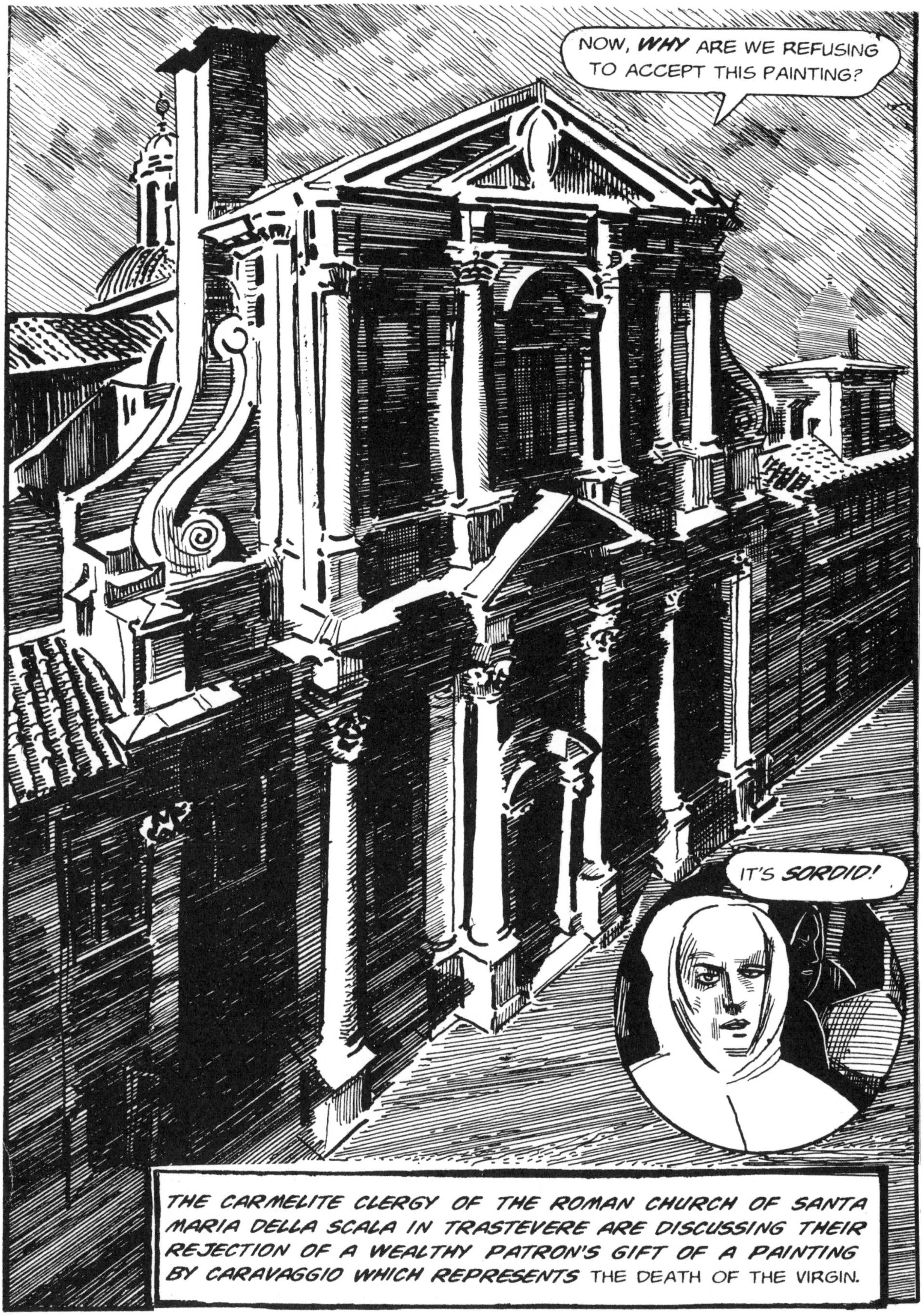
NOW, WHY ARE WE REFUSING TO ACCEPT THIS PAINTING?
IT'S SORDID!
THE CARMELITE CLERGY OF THE ROMAN CHURCH OF SANTA MARIA DELLA SCALA IN TRASTEVERE ARE DISCUSSING THEIR REJECTION OF A WEALTHY PATRON'S GIFT OF A PAINTING BY CARAVAGGIO WHICH REPRESENTS THE DEATH OF THE VIRGIN.

BUT IT'S MAGNIFICENT! HIS BEST SINCE THE CHIESA NUOVA *ENTOMBMENT*. I THINK WE SHOULD TAKE IT.

HUMPH!

MUTTER

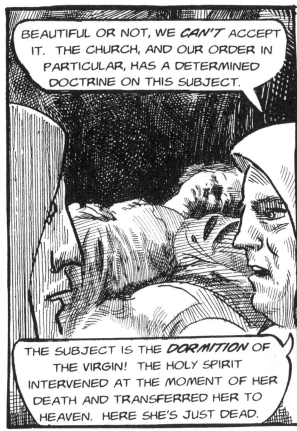

BEAUTIFUL OR NOT, WE *CAN'T* ACCEPT IT. THE CHURCH, AND OUR ORDER IN PARTICULAR, HAS A DETERMINED DOCTRINE ON THIS SUBJECT.

THE SUBJECT IS THE *DORMITION* OF THE VIRGIN! THE HOLY SPIRIT INTERVENED AT THE MOMENT OF HER DEATH AND TRANSFERRED HER TO HEAVEN. HERE SHE'S JUST DEAD.

BAREFOOT. LIVID. SWOLLEN. NOTHING HOLY OR SPIRITUAL ABOUT IT AT ALL.

HE NEVER CONSULTED US, OR *ANYONE*, ABOUT THEOLOGICAL PROPRIETY.

HE KNEW BETTER THAN THAT!

HE'S SUCH A SWINE ANYWAY. HE CAN'T DO ANYTHING BUT COPY FROM A MODEL. HE ALWAYS PAINTS THE SAINTS, THE VIRGIN, OUR DEAR LORD HIMSELF, FROM STREET BUMS AND BARFLIES. I EVEN *RECOGNIZE* SOME OF THEM!

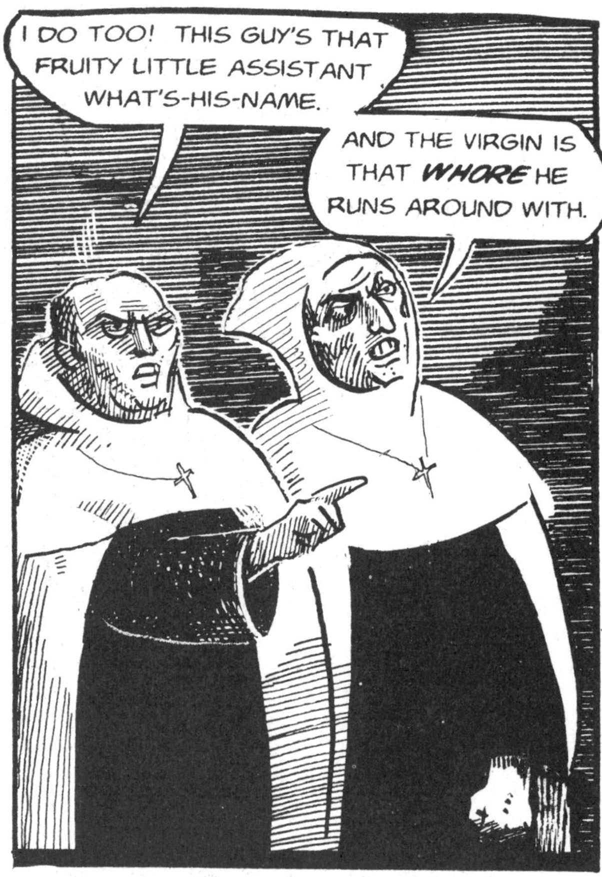
I DO TOO! THIS GUY'S THAT FRUITY LITTLE ASSISTANT WHAT'S-HIS-NAME.
AND THE VIRGIN IS THAT WHORE HE RUNS AROUND WITH.

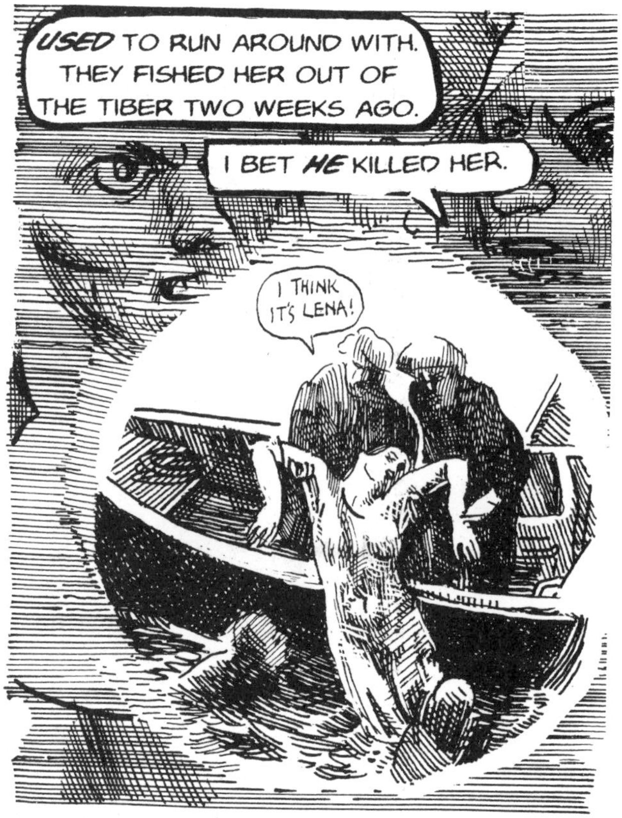
USED TO RUN AROUND WITH. THEY FISHED HER OUT OF THE TIBER TWO WEEKS AGO.
I BET HE KILLED HER.
I THINK IT'S LENA!

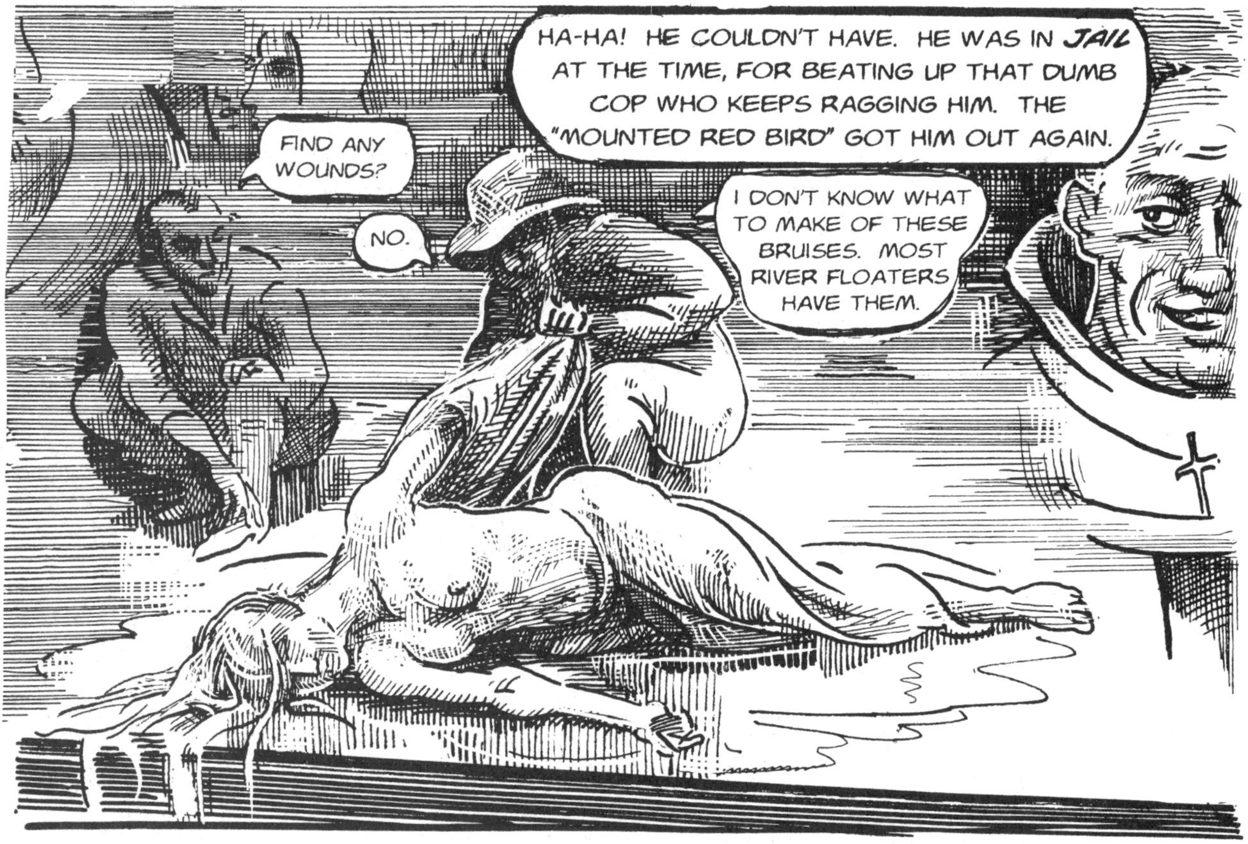
HA-HA! HE COULDN'T HAVE. HE WAS IN JAIL AT THE TIME, FOR BEATING UP THAT DUMB COP WHO KEEPS RAGGING HIM. THE "MOUNTED RED BIRD" GOT HIM OUT AGAIN.
FIND ANY WOUNDS?
NO.
I DON'T KNOW WHAT TO MAKE OF THESE BRUISES. MOST RIVER FLOATERS HAVE THEM.

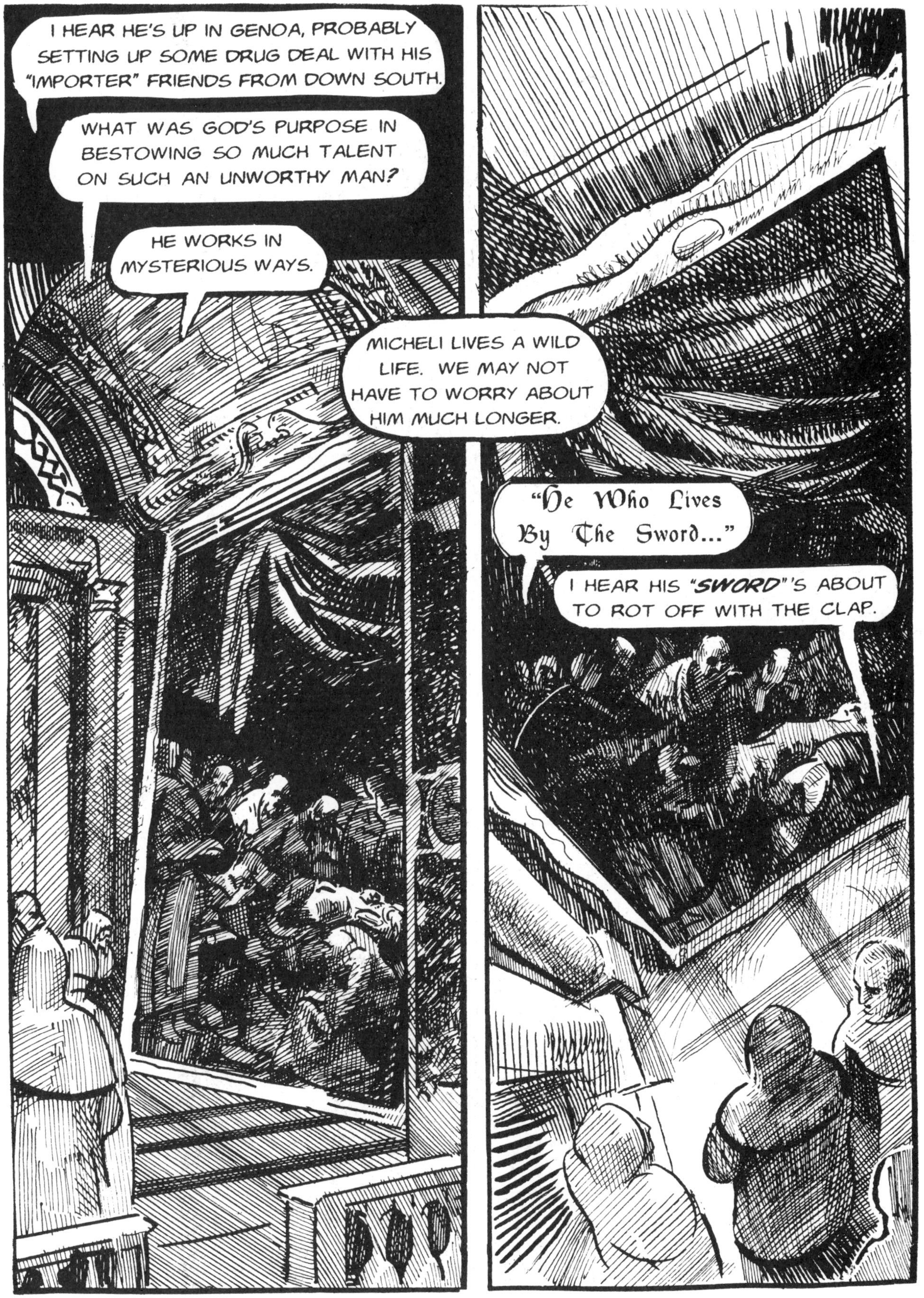

I HEAR HE'S UP IN GENOA, PROBABLY SETTING UP SOME DRUG DEAL WITH HIS "IMPORTER" FRIENDS FROM DOWN SOUTH.
WHAT WAS GOD'S PURPOSE IN BESTOWING SO MUCH TALENT ON SUCH AN UNWORTHY MAN?
HE WORKS IN MYSTERIOUS WAYS.
MICHELI LIVES A WILD LIFE. WE MAY NOT HAVE TO WORRY ABOUT HIM MUCH LONGER.
"He Who Lives By The Sword..."
I HEAR HIS "SWORD"'S ABOUT TO ROT OFF WITH THE CLAP.

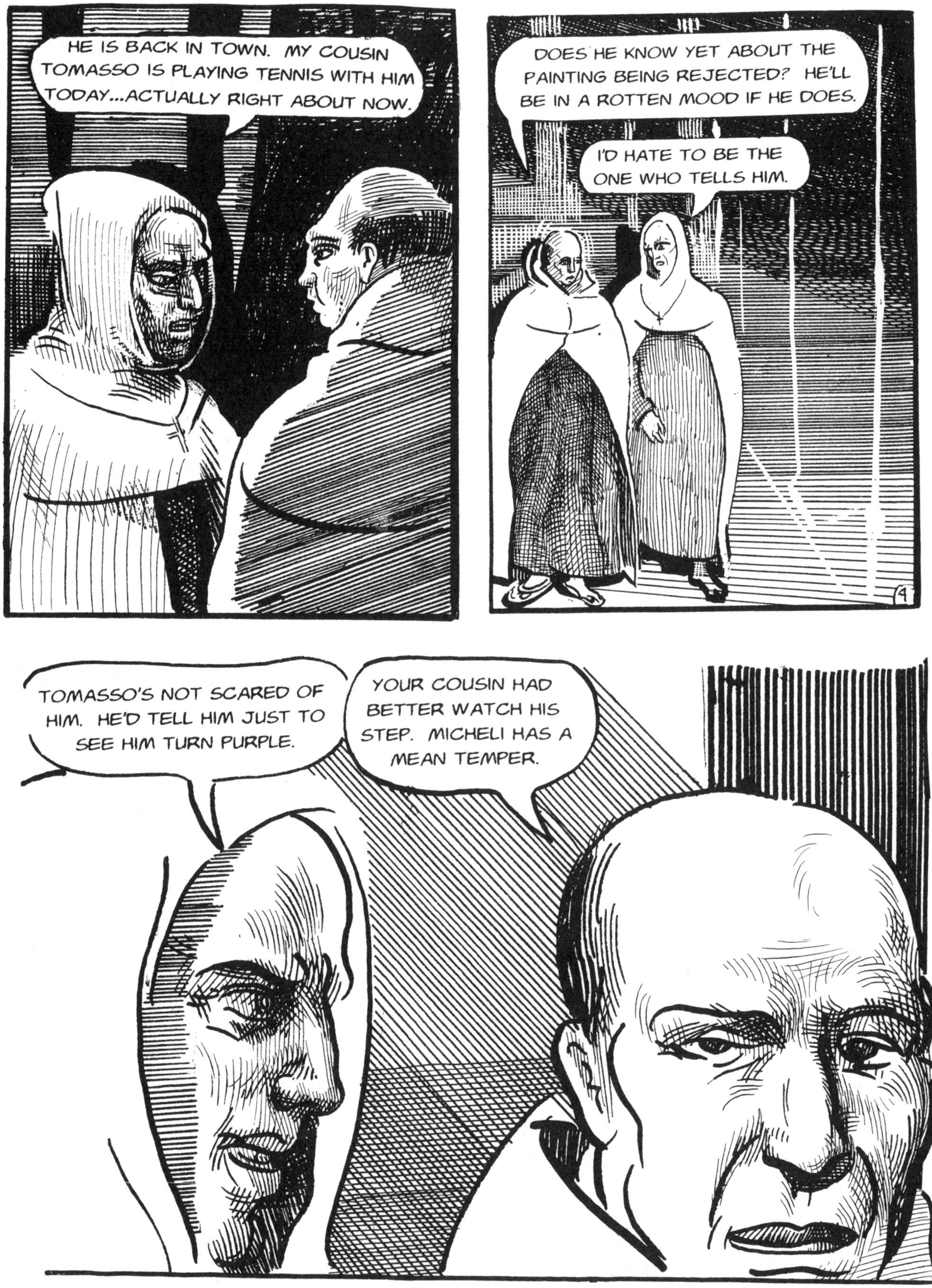
HE IS BACK IN TOWN. MY COUSIN TOMASSO IS PLAYING TENNIS WITH HIM TODAY...ACTUALLY RIGHT ABOUT NOW.
DOES HE KNOW YET ABOUT THE PAINTING BEING REJECTED? HE'LL BE IN A ROTTEN MOOD IF HE DOES.
I'D HATE TO BE THE ONE WHO TELLS HIM.
TOMASSO'S NOT SCARED OF HIM. HE'D TELL HIM JUST TO SEE HIM TURN PURPLE.
YOUR COUSIN HAD BETTER WATCH HIS STEP. MICHELI HAS A MEAN TEMPER.

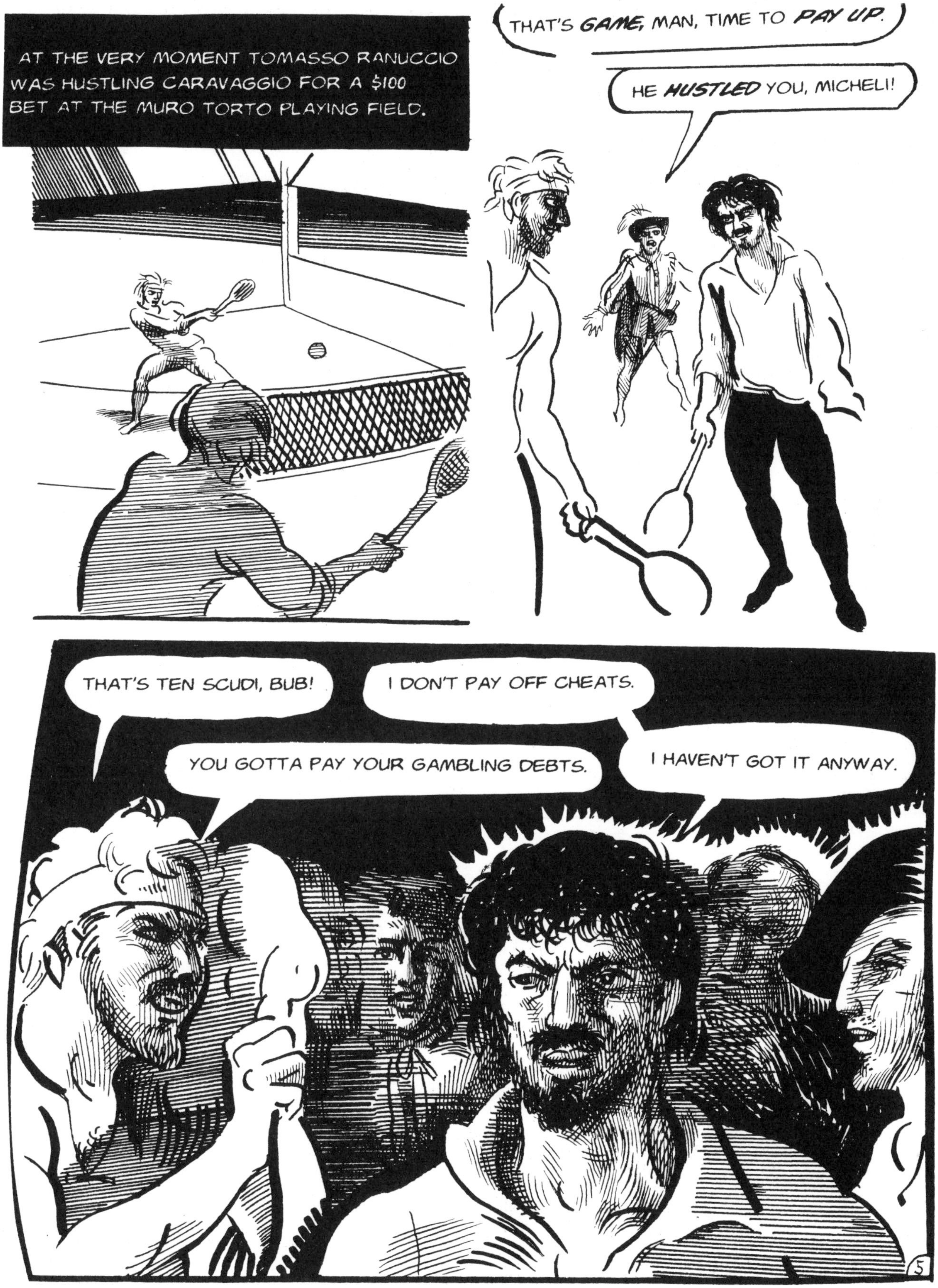
AT THE VERY MOMENT TOMASSO RANUCCIO WAS HUSTLING CARAVAGGIO FOR A $100 BET AT THE MURO TORTO PLAYING FIELD.
THAT'S GAME, MAN, TIME TO PAY UP.
HE HUSTLED YOU, MICHELI!
THAT'S TEN SCUDI, BUB!
YOU GOTTA PAY YOUR GAMBLING DEBTS.
I DON'T PAY OFF CHEATS.
I HAVEN'T GOT IT ANYWAY.
5

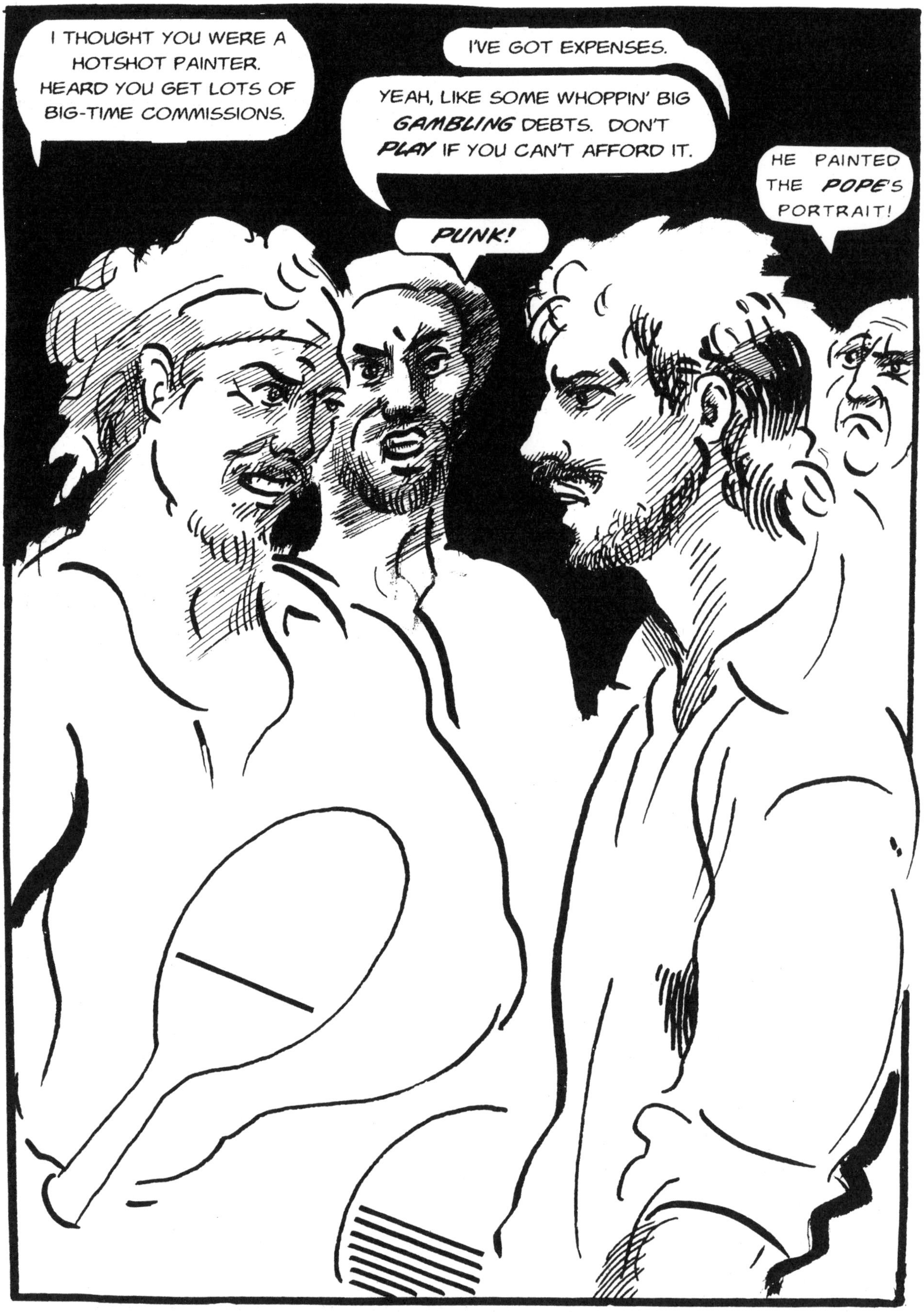
I THOUGHT YOU WERE A HOTSHOT PAINTER. HEARD YOU GET LOTS OF BIG-TIME COMMISSIONS.
I'VE GOT EXPENSES.
YEAH, LIKE SOME WHOPPIN' BIG *GAMBLING* DEBTS. DON'T *PLAY* IF YOU CAN'T AFFORD IT.
PUNK!
HE PAINTED THE *POPE*'S PORTRAIT!

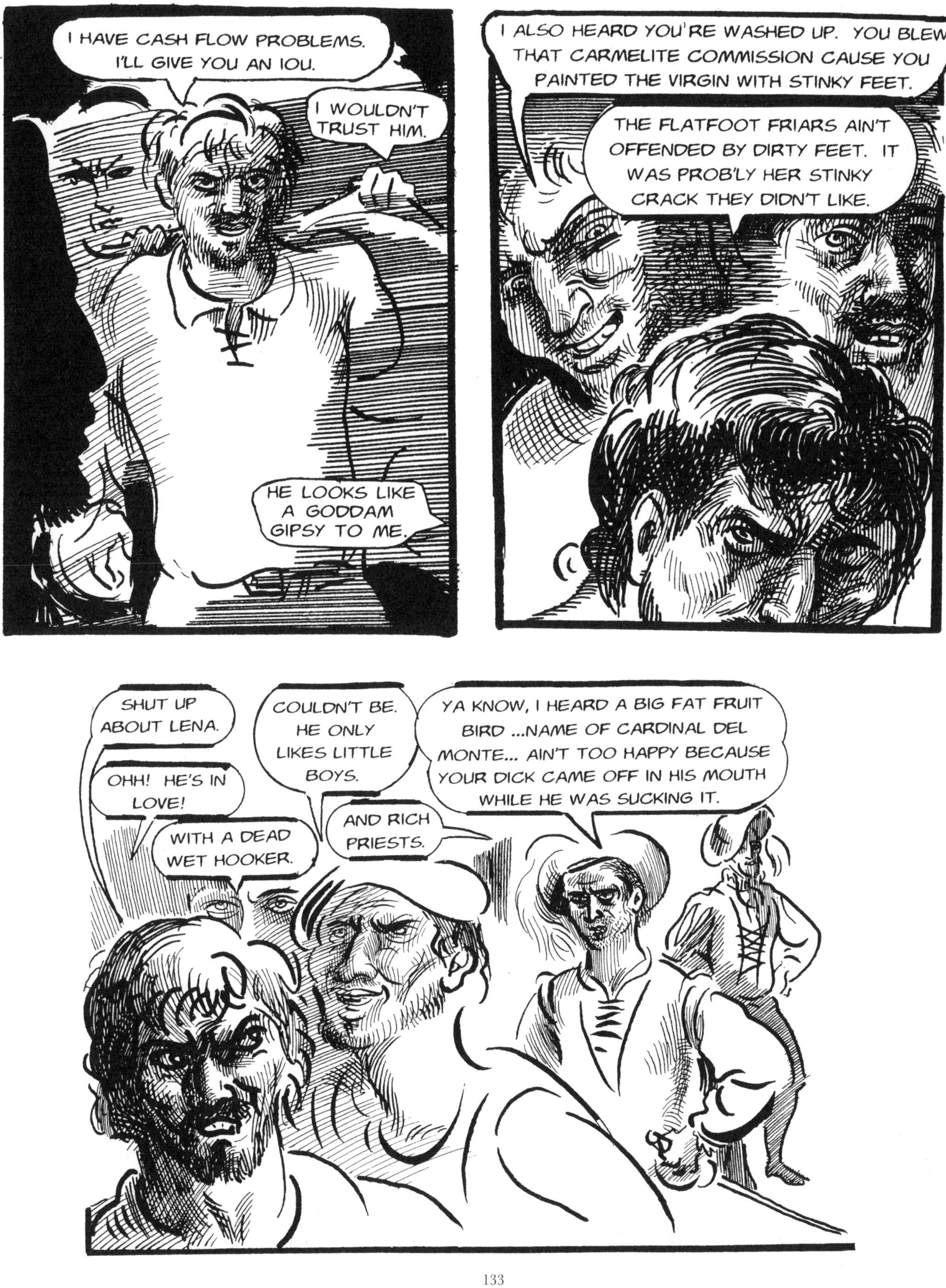
I HAVE CASH FLOW PROBLEMS. I'LL GIVE YOU AN IOU.
I WOULDN'T TRUST HIM.
HE LOOKS LIKE A GODDAM GIPSY TO ME.
I ALSO HEARD YOU'RE WASHED UP. YOU BLEW THAT CARMELITE COMMISSION CAUSE YOU PAINTED THE VIRGIN WITH STINKY FEET.
THE FLATFOOT FRIARS AIN'T OFFENDED BY DIRTY FEET. IT WAS PROB'LY HER STINKY CRACK THEY DIDN'T LIKE.
YA KNOW, I HEARD A BIG FAT FRUIT BIRD ...NAME OF CARDINAL DEL MONTE... AIN'T TOO HAPPY BECAUSE YOUR DICK CAME OFF IN HIS MOUTH WHILE HE WAS SUCKING IT.
COULDN'T BE. HE ONLY LIKES LITTLE BOYS.
AND RICH PRIESTS.
SHUT UP ABOUT LENA.
OHH! HE'S IN LOVE!
WITH A DEAD WET HOOKER.

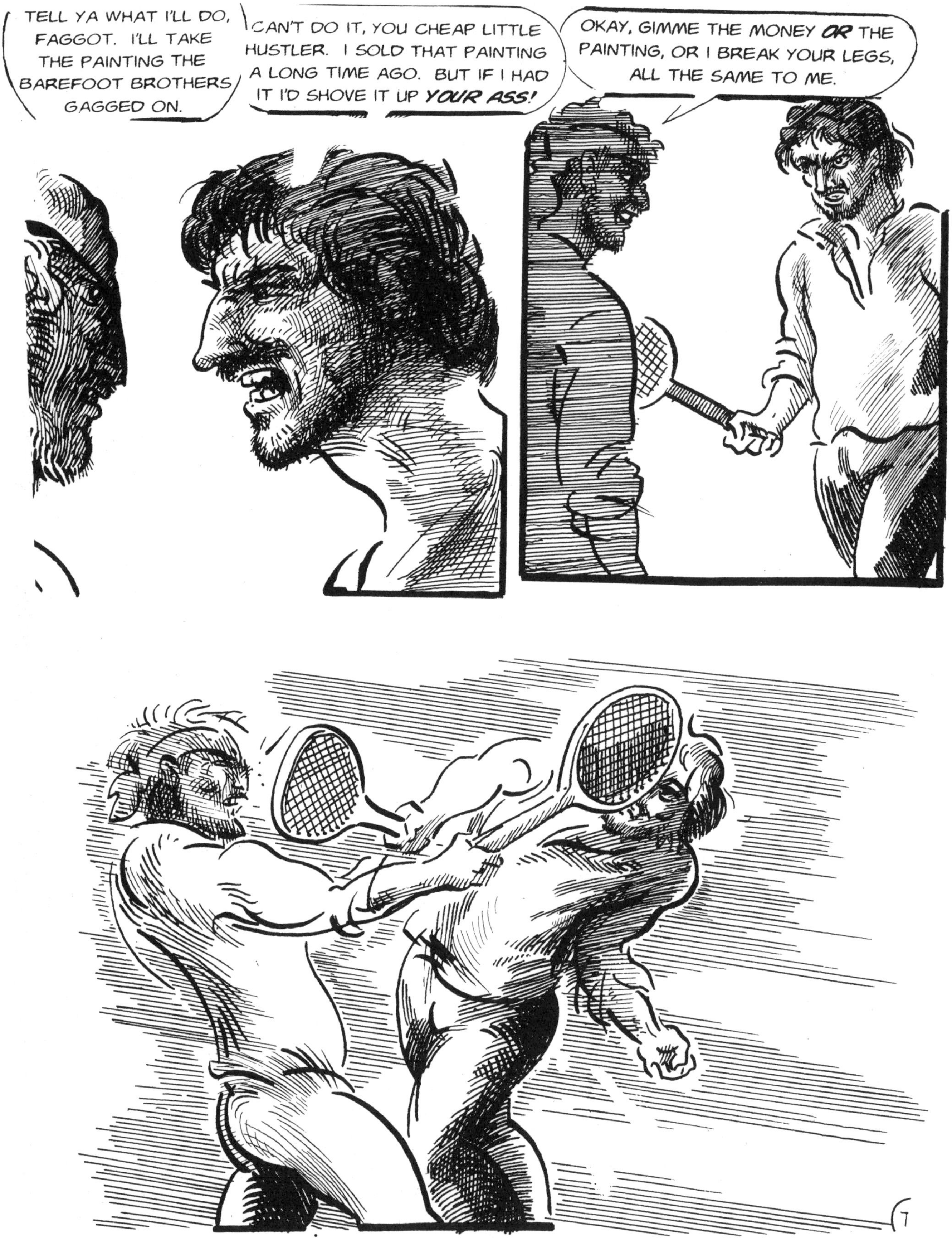
TELL YA WHAT I'LL DO, FAGGOT. I'LL TAKE THE PAINTING THE BAREFOOT BROTHERS GAGGED ON.
CAN'T DO IT, YOU CHEAP LITTLE HUSTLER. I SOLD THAT PAINTING A LONG TIME AGO. BUT IF I HAD IT I'D SHOVE IT UP YOUR ASS!
OKAY, GIMME THE MONEY OR THE PAINTING, OR I BREAK YOUR LEGS, ALL THE SAME TO ME.
7

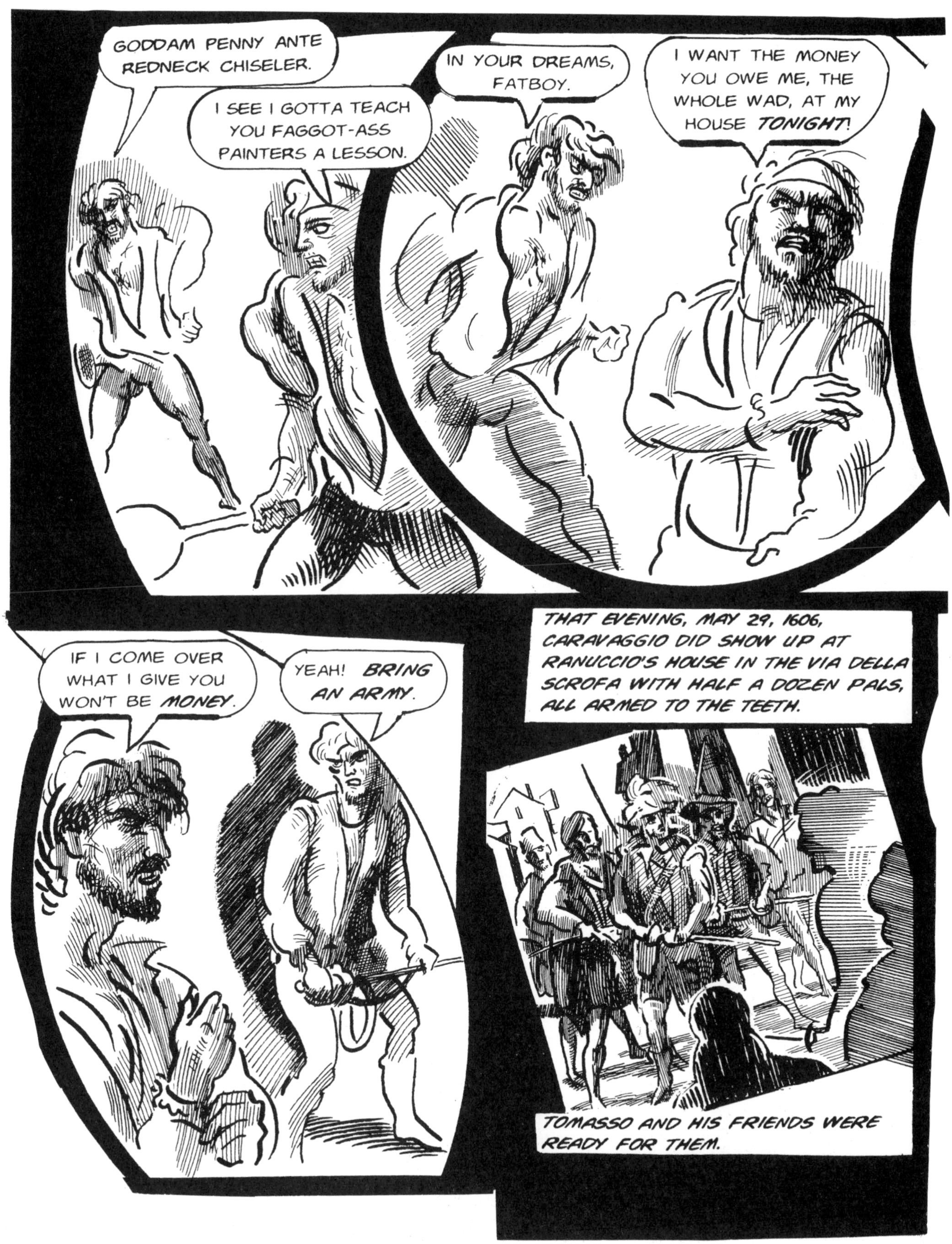
GODDAM PENNY ANTE REDNECK CHISELER.
I SEE I GOTTA TEACH YOU FAGGOT-ASS PAINTERS A LESSON.
IN YOUR DREAMS, FATBOY.
I WANT THE MONEY YOU OWE ME, THE WHOLE WAD, AT MY HOUSE *TONIGHT*!
IF I COME OVER WHAT I GIVE YOU WON'T BE *MONEY*.
YEAH! *BRING AN ARMY*.
THAT EVENING, MAY 29, 1606, CARAVAGGIO DID SHOW UP AT RANUCCIO'S HOUSE IN THE VIA DELLA SCROFA WITH HALF A DOZEN PALS, ALL ARMED TO THE TEETH.
TOMASSO AND HIS FRIENDS WERE READY FOR THEM.

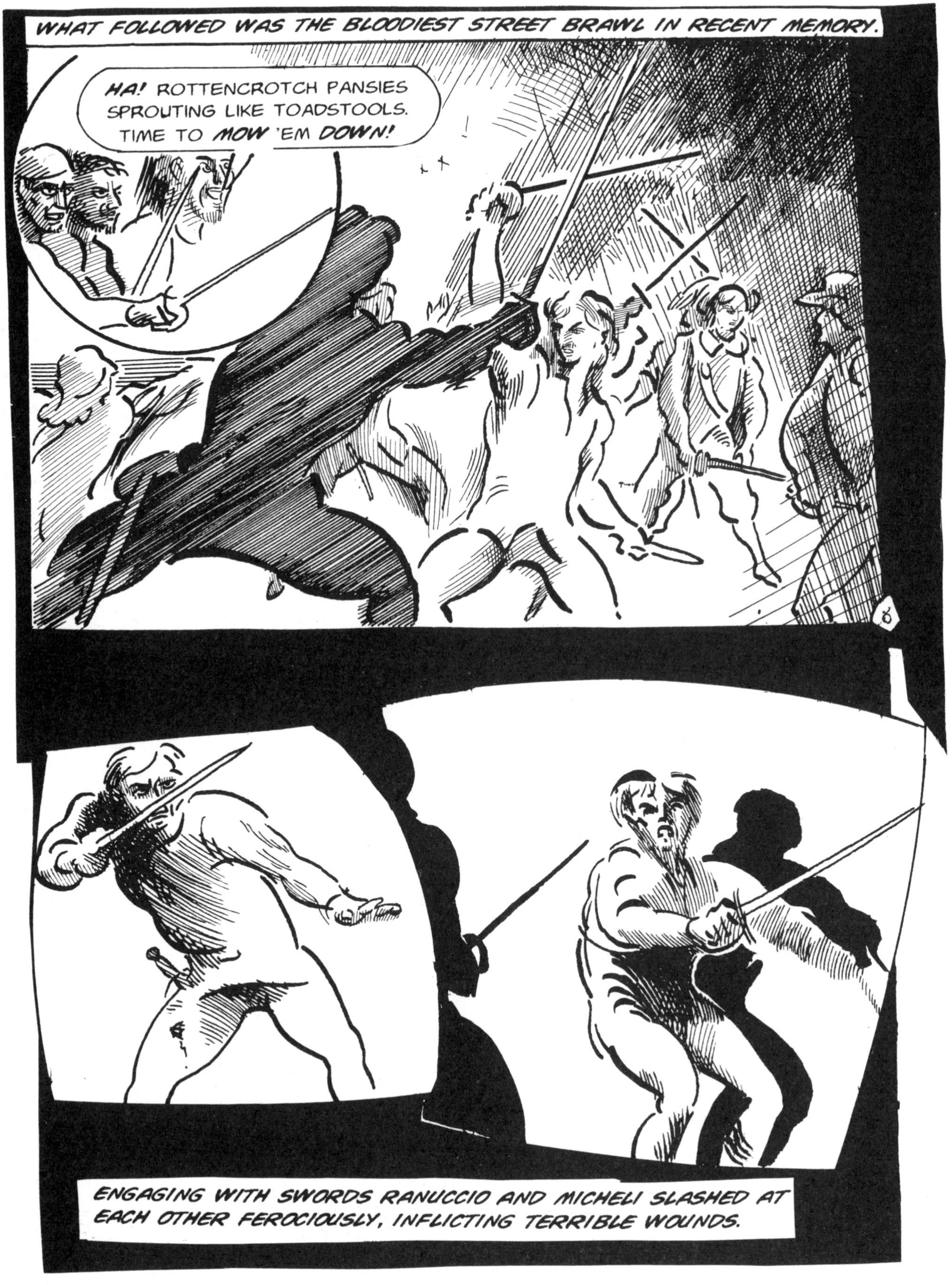
WHAT FOLLOWED WAS THE BLOODIEST STREET BRAWL IN RECENT MEMORY.
HA! ROTTENCROTCH PANSIES SPROUTING LIKE TOADSTOOLS. TIME TO MOW 'EM DOWN!
ENGAGING WITH SWORDS RANUCCIO AND MICHELI SLASHED AT EACH OTHER FEROCIOUSLY, INFLICTING TERRIBLE WOUNDS.

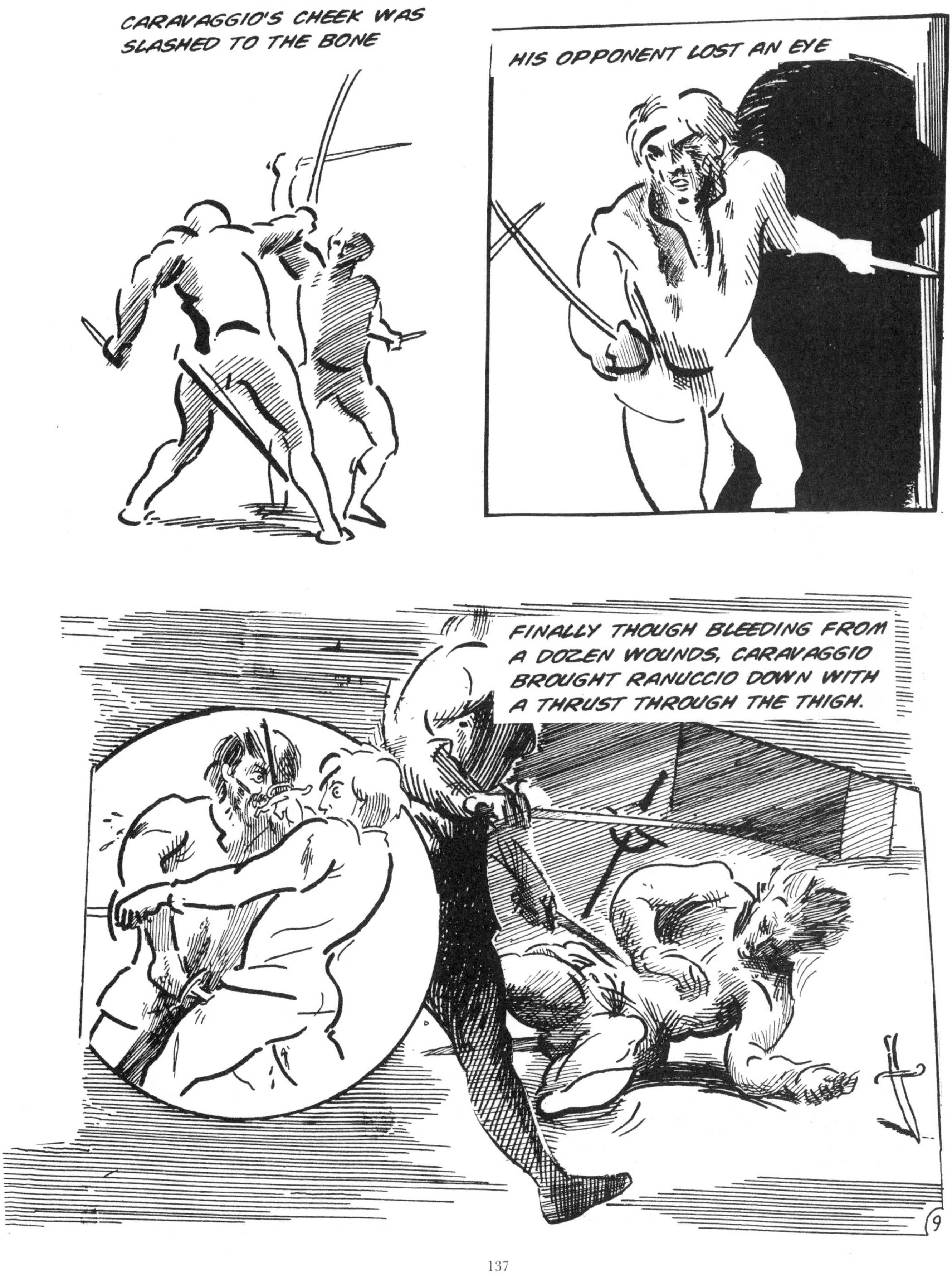
CARAVAGGIO'S CHEEK WAS SLASHED TO THE BONE
HIS OPPONENT LOST AN EYE
FINALLY THOUGH BLEEDING FROM A DOZEN WOUNDS, CARAVAGGIO BROUGHT RANUCCIO DOWN WITH A THRUST THROUGH THE THIGH.
9

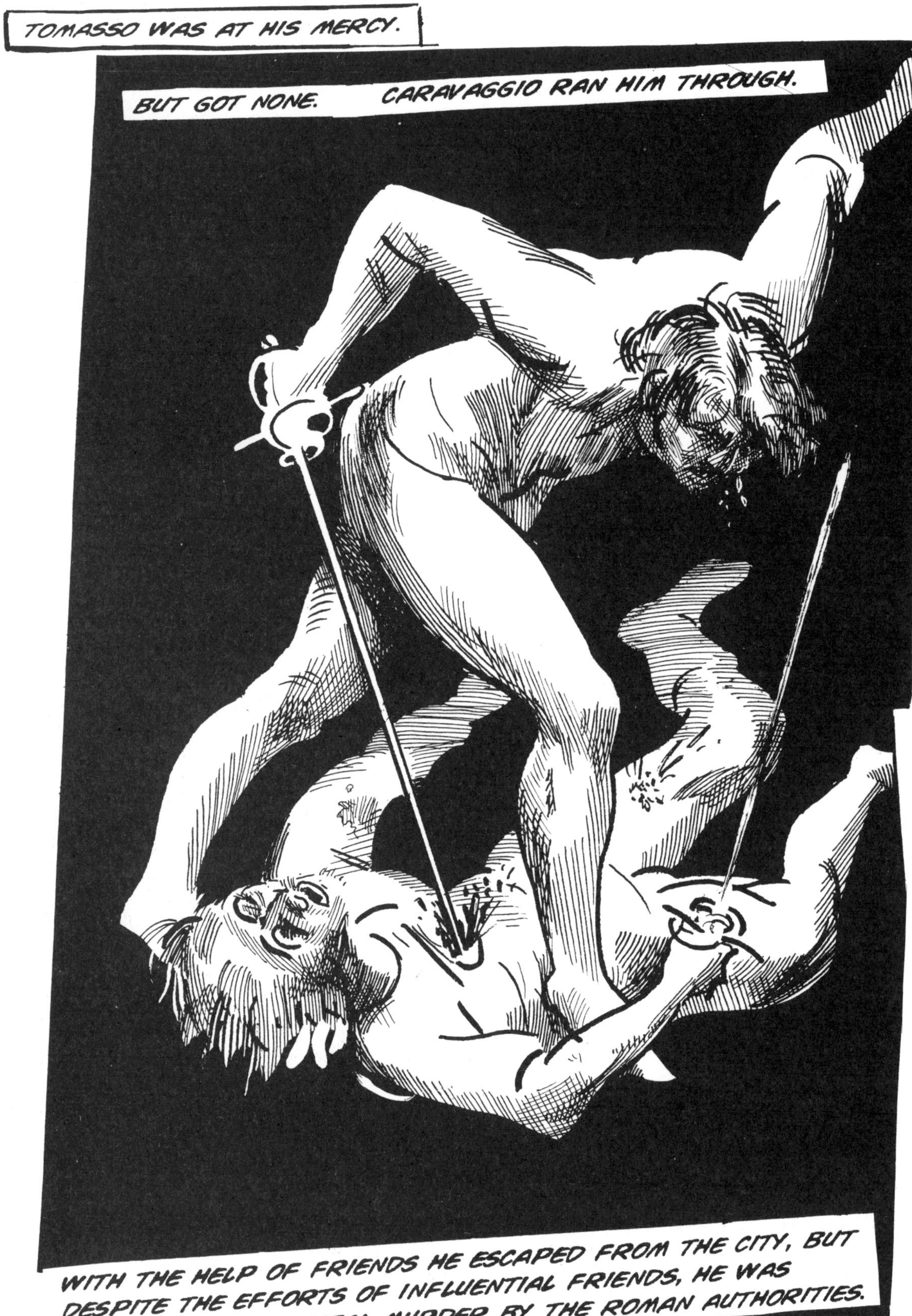
TOMASSO WAS AT HIS MERCY.
BUT GOT NONE.
CARAVAGGIO RAN HIM THROUGH.
WITH THE HELP OF FRIENDS HE ESCAPED FROM THE CITY, BUT DESPITE THE EFFORTS OF INFLUENTIAL FRIENDS, HE WAS CHARGED WITH CAPITAL MURDER BY THE ROMAN AUTHORITIES.

THE NEXT MORNING

MICHELI'S FINALLY DONE IT. HE *KILLED* TOMASSO IN A BRAWL LAST NIGHT.

CRAZY BASTARD. NOBODY CAN GET HIM OFF OF *THIS* RAP!

WELL, THE COP'S DON'T HAVE HIM YET. HE'S CUT UP REAL BAD, BUT HE BLEW TOWN AND NOBODY KNOWS *WHERE* HE IS.

HIGHLIGHTS OF CARAVAGGIO'S POLICE RECORD

1600

OCT 25   HE WAS INJURED IN A BRAWL.

NOV 19   ARRESTED FOR ASSAULT.

1601

FEB 7   CHARGED WITH ASSAULT ON A GUARD SERGEANT, PROCEEDINGS CANCELED.

1603

JUNE 11   IN PRISON FOR TWO WEEKS AT TOR DI NONA. RELEASED AT THE INTERVENTION OF THE FRENCH AMBASSADOR.

AUG 28   INVOLVED IN A LIBEL TRIAL.

1604

APRIL 4   ARRESTED FOR ASSAULT. HE THREW A PLATE OF FOOD IN A WAITER'S FACE.

OCT 20   ARRESTED FOR THROWING ROCKS IN THE STREET; RELEASED AFTER INTERCESSION OF HIS PATRON CARDINAL DEL MONTE.

NOV 18   JAILED FOR CURSING POLICE OFFICERS.

1605

FEB 15   SUES HIS LANDLADY FOR RETURN OF A RUG.

MAY 28   ARRESTED FOR CARRYING WEAPONS ILLEGALLY.

JULY 20   JAILED FOR HARASSING TWO WOMEN, BAILED OUT BY ARTIST FRIENDS.

JULY 29   IN JAIL FOR A WEEK FOR ATTACKING THE NOTARY MARIANO PASQUALONE IN A QUARREL OVER A WOMAN NAMED LENA.

SEPT 1   ARRESTED FOR THROWING ROCKS AT HIS FORMER LANDLADY'S WINDOW; HAS NO FIXED ADDRESS.

OCT 24   REPORTED RECOVERING FROM SWORD WOUNDS, WHICH HE CLAIMED WERE SELF-INFLICTED.

WHILE RECUPERATING IN HIDING HE WAS CONVICTED AND SENTENCED TO DEATH. USING HIS UNDERWORLD CONNECTIONS HE FLED TO NAPLES TO ESCAPE PAPAL AUTHORITY. THERE HE FOUND NEW PATRONS AND OPPORTUNITIES.
THE MOST PROMISING CHANCE WAS AN INVITATION TO WORK FOR THE MILITARY ORDER OF THE KNIGHTS OF SAINT JOHN ON THE FORTRESS ISLAND OF MALTA.

HE PAINTED AN OFFICIAL PORTRAIT OF GRAND MASTER ALOF DI WIGANCOURT, AND A MAGNIFICENT, HUGE BEHEADING OF JOHN THE BAPTIST *AS AN ALTARPIECE FOR THE CATHEDRAL OF VALLETTA. THE ORDER WAS SO PLEASED THAT CARAVAGGIO WAS INDUCTED INTO THE BROTHERHOOD.*

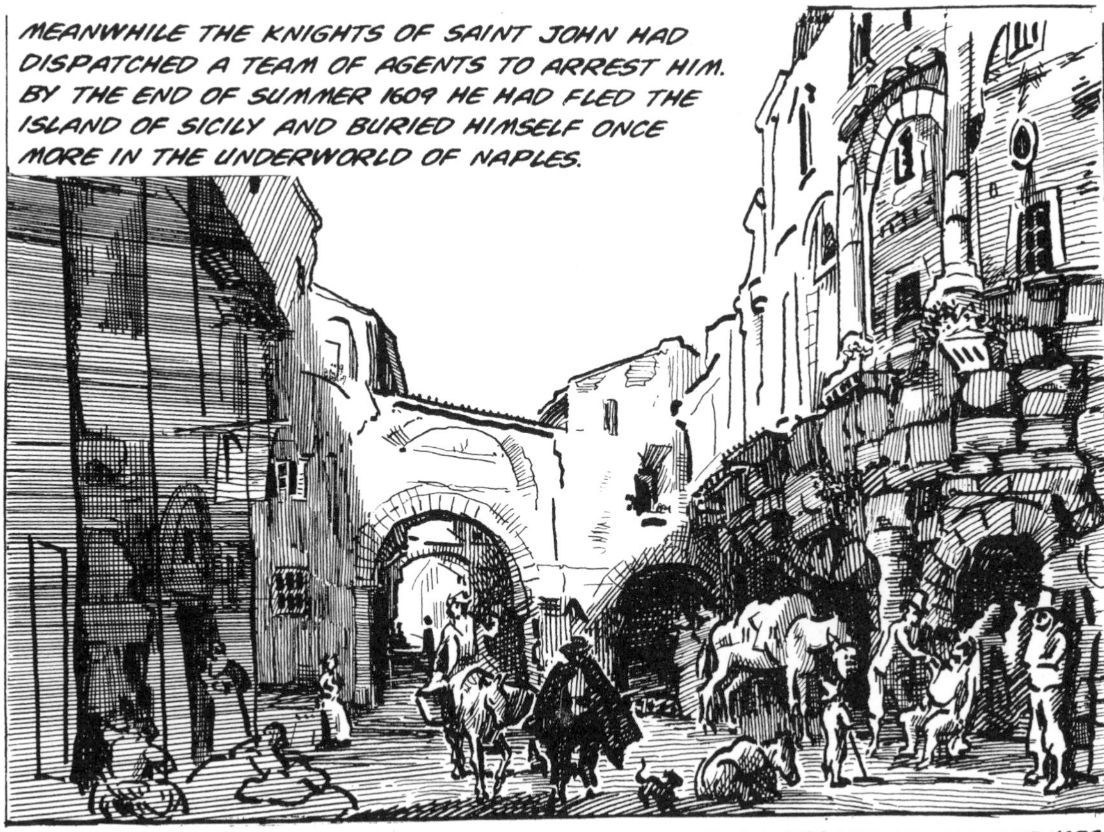
MEANWHILE THE KNIGHTS OF SAINT JOHN HAD DISPATCHED A TEAM OF AGENTS TO ARREST HIM. BY THE END OF SUMMER 1609 HE HAD FLED THE ISLAND OF SICILY AND BURIED HIMSELF ONCE MORE IN THE UNDERWORLD OF NAPLES.
BUT HE WAS NOT SUCCESSFUL IN ESCAPING HIS ENEMIES.

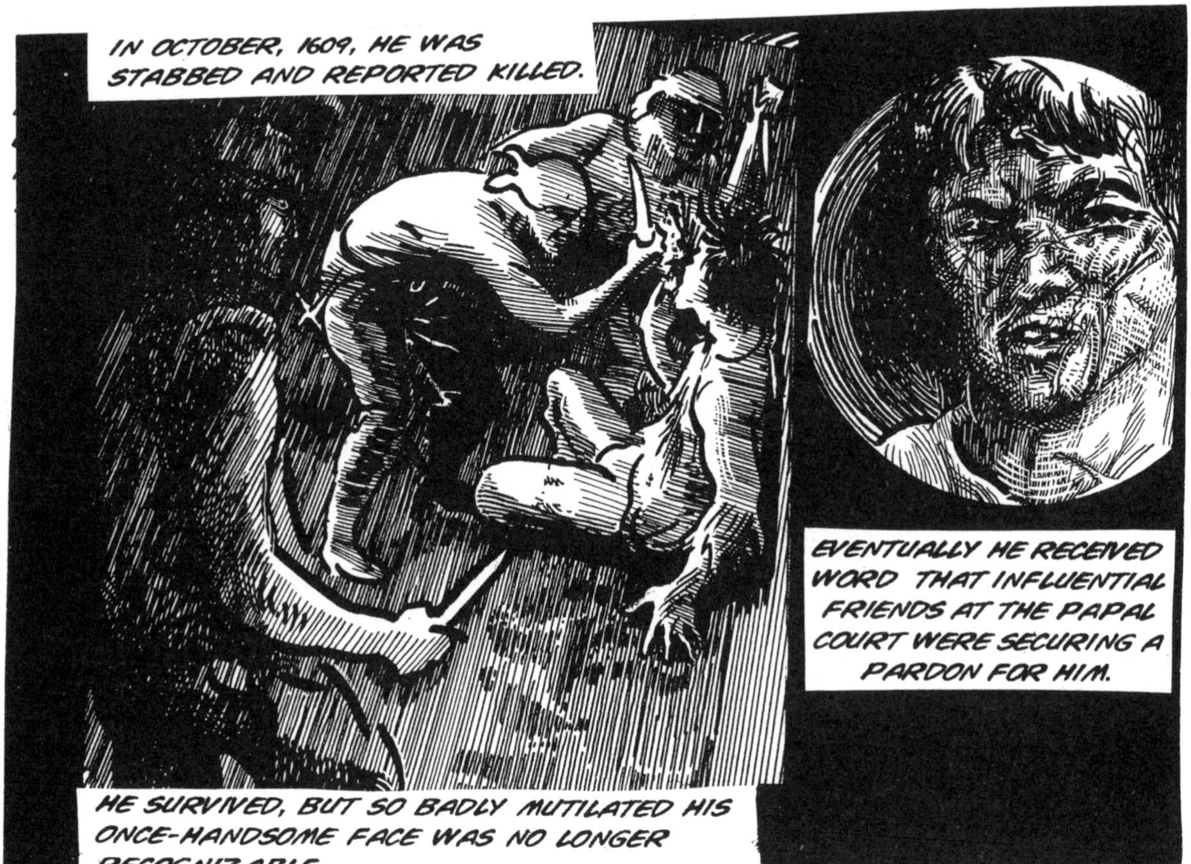
IN OCTOBER, 1609, HE WAS STABBED AND REPORTED KILLED.
HE SURVIVED, BUT SO BADLY MUTILATED HIS ONCE-HANDSOME FACE WAS NO LONGER RECOGNIZABLE.
EVENTUALLY HE RECEIVED WORD THAT INFLUENTIAL FRIENDS AT THE PAPAL COURT WERE SECURING A PARDON FOR HIM.

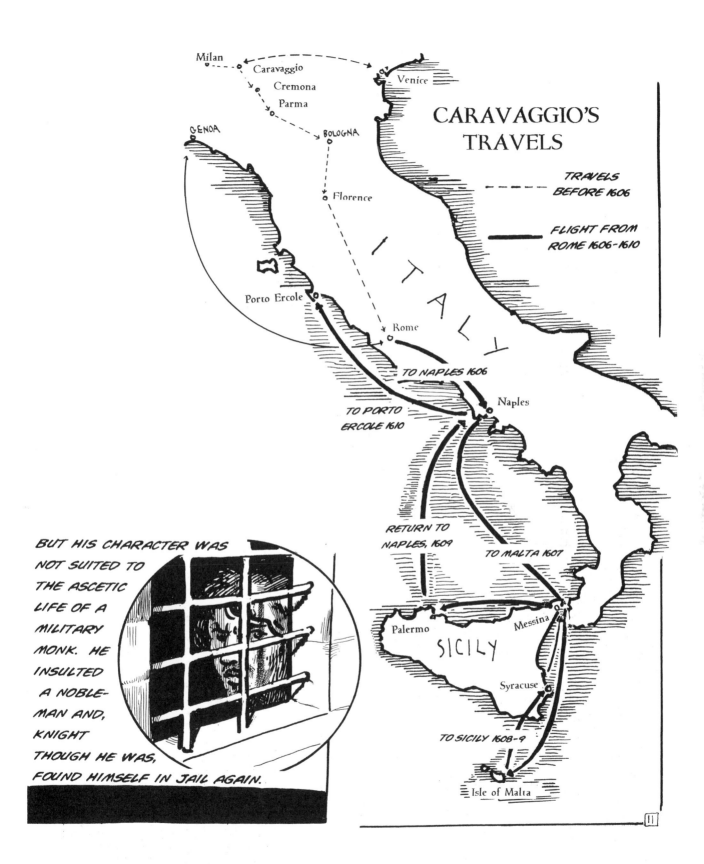

CARAVAGGIO'S TRAVELS

Milan
Caravaggio
Cremona
Parma
Venice
GENOA
BOLOGNA
Florence
Porto Ercole
Rome

I T A L Y

TRAVELS
BEFORE 1606

FLIGHT FROM
ROME 1606-1610

TO NAPLES 1606

TO PORTO
ERCOLE 1610

Naples

RETURN TO
NAPLES, 1609

TO MALTA 1607

Palermo
Messina

SICILY

Syracuse

TO SICILY 1608-9

Isle of Malta

BUT HIS CHARACTER WAS NOT SUITED TO THE ASCETIC LIFE OF A MILITARY MONK. HE INSULTED A NOBLE-MAN AND, KNIGHT THOUGH HE WAS, FOUND HIMSELF IN JAIL AGAIN.

11

IN OCTOBER 1608 HE ESCAPED FROM PRISON ON MALTA AND MADE HIS WAY TO SYRACUSE IN SICILY. THE KNIGHTS OF SAINT JOHN CONVICTED HIM, IN ABSENTIA, OF CRIMES AGAINST THE ORDER AND EXPELLED HIM FROM THEIR RANKS.

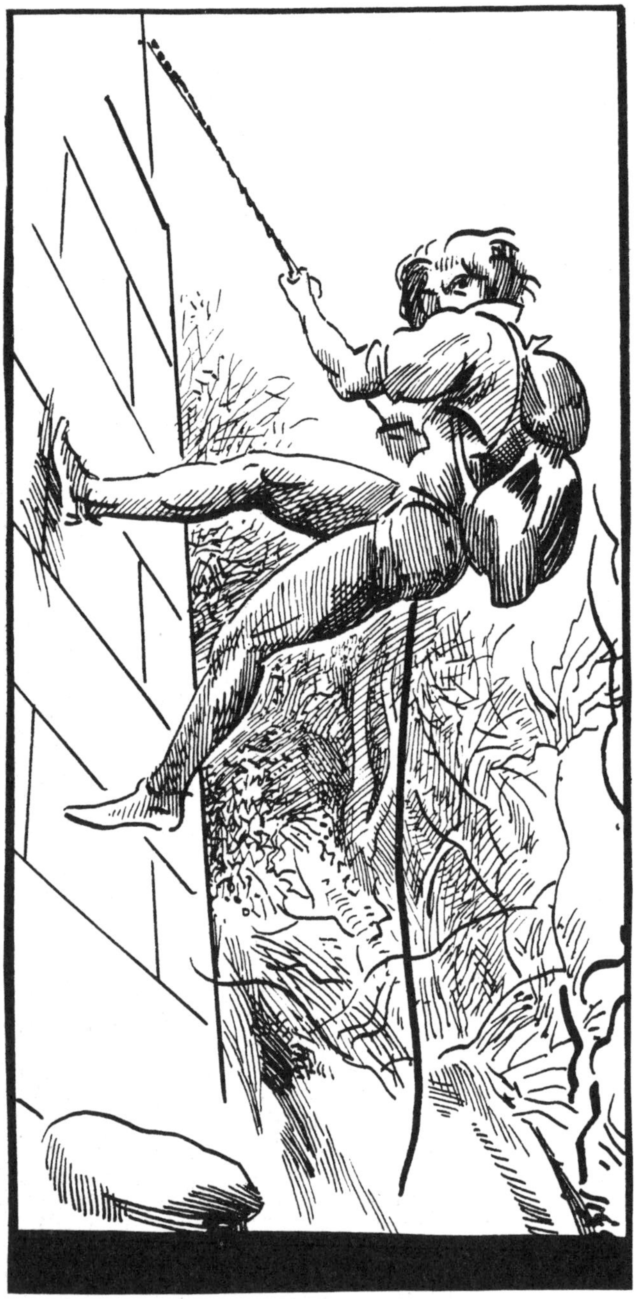

HE FOUND REFUGE WITH THE SICILIAN PAINTER MARIO MINNITI, HIS OLD ROOMMATE FROM ROME, WHO FOUND HIM COMMISSIONS, MODELS AND A PLACE TO WORK.

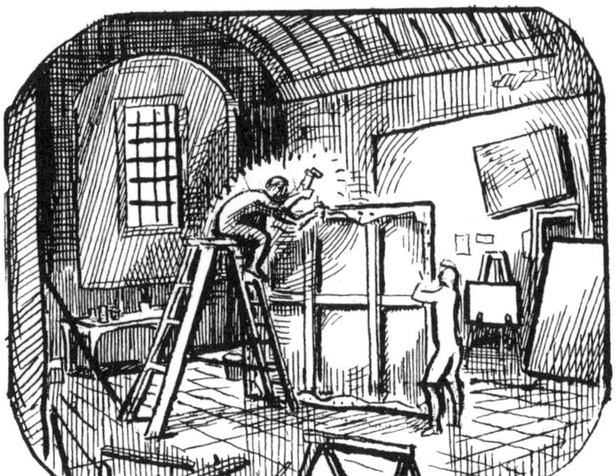

BUT HE WAS SO ANGRY AND VOLATILE THE SICILIANS THOUGHT HE WAS MAD. HE CONTINUED TO CLAIM THE TITLE OF KNIGHT OF ST JOHN.

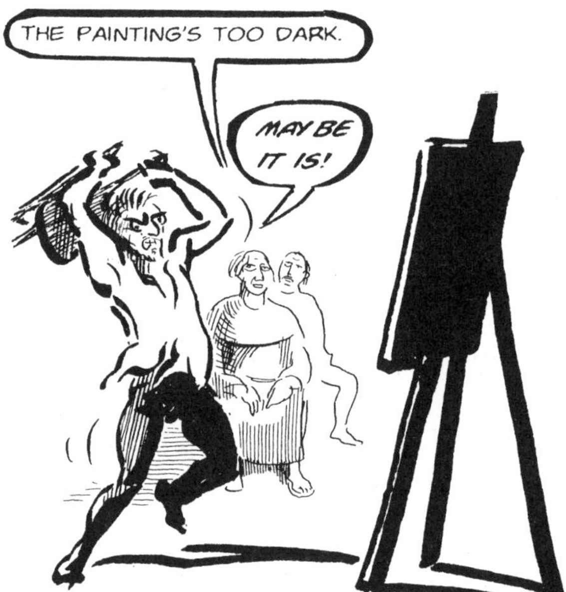
THE PAINTING'S TOO DARK.
MAYBE IT IS!

THOUGH HE WAS A FUGITIVE, CARAVAGGIO WAS ALSO A WORLD FAMOUS MASTER PAINTER, COMMANDING FANTASTIC PRICES FOR HIS PICTURES. THE NEW WORK FOR CHURCHES IN SYRACUSE, MESSINA AND PALERMO WAS SOME OF THE BEST OF HIS LIFE.

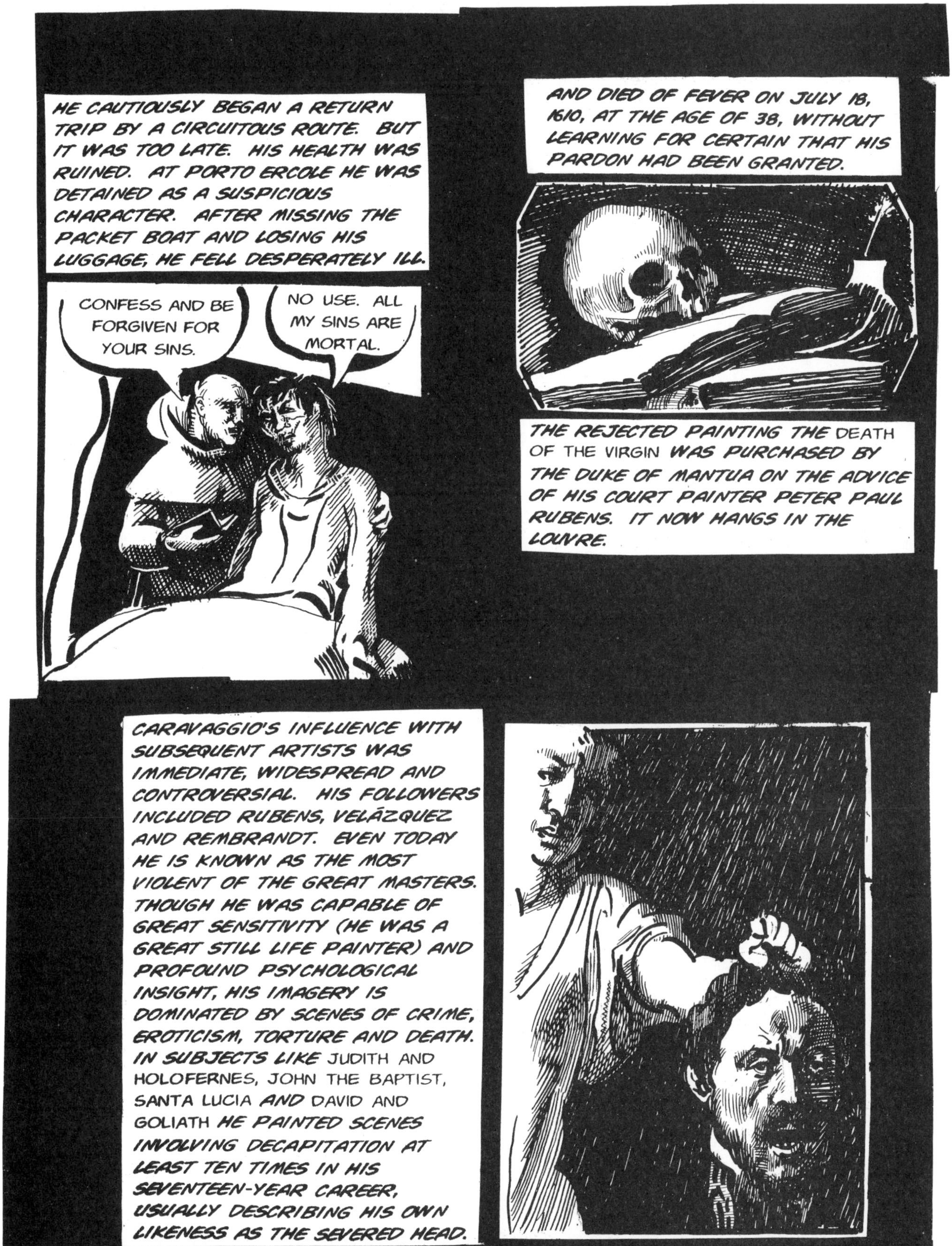
HE CAUTIOUSLY BEGAN A RETURN TRIP BY A CIRCUITOUS ROUTE. BUT IT WAS TOO LATE. HIS HEALTH WAS RUINED. AT PORTO ERCOLE HE WAS DETAINED AS A SUSPICIOUS CHARACTER. AFTER MISSING THE PACKET BOAT AND LOSING HIS LUGGAGE, HE FELL DESPERATELY ILL.
CONFESS AND BE FORGIVEN FOR YOUR SINS.
NO USE. ALL MY SINS ARE MORTAL.
AND DIED OF FEVER ON JULY 18, 1610, AT THE AGE OF 38, WITHOUT LEARNING FOR CERTAIN THAT HIS PARDON HAD BEEN GRANTED.
THE REJECTED PAINTING THE DEATH OF THE VIRGIN WAS PURCHASED BY THE DUKE OF MANTUA ON THE ADVICE OF HIS COURT PAINTER PETER PAUL RUBENS. IT NOW HANGS IN THE LOUVRE.
CARAVAGGIO'S INFLUENCE WITH SUBSEQUENT ARTISTS WAS IMMEDIATE, WIDESPREAD AND CONTROVERSIAL. HIS FOLLOWERS INCLUDED RUBENS, VELÁZQUEZ AND REMBRANDT. EVEN TODAY HE IS KNOWN AS THE MOST VIOLENT OF THE GREAT MASTERS. THOUGH HE WAS CAPABLE OF GREAT SENSITIVITY (HE WAS A GREAT STILL LIFE PAINTER) AND PROFOUND PSYCHOLOGICAL INSIGHT, HIS IMAGERY IS DOMINATED BY SCENES OF CRIME, EROTICISM, TORTURE AND DEATH. IN SUBJECTS LIKE JUDITH AND HOLOFERNES, JOHN THE BAPTIST, SANTA LUCIA AND DAVID AND GOLIATH HE PAINTED SCENES INVOLVING DECAPITATION AT LEAST TEN TIMES IN HIS SEVENTEEN-YEAR CAREER, USUALLY DESCRIBING HIS OWN LIKENESS AS THE SEVERED HEAD.

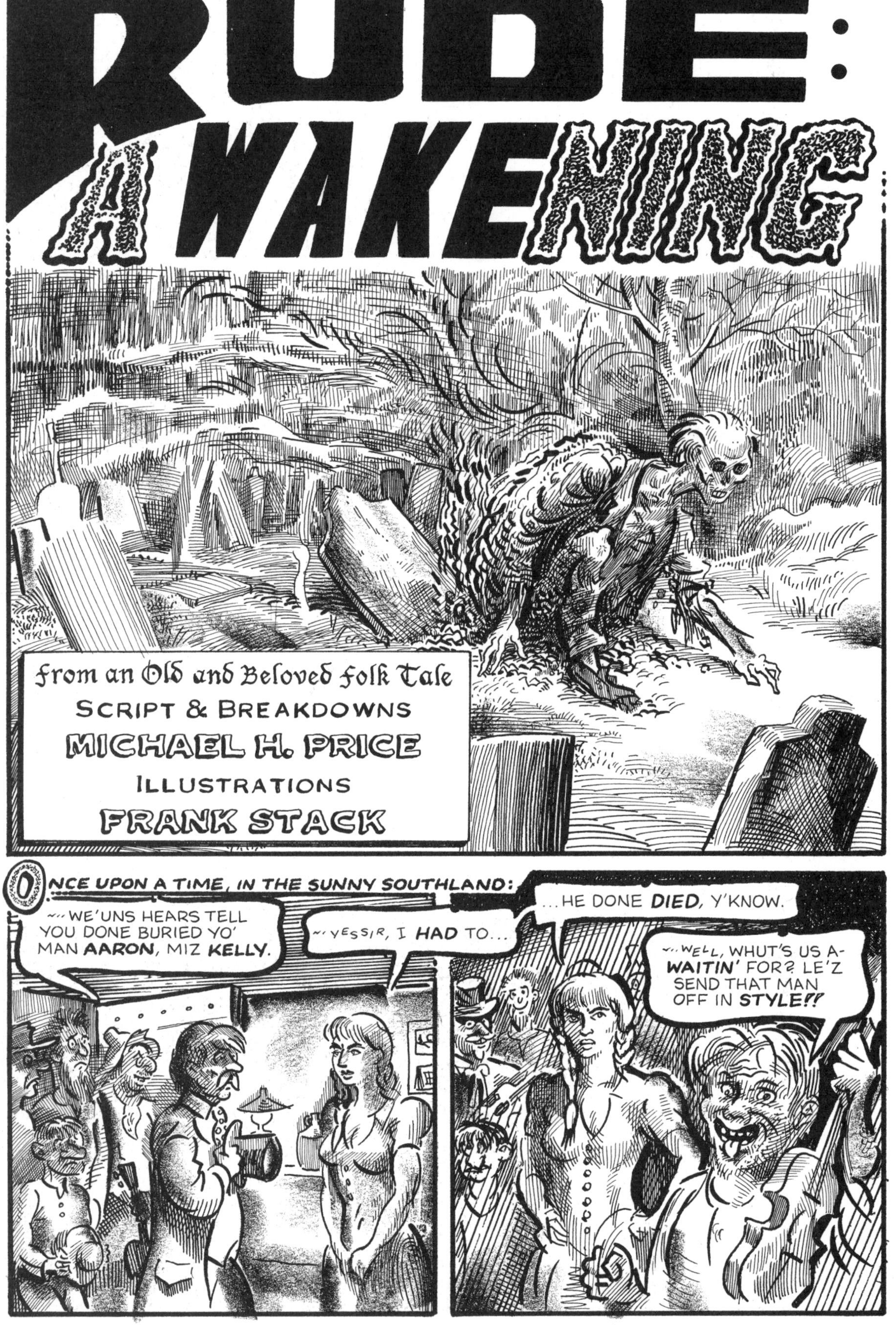
RUDE: A WAKENING
From an Old and Beloved Folk Tale
SCRIPT & BREAKDOWNS
MICHAEL H. PRICE
ILLUSTRATIONS
FRANK STACK
ONCE UPON A TIME, IN THE SUNNY SOUTHLAND:
~... WE'UNS HEARS TELL YOU DONE BURIED YO' MAN AARON, MIZ KELLY.
~... YESSIR, I HAD TO...
... HE DONE DIED, Y'KNOW.
~... WELL, WHUT'S US A-WAITIN' FOR? LE'Z SEND THAT MAN OFF IN STYLE!!

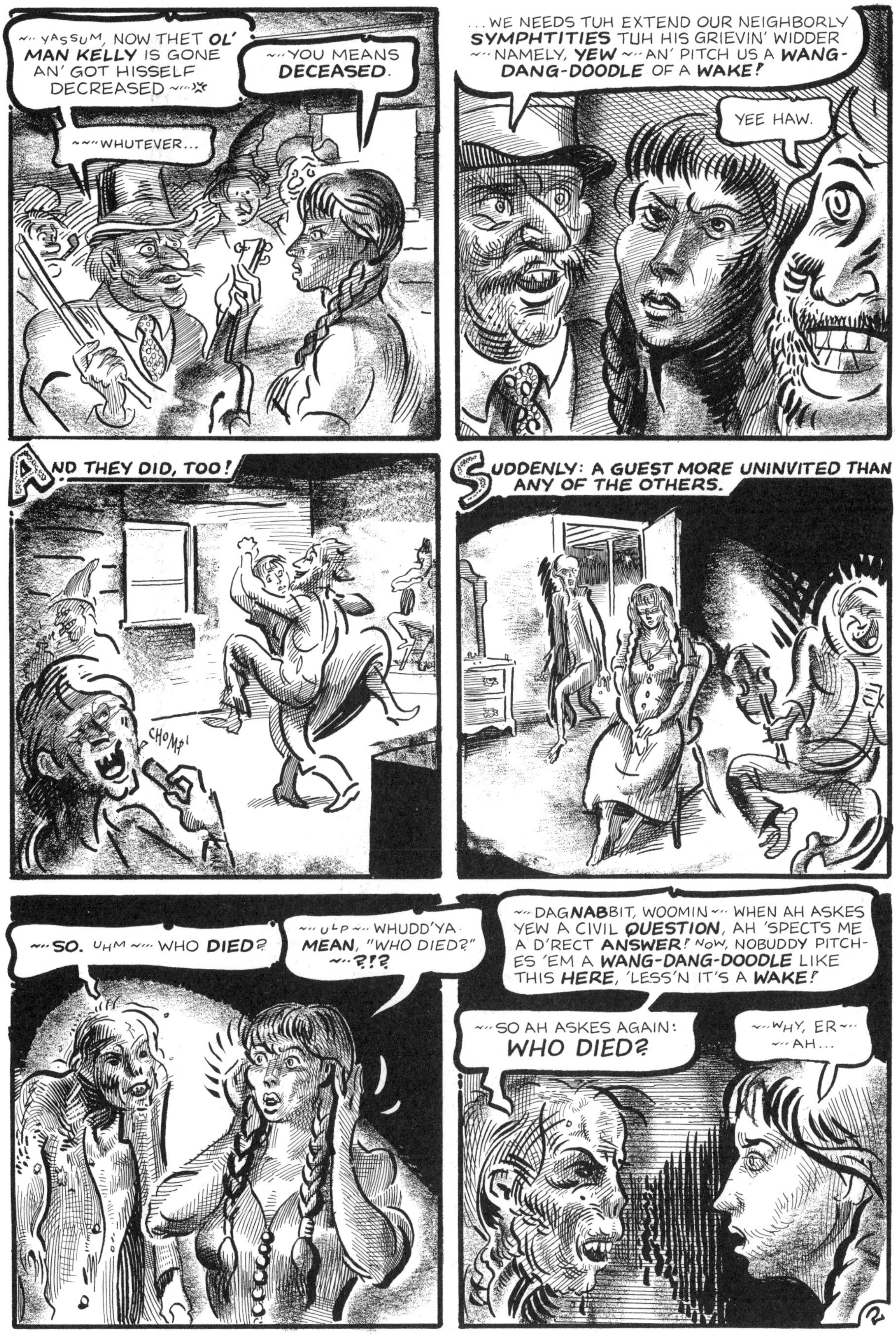
~·· YASSUM, NOW THET OL' MAN KELLY IS GONE AN' GOT HISSELF DECREASED ~··
~·· YOU MEANS DECEASED.
~~·· WHUTEVER...
. . . WE NEEDS TUH EXTEND OUR NEIGHBORLY SYMPHTITIES TUH HIS GRIEVIN' WIDDER ~·· NAMELY, YEW ~·· AN' PITCH US A WANG-DANG-DOODLE OF A WAKE!
YEE HAW.
AND THEY DID, TOO!
CHOMP!
SUDDENLY: A GUEST MORE UNINVITED THAN ANY OF THE OTHERS.
~·· SO. UHM ~·· WHO DIED?
~·· ULP ~·· WHUDD'YA MEAN, "WHO DIED?" ~·· ?!?
~·· DAGNABBIT, WOOMIN ~·· WHEN AH ASKES YEW A CIVIL QUESTION, AH 'SPECTS ME A D'RECT ANSWER! NOW, NOBUDDY PITCHES 'EM A WANG-DANG-DOODLE LIKE THIS HERE, 'LESS'N IT'S A WAKE!
~·· SO AH ASKES AGAIN: WHO DIED?
~·· WHY, ER ~·· ~·· AH...
2

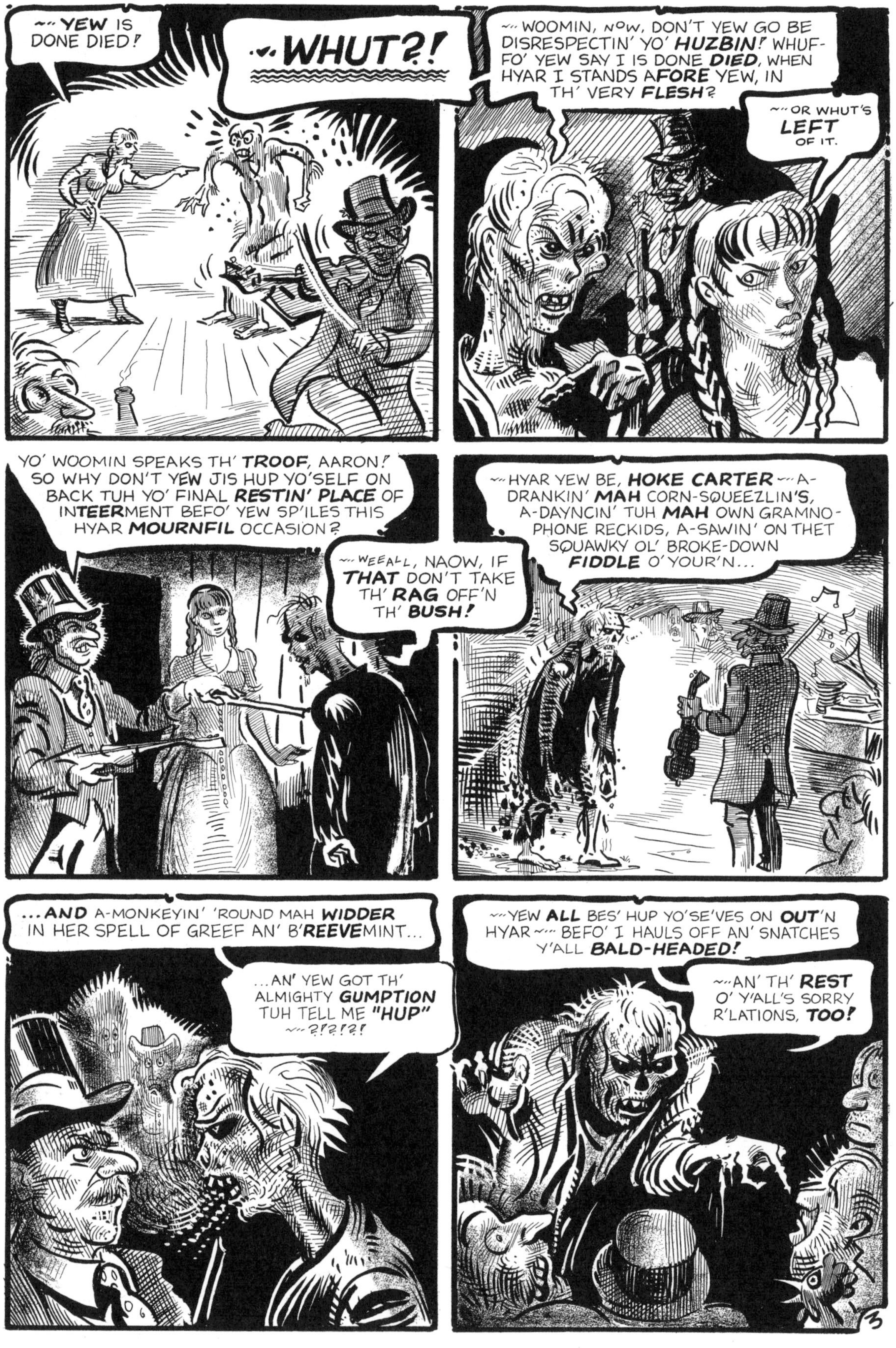
YEW IS DONE DIED!
WHUT?!
WOOMIN, NOW, DON'T YEW GO BE DISRESPECTIN' YO' HUZBIN! WHUFF-FO' YEW SAY I IS DONE DIED, WHEN HYAR I STANDS AFORE YEW, IN TH' VERY FLESH?
OR WHUT'S LEFT OF IT.
YO' WOOMIN SPEAKS TH' TROOF, AARON! SO WHY DON'T YEW JIS HUP YO'SELF ON BACK TUH YO' FINAL RESTIN' PLACE OF INTEERMENT BEFO' YEW SP'ILES THIS HYAR MOURNFIL OCCASION?
WEEALL, NAOW, IF THAT DON'T TAKE TH' RAG OFF'N TH' BUSH!
HYAR YEW BE, HOKE CARTER — A-DRANKIN' MAH CORN-SQUEEZLIN'S, A-DAYNCIN' TUH MAH OWN GRAMNO-PHONE RECKIDS, A-SAWIN' ON THET SQUAWKY OL' BROKE-DOWN FIDDLE O'YOUR'N...
...AND A-MONKEYIN' 'ROUND MAH WIDDER IN HER SPELL OF GREEF AN' B'REEVEMINT...
...AN' YEW GOT TH' ALMIGHTY GUMPTION TUH TELL ME "HUP" ?!?!?!
YEW ALL BES' HUP YO'SE'VES ON OUT'N HYAR — BEFO' I HAULS OFF AN' SNATCHES Y'ALL BALD-HEADED!
AN' TH' REST O' Y'ALL'S SORRY R'LATIONS, TOO!

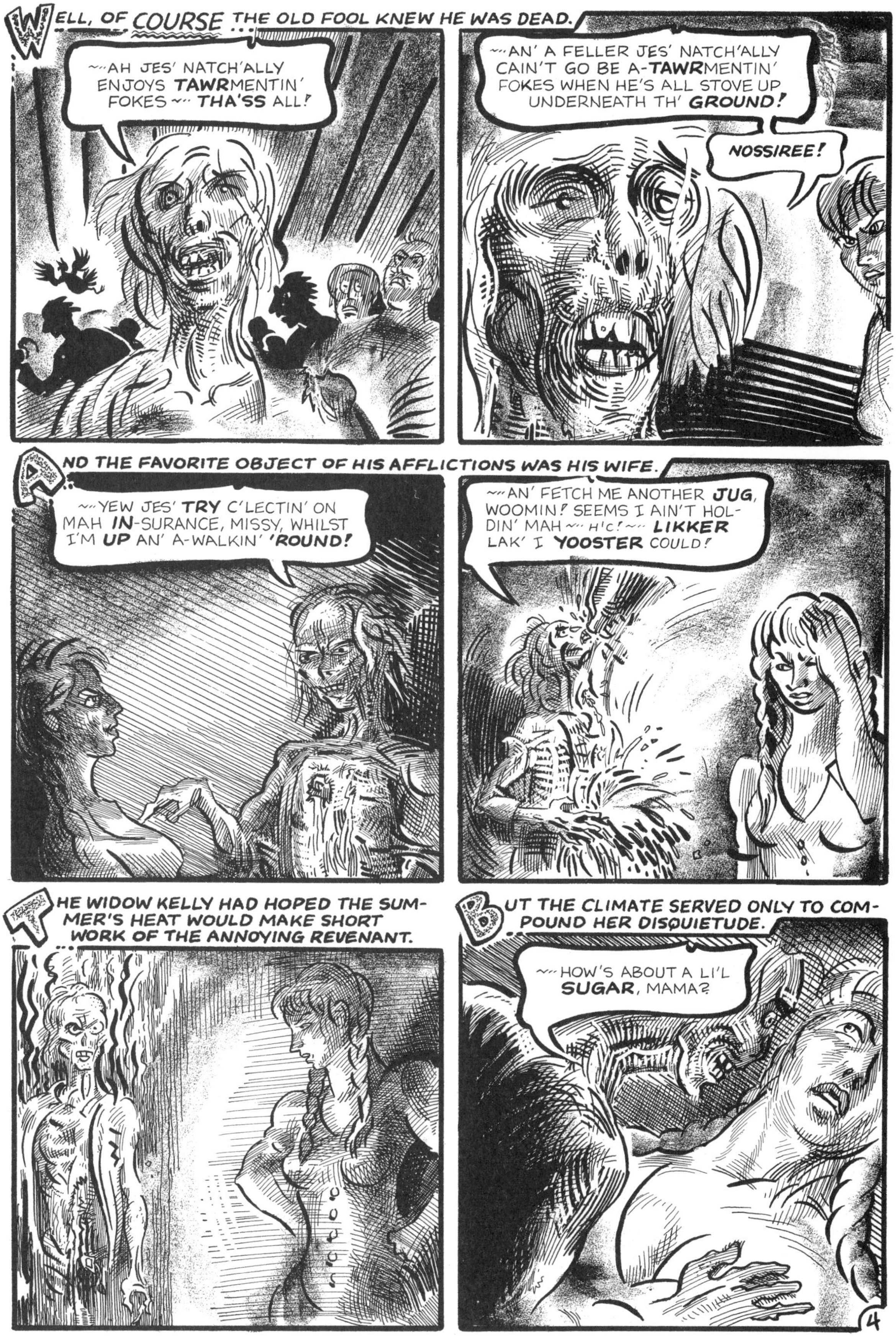
WELL, OF COURSE THE OLD FOOL KNEW HE WAS DEAD.
~...AH JES' NATCH'ALLY ENJOYS TAWRMENTIN' FOKES ~... THA'SS ALL!
~...AN' A FELLER JES' NATCH'ALLY CAIN'T GO BE A-TAWRMENTIN' FOKES WHEN HE'S ALL STOVE UP UNDERNEATH TH' GROUND!
NOSSIREE!
AND THE FAVORITE OBJECT OF HIS AFFLICTIONS WAS HIS WIFE.
~...YEW JES' TRY C'LECTIN' ON MAH IN-SURANCE, MISSY, WHILST I'M UP AN' A-WALKIN' 'ROUND!
~...AN' FETCH ME ANOTHER JUG, WOOMIN! SEEMS I AIN'T HOL-DIN' MAH ~... HIC! ~... LIKKER LAK' I YOOSTER COULD!
THE WIDOW KELLY HAD HOPED THE SUM-MER'S HEAT WOULD MAKE SHORT WORK OF THE ANNOYING REVENANT.
BUT THE CLIMATE SERVED ONLY TO COM-POUND HER DISQUIETUDE.
~...HOW'S ABOUT A LI'L SUGAR, MAMA?
4

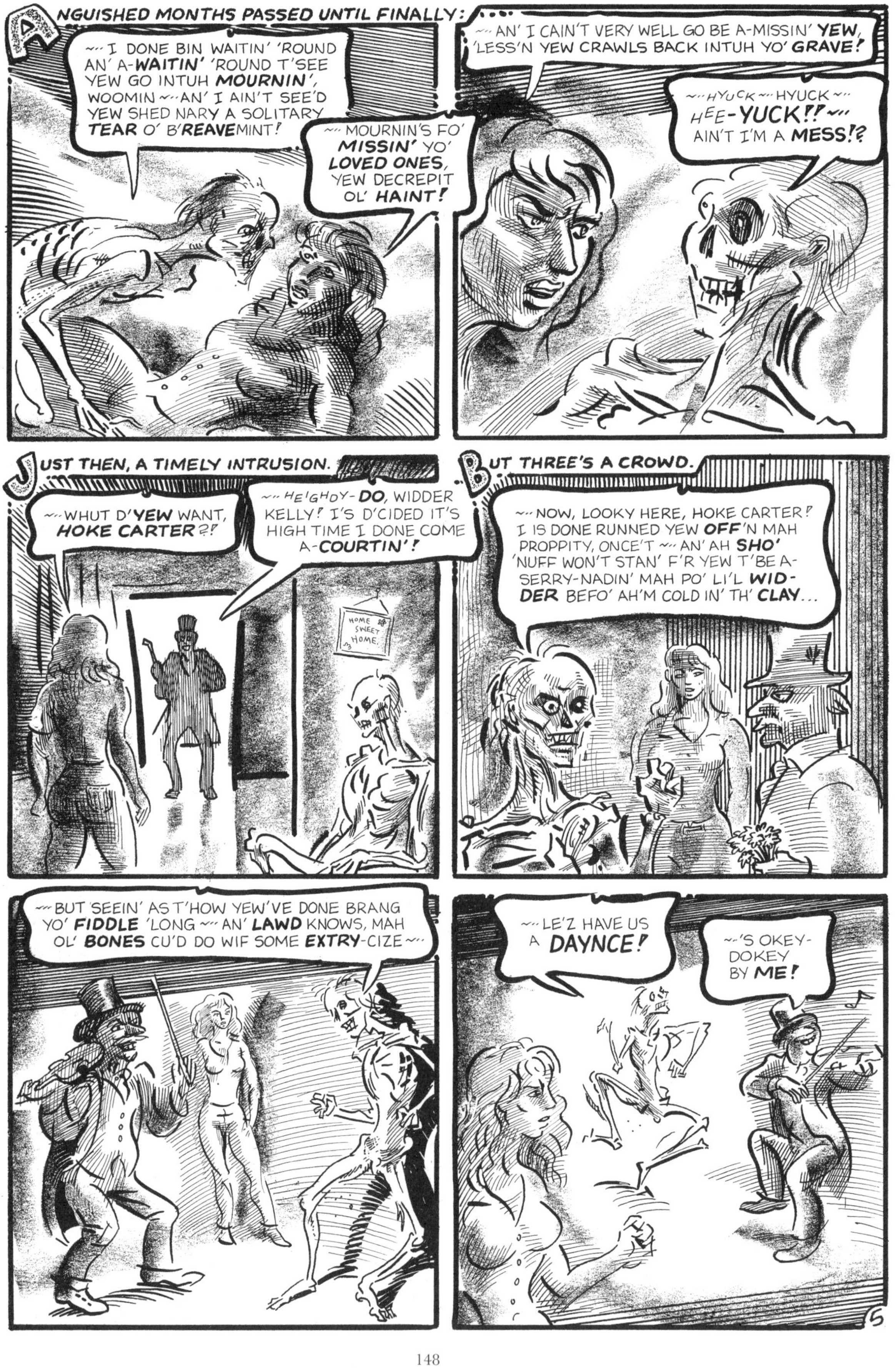
ANGUISHED MONTHS PASSED UNTIL FINALLY:
~··· I DONE BIN WAITIN' 'ROUND AN' A-WAITIN' 'ROUND T'SEE YEW GO INTUH MOURNIN', WOOMIN ~··· AN' I AIN'T SEE'D YEW SHED NARY A SOLITARY TEAR O' B'REAVEMINT!
~··· MOURNIN'S FO' MISSIN' YO' LOVED ONES, YEW DECREPIT OL' HAINT!
····· ~··· AN' I CAIN'T VERY WELL GO BE A-MISSIN' YEW, 'LESS'N YEW CRAWLS BACK INTUH YO' GRAVE!
~··· HYUCK ~··· HYUCK ~··· HEE-YUCK!?! ~··· AIN'T I'M A MESS!?
JUST THEN, A TIMELY INTRUSION.
~··· WHUT D'YEW WANT, HOKE CARTER?!?
~··· HEIGHDY-DO, WIDDER KELLY! I'S D'CIDED IT'S HIGH TIME I DONE COME A-COURTIN'!
HOME SWEET HOME
BUT THREE'S A CROWD.
~··· NOW, LOOKY HERE, HOKE CARTER! I IS DONE RUNNED YEW OFF'N MAH PROPPITY, ONCE'T ~··· AN' AH SHO' 'NUFF WON'T STAN' F'R YEW T'BE A-SERRY-NADIN' MAH PO' LI'L WIDDER BEFO' AH'M COLD IN' TH' CLAY...
~··· BUT 'SEEIN' AS T'HOW YEW'VE DONE BRANG YO' FIDDLE 'LONG ~··· AN' LAWD KNOWS, MAH OL' BONES CU'D DO WIF SOME EXTRY-CIZE ~···
~··· LE'Z HAVE US A DAYNCE!
~··· 'S OKEY-DOKEY BY ME!
5

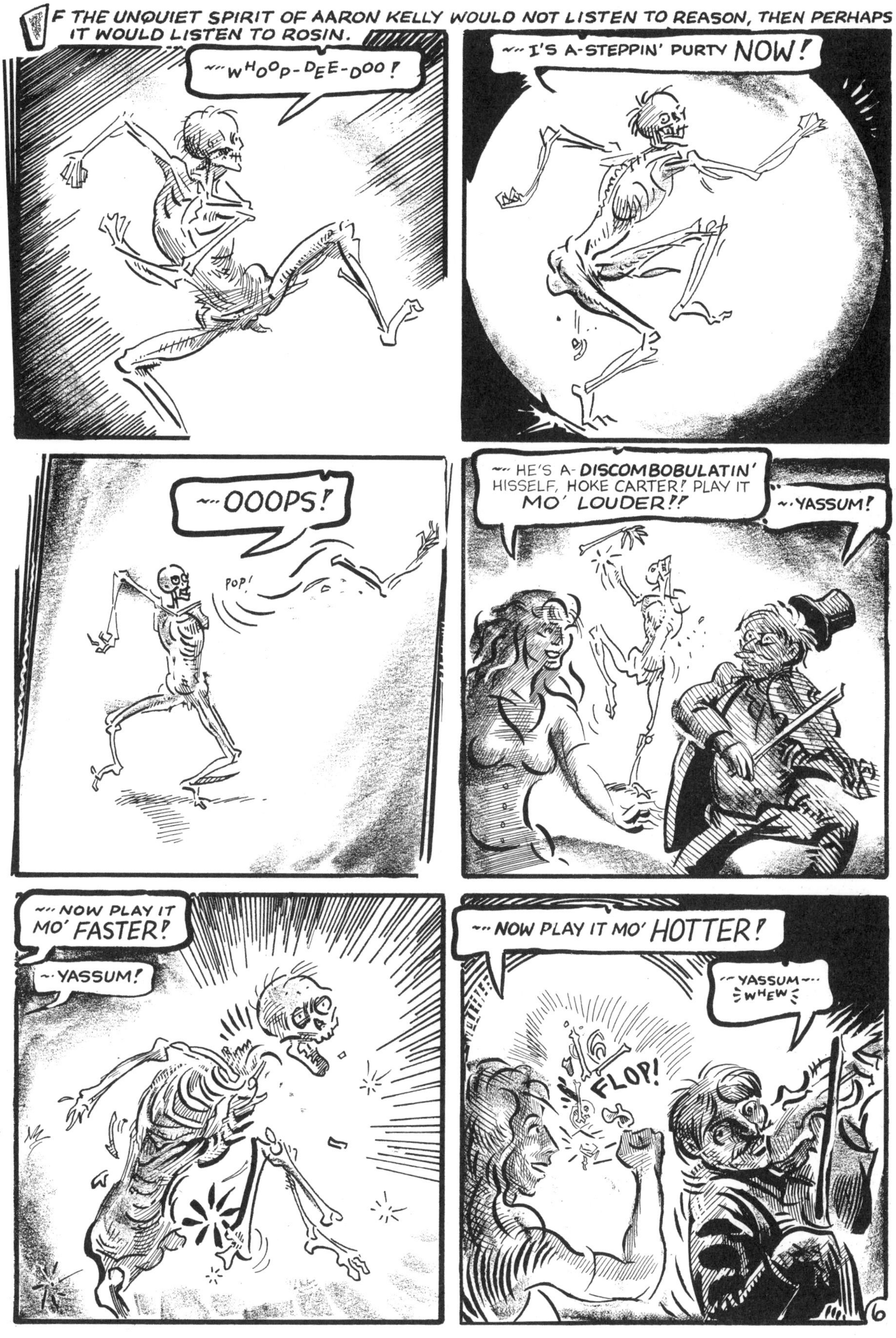
IF THE UNQUIET SPIRIT OF AARON KELLY WOULD NOT LISTEN TO REASON, THEN PERHAPS IT WOULD LISTEN TO ROSIN.
~WHOOP-DEE-DOO!
~I'S A-STEPPIN' PURTY NOW!
~OOOPS!
POP!
~HE'S A-DISCOMBOBULATIN' HISSELF, HOKE CARTER! PLAY IT MO' LOUDER!!
~YASSUM!
~NOW PLAY IT MO' FASTER!
~YASSUM!
~NOW PLAY IT MO' HOTTER!
~YASSUM~ WHEW
FLOP!
6

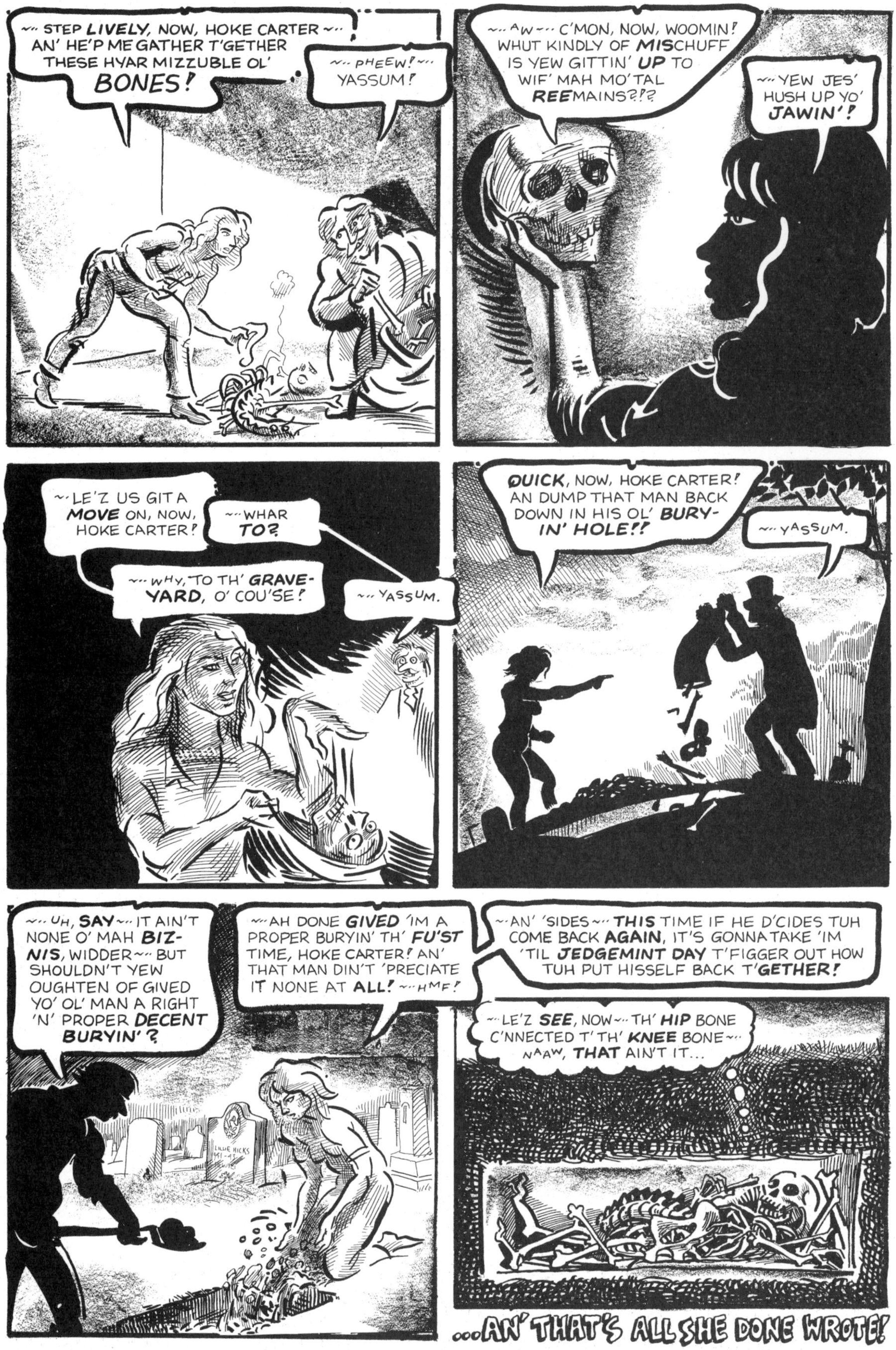
~.. STEP LIVELY, NOW, HOKE CARTER ~.. AN' HE'P ME GATHER T'GETHER THESE HYAR MIZZUBLE OL' BONES!
~.. PHEEW! ~.. YASSUM!
~.. AW ~.. C'MON, NOW, WOOMIN! WHUT KINDLY OF MISCHUFF IS YEW GITTIN' UP TO WIF' MAH MO'TAL REEMAINS?!?
~.. YEW JES' HUSH UP YO' JAWIN'!
~.. LE'Z US GIT A MOVE ON, NOW, HOKE CARTER!
~.. WHAR TO?
~.. WHY, TO TH' GRAVE-YARD, O' COU'SE!
~.. YASSUM.
QUICK, NOW, HOKE CARTER! AN DUMP THAT MAN BACK DOWN IN HIS OL' BURY-IN' HOLE!!
~.. YASSUM.
~.. UH, SAY ~.. IT AIN'T NONE O' MAH BIZ-NIS, WIDDER ~.. BUT SHOULDN'T YEW OUGHTEN OF GIVED YO' OL' MAN A RIGHT 'N' PROPER DECENT BURYIN'?
~.. AH DONE GIVED 'IM A PROPER BURYIN' TH' FU'ST TIME, HOKE CARTER! AN' THAT MAN DIN'T 'PRECIATE IT NONE AT ALL! ~.. HMF!
~.. AN' 'SIDES ~.. THIS TIME IF HE D'CIDES TUH COME BACK AGAIN, IT'S GONNA TAKE 'IM 'TIL JEDGEMINT DAY T'FIGGER OUT HOW TUH PUT HISSELF BACK T'GETHER!
~.. LE'Z SEE, NOW ~.. TH' HIP BONE C'NNECTED T' TH' KNEE BONE ~.. NAAW, THAT AIN'T IT...
LILLIE HICKS
...AN' THAT'S ALL SHE DONE WROTE!

Adventurers
and
Amazons

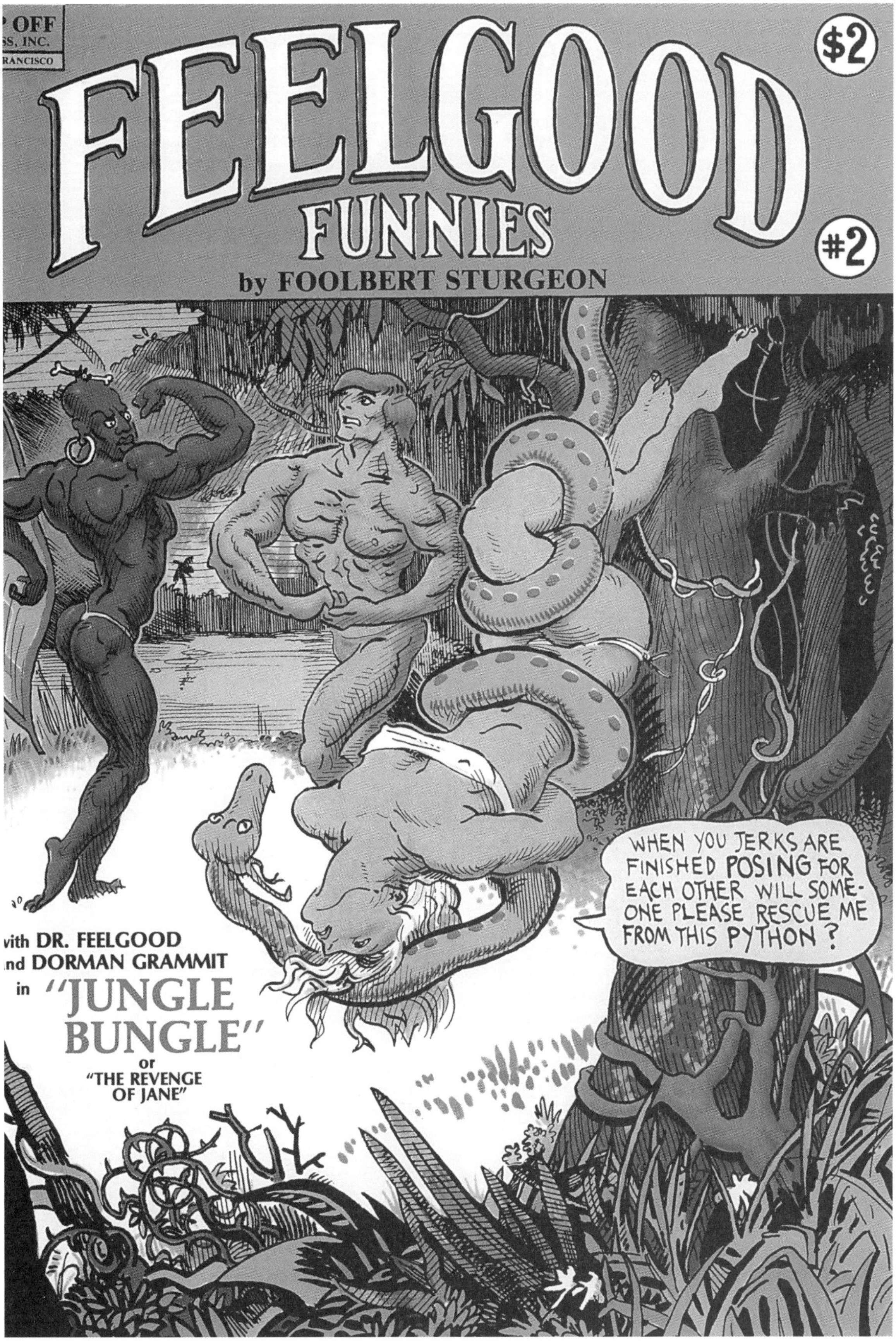

P OFF
SS, INC.
RANCISCO
$2
FEELGOOD
FUNNIES
#2
by FOOLBERT STURGEON
WHEN YOU JERKS ARE FINISHED POSING FOR EACH OTHER WILL SOME-ONE PLEASE RESCUE ME FROM THIS PYTHON?
with DR. FEELGOOD
and DORMAN GRAMMIT
in "JUNGLE BUNGLE"
or
"THE REVENGE OF JANE"

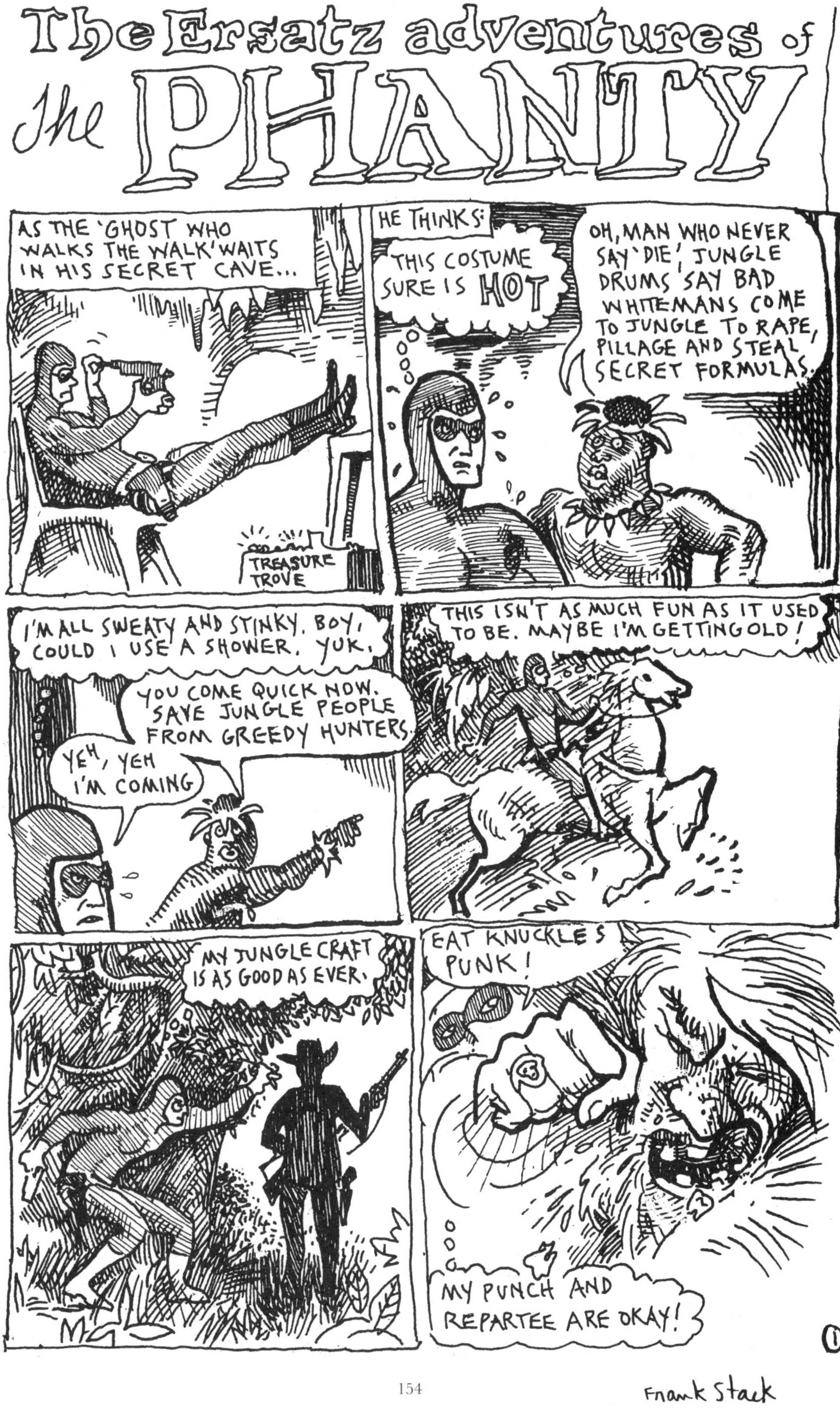
The Ersatz adventures of
The PHANTY
AS THE 'GHOST WHO WALKS THE WALK' WAITS IN HIS SECRET CAVE...
TREASURE TROVE
HE THINKS:
THIS COSTUME SURE IS HOT
OH, MAN WHO NEVER SAY 'DIE', JUNGLE DRUMS SAY BAD WHITEMANS COME TO JUNGLE TO RAPE, PILLAGE AND STEAL SECRET FORMULAS.
I'M ALL SWEATY AND STINKY. BOY, COULD I USE A SHOWER. YUK.
YOU COME QUICK NOW. SAVE JUNGLE PEOPLE FROM GREEDY HUNTERS.
YEH, YEH I'M COMING
THIS ISN'T AS MUCH FUN AS IT USED TO BE. MAYBE I'M GETTING OLD!
MY JUNGLE CRAFT IS AS GOOD AS EVER.
EAT KNUCKLES PUNK!
MY PUNCH AND REPARTEE ARE OKAY!
1
Frank Stack

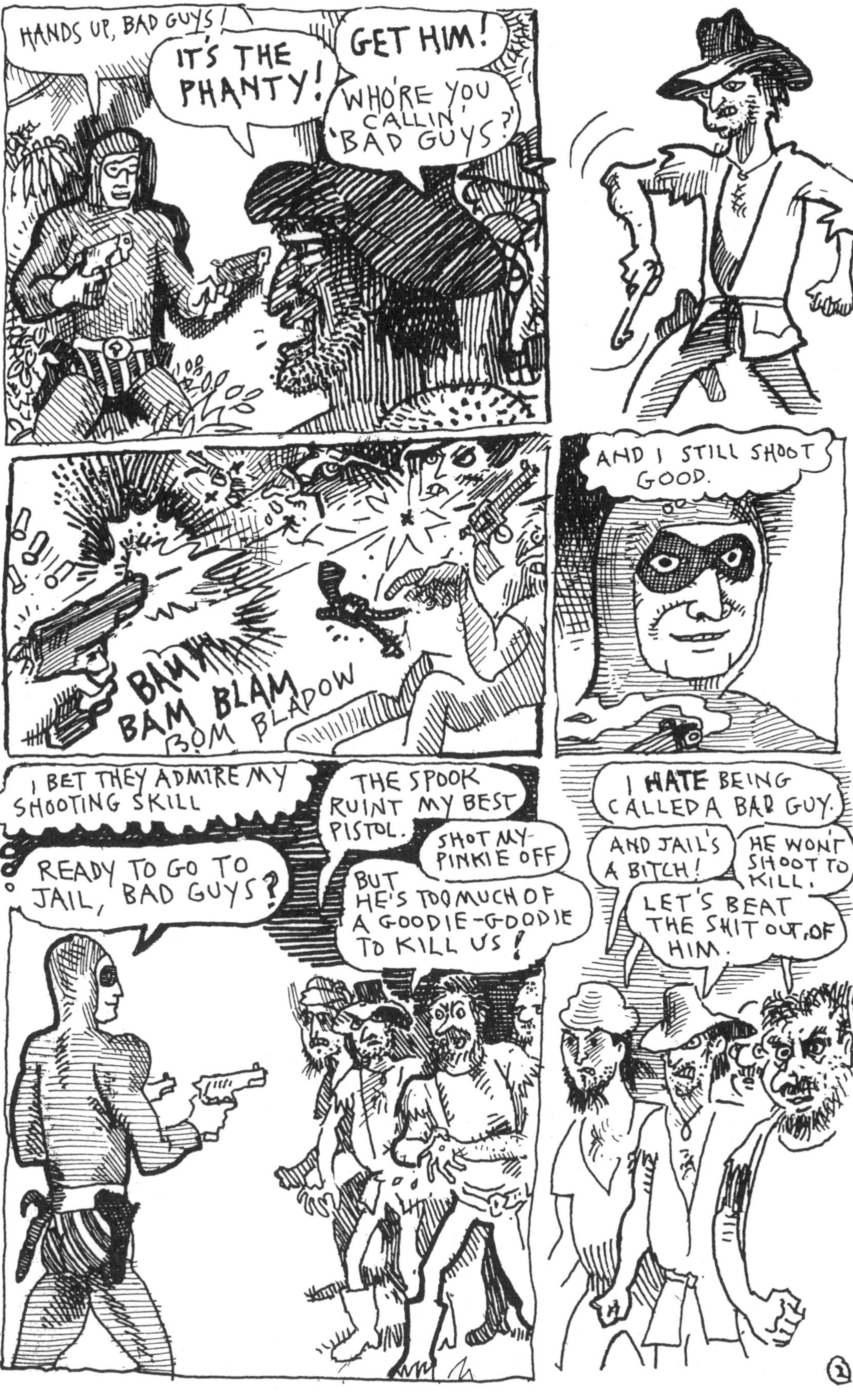
HANDS UP, BAD GUYS!
IT'S THE PHANTY!
GET HIM!
WHO'RE YOU CALLIN' 'BAD GUYS'?
BAM BAM BLAM BOM BLADOW
AND I STILL SHOOT GOOD.
I BET THEY ADMIRE MY SHOOTING SKILL
READY TO GO TO JAIL, BAD GUYS?
THE SPOOK RUINT MY BEST PISTOL.
SHOT MY PINKIE OFF
BUT HE'S TOO MUCH OF A GOODIE-GOODIE TO KILL US!
I HATE BEING CALLED A BAD GUY.
AND JAIL'S A BITCH!
HE WON'T SHOOT TO KILL.
LET'S BEAT THE SHIT OUT OF HIM.
2

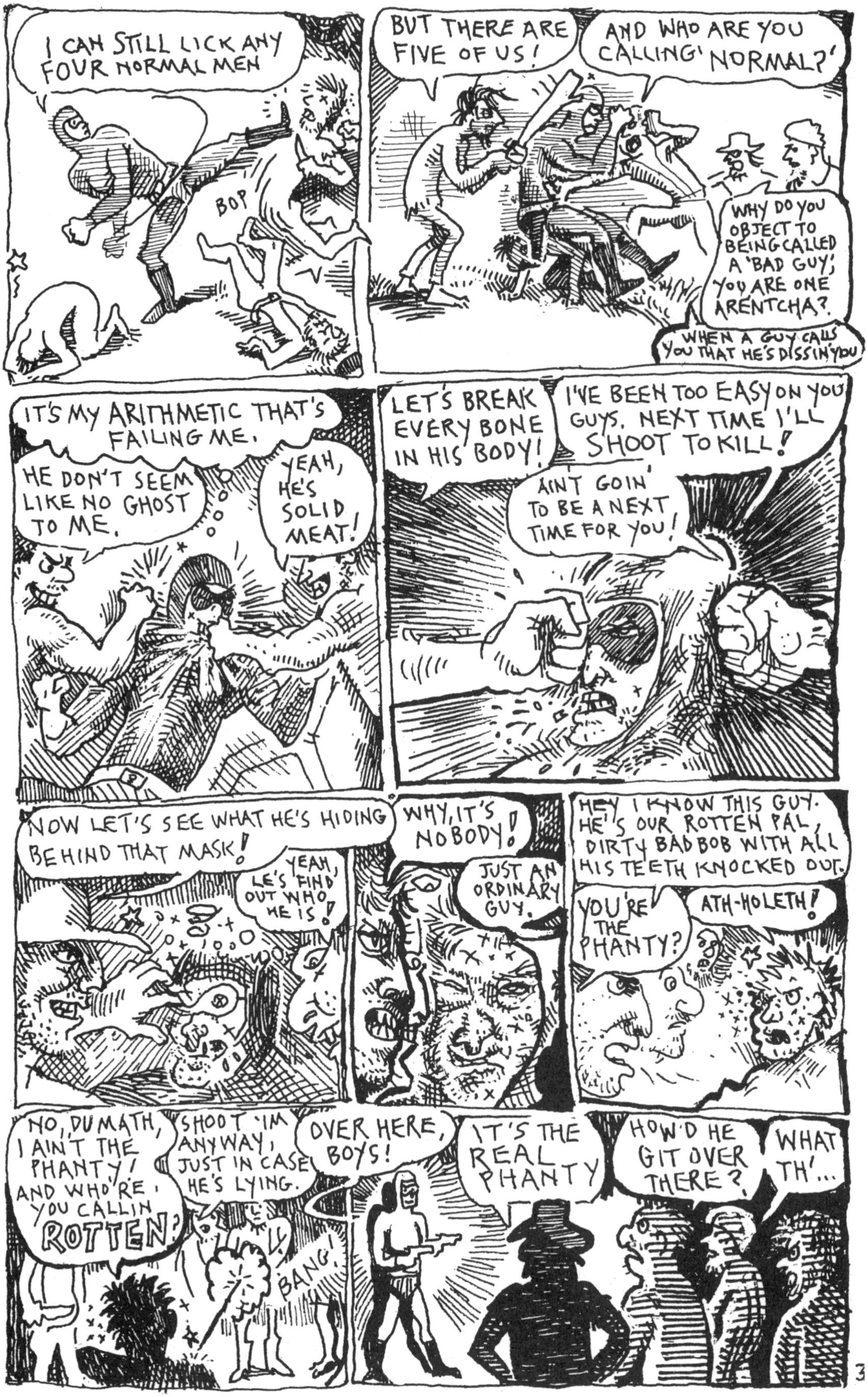
I CAN STILL LICK ANY FOUR NORMAL MEN
BOP
BUT THERE ARE FIVE OF US!
AND WHO ARE YOU CALLING 'NORMAL?'
WHY DO YOU OBJECT TO BEING CALLED A 'BAD GUY,' YOU ARE ONE ARENTCHA?
WHEN A GUY CALLS YOU THAT HE'S DISSIN'YOU
IT'S MY ARITHMETIC THAT'S FAILING ME.
HE DON'T SEEM LIKE NO GHOST TO ME.
YEAH, HE'S SOLID MEAT!
LET'S BREAK EVERY BONE IN HIS BODY!
I'VE BEEN TOO EASY ON YOU GUYS. NEXT TIME I'LL SHOOT TO KILL!
AINT GOIN' TO BE A NEXT TIME FOR YOU!
NOW LET'S SEE WHAT HE'S HIDING BEHIND THAT MASK!
YEAH, LE'S FIND OUT WHO HE IS!
WHY, IT'S NOBODY!
JUST AN ORDINARY GUY.
HEY I KNOW THIS GUY. HE'S OUR ROTTEN PAL, DIRTY BAD BOB WITH ALL HIS TEETH KNOCKED OUT.
YOU'RE THE PHANTY?
ATH-HOLETH!
NO, DUMATH, I AIN'T THE PHANTY! AND WHO'RE YOU CALLIN ROTTEN?
SHOOT 'IM ANYWAY, JUST IN CASE HE'S LYING.
OVER HERE, BOYS!
BANG!
IT'S THE REAL PHANTY
HOW'D HE GIT OVER THERE?
WHAT TH'...
3

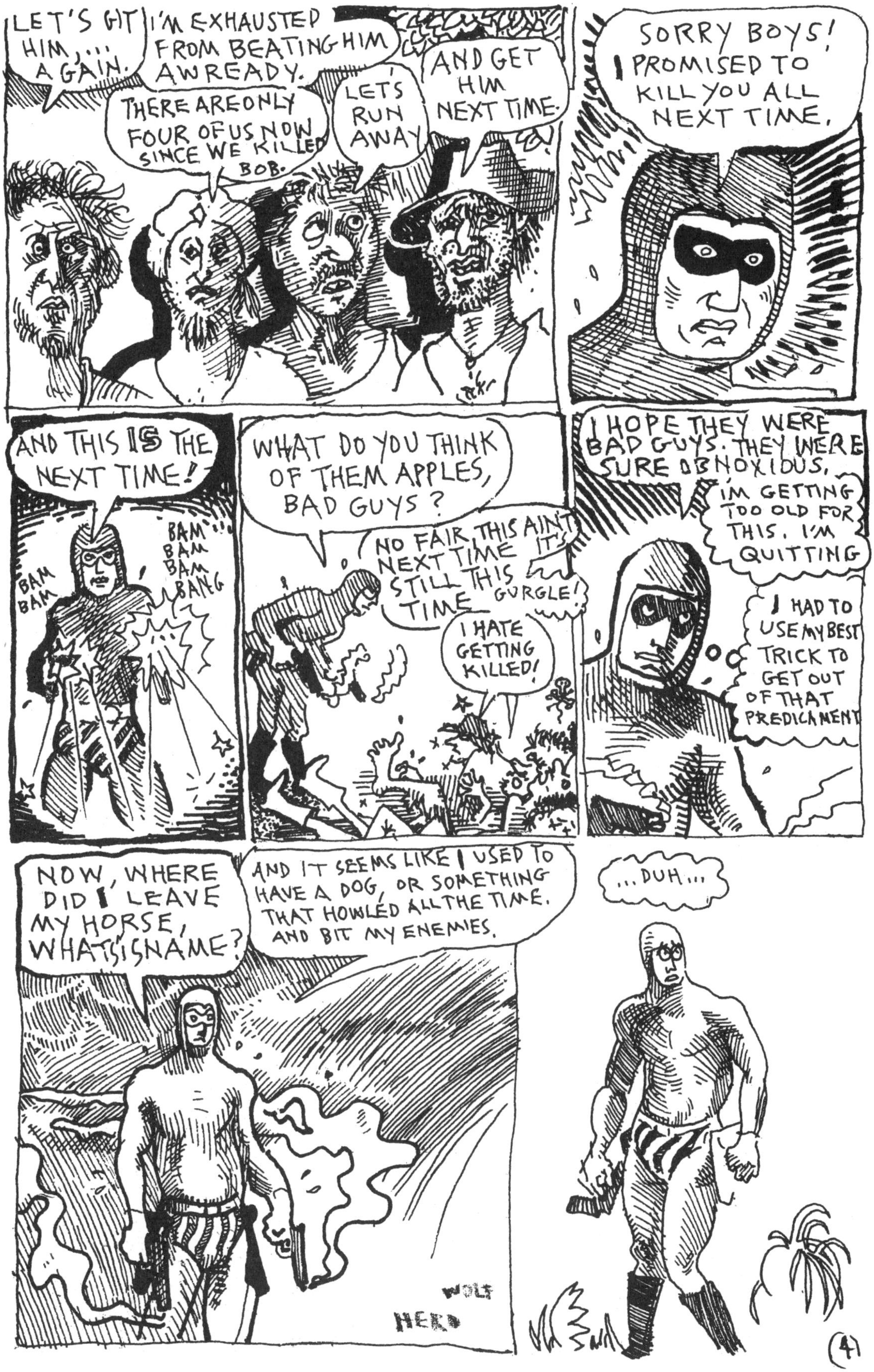
LET'S GIT HIM,... AGAIN.
I'M EXHAUSTED FROM BEATING HIM AWREADY.
THERE ARE ONLY FOUR OF US NOW SINCE WE KILLED BOB.
LET'S RUN AWAY
AND GET HIM NEXT TIME.
SORRY BOYS! I PROMISED TO KILL YOU ALL NEXT TIME.
AND THIS IS THE NEXT TIME!
BAM BAM
BAM BAM BAM BANG
WHAT DO YOU THINK OF THEM APPLES, BAD GUYS?
NO FAIR THIS AIN'T NEXT TIME IT'S STILL THIS TIME
GURGLE!
I HATE GETTING KILLED!
I HOPE THEY WERE BAD GUYS. THEY WERE SURE OBNOXIOUS.
I'M GETTING TOO OLD FOR THIS. I'M QUITTING
I HAD TO USE MY BEST TRICK TO GET OUT OF THAT PREDICAMENT
NOW, WHERE DID I LEAVE MY HORSE, WHATSISNAME?
AND IT SEEMS LIKE I USED TO HAVE A DOG, OR SOMETHING THAT HOWLED ALL THE TIME. AND BIT MY ENEMIES.
WOLF HERD
...DUH...
(4)

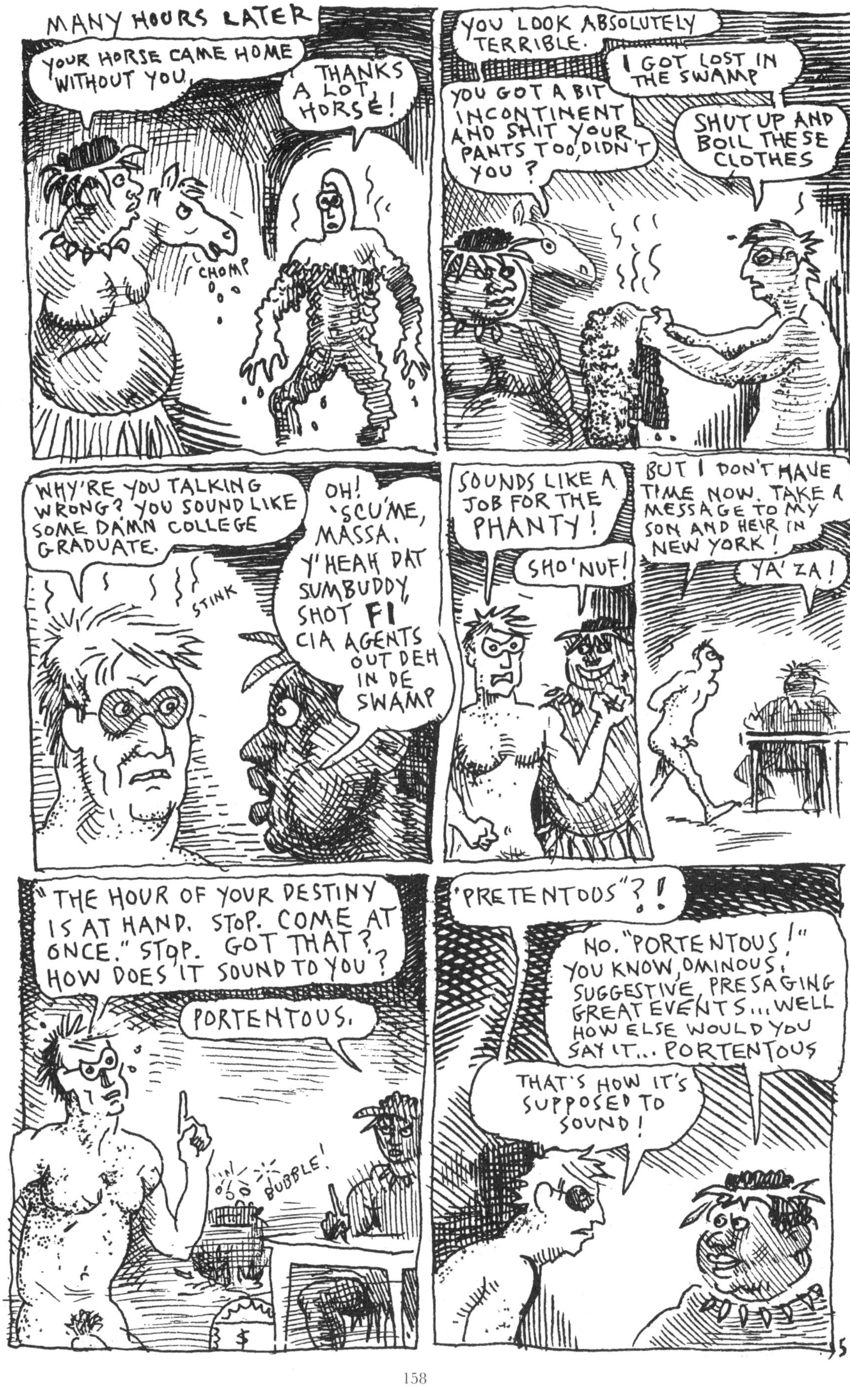
MANY HOURS LATER
YOUR HORSE CAME HOME WITHOUT YOU.
THANKS A LOT, HORSE!
CHOMP
YOU LOOK ABSOLUTELY TERRIBLE.
I GOT LOST IN THE SWAMP
YOU GOT A BIT INCONTINENT AND SHIT YOUR PANTS TOO, DIDN'T YOU?
SHUT UP AND BOIL THESE CLOTHES
WHY'RE YOU TALKING WRONG? YOU SOUND LIKE SOME DAMN COLLEGE GRADUATE.
OH! 'SCU'ME, MASSA. Y'HEAH DAT SUMBUDDY SHOT FI' CIA AGENTS OUT DEH IN DE SWAMP
STINK
SOUNDS LIKE A JOB FOR THE PHANTY!
SHO'NUF!
BUT I DON'T HAVE TIME NOW. TAKE A MESSAGE TO MY SON AND HEIR IN NEW YORK!
YA'ZA!
"THE HOUR OF YOUR DESTINY IS AT HAND. STOP. COME AT ONCE." STOP. GOT THAT? HOW DOES IT SOUND TO YOU?
PORTENTOUS.
BUBBLE!
"PRETENTOUS"?!
NO. "PORTENTOUS!" YOU KNOW, OMINOUS, SUGGESTIVE, PRESAGING GREAT EVENTS... WELL HOW ELSE WOULD YOU SAY IT... PORTENTOUS
THAT'S HOW IT'S SUPPOSED TO SOUND!
5

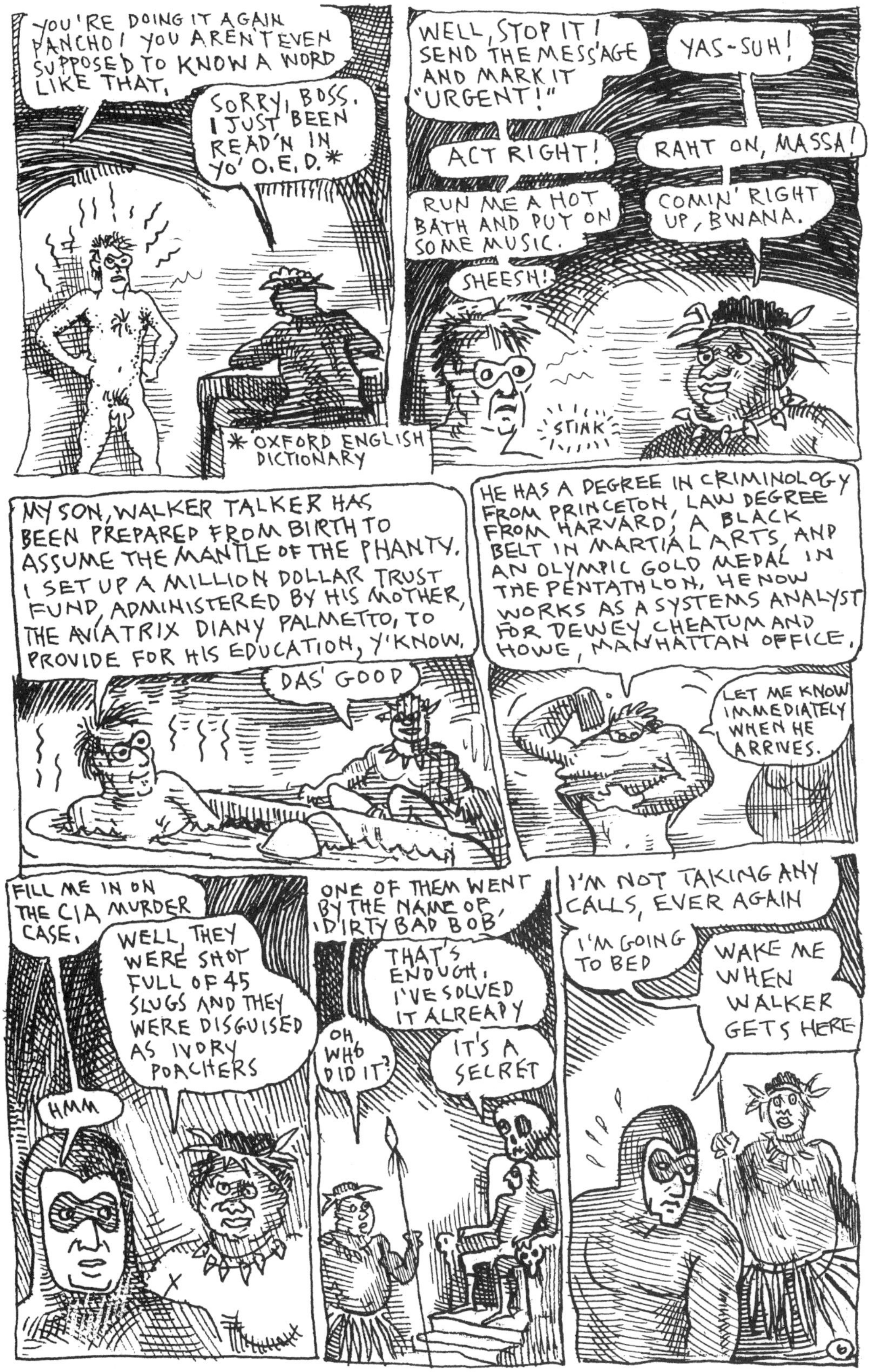

YOU'RE DOING IT AGAIN PANCHO! YOU AREN'T EVEN SUPPOSED TO KNOW A WORD LIKE THAT,
SORRY, BOSS. I JUST BEEN READ'N IN YO' O.E.D.*
* OXFORD ENGLISH DICTIONARY
WELL, STOP IT! SEND THE MESSAGE AND MARK IT "URGENT!"
YAS-SUH!
ACT RIGHT!
RAHT ON, MASSA!
RUN ME A HOT BATH AND PUT ON SOME MUSIC.
COMIN' RIGHT UP, BWANA.
SHEESH!
STINK
MY SON, WALKER TALKER HAS BEEN PREPARED FROM BIRTH TO ASSUME THE MANTLE OF THE PHANTY. I SET UP A MILLION DOLLAR TRUST FUND, ADMINISTERED BY HIS MOTHER, THE AVIATRIX DIANY PALMETTO, TO PROVIDE FOR HIS EDUCATION, Y'KNOW.
DAS' GOOD
HE HAS A DEGREE IN CRIMINOLOGY FROM PRINCETON, LAW DEGREE FROM HARVARD, A BLACK BELT IN MARTIAL ARTS, AND AN OLYMPIC GOLD MEDAL IN THE PENTATHLON. HE NOW WORKS AS A SYSTEMS ANALYST FOR DEWEY CHEATUM AND HOWE, MANHATTAN OFFICE.
LET ME KNOW IMMEDIATELY WHEN HE ARRIVES.
FILL ME IN ON THE CIA MURDER CASE.
WELL, THEY WERE SHOT FULL OF 45 SLUGS AND THEY WERE DISGUISED AS IVORY POACHERS
HMM
ONE OF THEM WENT BY THE NAME OF 'DIRTY BAD BOB'
THAT'S ENOUGH. I'VE SOLVED IT ALREADY
OH WHO DID IT?
IT'S A SECRET
I'M NOT TAKING ANY CALLS, EVER AGAIN
I'M GOING TO BED
WAKE ME WHEN WALKER GETS HERE
6

Will Walker wear the purple tights?! What will the Phanty find in Paris?! Stay tuned next issue for the unforgettable conclusion of "The Ersatz Adventures of the Phanty" by F.S.!

After a thrilling gunbattle the Purple Paradigm of Justice wipes out Bob's Badass Jungle Raiders, a wolfpack of loathsome marauding bandits who turn out to be adjunct CIA agents doing contract work as undercover ivory-poaching terrorists. He decides to retire as the Wraith Who Walks the Walk and summons his son and heir Walker Talker to succeed him as Masked Avenger of the Boondocks. Now he idles impatiently as he awaits the arrival of the

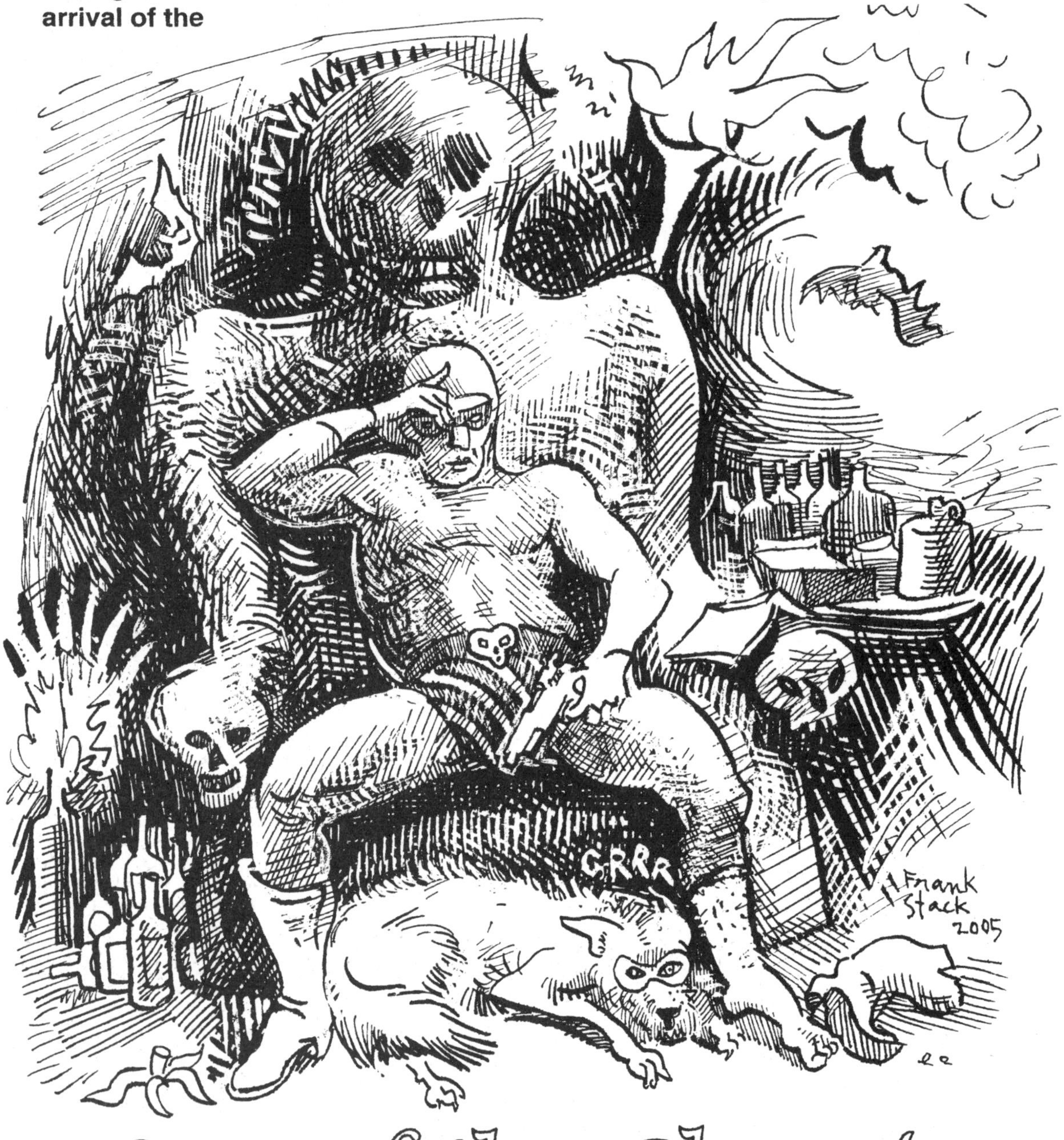
GRRR
Frank Stack 2005

Son of the Phanty

The Second and Final Astonishing Chapter of The Ersatz Adventures of the Phanty!

From the DryHole Entertainment Company

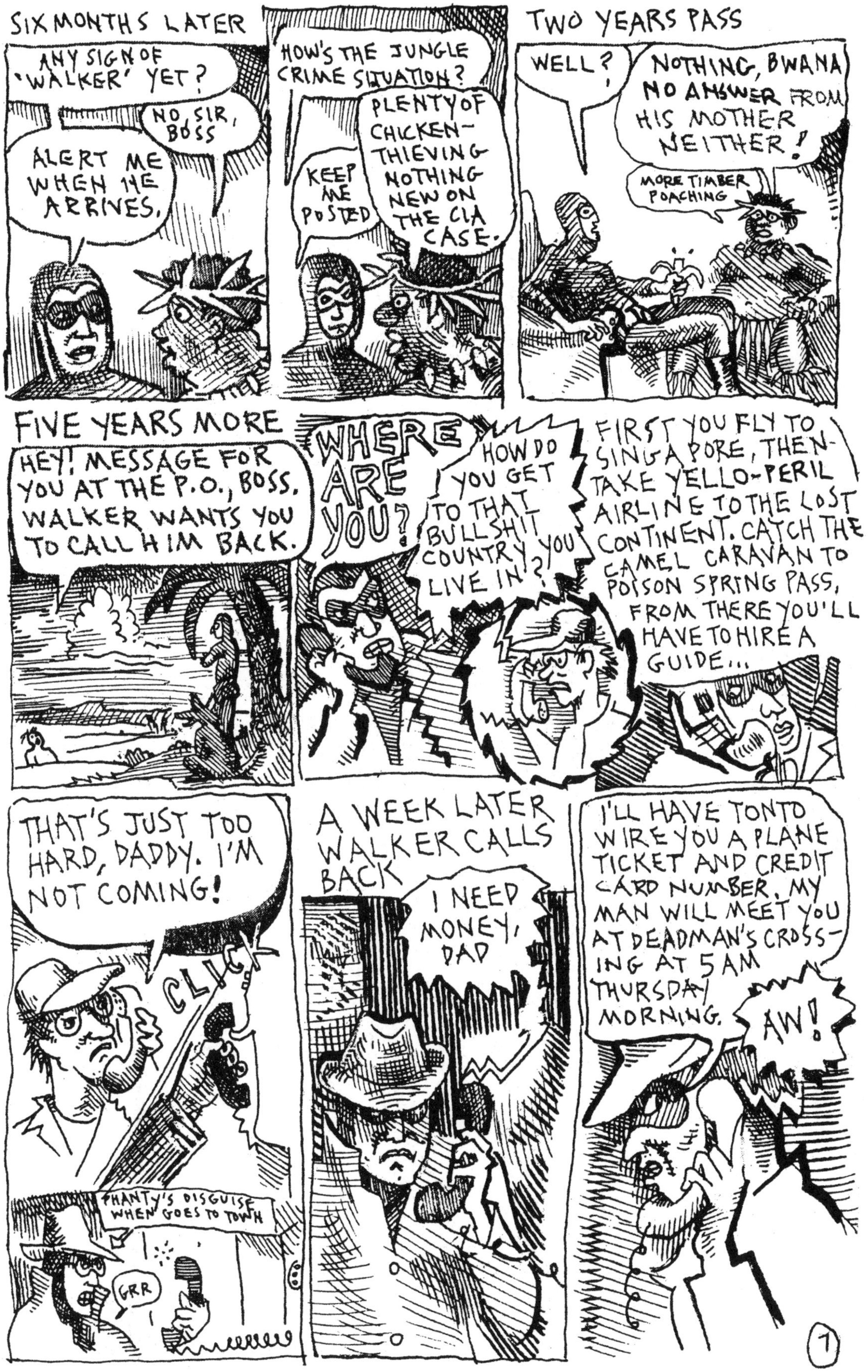
SIX MONTHS LATER
ANY SIGN OF 'WALKER' YET?
NO SIR, BOSS
ALERT ME WHEN HE ARRIVES.
HOW'S THE JUNGLE CRIME SITUATION?
PLENTY OF CHICKEN-THIEVING NOTHING NEW ON THE CIA CASE.
KEEP ME POSTED
TWO YEARS PASS
WELL?
NOTHING, BWANA NO ANSWER FROM HIS MOTHER NEITHER!
MORE TIMBER POACHING
FIVE YEARS MORE
HEY! MESSAGE FOR YOU AT THE P.O., BOSS. WALKER WANTS YOU TO CALL HIM BACK.
WHERE ARE YOU?
HOW DO YOU GET TO THAT BULLSHIT COUNTRY YOU LIVE IN?
FIRST YOU FLY TO SINGAPORE, THEN TAKE YELLO-PERIL AIRLINE TO THE LOST CONTINENT. CATCH THE CAMEL CARAVAN TO POISON SPRING PASS. FROM THERE YOU'LL HAVE TO HIRE A GUIDE...
THAT'S JUST TOO HARD, DADDY. I'M NOT COMING!
CLICK
PHANTY'S DISGUISE WHEN GOES TO TOWN
GRR
A WEEK LATER WALKER CALLS BACK
I NEED MONEY, DAD
I'LL HAVE TONTO WIRE YOU A PLANE TICKET AND CREDIT CARD NUMBER. MY MAN WILL MEET YOU AT DEADMAN'S CROSSING AT 5 AM THURSDAY MORNING.
AW!
7

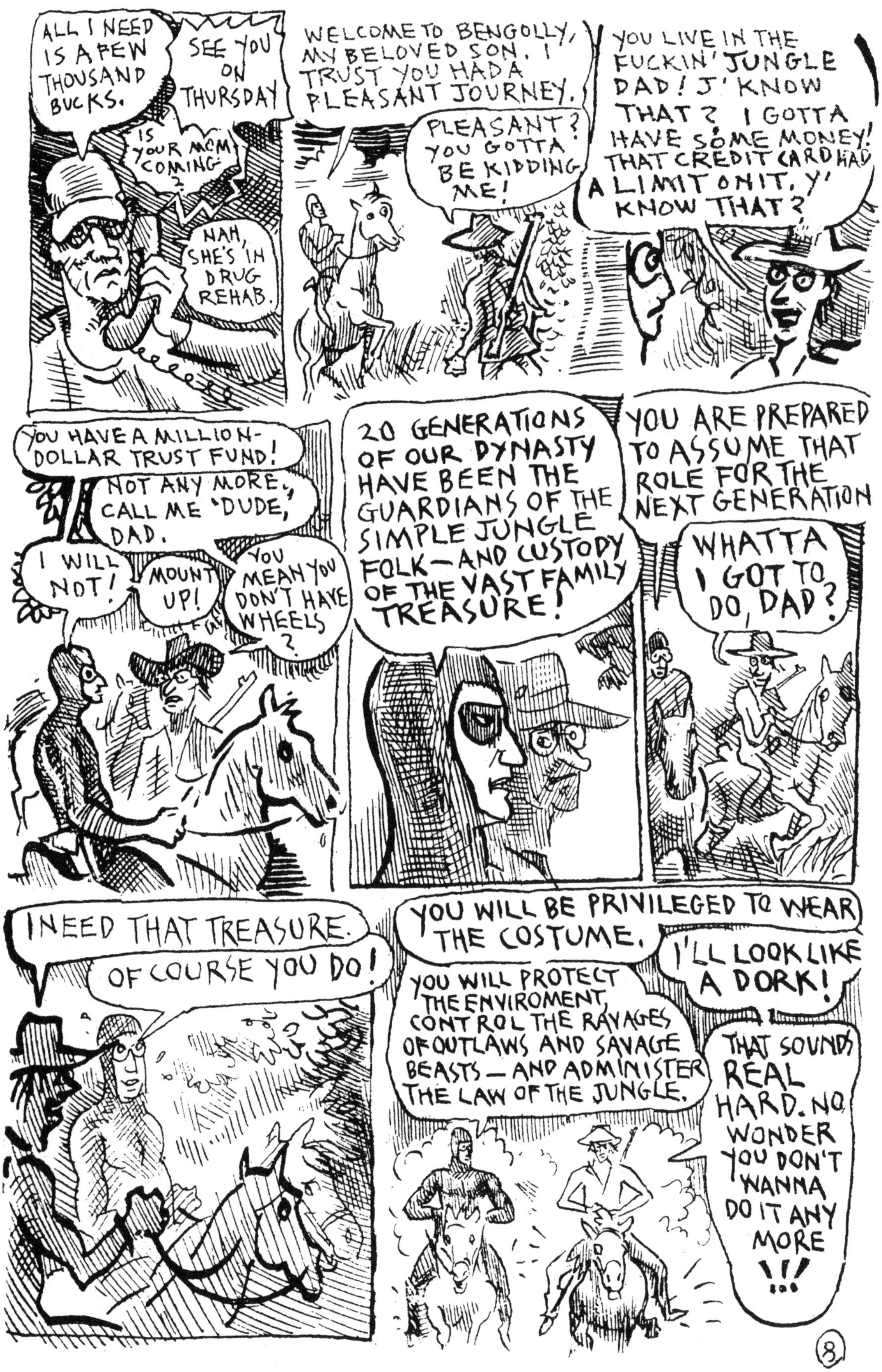
ALL I NEED IS A FEW THOUSAND BUCKS.
SEE YOU ON THURSDAY
IS YOUR MOM COMING?
NAH, SHE'S IN DRUG REHAB.
WELCOME TO BENGOLLY, MY BELOVED SON. I TRUST YOU HAD A PLEASANT JOURNEY.
PLEASANT? YOU GOTTA BE KIDDING ME!
YOU LIVE IN THE FUCKIN' JUNGLE DAD! J' KNOW THAT? I GOTTA HAVE SOME MONEY! THAT CREDIT CARD HAD A LIMIT ON IT, Y' KNOW THAT?
YOU HAVE A MILLION-DOLLAR TRUST FUND!
NOT ANY MORE. CALL ME 'DUDE,' DAD.
I WILL NOT!
MOUNT UP!
YOU MEAN YOU DON'T HAVE WHEELS?
20 GENERATIONS OF OUR DYNASTY HAVE BEEN THE GUARDIANS OF THE SIMPLE JUNGLE FOLK—AND CUSTODY OF THE VAST FAMILY TREASURE!
YOU ARE PREPARED TO ASSUME THAT ROLE FOR THE NEXT GENERATION
WHATTA I GOT TO DO, DAD?
I NEED THAT TREASURE.
OF COURSE YOU DO!
YOU WILL BE PRIVILEGED TO WEAR THE COSTUME.
I'LL LOOK LIKE A DORK!
YOU WILL PROTECT THE ENVIROMENT, CONTROL THE RAVAGES OF OUTLAWS AND SAVAGE BEASTS—AND ADMINISTER THE LAW OF THE JUNGLE.
THAT SOUNDS REAL HARD. NO WONDER YOU DON'T WANNA DO IT ANY MORE!!!
8

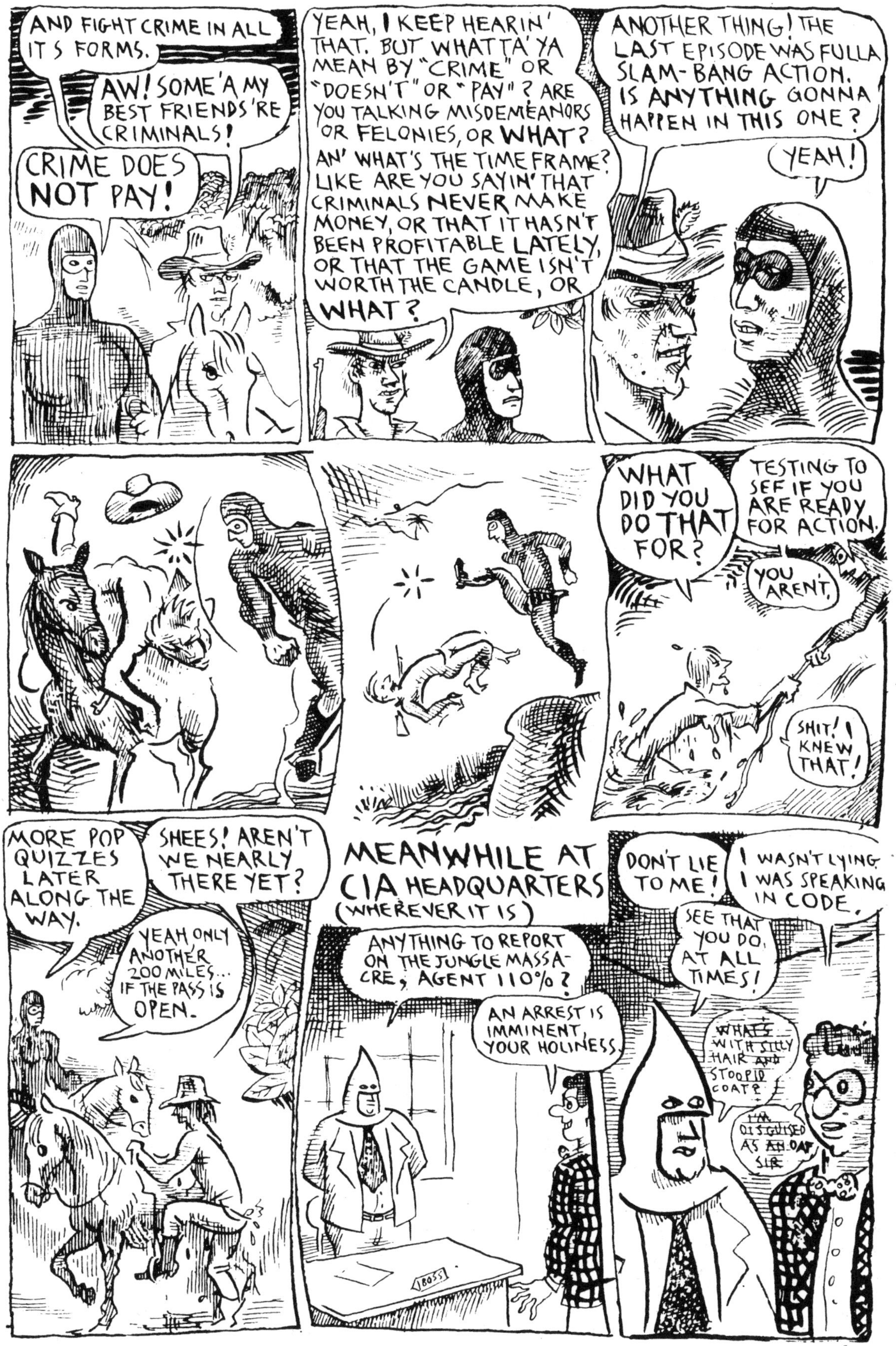
AND FIGHT CRIME IN ALL ITS FORMS.
AW! SOME 'A MY BEST FRIENDS 'RE CRIMINALS!
CRIME DOES NOT PAY!
YEAH, I KEEP HEARIN' THAT. BUT WHATTA' YA MEAN BY "CRIME" OR "DOESN'T" OR "PAY"? ARE YOU TALKING MISDEMEANORS OR FELONIES, OR WHAT? AN' WHAT'S THE TIME FRAME? LIKE ARE YOU SAYIN' THAT CRIMINALS NEVER MAKE MONEY, OR THAT IT HASN'T BEEN PROFITABLE LATELY, OR THAT THE GAME ISN'T WORTH THE CANDLE, OR WHAT?
ANOTHER THING! THE LAST EPISODE WAS FULLA SLAM-BANG ACTION. IS ANYTHING GONNA HAPPEN IN THIS ONE?
YEAH!
WHAT DID YOU DO THAT FOR?
TESTING TO SEE IF YOU ARE READY FOR ACTION.
YOU AREN'T.
SHIT! I KNEW THAT!
MORE POP QUIZZES LATER ALONG THE WAY.
SHEES! AREN'T WE NEARLY THERE YET?
YEAH ONLY ANOTHER 200 MILES... IF THE PASS IS OPEN.
MEANWHILE AT CIA HEADQUARTERS (WHEREVER IT IS)
ANYTHING TO REPORT ON THE JUNGLE MASSACRE, AGENT 110%?
AN ARREST IS IMMINENT, YOUR HOLINESS.
BOSS
DON'T LIE TO ME!
I WASN'T LYING. I WAS SPEAKING IN CODE.
SEE THAT YOU DO, AT ALL TIMES!
WHAT'S WITH SILLY HAIR AND STOOPID COAT?
I'M DISGUISED AS AN OAF SIR

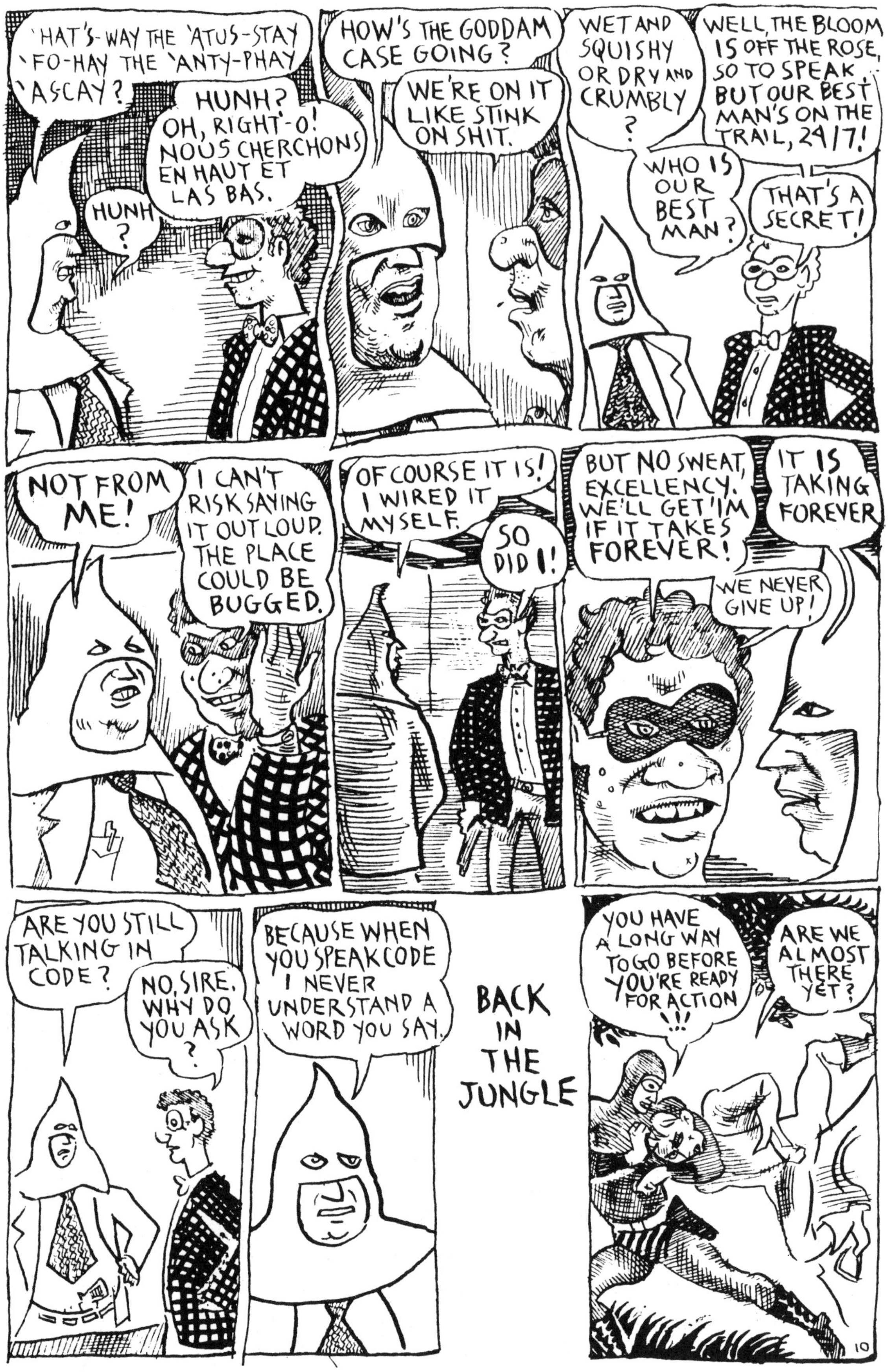
`HAT'S-WAY THE `ATUS-STAY `FO-HAY THE `ANTY-PHAY `ASCAY?
HUNH?
HUNH? OH, RIGHT-O! NOUS CHERCHONS EN HAUT ET LAS BAS.
HOW'S THE GODDAM CASE GOING?
WE'RE ON IT LIKE STINK ON SHIT.
WET AND SQUISHY OR DRY AND CRUMBLY?
WELL, THE BLOOM IS OFF THE ROSE, SO TO SPEAK... BUT OUR BEST MAN'S ON THE TRAIL, 24/7!
WHO IS OUR BEST MAN?
THAT'S A SECRET!
NOT FROM ME!
I CAN'T RISK SAYING IT OUT LOUD. THE PLACE COULD BE BUGGED.
OF COURSE IT IS! I WIRED IT MYSELF.
SO DID I!
BUT NO SWEAT, EXCELLENCY. WE'LL GET 'IM IF IT TAKES FOREVER!
IT IS TAKING FOREVER
WE NEVER GIVE UP!
ARE YOU STILL TALKING IN CODE?
NO, SIRE. WHY DO YOU ASK?
BECAUSE WHEN YOU SPEAK CODE I NEVER UNDERSTAND A WORD YOU SAY.
BACK IN THE JUNGLE
YOU HAVE A LONG WAY TO GO BEFORE YOU'RE READY FOR ACTION !!!
ARE WE ALMOST THERE YET?
10

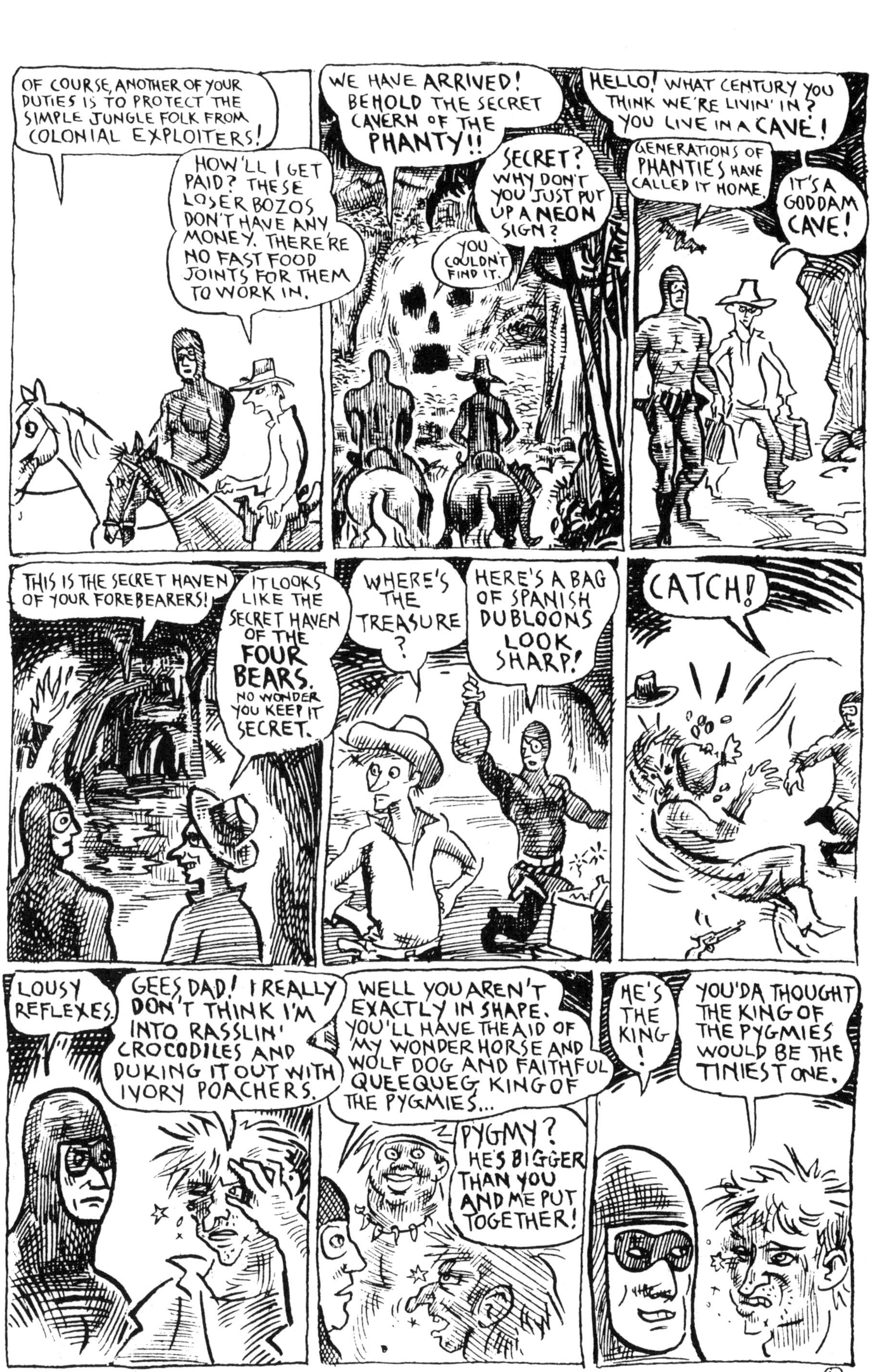
OF COURSE, ANOTHER OF YOUR DUTIES IS TO PROTECT THE SIMPLE JUNGLE FOLK FROM COLONIAL EXPLOITERS!
HOW'LL I GET PAID? THESE LOSER BOZOS DON'T HAVE ANY MONEY. THERE'RE NO FAST FOOD JOINTS FOR THEM TO WORK IN.
WE HAVE ARRIVED! BEHOLD THE SECRET CAVERN OF THE PHANTY!!
SECRET? WHY DON'T YOU JUST PUT UP A NEON SIGN?
YOU COULDN'T FIND IT.
HELLO! WHAT CENTURY YOU THINK WE'RE LIVIN' IN? YOU LIVE IN A CAVE!
GENERATIONS OF PHANTIE'S HAVE CALLED IT HOME.
IT'S A GODDAM CAVE!
THIS IS THE SECRET HAVEN OF YOUR FOREBEARERS!
IT LOOKS LIKE THE SECRET HAVEN OF THE FOUR BEARS. NO WONDER YOU KEEP IT SECRET.
WHERE'S THE TREASURE?
HERE'S A BAG OF SPANISH DUBLOONS LOOK SHARP!
CATCH!
LOUSY REFLEXES.
GEES, DAD! I REALLY DON'T THINK I'M INTO RASSLIN' CROCODILES AND DUKING IT OUT WITH IVORY POACHERS.
WELL YOU AREN'T EXACTLY IN SHAPE. YOU'LL HAVE THE AID OF MY WONDER HORSE AND WOLF DOG AND FAITHFUL QUEEQUEG KING OF THE PYGMIES...
PYGMY? HE'S BIGGER THAN YOU AND ME PUT TOGETHER!
HE'S THE KING!
YOU'DA THOUGHT THE KING OF THE PYGMIES WOULD BE THE TINIEST ONE.
11

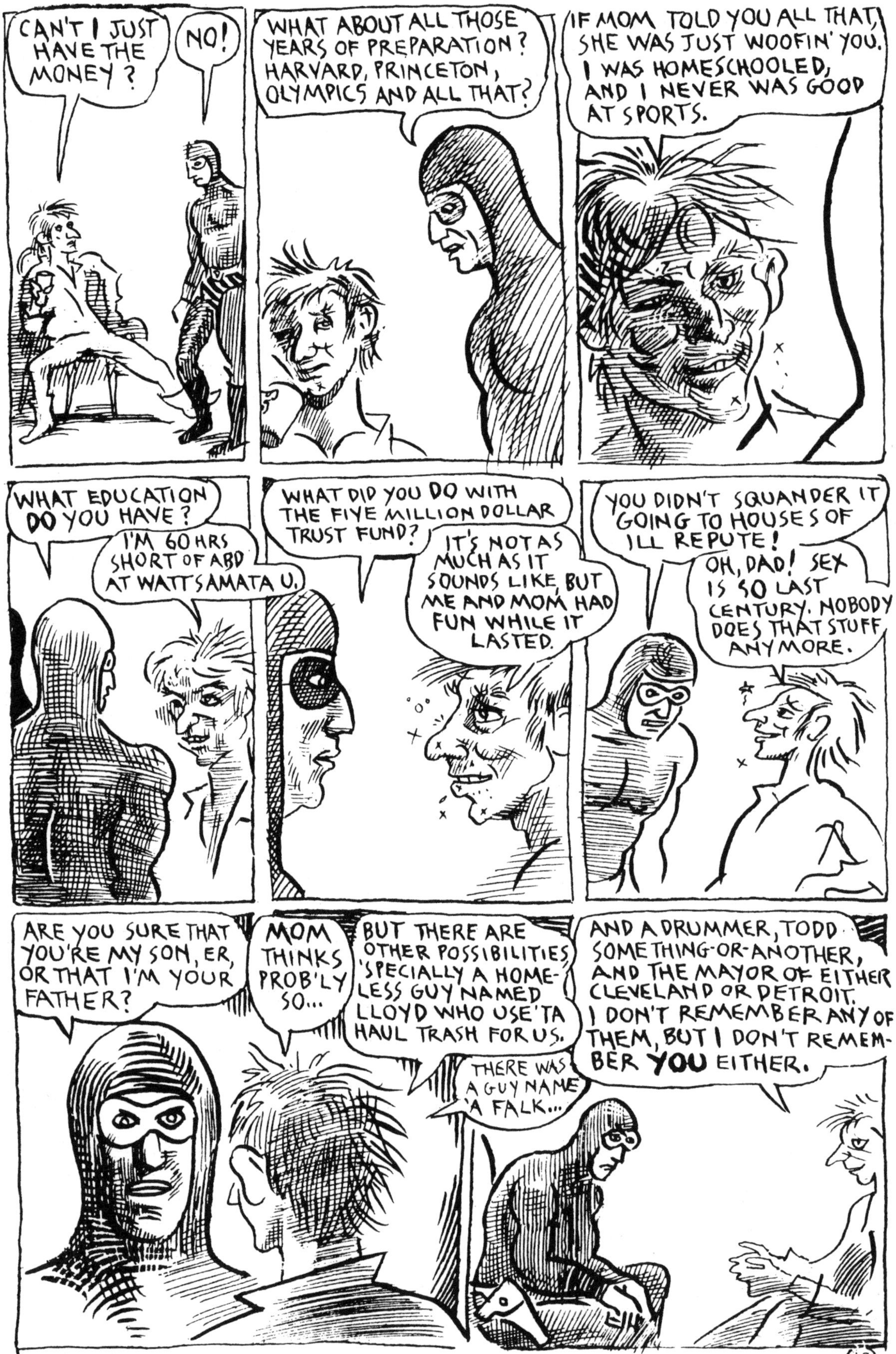

CAN'T I JUST HAVE THE MONEY?
NO!
WHAT ABOUT ALL THOSE YEARS OF PREPARATION? HARVARD, PRINCETON, OLYMPICS AND ALL THAT?
IF MOM TOLD YOU ALL THAT, SHE WAS JUST WOOFIN' YOU. I WAS HOMESCHOOLED, AND I NEVER WAS GOOD AT SPORTS.
WHAT EDUCATION DO YOU HAVE?
I'M 60 HRS SHORT OF ABD AT WATTSAMATA U.
WHAT DID YOU DO WITH THE FIVE MILLION DOLLAR TRUST FUND?
IT'S NOT AS MUCH AS IT SOUNDS LIKE, BUT ME AND MOM HAD FUN WHILE IT LASTED.
YOU DIDN'T SQUANDER IT GOING TO HOUSES OF ILL REPUTE!
OH, DAD! SEX IS SO LAST CENTURY. NOBODY DOES THAT STUFF ANYMORE.
ARE YOU SURE THAT YOU'RE MY SON, ER, OR THAT I'M YOUR FATHER?
MOM THINKS PROB'LY SO...
BUT THERE ARE OTHER POSSIBILITIES, 'SPECIALLY A HOMELESS GUY NAMED LLOYD WHO USE'TA HAUL TRASH FOR US.
THERE WAS A GUY NAME 'A FALK...
AND A DRUMMER, TODD SOMETHING-OR-ANOTHER, AND THE MAYOR OF EITHER CLEVELAND OR DETROIT. I DON'T REMEMBER ANY OF THEM, BUT I DON'T REMEMBER YOU EITHER.
12

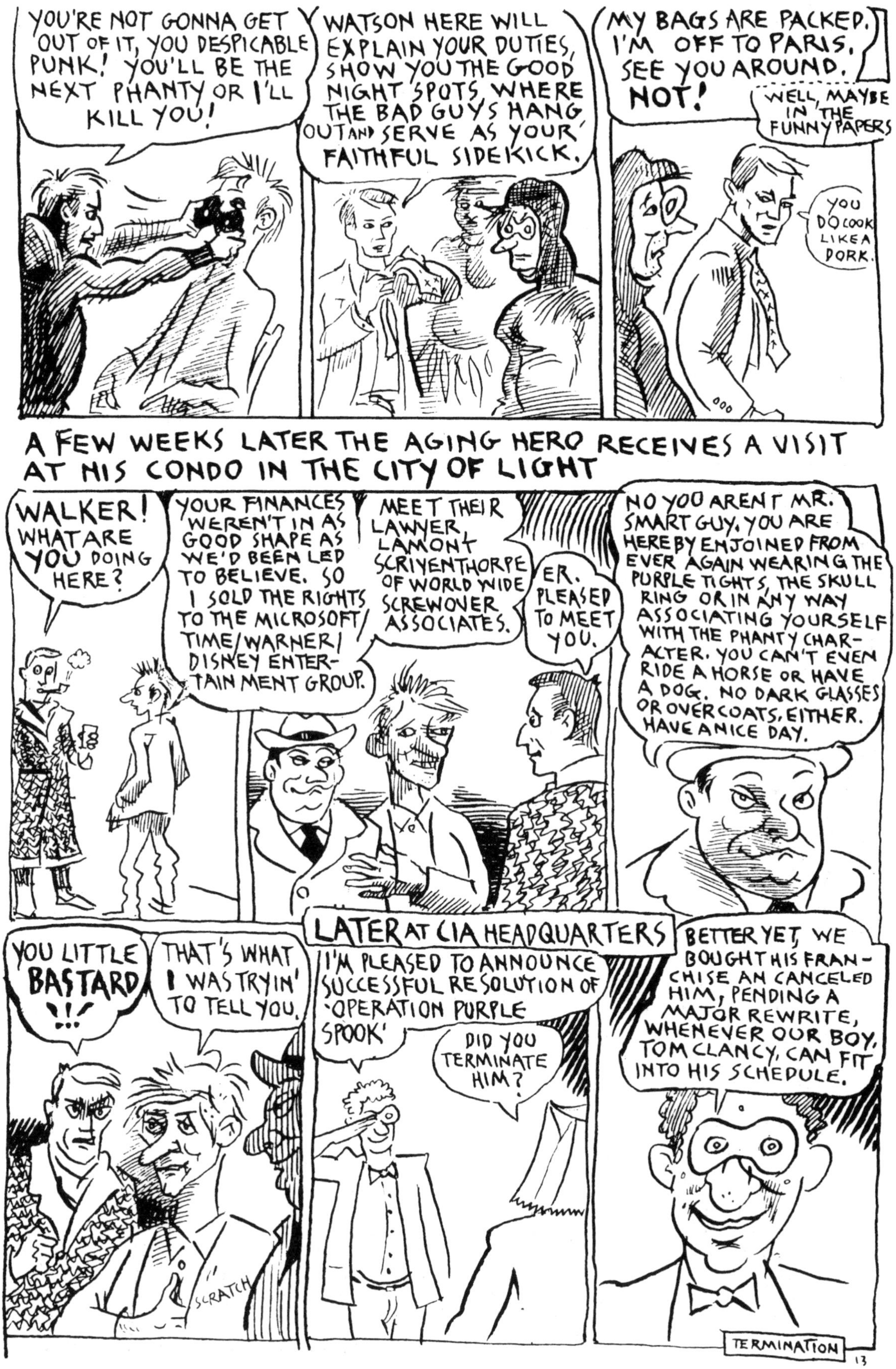
YOU'RE NOT GONNA GET OUT OF IT, YOU DESPICABLE PUNK! YOU'LL BE THE NEXT PHANTY OR I'LL KILL YOU!
WATSON HERE WILL EXPLAIN YOUR DUTIES, SHOW YOU THE GOOD NIGHT SPOTS WHERE THE BAD GUYS HANG OUT AND SERVE AS YOUR FAITHFUL SIDEKICK.
MY BAGS ARE PACKED. I'M OFF TO PARIS. SEE YOU AROUND. NOT!
WELL, MAYBE IN THE FUNNY PAPERS
YOU DO LOOK LIKE A DORK.
A FEW WEEKS LATER THE AGING HERO RECEIVES A VISIT AT HIS CONDO IN THE CITY OF LIGHT
WALKER! WHAT ARE YOU DOING HERE?
YOUR FINANCES WEREN'T IN AS GOOD SHAPE AS WE'D BEEN LED TO BELIEVE. SO I SOLD THE RIGHTS TO THE MICROSOFT/TIME/WARNER/DISNEY ENTERTAINMENT GROUP.
MEET THEIR LAWYER, LAMONT SCRIVENTHORPE OF WORLD WIDE SCREWOVER ASSOCIATES.
ER. PLEASED TO MEET YOU.
NO YOU AREN'T MR. SMART GUY, YOU ARE HEREBY ENJOINED FROM EVER AGAIN WEARING THE PURPLE TIGHTS, THE SKULL RING OR IN ANY WAY ASSOCIATING YOURSELF WITH THE PHANTY CHARACTER. YOU CAN'T EVEN RIDE A HORSE OR HAVE A DOG. NO DARK GLASSES OR OVERCOATS, EITHER. HAVE A NICE DAY.
YOU LITTLE BASTARD !!!
THAT'S WHAT I WAS TRYIN' TO TELL YOU.
SCRATCH
LATER AT CIA HEADQUARTERS
I'M PLEASED TO ANNOUNCE SUCCESSFUL RESOLUTION OF 'OPERATION PURPLE SPOOK'
DID YOU TERMINATE HIM?
BETTER YET, WE BOUGHT HIS FRANCHISE AN CANCELED HIM, PENDING A MAJOR REWRITE, WHENEVER OUR BOY, TOM CLANCY, CAN FIT INTO HIS SCHEDULE.
TERMINATION
13

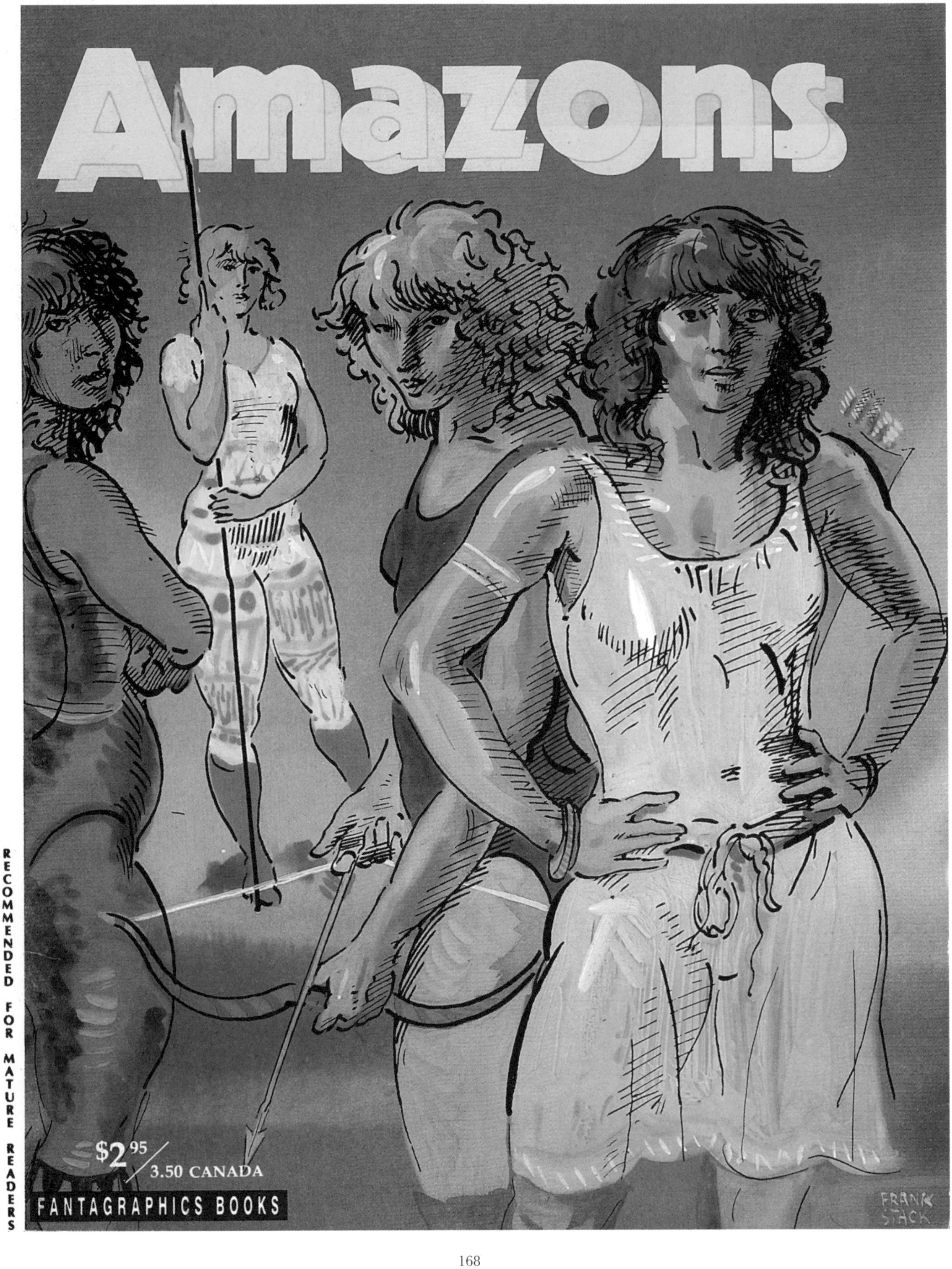
Amazons
$2.95/3.50 CANADA
FANTAGRAPHICS BOOKS
FRANK STACK
RECOMMENDED FOR MATURE READERS

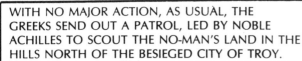

WITH NO MAJOR ACTION, AS USUAL, THE GREEKS SEND OUT A PATROL, LED BY NOBLE ACHILLES TO SCOUT THE NO-MAN'S LAND IN THE HILLS NORTH OF THE BESIEGED CITY OF TROY.

IT'S HOT! MY FEET HURT!

SHUTUP THE BITCHING AND KEEP YOUR EYES PEELED FOR **TROJANS**

I HATE THIS HUMPIN' SHIT!

I GOT A HEADACHE

I WANT TO GO HOME!

I GOTTA TAKE A PISS!

DO IT THEN.

HEY! SHUDDUP IN THE RANKS!

KEEP THEM SPEAR POINTS **UP**, MEN!

LOOKS LIKE THERE AIN'T ANY **TROJANS** OUT TODAY!

PROB'LY SAW US COMIN' SO THEY STAYED IN!

OH, YEAH. THEY'RE SCARED OF **YOU**!

FINE WITH **ME**. YOU CAN GET **KILLED** REAL DEAD IN ONE'A THOSE FREE-FER-ALL BRAWLS!

I FUCKED UP MY KNEE IN THE LAST ONE

LONG AS NOTHIN'S DOING WHAT SAY WE CUT IT SHORT TODAY, PRINCE ACHILLES?

WHAT FOR? GET BACK EARLY AND THEY'LL FIND SOME SHIT DETAIL FOR US.

TAKE FIVE, YOU GUYS

I DON'T LIKE THIS WAR! IT'S NO FUN!

I WISH I HAD SOME LOCO WEED.

BULL SHIT

IT'S BORING. WE AIN'T GOT TO LOOT A TOWN IN **MONTHS**!

DULLSBURGER!

THIS WIND CHAPS MY ASS!

OH-OH! LOOKA THERE!

A TROJAN SCOUTING PARTY, ON **HORSEBACK!**

CRAP! I HOPE THEY DON'T SPOT US.

FAT CHANCE. THEY AWREADY HAVE!

169

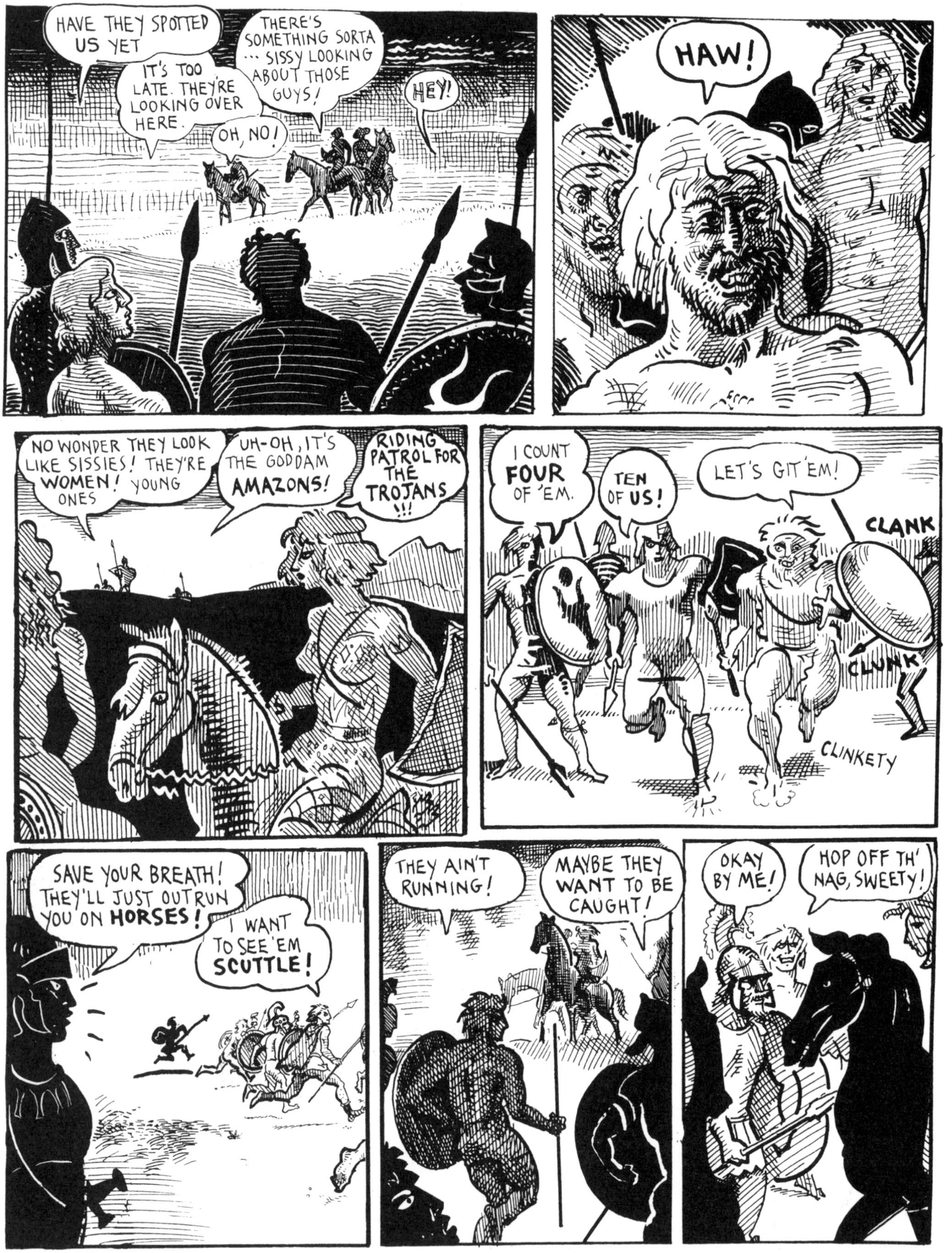
HAVE THEY SPOTTED US YET
IT'S TOO LATE. THEY'RE LOOKING OVER HERE.
THERE'S SOMETHING SORTA ... SISSY LOOKING ABOUT THOSE GUYS!
OH, NO!
HEY!
HAW!
NO WONDER THEY LOOK LIKE SISSIES! THEY'RE WOMEN! YOUNG ONES
UH-OH, IT'S THE GODDAM AMAZONS!
RIDING PATROL FOR THE TROJANS !!!
I COUNT FOUR OF 'EM.
TEN OF US!
LET'S GIT 'EM!
CLANK
CLUNK
CLINKETY
SAVE YOUR BREATH! THEY'LL JUST OUTRUN YOU ON HORSES!
I WANT TO SEE 'EM SCUTTLE!
THEY AIN'T RUNNING!
MAYBE THEY WANT TO BE CAUGHT!
OKAY BY ME!
HOP OFF TH' NAG, SWEETY!

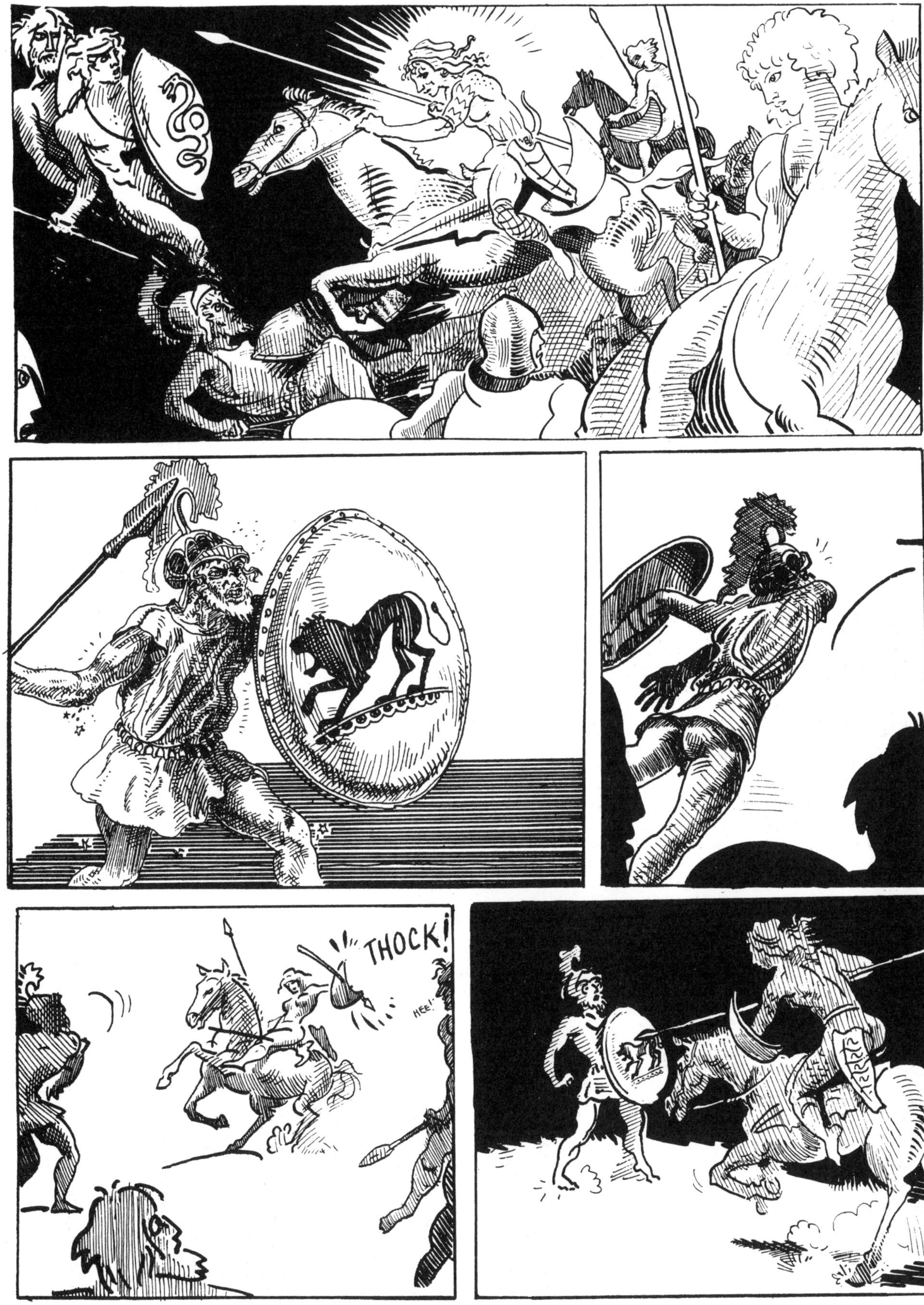
THOCK!
HEE!

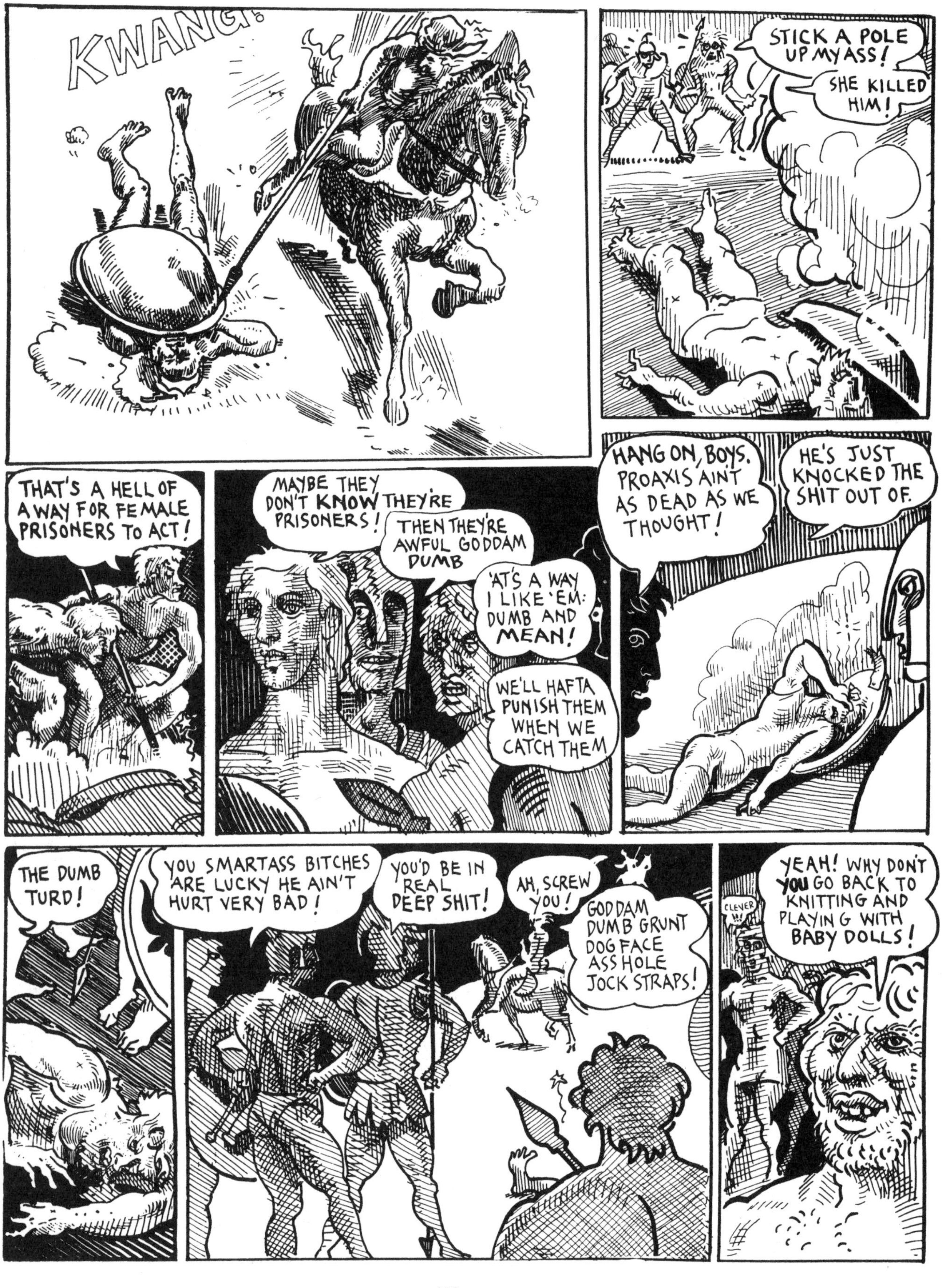

KWANG!
STICK A POLE UP MY ASS!
SHE KILLED HIM!
THAT'S A HELL OF A WAY FOR FEMALE PRISONERS TO ACT!
MAYBE THEY DON'T KNOW THEY'RE PRISONERS!
THEN THEY'RE AWFUL GODDAM DUMB
'AT'S A WAY I LIKE 'EM: DUMB AND MEAN!
WE'LL HAFTA PUNISH THEM WHEN WE CATCH THEM
HANG ON, BOYS. PROAXIS AIN'T AS DEAD AS WE THOUGHT!
HE'S JUST KNOCKED THE SHIT OUT OF.
THE DUMB TURD!
YOU SMARTASS BITCHES ARE LUCKY HE AIN'T HURT VERY BAD!
YOU'D BE IN REAL DEEP SHIT!
AH, SCREW YOU!
GODDAM DUMB GRUNT DOG FACE ASSHOLE JOCK STRAPS!
CLEVER!!!
YEAH! WHY DON'T YOU GO BACK TO KNITTING AND PLAYING WITH BABY DOLLS!

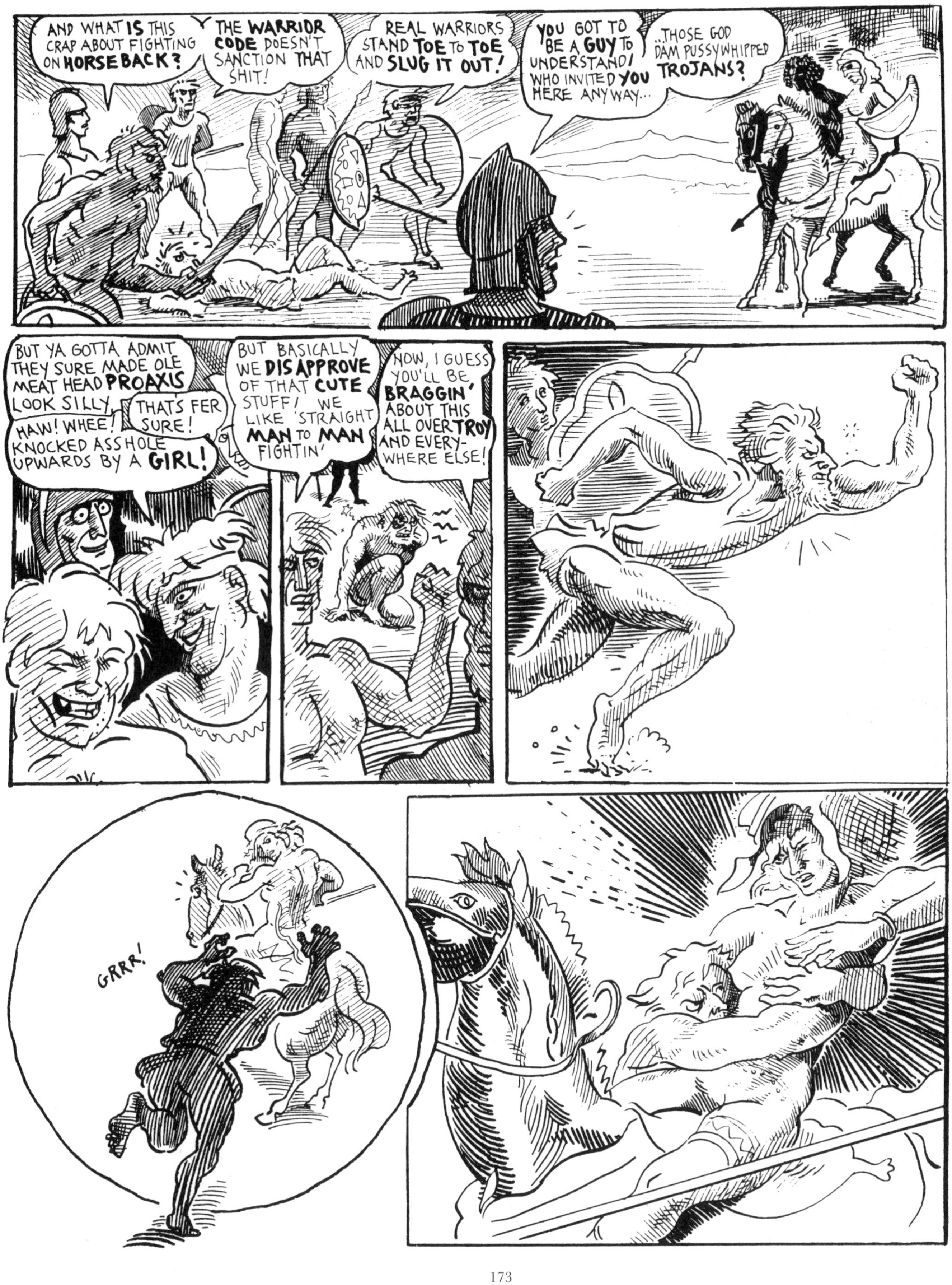
AND WHAT IS THIS CRAP ABOUT FIGHTING ON HORSEBACK?
THE WARRIOR CODE DOESN'T SANCTION THAT SHIT!
REAL WARRIORS STAND TOE TO TOE AND SLUG IT OUT!
YOU GOT TO BE A GUY TO UNDERSTAND! WHO INVITED YOU HERE ANYWAY...
..THOSE GOD DAM PUSSYWHIPPED TROJANS?
BUT YA GOTTA ADMIT THEY SURE MADE OLE MEAT HEAD PROAXIS LOOK SILLY,
THAT'S FER SURE!
HAW! WHEE! KNOCKED ASSHOLE UPWARDS BY A GIRL!
BUT BASICALLY WE DISAPPROVE OF THAT CUTE STUFF! WE LIKE 'STRAIGHT MAN TO MAN FIGHTIN'
NOW, I GUESS YOU'LL BE BRAGGIN' ABOUT THIS ALL OVER TROY AND EVERYWHERE ELSE!
GRRR!

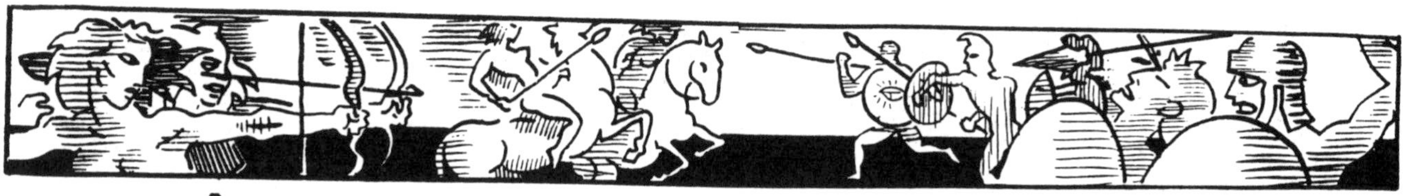

Amazons

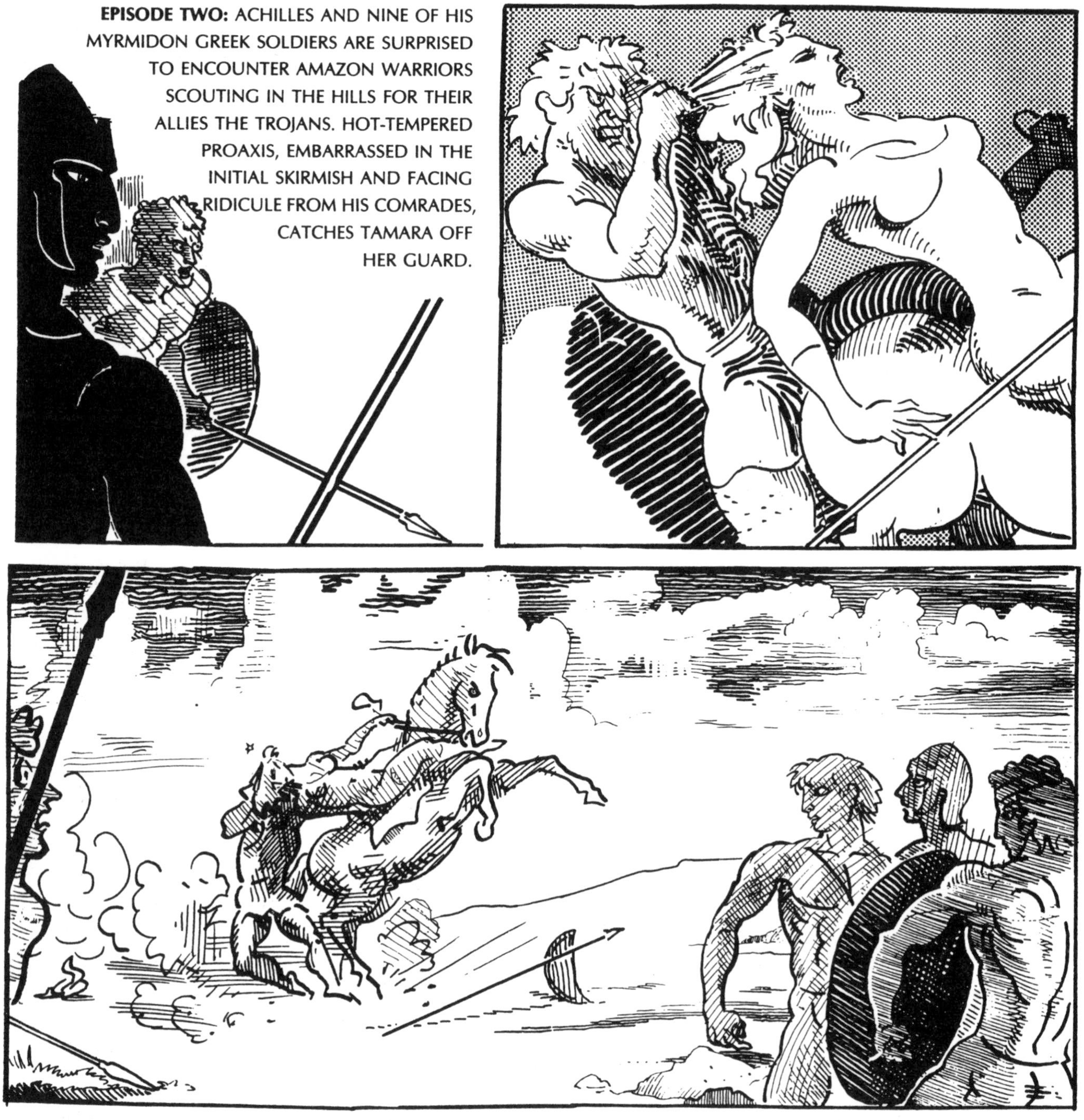
EPISODE TWO: ACHILLES AND NINE OF HIS MYRMIDON GREEK SOLDIERS ARE SURPRISED TO ENCOUNTER AMAZON WARRIORS SCOUTING IN THE HILLS FOR THEIR ALLIES THE TROJANS. HOT-TEMPERED PROAXIS, EMBARRASSED IN THE INITIAL SKIRMISH AND FACING RIDICULE FROM HIS COMRADES, CATCHES TAMARA OFF HER GUARD.

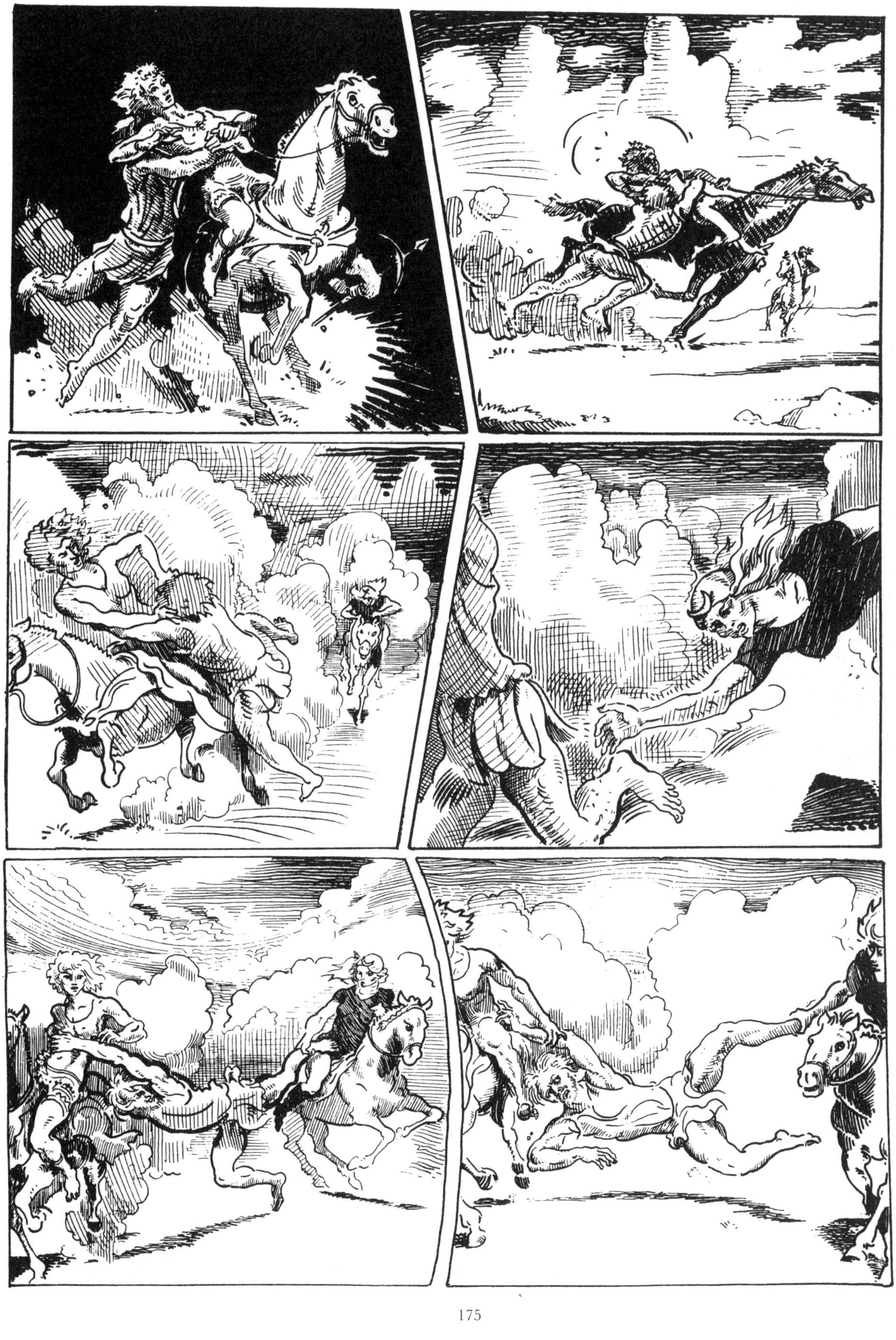

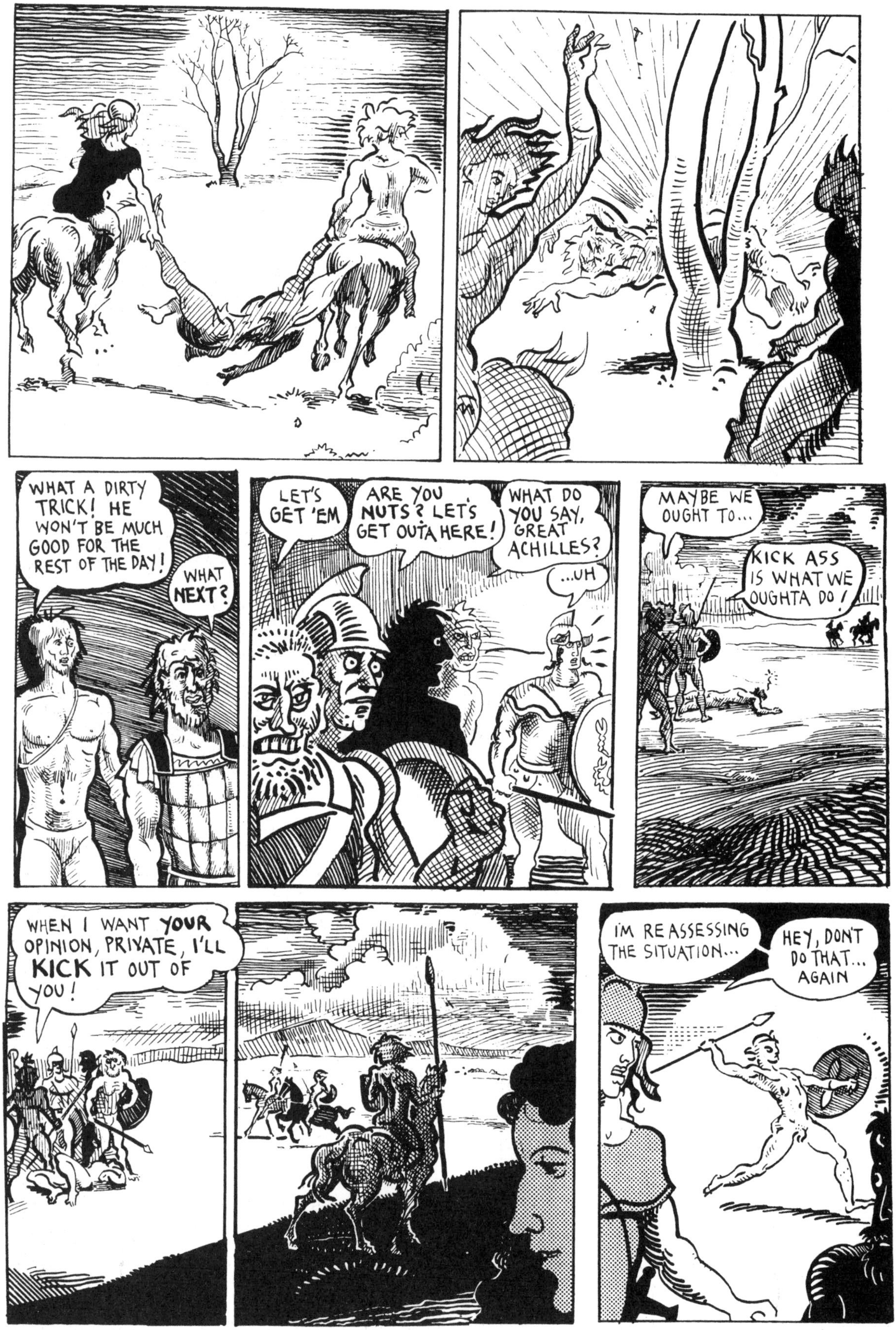
WHAT A DIRTY TRICK! HE WON'T BE MUCH GOOD FOR THE REST OF THE DAY!
WHAT NEXT?
LET'S GET 'EM
ARE YOU NUTS? LET'S GET OUTA HERE!
WHAT DO YOU SAY, GREAT ACHILLES?
...UH
MAYBE WE OUGHT TO...
KICK ASS IS WHAT WE OUGHTA DO!
WHEN I WANT YOUR OPINION, PRIVATE, I'LL KICK IT OUT OF YOU!
I'M REASSESSING THE SITUATION...
HEY, DON'T DO THAT... AGAIN

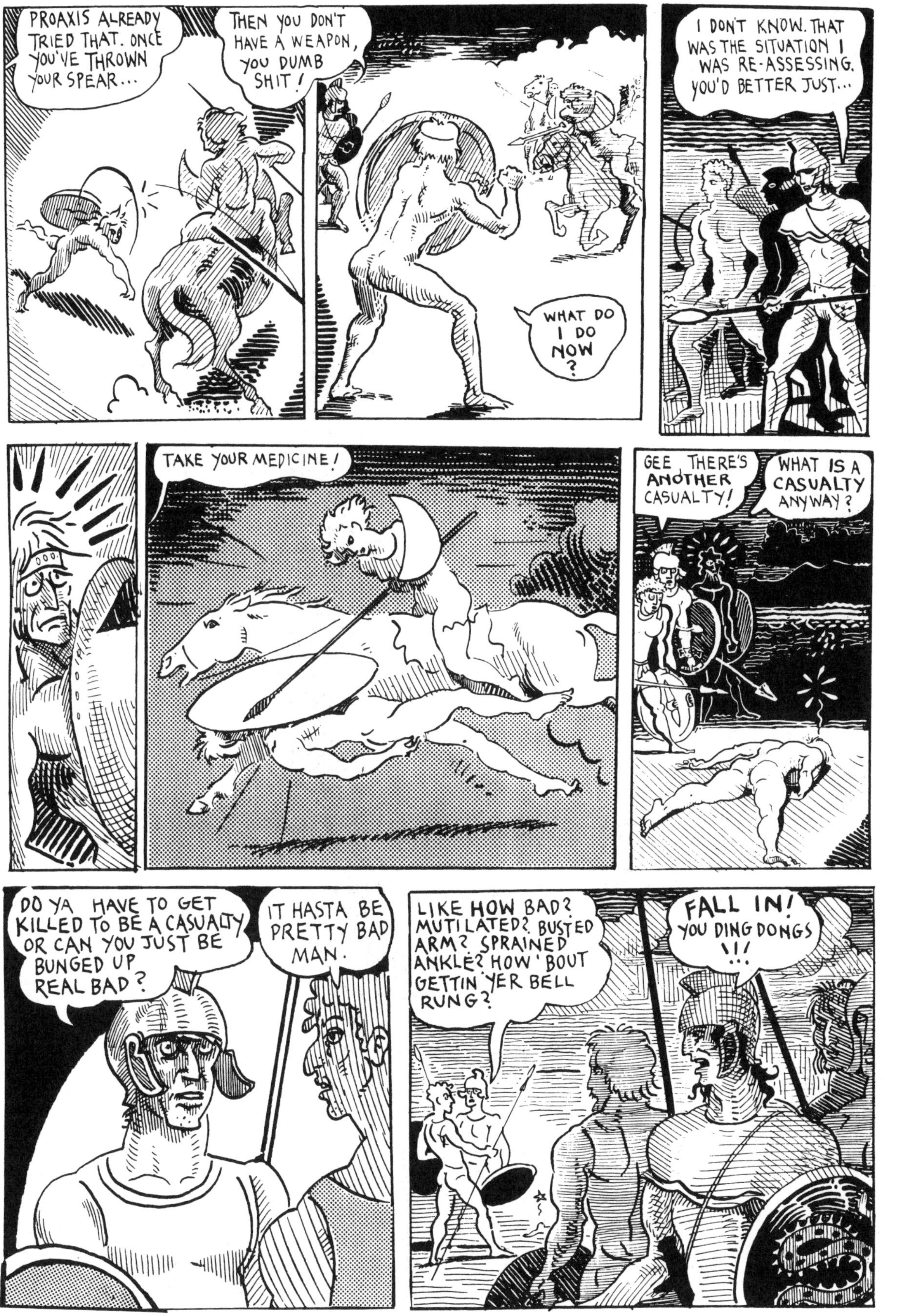
PROAXIS ALREADY TRIED THAT. ONCE YOU'VE THROWN YOUR SPEAR...
THEN YOU DON'T HAVE A WEAPON, YOU DUMB SHIT!
WHAT DO I DO NOW?
I DON'T KNOW. THAT WAS THE SITUATION I WAS RE-ASSESSING. YOU'D BETTER JUST...
TAKE YOUR MEDICINE!
GEE THERE'S ANOTHER CASUALTY!
WHAT IS A CASUALTY ANYWAY?
DO YA HAVE TO GET KILLED TO BE A CASUALTY OR CAN YOU JUST BE BUNGED UP REAL BAD?
IT HASTA BE PRETTY BAD MAN.
LIKE HOW BAD? MUTILATED? BUSTED ARM? SPRAINED ANKLE? HOW 'BOUT GETTIN' YER BELL RUNG?
FALL IN! YOU DING DONGS !!!

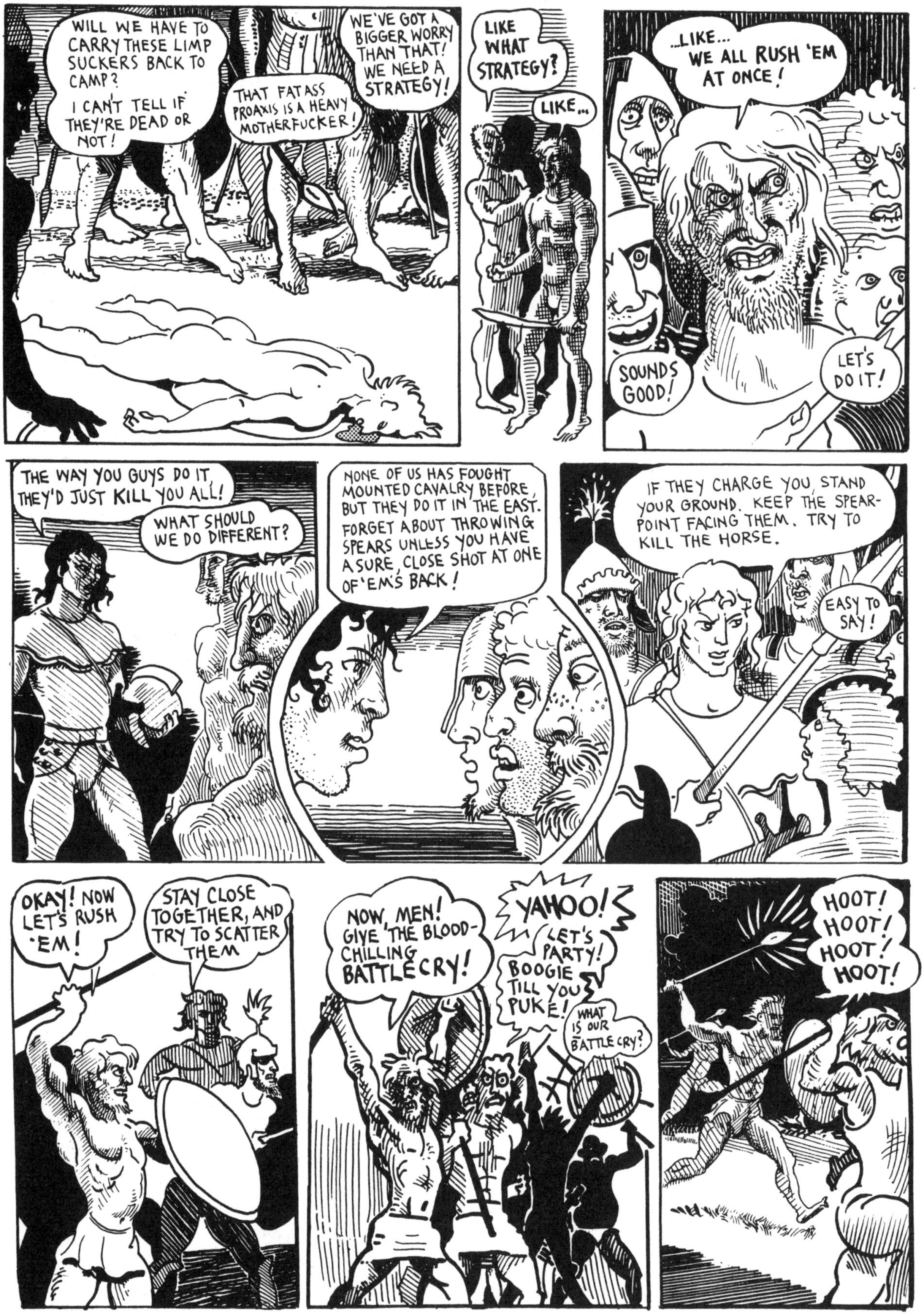
WILL WE HAVE TO CARRY THESE LIMP SUCKERS BACK TO CAMP?
I CAN'T TELL IF THEY'RE DEAD OR NOT!
THAT FATASS PROAXIS IS A HEAVY MOTHERFUCKER!
WE'VE GOT A BIGGER WORRY THAN THAT! WE NEED A STRATEGY!
LIKE WHAT STRATEGY?
LIKE...
...LIKE... WE ALL RUSH 'EM AT ONCE!
SOUNDS GOOD!
LET'S DO IT!
THE WAY YOU GUYS DO IT, THEY'D JUST KILL YOU ALL!
WHAT SHOULD WE DO DIFFERENT?
NONE OF US HAS FOUGHT MOUNTED CAVALRY BEFORE, BUT THEY DO IT IN THE EAST. FORGET ABOUT THROWING SPEARS UNLESS YOU HAVE A SURE, CLOSE SHOT AT ONE OF 'EM'S BACK!
IF THEY CHARGE YOU, STAND YOUR GROUND. KEEP THE SPEARPOINT FACING THEM. TRY TO KILL THE HORSE.
EASY TO SAY!
OKAY! NOW LET'S RUSH 'EM!
STAY CLOSE TOGETHER, AND TRY TO SCATTER THEM
NOW, MEN! GIVE THE BLOOD-CHILLING BATTLECRY!
YAHOO!
LET'S PARTY!
BOOGIE TILL YOU PUKE!
WHAT IS OUR BATTLE CRY?
HOOT! HOOT! HOOT! HOOT!

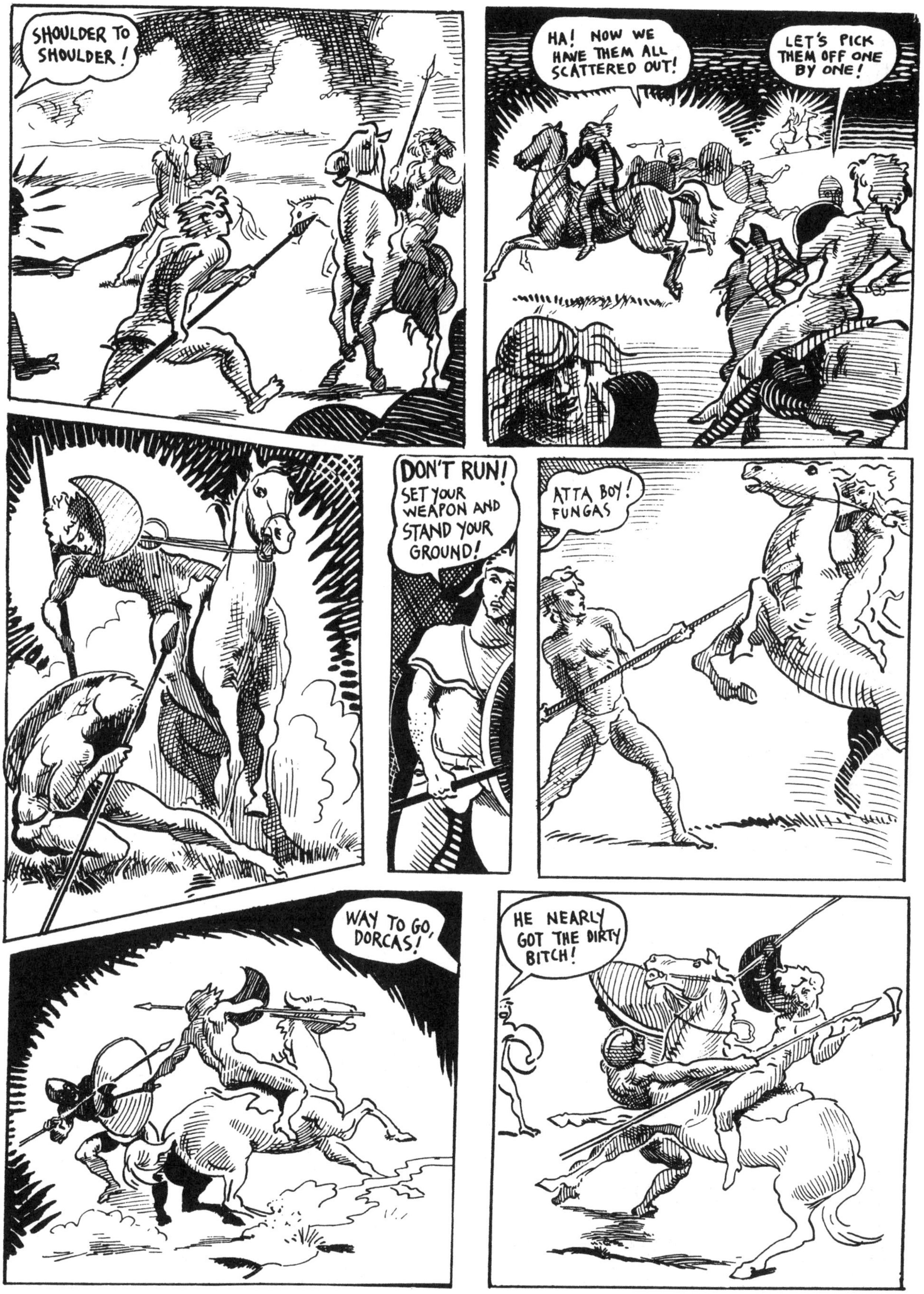
SHOULDER TO SHOULDER!
HA! NOW WE HAVE THEM ALL SCATTERED OUT!
LET'S PICK THEM OFF ONE BY ONE!
DON'T RUN! SET YOUR WEAPON AND STAND YOUR GROUND!
ATTA BOY! FUNGAS
WAY TO GO, DORCAS!
HE NEARLY GOT THE DIRTY BITCH!

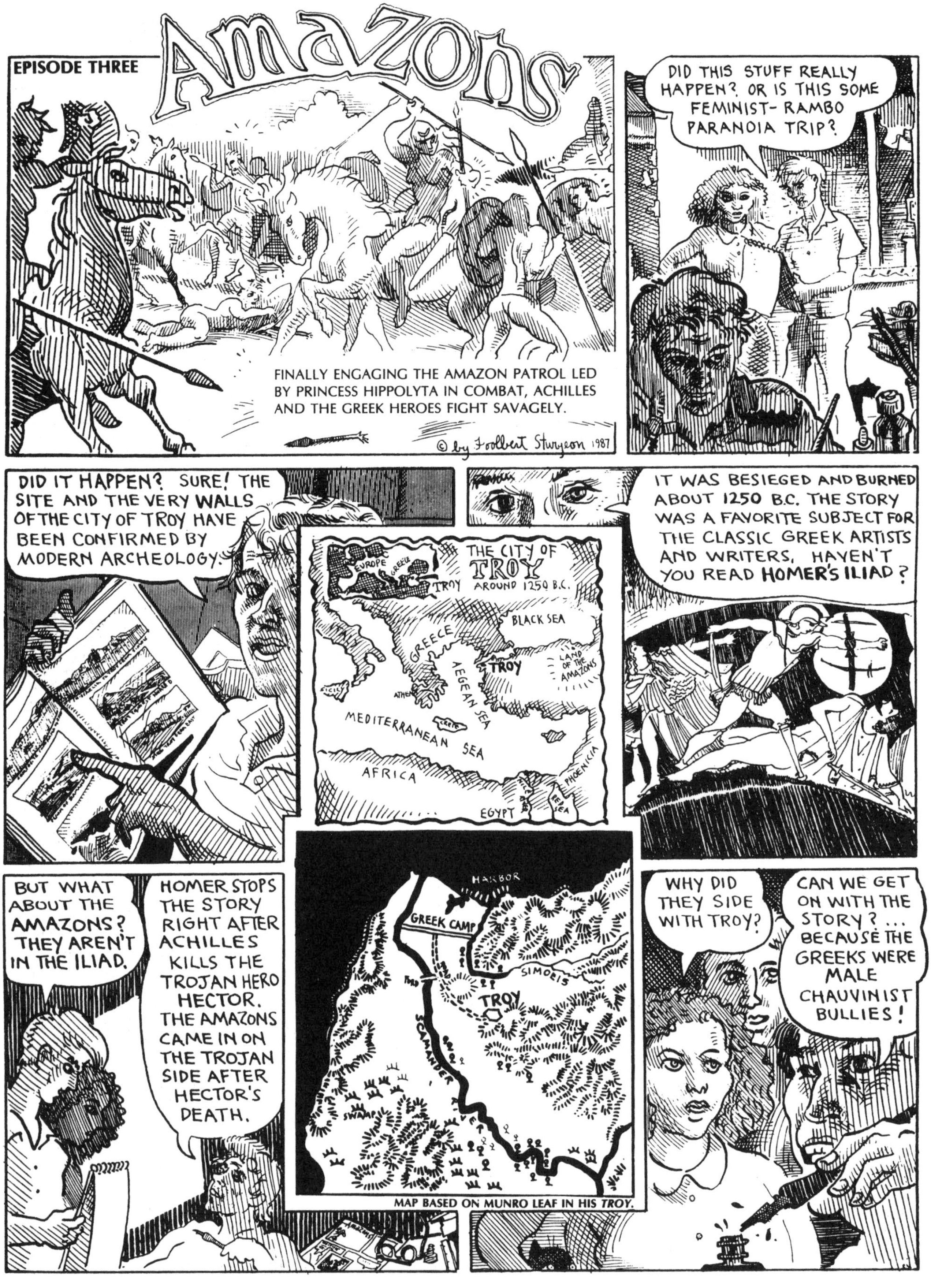
EPISODE THREE
AMAZONS
FINALLY ENGAGING THE AMAZON PATROL LED BY PRINCESS HIPPOLYTA IN COMBAT, ACHILLES AND THE GREEK HEROES FIGHT SAVAGELY.
© by Foolbert Sturgeon 1987
DID THIS STUFF REALLY HAPPEN? OR IS THIS SOME FEMINIST- RAMBO PARANOIA TRIP?
DID IT HAPPEN? SURE! THE SITE AND THE VERY WALLS OF THE CITY OF TROY HAVE BEEN CONFIRMED BY MODERN ARCHEOLOGY.
IT WAS BESIEGED AND BURNED ABOUT 1250 B.C. THE STORY WAS A FAVORITE SUBJECT FOR THE CLASSIC GREEK ARTISTS AND WRITERS, HAVEN'T YOU READ HOMER'S ILIAD?
THE CITY OF TROY AROUND 1250 B.C.
EUROPE
GREECE
TROY
BLACK SEA
GREECE
TROY
LAND OF THE AMAZONS
ATHENS
AEGEAN SEA
SICILY
CRETE
MEDITERRANEAN SEA
AFRICA
PHOENICIA
EGYPT
RED SEA
BUT WHAT ABOUT THE AMAZONS? THEY AREN'T IN THE ILIAD.
HOMER STOPS THE STORY RIGHT AFTER ACHILLES KILLS THE TROJAN HERO HECTOR. THE AMAZONS CAME IN ON THE TROJAN SIDE AFTER HECTOR'S DEATH.
HARBOR
GREEK CAMP
SIMOEIS
TROY
SCAMANDER RIVER
SWAMP
MAP BASED ON MUNRO LEAF IN HIS TROY.
WHY DID THEY SIDE WITH TROY?
CAN WE GET ON WITH THE STORY? ... BECAUSE THE GREEKS WERE MALE CHAUVINIST BULLIES!

THE TOUGH EXPERIENCED GREEK INFANTRY ARMED WITH LONG STURDY WAR SPEARS PROVE TOO STRONG FOR THE LIGHTLY ARMED FEMALE WARRIORS. **HIPPOLYTA** HERSELF IS UNHORSED IN THE MELEE.

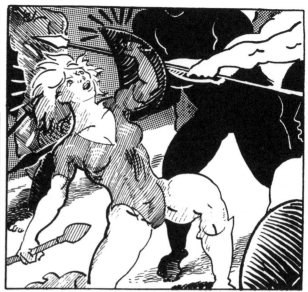

GET OUT OF THERE! RUN!

WE'LL COVER YOU!

THROW YOUR SPEAR NOW, QUICK! WHAT'S WRONG WITH YOU?

YOU JUST TOLD ME NOT TO THROW IT!

SHIT!

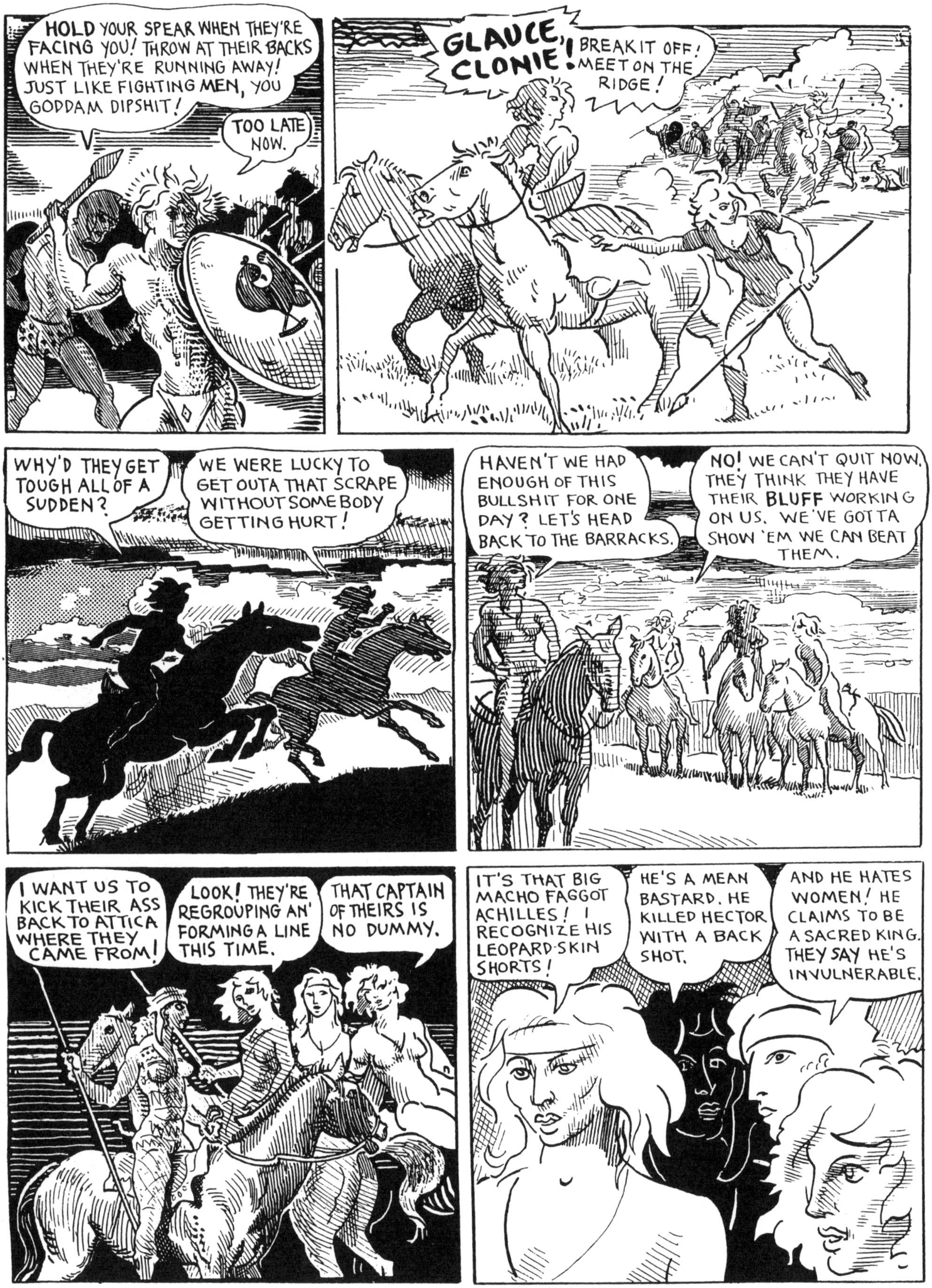
HOLD YOUR SPEAR WHEN THEY'RE FACING YOU! THROW AT THEIR BACKS WHEN THEY'RE RUNNING AWAY! JUST LIKE FIGHTING MEN, YOU GODDAM DIPSHIT!
TOO LATE NOW.
GLAUCE, CLONIE!
BREAK IT OFF! MEET ON THE RIDGE!
WHY'D THEY GET TOUGH ALL OF A SUDDEN?
WE WERE LUCKY TO GET OUTA THAT SCRAPE WITHOUT SOMEBODY GETTING HURT!
HAVEN'T WE HAD ENOUGH OF THIS BULLSHIT FOR ONE DAY? LET'S HEAD BACK TO THE BARRACKS.
NO! WE CAN'T QUIT NOW. THEY THINK THEY HAVE THEIR BLUFF WORKING ON US. WE'VE GOTTA SHOW 'EM WE CAN BEAT THEM.
I WANT US TO KICK THEIR ASS BACK TO ATTICA WHERE THEY CAME FROM!
LOOK! THEY'RE REGROUPING AN' FORMING A LINE THIS TIME.
THAT CAPTAIN OF THEIRS IS NO DUMMY.
IT'S THAT BIG MACHO FAGGOT ACHILLES! I RECOGNIZE HIS LEOPARD-SKIN SHORTS!
HE'S A MEAN BASTARD. HE KILLED HECTOR WITH A BACK SHOT.
AND HE HATES WOMEN! HE CLAIMS TO BE A SACRED KING. THEY SAY HE'S INVULNERABLE.

INVULNERABLE SACRED KING! HORSESHIT! EVERY PETTY SHEEPHERDER WHO CAN HIRE A DOZEN THUGS TO STRONGARM FOR HIM CLAIMS HE'S A SACRED KING!

I'M A SACRED QUEEN TOO! LET'S KICK HIS INVULNERABLE ASS! WE'LL FAKE A CHARGE AT THEIR CENTER...

THEN WE VEER OFF AND DOUBLE TEAM THE GUYS ON BOTH FLANKS.

GOOD PLAN! CLONIE AND TAMARA TAKE THE RIGHT. GLAUCE'N I'LL GO LEFT.

SWING WIDE ON THE FLANK. DON'T GIVE HIS BUDDY ON THE INSIDE A FREE SHOT AT YOUR UNPROTECTED SIDE.

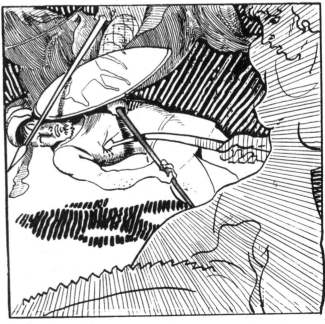

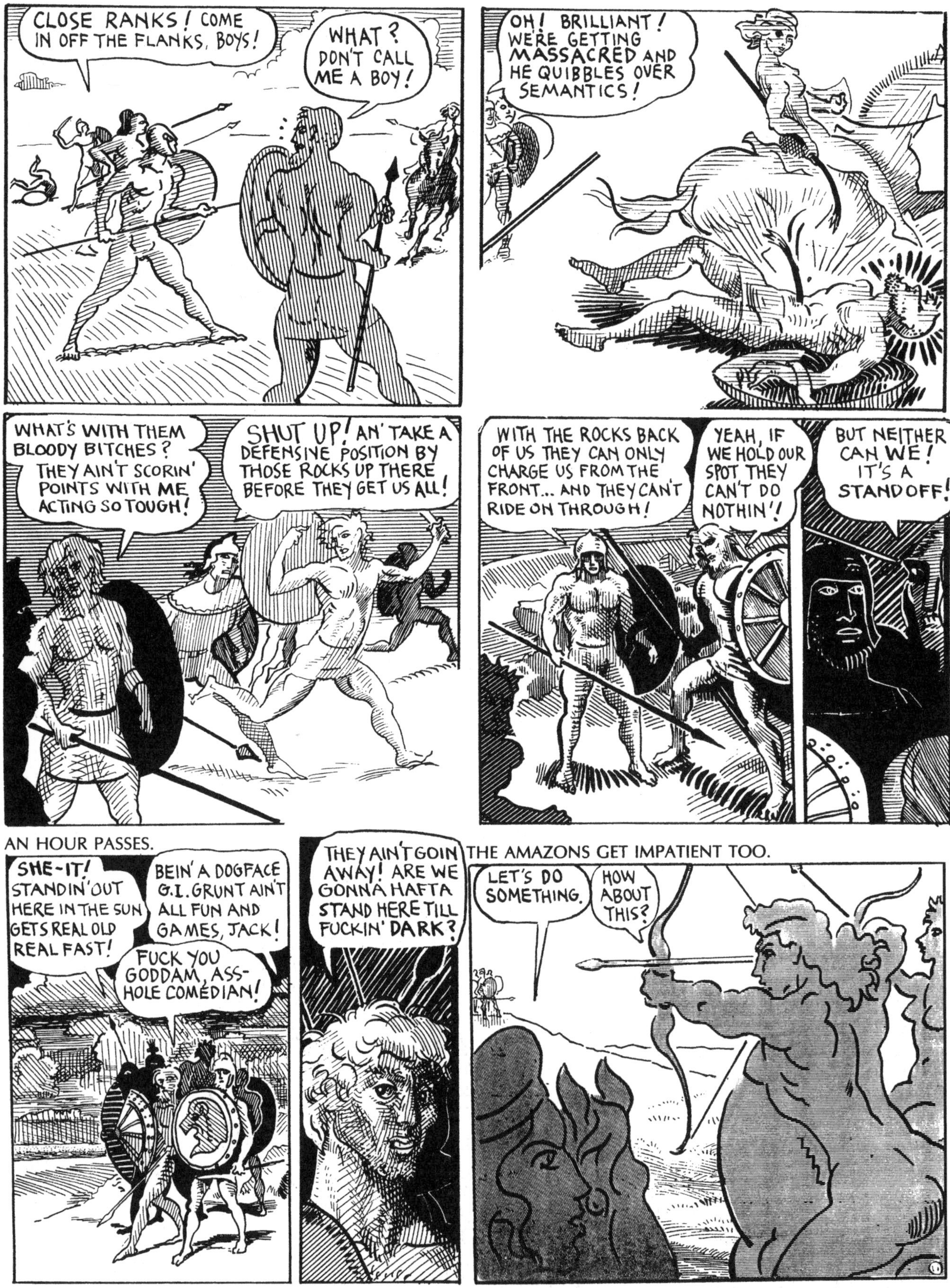
CLOSE RANKS! COME IN OFF THE FLANKS, BOYS!
WHAT? DON'T CALL ME A BOY!
OH! BRILLIANT! WE'RE GETTING MASSACRED AND HE QUIBBLES OVER SEMANTICS!
WHAT'S WITH THEM BLOODY BITCHES? THEY AIN'T SCORIN' POINTS WITH ME ACTING SO TOUGH!
SHUT UP! AN' TAKE A DEFENSIVE POSITION BY THOSE ROCKS UP THERE BEFORE THEY GET US ALL!
WITH THE ROCKS BACK OF US THEY CAN ONLY CHARGE US FROM THE FRONT... AND THEY CAN'T RIDE ON THROUGH!
YEAH, IF WE HOLD OUR SPOT THEY CAN'T DO NOTHIN'!
BUT NEITHER CAN WE! IT'S A STANDOFF!
AN HOUR PASSES.
SHE-IT! STANDIN' OUT HERE IN THE SUN GETS REAL OLD REAL FAST!
BEIN' A DOGFACE G.I. GRUNT AIN'T ALL FUN AND GAMES, JACK!
FUCK YOU GODDAM, ASS-HOLE COMÉDIAN!
THEY AIN'T GOIN AWAY! ARE WE GONNA HAFTA STAND HERE TILL FUCKIN' DARK?
THE AMAZONS GET IMPATIENT TOO.
LET'S DO SOMETHING.
HOW ABOUT THIS?

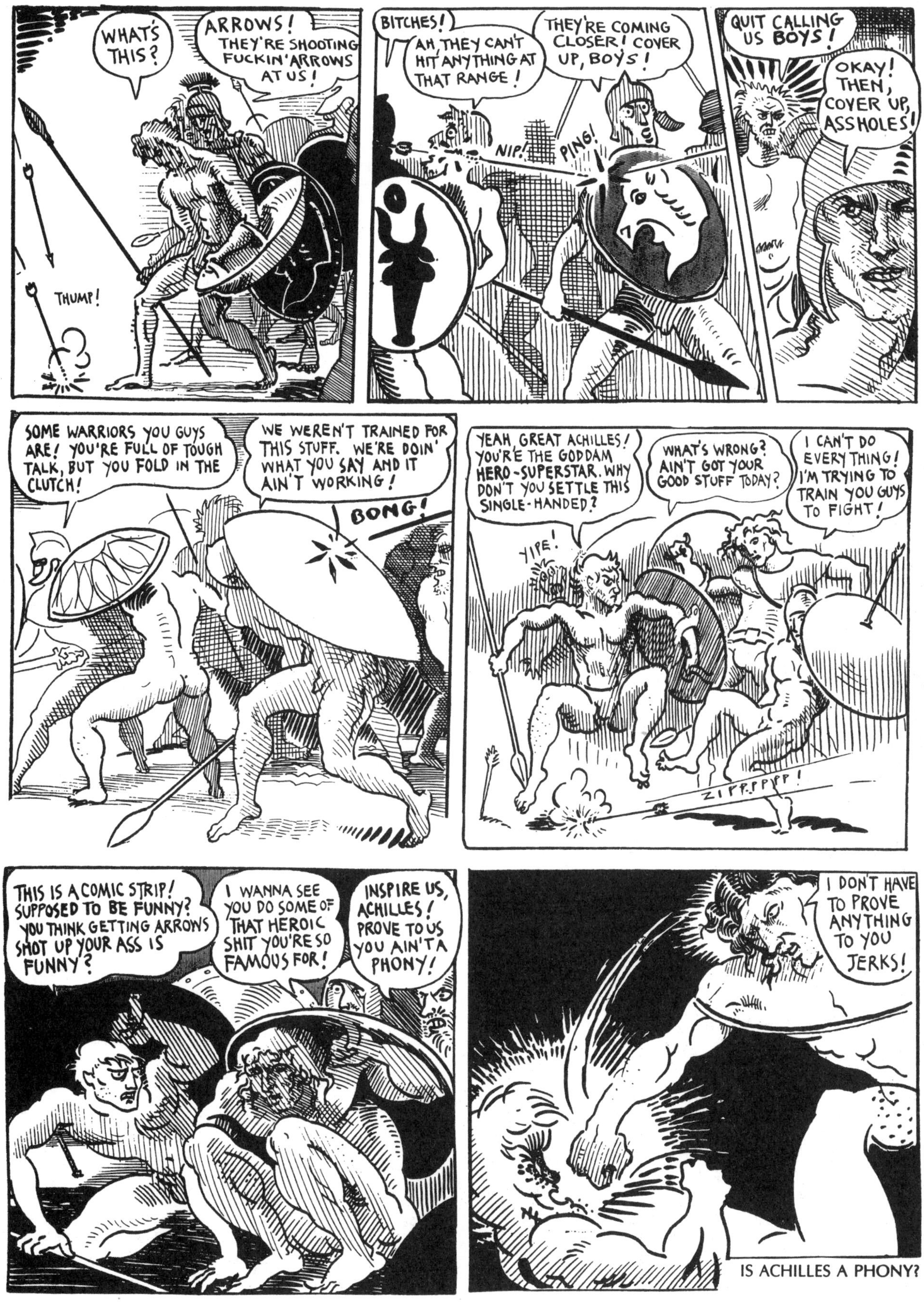
WHAT'S THIS?
ARROWS! THEY'RE SHOOTING FUCKIN' ARROWS AT US!
THUMP!
BITCHES!
AH, THEY CAN'T HIT ANYTHING AT THAT RANGE!
THEY'RE COMING CLOSER! COVER UP, BOYS!
NIP!
PING!
QUIT CALLING US BOYS!
OKAY! THEN, COVER UP, ASSHOLES!
SOME WARRIORS YOU GUYS ARE! YOU'RE FULL OF TOUGH TALK, BUT YOU FOLD IN THE CLUTCH!
WE WEREN'T TRAINED FOR THIS STUFF. WE'RE DOIN' WHAT YOU SAY AND IT AIN'T WORKING!
BONG!
YEAH, GREAT ACHILLES! YOU'RE THE GODDAM HERO-SUPERSTAR. WHY DON'T YOU SETTLE THIS SINGLE-HANDED?
WHAT'S WRONG? AIN'T GOT YOUR GOOD STUFF TODAY?
I CAN'T DO EVERYTHING! I'M TRYING TO TRAIN YOU GUYS TO FIGHT!
YIPE!
ZIPPPPPPP!
THIS IS A COMIC STRIP! SUPPOSED TO BE FUNNY? YOU THINK GETTING ARROWS SHOT UP YOUR ASS IS FUNNY?
I WANNA SEE YOU DO SOME OF THAT HEROIC SHIT YOU'RE SO FAMOUS FOR!
INSPIRE US, ACHILLES! PROVE TO US YOU AIN'T A PHONY!
I DON'T HAVE TO PROVE ANYTHING TO YOU JERKS!
IS ACHILLES A PHONY?

AMAZONS

EPISODE FOUR
BY FOOLBERT STURGEON

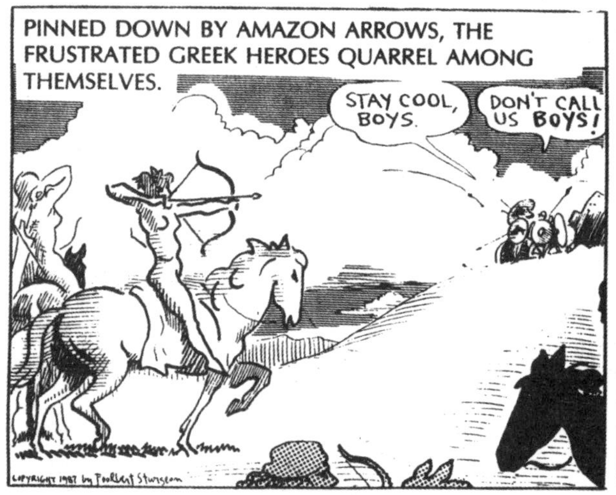
PINNED DOWN BY AMAZON ARROWS, THE FRUSTRATED GREEK HEROES QUARREL AMONG THEMSELVES.
STAY COOL, BOYS.
DON'T CALL US BOYS!
COPYRIGHT 1987 by Foolbert Sturgeon

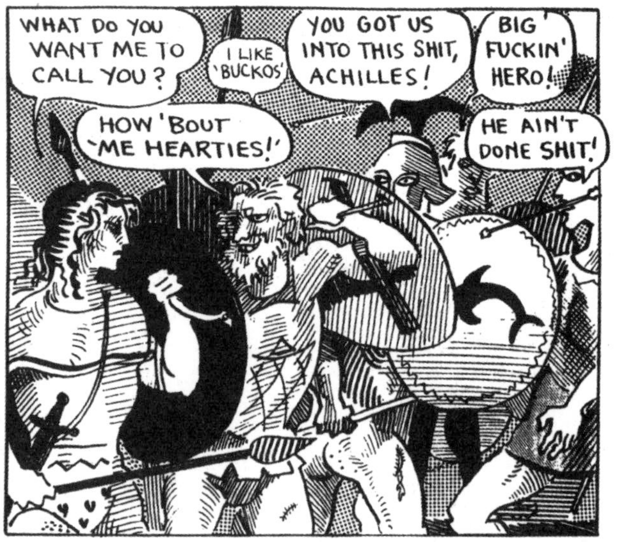
WHAT DO YOU WANT ME TO CALL YOU?
I LIKE 'BUCKOS'
YOU GOT US INTO THIS SHIT, ACHILLES!
BIG FUCKIN' HERO!
HOW 'BOUT 'ME HEARTIES!'
HE AIN'T DONE SHIT!

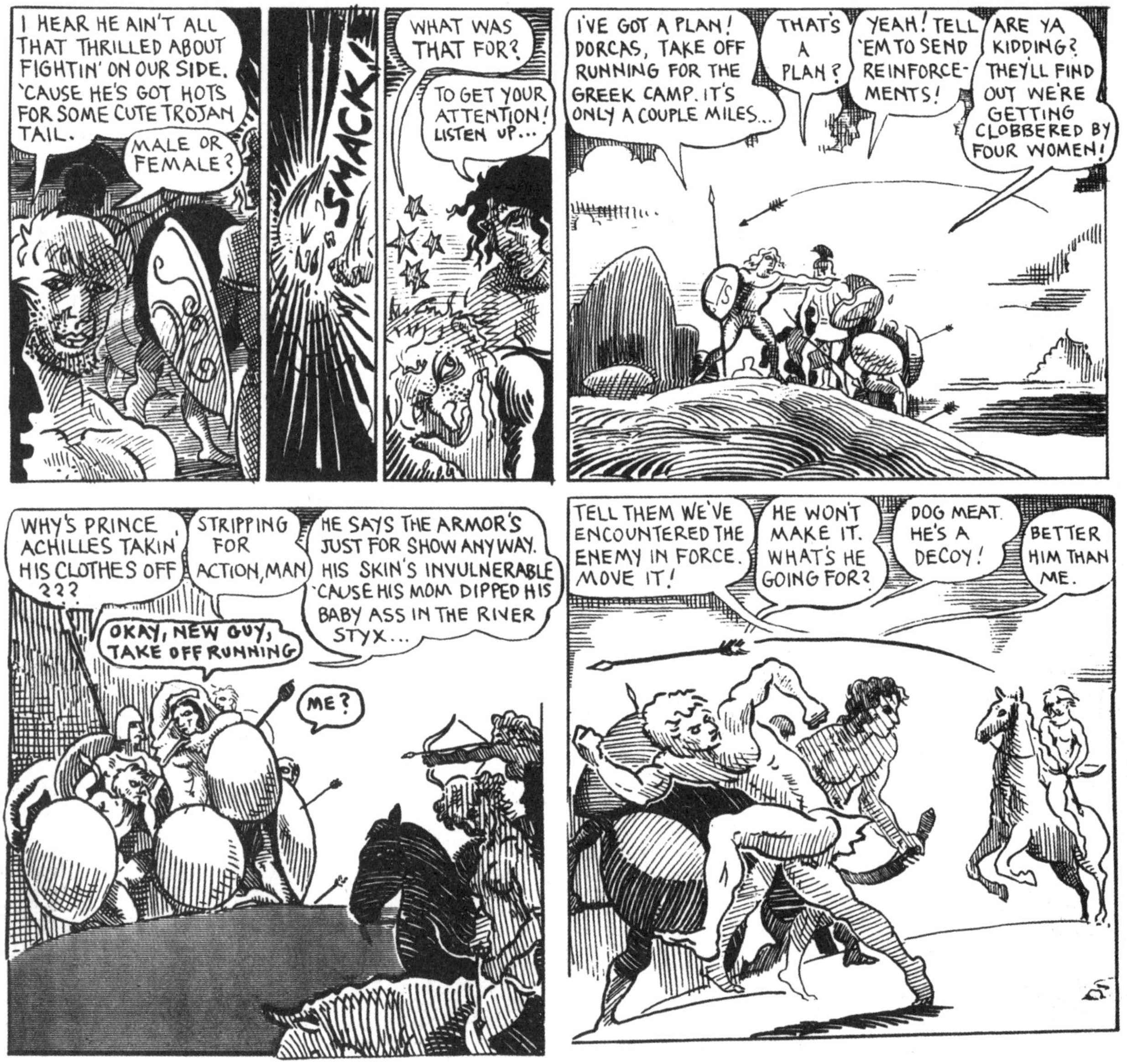
I HEAR HE AIN'T ALL THAT THRILLED ABOUT FIGHTIN' ON OUR SIDE. 'CAUSE HE'S GOT HOTS FOR SOME CUTE TROJAN TAIL.
MALE OR FEMALE?
SMACK!
WHAT WAS THAT FOR?
TO GET YOUR ATTENTION! LISTEN UP...
I'VE GOT A PLAN! DORCAS, TAKE OFF RUNNING FOR THE GREEK CAMP. IT'S ONLY A COUPLE MILES...
THAT'S A PLAN?
YEAH! TELL 'EM TO SEND REINFORCEMENTS!
ARE YA KIDDING? THEY'LL FIND OUT WE'RE GETTING CLOBBERED BY FOUR WOMEN!
WHY'S PRINCE ACHILLES TAKIN' HIS CLOTHES OFF ???
STRIPPING FOR ACTION, MAN
HE SAYS THE ARMOR'S JUST FOR SHOW ANYWAY. HIS SKIN'S INVULNERABLE 'CAUSE HIS MOM DIPPED HIS BABY ASS IN THE RIVER STYX...
OKAY, NEW GUY, TAKE OFF RUNNING
ME?
TELL THEM WE'VE ENCOUNTERED THE ENEMY IN FORCE. MOVE IT!
HE WON'T MAKE IT. WHAT'S HE GOING FOR?
DOG MEAT. HE'S A DECOY!
BETTER HIM THAN ME.

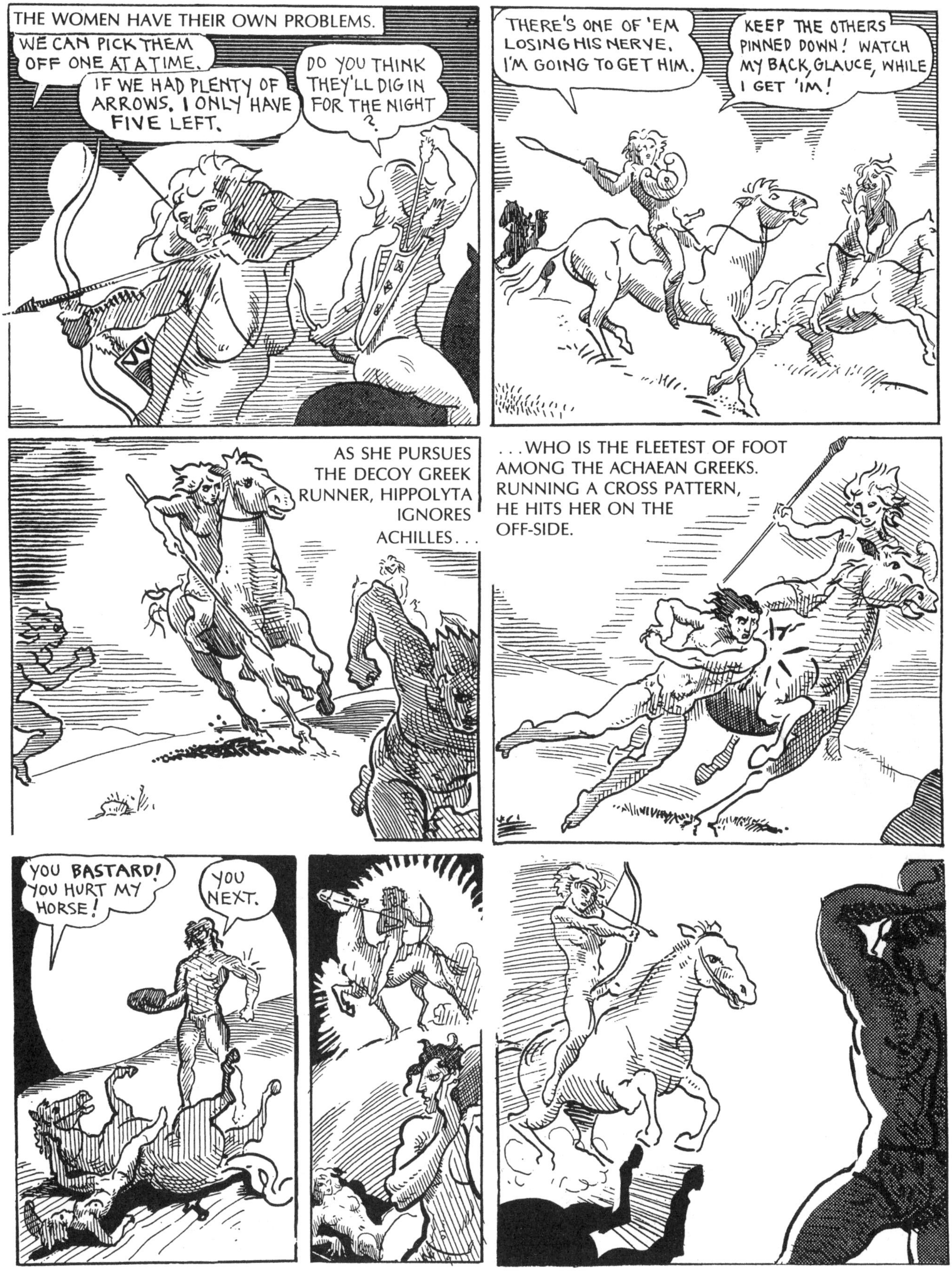
THE WOMEN HAVE THEIR OWN PROBLEMS.
WE CAN PICK THEM OFF ONE AT A TIME.
IF WE HAD PLENTY OF ARROWS. I ONLY HAVE FIVE LEFT.
DO YOU THINK THEY'LL DIG IN FOR THE NIGHT ?
THERE'S ONE OF 'EM LOSING HIS NERVE. I'M GOING TO GET HIM.
KEEP THE OTHERS PINNED DOWN! WATCH MY BACK, GLAUCE, WHILE I GET 'IM!
AS SHE PURSUES THE DECOY GREEK RUNNER, HIPPOLYTA IGNORES ACHILLES...
...WHO IS THE FLEETEST OF FOOT AMONG THE ACHAEAN GREEKS. RUNNING A CROSS PATTERN, HE HITS HER ON THE OFF-SIDE.
YOU BASTARD! YOU HURT MY HORSE!
YOU NEXT.

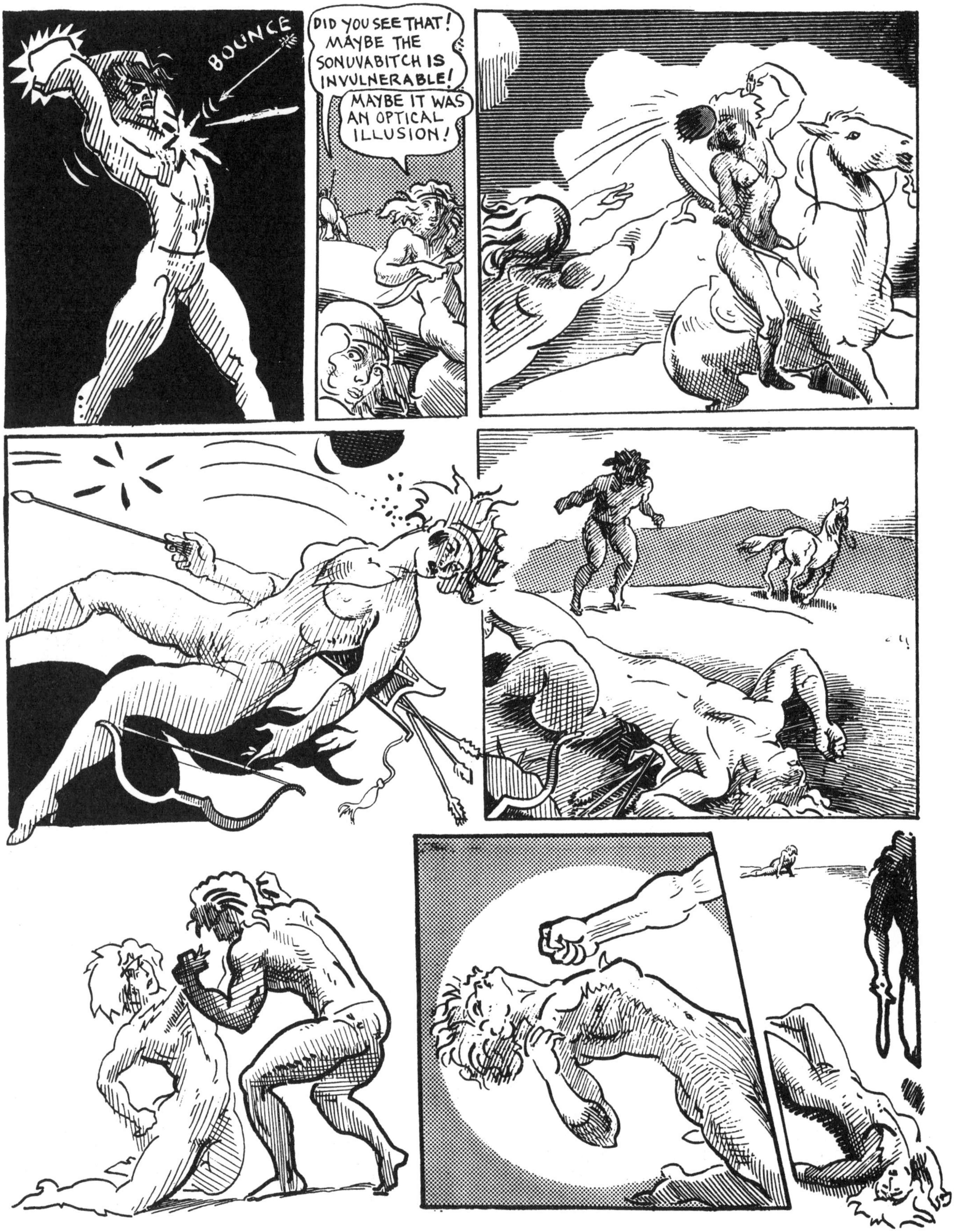
BOUNCE
DID YOU SEE THAT! MAYBE THE SONUVABITCH IS INVULNERABLE!
MAYBE IT WAS AN OPTICAL ILLUSION!

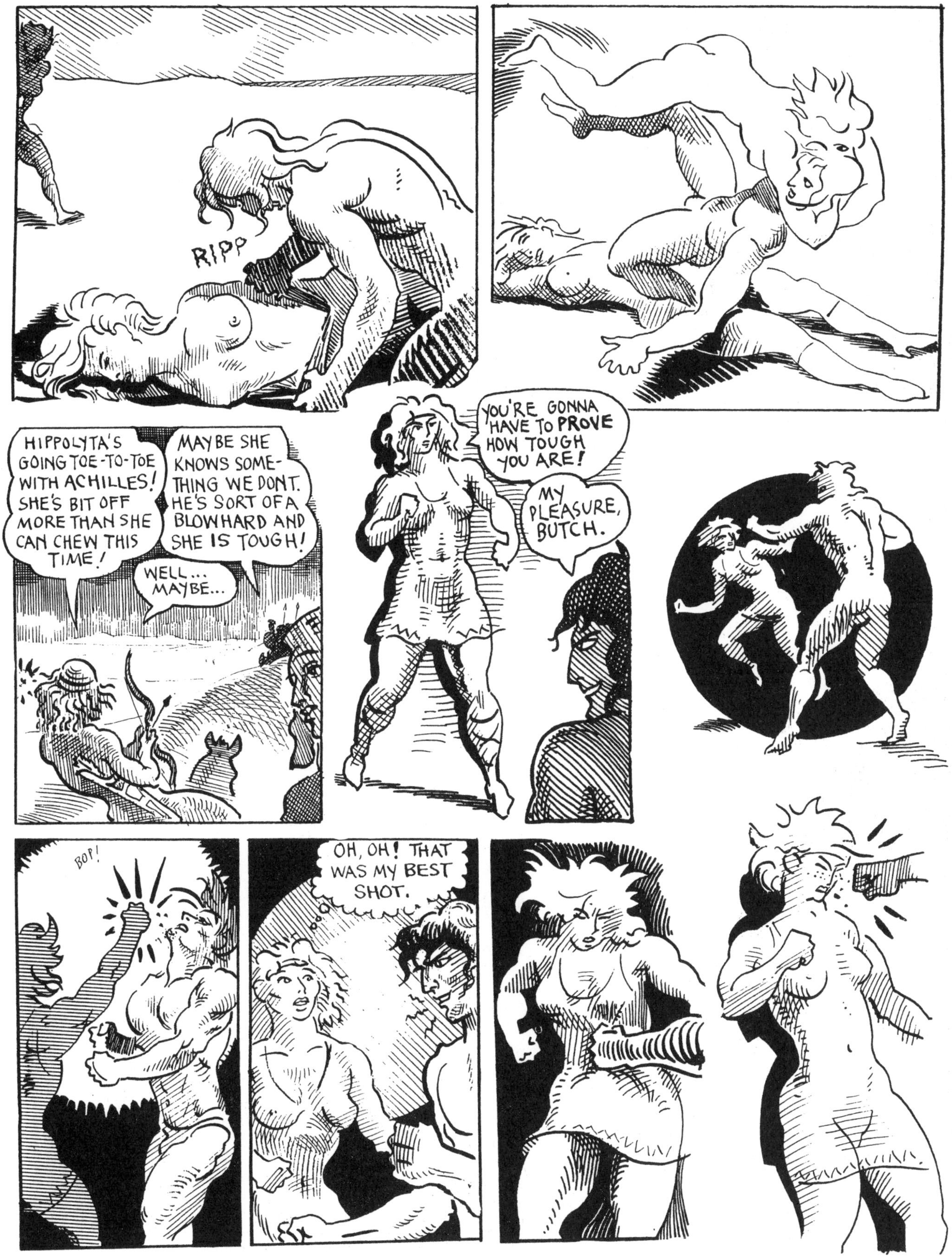
RIPP
HIPPOLYTA'S GOING TOE-TO-TOE WITH ACHILLES! SHE'S BIT OFF MORE THAN SHE CAN CHEW THIS TIME!
MAYBE SHE KNOWS SOME-THING WE DONT. HE'S SORT OF A BLOWHARD AND SHE IS TOUGH!
WELL... MAYBE...
YOU'RE GONNA HAVE TO PROVE HOW TOUGH YOU ARE!
MY PLEASURE, BUTCH.
BOP!
OH, OH! THAT WAS MY BEST SHOT.

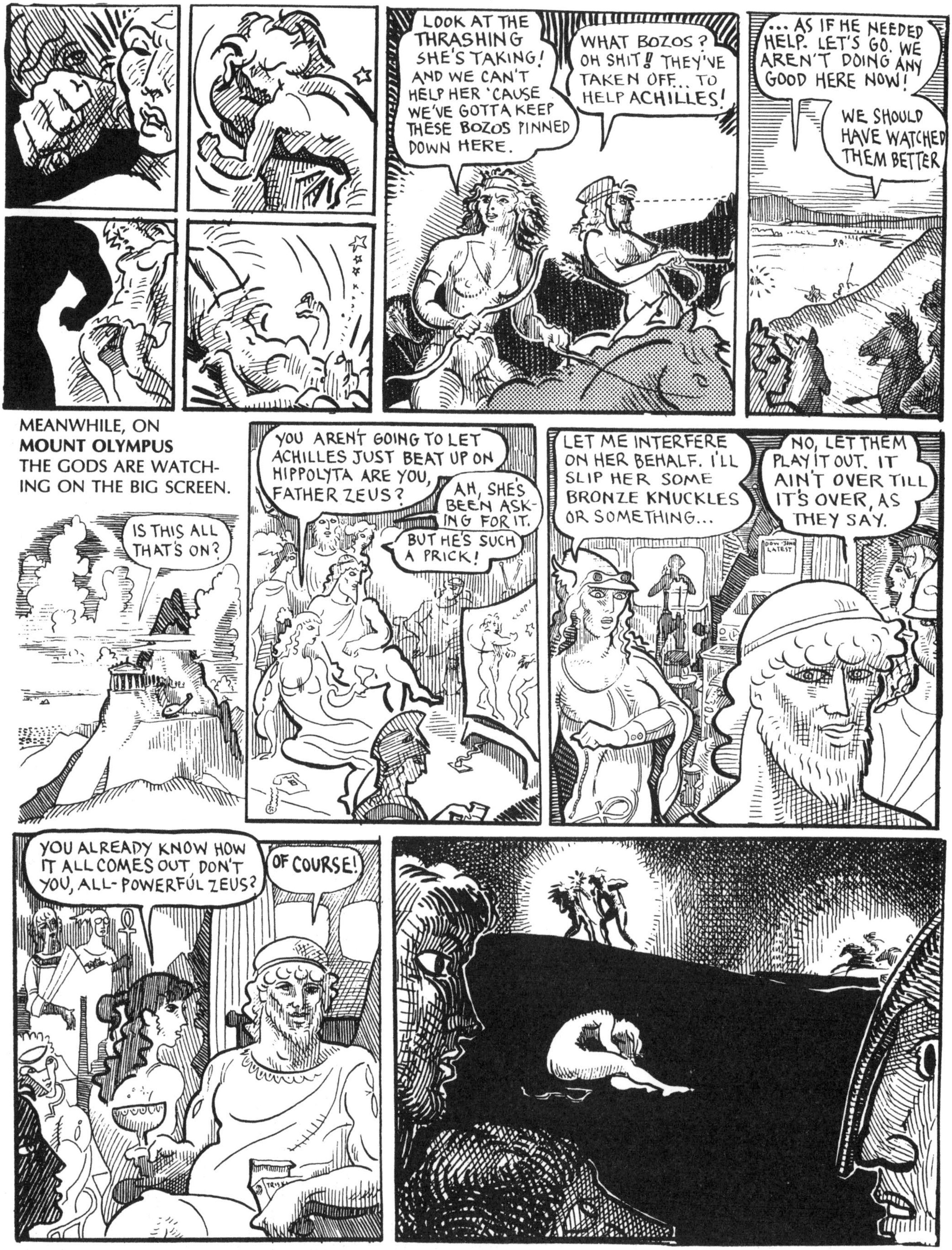
LOOK AT THE THRASHING SHE'S TAKING! AND WE CAN'T HELP HER 'CAUSE WE'VE GOTTA KEEP THESE BOZOS PINNED DOWN HERE.
WHAT BOZOS? OH SHIT! THEY'VE TAKEN OFF... TO HELP ACHILLES!
... AS IF HE NEEDED HELP. LET'S GO. WE AREN'T DOING ANY GOOD HERE NOW!
WE SHOULD HAVE WATCHED THEM BETTER
MEANWHILE, ON MOUNT OLYMPUS THE GODS ARE WATCHING ON THE BIG SCREEN.
IS THIS ALL THAT'S ON?
YOU AREN'T GOING TO LET ACHILLES JUST BEAT UP ON HIPPOLYTA ARE YOU, FATHER ZEUS?
AH, SHE'S BEEN ASKING FOR IT.
BUT HE'S SUCH A PRICK!
LET ME INTERFERE ON HER BEHALF. I'LL SLIP HER SOME BRONZE KNUCKLES OR SOMETHING...
NO, LET THEM PLAY IT OUT. IT AIN'T OVER TILL IT'S OVER, AS THEY SAY.
YOU ALREADY KNOW HOW IT ALL COMES OUT, DON'T YOU, ALL-POWERFUL ZEUS?
OF COURSE!

AMAZONS

by Foolbert Sturgeon

FINAL CHAPTER

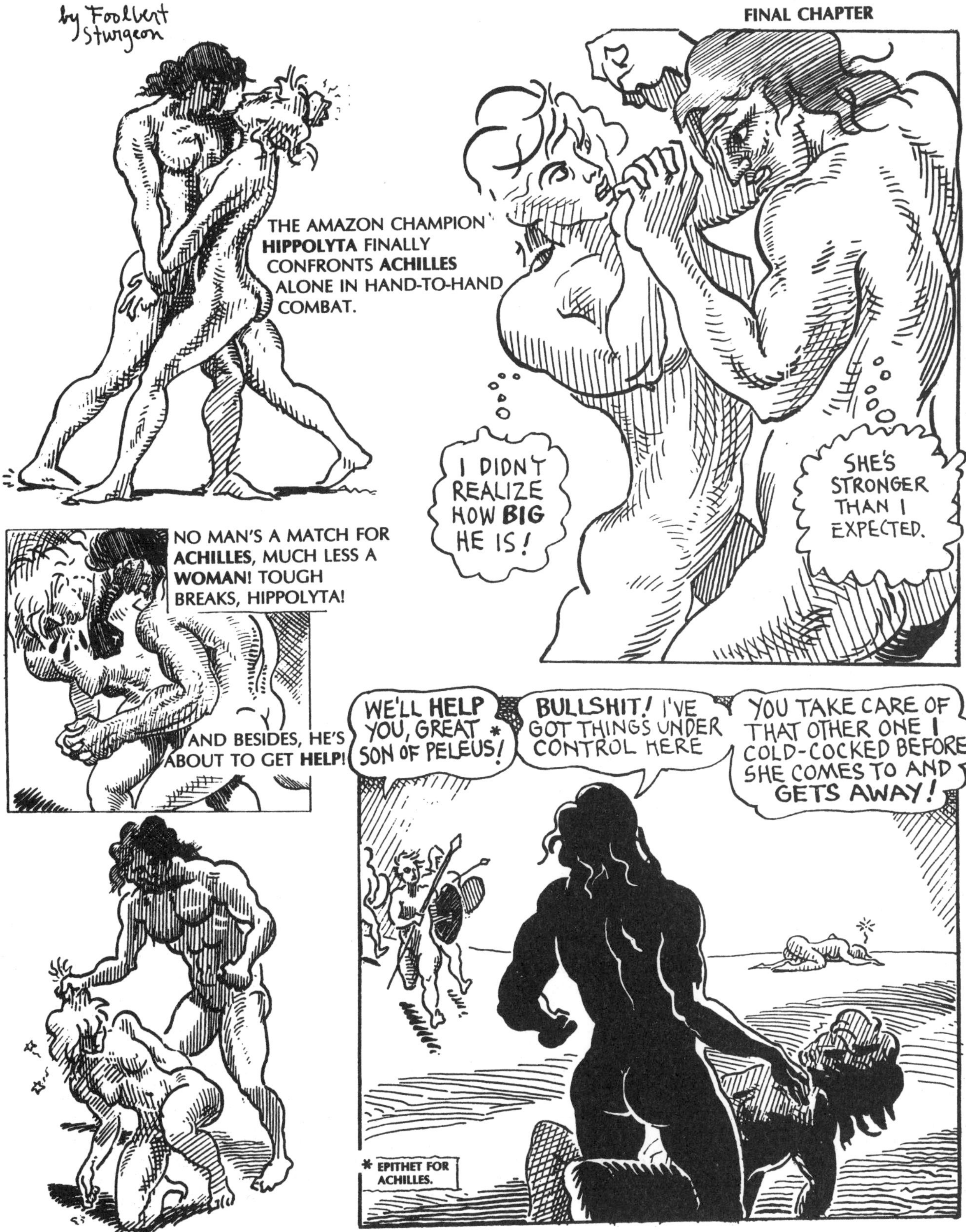

THE AMAZON CHAMPION **HIPPOLYTA** FINALLY CONFRONTS **ACHILLES** ALONE IN HAND-TO-HAND COMBAT.
I DIDN'T REALIZE HOW **BIG** HE IS!
SHE'S STRONGER THAN I EXPECTED.
NO MAN'S A MATCH FOR **ACHILLES**, MUCH LESS A **WOMAN**! TOUGH BREAKS, HIPPOLYTA!
AND BESIDES, HE'S ABOUT TO GET **HELP**!
WE'LL **HELP** YOU, GREAT SON OF PELEUS! *
BULLSHIT! I'VE GOT THINGS UNDER CONTROL HERE
YOU TAKE CARE OF THAT OTHER ONE I COLD-COCKED BEFORE SHE COMES TO AND **GETS AWAY**!
* EPITHET FOR ACHILLES.

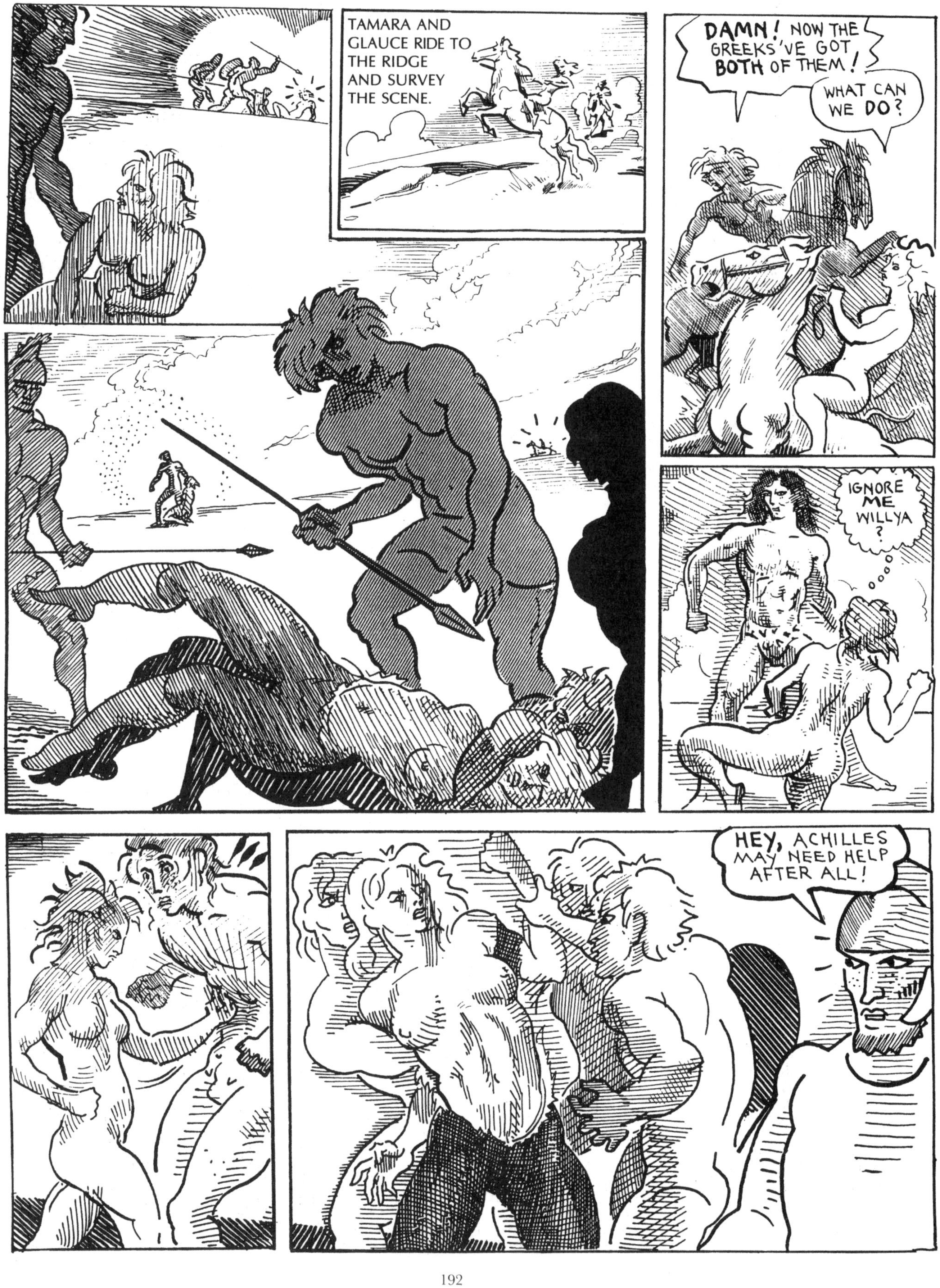
TAMARA AND GLAUCE RIDE TO THE RIDGE AND SURVEY THE SCENE.
DAMN! NOW THE GREEKS'VE GOT BOTH OF THEM!
WHAT CAN WE DO?
IGNORE ME WILLYA?
HEY, ACHILLES MAY NEED HELP AFTER ALL!

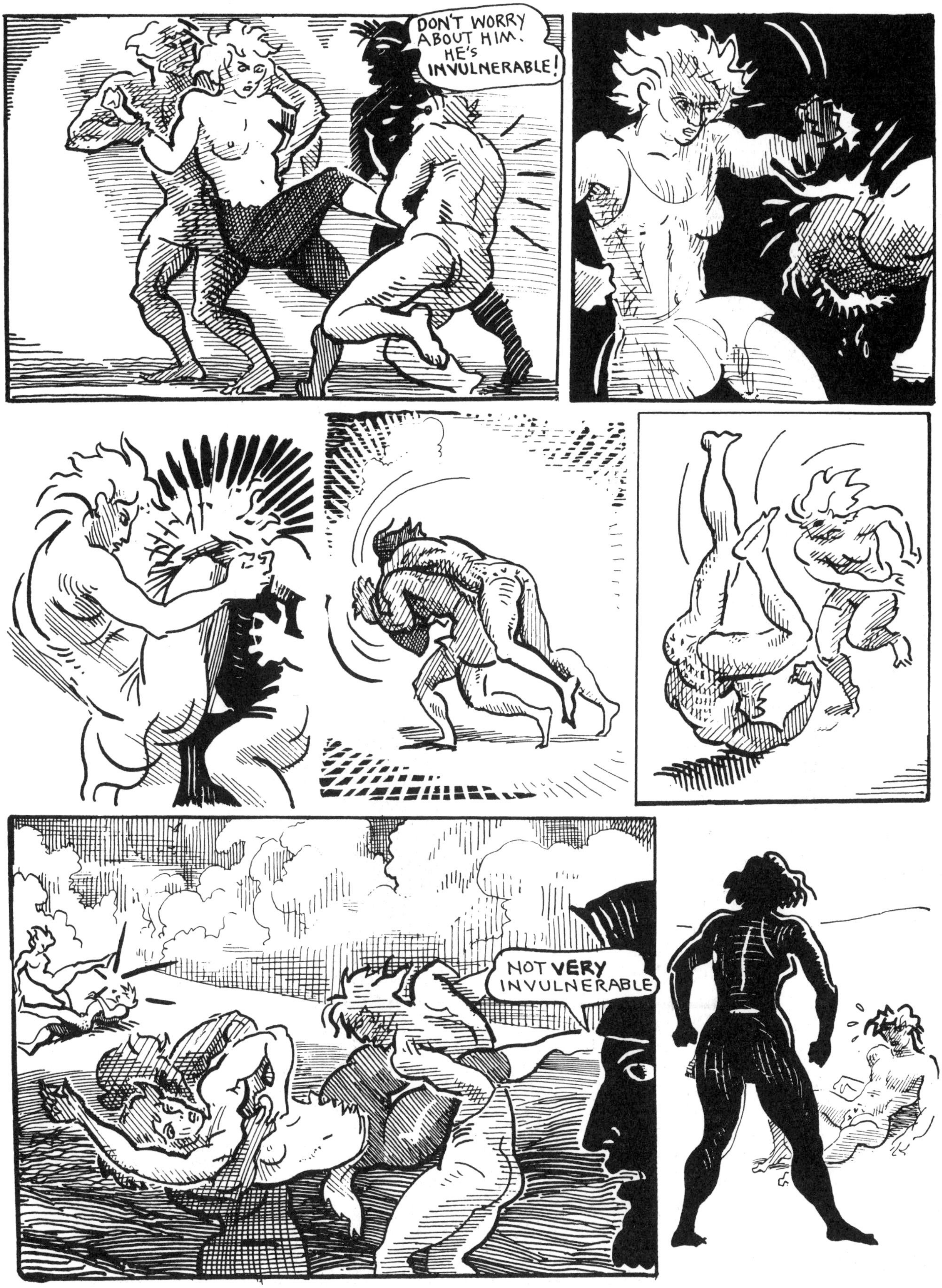
DON'T WORRY ABOUT HIM. HE'S INVULNERABLE!
NOT VERY INVULNERABLE

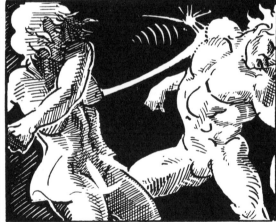

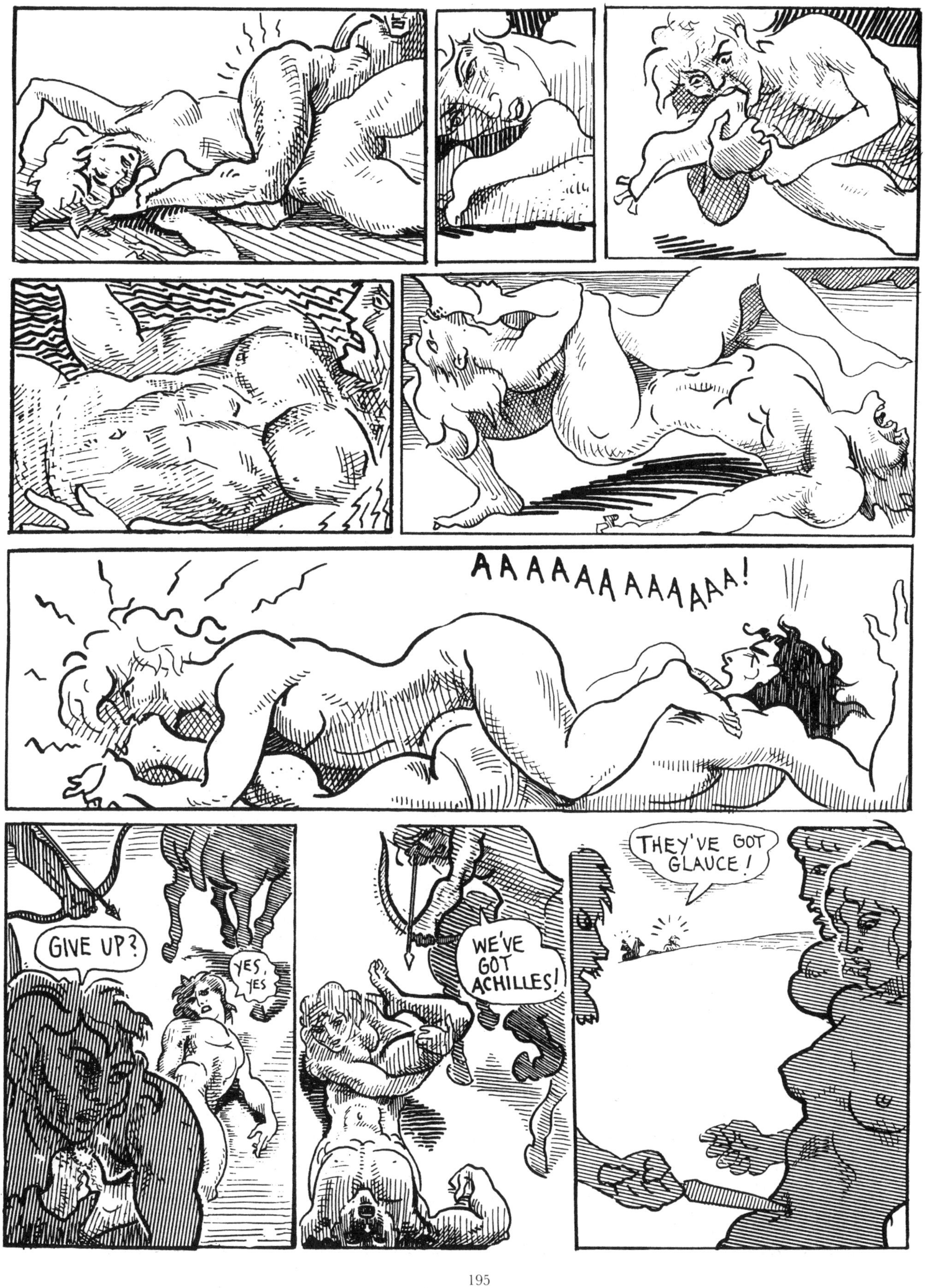
AAAAAAAAAAAAA!
GIVE UP?
YES, YES
WE'VE GOT ACHILLES!
THEY'VE GOT GLAUCE!

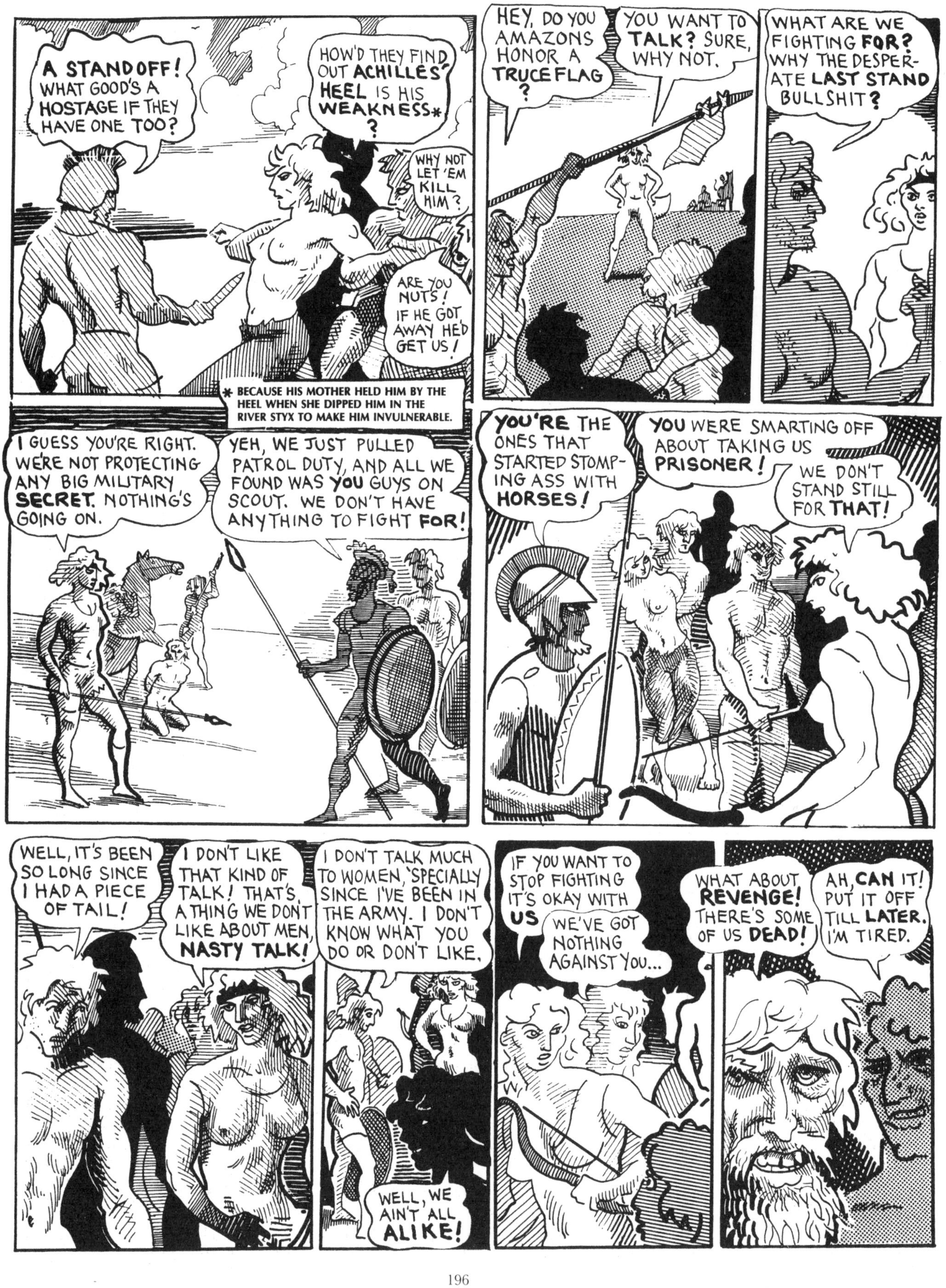

A STANDOFF! WHAT GOOD'S A HOSTAGE IF THEY HAVE ONE TOO?
HOW'D THEY FIND OUT ACHILLES' HEEL IS HIS WEAKNESS*?
WHY NOT LET 'EM KILL HIM?
ARE YOU NUTS! IF HE GOT AWAY HE'D GET US!
* BECAUSE HIS MOTHER HELD HIM BY THE HEEL WHEN SHE DIPPED HIM IN THE RIVER STYX TO MAKE HIM INVULNERABLE.
HEY, DO YOU AMAZONS HONOR A TRUCE FLAG?
YOU WANT TO TALK? SURE, WHY NOT.
WHAT ARE WE FIGHTING FOR? WHY THE DESPERATE LAST STAND BULLSHIT?
I GUESS YOU'RE RIGHT. WE'RE NOT PROTECTING ANY BIG MILITARY SECRET. NOTHING'S GOING ON.
YEH, WE JUST PULLED PATROL DUTY, AND ALL WE FOUND WAS YOU GUYS ON SCOUT. WE DON'T HAVE ANYTHING TO FIGHT FOR!
YOU'RE THE ONES THAT STARTED STOMPING ASS WITH HORSES!
YOU WERE SMARTING OFF ABOUT TAKING US PRISONER!
WE DON'T STAND STILL FOR THAT!
WELL, IT'S BEEN SO LONG SINCE I HAD A PIECE OF TAIL!
I DON'T LIKE THAT KIND OF TALK! THAT'S A THING WE DON'T LIKE ABOUT MEN, NASTY TALK!
I DON'T TALK MUCH TO WOMEN, 'SPECIALLY SINCE I'VE BEEN IN THE ARMY. I DON'T KNOW WHAT YOU DO OR DON'T LIKE.
WELL, WE AIN'T ALL ALIKE!
IF YOU WANT TO STOP FIGHTING IT'S OKAY WITH US
WE'VE GOT NOTHING AGAINST YOU...
WHAT ABOUT REVENGE! THERE'S SOME OF US DEAD!
AH, CAN IT! PUT IT OFF TILL LATER. I'M TIRED.

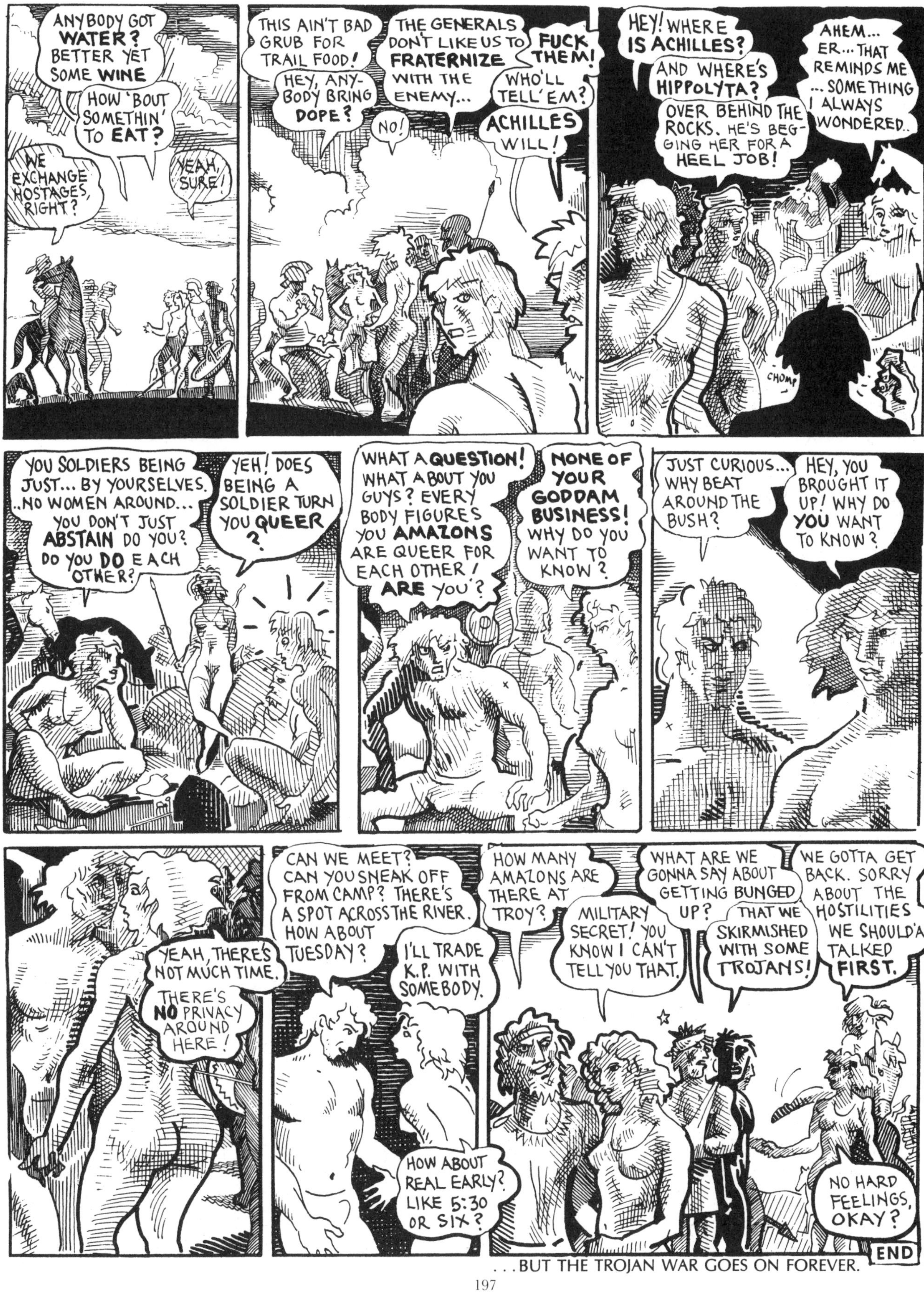
ANYBODY GOT WATER? BETTER YET SOME WINE
HOW 'BOUT SOMETHIN' TO EAT?
WE EXCHANGE HOSTAGES, RIGHT?
YEAH, SURE!
THIS AIN'T BAD GRUB FOR TRAIL FOOD!
HEY, ANY-BODY BRING DOPE?
NO!
THE GENERALS DON'T LIKE US TO FRATERNIZE WITH THE ENEMY...
FUCK THEM!
WHO'LL TELL 'EM?
ACHILLES WILL!
HEY! WHERE IS ACHILLES?
AND WHERE'S HIPPOLYTA?
OVER BEHIND THE ROCKS. HE'S BEG-GING HER FOR A HEEL JOB!
AHEM... ER... THAT REMINDS ME ...SOMETHING I ALWAYS WONDERED..
CHOMP
YOU SOLDIERS BEING JUST... BY YOURSELVES. ..NO WOMEN AROUND... YOU DON'T JUST ABSTAIN DO YOU? DO YOU DO EACH OTHER?
YEH! DOES BEING A SOLDIER TURN YOU QUEER?
WHAT A QUESTION! WHAT ABOUT YOU GUYS? EVERY BODY FIGURES YOU AMAZONS ARE QUEER FOR EACH OTHER! ARE YOU?
NONE OF YOUR GODDAM BUSINESS! WHY DO YOU WANT TO KNOW?
JUST CURIOUS... WHY BEAT AROUND THE BUSH?
HEY, YOU BROUGHT IT UP! WHY DO YOU WANT TO KNOW?
YEAH, THERE'S NOT MUCH TIME.
THERE'S NO PRIVACY AROUND HERE!
CAN WE MEET? CAN YOU SNEAK OFF FROM CAMP? THERE'S A SPOT ACROSS THE RIVER. HOW ABOUT TUESDAY?
I'LL TRADE K.P. WITH SOMEBODY.
HOW ABOUT REAL EARLY? LIKE 5:30 OR SIX?
HOW MANY AMAZONS ARE THERE AT TROY?
MILITARY SECRET! YOU KNOW I CAN'T TELL YOU THAT.
WHAT ARE WE GONNA SAY ABOUT GETTING BUNGED UP?
THAT WE SKIRMISHED WITH SOME TROJANS!
WE GOTTA GET BACK. SORRY ABOUT THE HOSTILITIES WE SHOULD'A TALKED FIRST.
NO HARD FEELINGS, OKAY?
END

...BUT THE TROJAN WAR GOES ON FOREVER.

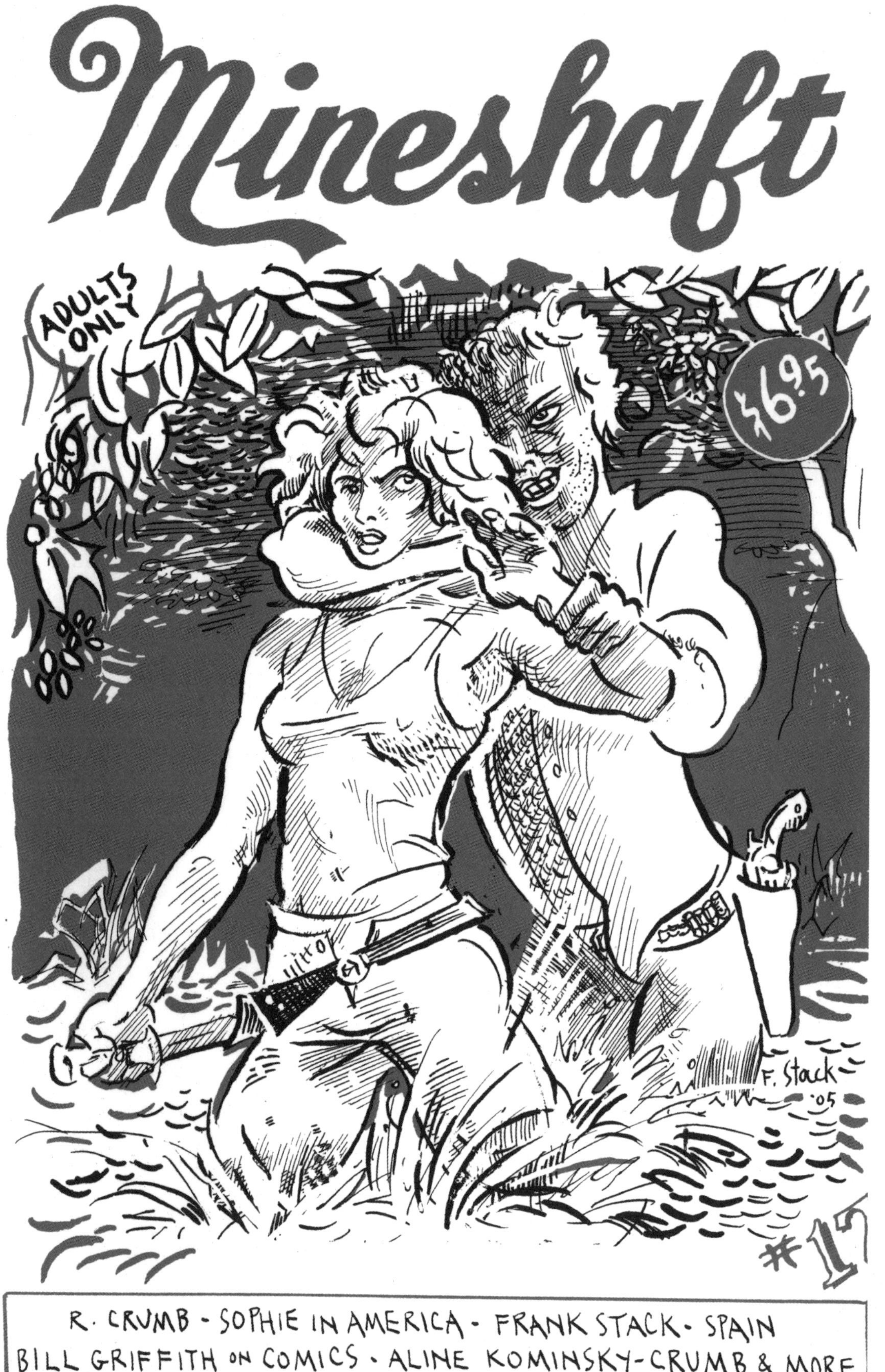

Mineshaft
ADULTS ONLY
$6.95
F. Stack '05
#17
R. CRUMB - SOPHIE IN AMERICA - FRANK STACK - SPAIN
BILL GRIFFITH ON COMICS - ALINE KOMINSKY-CRUMB & MORE

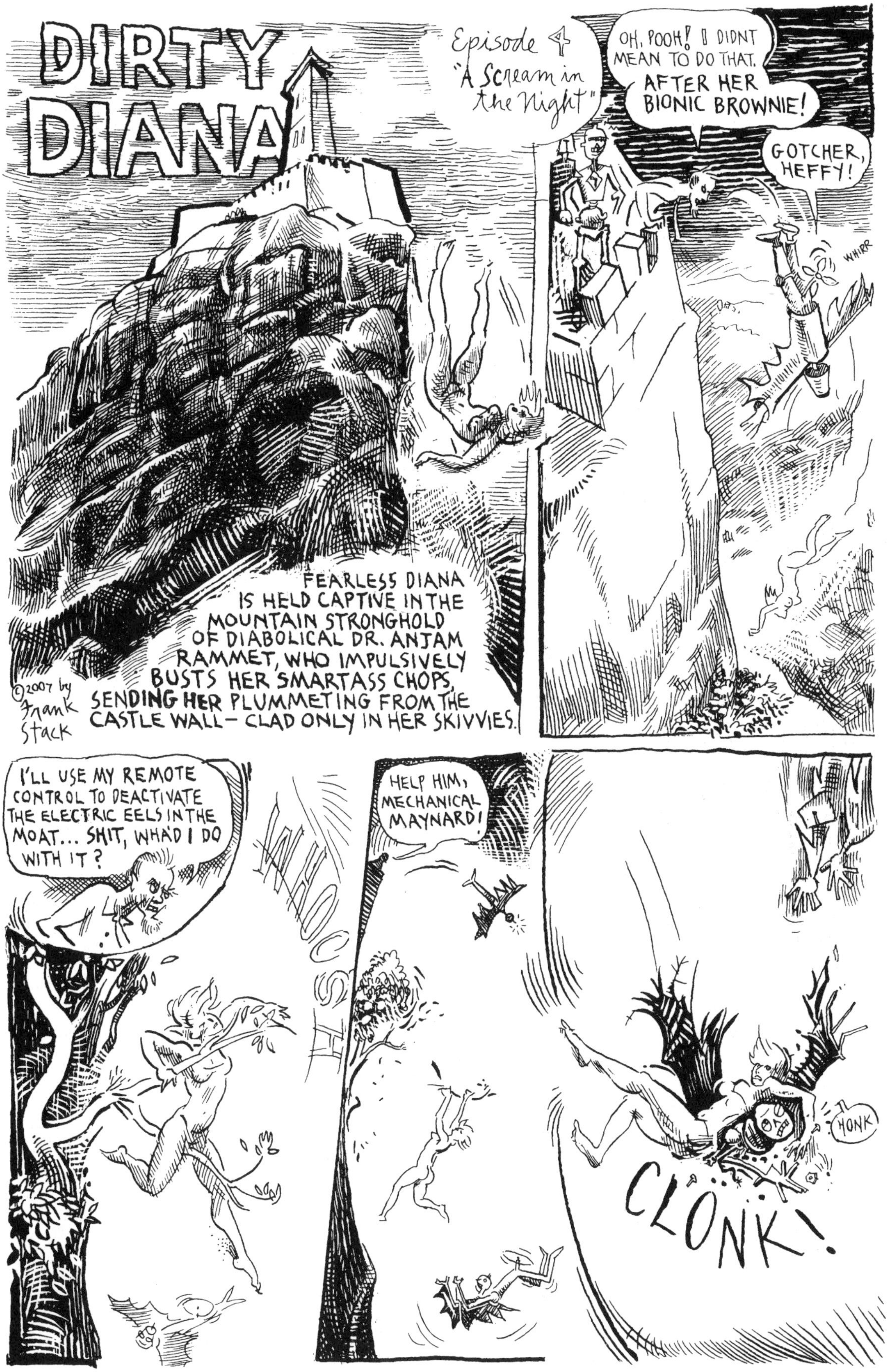
DIRTY DIANA
Episode 4 "A Scream in the Night"
OH, POOH! I DIDNT MEAN TO DO THAT. AFTER HER BIONIC BROWNIE!
GOTCHER, HEFFY!
WHIRR
FEARLESS DIANA IS HELD CAPTIVE IN THE MOUNTAIN STRONGHOLD OF DIABOLICAL DR. ANJAM RAMMET, WHO IMPULSIVELY BUSTS HER SMARTASS CHOPS, SENDING HER PLUMMETING FROM THE CASTLE WALL — CLAD ONLY IN HER SKIVVIES.
©2007 by Frank Stack
I'LL USE MY REMOTE CONTROL TO DEACTIVATE THE ELECTRIC EELS IN THE MOAT... SHIT, WHAD'I DO WITH IT?
HELP HIM, MECHANICAL MAYNARD!
HONK
CLONK!

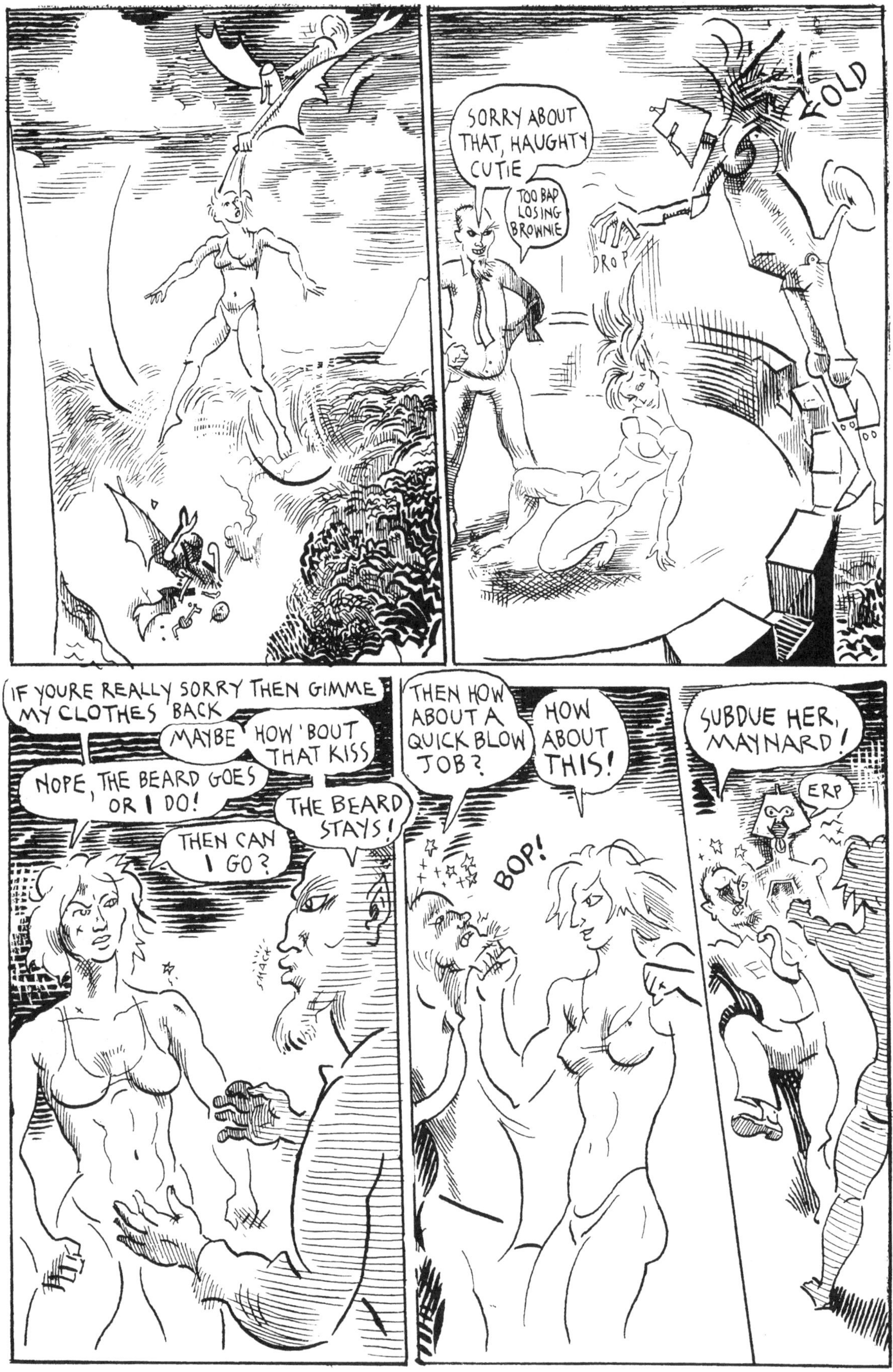
SORRY ABOUT THAT, HAUGHTY CUTIE
TOO BAD LOSING BROWNIE
DROP
FOLD
IF YOURE REALLY SORRY THEN GIMME MY CLOTHES BACK
MAYBE
HOW 'BOUT THAT KISS
NOPE, THE BEARD GOES OR I DO!
THE BEARD STAYS!
THEN CAN I GO?
SMACK
THEN HOW ABOUT A QUICK BLOW JOB?
HOW ABOUT THIS!
BOP!
SUBDUE HER, MAYNARD!
ERP
DIRTY DIANA EPISODE 4 PAGE 2 OF 7

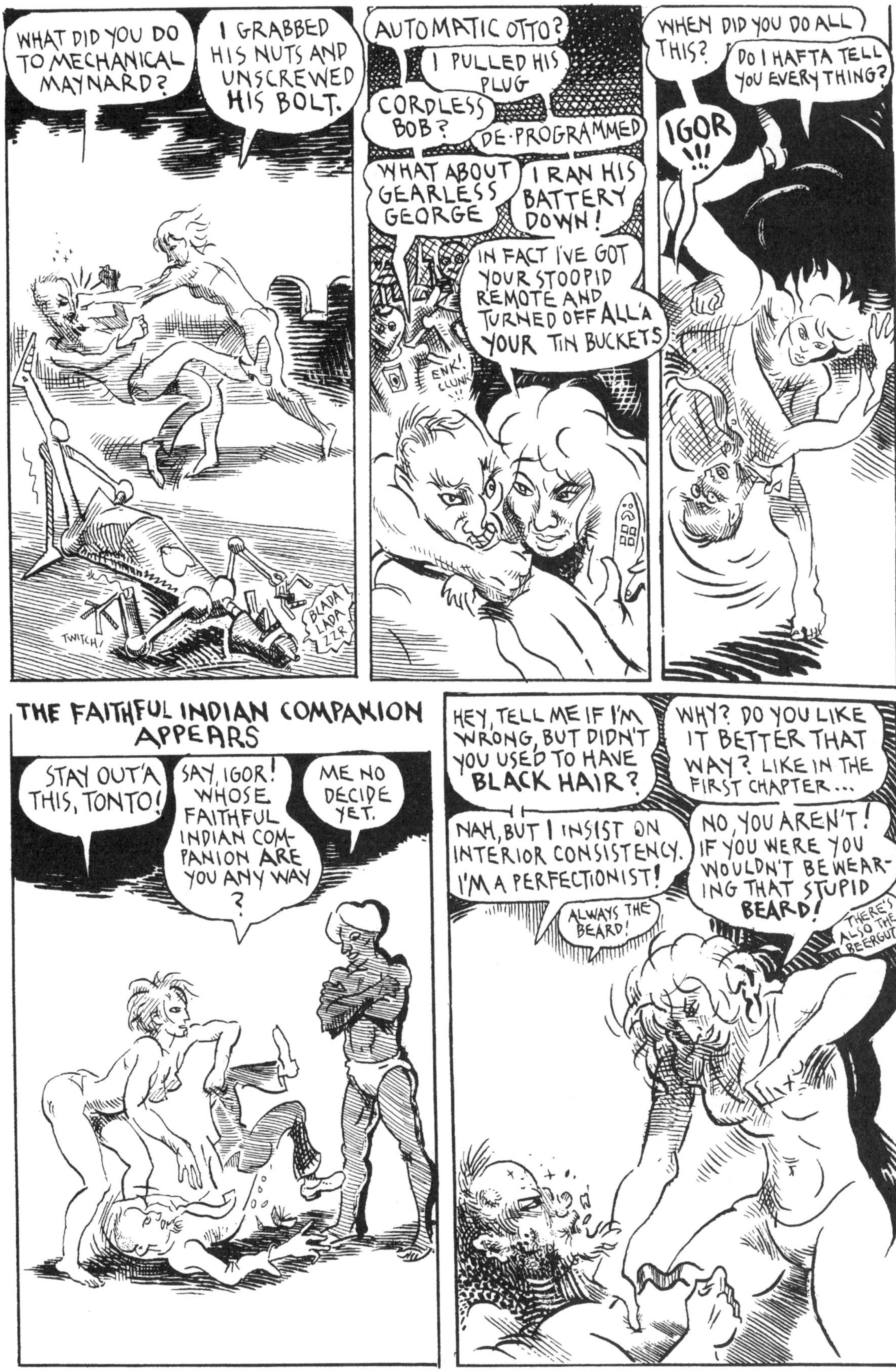
WHAT DID YOU DO TO MECHANICAL MAYNARD?
I GRABBED HIS NUTS AND UNSCREWED HIS BOLT.
TWITCH!
BLADA LADA ZZZR
AUTOMATIC OTTO?
I PULLED HIS PLUG
CORDLESS BOB?
DE-PROGRAMMED
WHAT ABOUT GEARLESS GEORGE
I RAN HIS BATTERY DOWN!
IN FACT I'VE GOT YOUR STOOPID REMOTE AND TURNED OFF ALL'A YOUR TIN BUCKETS
ENK! CLUNK !!!
WHEN DID YOU DO ALL THIS?
DO I HAFTA TELL YOU EVERYTHING?
IGOR !!!
THE FAITHFUL INDIAN COMPANION APPEARS
STAY OUT'A THIS, TONTO!
SAY, IGOR! WHOSE FAITHFUL INDIAN COMPANION ARE YOU ANY WAY ?
ME NO DECIDE YET.
HEY, TELL ME IF I'M WRONG, BUT DIDN'T YOU USED TO HAVE BLACK HAIR?
WHY? DO YOU LIKE IT BETTER THAT WAY? LIKE IN THE FIRST CHAPTER...
NAH, BUT I INSIST ON INTERIOR CONSISTENCY. I'M A PERFECTIONIST!
ALWAYS THE BEARD!
NO, YOU AREN'T! IF YOU WERE YOU WOULDN'T BE WEARING THAT STUPID BEARD!
THERE'S ALSO THE BEERGUT
DIRTY DIANA EPISODE 4 PAGE 3 OF 7

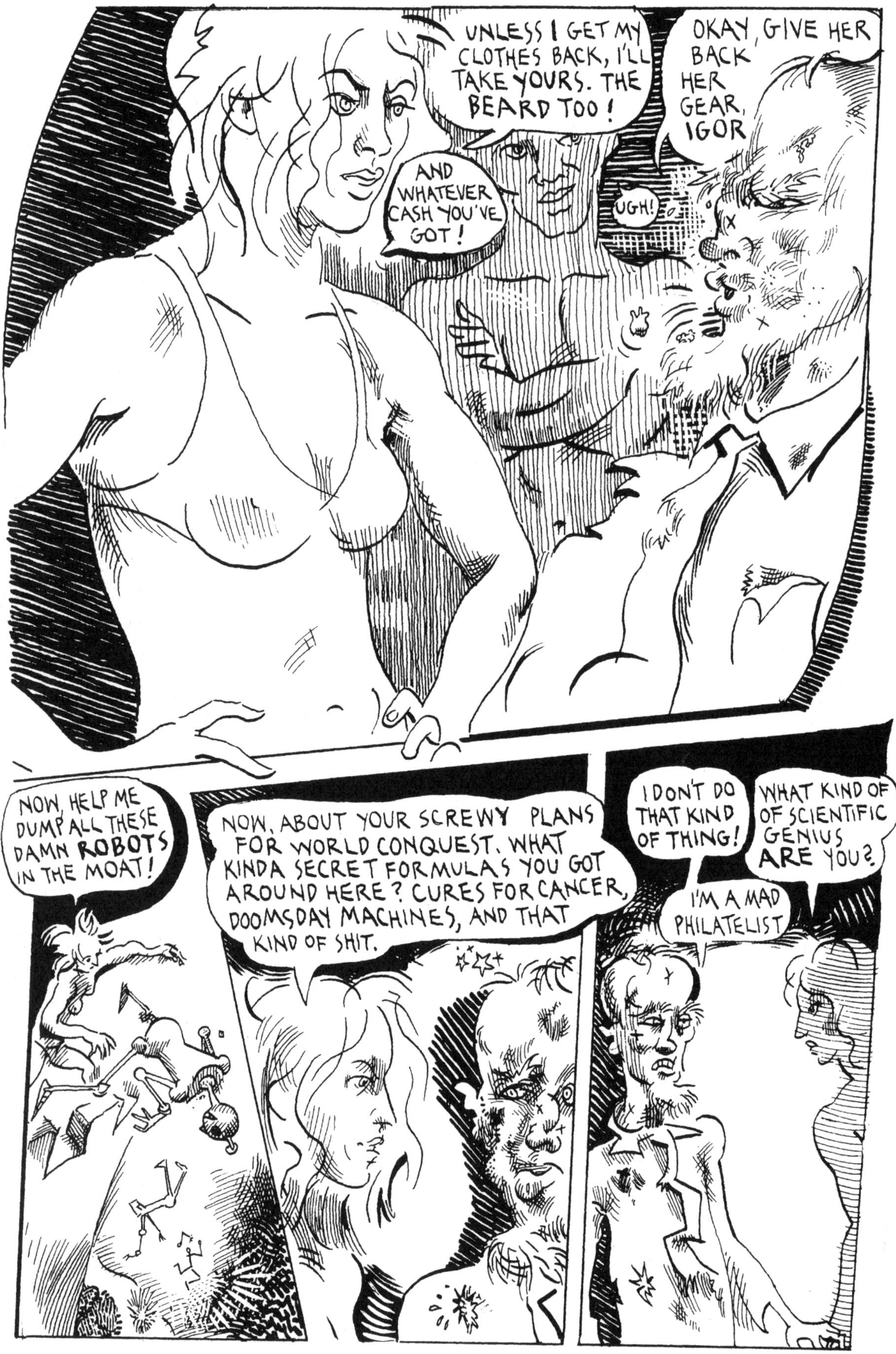
UNLESS I GET MY CLOTHES BACK, I'LL TAKE YOURS. THE BEARD TOO!
AND WHATEVER CASH YOU'VE GOT!
OKAY, GIVE HER BACK HER GEAR, IGOR
UGH!
NOW, HELP ME DUMP ALL THESE DAMN ROBOTS IN THE MOAT!
NOW, ABOUT YOUR SCREWY PLANS FOR WORLD CONQUEST. WHAT KINDA SECRET FORMULAS YOU GOT AROUND HERE? CURES FOR CANCER, DOOMSDAY MACHINES, AND THAT KIND OF SHIT.
I DON'T DO THAT KIND OF THING!
WHAT KIND OF OF SCIENTIFIC GENIUS ARE YOU?
I'M A MAD PHILATELIST

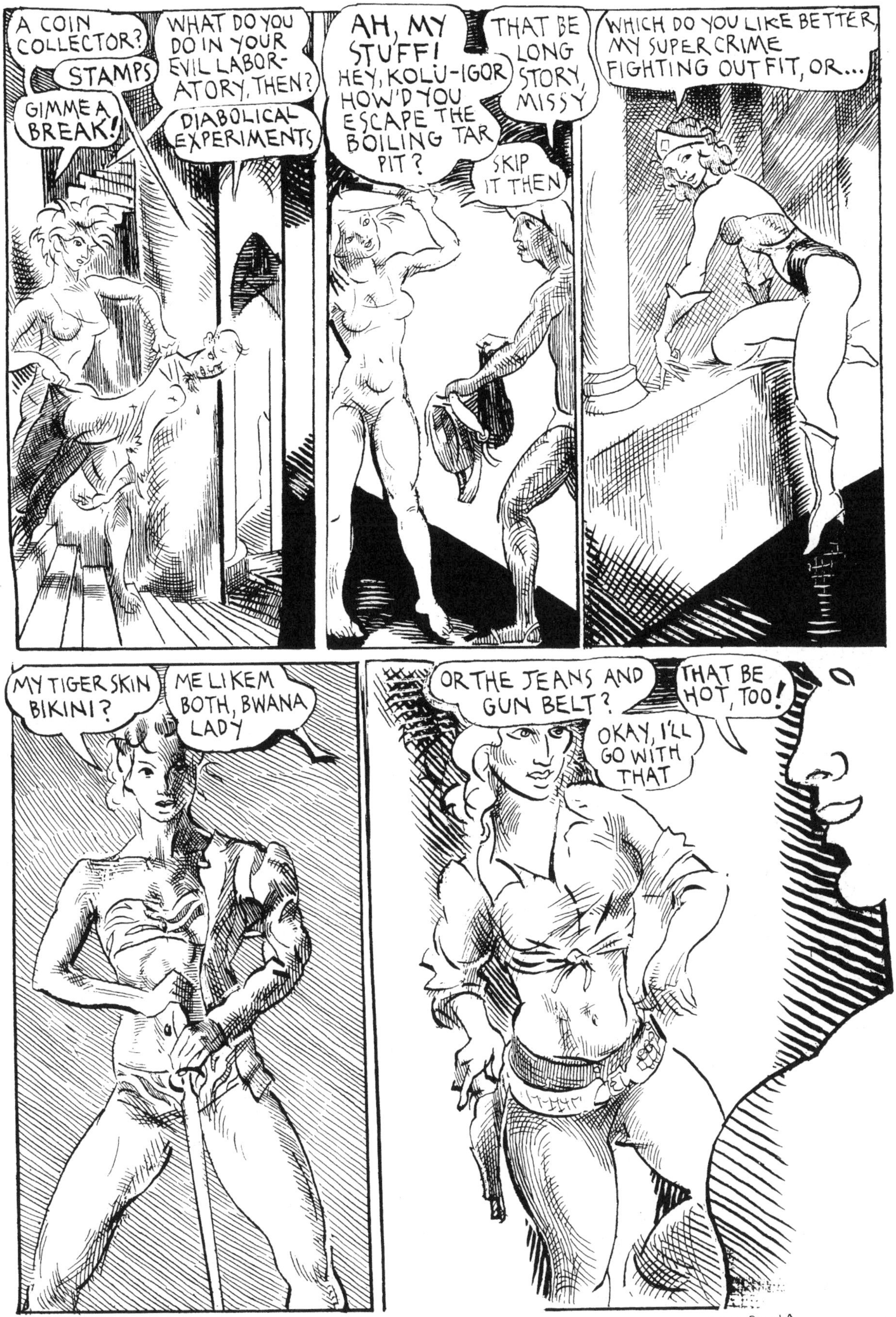
A COIN COLLECTOR?
STAMPS
GIMME A BREAK!
WHAT DO YOU DO IN YOUR EVIL LABORATORY, THEN?
DIABOLICAL EXPERIMENTS
AH, MY STUFF! HEY, KOLU-IGOR HOW'D YOU ESCAPE THE BOILING TAR PIT?
THAT BE LONG STORY, MISSY
SKIP IT THEN
WHICH DO YOU LIKE BETTER, MY SUPER CRIME FIGHTING OUTFIT, OR...
MY TIGER SKIN BIKINI?
ME LIKEM BOTH, BWANA LADY
OR THE JEANS AND GUN BELT?
THAT BE HOT, TOO!
OKAY, I'LL GO WITH THAT
DIRTY DIANA EPISODE 4
PAGE 5 OF 7

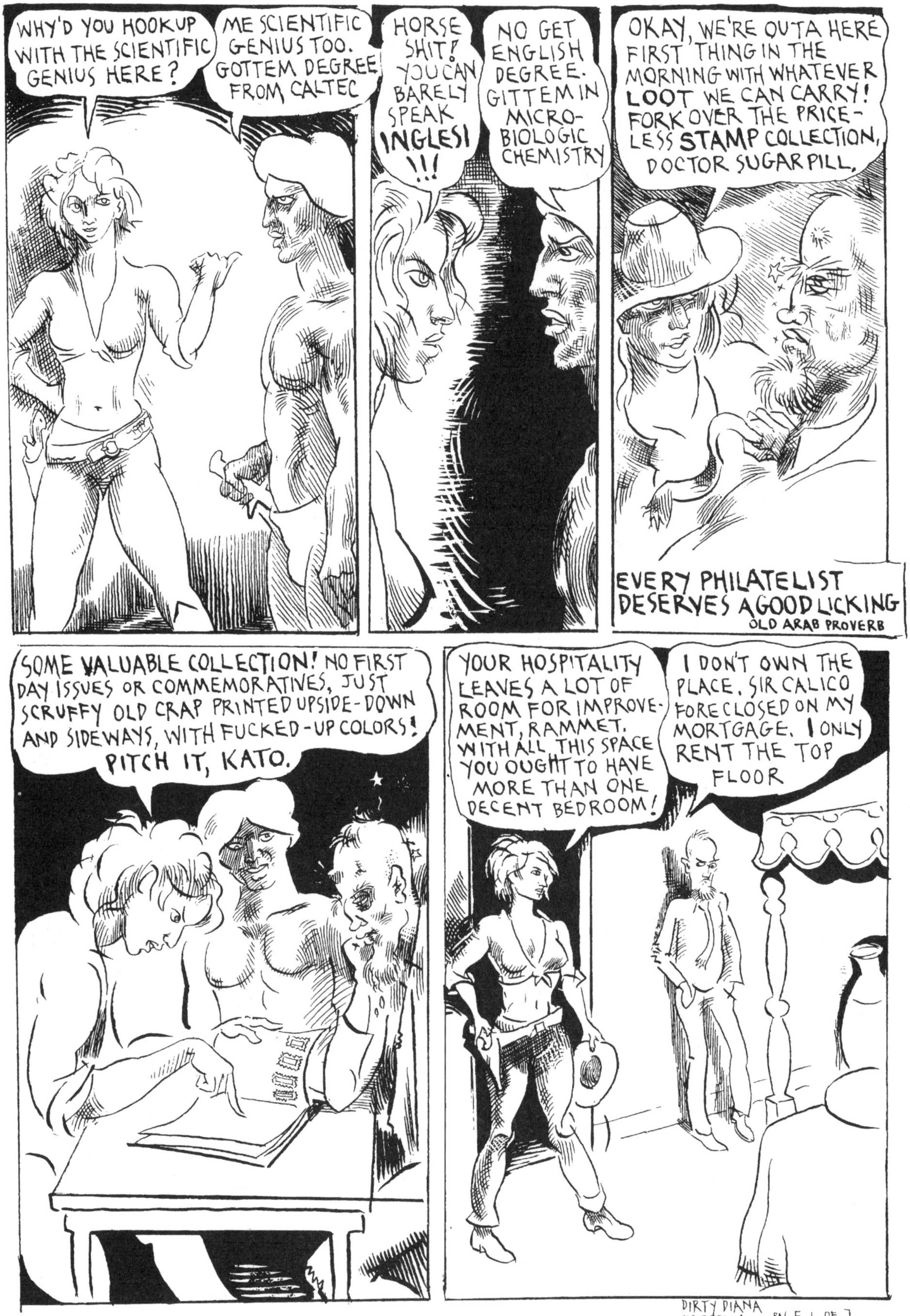
WHY'D YOU HOOKUP WITH THE SCIENTIFIC GENIUS HERE?
ME SCIENTIFIC GENIUS TOO. GOTTEM DEGREE FROM CALTEC
HORSE SHIT! YOU CAN BARELY SPEAK INGLESI !!!
NO GET ENGLISH DEGREE. GITTEM IN MICRO-BIOLOGIC CHEMISTRY
OKAY, WE'RE OUTA HERE FIRST THING IN THE MORNING WITH WHATEVER LOOT WE CAN CARRY! FORK OVER THE PRICE-LESS STAMP COLLECTION, DOCTOR SUGARPILL.
EVERY PHILATELIST DESERVES A GOOD LICKING
OLD ARAB PROVERB
SOME VALUABLE COLLECTION! NO FIRST DAY ISSUES OR COMMEMORATIVES, JUST SCRUFFY OLD CRAP PRINTED UPSIDE-DOWN AND SIDEWAYS, WITH FUCKED-UP COLORS! PITCH IT, KATO.
YOUR HOSPITALITY LEAVES A LOT OF ROOM FOR IMPROVE-MENT, RAMMET. WITH ALL THIS SPACE YOU OUGHT TO HAVE MORE THAN ONE DECENT BEDROOM!
I DON'T OWN THE PLACE. SIR CALICO FORECLOSED ON MY MORTGAGE. I ONLY RENT THE TOP FLOOR
DIRTY DIANA EPISODE 4 PAGE 6 OF 7

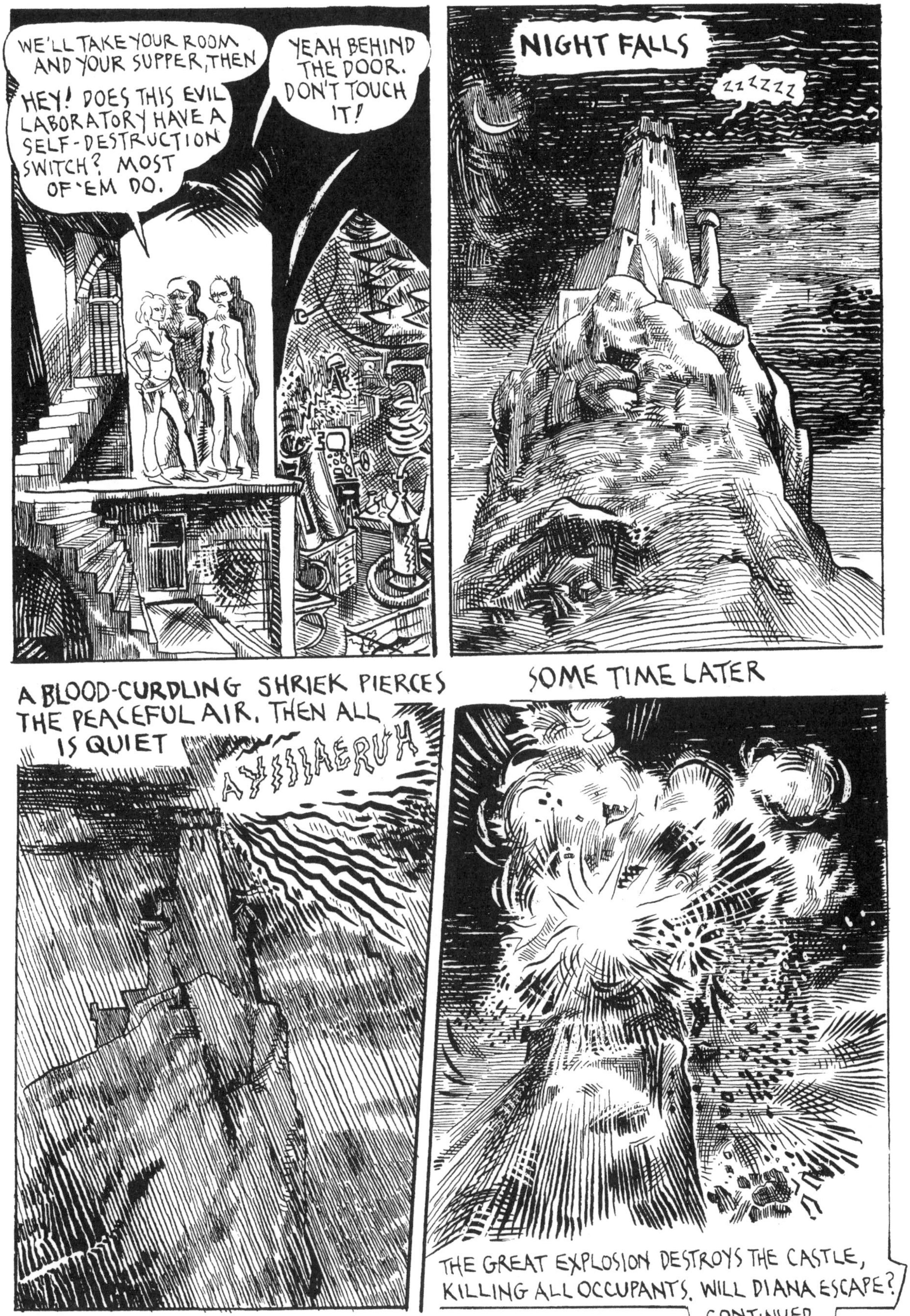
WE'LL TAKE YOUR ROOM AND YOUR SUPPER, THEN
YEAH BEHIND THE DOOR. DON'T TOUCH IT!
HEY! DOES THIS EVIL LABORATORY HAVE A SELF-DESTRUCTION SWITCH? MOST OF 'EM DO.
NIGHT FALLS
ZZZZZZ
A BLOOD-CURDLING SHRIEK PIERCES THE PEACEFUL AIR. THEN ALL IS QUIET
AYIIIIAERUH
SOME TIME LATER
THE GREAT EXPLOSION DESTROYS THE CASTLE, KILLING ALL OCCUPANTS. WILL DIANA ESCAPE?
CONTINUED

Political

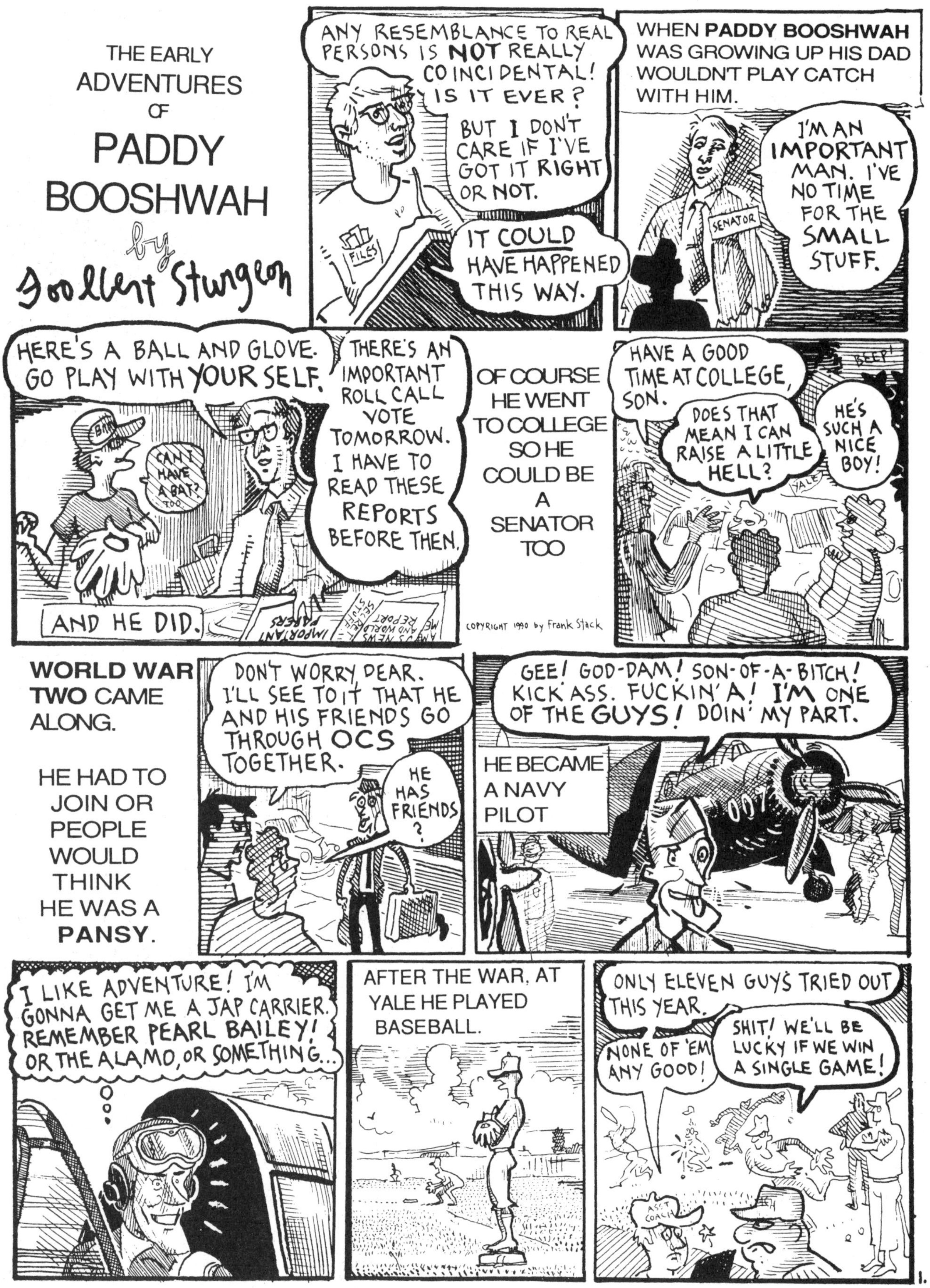
THE EARLY ADVENTURES OF PADDY BOOSHWAH
by Joolbert Sturgeon
ANY RESEMBLANCE TO REAL PERSONS IS NOT REALLY COINCIDENTAL! IS IT EVER?
BUT I DON'T CARE IF I'VE GOT IT RIGHT OR NOT.
IT COULD HAVE HAPPENED THIS WAY.
FILES
WHEN PADDY BOOSHWAH WAS GROWING UP HIS DAD WOULDN'T PLAY CATCH WITH HIM.
I'M AN IMPORTANT MAN. I'VE NO TIME FOR THE SMALL STUFF.
SENATOR
HERE'S A BALL AND GLOVE. GO PLAY WITH YOURSELF.
CAN I HAVE A BAT? TOO
THERE'S AN IMPORTANT ROLL CALL VOTE TOMORROW. I HAVE TO READ THESE REPORTS BEFORE THEN.
AND HE DID.
IMPORTANT PAPERS
OF COURSE HE WENT TO COLLEGE SO HE COULD BE A SENATOR TOO
COPYRIGHT 1990 by Frank Stack
HAVE A GOOD TIME AT COLLEGE, SON.
DOES THAT MEAN I CAN RAISE A LITTLE HELL?
HE'S SUCH A NICE BOY!
BEEP!
YALE
WORLD WAR TWO CAME ALONG.
HE HAD TO JOIN OR PEOPLE WOULD THINK HE WAS A PANSY.
DON'T WORRY, DEAR. I'LL SEE TO IT THAT HE AND HIS FRIENDS GO THROUGH OCS TOGETHER.
HE HAS FRIENDS?
HE BECAME A NAVY PILOT
GEE! GOD-DAM! SON-OF-A-BITCH! KICK ASS. FUCKIN' A! I'M ONE OF THE GUYS! DOIN' MY PART.
I LIKE ADVENTURE! I'M GONNA GET ME A JAP CARRIER. REMEMBER PEARL BAILEY! OR THE ALAMO, OR SOMETHING...
AFTER THE WAR, AT YALE HE PLAYED BASEBALL.
ONLY ELEVEN GUYS TRIED OUT THIS YEAR.
NONE OF 'EM ANY GOOD!
SHIT! WE'LL BE LUCKY IF WE WIN A SINGLE GAME!
ASS'T COACH
1.

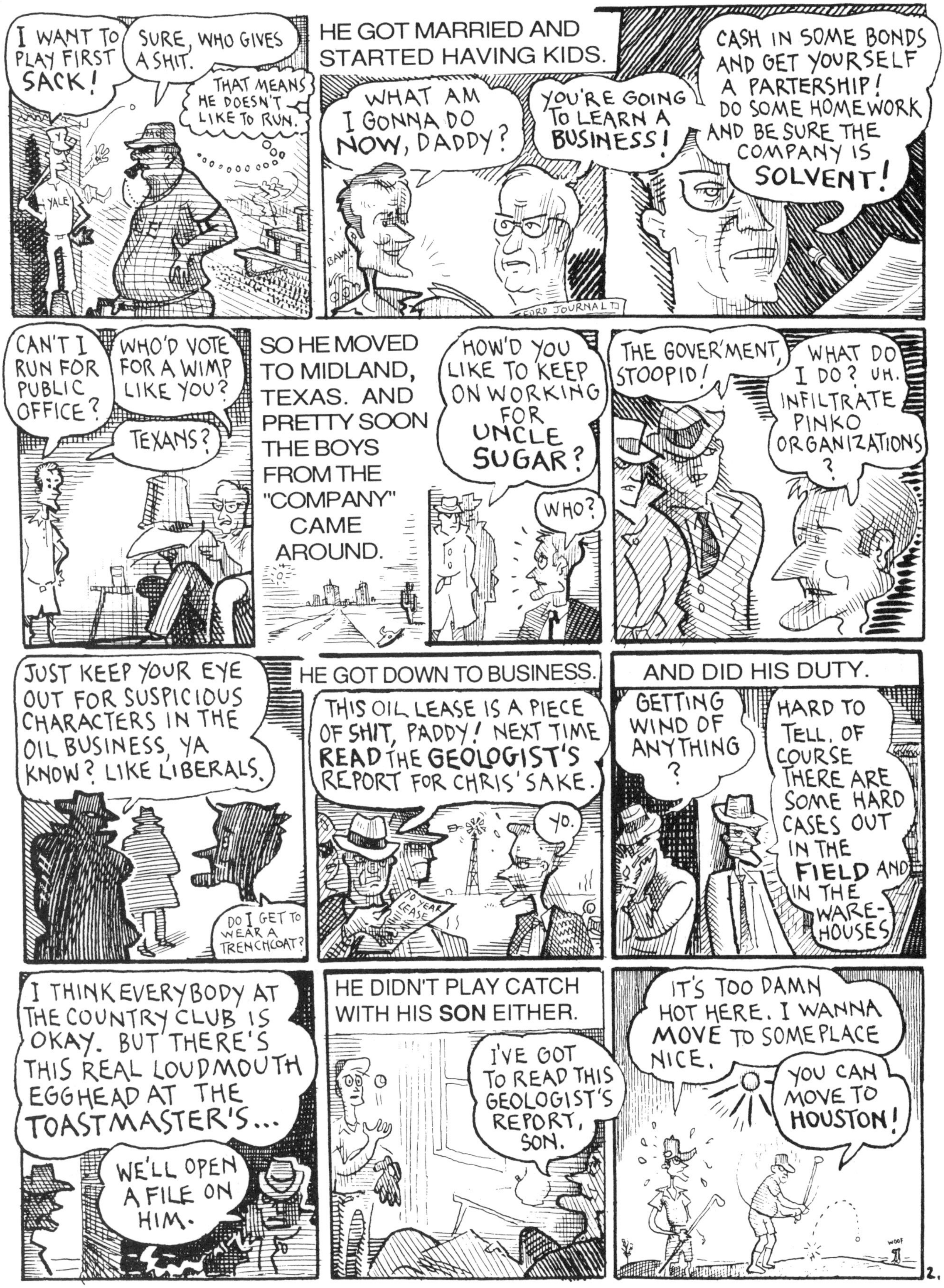
I WANT TO PLAY FIRST SACK!
SURE, WHO GIVES A SHIT.
THAT MEANS HE DOESN'T LIKE TO RUN.
HE GOT MARRIED AND STARTED HAVING KIDS.
WHAT AM I GONNA DO NOW, DADDY?
YOU'RE GOING TO LEARN A BUSINESS!
CASH IN SOME BONDS AND GET YOURSELF A PARTERSHIP! DO SOME HOMEWORK AND BE SURE THE COMPANY IS SOLVENT!
CAN'T I RUN FOR PUBLIC OFFICE?
WHO'D VOTE FOR A WIMP LIKE YOU?
TEXANS?
SO HE MOVED TO MIDLAND, TEXAS. AND PRETTY SOON THE BOYS FROM THE "COMPANY" CAME AROUND.
HOW'D YOU LIKE TO KEEP ON WORKING FOR UNCLE SUGAR?
WHO?
THE GOVER'MENT, STOOPID!
WHAT DO I DO? UH. INFILTRATE PINKO ORGANIZATIONS?
JUST KEEP YOUR EYE OUT FOR SUSPICIOUS CHARACTERS IN THE OIL BUSINESS, YA KNOW? LIKE LIBERALS.
DO I GET TO WEAR A TRENCHCOAT?
HE GOT DOWN TO BUSINESS.
THIS OIL LEASE IS A PIECE OF SHIT, PADDY! NEXT TIME READ THE GEOLOGIST'S REPORT FOR CHRIS' SAKE.
YO.
10 YEAR LEASE
AND DID HIS DUTY.
GETTING WIND OF ANYTHING?
HARD TO TELL. OF COURSE THERE ARE SOME HARD CASES OUT IN THE FIELD AND IN THE WARE-HOUSES
I THINK EVERYBODY AT THE COUNTRY CLUB IS OKAY. BUT THERE'S THIS REAL LOUDMOUTH EGGHEAD AT THE TOASTMASTER'S...
WE'LL OPEN A FILE ON HIM.
HE DIDN'T PLAY CATCH WITH HIS SON EITHER.
I'VE GOT TO READ THIS GEOLOGIST'S REPORT, SON.
IT'S TOO DAMN HOT HERE. I WANNA MOVE TO SOMEPLACE NICE.
YOU CAN MOVE TO HOUSTON!
2.

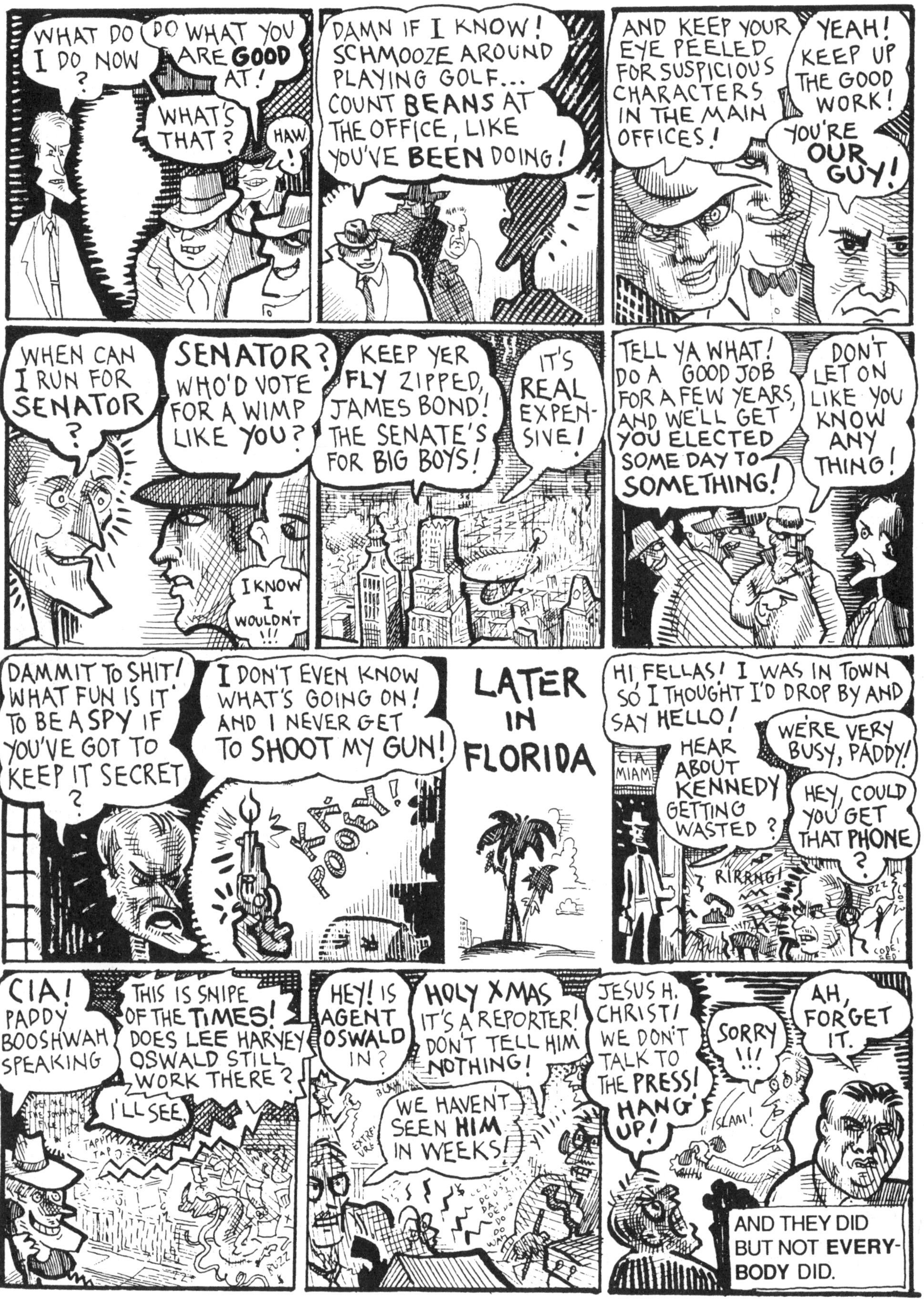
WHAT DO I DO NOW?
DO WHAT YOU ARE GOOD AT!
WHAT'S THAT?
HAW!
DAMN IF I KNOW! SCHMOOZE AROUND PLAYING GOLF... COUNT BEANS AT THE OFFICE, LIKE YOU'VE BEEN DOING!
AND KEEP YOUR EYE PEELED FOR SUSPICIOUS CHARACTERS IN THE MAIN OFFICES!
YEAH! KEEP UP THE GOOD WORK!
YOU'RE OUR GUY!
WHEN CAN I RUN FOR SENATOR?
SENATOR? WHO'D VOTE FOR A WIMP LIKE YOU?
I KNOW I WOULDN'T !!!
KEEP YER FLY ZIPPED, JAMES BOND! THE SENATE'S FOR BIG BOYS!
IT'S REAL EXPEN-SIVE!
TELL YA WHAT! DO A GOOD JOB FOR A FEW YEARS, AND WE'LL GET YOU ELECTED SOME DAY TO SOMETHING!
DON'T LET ON LIKE YOU KNOW ANY THING!
DAMMIT TO SHIT! WHAT FUN IS IT TO BE A SPY IF YOU'VE GOT TO KEEP IT SECRET?
I DON'T EVEN KNOW WHAT'S GOING ON! AND I NEVER GET TO SHOOT MY GUN!
KA-POOEY!
LATER IN FLORIDA
HI, FELLAS! I WAS IN TOWN SO I THOUGHT I'D DROP BY AND SAY HELLO!
CIA MIAMI
HEAR ABOUT KENNEDY GETTING WASTED?
WE'RE VERY BUSY, PADDY!
HEY, COULD YOU GET THAT PHONE?
RIRRNG!
BZZ
CODE RED
CIA! PADDY BOOSHWAH SPEAKING
THIS IS SNIPE OF THE TIMES! DOES LEE HARVEY OSWALD STILL WORK THERE?
I'LL SEE.
TAPPITY TAP
HEY! IS AGENT OSWALD IN?
HOLY XMAS IT'S A REPORTER! DON'T TELL HIM NOTHING!
WE HAVEN'T SEEN HIM IN WEEKS!
JESUS H. CHRIST! WE DON'T TALK TO THE PRESS! HANG UP!
SORRY !!!
SLAM!
AH, FORGET IT.
AND THEY DID BUT NOT EVERY-BODY DID.

The Further Adventures of

Paddy Booshwah

Undercover Executive

By Foolbert Sturgeon

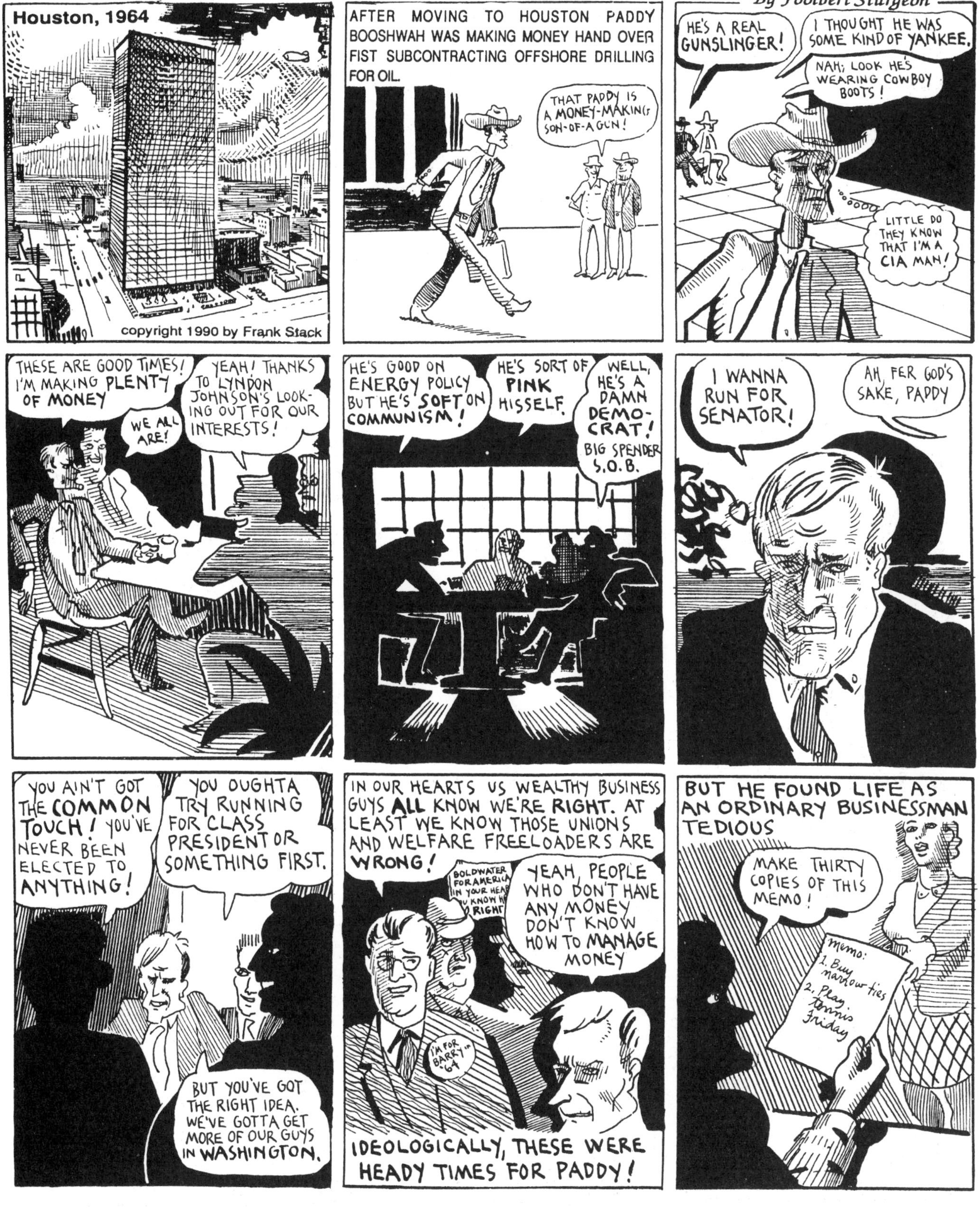

Houston, 1964
copyright 1990 by Frank Stack
AFTER MOVING TO HOUSTON PADDY BOOSHWAH WAS MAKING MONEY HAND OVER FIST SUBCONTRACTING OFFSHORE DRILLING FOR OIL.
THAT PADDY IS A MONEY-MAKING SON-OF-A GUN!
HE'S A REAL GUNSLINGER!
I THOUGHT HE WAS SOME KIND OF YANKEE.
NAH; LOOK HE'S WEARING COWBOY BOOTS!
LITTLE DO THEY KNOW THAT I'M A CIA MAN!
THESE ARE GOOD TIMES! I'M MAKING PLENTY OF MONEY
YEAH! THANKS TO LYNDON JOHNSON'S LOOKING OUT FOR OUR INTERESTS!
WE ALL ARE!
HE'S GOOD ON ENERGY POLICY BUT HE'S SOFT ON COMMUNISM!
HE'S SORT OF PINK HISSELF.
WELL, HE'S A DAMN DEMOCRAT!
BIG SPENDER S.O.B.
I WANNA RUN FOR SENATOR!
AH, FER GOD'S SAKE, PADDY
YOU AIN'T GOT THE COMMON TOUCH! YOU'VE NEVER BEEN ELECTED TO ANYTHING!
YOU OUGHTA TRY RUNNING FOR CLASS PRESIDENT OR SOMETHING FIRST.
BUT YOU'VE GOT THE RIGHT IDEA. WE'VE GOTTA GET MORE OF OUR GUYS IN WASHINGTON.
IN OUR HEARTS US WEALTHY BUSINESS GUYS ALL KNOW WE'RE RIGHT. AT LEAST WE KNOW THOSE UNIONS AND WELFARE FREELOADERS ARE WRONG!
BOLDWATER FOR AMERICA
YEAH, PEOPLE WHO DON'T HAVE ANY MONEY DON'T KNOW HOW TO MANAGE MONEY
I'M FOR BARRY IN '64
IDEOLOGICALLY, THESE WERE HEADY TIMES FOR PADDY!
BUT HE FOUND LIFE AS AN ORDINARY BUSINESSMAN TEDIOUS
MAKE THIRTY COPIES OF THIS MEMO!
memo:
1. Buy narrow ties
2. Play tennis Friday

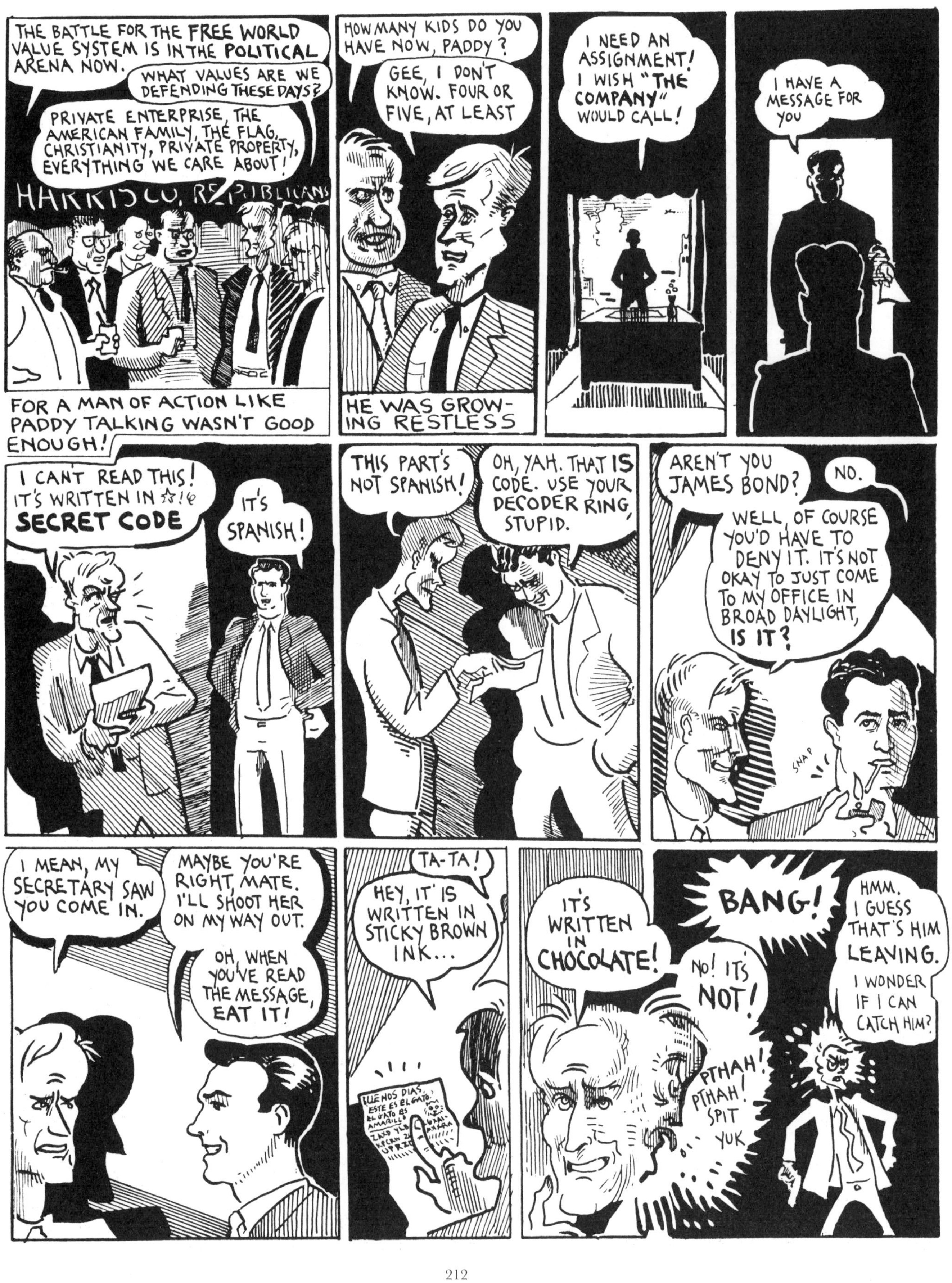
THE BATTLE FOR THE FREE WORLD VALUE SYSTEM IS IN THE POLITICAL ARENA NOW.
WHAT VALUES ARE WE DEFENDING THESE DAYS?
PRIVATE ENTERPRISE, THE AMERICAN FAMILY, THE FLAG, CHRISTIANITY, PRIVATE PROPERTY, EVERYTHING WE CARE ABOUT!
HARRIS CO. REPUBLICANS
FOR A MAN OF ACTION LIKE PADDY TALKING WASN'T GOOD ENOUGH!
HOW MANY KIDS DO YOU HAVE NOW, PADDY?
GEE, I DON'T KNOW. FOUR OR FIVE, AT LEAST
HE WAS GROWING RESTLESS
I NEED AN ASSIGNMENT! I WISH "THE COMPANY" WOULD CALL!
I HAVE A MESSAGE FOR YOU
I CAN'T READ THIS! IT'S WRITTEN IN ☆!¢ SECRET CODE
IT'S SPANISH!
THIS PART'S NOT SPANISH!
OH, YAH. THAT IS CODE. USE YOUR DECODER RING, STUPID.
AREN'T YOU JAMES BOND?
NO.
WELL, OF COURSE YOU'D HAVE TO DENY IT. IT'S NOT OKAY TO JUST COME TO MY OFFICE IN BROAD DAYLIGHT, IS IT?
SNAP
I MEAN, MY SECRETARY SAW YOU COME IN.
MAYBE YOU'RE RIGHT, MATE. I'LL SHOOT HER ON MY WAY OUT.
OH, WHEN YOU'VE READ THE MESSAGE, EAT IT!
TA-TA!
HEY, IT IS WRITTEN IN STICKY BROWN INK...
BUENOS DIAS. ESTE ES EL GATO. EL GATO ES AMARILLO
IT'S WRITTEN IN CHOCOLATE!
NO! IT'S NOT!
PTHAH! PTHAH! SPIT YUK
BANG!
HMM. I GUESS THAT'S HIM LEAVING.
I WONDER IF I CAN CATCH HIM?

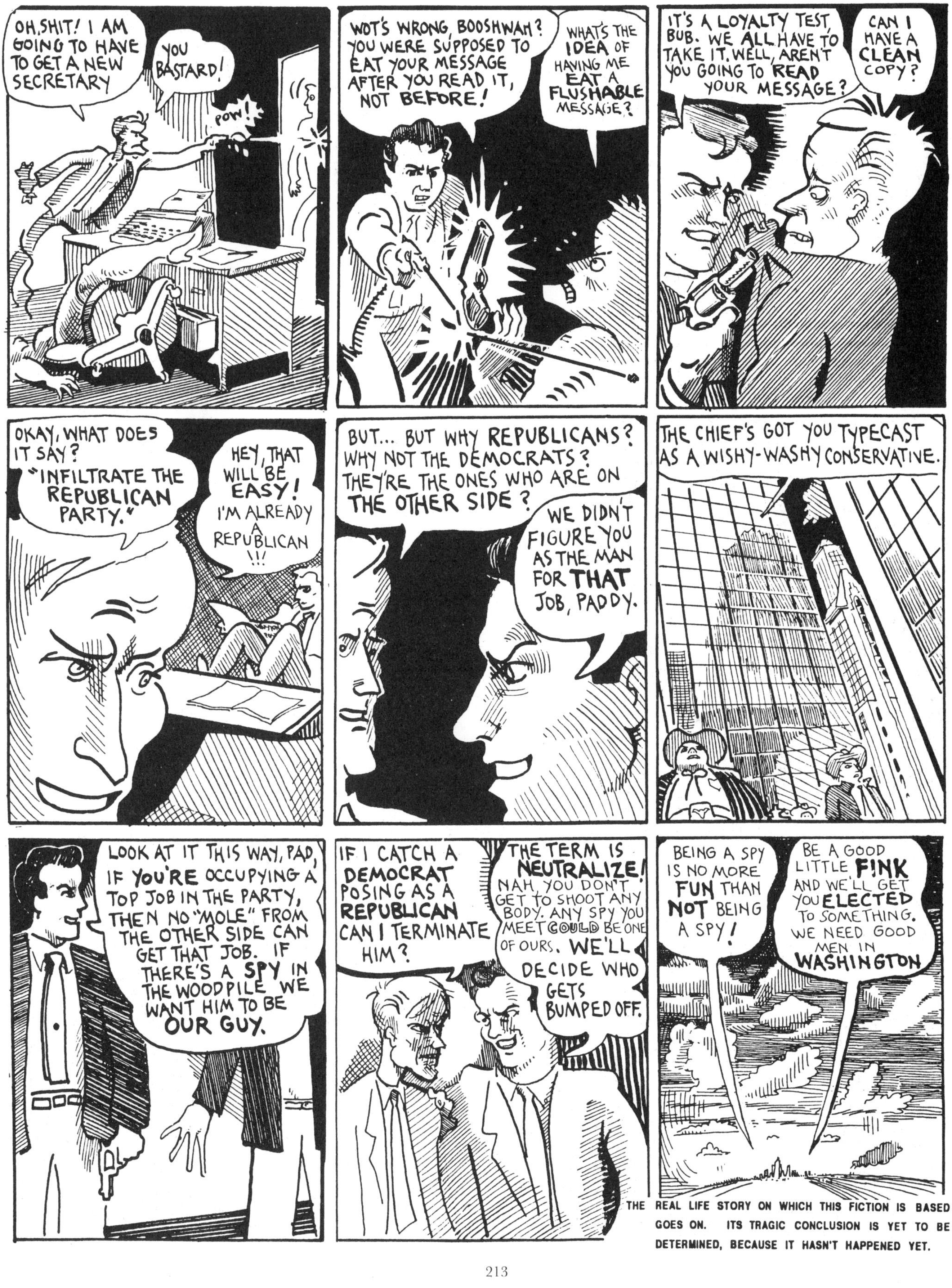
OH, SHIT! I AM GOING TO HAVE TO GET A NEW SECRETARY
YOU BASTARD!
POW!
WOT'S WRONG, BOOSHWAH? YOU WERE SUPPOSED TO EAT YOUR MESSAGE AFTER YOU READ IT, NOT BEFORE!
WHAT'S THE IDEA OF HAVING ME EAT A FLUSHABLE MESSAGE?
IT'S A LOYALTY TEST, BUB. WE ALL HAVE TO TAKE IT. WELL, AREN'T YOU GOING TO READ YOUR MESSAGE?
CAN I HAVE A CLEAN COPY?
OKAY, WHAT DOES IT SAY? "INFILTRATE THE REPUBLICAN PARTY."
HEY, THAT WILL BE EASY! I'M ALREADY A REPUBLICAN !!!
BUT... BUT WHY REPUBLICANS? WHY NOT THE DEMOCRATS? THEY'RE THE ONES WHO ARE ON THE OTHER SIDE?
WE DIDN'T FIGURE YOU AS THE MAN FOR THAT JOB, PADDY.
THE CHIEF'S GOT YOU TYPECAST AS A WISHY-WASHY CONSERVATIVE.
LOOK AT IT THIS WAY, PAD, IF YOU'RE OCCUPYING A TOP JOB IN THE PARTY, THEN NO "MOLE" FROM THE OTHER SIDE CAN GET THAT JOB. IF THERE'S A SPY IN THE WOODPILE WE WANT HIM TO BE OUR GUY.
IF I CATCH A DEMOCRAT POSING AS A REPUBLICAN CAN I TERMINATE HIM?
THE TERM IS NEUTRALIZE! NAH, YOU DON'T GET TO SHOOT ANY BODY. ANY SPY YOU MEET COULD BE ONE OF OURS. WE'LL DECIDE WHO GETS BUMPED OFF.
BEING A SPY IS NO MORE FUN THAN NOT BEING A SPY!
BE A GOOD LITTLE FINK AND WE'LL GET YOU ELECTED TO SOMETHING. WE NEED GOOD MEN IN WASHINGTON

THE REAL LIFE STORY ON WHICH THIS FICTION IS BASED GOES ON. ITS TRAGIC CONCLUSION IS YET TO BE DETERMINED, BECAUSE IT HASN'T HAPPENED YET.

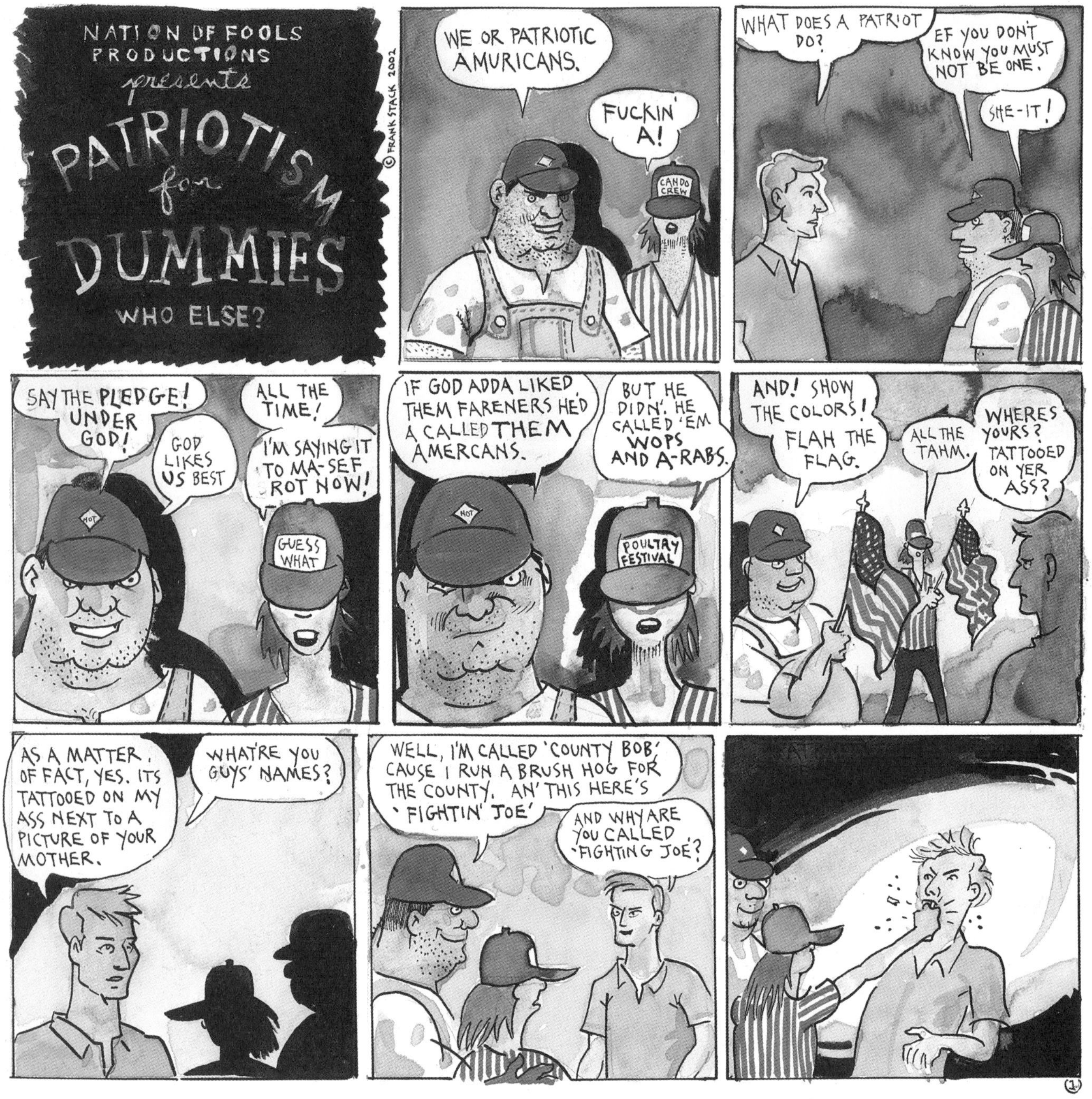
NATION OF FOOLS PRODUCTIONS
presents
PATRIOTISM for DUMMIES
WHO ELSE?
© FRANK STACK 2002
WE OR PATRIOTIC AMURICANS.
FUCKIN' A!
CAN DO CREW
WHAT DOES A PATRIOT DO?
EF YOU DON'T KNOW YOU MUST NOT BE ONE.
SHE-IT!
SAY THE PLEDGE! UNDER GOD!
GOD LIKES US BEST
ALL THE TIME!
I'M SAYING IT TO MA-SEF ROT NOW!
HOT
GUESS WHAT
IF GOD ADDA LIKED THEM FARENERS HE'D A CALLED THEM AMERCANS.
BUT HE DIDN'. HE CALLED 'EM WOPS AND A-RABS.
POULTRY FESTIVAL
AND! SHOW THE COLORS!
FLAH THE FLAG.
ALL THE TAHM.
WHERES YOURS? TATTOOED ON YER ASS?
AS A MATTER OF FACT, YES. ITS TATTOOED ON MY ASS NEXT TO A PICTURE OF YOUR MOTHER.
WHAT'RE YOU GUYS' NAMES?
WELL, I'M CALLED 'COUNTY BOB' CAUSE I RUN A BRUSH HOG FOR THE COUNTY. AN' THIS HERE'S 'FIGHTIN' JOE'
AND WHY ARE YOU CALLED 'FIGHTING JOE'?
1

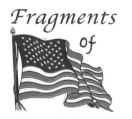

Fragments of
REAL AMERICA
HAND DRAWN BY THAT SUPER PATRIOT
Frank O'Phile Stack
LISTEN UP, WORLD! HERE'S WHAT AMERICA HAS TO SAY.
HAIL
SHEEE THEY AIN'T GOT NOTHIN' MY SIZE.
THE BIG SALE
HI, HOW ARE YA?
LIVING BRAVE
HOW'S YOURS?
I'VE HAD WORSE
WANT A BITE?
WHAT YOU THINK ABOUT IRAQ?
WHAT ROCK?
I-RAQ.
SINCE WHEN?
I JUST WANT A STRAIGHT ANSWER.
YOU AREN'T GETTING IT. SAYS HERE...
BUT NOW A BREAK FOR MORE HOMESPUN COMMON SENSE FROM OUR OWN BELOVED COUNTY BOB...
YOU CAN'T CALL ME 'COUNTY BOB' NO MORE. UH WORK IN TOWN NOW. I'M CITY BOB.
WHAT DO YOU HAVE FOR US, BOB?
I'M GONNA FART.
UNH
PSHEESHshuuu
UH-OH
IT WAS A WET ONE.
UM. WELL COME BACK REAL SOON, CITY BOB.
ACKSHALLY, AH LOST MA CITY JOB TOO. CALL ME JOBLESS BOB.
2

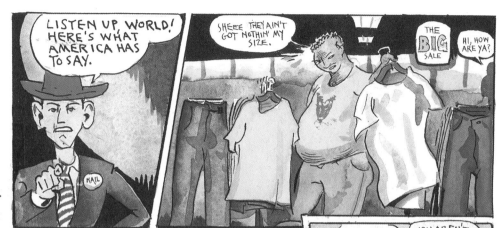

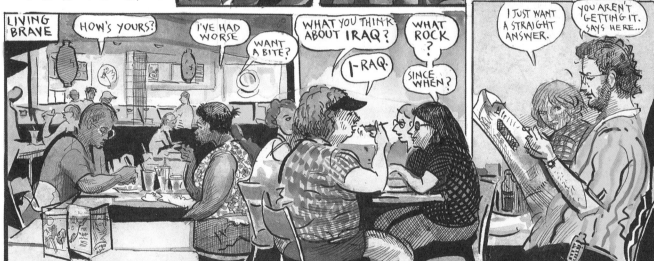

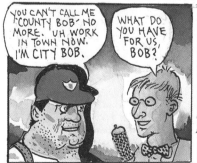

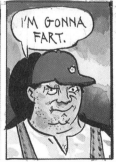

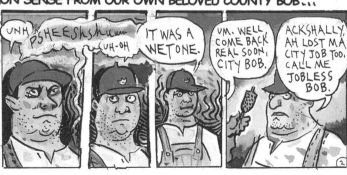

AND NOW, BACK TO OUR STORY

EATING MY LUNCH. YEP.

GOT ANY MONEY LEFT?

COUPLE BUCKS

NEED IT FOR TOLLS

I NEED TO GO BATHROOM

KNOW WHERE IT IS?

SHE'S WEIRD, MAN.

WEIRDER 'N YOU?

NO TELLIN'

HOW YA DOIN?

DON'T BE LOOKING AT ME ALL PSYCHO!

UNITED WE STAND

WHERE YOU GOING?

WHAT YOU WANT TO KNOW FOR?

HEY, PEOPLE! THE WORLD NEEDS TO KNOW WHAT YOU REALLY THINK. GET SERIOUS.

LIKE, YOU KNOW... NASHNUL PRIDE!

HEY, MAN, HOW YA DOIN'?

DUDE!

NOT BAD. YOU?

PRETTY GOOD,

WHATTAYA SAY?

NEVER FORGET!

NEVER FORGET WHAT?

YOU FORGOT!

I NEVER.

YOU DID.

TERRORISM! THERE'S NOTHING I CAN DO ABOUT IT.

YES, THERE IS! YOU CAN WEAR YOUR RED, WHITE AND BLUE UNCLE SAM SUIT!

WHAT REALLY SHOCKED ME ABOUT THE TERRORIST ATTACKS WAS THE REALIZATION OF HOW MUCH WE, AS AMERICANS, ARE DESPISED.

I'M NOT SO DESPICABLE. NEITHER ARE YOU,

GEORGE BUSH IS.

CHEAP SHOT!

IS THIS STILL REAL AMERICA?

Upshot

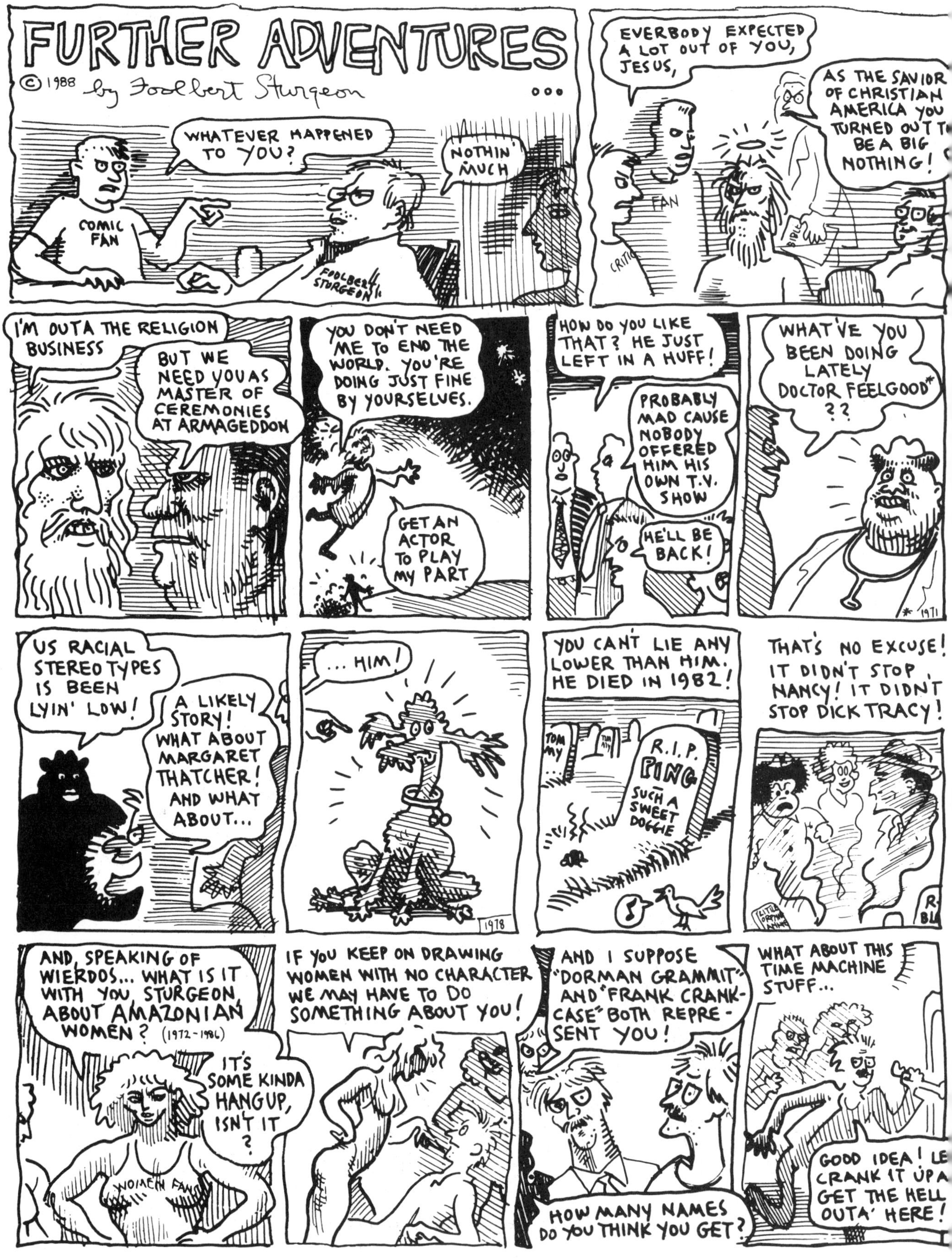
FURTHER ADVENTURES
©1988 by Foolbert Sturgeon
...
WHATEVER HAPPENED TO YOU?
COMIC FAN
NOTHIN' MUCH
FOOLBERT STURGEON
EVERBODY EXPECTED A LOT OUT OF YOU, JESUS,
AS THE SAVIOR OF CHRISTIAN AMERICA YOU TURNED OUT T BE A BIG NOTHING!
FAN
CRITIC
BIBLE
I'M OUTA THE RELIGION BUSINESS
BUT WE NEED YOU AS MASTER OF CEREMONIES AT ARMAGEDDON
YOU DON'T NEED ME TO END THE WORLD. YOU'RE DOING JUST FINE BY YOURSELVES.
GET AN ACTOR TO PLAY MY PART
HOW DO YOU LIKE THAT? HE JUST LEFT IN A HUFF!
PROBABLY MAD CAUSE NOBODY OFFERED HIM HIS OWN T.V. SHOW
HE'LL BE BACK!
WHAT'VE YOU BEEN DOING LATELY DOCTOR FEELGOOD* ??
* 1971
US RACIAL STEREOTYPES IS BEEN LYIN' LOW!
A LIKELY STORY! WHAT ABOUT MARGARET THATCHER! AND WHAT ABOUT...
... HIM!
1978
YOU CAN'T LIE ANY LOWER THAN HIM. HE DIED IN 1982!
R.I.P. PING SUCH A SWEET DOGGIE
THAT'S NO EXCUSE! IT DIDN'T STOP NANCY! IT DIDN'T STOP DICK TRACY!
AND, SPEAKING OF WIERDOS... WHAT IS IT WITH YOU, STURGEON, ABOUT AMAZONIAN WOMEN? (1972-1986)
IT'S SOME KINDA HANGUP, ISN'T IT ?
WOMEN FAN
IF YOU KEEP ON DRAWING WOMEN WITH NO CHARACTER WE MAY HAVE TO DO SOMETHING ABOUT YOU!
AND I SUPPOSE "DORMAN GRAMMIT" AND "FRANK CRANKCASE" BOTH REPRESENT YOU!
HOW MANY NAMES DO YOU THINK YOU GET?
WHAT ABOUT THIS TIME MACHINE STUFF...
GOOD IDEA! LE CRANK IT UP A GET THE HELL OUTA' HERE!

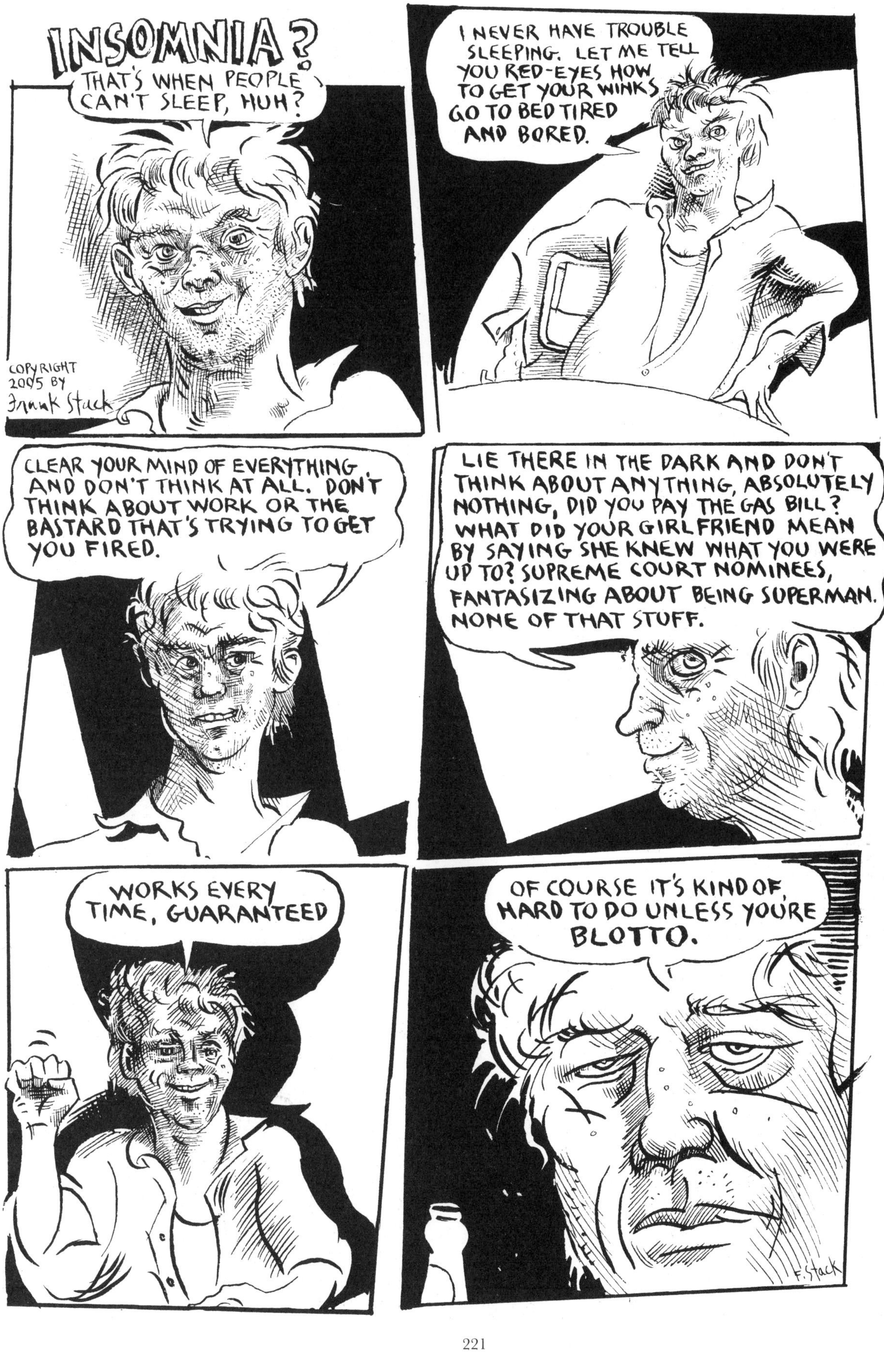
INSOMNIA?
THAT'S WHEN PEOPLE CAN'T SLEEP, HUH?
COPYRIGHT 2005 BY Frank Stack
I NEVER HAVE TROUBLE SLEEPING. LET ME TELL YOU RED-EYES HOW TO GET YOUR WINKS GO TO BED TIRED AND BORED.
CLEAR YOUR MIND OF EVERYTHING AND DON'T THINK AT ALL. DON'T THINK ABOUT WORK OR THE BASTARD THAT'S TRYING TO GET YOU FIRED.
LIE THERE IN THE DARK AND DON'T THINK ABOUT ANYTHING, ABSOLUTELY NOTHING, DID YOU PAY THE GAS BILL? WHAT DID YOUR GIRLFRIEND MEAN BY SAYING SHE KNEW WHAT YOU WERE UP TO? SUPREME COURT NOMINEES, FANTASIZING ABOUT BEING SUPERMAN. NONE OF THAT STUFF.
WORKS EVERY TIME, GUARANTEED
OF COURSE IT'S KIND OF HARD TO DO UNLESS YOU'RE BLOTTO.
F. Stack

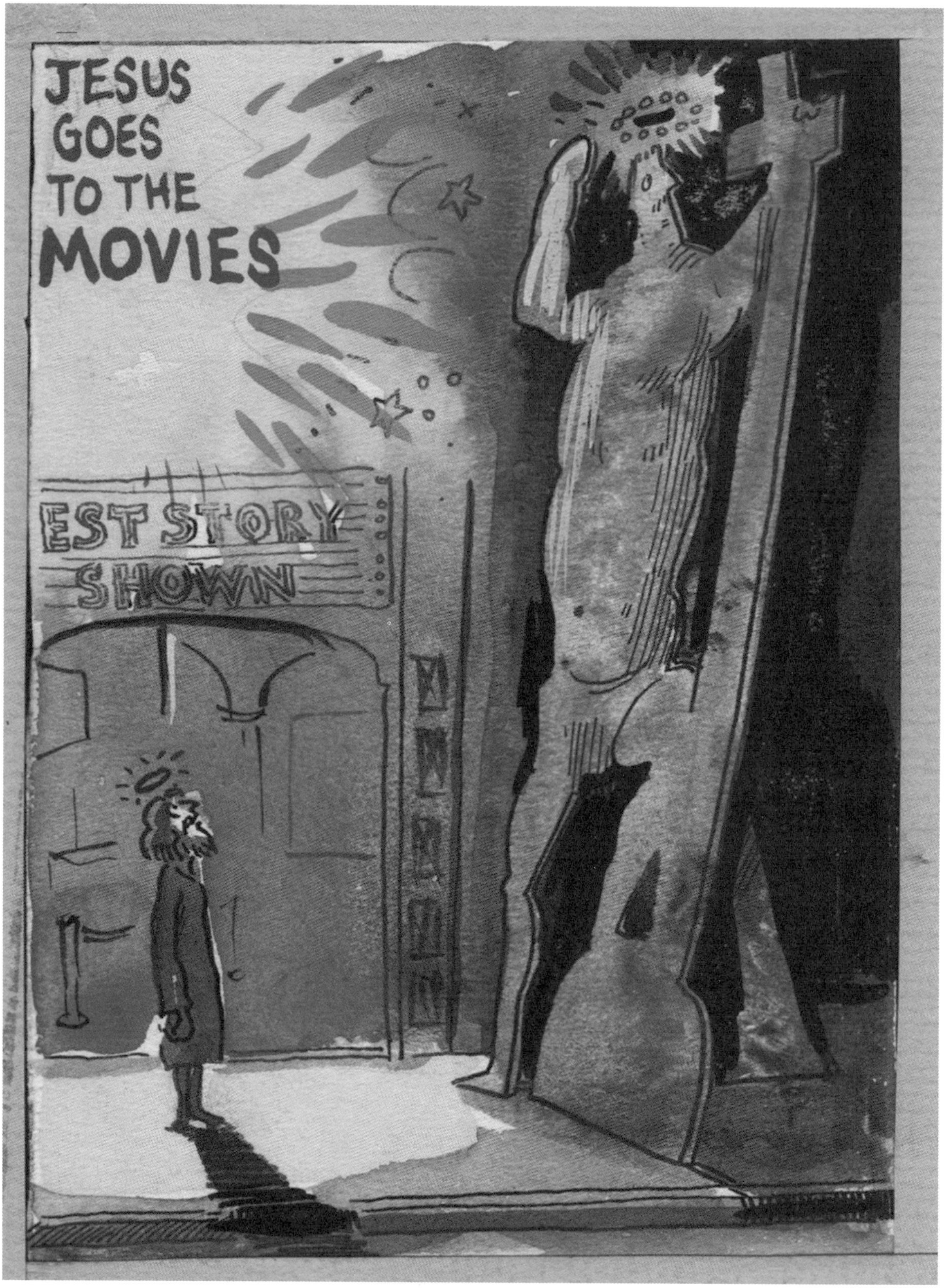
JESUS GOES TO THE MOVIES
EST STORY SHOWN

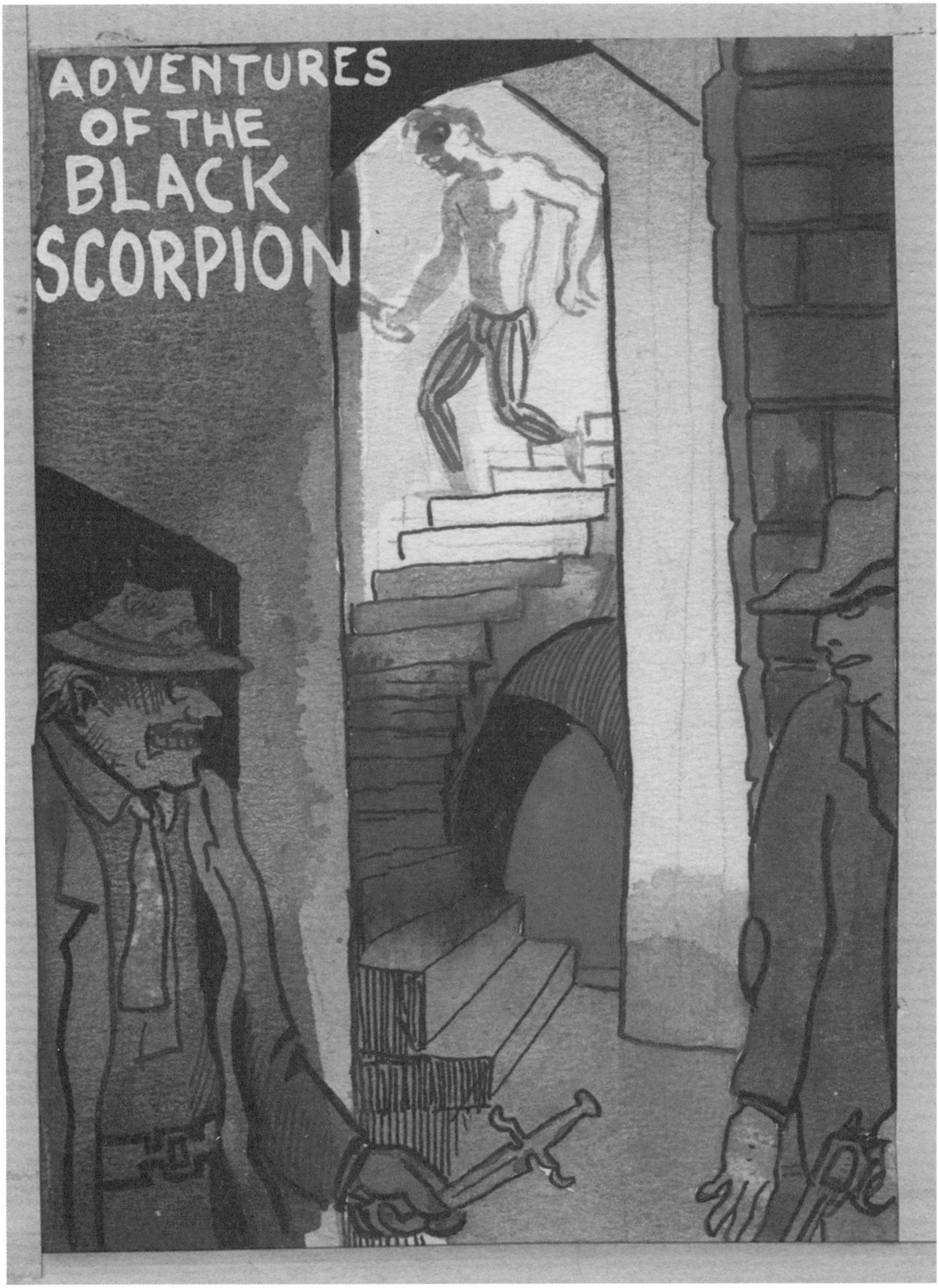
ADVENTURES OF THE BLACK SCORPION